Samuel Johnson
The Lives of the Poets

SAMUEL JOHNSON

THE LIVES OF THE MOST EMINENT ENGLISH POETS; WITH CRITICAL OBSERVATIONS ON THEIR WORKS

With an Introduction and Notes by
ROGER LONSDALE

Volume IV

CLARENDON PRESS · OXFORD

OXFORD
UNIVERSITY PRESS

Great Clarendon Street, Oxford OX2 6DP

Oxford University Press is a department of the University of Oxford.
It furthers the University's objective of excellence in research, scholarship,
and education by publishing worldwide in

Oxford New York

Auckland Cape Town Dar es Salaam Hong Kong Karachi
Kuala Lumpur Madrid Melbourne Mexico City Nairobi
New Delhi Shanghai Taipei Toronto

With offices in

Argentina Austria Brazil Chile Czech Republic France Greece
Guatemala Hungary Italy Japan Poland Portugal Singapore
South Korea Switzerland Thailand Turkey Ukraine Vietnam

Oxford is a registered trade mark of Oxford University Press
in the UK and in certain other countries

Published in the United States
by Oxford University Press Inc., New York

© Roger Lonsdale 2006

British Library Cataloguing in Publication Data

Data available

Library of Congress Cataloguing in Publication Data

Data available

Typeset by SPI Publisher Services, Pondicherry, India
Printed in Great Britain
on acid-free paper by

ISBN 0-19-927897-0 978-0-19-927897-8 (Set)
ISBN 0-19-928479-2 978-0-19-928479-5 (Volume i)
ISBN 0-19-928480-6 978-0-19-928480-1 (Volume ii)
ISBN 0-19-928481-4 978-0-19-928481-8 (Volume iii)
ISBN 0-19-928482-2 978-0-19-928482-5 (Volume iv)

1 3 5 7 9 10 8 6 4 2

Burney, *Early Journals*
The Early Journals and Letters of Fanny Burney, ed. Lars E. Troide et al., vols. i–
(Oxford, 1988–   ).

Carnie (1956)
R. H. Carnie, 'Lord Hailes's Notes on Johnson's "Lives of the Poets" ', *N & Q*
201 (1956), 73–5, 106–8, 174–6, 343–6, 486–9

Chesterfield, *Letters*
Earl of Chesterfield, *Letters*, ed. Bonamy Dobrée (6 vols., 1932)

Clifford (1955)
James L. Clifford, *Young Sam Johnson* (New York, 1955)

Clifford (1979)
James L. Clifford, *Dictionary Johnson: Samuel Johnson's Middle Years* (New
York, 1979)

Clifford, *Mrs. Thrale*
James L. Clifford, *Hester Lynch Piozzi (Mrs. Thrale)* (Oxford, 1941)

Cokayne
G. E. Cokayne, *The Complete Peerage* (rev. edn., 13 vols., 1910–59)

Cokayne, *Baronetage*
G. E. Cokayne, *The Complete Baronetage* (6 vols., Exeter, 1900–9)

Cowper, *Letters*
William Cowper, *Letters and Prose Writings*, ed. James King and Charles
Ryskamp (5 vols., Oxford, 1979–86)

Cunningham, *Lives* (1854)
Lives of the Most Eminent English Poets ... By Samuel Johnson, ed. Peter
Cunningham (3 vols., 1854)

Damrosch (1976)
Leopold Damrosch, Jr., *The Uses of Johnson's Criticism* (Charlottesville, Va.,
1976)

DeMaria (1986)
Robert DeMaria, Jr., *Johnson's Dictionary and the Language of Learning* (Oxford,
1986)

Dennis, *Works*
The Critical Works of John Dennis, ed. Edward Niles Hooker (2 vols., Baltimore,
1939–43)

Dict.
Samuel Johnson, *A Dictionary of the English Language* (2 vols., 1755; 4th edn.,
1773)

Doddridge, *Corresp.*
Calendar of the Correspondence of Philip Doddridge, D. D. (1702–1751), ed. G. F.
Nuttall (London, 1979)

Dodsley, *Collection*
A Collection of Poems by Several Hands, ed. Robert Dodsley (6 vols., 1748–58)

Dodsley, *Corresp.*
The Correspondence of Robert Dodsley 1733–64, ed. James E. Tierney
(Cambridge, 1988)

SHORT TITLES

Place of publication is London unless otherwise stated.

Bate (1978)
> W. Jackson Bate, *Samuel Johnson* (1978)

BB
> William Oldys et al. (eds.), *Biographia Britannica* (7 vols., 1747–66); 2nd edn., ed. Andrew Kippis (6 vols., 1778–93)

Bibliography
> J. D. Fleeman (comp.), *A Bibliography of the Works of Samuel Johnson*, prepared for publication by James McLaverty (2 vols., Oxford, 2000)

Boswell, *Applause*
> *Boswell: The Applause of the Jury 1782–85*, ed. Irma S. Lustig and Frederick A. Pottle (New York, 1981)

Boswell, *Catalogue*
> *Catalogue of the Papers of James Boswell at Yale University*, ed. Marion Pottle et al. (3 vols., New Haven, 1993)

Boswell in Extremes
> *Boswell in Extremes 1776–1778*, ed. Charles McC. Weis and Frederick A. Pottle (New York, 1970)

Boswell, Laird of Auchinleck
> *Boswell: Laird of Auchinleck 1778–1782*, ed. Joseph W. Reed and Frederick A. Pottle (New York, 1977)

Boswell, *Making of the Life*
> *The Correspondence and Other Papers of James Boswell Relating to the Making of the Life of Johnson*, ed. Marshall Waingrow (1969; 2nd edn., Edinburgh, 2001)

Boswell, *Members of the Club*
> *The Correspondence of James Boswell with Certain Members of the Club*, ed. Charles N. Fifer (1976)

Boswell, *Ominous Years*
> Boswell: The Ominous Years 1774–1776, *ed. Charles Ryskamp and Frederick A. Pottle (New York, 1963)*

Brown, *Critical Opinions*
> *The Critical Opinions of Samuel Johnson*, ed. Joseph Epes Brown (Princeton, 1926; New York, 1961)

Burke, *Corresp.*
> Edmund Burke, *Correspondence*, ed. Thomas W. Copeland et al. (10 vols., Cambridge, 1958–78)

Burke, *Enquiry*
> Edmund Burke, *A Philosophical Enquiry into our Ideas of the Sublime and Beautiful* (1757), ed. James T. Boulton (1958)

Burney, *Diary and Letters*
> *The Diary and Letters of Madame d'Arblay*, ed. Austin Dobson (6 vols., 1904–5)

LIVES OF THE ENGLISH POETS
IN ALPHABETICAL ORDER

CONTENTS TO VOLUME IV

Early Biographies (1974)
  The Early Biographies of Samuel Johnson, ed. O. M. Brack, Jr., and Robert E. Kelley (Iowa City, 1974)
Early Biog. Writings (1973)
  Early Biographical Writings of Dr. Johnson, ed. J. D. Fleeman (Westmead, 1973)
Edinger (1977)
  William Edinger, *Samuel Johnson and Poetic Style* (Chicago, 1977)
Eng. Poets (1779)
  The Works of the English Poets. With Prefaces, Biographical and Critical, By Samuel Johnson (58 vols., 1779; 2nd edn., 75 vols., 1790)
Evelyn, *Diary*
  The Diary of John Evelyn, ed. E. S. de Beer (6 vols., Oxford, 1955)
Fleeman, *Handlist* (1967)
  J. D. Fleeman (ed.), *A Preliminary Handlist of Documents & Manuscripts of Samuel Johnson* (Oxford, 1967)
Fleeman, *Handlist* (1984)
  J. D. Fleeman, *A Preliminary Handlist of Copies of Books Associated with Dr. Samuel Johnson* (Oxford, 1984)
Fleeman (1962)
  J. D. Fleeman, 'Some Proofs of Johnson's *Prefaces to the Poets*', *Library*, 5th ser. 17 (1962), 213–30
Folkenflik
  Robert Folkenflik, *Samuel Johnson, Biographer* (Ithaca, NY, 1978)
Foster, *Alumni Oxon.*
  Joseph Foster, *Alumni Oxonienses: The Members of the University of Oxford, 1500–1714* (4 vols., 1891–2); *1715–1886* (4 vols., 1887–8)
Foxon, *English Verse*
  D. F. Foxon, *English Verse, 1701–1750: A Catalogue of Separately Printed Poems* (2 vols., Cambridge, 1975)
Garrick, *Letters*
  The Letters of David Garrick, ed. David M. Little and George M. Kahrl (3 vols., 1963)
GD
  Thomas Birch, John Peter Bernard, and John Lockman, *A General Dictionary, Historical and Critical* (10 vols., 1734–41)
Gent. Mag.
  Gentleman's Magazine (1731–   )
Gleanings
  A. L. Reade, *Johnsonian Gleanings* (11 vols., 1909–52)
Goldsmith, *Coll. Works*
  Oliver Goldsmith, *Collected Works*, ed. Arthur Friedman (5 vols., Oxford, 1966)
Gray, *Corresp.*
  The Correspondence of Thomas Gray, ed. Paget Toynbee and Leonard Whibley (3 vols., Oxford, 1935; corrected edn. by H. W. Starr, 1971)

Guardian
    The Guardian, ed. John Calhoun Stephens (Lexington, Mass., 1982)
Hagstrum (1952)
    Jean H. Hagstrum, *Samuel Johnson's Literary Criticism* (Chicago, 1952)
Hart (1950)
    E. L. Hart, 'Some New Sources of Johnson's *Lives*', *PMLA* 65 (1950), 1088–111
Hawkins, *J's Works* (1787)
    The Works of Samuel Johnson, ed. Sir John Hawkins (11 vols., 1787)
Hawkins, *Life*
    The Life of Samuel Johnson (1787) (also as vol. i of the preceding)
Hazen
    Allen T. Hazen, *Samuel Johnson's Prefaces and Dedications* (New Haven, 1937)
Henson
    Eithne Henson, *'The Fictions of Romantick Chivalry': Samuel Johnson and Romance* (1992)
Highfill, *Dictionary*
    Philip H. Highfill et al., *A Biographical Dictionary of Actors, Actresses, Musicians ... 1660–1800* (16 vols., Carbondale, Ill., 1973–93)
Hill (1905)
    Lives of the English Poets by Samuel Johnson, ed. George Birkbeck Hill (3 vols., Oxford, 1905)
Jacob
    Giles Jacob, *The Poetical Register: or, The Lives and Characters of the English Dramatick Poets* (1719); *An Historical Account of the Lives and Writings of our Most Considerable English Poets* (1720); 2nd edn. as *The Poetical Register* (2 vols., 1723)
J. Misc.
    Johnsonian Miscellanies, ed. George Birkbeck Hill (2 vols., Oxford, 1897)
Journey (1985)
    Samuel Johnson, *A Journey to the Western Islands of Scotland*, ed. J. D. Fleeman (Oxford, 1985)
Kaminski
    Thomas Kaminski, *The Early Career of Samuel Johnson* (New York, 1987)
L81–L83
    Samuel Johnson, *The Lives of the Most Eminent English Poets* (4 vols., 1781; 4 vols., 1783)
Letters
    The Letters of Samuel Johnson, ed. Bruce Redford (5 vols., Oxford, 1992–94)
Letters (1788)
    Letters to and from the Late Samuel Johnson, LL.D. ... Published from the Original MSS. in her Possession, by Hester Lynch Piozzi (2 vols., 1788)
Letters, ed. Chapman
    The Letters of Samuel Johnson, with Mrs. Thrale's Genuine Letters to Him, ed. R. W. Chapman (3 vols., Oxford, 1952)

Life
 Boswell's Life of Johnson, Together with Boswell's Journal of a Tour to the Hebrides, ed. George Birkbeck Hill, rev. L. F. Powell (6 vols., 1934–50; vols. v and vi, 2nd edn., 1964)
Lipking (1970)
 Lawrence Lipking, *The Ordering of the Arts in Eighteenth-Century England* (Princeton, 1970)
Lipking (1998)
 Lawrence Lipking, *Samuel Johnson: The Life of an Author* (Cambridge, Mass., 1998)
Lobban
 J. H. Lobban, *Dr. Johnson's Mrs. Thrale* (Edinburgh, 1910)
London Stage
 The London Stage 1660–1800: Pt. i: *1660–1700*, ed. W. Van Lennep (Carbondale, Ill., 1965); Pt. ii: *1700–1729*, ed. E. L. Avery (1960); Pt. iii: *1729–1747*, ed. A. H. Scouten (1961); Pt. iv: *1747–1776*, ed. G. W. Stone, Jr. (1962); Pt. v: *1776–1800*, ed. C. B. Hogan (1968)
McCarthy
 W. McCarthy, 'The Composition of Johnson's *Lives*: A Calendar', *PQ* 60 (1981), 53–67
McGuffie
 Helen L. McGuffie, *Samuel Johnson in the British Press 1749–84: A Chronological Checklist* (New York, 1976)
MR
 Monthly Review (1749–)
NCBEL
 George Watson (ed.), *The New Cambridge Bibliography of English Literature* (5 vols., Cambridge, 1969–77)
Nichols, *Lit. Anec.*
 John Nichols, *Literary Anecdotes of the Eighteenth Century* (9 vols., 1812–16)
Nichols, *Lit. Ill.*
 John Nichols, *Illustrations of the Literary History of the Eighteenth Century* (8 vols., 1817–58)
Nichols, *Minor Lives*
 Minor Lives: A Collection of Biographies by John Nichols, ed. E. L. Hart (Cambridge, Mass., 1971)
Nichols, *Sel. Collection*
 John Nichols (ed.), *A Select Collection of Poems* (8 vols., 1780–2)
OASJ
 Samuel Johnson (The Oxford Authors), ed. Donald Greene (Oxford, 1984); reissued as *The Major Works* (World's Classics, Oxford, 2000).
P79–P81
 Samuel Johnson, *Prefaces, Biographical and Critical, to the Works of the English Poets*, vols. i–iv (1779); vols. v–x (1781)

Pepys

The Diary of Samuel Pepys, ed. Robert Latham and William Matthews (11 vols., 1970–83)

Percy, *Corresp.*

The Percy Letters, ed. David Nichol Smith, Cleanth Brooks and A. F. Falconar (9 vols., Baton Rouge, a. 1944–88), incl. Thomas Percy's *Corresp.* with: i *Edmond Malone*, ed. A. Tillotson (1944); ii *Richard Farmer*, ed. C. Brooks (1946); iii *Thomas Warton*, ed. M. G. Robinson and L. Dennis (1951); iv *David Dalrymple, Lord Hades*, ed. H. F. Falconer (1954); v *Evan Evans*, ed. A. Lewis (195); vii *William Shenstone*, ed. C. Brooks (1977); ix *Robert Anderson*, ed. W. E. K. Anderson (1988)

POAS

George deForest Lord (ed.), *Poems on Affairs of State* (7 vols., New Haven, 1963–75)

Poems

The Poems of Samuel Johnson, ed. David Nichol Smith and E. L. McAdam, Jr. (1941), rev. J. D. Fleeman (Oxford, 1974)

Pope, *Corresp.*

The Correspondence of Alexander Pope, ed. George Sherburn (5 vols., Oxford, 1956)

Pope, *TE*

The Twickenham Edition of the Poems of Alexander Pope, ed. John Butt et al. (10 vols., 1938–67)

Potter, *Inquiry*

Robert Potter, *An Inquiry into Some Passages in Dr. Johnson's Lives of the Poets* (1783)

Prior, *Lit. Works*

The Literary Works of Matthew Prior, ed. H. Bunker Wright and Monroe K. Spears (2 vols., Oxford, 1959; 2nd edn., 1971)

Queeney Letters

The Queeney Letters: Being Letters Addressed to Hester Maria Thrale by Doctor Johnson, Fanny Burney and Mrs. Thrale-Piozzi, ed. Marquis of Lansdowne (1934)

Reddick

Allen Reddick, *The Making of Johnson's Dictionary, 1746–73* (Cambridge, 1990)

Reynolds, *Discourses*

Sir Joshua Reynolds, *Discourses*, ed. Pat Rogers (1992)

Reynolds, *Portraits*

Sir Joshua Reynolds, *Portraits*, ed. F. W. Hilles (1952)

Rogers (1980)

Pat Rogers, 'Samuel Johnson and the Biographic Dictionaries', *RES* 31 (1980), 149–71

Rymer, *Critical Works*

Thomas Rymer, *Critical Works*, ed. C. A. Zimansky (New Haven, 1956)

Shenstone, *Letters*
  Letters of William Shenstone, ed. Marjorie Williams (Oxford, 1939)
Shiels, *Lives*
  [Robert Shiels or Shiells], *The Lives of the Poets of Great Britain and Ireland, to the Time of Dean Swift. By Mr. Cibber* (5 vols., 1753)
Spectator
  Donald F. Bond (ed.), *The Spectator* (5 vols., Oxford, 1965)
Spence
  Joseph Spence, *Observations, Anecdotes, and Characters of Books and Men*, ed. James M. Osborn (2 vols., Oxford, 1966)
Spingarn
  J. E. Spingarn (ed.), *Critical Essays of the Seventeenth Century* (3 vols., Oxford, 1908)
Swift, *Corresp.*
  The Correspondence of Jonathan Swift, ed. Harold Williams (5 vols., Oxford, 1963–5)
Swift, *Jnl. to Stella*
  Jonathan Swift, *Journal to Stella*, ed. Harold Williams (2 vols., Oxford, 1948; also as vols. xv–xvi of *Prose Writings* below
Swift, *Poems*
  Jonathan Swift, *Poems*, ed. H. Williams (3 vols., Oxford, 1937; 2nd edn. Oxford, 1958, cited)
Swift, *PW*
  Jonathan Swift, *Prose Writings*, ed. Herbert Davis (14 vols., Oxford, 1939–68)
Tatler
  Donald F. Bond (ed.), *The Tatler* (3 vols., Oxford, 1987)
Thomson, *Letters*
  James Thomson (1700–1748): Letters and Documents, ed. A. D. McKillop (Lawrence, Kan., 1958)
Thrale-Piozzi, *Anecdotes*
  Anecdotes of the Late Samuel Johnson (1786) (cited from *J. Misc.*, i. 144–351)
Thraliana
  Thraliana: The Diary of Mrs. Hester Lynch Thrale, ed. K. C. Balderston (2 vols., Oxford, 1942; rev. edn., 1951, cited)
Venn, *Alumni Cantab.*
  Alumni Cantabrigienses, Pt. i: *To 1751*, ed. John Venn and J. A. Venn (4 vols., Cambridge, 1922–7); Pt. ii: *1752–1900*, ed. J. A. Venn (6 vols., Cambridge, 1940–54)
Walpole, *Corresp.*
  The Yale Edition of Horace Walpole's Correspondence, ed. W. S. Lewis et al. (48 vols., New Haven, 1937–83)

Warton, *Essay*
    An Essay on the Writings and Genius of Pope (1756; 2nd edn., 1762, as *Essay on the Genius and Writings* etc.; vol. ii, 1782; 5th edn., 2 vols., 1806)

Watson
    John Dryden, *Of Dramatic Poesy and Other Critical Essays*, ed. George Watson (2 vols., 1962)

Wood
    Anthony Wood, *Athenae Oxonienses ... To which are added, the Fasti, or Annals, of the said University* (2 vols., 1691–2; 2nd edn., 2 vols., 1721, cited)

Wordsworth, *Prose Works*
    William Wordsworth, *Prose Works*, ed. W. J. B. Owen and J. W. Smyser (3 vols., Oxford, 1974)

YW
    The Yale Edition of the Works of Samuel Johnson, general editor, J. H. Middendorf: i: *Diaries, Prayers, and Annals*, ed. E. L. McAdam, Jr., with Donald and Mary Hyde (1958); ii: *The Idler* and *The Adventurer*, ed. W. J. Bate, J. Bullitt, and L. F. Powell (1963); iii–v: *The Rambler*, ed. W. J. Bate and A. B. Strauss (1969); vi: *Poems*, ed. E. L. McAdam, Jr. with G. Milne (1964); vii–viii: *Johnson on Shakespeare*, ed. A. Sherbo (1968); ix: *A Journey to the Western Isles of Scotland*, ed. M. Lascelles (1971); x: *Political Writings*, ed. D. J. Greene (1977); xiv: *Sermons*, ed. J. H. Hagstrum and J. Gray (1978); xv: *A Voyage to Abyssinia*, ed. J. J. Gold (1985); xvi: *Rasselas and Other Tales*, ed. G. J. Kolb (1990)

PERIODICALS

Age of J	*Age of Johnson*
BJECS	*British Journal for Eighteenth-Century Studies*
BLR	*Bodleian Library Record*
BNYPL	*Bulletin of the New York Public Library*
BRH	*Bulletin of Research in the Humanities*
DUJ	*Durham University Journal*
EC	*Essays in Criticism*
ECL	*Eighteenth-Century Life*
ECS	*Eighteenth-Century Studies*
ELH	*Journal of English Literary History*
ELN	*English Language Notes*
ES	*English Studies*
HLQ	*Huntington Library Quarterly*
JEGP	*Journal of English and Germanic Philology*
JNL	*Johnsonian News Letter*
MLN	*Modern Language Notes*
MLQ	*Modern Language Quarterly*
MP	*Modern Philology*

N & Q	*Notes and Queries*
PBSA	*Publications of the Bibliographical Society of America*
PMLA	*Publications of the Modern Language Association of America*
PQ	*Philological Quarterly*
RES	*Review of English Studies*
SB	*Studies in Bibliography*
SEC	*Studies in Eighteenth-Century Culture*
SEL	*Studies in English Literature*
SP	*Studies in Philology*
TLS	*Times Literary Supplement*

POPE

ALEXANDER POPE was born in London, May 21, 1688, of parents whose 1
rank or station was never ascertained: we are informed that they were of
gentle blood; that his father was of a family of which the Earl of Downe was
the head, and that his mother was the daughter of William Turner, Esquire,
of York, who had likewise three sons, one of whom had the honour of being
killed, and the other of dying, in the service of Charles the First; the third
was made a general officer in Spain, from whom the sister inherited what
sequestrations and forfeitures had left in the family.

This, and this only, is told by Pope; who is more willing, as I have heard 2
observed, to shew what his father was not, than what he was. It is allowed
that he grew rich by trade; but whether in a shop or on the Exchange was
never discovered, till Mr. Tyers told, on the authority of Mrs. Racket, that
he was a linen-draper in the Strand. Both parents were papists.

Pope was from his birth of a constitution tender and delicate; but is said 3
to have shewn remarkable gentleness and sweetness of disposition. The
weakness of his body continued through his life, but the mildness of his
mind perhaps ended with his childhood. His voice, when he was young, was
so pleasing, that he was called in fondness the *little Nightingale*.

Being not sent early to school, he was taught to read by an aunt; and when 4
he was seven or eight years old, became a lover of books. He first learned to
write by imitating printed books; a species of penmanship in which he
retained great excellence through his whole life, though his ordinary hand
was not elegant.

When he was about eight, he was placed in Hampshire under Taverner, a 5
Romish priest, who, by a method very rarely practised, taught him the
Greek and Latin rudiments together. He was now first regularly initiated in
poetry by the perusal of Ogylby's *Homer*, and Sandys's *Ovid*: Ogylby's
assistance he never repaid with any praise; but of Sandys he declared, in his
notes to the *Iliad*, that English poetry owed much of its present beauty to
his translations. Sandys very rarely attempted original composition.

From the care of Taverner, under whom his proficiency was consider- 6
able, he was removed to a school at Twyford near Winchester, and again to
another school about Hyde-park Corner; from which he used sometimes to
stroll to the playhouse, and was so delighted with theatrical exhibitions, that
he formed a kind of play from Ogylby's *Iliad*, with some verses of his own

intermixed, which he persuaded his schoolfellows to act, with the addition of his master's gardener, who personated *Ajax*.

7   At the two last schools he used to represent himself as having lost part of what Taverner had taught him, and on his master at Twyford he had already exercised his poetry in a lampoon. Yet under those masters he translated more than a fourth part of the *Metamorphoses*. If he kept the same proportion in his other exercises, it cannot be thought that his loss was great.

8   He tells of himself, in his poems, that *he lisp'd in numbers*; and used to say that he could not remember the time when he began to make verses. In the style of fiction it might have been said of him as of Pindar, that when he lay in his cradle, *the bees swarmed about his mouth*.

9   About the time of the Revolution his father, who was undoubtedly disappointed by the sudden blast of popish prosperity, quitted his trade, and retired to Binfield in Windsor Forest, with about twenty thousand pounds; for which, being conscientiously determined not to entrust it to the government, he found no better use than that of locking it up in a chest, and taking from it what his expences required; and his life was long enough to consume a great part of it, before his son came to the inheritance.

10   To Binfield Pope was called by his father when he was about twelve years old; and there he had for a few months the assistance of one Deane, another priest, of whom he learned only to construe a little of *Tully's Offices*. How Mr. Deane could spend, with a boy who had translated so much of *Ovid*, some months over a small part of *Tully's Offices*, it is now vain to enquire.

11   Of a youth so successfully employed, and so conspicuously improved, a minute account must be naturally desired; but curiosity must be contented with confused, imperfect, and sometimes improbable intelligence. Pope, finding little advantage from external help, resolved thenceforward to direct himself, and at twelve formed a plan of study which he completed with little other incitement than the desire of excellence.

12   His primary and principal purpose was to be a poet, with which his father accidentally concurred, by proposing subjects, and obliging him to correct his performances by many revisals; after which the old gentleman, when he was satisfied, would say, *these are good rhymes*.

13   In his perusal of the English poets he soon distinguished the versification of Dryden, which he considered as the model to be studied, and was impressed with such veneration for his instructer, that he persuaded some friend to take him to the coffee-house which Dryden frequented, and pleased himself with having seen him.

14   Dryden died May 1, 1701, some days before Pope was twelve; so early must he therefore have felt the power of harmony, and the zeal of genius.

Who does not wish that Dryden could have known the value of the homage that was paid him, and foreseen the greatness of his young admirer?

The earliest of Pope's productions is his *Ode on Solitude*, written before he was twelve, in which there is nothing more than other forward boys have attained, and which is not equal to Cowley's performances at the same age.

His time was now spent wholly in reading and writing. As he read the Classicks, he amused himself with translating them; and at fourteen made a version of the first book of the *Thebais*, which, with some revision, he afterwards published. He must have been at this time, if he had no help, a considerable proficient in the Latin tongue.

By Dryden's Fables, which had then been not long published, and were much in the hands of poetical readers, he was tempted to try his own skill in giving Chaucer a more fashionable appearance, and put *January and May*, and the *Prologue of the Wife of Bath*, into modern English. He translated likewise the Epistle of *Sappho to Phaon* from Ovid, to complete the version, which was before imperfect; and wrote some other small pieces, which he afterwards printed.

He sometimes imitated the English poets, and professed to have written at fourteen his poem upon *Silence*, after Rochester's *Nothing*. He had now formed his versification, and in the smoothness of his numbers surpassed his original: but this is a small part of his praise; he discovers such acquaintance both with human life and public affairs, as is not easily conceived to have been attainable by a boy of fourteen in *Windsor Forest*.

Next year he was desirous of opening to himself new sources of knowledge, by making himself acquainted with modern languages; and removed for a time to London, that he might study French and Italian, which, as he desired nothing more than to read them, were by diligent application soon dispatched. Of Italian learning he does not appear to have ever made much use in his subsequent studies.

He then returned to Binfield, and delighted himself with his own poetry. He tried all styles, and many subjects. He wrote a comedy, a tragedy, an epick poem, with panegyricks on all the princes of Europe; and, as he confesses, *thought himself the greatest genius that ever was*. Self-confidence is the first requisite to great undertakings; he, indeed, who forms his opinion of himself in solitude, without knowing the powers of other men, is very liable to errour; but it was the felicity of Pope to rate himself at his real value.

Most of his puerile productions were, by his maturer judgement, afterwards destroyed; *Alcander*, the epick poem, was burnt by the persuasion of Atterbury. The tragedy was founded on the legend of *St. Genevieve*. Of the comedy there is no account.

22   Concerning his studies it is related, that he translated Tully *on old Age*; and that, besides his books of poetry and criticism, he read *Temple's Essays* and *Locke on human Understanding*. His reading, though his favourite authors are not known, appears to have been sufficiently extensive and multifarious; for his early pieces shew, with sufficient evidence, his knowledge of books.

23   He that is pleased with himself, easily imagines that he shall please others. Sir William Trumbal, who had been ambassador at Constantinople, and secretary of state, when he retired from business, fixed his residence in the neighbourhood of Binfield. Pope, not yet sixteen, was introduced to the statesman of sixty, and so distinguished himself, that their interviews ended in friendship and correspondence. Pope was, through his whole life, ambitious of splendid acquaintance, and he seems to have wanted neither diligence nor success in attracting the notice of the great; for from his first entrance into the world, and his entrance was very early, he was admitted to familiarity with those whose rank or station made them most conspicuous.

24   From the age of sixteen the life of Pope, as an author, may be properly computed. He now wrote his pastorals, which were shewn to the Poets and Criticks of that time; as they well deserved, they were read with admiration, and many praises were bestowed upon them and upon the Preface, which is both elegant and learned in a high degree: they were, however, not published till five years afterwards.

25   Cowley, Milton, and Pope, are distinguished among the English Poets by the early exertion of their powers; but the works of Cowley alone were published in his childhood, and therefore of him only can it be certain that his puerile performances received no improvement from his maturer studies.

26   At this time began his acquaintance with Wycherley, a man who seems to have had among his contemporaries his full share of reputation, to have been esteemed without virtue, and caressed without good-humour. Pope was proud of his notice; Wycherley wrote verses in his praise, which he was charged by Dennis with writing to himself, and they agreed for a while to flatter one another. It is pleasant to remark how soon Pope learned the cant of an author, and began to treat criticks with contempt, though he had yet suffered nothing from them.

27   But the fondness of Wycherley was too violent to last. His esteem of Pope was such, that he submitted some poems to his revision; and when Pope, perhaps proud of such confidence, was sufficiently bold in his criticisms, and liberal in his alterations, the old scribbler was angry to see his pages defaced, and felt more pain from the detection than content from the amendment of his faults. They parted; but Pope always considered him with kindness, and visited him a little time before he died.

Another of his early correspondents was Mr. Cromwell, of whom I have 28
learned nothing particular but that he used to ride a-hunting in a tye-wig.
He was fond, and perhaps vain, of amusing himself with poetry and
criticism; and sometimes sent his performances to Pope, who did not
forbear such remarks as were now-and-then unwelcome. Pope, in his
turn, put the juvenile version of *Statius* into his hands for correction.

Their correspondence afforded the publick its first knowledge of Pope's 29
Epistolary Powers; for his Letters were given by Cromwell to one Mrs.
Thomas, and she many years afterwards sold them to Curll, who inserted
them in a volume of his Miscellanies.

Walsh, a name yet preserved among the minor poets, was one of his first 30
encouragers. His regard was gained by the Pastorals, and from him Pope
received the counsel by which he seems to have regulated his studies. Walsh
advised him to correctness, which, as he told him, the English poets had
hitherto neglected, and which therefore was left to him as a basis of fame;
and, being delighted with rural poems, recommended to him to write a
pastoral comedy, like those which are read so eagerly in Italy; a design
which Pope probably did not approve, as he did not follow it.

Pope had now declared himself a poet; and, thinking himself entitled to 31
poetical conversation, began at seventeen to frequent Will's, a coffee-house
on the north side of Russel-street in Covent-garden, where the wits of that
time used to assemble, and where Dryden had, when he lived, been
accustomed to preside.

During this period of his life he was indefatigably diligent, and insatiably 32
curious; wanting health for violent, and money for expensive pleasures, and
having certainly excited in himself very strong desires of intellectual eminence, he spent much of his time over his books; but he read only to store
his mind with facts and images, seizing all that his authors presented with
undistinguishing voracity, and with an appetite for knowledge too eager to
be nice. In a mind like his, however, all the faculties were at once involun-
tarily improving. Judgement is forced upon us by experience. He that reads
many books must compare one opinion or one style with another; and when
he compares, must necessarily distinguish, reject, and prefer. But the
account given by himself of his studies was, that from fourteen to twenty
he read only for amusement, from twenty to twenty-seven for improvement
and instruction; that in the first part of this time he desired only to know,
and in the second he endeavoured to judge.

The Pastorals, which had been for some time handed about among 33
poets and criticks, were at last printed (1709) in Tonson's Miscellany, in
a volume which began with the Pastorals of Philips, and ended with those
of Pope.

34   The same year was written the *Essay on Criticism*; a work which displays such extent of comprehension, such nicety of distinction, such acquaintance with mankind, and such knowledge both of ancient and modern learning, as are not often attained by the maturest age and longest experience. It was published about two years afterwards, and being praised by Addison in the *Spectator* with sufficient liberality, met with so much favour as enraged Dennis, "who," he says, "found himself attacked, without any manner of provocation on his side, and attacked in his person, instead of his writings, by one who was wholly a stranger to him, at a time when all the world knew he was persecuted by fortune; and not only saw that this was attempted in a clandestine manner, with the utmost falsehood and calumny, but found that all this was done by a little affected hypocrite, who had nothing in his mouth at the same time but truth, candour, friendship, good-nature, humanity, and magnanimity."

35   How the attack was clandestine is not easily perceived, nor how his person is depreciated; but he seems to have known something of Pope's character, in whom may be discovered an appetite to talk too frequently of his own virtues.

36   The pamphlet is such as rage might be expected to dictate. He supposes himself to be asked two questions; whether the Essay will succeed, and who or what is the author.

37   Its success he admits to be secured by the false opinions then prevalent; the author he concludes to be *young and raw*.

    "First, because he discovers a sufficiency beyond his little ability, and hath rashly undertaken a task infinitely above his force. Secondly, while this little author struts, and affects the dictatorian air, he plainly shews that at the same time he is under the rod; and while he pretends to give laws to others, is a pedantick slave to authority and opinion. Thirdly, he hath, like schoolboys, borrowed both from living and dead. Fourthly, he knows not his own mind, and frequently contradicts himself. Fifthly, he is almost perpetually in the wrong."

38   All these positions he attempts to prove by quotations and remarks; but his desire to do mischief is greater than his power. He has, however, justly criticised some passages. In these lines,

> There are whom heaven has bless'd with store of wit,
> Yet want as much again to manage it;
> For wit and judgment ever are at strife—

it is apparent that *wit* has two meanings, and that what is wanted, though called *wit*, is truly judgment. So far Dennis is undoubtedly right; but, not content with argument, he will have a little mirth, and triumphs over the first couplet in terms too elegant to be forgotten. "By the way, what rare numbers are here! Would not one swear that this youngster had espoused some antiquated Muse, who had sued out a divorce on account of impotence from some superannuated sinner; and, having been p—xed by her former spouse, has got the gout in her decrepit age, which makes her hobble so damnably." This was the man who would reform a nation sinking into barbarity.

In another place Pope himself allowed that Dennis had detected one of 39 those blunders which are called *bulls*. The first edition had this line:

> What is this wit—
> Where wanted, scorn'd; and envied where acquir'd?

"How," says the critick, "can wit be *scorn'd* where it is not? Is not this a figure frequently employed in Hibernian land? The person that wants this wit may indeed be scorned, but the scorn shews the honour which the contemner has for wit." Of this remark Pope made the proper use, by correcting the passage.

I have preserved, I think, all that is reasonable in Dennis's criticism; it 40 remains that justice be done to his delicacy. "For his acquaintance (says Dennis) he names Mr. Walsh, who had by no means the qualification which this author reckons absolutely necessary to a critick, it being very certain that he was, like this Essayer, a very indifferent poet; he loved to be well-dressed; and I remember a little young gentleman whom Mr. Walsh used to take into his company, as a double foil to his person and capacity.—Enquire between *Sunninghill* and *Oakingham* for a young, short, squab gentleman, the very bow of the God of Love, and tell me whether he be a proper author to make personal reflections?—He may extol the antients, but he has reason to thank the gods that he was born a modern; for had he been born of Grecian parents, and his father consequently had by law had the absolute disposal of him, his life had been no longer than that of one of his poems, the life of half a day.—Let the person of a gentleman of his parts be never so contemptible, his inward man is ten times more ridiculous; it being impossible that his outward form, though it be that of downright monkey, should differ so much from human shape, as his unthinking immaterial part does from human understanding." Thus began the hostility between Pope and Dennis, which, though it was suspended for a short time, never was appeased. Pope seems, at first, to have attacked him wantonly; but though he always professed to despise him, he discovers, by mentioning him very often, that he felt his force or his venom.

Of this Essay Pope declared that he did not expect the sale to be quick, 41 because *not one gentleman in sixty, even of liberal education, could understand it*. The gentlemen, and the education of that time, seem to have been of a lower character than they are of this. He mentioned a thousand copies as a numerous impression.

42   Dennis was not his only censurer; the zealous papists thought the monks treated with too much contempt, and Erasmus too studiously praised; but to these objections he had not much regard.

43   The *Essay* has been translated into French by *Hamilton*, author of the *Comte de Grammont*, whose version was never printed, by *Robotham*, secretary to the King for Hanover, and by *Resnel*; and commented by Dr. Warburton, who has discovered in it such order and connection as was not perceived by Addison, nor, as is said, intended by the author.

44   Almost every poem, consisting of precepts, is so far arbitrary and immethodical, that many of the paragraphs may change places with no apparent inconvenience; for of two or more positions, depending upon some remote and general principle, there is seldom any cogent reason why one should precede the other. But for the order in which they stand, whatever it be, a little ingenuity may easily give a reason. *It is possible*, says Hooker, *that by long circumduction, from any one truth all truth may be inferred*. Of all homogeneous truths at least, of all truths respecting the same general end, in whatever series they may be produced, a concatenation by intermediate ideas may be formed, such as, when it is once shewn, shall appear natural; but if this order be reversed, another mode of connection equally specious may be found or made. Aristotle is praised for naming Fortitude first of the cardinal virtues, as that without which no other virtue can steadily be practised; but he might, with equal propriety, have placed Prudence and Justice before it, since without Prudence Fortitude is mad; without Justice, it is mischievous.

45   As the end of method is perspicuity, that series is sufficiently regular that avoids obscurity; and where there is no obscurity it will not be difficult to discover method.

46   In the *Spectator* was published the *Messiah*, which he first submitted to the perusal of Steele, and corrected in compliance with his criticisms.

47   It is reasonable to infer, from his Letters, that the verses on the *Unfortunate Lady* were written about the time when his *Essay* was published. The Lady's name and adventures I have sought with fruitless enquiry.

48   I can therefore tell no more than I have learned from Mr. Ruffhead, who writes with the confidence of one who could trust his information. She was a woman of eminent rank and large fortune, the ward of an unkle, who, having given her a proper education, expected like other guardians that she should make at least an equal match; and such he proposed to her, but found it rejected in favour of a young gentleman of inferior condition.

Having discovered the correspondence between the two lovers, and ₄₉ finding the young lady determined to abide by her own choice, he supposed that separation might do what can rarely be done by arguments, and sent her into a foreign country, where she was obliged to converse only with those from whom her unkle had nothing to fear.

Her lover took care to repeat his vows; but his letters were intercepted ₅₀ and carried to her guardian, who directed her to be watched with still greater vigilance; till of this restraint she grew so impatient, that she bribed a woman-servant to procure her a sword, which she directed to her heart.

From this account, given with evident intention to raise the Lady's ₅₁ character, it does not appear that she had any claim to praise, nor much to compassion. She seems to have been impatient, violent, and ungovernable. Her unkle's power could not have lasted long; the hour of liberty and choice would have come in time. But her desires were too hot for delay, and she liked self-murder better than suspence.

Nor is it discovered that the unkle, whoever he was, is with much justice ₅₂ delivered to posterity as a *false Guardian*; he seems to have done only that for which a guardian is appointed; he endeavoured to direct his niece till she should be able to direct herself. Poetry has not often been worse employed than in dignifying the amorous fury of a raving girl.

Not long after, he wrote the *Rape of the Lock*, the most airy, the most ₅₃ ingenious, and the most delightful of all his compositions, occasioned by a frolick of gallantry, rather too familiar, in which Lord Petre cut off a lock of Mrs. Arabella Fermor's hair. This, whether stealth or violence, was so much resented, that the commerce of the two families, before very friendly, was interrupted. Mr. Caryl, a gentleman who, being secretary to King James's Queen, had followed his Mistress into France, and who being the author of *Sir Solomon Single*, a comedy, and some translations, was entitled to the notice of a Wit, solicited Pope to endeavour a reconciliation by a ludicrous poem, which might bring both the parties to a better temper. In compliance with Caryl's request, though his name was for a long time marked only by the first and last letter, C—l, a poem of two cantos was written (1711), as is said, in a fortnight, and sent to the offended Lady, who liked it well enough to shew it; and, with the usual process of literary transactions, the author, dreading a surreptitious edition, was forced to publish it.

The event is said to have been such as was desired; the pacification and ₅₄ diversion of all to whom it related, except Sir *George Brown*, who complained with some bitterness that, in the character of *Sir Plume*, he was made to talk nonsense. Whether all this be true, I have some doubt; for at Paris, a few years ago, a niece of Mrs. Fermor, who presided in an English

Convent, mentioned Pope's work with very little gratitude, rather as an insult than an honour; and she may be supposed to have inherited the opinion of her family.

55   At its first appearance it was termed by Addison *merum sal.* Pope, however, saw that it was capable of improvement; and, having luckily contrived to borrow his machinery from the *Rosicrucians*, imparted the scheme with which his head was teeming to Addison, who told him that his work, as it stood, was *a delicious little thing*, and gave him no encouragement to retouch it.

56   This has been too hastily considered as an instance of Addison's jealousy; for as he could not guess the conduct of the new design, or the possibilities of pleasure comprised in a fiction of which there had been no examples, he might very reasonably and kindly persuade the author to acquiesce in his own prosperity, and forbear an attempt which he considered as an unnecessary hazard.

57   Addison's counsel was happily rejected. Pope foresaw the future efflorescence of imagery then budding in his mind, and resolved to spare no art, or industry of cultivation. The soft luxuriance of his fancy was already shooting, and all the gay varieties of diction were ready at his hand to colour and embellish it.

58   His attempt was justified by its success. The *Rape of the Lock* stands forward, in the classes of literature, as the most exquisite example of ludicrous poetry. Berkeley congratulated him upon the display of powers more truly poetical than he had shewn before; with elegance of description and justness of precepts, he had now exhibited boundless fertility of invention.

59   He always considered the intertexture of the machinery with the action as his most successful exertion of poetical art. He indeed could never afterwards produce any thing of such unexampled excellence. Those performances, which strike with wonder, are combinations of skilful genius with happy casualty; and it is not likely that any felicity, like the discovery of a new race of preternatural agents, should happen twice to the same man.

60   Of this poem the author was, I think, allowed to enjoy the praise for a long time without disturbance. Many years afterwards Dennis published some remarks upon it, with very little force, and with no effect; for the opinion of the publick was already settled, and it was no longer at the mercy of criticism.

61   About this time he published the *Temple of Fame*, which, as he tells Steele in their correspondence, he had written two years before; that is, when he was only twenty-two years old, an early time of life for so much learning and so much observation as that work exhibits.

On this poem Dennis afterwards published some remarks, of which the most reasonable is, that some of the lines represent *motion* as exhibited by *sculpture*. 62

Of the Epistle from *Eloisa to Abelard*, I do not know the date. His first inclination to attempt a composition of that tender kind arose, as Mr. Savage told me, from his perusal of Prior's *Nut-brown Maid*. How much he has surpassed Prior's work it is not necessary to mention, when perhaps it may be said with justice, that he has excelled every composition of the same kind. The mixture of religious hope and resignation gives an elevation and dignity to disappointed love, which images merely natural cannot bestow. The gloom of a convent strikes the imagination with far greater force than the solitude of a grove. 63

This piece was, however, not much his favourite in his latter years, though I never heard upon what principle he slighted it. 64

In the next year (1713) he published *Windsor Forest*; of which part was, as he relates, written at sixteen, about the same time as his Pastorals, and the latter part was added afterwards: where the addition begins, we are not told. The lines relating to the Peace confess their own date. It is dedicated to Lord Lansdowne, who was then high in reputation and influence among the Tories; and it is said, that the conclusion of the poem gave great pain to Addison, both as a poet and a politician. Reports like this are often spread with boldness very disproportionate to their evidence. Why should Addison receive any particular disturbance from the last lines of *Windsor Forest?* If contrariety of opinion could poison a politician, he would not live a day; and, as a poet, he must have felt Pope's force of genius much more from many other parts of his works. 65

The pain that Addison might feel it is not likely that he would confess; and it is certain that he so well suppressed his discontent, that Pope now thought himself his favourite; for having been consulted in the revisal of *Cato*, he introduced it by a Prologue; and, when Dennis published his Remarks, undertook not indeed to vindicate but to revenge his friend, by a *Narrative of the Frenzy of John Dennis*. 66

There is reason to believe that Addison gave no encouragement to this disingenuous hostility; for, says Pope, in a Letter to him, "indeed your opinion, that 'tis entirely to be neglected, would be my own in my own case; but I felt more warmth here than I did when I first saw his book against myself (though indeed in two minutes it made me heartily merry)." Addison was not a man on whom such cant of sensibility could make much impression. He left the pamphlet to itself, having disowned it to Dennis, and perhaps did not think Pope to have deserved much by his officiousness. 67

68   This year was printed in the *Guardian* the ironical comparison between the Pastorals of Philips and Pope; a composition of artifice, criticism, and literature, to which nothing equal will easily be found. The superiority of Pope is so ingeniously dissembled, and the feeble lines of Philips so skilfully preferred, that Steele, being deceived, was unwilling to print the paper lest Pope should be offended. Addison immediately saw the writer's design; and, as it seems, had malice enough to conceal his discovery, and to permit a publication which, by making his friend Philips ridiculous, made him for ever an enemy to Pope.

69   It appears that about this time Pope had a strong inclination to unite the art of Painting with that of Poetry, and put himself under the tuition of Jervas. He was near-sighted, and therefore not formed by nature for a painter: he tried, however, how far he could advance, and sometimes persuaded his friends to sit. A picture of Betterton, supposed to be drawn by him, was in the possession of Lord Mansfield: if this was taken from the life, he must have begun to paint earlier; for Betterton was now dead. Pope's ambition of this new art produced some encomiastick verses to Jervas, which certainly shew his power as a poet, but I have been told that they betray his ignorance of painting.

70   He appears to have regarded Betterton with kindness and esteem; and after his death published, under his name, a version into modern English of Chaucer's Prologues, and one of his Tales, which, as was related by Mr. Harte, were believed to have been the performance of Pope himself by Fenton, who made him a gay offer of five pounds, if he would shew them in the hand of Betterton.

71   The next year (1713) produced a bolder attempt, by which profit was sought as well as praise. The poems which he had hitherto written, however they might have diffused his name, had made very little addition to his fortune. The allowance which his father made him, though, proportioned to what he had, it might be liberal, could not be large; his religion hindered him from the occupation of any civil employment, and he complained that he wanted even money to buy books*.

72   He therefore resolved to try how far the favour of the publick extended, by soliciting a subscription to a version of the *Iliad*, with large notes.

73   To print by subscription was, for some time, a practice peculiar to the English. The first considerable work for which this expedient was employed is said to have been Dryden's *Virgil*; and it had been tried again with great success when the *Tatlers* were collected into volumes.

* Spence.

There was reason to believe that Pope's attempt would be successful. He 74 was in the full bloom of reputation, and was personally known to almost all whom dignity of employment or splendour of reputation had made eminent; he conversed indifferently with both parties, and never disturbed the publick with his political opinions; and it might be naturally expected, as each faction then boasted its literary zeal, that the great men, who on other occasions practised all the violence of opposition, would emulate each other in their encouragement of a poet who had delighted all, and by whom none had been offended.

With those hopes, he offered an English *Iliad* to subscribers, in six 75 volumes in quarto, for six guineas; a sum, according to the value of money at that time, by no means inconsiderable, and greater than I believe to have been ever asked before. His proposal, however, was very favourably received, and the patrons of literature were busy to recommend his undertaking, and promote his interest. Lord Oxford, indeed, lamented that such a genius should be wasted upon a work not original; but proposed no means by which he might live without it: Addison recommended caution and moderation, and advised him not to be content with the praise of half the nation, when he might be universally favoured.

The greatness of the design, the popularity of the author, and the 76 attention of the literary world, naturally raised such expectations of the future sale, that the booksellers made their offers with great eagerness; but the highest bidder was *Bernard Lintot*, who became proprietor on condition of supplying, at his own expence, all the copies which were to be delivered to subscribers, or presented to friends, and paying two hundred pounds for every volume.

Of the Quartos it was, I believe, stipulated that none should be printed 77 but for the author, that the subscription might not be depreciated; but Lintot impressed the same pages upon a small Folio, and paper perhaps a little thinner; and sold exactly at half the price, for half a guinea each volume, books so little inferior to the Quartos, that, by a fraud of trade, those Folios, being afterwards shortened by cutting away the top and bottom, were sold as copies printed for the subscribers.

Lintot printed two hundred and fifty on royal paper in Folio for two 78 guineas a volume; of the small Folio, having printed seventeen hundred and fifty copies of the first volume, he reduced the number in the other volumes to a thousand.

It is unpleasant to relate that the bookseller, after all his hopes and all his 79 liberality, was, by a very unjust and illegal action, defrauded of his profit. An edition of the English *Iliad* was printed in Holland in Duodecimo, and imported clandestinely for the gratification of those who were impatient to read what they could not yet afford to buy. This fraud could only be counteracted by an edition equally cheap and more commodious; and Lintot was compelled to contract his Folio at once into a Duodecimo, and lose the advantage of an intermediate gradation. The notes, which in the Dutch copies were placed at the end of each book, as they had been in the large volumes, were now subjoined to the text in the same page, and are therefore more easily consulted. Of this edition two thousand five hundred were first printed, and five thousand a few weeks afterwards; but indeed great numbers were necessary to produce considerable profit.

80   Pope, having now emitted his proposals, and engaged not only his own reputation, but in some degree that of his friends who patronised his subscription, began to be frighted at his own undertaking; and finding himself at first embarrassed with difficulties, which retarded and oppressed him, he was for a time timorous and uneasy; had his nights disturbed by dreams of long journeys through unknown ways, and wished, as he said, *that somebody would hang him**.

81   This misery, however, was not of long continuance; he grew by degrees more acquainted with Homer's images and expressions, and practice increased his facility of versification. In a short time he represents himself as dispatching regularly fifty verses a day, which would shew him by an easy computation the termination of his labour.

82   His own diffidence was not his only vexation. He that asks a subscription soon finds that he has enemies. All who do not encourage him defame him. He that wants money will rather be thought angry than poor, and he that wishes to save his money conceals his avarice by his malice. Addison had hinted his suspicion that Pope was too much a Tory; and some of the Tories suspected his principles because he had contributed to the *Guardian*, which was carried on by *Steele*.

83   To those who censured his politicks were added enemies yet more dangerous, who called in question his knowledge of Greek, and his qualifications for a translator of Homer. To these he made no publick opposition; but in one of his Letters escapes from them as well as he can. At an age like his, for he was not more than twenty-five, with an irregular education, and a course of life of which much seems to have passed in conversation, it is not very likely that he overflowed with Greek. But when he felt himself deficient he sought assistance; and what man of learning would refuse to help him? Minute enquiries into the force of words are less necessary in translating Homer than other poets, because his positions are general, and his representations natural, with very little dependence on local or

* Spence.

temporary customs, on those changeable scenes of artificial life, which, by mingling original with accidental notions, and crowding the mind with images which time effaces, produce ambiguity in diction, and obscurity in books. To this open display of unadulterated nature it must be ascribed, that Homer has fewer passages of doubtful meaning than any other poet either in the learned or in modern languages. I have read of a man, who being, by his ignorance of Greek, compelled to gratify his curiosity with the Latin printed on the opposite page, declared that from the rude simplicity of the lines literally rendered, he formed nobler ideas of the Homeric majesty than from the laboured elegance of polished versions.

Those literal translations were always at hand, and from them he could 84 easily obtain his author's sense with sufficient certainty; and among the readers of Homer the number is very small of those who find much in the Greek more than in the Latin, except the musick of the numbers.

If more help was wanting, he had the poetical translation of *Eobanus* 85 *Hessus*, an unwearied writer of Latin verses; he had the French Homers of *La Valterie* and *Dacier*, and the English of *Chapman, Hobbes*, and *Ogylby*. With Chapman, whose work, though now totally neglected, seems to have been popular almost to the end of the last century, he had very frequent consultations, and perhaps never translated any passage till he had read his version, which indeed he has been sometimes suspected of using instead of the original.

Notes were likewise to be provided; for the six volumes would have been 86 very little more than six pamphlets without them. What the mere perusal of the text could suggest, Pope wanted no assistance to collect or methodize; but more was necessary; many pages were to be filled, and learning must supply materials to wit and judgment. Something might be gathered from Dacier; but no man loves to be indebted to his contemporaries, and Dacier was accessible to common readers. Eustathius was therefore necessarily consulted. To read Eustathius, of whose work there was then no Latin version, I suspect Pope, if he had been willing, not to have been able; some other was therefore to be found, who had leisure as well as abilities, and he was doubtless most readily employed who would do much work for little money.

The history of the notes has never been traced. Broome, in his preface to 87 his poems, declares himself the commentator *in part upon the Iliad*; and it appears from Fenton's Letter, preserved in the Museum, that Broome was at first engaged in consulting Eustathius; but that after a time, whatever was the reason, he desisted: another man of Cambridge was them employed, who soon grew weary of the work; and a third, that was recommended by *Thirlby*, is now discovered to have been *Jortin*, a man since well known to the learned world, who complained that Pope, having accepted and approved his performance, never testified any curiosity to see him, and who professed to have forgotten the terms on which he worked. The terms which Fenton uses are very mercantile: *I think at first sight that his performance is very commendable, and have sent word for him to finish the 17th book, and to send it with his demands for his trouble. I have here enclosed the specimen; if the rest come before you return, I will keep them till I receive your order.*

88   Broome then offered his service a second time, which was probably accepted, as they had afterwards a closer correspondence. Parnell contributed the Life of Homer, which Pope found so harsh, that he took great pains in correcting it; and by his own diligence, with such help as kindness or money could procure him, in somewhat more than five years he completed his version of the *Iliad*, with the notes. He began it in 1712, his twenty-fifth year, and concluded it in 1718, his thirtieth year.

89   When we find him translating fifty lines a day, it is natural to suppose that he would have brought his work to a more speedy conclusion. The *Iliad*, containing less than sixteen thousand verses, might have been despatched in less than three hundred and twenty days by fifty verses in a day. The notes, compiled with the assistance of his mercenaries, could not be supposed to require more time than the text. According to this calculation, the progress of Pope may seem to have been slow; but the distance is commonly very great between actual performances and speculative possibility. It is natural to suppose, that as much as has been done to-day may be done to-morrow; but on the morrow some difficulty emerges, or some external impediment obstructs. Indolence, interruption, business, and pleasure, all take their turns of retardation; and every long work is lengthened by a thousand causes that can, and ten thousand that cannot, be recounted. Perhaps no extensive and multifarious performance was ever effected within the term originally fixed in the undertaker's mind. He that runs against Time, has an antagonist not subject to casualties.

90   The encouragement given to this translation, though report seems to have over-rated it, was such as the world has not often seen. The subscribers were five hundred and seventy-five. The copies for which subscriptions were given were six hundred and fifty-four; and only six hundred and sixty were printed. For those copies Pope had nothing to pay; he therefore received, including the two hundred pounds a volume, five thousand three hundred and twenty pounds four shillings, without deduction, as the books were supplied by Lintot.

91   By the success of his subscription Pope was relieved from those pecuniary distresses with which, notwithstanding his popularity, he had hitherto struggled. Lord Oxford had often lamented his disqualification for publick

employment, but never proposed a pension. While the translation of *Homer* was in its progress, Mr. Craggs, then secretary of state, offered to procure him a pension, which, at least during his ministry, might be enjoyed with secrecy. This was not accepted by Pope, who told him, however, that, if he should be pressed with want of money, he would send to him for occasional supplies. Craggs was not long in power, and was never solicited for money by Pope, who disdained to beg what he did not want.

With the product of this subscription, which he had too much discretion to squander, he secured his future life from want, by considerable annuities. The estate of the Duke of Buckingham was found to have been charged with five hundred pounds a year, payable to Pope, which doubtless his translation enabled him to purchase.   92

It cannot be unwelcome to literary curiosity, that I deduce thus minutely the history of the English *Iliad*. It is certainly the noblest version of poetry which the world has ever seen; and its publication must therefore be considered as one of the great events in the annals of Learning.   93

To those who have skill to estimate the excellence and difficulty of this great work, it must be very desirable to know how it was performed, and by what gradations it advanced to correctness. Of such an intellectual process the knowledge has very rarely been attainable; but happily there remains the original copy of the *Iliad*, which, being obtained by Bolingbroke as a curiosity, descended from him to Mallet, and is now by the solicitation of the late Dr. Maty reposited in the Museum.   94

Between this manuscript, which is written upon accidental fragments of paper, and the printed edition, there must have been an intermediate copy, that was perhaps destroyed as it returned from the press.   95

From the first copy I have procured a few transcripts, and shall exhibit first the printed lines; then, in a smaller print, those of the manuscripts, with all their variations. Those words in the small print which are given in Italicks, are cancelled in the copy, and the words placed under them adopted in their stead.   96

The beginning of the first book stands thus: 97

> The wrath of Peleus' son, the direful spring
> Of all the Grecian woes, O Goddess, sing;
> That wrath which hurl'd to Pluto's gloomy reign
> The souls of mighty chiefs untimely slain.
>
> The stern Pelides' *rage*, O Goddess, sing,
>   wrath
> Of all the woes *of Greece* the fatal spring,
>   Grecian
> That strew'd with *warriors* dead the Phrygian plain,
>   heroes

And *peopled the dark hell with heroes* slain;
  fill'd the shady hell with chiefs untimely

Whose limbs, unburied on the naked shore,
Devouring dogs and hungry vultures tore,
Since great Achilles and Atrides strove;
Such was the sovereign doom, and such the will of Jove.

Whose limbs, unburied on the hostile shore,
Devouring dogs and greedy vultures tore,
Since first *Atrides* and *Achilles* strove;
Such was the sovereign doom, and such the will of Jove.

Declare, O Muse, in what ill-fated hour
Sprung the fierce strife, from what offended Power!
Latona's son a dire contagion spread,
And heap'd the camp with mountains of the dead;
The King of Men his reverend priest defy'd,
And for the King's offence the people dy'd.

Declare, O Goddess, what offended Power
Enflam'd their *rage*, in that *ill-omen'd* hour;
       anger   fatal, hapless
Phœbus himself the *dire* debate procur'd,
         fierce
'T' avenge the wrongs his injur'd priest endur'd;
For this the God a dire infection spread,
And heap'd the camp with millions of the dead:
The King of Men the sacred Sire defy'd,
And for the King's offence the people dy'd.

For Chryses sought with costly gifts to gain
His captive daughter from the Victor's chain;
Suppliant the venerable Father stands,
Apollo's awful ensigns grace his hands,
By these he begs, and, lowly bending down,
Extends the sceptre and the laurel crown.

For Chryses sought by *presents to regain*
              costly gifts to gain
His captive daughter from the Victor's chain;
Suppliant the venerable Father stands,
Apollo's awful ensigns grac'd his hands,
By these he begs, and lowly bending down
The golden sceptre and the laurel crown,
Presents the sceptre
For these as ensigns of his God he bare,
The God that sends his golden shafts afar;
Then low on earth, the venerable man,
Suppliant before the brother kings began.

He sued to all, but chief implor'd for grace
The brother kings of Atreus' royal race;
Ye kings and warriors, may your vows be crown'd,

And Troy's proud walls lie level with the ground;
May Jove restore you, when your toils are o'er,
Safe to the pleasures of your native shore.

To all he sued, but chief implor'd for grace
The brother kings of Atreus' royal race.
Ye *sons of Atreus*, may your vows be crown'd,
    Kings and warriors
Your labours, by the Gods be all your labours crown'd;
So may the Gods your arms with conquest bless,
And Troy's proud walls lie level with the ground;
Till   *laid*
And crown your labours with deserv'd success;
May Jove restore you, when your toils are o'er,
Safe to the pleasures of your native shore.

But, oh! relieve a wretched parent's pain,
And give Chryseis to these arms again;
If mercy fail, yet let my present move,
And dread avenging Phœbus, son of Jove.

But, oh! relieve a hapless parent's pain,
And give my daughter to these arms again;
Receive my gifts; if mercy fails, yet let my present move,
And fear *the God that deals his darts around,*
        avenging Phœbus, son of Jove.

The Greeks, in shouts, their joint assent declare
The priest to reverence, and release the fair.
Not so Atrides; he, with kingly pride,
Repuls'd the sacred Sire, and thus reply'd.

He said, the Greeks their joint assent declare.
The father said, the gen'rous Greeks relent,
T'accept the ransom, and release the fair:
Revere the priest, and speak their joint assent:
Not so *the tyrant*, he, with kingly pride,
    Atrides,
Repuls'd the sacred Sire, and thus reply'd.
    [Not so the tyrant. DRYDEN.]

Of these lines, and of the whole first book, I am told that there was yet a   97*a*
former copy, more varied, and more deformed with interlineations.

The beginning of the second book varies very little from the printed   98
page, and is therefore set down without any parallel: the few slight differ-
ences do not require to be elaborately displayed.

Now pleasing sleep had seal'd each mortal eye;
Stretch'd in their tents the Grecian leaders lie;
Th' Immortals slumber'd on their thrones above,
All but the ever-watchful eye of Jove.
To honour Thetis' son he bends his care,
And plunge the Greeks in all the woes of war.

Then bids an empty phantom rise to sight,
And thus *commands* the vision of the night:
      directs
Fly hence, delusive dream, and, light as air,
To Agamemnon's royal tent repair;
Bid him in arms draw forth th' embattled train,
March all his legions to the dusty plain.
Now tell the King 'tis given him to destroy
Declare ev'n now
The lofty *walls* of wide-extended Troy;
      tow'rs
For now no more the Gods with Fate contend;
At Juno's suit the heavenly factions end.
Destruction *hovers* o'er yon devoted wall,
      hangs
And nodding Ilium waits th' impending fall.

Invocation to the Catalogue of Ships.

  Say, Virgins, seated round the throne divine,
All-knowing Goddesses! immortal Nine!
Since earth's wide regions, heaven's unmeasur'd height,
And hell's abyss, hide nothing from your sight,
(We, wretched mortals! lost in doubts below,
But guess by rumour, and but boast we know)
Oh say what heroes, fir'd by thirst of fame,
Or urg'd by wrongs, to Troy's destruction came!
To count them all, demands a thousand tongues,
A throat of brass and adamantine lungs.

  Now, Virgin Goddesses, immortal Nine!
That round Olympus' heavenly summit shine,
Who see through heaven and earth, and hell profound,
And all things know, and all things can resound;
Relate what armies sought the Trojan land,
What nations follow'd, and what chiefs command;
(For doubtful Fame distracts mankind below,
And nothing can we tell, and nothing know)
Without your aid, to count th' unnumber'd train,
A thousand mouths, a thousand tongues were vain.

Book V. *v.* i.

  But Pallas now Tydides' soul inspires,
Fills with her force, and warms with all her fires:
Above the Greeks his deathless fame to raise,
And crown her hero with distinguish'd praise,
High on his helm celestial lightnings play,
His beamy shield emits a living ray;
Th' unwearied blaze incessant streams supplies,
Like the red star that fires th' autumnal skies.

But Pallas now Tydides' soul inspires,
Fills with her *rage*, and warms with all her fires;
         force,
O'er all the Greeks decrees his fame to raise,
Above the Greeks *her warrior's* fame to raise,
         his deathless
And crown her hero with *immortal* praise:
            distinguish'd
Bright from his beamy *crest* the lightnings play,
High on   helm
From his broad buckler flash'd the living ray,
High on his helm celestial lightnings play,
His beamy shield emits a living ray.
The Goddess with her breath the flame supplies,
Bright as the star whose fires in Autumn rise;
Her breath divine thick streaming flames supplies,
Bright as the star that fires the autumnal skies:
Th' unwearied blaze incessant streams supplies,
Like the red star that fires th' autumnal skies.

When first he rears his radiant orb to sight,
And bath'd in ocean shoots a keener light.
Such glories Pallas on the chief bestow'd,
Such from his arms the fierce effulgence flow'd;
Onward she drives him furious to engage,
Where the fight burns, and where the thickest rage.

When fresh he rears his radiant orb to sight,
And gilds old Ocean with a blaze of light,
Bright as the star that fires th' autumnal skies,
Fresh from the deep, and gilds the seas and skies.
Such glories Pallas on her chief bestow'd,
Such sparkling rays from his bright armour flow'd,
Such from his arms the fierce effulgence flow'd.
Onward she drives him *headlong* to engage,
         furious
Where the *war bleeds*, and where the *fiercest* rage.
     fight burns,   thickest

The sons of Dares first the combat sought,
A wealthy priest, but rich without a fault;
In Vulcan's fane the father's days were led,
The sons to toils of glorious battle bred;

There liv'd a Trojan—Dares was his name,
The priest of Vulcan, rich, yet void of blame;
The sons of Dares first the combat sought,
A wealthy priest, but rich without a fault.

Conclusion of Book VIII. *v.* 687.

As when the moon, refulgent lamp of night,
O'er heaven's clear azure spreads her sacred light;
When not a breath disturbs the deep serene,
And not a cloud o'ercasts the solemn scene;

Around her throne the vivid planets roll,
And stars unnumber'd gild the glowing pole:
O'er the dark trees a yellower verdure shed,
And tip with silver every mountain's head;
Then shine the vales—the rocks in prospect rise,
A flood of glory bursts from all the skies;
The conscious swains, rejoicing in the sight,
Eye the blue vault, and bless the useful light.
So many flames before proud Ilion blaze,
And lighten glimmering Xanthus with their rays;
The long reflexion of the distant fires
Gleam on the walls, and tremble on the spires:
A thousand piles the dusky horrors gild,
And shoot a shady lustre o'er the field;
Full fifty guards each flaming pile attend,
Whose umber'd arms by fits thick flashes send;
Loud neigh the coursers o'er their heaps of corn,
And ardent warriors wait the rising morn.

As when in stillness of the silent night,
As when the moon in all her lustre bright,
As when the moon, refulgent lamp of night,
O'er heaven's *clear* azure *sheds* her *silver* light;
         pure   spreads   sacred
As still in air the trembling lustre stood,
And o'er its golden border shoots a flood;
When *no loose gale* disturbs the deep serene,
    not a breath
And *no dim* cloud o'ercasts the solemn scene;
    not a
Around her silver throne the planets glow,
And stars unnumber'd trembling beams bestow;
Around her throne the vivid planets roll,
And stars unnumber'd gild the glowing pole:
Clear gleams of light o'er the dark trees are seen,
           o'er the dark trees a yellow sheds,
O'er the dark trees a yellower *green* they shed,
          gleam
          verdure
And tip with silver all the *mountain* heads:
        forest
And tip with silver every mountain's head.
The vallies open, and the forests rise,
The vales appear, the rocks in prospect rise,
Then shine the vales, the rocks in prospect rise,
All Nature stands reveal'd before our eyes;
A flood of glory bursts from all the skies.
The conscious shepherd, joyful at the sight,
Eyes the blue vault, and numbers every light.

The conscious *swains rejoicing at the* sight
                shepherds gazing with delight
Eye the blue vault, and bless the *vivid* light.
                glorious
                useful
So many flames before *the navy* blaze,
                proud Ilion
And lighten glimmering Xanthus with their rays,
Wide o'er the fields to Troy extend the gleams,
And tip the distant spires with fainter beams;
The long reflexions of the distant fires
Gild the high walls, and tremble on the spires,
Gleam on the walls, and tremble on the spires;
A thousand fires at distant stations bright,
Gild the dark prospect, and dispel the night.

Of these specimens every man who has cultivated poetry, or who delights   99
to trace the mind from the rudeness of its first conceptions to the elegance of
its last, will naturally desire a greater number; but most other readers are
already tired, and I am not writing only to poets and philosophers.

The *Iliad* was published volume by volume, as the translation proceeded;   100
the four first books appeared in 1715. The expectation of this work was
undoubtedly high, and every man who had connected his name with
criticism, or poetry, was desirous of such intelligence as might enable him
to talk upon the popular topick. Halifax, who, by having been first a poet,
and then a patron of poetry, had acquired the right of being a judge, was
willing to hear some books while they were yet unpublished. Of this
rehearsal Pope afterwards gave the following account*.

"The famous Lord Halifax was rather a pretender to taste than really
possessed of it.—When I had finished the two or three first books of my
translation of the *Iliad*, that Lord desired to have the pleasure of hearing
them read at his house.—Addison, Congreve, and Garth, were there at the
reading. In four or five places, Lord Halifax stopt me very civilly, and with a
speech each time, much of the same kind, 'I beg your pardon, Mr. Pope; but
there is something in that passage that does not quite please me.—Be so
good as to mark the place, and consider it a little at your leisure.—I'm sure
you can give it a little turn.' I returned from Lord Halifax's with Dr. Garth,
in his chariot; and, as we were going along, was saying to the Doctor, that my
Lord had laid me under a good deal of difficulty by such loose and general
observations; that I had been thinking over the passages almost ever since,
and could not guess at what it was that offended his Lordship in either of
them. Garth laughed heartily at my embarrassment; said, I had not been

* Spence.

long enough acquainted with Lord Halifax to know his way yet; that I need not puzzle myself about looking those places over and over, when I got home. 'All you need do (says he) is to leave them just as they are; call on Lord Halifax two or three months hence, thank him for his kind observations on those passages, and then read them to him as altered. I have known him much longer than you have, and will be answerable for the event.' I followed his advice; waited on Lord Halifax some time after; said, I hoped he would find his objections to those passages removed; read them to him exactly as they were at first: and his Lordship was extremely pleased with them, and cried out, *Ay, now they are perfectly right: nothing can be better.*"

101   It is seldom that the great or the wise suspect that they are despised or cheated. Halifax, thinking this a lucky opportunity of securing immortality, made some advances of favour and some overtures of advantage to Pope, which he seems to have received with sullen coldness. All our knowledge of this transaction is derived from a single Letter (Dec. 1, 1714), in which Pope says, "I am obliged to you, both for the favours you have done me, and those you intend me. I distrust neither your will nor your memory, when it is to do good; and if I ever become troublesome or solicitous, it must not be out of expectation, but out of gratitude. Your Lordship may cause me to live agreeably in the town, or contentedly in the country, which is really all the difference I set between an easy fortune and a small one. It is indeed a high strain of generosity in you to think of making me easy all my life, only because I have been so happy as to divert you some few hours; but, if I may have leave to add it is because you think me no enemy to my native country, there will appear a better reason; for I must of consequence be very much (as I sincerely am) yours &c."

102   These voluntary offers, and this faint acceptance, ended without effect. The patron was not accustomed to such frigid gratitude, and the poet fed his own pride with the dignity of independence. They probably were suspicious of each other. Pope would not dedicate till he saw at what rate his praise was valued; he would be *troublesome out of gratitude, not expectation.* Halifax thought himself entitled to confidence; and would give nothing, unless he knew what he should receive. Their commerce had its beginning in hope of praise on one side, and of money on the other, and ended because Pope was less eager of money than Halifax of praise. It is not likely that Halifax had any personal benevolence to Pope; it is evident that Pope looked on Halifax with scorn and hatred.

103   The reputation of this great work failed of gaining him a patron; but it deprived him of a friend. Addison and he were now at the head of poetry and criticism; and both in such a state of elevation, that, like the two rivals in the Roman state, one could no longer bear an equal, nor the other a

superior. Of the gradual abatement of kindness between friends, the beginning is often scarcely discernible by themselves, and the process is continued by petty provocations, and incivilities sometimes peevishly returned, and sometimes contemptuously neglected, which would escape all attention but that of pride, and drop from any memory but that of resentment. That the quarrel of those two wits should be minutely deduced, is not to be expected from a writer to whom, as Homer says, *nothing but rumour has reached, and who has no personal knowledge.*

Pope doubtless approached Addison, when the reputation of their wit   104 first brought them together, with the respect due to a man whose abilities were acknowledged, and who, having attained that eminence to which he was himself aspiring, had in his hands the distribution of literary fame. He paid court with sufficient diligence by his Prologue to *Cato*, by his abuse of Dennis, and, with praise yet more direct, by his poem on the *Dialogues on Medals*, of which the immediate publication was then intended. In all this there was no hypocrisy; for he confessed that he found in Addison something more pleasing than in any other man.

It may be supposed, that as Pope saw himself favoured by the world, and   105 more frequently compared his own powers with those of others, his confidence increased, and his submission lessened; and that Addison felt no delight from the advances of a young wit, who might soon contend with him for the highest place. Every great man, of whatever kind be his greatness, has among his friends those who officiously, or insidiously, quicken his attention to offences, heighten his disgust, and stimulate his resentment. Of such adherents Addison doubtless had many, and Pope was now too high to be without them.

From the emission and reception of the Proposals for the *Iliad*, the   106 kindness of Addison seems to have abated. Jervas the painter once pleased himself (Aug. 20, 1714) with imagining that he had re-established their friendship; and wrote to Pope that Addison once suspected him of too close a confederacy with Swift, but was now satisfied with his conduct. To this Pope answered, a week after, that his engagements to Swift were such as his services in regard to the subscription demanded, and that the Tories never put him under the necessity of asking leave to be grateful. *But*, says he, *as Mr. Addison must be* the judge *in what regards himself, and seems to be no very just one in regard to me, so I must own to you I expect nothing but civility from him.* In the same Letter he mentions Philips, as having been busy to kindle animosity between them; but, in a Letter to Addison, he expresses some consciousness of behaviour, inattentively deficient in respect.

Of Swift's industry in promoting the subscription there remains the   107 testimony of Kennet, no friend to either him or Pope.

"Nov. 2, 1713, Dr. Swift came into the coffee-house, and had a bow from every body but me, who, I confess, could not but despise him. When I came to the anti-chamber to wait, before prayers, Dr. Swift was the principal man of talk and business, and acted as master of requests.—Then he instructed a young nobleman that the *best Poet in England* was *Mr. Pope* (a papist), who had begun a translation of *Homer* into English verse, for which *he must have them all subscribe*; for, says he, the author *shall not* begin to print till *I have* a thousand guineas for him."

108   About this time it is likely that Steele, who was, with all his political fury, good-natured and officious, procured an interview between these angry rivals, which ended in aggravated malevolence. On this occasion, if the reports be true, Pope made his complaint with frankness and spirit, as a man undeservedly neglected or opposed; and Addison affected a contemptuous unconcern, and, in a calm even voice, reproached Pope with his vanity, and, telling him of the improvements which his early works had received from his own remarks and those of Steele, said, that he, being now engaged in publick business, had no longer any care for his poetical reputation; nor had any other desire, with regard to Pope, than that his should not, by too much arrogance, alienate the publick.

109   To this Pope is said to have replied with great keenness and severity, upbraiding Addison with perpetual dependance, and with the abuse of those qualifications which he had obtained at the publick cost, and charging him with mean endeavours to obstruct the progress of rising merit. The contest rose so high, that they parted at last without any interchange of civility.

110   The first volume of *Homer* was (1715) in time published; and a rival version of the first *Iliad*, for rivals the time of their appearance inevitably made them, was immediately printed, with the name of Tickell. It was soon perceived that, among the followers of Addison, Tickell had the preference, and the criticks and poets divided into factions. *I*, says Pope, *have the town, that is, the mob, on my side; but it is not uncommon for the smaller party to supply by industry what it wants in numbers.—I appeal to the people as my rightful judges, and, while they are not inclined to condemn me, shall not fear the high-flyers at Button's*. This opposition he immediately imputed to Addison, and complained of it in terms sufficiently resentful to Craggs, their common friend.

111   When Addison's opinion was asked, he declared the versions to be both good, but Tickell's the best that had ever been written; and sometimes said that they were both good, but that Tickell had more of *Homer*.

112   Pope was now sufficiently irritated; his reputation and his interest were at hazard. He once intended to print together the four versions of Dryden,

Maynwaring, Pope, and Tickell, that they might be readily compared, and fairly estimated. This design seems to have been defeated by the refusal of Tonson, who was the proprietor of the other three versions.

Pope intended at another time a rigorous criticism of Tickell's transla- 113 tion, and had marked a copy, which I have seen, in all places that appeared defective. But while he was thus meditating defence or revenge, his adversary sunk before him without a blow; the voice of the publick was not long divided, and the preference was universally given to Pope's performance.

He was convinced, by adding one circumstance to another, that the other 114 translation was the work of Addison himself; but if he knew it in Addison's life-time, it does not appear that he told it. He left his illustrious antagonist to be punished by what has been considered as the most painful of all reflections, the remembrance of a crime perpetrated in vain.

The other circumstances of their quarrel were thus related by Pope*. 115

"Philips seemed to have been encouraged to abuse me in coffee-houses, and conversations: and Gildon wrote a thing about Wycherley, in which he had abused both me and my relations very grossly. Lord Warwick himself told me one day, that it was in vain for me to endeavour to be well with Mr. Addison; that his jealous temper would never admit of a settled friendship between us: and, to convince me of what he had said, assured me, that Addison had encouraged Gildon to publish those scandals, and had given him ten guineas after they were published. The next day, while I was heated with what I had heard, I wrote a Letter to Mr. Addison, to let him know that I was not unacquainted with this behaviour of his; that if I was to speak severely of him, in return for it, it should not be in such a dirty way, that I should rather tell him, himself, fairly of his faults, and allow his good qualities; and that it should be something in the following manner: I then adjoined the first sketch of what has since been called my satire on Addison. Mr. Addison used me very civilly ever after."

The verses on Addison, when they were sent to Atterbury, were con- 116 sidered by him as the most excellent of Pope's performances; and the writer was advised, since he knew where his strength lay, not to suffer it to remain unemployed.

This year (1715) being, by the subscription, enabled to live more by 117 choice, having persuaded his father to sell their estate at Binfield, he purchased, I think only for his life, that house at Twickenham to which his residence afterwards procured so much celebration, and removed thither with his father and mother.

* Spence.

118   Here he planted the vines and the quincunx which his verses mention; and being under the necessity of making a subterraneous passage to a garden on the other side of the road, he adorned it with fossile bodies, and dignified it with the title of a grotto; a place of silence and retreat, from which he endeavoured to persuade his friends and himself that cares and passions could be excluded.

119   A grotto is not often the wish or pleasure of an Englishman, who has more frequent need to solicit than exclude the sun; but Pope's excavation was requisite as an entrance to his garden, and, as some men try to be proud of their defects, he extracted an ornament from an inconvenience, and vanity produced a grotto where necessity enforced a passage. It may be frequently remarked of the studious and speculative, that they are proud of trifles, and that their amusements seem frivolous and childish; whether it be that men conscious of great reputation think themselves above the reach of censure, and safe in the admission of negligent indulgences, or that mankind expect from elevated genius an uniformity of greatness, and watch its degradation with malicious wonder; like him who having followed with his eye an eagle into the clouds, should lament that she ever descended to a perch.

120   While the volumes of his *Homer* were annually published, he collected his former works (1717) into one quarto volume, to which he prefixed a Preface, written with great spriteliness and elegance, which was afterwards reprinted, with some passages subjoined that he at first omitted; other marginal additions of the same kind he made in the later editions of his poems. Waller remarks, that poets lose half their praise, because the reader knows not what they have blotted. Pope's voracity of fame taught him the art of obtaining the accumulated honour both of what he had published, and of what he had suppressed.

121   In this year his father died suddenly, in his seventy-fifth year, having passed twenty-nine years in privacy. He is not known but by the character which his son has given him. If the money with which he retired was all gotten by himself, he had traded very successfully in times when sudden riches were rarely attainable.

122   The publication of the *Iliad* was at last completed in 1720. The splendor and success of this work raised Pope many enemies, that endeavoured to depreciate his abilities; Burnet, who was afterwards a Judge of no mean reputation, censured him in a piece called *Homerides* before it was published; Ducket likewise endeavoured to make him ridiculous. Dennis was the perpetual persecutor of all his studies. But, whoever his criticks were, their writings are lost, and the names which are preserved, are preserved in the *Dunciad*.

In this disastrous year (1720) of national infatuation, when more riches 123 than Peru can boast were expected from the South Sea, when the contagion of avarice tainted every mind, and even poets panted after wealth, Pope was seized with the universal passion, and ventured some of his money. The stock rose in its price; and he for a while thought himself *the Lord of thousands*. But this dream of happiness did not last long, and he seems to have waked soon enough to get clear with the loss only of what he once thought himself to have won, and perhaps not wholly of that.

Next year he published some select poems of his friend Dr. Parnell, with 124 a very elegant Dedication to the Earl of Oxford; who, after all his struggles and dangers, then lived in retirement, still under the frown of a victorious faction, who could take no pleasure in hearing his praise.

He gave the same year (1721) an edition of *Shakspeare*. His name was now 125 of so much authority, that Tonson thought himself entitled, by annexing it, to demand a subscription of six guineas for Shakspeare's plays in six quarto volumes; nor did his expectation much deceive him; for of seven hundred and fifty which he printed, he dispersed a great number at the price proposed. The reputation of that edition indeed sunk afterwards so low, that one hundred and forty copies were sold at sixteen shillings each.

On this undertaking, to which Pope was induced by a reward of two 126 hundred and seventeen pounds twelve shillings, he seems never to have reflected afterwards without vexation; for Theobald, a man of heavy diligence, with very slender powers, first, in a book called *Shakespeare Restored*, and then in a formal edition, detected his deficiencies with all the insolence of victory; and, as he was now high enough to be feared and hated, Theobald had from others all the help that could be supplied, by the desire of humbling a haughty character.

From this time Pope became an enemy to editors, collaters, commenta- 127 tors, and verbal criticks; and hoped to persuade the world, that he miscarried in this undertaking only by having a mind too great for such minute employment.

Pope in his edition undoubtedly did many things wrong, and left many 128 things undone; but let him not be defrauded of his due praise. He was the first that knew, at least the first that told, by what helps the text might be improved. If he inspected the early editions negligently, he taught others to be more accurate. In his Preface he expanded with great skill and elegance the character which had been given of Shakspeare by Dryden; and he drew the publick attention upon his works, which, though often mentioned, had been little read.

Soon after the appearance of the *Iliad*, resolving not to let the general 129 kindness cool, he published proposals for a translation of the *Odyssey*, in five volumes, for five guineas. He was willing, however, now to have associates in his labour, being either weary with toiling upon another's thoughts, or having heard, as Ruffhead relates, that Fenton and Broome had already begun the work, and liking better to have them confederates than rivals.

130 In the patent, instead of saying that he had *translated* the *Odyssey*, as he had said of the *Iliad*, he says that he had *undertaken* a translation; and in the proposals the subscription is said to be not solely for his own use, but for that of *two of his friends who have assisted him in this work*.

131 In 1723, while he was engaged in this new version, he appeared before the Lords at the memorable trial of Bishop Atterbury, with whom he had lived in great familiarity, and frequent correspondence. Atterbury had honestly recommended to him the study of the popish controversy, in hope of his conversion; to which Pope answered in a manner that cannot much recommend his principles, or his judgement. In questions and projects of learning, they agreed better. He was called at the trial to give an account of Atterbury's domestick life, and private employment, that it might appear how little time he had left for plots. Pope had but few words to utter, and in those few he made several blunders.

132 His Letters to Atterbury express the utmost esteem, tenderness, and gratitude: *perhaps*, says he, *it is not only in this world that I may have cause to remember the Bishop of Rochester*. At their last interview in the Tower, Atterbury presented him with a Bible.

133 Of the *Odyssey* Pope translated only twelve books; the rest were the work of Broome and Fenton: the notes were written wholly by Broome, who was not over-liberally rewarded. The Public was carefully kept ignorant of the several shares; and an account was subjoined at the conclusion, which is now known not to be true.

134 The first copy of Pope's books, with those of Fenton, are to be seen in the Museum. The parts of Pope are less interlined than the *Iliad*, and the latter books of the *Iliad* less than the former. He grew dexterous by practice, and every sheet enabled him to write the next with more facility. The books of Fenton have very few alterations by the hand of Pope. Those of Broome have not been found; but Pope complained, as it is reported, that he had much trouble in correcting them.

135 His contract with Lintot was the same as for the *Iliad*, except that only one hundred pounds were to be paid him for each volume. The number of subscribers was five hundred and seventy-four, and of copies eight hundred and nineteen; so that his profit, when he had paid his assistants, was still very considerable. The work was finished in 1725, and from that time he resolved to make no more translations.

The sale did not answer Lintot's expectation, and he then pretended to discover something of fraud in Pope, and commenced, or threatened, a suit in Chancery. 136

On the English *Odyssey* a criticism was published by Spence, at that time Prelector of Poetry at Oxford; a man whose learning was not very great, and whose mind was not very powerful. His criticism, however, was commonly just; what he thought, he thought rightly; and his remarks were recommended by his coolness and candour. In him Pope had the first experience of a critick without malevolence, who thought it as much his duty to display beauties as expose faults; who censured with respect, and praised with alacrity. 137

With this criticism Pope was so little offended, that he sought the acquaintance of the writer, who lived with him from that time in great familiarity, attended him in his last hours, and compiled memorials of his conversation. The regard of Pope recommended him to the great and powerful, and he obtained very valuable preferments in the Church. 138

Not long after Pope was returning home from a visit in a friend's coach, which, in passing a bridge, was overturned into the water; the windows were closed, and being unable to force them open, he was in danger of immediate death, when the postilion snatched him out by breaking the glass, of which the fragments cut two of his fingers in such a manner, that he lost their use. 139

Voltaire, who was then in England, sent him a Letter of Consolation. He had been entertained by Pope at his table, where he talked with so much grossness that Mrs. Pope was driven from the room. Pope discovered, by a trick, that he was a spy for the Court, and never considered him as a man worthy of confidence. 140

He soon afterwards (1727) joined with Swift, who was then in England, to publish three volumes of Miscellanies, in which amongst other things he inserted the *Memoirs of a Parish Clerk*, in ridicule of Burnet's importance in his own History, and a *Debate upon Black and White Horses*, written in all the formalities of a legal process by the assistance, as is said, of Mr. Fortescue, afterwards Master of the Rolls. Before these Miscellanies is a preface signed by Swift and Pope, but apparently written by Pope; in which he makes a ridiculous and romantick complaint of the robberies committed upon authors by the clandestine seizure and sale of their papers. He tells, in tragick strains, how *the cabinets of the Sick and the closets of the Dead have been broke open and ransacked*; as if those violences were often committed for papers of uncertain and accidental value, which are rarely provoked by real treasures; as if epigrams and essays were in danger where gold and diamonds are safe. A cat, hunted for his 141 musk, is, according to Pope's account, but the emblem of a wit winded by booksellers.

142   His complaint, however, received some attestation; for the same year the Letters written by him to Mr. Cromwell, in his youth, were sold by Mrs. Thomas to Curll, who printed them.

143   In these Miscellanies was first published the *Art of Sinking in Poetry*, which, by such a train of consequences as usually passes in literary quarrels, gave in a short time, according to Pope's account, occasion to the *Dunciad*.

144   In the following year (1728) he began to put Atterbury's advice in practice; and shewed his satirical powers by publishing the *Dunciad*, one of his greatest and most elaborate performances, in which he endeavoured to sink into contempt all the writers by whom he had been attacked, and some others whom he thought unable to defend themselves.

145   At the head of the Dunces he placed poor Theobald, whom he accused of ingratitude; but whose real crime was supposed to be that of having revised *Shakspeare* more happily than himself. This satire had the effect which he intended, by blasting the characters which it touched. Ralph, who, unnecessarily interposing in the quarrel, got a place in a subsequent edition, complained that for a time he was in danger of starving, as the booksellers had no longer any confidence in his capacity.

146   The prevalence of this poem was gradual and slow: the plan, if not wholly new, was little understood by common readers. Many of the allusions required illustration; the names were often expressed only by the initial and final letters, and, if they had been printed at length, were such as few had known or recollected. The subject itself had nothing generally interesting, for whom did it concern to know that one or another scribbler was a dunce? If therefore it had been possible for those who were attacked to conceal their pain and their resentment, the *Dunciad* might have made its way very slowly in the world.

147   This, however, was not to be expected: every man is of importance to himself, and therefore, in his own opinion, to others; and, supposing the world already acquainted with all his pleasures and his pains, is perhaps the first to publish injuries or misfortunes, which had never been known unless related by himself, and at which those that hear them will only laugh; for no man sympathises with the sorrows of vanity.

148   The history of the *Dunciad* is very minutely related by Pope himself, in a Dedication which he wrote to Lord Middlesex in the name of Savage.

"I will relate the war of the *Dunces* (for so it has been commonly called), which began in the year 1727, and ended in 1730.

"When Dr. Swift and Mr. Pope thought it proper, for reasons specified in the Preface to their Miscellanies, to publish such little pieces of theirs as had casually got abroad, there was added to them the *Treatise of the Bathos*, or the *Art of Sinking in Poetry*. It happened that in one chapter of this piece the several species of bad poets were ranged in classes, to which were prefixed almost all the letters of the alphabet (the greatest part of them at random); but such was the number of poets eminent in that art, that some one or other took every letter to himself: all fell into so violent a fury, that, for half a year or more, the common newspapers (in most of which they had some property, as being hired writers) were filled with the most abusive falshoods and scurrilities they could possibly devise. A liberty no way to be wondered at in those people, and in those papers, that for many years, during the uncontrouled license of the press, had aspersed almost all the great characters of the age; and this with impunity, their own persons and names being utterly secret and obscure.

"This gave Mr. Pope the thought, that he had now some opportunity of doing good, by detecting and dragging into light these common enemies of mankind; since to invalidate this universal slander, it sufficed to shew what contemptible men were the authors of it. He was not without hopes, that, by manifesting the dulness of those who had only malice to recommend them, either the booksellers would not find their account in employing them, or the men themselves, when discovered, want courage to proceed in so unlawful an occupation. This it was that gave birth to the *Dunciad*; and he thought it an happiness, that, by the late flood of slander on himself, he had acquired such a peculiar right over their names as was necessary to this design.

"On the 12th of March, 1729, at St. James's, that poem was presented to the King and Queen (who had before been pleased to read it) by the right honourable Sir Robert Walpole; and some days after the whole impression was taken and dispersed by several noblemen and persons of the first distinction.

"It is certainly a true observation, that no people are so impatient of censure as those who are the greatest slanderers, which was wonderfully exemplified on this occasion. On the day the book was first vended, a crowd of authors besieged the shop; intreaties, advices, threats of law and battery, nay cries of treason, were all employed to hinder the coming-out of the *Dunciad*: on the other side, the booksellers and hawkers made as great efforts to procure it. What could a few poor authors do against so great a majority as the publick? There was no stopping a torrent with a finger, so out it came.

"Many ludicrous circumstances attended it. The *Dunces* (for by this name they were called) held weekly clubs, to consult of hostilities against the author: one wrote a Letter to a great minister, assuring him Mr. Pope was the greatest enemy the government had; and another bought his image in clay, to execute him in effigy, with which sad sort of satisfactions the gentlemen were a little comforted.

"Some false editions of the book having an owl in their frontispiece, the true one, to distinguish it, fixed in its stead an ass laden with authors. Then another surreptitious one being printed with the same ass, the new edition in octavo returned for distinction to the owl again. Hence arose a great contest of booksellers against booksellers, and advertisements against advertisements; some recommending the edition of the owl, and others the edition of the ass; by which names they came to be distinguished, to the great honour also of the gentlemen of the *Dunciad*."

149   Pope appears by this narrative to have contemplated his victory over the *Dunces* with great exultation; and such was his delight in the tumult which he had raised, that for a while his natural sensibility was suspended, and he read reproaches and invectives without emotion, considering them only as the necessary effects of that pain which he rejoiced in having given.

150   It cannot however be concealed that, by his own confession, he was the aggressor; for nobody believes that the letters in the *Bathos* were placed at random; and it may be discovered that, when he thinks himself concealed, he indulges the common vanity of common men, and triumphs in those distinctions which he had affected to despise. He is proud that his book was presented to the King and Queen by the right honourable Sir Robert Walpole; he is proud that they had read it before; he is proud that the edition was taken off by the nobility and persons of the first distinction.

151   The edition of which he speaks was, I believe, that, which by telling in the text the names and in the notes the characters of those whom he had satirised, was made intelligible and diverting. The criticks had now declared their approbation of the plan, and the common reader began to like it without fear; those who were strangers to petty literature, and therefore unable to decypher initials and blanks, had now names and persons brought within their view; and delighted in the visible effect of those shafts of malice, which they had hitherto contemplated, as shot into the air.

152   Dennis, upon the fresh provocation now given him, renewed the enmity which had for a time been appeased by mutual civilities; and published remarks, which he had till then suppressed, upon the *Rape of the Lock*. Many more grumbled in secret, or vented their resentment in the newspapers by epigrams or invectives.

153   Ducket, indeed, being mentioned as loving Burnet with *pious passion*, pretended that his moral character was injured, and for some time declared his resolution to take vengeance with a cudgel. But Pope appeased him, by changing *pious passion* to *cordial friendship*, and by a note, in which

he vehemently disclaims the malignity of meaning imputed to the first expression.

Aaron Hill, who was represented as diving for the prize, expostulated 154 with Pope in a manner so much superior to all mean solicitation, that Pope was reduced to sneak and shuffle, sometimes to deny, and sometimes to apologize; he first endeavours to wound, and is then afraid to own that he meant a blow.

The *Dunciad*, in the complete edition, is addressed to Dr. Swift: of the 155 notes, part was written by Dr. Arbuthnot, and an apologetical Letter was prefixed, signed by Cleland, but supposed to have been written by Pope.

After this general war upon dulness, he seems to have indulged himself 156 awhile in tranquillity; but his subsequent productions prove that he was not idle. He published (1731) a poem on *Taste*, in which he very particularly and severely criticises the house, the furniture, the gardens, and the entertainments of *Timon*, a man of great wealth and little taste. By *Timon* he was universally supposed, and by the Earl of Burlington, to whom the poem is addressed, was privately said, to mean the Duke of Chandos; a man perhaps too much delighted with pomp and show, but of a temper kind and beneficent, and who had consequently the voice of the publick in his favour.

A violent outcry was therefore raised against the ingratitude and trea- 157 chery of Pope, who was said to have been indebted to the patronage of Chandos for a present of a thousand pounds, and who gained the opportunity of insulting him by the kindness of his invitation.

The receipt of the thousand pounds Pope publickly denied; but from the 158 reproach which the attack on a character so amiable brought upon him, he tried all means of escaping. The name of Cleland was again employed in an apology, by which no man was satisfied; and he was at last reduced to shelter his temerity behind dissimulation, and endeavour to make that disbelieved which he never had confidence openly to deny. He wrote an exculpatory letter to the Duke, which was answered with great magnanimity, as by a man who accepted his excuse without believing his professions. He said, that to have ridiculed his taste, or his buildings, had been an indifferent action in another man; but that in Pope, after the reciprocal kindness that had been exchanged between them, it had been less easily excused.

Pope, in one of his Letters, complaining of the treatment which his poem 159 had found, *owns that such criticks can intimidate him, nay almost persuade him to write no more, which is a compliment this age deserves*. The man who threatens the world is always ridiculous; for the world can easily go on without him, and in a short time will cease to miss him. I have heard of an idiot, who used to revenge his vexations by lying all night upon the bridge. *There is nothing*, says Juvenal, *that a man will not believe in his own favour*.

Pope had been flattered till he thought himself one of the moving powers in the system of life. When he talked of laying down his pen, those who sat round him intreated and implored, and self-love did not suffer him to suspect that they went away and laughed.

160   The following year deprived him of Gay, a man whom he had known early, and whom he seemed to love with more tenderness than any other of his literary friends. Pope was now forty-four years old; an age at which the mind begins less easily to admit new confidence, and the will to grow less flexible, and when therefore the departure of an old friend is very acutely felt.

161   In the next year he lost his mother, not by an unexpected death, for she had lasted to the age of ninety-three; but she did not die unlamented. The filial piety of Pope was in the highest degree amiable and exemplary; his parents had the happiness of living till he was at the summit of poetical reputation, till he was at ease in his fortune, and without a rival in his fame, and found no diminution of his respect or tenderness. Whatever was his pride, to them he was obedient; and whatever was his irritability, to them he was gentle. Life has, among its soothing and quiet comforts, few things better to give than such a son.

162   One of the passages of Pope's life, which seems to deserve some enquiry, was a publication of Letters between him and many of his friends, which falling into the hands of *Curll*, a rapacious bookseller of no good fame, were by him printed and sold. This volume containing some Letters from noblemen, Pope incited a prosecution against him in the House of Lords for breach of privilege, and attended himself to stimulate the resentment of his friends. *Curll* appeared at the bar, and, knowing himself in no great danger, spoke of Pope with very little reverence. *He has*, said Curll, *a knack at versifying, but in prose I think myself a match for him.* When the orders of the House were examined, none of them appeared to have been infringed; Curll went away triumphant, and Pope was left to seek some other remedy.

163   Curll's account was, that one evening a man in a clergyman's gown, but with a lawyer's band, brought and offered to sale a number of printed volumes, which he found to be Pope's epistolary correspondence; that he asked no name, and was told none, but gave the price demanded, and thought himself authorised to use his purchase to his own advantage.

164   That Curll gave a true account of the transaction, it is reasonable to believe, because no falshood was ever detected; and when some years afterwards I mentioned it to Lintot, the son of Bernard, he declared his opinion to be, that Pope knew better than any body else how Curll obtained the copies, because another parcel was at the same time sent to himself, for

which no price had ever been demanded, as he made known his resolution not to pay a porter, and consequently not to deal with a nameless agent.

Such care had been taken to make them publick, that they were sent at 165 once to two booksellers; to Curll, who was likely to seize them as a prey, and to Lintot, who might be expected to give Pope information of the seeming injury. Lintot, I believe, did nothing; and Curll did what was expected. That to make them publick was the only purpose may be reasonably supposed, because the numbers offered to sale by the private messengers shewed that hope of gain could not have been the motive of the impression.

It seems that Pope, being desirous of printing his Letters, and not 166 knowing how to do, without imputation of vanity, what has in this country been done very rarely, contrived an appearance of compulsion; that when he could complain that his Letters were surreptitiously published, he might decently and defensively publish them himself.

Pope's private correspondence, thus promulgated, filled the nation with 167 praises of his candour, tenderness, and benevolence, the purity of his purposes, and the fidelity of his friendship. There were some Letters which a very good or a very wise man would wish suppressed; but, as they had been already exposed, it was impracticable now to retract them.

From the perusal of those Letters, Mr. Allen first conceived the desire of 168 knowing him; and with so much zeal did he cultivate the friendship which he had newly formed, that when Pope told his purpose of vindicating his own property by a genuine edition, he offered to pay the cost.

This however Pope did not accept; but in time solicited a subscription for 169 a Quarto volume, which appeared (1737) I believe, with sufficient profit. In the Preface he tells that his Letters were reposited in a friend's library, said to be the Earl of Oxford's, and that the copy thence stolen was sent to the press. The story was doubtless received with different degrees of credit. It may be suspected that the Preface to the Miscellanies was written to prepare the publick for such an incident; and to strengthen this opinion, James Worsdale, a painter, who was employed in clandestine negotiations, but whose veracity was very doubtful, declared that he was the messenger who carried, by Pope's direction, the books to Curll.

When they were thus published and avowed, as they had relation to 170 recent facts, and persons either then living or not yet forgotten, they may be supposed to have found readers ; but as the facts were minute, and the characters being either private or literary, were little known, or little regarded, they awakened no popular kindness or resentment: the book never became much the subject of conversation; some read it as contemporary history, and some perhaps as a model of epistolary language; but those who read it did not talk of it. Not much therefore was added by it to fame or envy; nor do I remember that it produced either publick praise, or publick censure.

171 It had however, in some degree, the recommendation of novelty. Our language has few Letters, except those of statesmen. Howel indeed, about a century ago, published his Letters, which are commended by *Morhoff*, and which alone of his hundred volumes continue his memory. Loveday's Letters were printed only once; those of Herbert and Suckling are hardly known. Mrs. Phillips's [*Orinda's*] are equally neglected; and those of Walsh seem written as exercises, and were never sent to any living mistress or friend. Pope's epistolary excellence had an open field; he had no English rival, living or dead.

172 Pope is seen in this collection as connected with the other contemporary wits, and certainly suffers no disgrace in the comparison; but it must be remembered, that he had the power of favouring himself: he might have originally had publication in his mind, and have written with care, or have afterwards selected those which he had most happily conceived, or most diligently laboured; and I know not whether there does not appear something more studied and artificial in his productions than the rest, except one long Letter by Bolingbroke, composed with all the skill and industry of a professed author. It is indeed not easy to distinguish affectation from habit; he that has once studiously formed a style, rarely writes afterwards with complete ease. Pope may be said to write always with his reputation in his head; Swift perhaps like a man who remembered that he was writing to Pope; but Arbuthnot like one who lets thoughts drop from his pen as they rise into his mind.

173 Before these Letters appeared, he published the first part of what he persuaded himself to think a system of Ethicks, under the title of an *Essay on Man*; which, if his Letter to Swift (of Sept. 14, 1725) be rightly explained by the commentator, had been eight years under his consideration, and of which he seems to have desired the success with great solicitude. He had now many open and doubtless many secret enemies. The *Dunces* were yet smarting with the war; and the superiority which he publickly arrogated, disposed the world to wish his humiliation.

174 All this he knew, and against all this he provided. His own name, and that of his friend to whom the work is inscribed, were in the first editions carefully suppressed; and the poem, being of a new kind, was ascribed to one or another, as favour determined, or conjecture wandered; it was given, says Warburton, to every man, except him only who could write it. Those who like only when they like the author, and who are under the dominion of a name, condemned it; and those admired it who are willing to scatter praise at random, which while it is unappropriated excites no envy. Those friends

of Pope, that were trusted with the secret, went about lavishing honours on the new-born poet, and hinting that Pope was never so much in danger from any former rival.

To those authors whom he had personally offended, and to those whose 175 opinion the world considered as decisive, and whom he suspected of envy or malevolence, he sent his essay as a present before publication, that they might defeat their own enmity by praises, which they could not afterwards decently retract.

With these precautions, in 1733 was published the first part of the *Essay* 176 *on Man*. There had been for some time a report that Pope was busy upon a System of Morality; but this design was not discovered in the new poem, which had a form and a title with which its readers were unacquainted. Its reception was not uniform; some thought it a very imperfect piece, though not without good lines. While the author was unknown, some, as will always happen, favoured him as an adventurer, and some censured him as an intruder; but all thought him above neglect; the sale increased, and editions were multiplied.

The subsequent editions of the first Epistle exhibited two memorable 177 corrections. At first, the poet and his friend

> Expatiate free o'er all this scene of man,
> A mighty maze *of walks without a plan*.

For which he wrote afterwards,

> A mighty maze, *but not without a plan:*

for, if there were no plan, it was in vain to describe or to trace the maze. The other alteration was of these lines;

> And spite of pride, *and in thy reason's spite*,
> One truth is clear, whatever is, is right:

but having afterwards discovered, or been shewn, that the *truth* which subsisted *in spite of reason* could not be very *clear*, he substituted

> And spite of pride, *in erring reason's spite*.

To such oversights will the most vigorous mind be liable, when it is employed at once upon argument and poetry.

The second and third Epistles were published; and Pope was, I believe, 178 more and more suspected of writing them; at last, in 1734, he avowed the fourth, and claimed the honour of a moral poet.

In the conclusion it is sufficiently acknowledged, that the doctrine of the 179 *Essay on Man* was received from Bolingbroke, who is said to have ridiculed

Pope, among those who enjoyed his confidence, as having adopted and advanced principles of which he did not perceive the consequence, and as blindly propagating opinions contrary to his own. That those communications had been consolidated into a scheme regularly drawn, and delivered to Pope, from whom it returned only transformed from prose to verse, has been reported, but hardly can be true. The Essay plainly appears the fabrick of a poet: what Bolingbroke supplied could be only the first principles; the order, illustration, and embellishments must all be Pope's.

180   These principles it is not my business to clear from obscurity, dogmatism, or falsehood; but they were not immediately examined; philosophy and poetry have not often the same readers; and the Essay abounded in splendid amplifications and sparkling sentences, which were read and admired, with no great attention to their ultimate purpose; its flowers caught the eye, which did not see what the gay foliage concealed, and for a time flourished in the sunshine of universal approbation. So little was any evil tendency discovered, that, as innocence is unsuspicious, many read it for a manual of piety.

181   Its reputation soon invited a translator. It was first turned into French prose, and afterwards by Resnel into verse. Both translations fell into the hands of Crousaz, who first, when he had the version in prose, wrote a general censure, and afterwards reprinted Resnel's version, with particular remarks upon every paragraph.

182   Crousaz was a professor of Switzerland, eminent for his treatise of Logick, and his *Examen de Pyrrhonisme*, and, however little known or regarded here, was no mean antagonist. His mind was one of those in which philosophy and piety are happily united. He was accustomed to argument and disquisition, and perhaps was grown too desirous of detecting faults; but his intentions were always right, his opinions were solid, and his religion pure.

183   His incessant vigilance for the promotion of piety disposed him to look with distrust upon all metaphysical systems of Theology, and all schemes of virtue and happiness purely rational; and therefore it was not long before he was persuaded that the positions of Pope, as they terminated for the most part in natural religion, were intended to draw mankind away from revelation, and to represent the whole course of things as a necessary concatenation of indissoluble fatality; and it is undeniable, that in many passages a religious eye may easily discover expressions not very favourable to morals, or to liberty.

184   About this time Warburton began to make his appearance in the first ranks of learning. He was a man of vigorous faculties, a mind fervid and vehement, supplied by incessant and unlimited enquiry, with wonderful extent and

variety of knowledge, which yet had not oppressed his imagination, nor clouded his perspicacity. To every work he brought a memory full fraught, together with a fancy fertile of original combinations, and at once exerted the powers of the scholar, the reasoner, and the wit. But his knowledge was too multifarious to be always exact, and his pursuits were too eager to be always cautious. His abilities gave him an haughty confidence, which he disdained to conceal or mollify; and his impatience of opposition disposed him to treat his adversaries with such contemptuous superiority as made his readers commonly his enemies, and excited against the advocate the wishes of some who favoured the cause. He seems to have adopted the Roman Emperor's determination, *oderint dum metuant*; he used no allurements of gentle language, but wished to compel rather than persuade.

His style is copious without selection, and forcible without neatness; he 185 took the words that presented themselves: his diction is coarse and impure, and his sentences are unmeasured.

He had, in the early part of his life, pleased himself with the notice of 186 inferior wits, and corresponded with the enemies of Pope. A Letter was produced, when he had perhaps himself forgotten it, in which he tells *Concanen*, "Dryden *I observe borrows for want of leasure, and* Pope *for want of genius:* Milton *out of pride, and* Addison *out of modesty.*" And when Theobald published *Shakespeare*, in opposition of Pope, the best notes were supplied by Warburton.

But the time was now come when Warburton was to change his opinion, 187 and Pope was to find a defender in him who had contributed so much to the exaltation of his rival.

The arrogance of Warburton excited against him every artifice of offence, 188 and therefore it may be supposed that his union with Pope was censured as hypocritical inconstancy; but surely to think differently, at different times, of poetical merit, may be easily allowed. Such opinions are often admitted, and dismissed, without nice examination. Who is there that has not found reason for changing his mind about questions of greater importance?

Warburton, whatever was his motive, undertook, without solicitation, to 189 rescue Pope from the talons of Crousaz, by freeing him from the imputation of favouring fatality, or rejecting revelation; and from month to month continued a vindication of the *Essay on Man*, in the literary journal of that time called *The Republick of Letters*.

Pope, who probably began to doubt the tendency of his own work, was 190 glad that the positions, of which he perceived himself not to know the full meaning, could by any mode of interpretation be made to mean well. How much he was pleased with his gratuitous defender, the following Letter evidently shews:

"SIR,   March 24, 1743.

I have just received from Mr. R. two more of your Letters. It is in the greatest hurry imaginable that I write this; but I cannot help thanking you in particular for your third Letter, which is so extremely clear, short, and full, that I think Mr. Crousaz ought never to have another answer, and deserved not so good an one, I can only say, you do him too much honour, and me too much right, so odd as the expression seems; for you have made my system as clear as I ought to have done, and could not. It is indeed the same system as mine, but illustrated with a ray of your own, as they say our natural body is the same still when it is glorified. I am sure I like it better than I did before, and so will every man else. I know I meant just what you explain; but I did not explain my own meaning so well as you. You understand me as well as I do myself; but you express me better than I could express myself. Pray accept the sincerest acknowledgements. I cannot but wish these Letters were put together in one Book, and intend (with your leave) to procure a translation of part, at least, of all of them into French; but I shall not proceed a step without your consent and opinion, &c."

191   By this fond and eager acceptance of an exculpatory comment, Pope testified that, whatever might be the seeming or real import of the principles which he had received from Bolingbroke, he had not intentionally attacked religion; and Bolingbroke, if he meant to make him without his own consent an instrument of mischief, found him now engaged with his eyes open on the side of truth.

192   It is known that Bolingbroke concealed from Pope his real opinions. He once discovered them to Mr. Hooke, who related them again to Pope, and was told by him that he must have mistaken the meaning of what he heard; and Bolingbroke, when Pope's uneasiness incited him to desire an explanation, declared that Hooke had misunderstood him.

193   Bolingbroke hated Warburton, who had drawn his pupil from him; and a little before Pope's death they had a dispute, from which they parted with mutual aversion.

194   From this time Pope lived in the closest intimacy with his commentator, and amply rewarded his kindness and his zeal; for he introduced him to Mr. Murray, by whose interest he became preacher at Lincoln's Inn, and to Mr. Allen, who gave him his niece and his estate, and by consequence a bishoprick. When he died, he left him the property of his works; a legacy which may be reasonably estimated at four thousand pounds.

195   Pope's fondness for the *Essay on Man* appeared by his desire of its propagation. Dobson, who had gained reputation by his version of Prior's *Solomon*, was employed by him to translate it into Latin verse, and was for that purpose some time at Twickenham; but he left his work, whatever was

the reason, unfinished; and, by Benson's invitation, undertook the longer task of *Paradise Lost*. Pope then desired his friend to find a scholar who should turn his Essay into Latin prose; but no such performance has ever appeared.

Pope lived at this time *among the great*, with that reception and respect to   196
which his works entitled him, and which he had not impaired by any private misconduct or factious partiality. Though Bolingbroke was his friend, Walpole was not his enemy; but treated him with so much consideration as, at his request, to solicit and obtain from the French Minister an abbey for Mr. Southcot, whom he considered himself as obliged to reward, by this exertion of his interest, for the benefit which he had received from his attendance in a long illness.

It was said, that, when the Court was at Richmond, Queen Caroline had   197
declared her intention to visit him. This may have been only a careless effusion, thought on no more: the report of such notice, however, was soon in many mouths; and, if I do not forget or misapprehend Savage's account, Pope, pretending to decline what was not yet offered, left his house for a time, not, I suppose, for any other reason than lest he should be thought to stay at home in expectation of an honour which would not be conferred. He was therefore angry at Swift, who represents him as *refusing the visits of a Queen*, because he knew that what had never been offered, had never been refused.

Beside the general system of morality supposed to be contained in the   198
Essay on Man, it was his intention to write distinct poems upon the different duties or conditions of life; one of which is the Epistle to Lord Bathurst (1733) on the *Use of Riches*, a piece on which he declared great labour to have been bestowed*.

Into this poem some incidents are historically thrown, and some known   199
characters are introduced, with others of which it is difficult to say how far they are real or fictitious; but the praise of *Kyrl*, the *Man of Ross*, deserves particular examination, who, after a long and pompous enumeration of his publick works and private charities, is said to have diffused all those blessings from *five hundred a year*. Wonders are willing told, and willingly heard. The truth is, that *Kyrl* was a man of known integrity, and active benevolence, by whose solicitation the wealthy were persuaded to pay contributions to his charitable schemes; this influence he obtained by an example of liberality exerted to the utmost extent of his power, and was thus enabled to give more than he had. This account *Mr. Victor* received from

* Spence.

the minister of the place, and I have preserved it, that the praise of a good man being made more credible, may be more solid. Narrations of romantick and impracticable virtue will be read with wonder, but that which is unattainable is recommended in vain; that good may be endeavoured, it must be shewn to be possible.

200   This is the only piece in which the author has given a hint of his religion, by ridiculing the ceremony of burning the pope, and by mentioning with some indignation the inscription on the Monument.

201   When this poem was first published, the dialogue, having no letters of direction, was perplexed and obscure. Pope seems to have written with no very distinct idea; for he calls that an *Epistle to Bathurst*, in which Bathurst is introduced as speaking.

202   He afterwards (1734) inscribed to Lord Cobham his *Characters of Men*, written with close attention to the operations of the mind and modifications of life. In this poem he has endeavoured to establish and exemplify his favourite theory of the *Ruling Passion*, by which he means an original direction of desire to some particular object, an innate affection which gives all action a determinate and invariable tendency, and operates upon the whole system of life, either openly, or more secretly by the intervention of some accidental or subordinate propension.

203   Of any passion, thus innate and irresistible, the existence may reasonably be doubted. Human characters are by no means constant; men change by change of place, of fortune, of acquaintance; he who is at one time a lover of pleasure, is at another a lover of money. Those indeed who attain any excellence, commonly spend life in one pursuit; for excellence is not often gained upon easier terms. But to the particular species of excellence men are directed, not by an ascendant planet or predominating humour, but by the first book which they read, some early conversation which they heard, or some accident which excited ardour and emulation.

204   It must be at least allowed that this *ruling Passion*, antecedent to reason and observation, must have an object independent on human contrivance; for there can be no natural desire of artificial good. No man therefore can be born, in the strict acceptation, a lover of money; for he may be born where money does not exist; nor can he be born, in a moral sense, a lover of his country; for society, politically regulated, is a state contradistinguished from a state of nature; and any attention to that coalition of interests which makes the happiness of a country, is possible only to those whom enquiry and reflection have enabled to comprehend it.

205   This doctrine is in itself pernicious as well as false: its tendency is to produce the belief of a kind of moral predestination, or over-ruling principle which cannot be resisted; he that admits it, is prepared to comply with

every desire that caprice or opportunity shall excite, and to flatter himself that he submits only to the lawful dominion of Nature, in obeying the resistless authority of his *ruling Passion*.

Pope has formed his theory with so little skill, that, in the examples by which he illustrates and confirms it, he has confounded, passions, appetites, and habits. 206

To the *Characters of Men* he added soon after, in an Epistle supposed to have been addressed to Martha Blount, but which the last edition has taken from her, the *Characters of Women*. This poem, which was laboured with great diligence, and in the author's opinion with great success, was neglected at its first publication, as the commentator supposes, because the publick was informed by an advertisement, that it contained *no Character drawn from the Life*; an assertion which Pope probably did not expect or wish to have been believed, and which he soon gave his readers sufficient reason to distrust, by telling them in a note, that the work was imperfect, because part of his subject was *Vice too high* to be yet exposed. 207

The time however soon came, in which it was safe to display the Dutchess of Marlborough under the name of *Atossa*; and her character was inserted with no great honour to the writer's gratitude. 208

He published from time (between 1730 and 1740) Imitations of different poems of Horace, generally with his name, and once as was suspected without it. What he was upon moral principles ashamed to own, he ought to have suppressed. Of these pieces it is useless to settle the dates, as they had seldom much relation to the times, and perhaps had been long in his hands. 209

This mode of imitation, in which the ancients are familiarised, by adapting their sentiments to modern topicks, by making Horace say of Shakspeare what he originally said of Ennius, and accommodating his satires on Pantolabus and Nomentanus to the flatterers and prodigals of our own time, was first practised in the reign of Charles the Second by Oldham and Rochester, at least I remember no instances more ancient. It is a kind of middle composition between translation and original design, which pleases when the thoughts are unexpectedly applicable, and the parallels lucky. It seems to have been Pope's favourite amusement; for he has carried it further than any former poet. 210

He published likewise a revival, in smoother numbers, of Dr. Donne's Satires, which was recommended to him by the Duke of Shrewsbury and the Earl of Oxford. They made no great impression on the publick. Pope seems to have known their imbecillity, and therefore suppressed them while he was yet contending to rise in reputation, but ventured them when he thought their deficiencies more likely to be imputed to Donne than to himself. 211

212   The Epistle to Dr. Arbuthnot, which seems to be derived in its first design from Boileau's Address *à son Esprit*, was published in January 1735, about a month before the death of him to whom it is inscribed. It is to be regretted that either honour or pleasure should have been missed by Arbuthnot; a man estimable for his learning, amiable for his life, and venerable for his piety.

213   Arbuthnot was a man of great comprehension, skilful in his profession, versed in the sciences, acquainted with ancient literature, and able to animate his mass of knowledge by a bright and active imagination; a scholar with great brilliancy of wit; a wit, who, in the crowd of life, retained and discovered a noble ardour of religious zeal.

214   In this poem Pope seems to reckon with the publick. He vindicates himself from censures; and with dignity, rather than arrogance, enforces his own claims to kindness and respect.

215   Into this poem are interwoven several paragraphs which had been before printed as a fragment, and among them the satirical lines upon Addison, of which the last couplet has been twice corrected. It was at first,

> Who would not smile if such a man there be?
> Who would not laugh if Addison were he?

Then,

> Who would not grieve if such a man there be?
> Who would not laugh if Addison were he?

At last it is,

> Who but must laugh if such a man there be?
> Who would not weep if Atticus were he?

216   He was at this time at open war with Lord Hervey, who had distinguished himself as a steady adherent to the Ministry; and, being offended with a contemptuous answer to one of his pamphlets, had summoned Pulteney to a duel. Whether he or Pope made the first attack, perhaps cannot now be easily known: he had written an invective against Pope, whom he calls, *Hard as thy heart, and as thy birth obscure*; and hints that his father was a *hatter*. To this Pope wrote a reply in verse and prose: the verses are in this poem; and the prose, though it was never sent, is printed among his Letters, but to a cool reader of the present time exhibits nothing but tedious malignity.

217   His last Satires, of the general kind, were two Dialogues, named from the year in which they were published *Seventeen Hundred and Thirty-eight*. In these poems many are praised and many are reproached. Pope was then

entangled in the opposition; a follower of the Prince of Wales, who dined at his house, and the friend of many who obstructed and censured the conduct of the Ministers. His political partiality was too plainly shewn; he forgot the prudence with which he passed, in his earlier years, uninjured and unoffending through much more violent conflicts of faction.

In the first Dialogue, having an opportunity of praising Allen of Bath, he asked his leave to mention him as a man not illustrious by any merit of his ancestors, and called him in his verses *low-born Allen*. Men are seldom satisfied with praise introduced or followed by any mention of defect. Allen seems not to have taken any pleasure in his epithet, which was afterwards softened into *humble Allen*. 218

In the second Dialogue he took some liberty with one of the *Foxes*, among others; which *Fox*, in a reply to Lyttelton, took an opportunity of repaying, by reproaching him with the friendship of a lampooner, who scattered his ink without fear or decency, and against whom he hoped the resentment of the Legislature would quickly be discharged. 219

About this time Paul Whitehead, a small poet, was summoned before the Lords for a poem called *Manners*, together with Dodsley his publisher. Whitehead, who hung loose upon society, sculked and escaped; but Dodsley's shop and family made his appearance necessary. He was, however, soon dismissed; and the whole process was probably intended rather to intimidate Pope than to punish Whitehead. 220

Pope never afterwards attempted to join the patriot with the poet, nor drew his pen upon statesmen. That he desisted from his attempts of reformation is imputed, by his commentator, to his despair of prevailing over the corruption of the time. He was not likely to have been ever of opinion that the dread of his satire would countervail the love of power or of money; he pleased himself with being important and formidable, and gratified sometimes his pride, and sometimes his resentment; till at last he began to think he should be more safe, if he were less busy. 221

The *Memoirs of Scriblerus*, published about this time, extend only to the first book of a work, projected in concert by Pope, Swift, and Arbuthnot, who used to meet in the time of Queen Anne, and denominated themselves the *Scriblerus Club*. Their purpose was to censure the abuses of learning by a fictitious Life of an infatuated scholar. They were dispersed; the design was never completed; and Warburton laments its miscarriage, as an event very disastrous to polite letters. 222

If the whole may be estimated by this specimen, which seems to be the production of Arbuthnot, with a few touches perhaps by Pope, the want of more will not be much lamented; for the follies which the writer ridicules are so little practised, that they are not known; nor can the satire be 223 understood but by the learned: he raises phantoms of absurdity, and then drives them away. He cures diseases that were never felt.

224   For this reason this joint production of three great writers has never obtained any notice from mankind; it has been little read, or when read has been forgotten, as no man could be wiser, better, or merrier, by remembering it.

225   The design cannot boast of much originality; for, besides its general resemblance to *Don Quixote*, there will be found in it particular imitations of the History of Mr. *Oufle*.

226   Swift carried so much of it into Ireland as supplied him with hints for his *Travels*; and with those the world might have been contented, though the rest had been suppressed.

227   Pope had sought for images and sentiments in a region not known to have been explored by many other of the English writers; he had consulted the modern writers of Latin poetry, a class of authors whom Boileau endeavoured to bring into contempt, and who are too generally neglected. Pope, however, was not ashamed of their acquaintance, nor ungrateful for the advantages which he might have derived from it. A small selection from the Italians who wrote in Latin had been published at London, about the latter end of the last century, by a man who concealed his name, but whom his Preface shews to have been well qualified for his undertaking. This collection Pope amplified by more than half, and (1740) published it in two volumes, but injuriously omitted his predecessor's preface. To these books, which had nothing but the mere text, no regard was paid, the authors were still neglected, and the editor was neither praised nor censured.

228   He did not sink into idleness; he had planned a work, which he considered as subsequent to his *Essay on Man*, of which he has given this account to Dr. Swift.

"March 25, 1736.

"If ever I write any more Epistles in verse, one of them shall be addressed to you. I have long concerted it, and begun it; but I would make what bears your name as finished as my last work ought to be, that is to say, more finished than any of the rest. The subject is large, and will divide into four Epistles, which naturally follow the *Essay on Man*, viz. 1. Of the Extent and Limits of Human Reason and Science. 2. A View of the useful and therefore attainable, and of the unuseful and therefore unattainable Arts. 3. Of the Nature, Ends, Application, and Use of different Capacities. 4. Of the Use of *Learning*, of the Science of the *World*, and of *Wit*. It will conclude with a satire against the Misapplication of all these, exemplified by Pictures, Characters, and Examples."

This work in its full extent, being now afflicted with an asthma, and   229
finding the powers of life gradually declining, he had no longer courage to
undertake; but, from the materials which he had provided, he added, at
Warburton's request, another book to the *Dunciad*, of which the design is to
ridicule such studies as are either hopeless or useless, as either pursue what
is unattainable, or what, if it be attained, is of no use.

When this book was printed (1742) the laurel had been for some time   230
upon the head of Cibber; a man whom it cannot be supposed that Pope
could regard with much kindness or esteem, though in one of the Imitations
of *Horace* he has liberally enough praised the *Careless Husband*. In the
Dunciad, among other worthless scribblers, he had mentioned Cibber;
who, in his *Apology*, complains of the great poet's unkindness as more
injurious, *because*, says he, *I never have offended him*.

It might have been expected that Pope should have been, in some degree,   231
mollified by this submissive gentleness; but no such consequence appeared.
Though he condescended to commend Cibber once, he mentioned him
afterwards contemptuously in one of his Satires, and again in his Epistle to
Arbuthnot; and in the fourth book of the *Dunciad* attacked him with
acrimony, to which the provocation is not easily discoverable. Perhaps he
imagined that, in ridiculing the Laureat, he satirised those by whom the
laurel had been given, and gratified that ambitious petulance with which he
affected to insult the great.

The severity of this satire left Cibber no longer any patience. He had   232
confidence enough in his own powers to believe that he could disturb the
quiet of his adversary, and doubtless did not want instigators, who, without
any care about the victory, desired to amuse themselves by looking on the
contest. He therefore gave the town a pamphlet, in which he declares his
resolution from that time never to bear another blow without returning it,
and to tire out his adversary by perseverance, if he cannot conquer him by
strength.

The incessant and unappeasable malignity of Pope he imputes to a very   233
distant cause. After the *Three Hours after Marriage* had been driven off the
stage, by the offence which the mummy and crocodile gave the audience,
while the exploded scene was yet fresh in memory, it happened that Cibber
played *Bayes* in the *Rehearsal*; and, as it had been usual to enliven the part
by the mention of any recent theatrical transactions, he said, that he once
thought to have introduced his lovers disguised in a Mummy and a Crocodile. "This," says he, "was received with loud claps, which indicated
contempt of the play." Pope, who was behind the scenes, meeting him as
he left the stage, attacked him, as he says, with all the virulence of a *Wit out
of his senses*; to which he replied, "that he would take no other notice of what

was said by so particular a man than to declare, that, as often as he played that part, he would repeat the same provocation."

234   He shews his opinion to be, that Pope was one of the authors of the play which he so zealously defended; and adds an idle story of Pope's behaviour at a tavern.

235   The pamphlet was written with little power of thought of language, and, if suffered to remain without notice, would have been very soon forgotten. Pope had now been enough acquainted with human life to know, if his passion had not been too powerful for his understanding, that, from a contention like his with Cibber, the world seeks nothing but diversion, which is given at the expence of the higher character. When Cibber lampooned Pope, curiosity was excited; what Pope would say of Cibber nobody enquired, but in hope that Pope's asperity might betray his pain and lessen his dignity.

236   He should therefore have suffered the pamphlet to flutter and die, without confessing that it stung him. The dishonour of being shewn as Cibber's antagonist could never be compensated by the victory. Cibber had nothing to lose; when Pope had exhausted all his malignity upon him, he would rise in the esteem both of his friends and his enemies. Silence only could have made him despicable; the blow which did not appear to be felt, would have been struck in vain.

237   But Pope's irascibility prevailed, and he resolved to tell the whole English world that he was at war with Cibber; and to shew that he thought him no common adversary, he prepared no common vengeance; he published a new edition of the *Dunciad*, in which he degraded *Theobald* from his painful pre-eminence, and enthroned *Cibber* in his stead. Unhappily the two heroes were of opposite characters, and Pope was unwilling to lose what he had already written; he has therefore depraved his poem by giving to Cibber the old books, the cold pedantry and sluggish pertinacity of Theobald.

238   Pope was ignorant enough of his own interest, to make another change, and introduced Osborne contending for the prize among the booksellers. Osborne was a man intirely destitute of shame, without sense of any disgrace but that of poverty. He told me, when he was doing that which raised Pope's resentment, that he should be put into the *Dunciad*; but he had the fate of *Cassandra*; I gave no credit to his prediction, till in time I saw it accomplished. The shafts of satire were directed equally in vain against Cibber and Osborne; being repelled by the impenetrable impudence of one, and deadened by the impassive dulness of the other. Pope confessed his own pain by his anger; but he gave no pain to those who had provoked him. He was able to hurt none but himself; by transferring the same ridicule from one to another, he destroyed its efficacy; for, by shewing that what he had

said of one he was ready to say of another, he reduced himself to the insignificance of his own magpye, who from his cage calls cuckold at a venture.

Cibber, according to his engagement, repaid the *Dunciad* with another pamphlet, which, Pope said, *would be as good as a dose of hartshorn to him*; but his tongue and his heart were at variance. I have heard Mr. Richardson relate, that he attended his father the painter on a visit, when one of Cibber's pamphlets came into the hands of Pope, who said, *These things are my diversion*. They sat by him while he perused it, and saw his features writhen with anguish; and young Richardson said to his father, when they returned, that he hoped to be preserved from such diversion as had been that day the lot of Pope. 239

From this time, finding his diseases more oppressive, and his vital powers gradually declining, he no longer strained his faculties with any original composition, nor proposed any other employment for his remaining life than the revisal and correction of his former works; in which he received advice and assistance from Warburton, whom he appears to have trusted and honoured in the highest degree. 240

He laid aside his Epick Poem, perhaps without much loss to mankind; for his hero was *Brutus* the Trojan, who, according to a ridiculous fiction, established a colony in Britain. The subject therefore was of the fabulous age; the actors were a race upon whom imagination has been exhausted, and attention wearied, and to whom the mind will not easily be recalled, when it is invited in blank verse, which Pope had adopted with great imprudence, and, I think, without due consideration of the nature of our language. The sketch is, at least in part, preserved by Ruffhead; by which it appears, that Pope was thoughtless enough to model the names of his heroes with terminations not consistent with the time or country in which he places them. 241

He lingered through the next year; but perceived himself, as he expresses it, *going down the hill*. He had for at least five years been afflicted with an asthma, and other disorders, which his physicians were unable to relieve. Towards the end of his life he consulted Dr. Thomson, a man who had, by large promises, and free censures of the common practice of physick, forced himself up into sudden reputation. Thomson declared his distemper to be a dropsy, and evacuated part of the water by tincture of jalap; but confessed that his belly did not subside. Thomson had many enemies, and Pope was persuaded to dismiss him. 242

While he was yet capable of amusement and conversation, as he was one day sitting in the air with Lord Bolingbroke and Lord Marchmont, he saw his favourite Martha Blount at the bottom of the terrace, and asked Lord 243

Bolingbroke to go and hand her up. Bolingbroke, not liking his errand, crossed his legs, and sat still; but Lord Marchmont, who was younger and less captious, waited on the Lady; who, when he came to her, asked, *What, is he not dead yet?* She is said to have neglected him, with shameful unkindness, in the latter time of his decay; yet, of the little which he had to leave, she had a very great part. Their acquaintance began early; the life of each was pictured on the other's mind; their conversation therefore was endearing, for when they met, there was an immediate coalition of congenial notions. Perhaps he considered her unwillingness to approach the chamber of sickness as female weakness, or human frailty; perhaps he was conscious to himself of peevishness and impatience, or, though he was offended by her inattention, might yet consider her merit as overbalancing her fault; and, if he had suffered his heart to be alienated from her, he could have found nothing that might fill her place; he could have only shrunk within himself; it was too late to transfer his confidence or fondness.

244   In May 1744, his death was approaching*; on the sixth, he was all day delirious, which he mentioned four days afterwards as a sufficient humiliation of the vanity of man; he afterwards complained of seeing things as through a curtain, and in false colours; and one day, in the presence of Dodsley, asked what arm it was that came out from the wall. He said that his greatest inconvenience was inability to think.

245   Bolingbroke sometimes wept over him in this state of helpless decay; and being told by Spence, that Pope, at the intermission of his deliriousness, was always saying something kind either of his present or absent friends, and that his humanity seemed to have survived his understanding, answered, *It has so.* And added, *I never in my life knew a man that had so tender a heart for his particular friends, or more general friendship for mankind.* At another time he said, *I have known Pope these thirty years, and value myself more in his friendship than*—his grief then suppressed his voice.

246   Pope expressed undoubting confidence of a future state. Being asked by his friend Mr. Hooke, a papist, whether he would not die like his father and mother, and whether a priest should not be called, he answered, *I do not think it essential, but it will be very right; and I thank you for putting me in mind of it.*

247   In the morning, after the priest had given him the last sacraments, he said, "There is nothing that is meritorious but virtue and friendship, and indeed friendship itself is only a part of virtue."

248   He died in the evening of the thirtieth day of May, 1744, so placidly, that the attendants did not discern the exact time of his expiration. He was

* Spence.

buried at Twickenham, near his father and mother, where a monument has been erected to him by his commentator, the Bishop of Gloucester.

He left the care of his papers to his executors, first to Lord Bolingbroke, 249 and if he should not be living to the Earl of Marchmont, undoubtedly expecting them to be proud of the trust, and eager to extend his fame. But let no man dream of influence beyond his life. After a decent time Dodsley the bookseller went to solicit preference as the publisher, and was told that the parcel had not been yet inspected; and whatever was the reason, the world has been disappointed of what was *reserved for the next age*.

He lost, indeed, the favour of Bolingbroke by a kind of posthumous 250 offence. The political pamphlet called *The Patriot King* had been put into his hands that he might procure the impression of a very few copies, to be distributed according to the author's direction among his friends, and Pope assured him that no more had been printed than were allowed; but, soon after his death, the printer brought and resigned a complete edition of fifteen hundred copies, which Pope had ordered him to print, and to retain in secret. He kept, as was observed, his engagement to Pope better than Pope had kept it to his friend; and nothing was known of the transaction, till, upon the death of his employer, he thought himself obliged to deliver the books to the right owner, who, with great indignation, made a fire in his yard, and delivered the whole impression to the flames.

Hitherto nothing had been done which was not naturally dictated by 251 resentment of violated faith; resentment more acrimonious, as the violator had been more loved or more trusted. But here the anger might have stopped; the injury was private, and there was little danger from the example.

Bolingbroke, however, was not yet satisfied; his thirst of vengeance 252 incited him to blast the memory of the man over whom he had wept in his last struggles; and he employed Mallet, another friend of Pope, to tell the tale to the publick, with all its aggravations. Warburton, whose heart was warm with his legacy, and tender by the recent separation, thought it proper for him to interpose; and undertook, not indeed to vindicate the action, for breach of trust has always something criminal, but to extenuate it by an apology. Having advanced, what cannot be denied, that moral obliquity is made more or less excusable by the motives that produce it, he enquires what evil purpose could have induced Pope to break his promise. He could not delight his vanity by usurping the work, which, though not sold in shops, had been shewn to a number more than sufficient to preserve the author's claim; he could not gratify his avarice; for he could not sell his plunder till Bolingbroke was dead; and even then, if the copy was left to another, his fraud would be defeated, and if left to himself, would be useless.

253   Warburton therefore supposes, with great appearance of reason, that the irregularity of his conduct proceeded wholly from his zeal for Bolingbroke, who might perhaps have destroyed the pamphlet, which Pope thought it his duty to preserve, even without its author's approbation. To this apology an answer was written in a *Letter to the most impudent man living.*

254   He brought some reproach upon his own memory by the petulant and contemptuous mention made in his will of Mr. Allen, and an affected repayment of his benefactions. Mrs. Blount, as the known friend and favourite of Pope, had been invited to the house of Allen, where she comported herself with such indecent arrogance, that she parted from Mrs. Allen in a state of irreconcileable dislike, and the door was for ever barred against her. This exclusion she resented with so much bitterness as to refuse any legacy from Pope, unless he left the world with a disavowal of obligation to Allen. Having been long under her dominion, now tottering in the decline of life, and unable to resist the violence of her temper, or, perhaps with the prejudice of a lover, persuaded that she had suffered improper treatment, he complied with her demand, and polluted his will with female resentment. Allen accepted the legacy, which he gave to the Hospital at Bath; observing that Pope was always a bad accomptant, and that if to 150*l.* he had put a cypher more, he had come nearer to the truth.

255   THE person of Pope is well known not to have been formed by the nicest model. He has, in his account of the *Little Club*, compared himself to a spider, and by another is described as protuberant behind and before. He is said to have been beautiful in his infancy; but he was of a constitution originally feeble and weak; and as bodies of a tender frame are easily distorted, his deformity was probably in part the effect of his application. His stature was so low, that, to bring him to a level with common tables, it was necessary to raise his seat. But his face was not displeasing, and his eyes were animated and vivid.

256   By natural deformity, or accidental distortion, his vital functions were so much disordered, that his life was a *long disease.* His most frequent assailant was the headach, which he used to relieve by inhaling the steam of coffee, which he very frequently required.

257   Most of what can be told concerning his petty peculiarities was communicated by a female domestick of the Earl of Oxford, who knew him perhaps after the middle of life. He was then so weak as to stand in perpetual need of female attendance; extremely sensible of cold, so that he wore a kind of fur doublet, under a shirt of very coarse warm linen with fine sleeves. When he rose, he was invested in boddice made of stiff canvass, being scarce able to hold himself erect till they were laced, and he then put on a flannel

waistcoat. One side was contracted. His legs were so slender, that he enlarged their bulk with three pair of stockings, which were drawn on and off by the maid; for he was not able to dress or undress himself, and neither went to bed nor rose without help. His weakness made it very difficult for him to be clean.

His hair had fallen almost all away; and he used to dine sometimes with Lord Oxford, privately, in a velvet cap. His dress of ceremony was black with a tye-wig, and a little sword. 258

The indulgence and accommodation which his sickness required, had taught him all the unpleasing and unsocial qualities of a valetudinary man. He expected that every thing should give way to his ease or humour, as a child, whose parents will not hear her cry, has an unresisted dominion in the nursery. 259

> C'est que l'enfant toûjours est homme,
> C'est que l'homme est toûjours enfant.

When he wanted to sleep he *nodded in company*; and once slumbered at his own table while the Prince of Wales was talking of poetry.

The reputation which his friendship gave, procured him many invitations; but he was a very troublesome inmate. He brought no servant, and had so many wants, that a numerous attendance was scarcely able to supply them. Wherever he was, he left no room for another, because he exacted the attention, and employed the activity of the whole family. His errands were so frequent and frivolous, that the footmen in time avoided and neglected him; and the Earl of Oxford discharged some of the servants for their resolute refusal of his messages. The maids, when they had neglected their business, alleged that they had been employed by Mr. Pope. One of his constant demands was of coffee in the night, and to the woman that waited on him in his chamber he was very burthensome; but he was careful to recompense her want of sleep; and Lord Oxford's servant declared, that in a house where her business was to answer his call, she would not ask for wages. 260

He had another fault, easily incident to those who, suffering much pain, think themselves entitled to whatever pleasures they can snatch. He was too indulgent to his appetite; he loved meat highly seasoned and of strong taste; and, at the intervals of the table, amused himself with biscuits and dry conserves. If he sat down to a variety of dishes, he would oppress his stomach with repletion, and though he seemed angry when a dram was offered him, did not forbear to drink it. His friends, who knew the avenues to his heart, pampered him with presents of luxury, which he did not suffer to stand neglected. The death of great men is not always proportioned to the lustre of their lives. Hannibal, says Juvenal, did not perish by a javelin or a 261 sword; the slaughters of Cannæ were revenged by a ring. The death of Pope was imputed by some of his friends to a silver saucepan, in which it was his delight to heat potted lampreys.

262   That he loved too well to eat, is certain; but that his sensuality shortened his life will not be hastily concluded, when it is remembered that a conformation so irregular lasted six and fifty years, notwithstanding such pertinacious diligence of study and meditation.

263   In all his intercourse with mankind, he had great delight in artifice, and endeavoured to attain all his purposes by indirect and unsuspected methods. *He hardly drank tea without a stratagem.* If, at the house of his friends, he wanted any accommodation, he was not willing to ask for it in plain terms, but would mention it remotely as something convenient; though, when it was procured, he soon made it appear for whose sake it had been recommended. Thus he teized Lord Orrery till he obtained a screen. He practised his arts on such small occasions, that Lady Bolingbroke used to say, in a French phrase, that *he plaid the politician about cabbages and turnips.* His unjustifiable impression of the *Patriot King*, as it can be imputed to no particular motive, must have proceeded from his general habit of secrecy and cunning; he caught an opportunity of a sly trick, and pleased himself with the thought of outwitting Bolingbroke.

264   In familiar or convivial conversation, it does not appear that he excelled. He may be said to have resembled Dryden, as being not one that was distinguished by vivacity in company. It is remarkable, that, so near his time, so much should be known of what he has written, and so little of what he has said: traditional memory retains no sallies of raillery, nor sentences of observation; nothing either pointed or solid, either wise or merry. One apophthegm only stands upon record. When an objection raised against his inscription for Shakspeare was defended by the authority of *Patrick*, he replied—*horresco referens*— that *he would allow the publisher of a Dictionary to know the meaning of a single word, but not of two words put together.*

265   He was fretful, and easily displeased, and allowed himself to be capriciously resentful. He would sometimes leave Lord Oxford silently, no one could tell why, and was to be courted back by more letters and messages than the footmen were willing to carry. The table was indeed infested by Lady Mary Wortley, who was the friend of Lady Oxford, and who, knowing his peevishness, could by no intreaties be restrained from contradicting him, till their disputes were sharpened to such asperity, that one or the other quitted the house.

266   He sometimes condescended to be jocular with servants or inferiors; but by no merriment, either of others or his own, was he ever seen excited to laughter.

Of his domestick character, frugality was a part eminently remarkable. 267
Having determined not to be dependent, he determined not to be in want,
and therefore wisely and magnanimously rejected all temptations to expence unsuitable to his fortune. This general care must be universally
approved; but it sometimes appeared in petty artifices of parsimony, such
as the practice of writing his compositions on the back of letters, as may be
seen in the remaining copy of the *Iliad*, by which perhaps in five years five
shillings were saved; or in a niggardly reception of his friends, and scantiness of entertainment, as, when he had two guests in his house, he would set
at supper a single pint upon the table; and having himself taken two small
glasses would retire, and say, *Gentlemen, I leave you to your wine.* Yet he tells
his friends, that *he has a heart for all, a house for all, and, whatever they may
think, a fortune for all.*

He sometimes, however, made a splendid dinner, and is said to have 268
wanted no part of the skill or elegance which such performances require.
That this magnificence should be often displayed, that obstinate prudence
with which he conducted his affairs would not permit; for his revenue,
certain and casual, amounted only to about eight hundred pounds a year, of
which however he declares himself able to assign one hundred to charity.

Of this fortune, which as it arose from publick approbation was very 269
honourably obtained, his imagination seems to have been too full: it would
be hard to find a man, so well entitled to notice by his wit, that ever
delighted so much in talking of his money. In his Letters, and in his
Poems, his garden and his grotto, his quincunx and his vines, or some
hints of his opulence, are always to be found. The great topick of his ridicule
is poverty; the crimes with which he reproaches his antagonists are their
debts, their habitation in the Mint, and their want of a dinner. He seems to
be of an opinion not very uncommon in the world, that to want money is to
want every thing.

Next to the pleasure of contemplating his possessions, seems to be that of 270
enumerating the men of high rank with whom he was acquainted, and
whose notice he loudly proclaims not to have been obtained by any practices
of meanness or servility; a boast which was never denied to be true, and to
which very few poets have ever aspired. Pope never set his genius to sale; he
never flattered those whom he did not love, or praised those whom he did
not esteem. Savage however remarked, that he began a little to relax his
dignity when he wrote a distich for *his Highness's dog.*

His admiration of the Great seems to have increased in the advance of 271
life. He passed over peers and statesmen to inscribe his *Iliad* to Congreve,
with a magnanimity of which the praise had been compleat, had his friend's
virtue been equal to his wit. Why he was chosen for so great an honour, it is

not now possible to know; there is no trace in literary history of any particular intimacy between them. The name of Congreve appears in the Letters among those of his other friends, but without any observable distinction or consequence.

272   To his latter works, however, he took care to annex names dignified with titles, but was not very happy in his choice; for, except Lord Bathurst, none of his noble friends were such as that a good man would wish to have his intimacy with them known to posterity: he can derive little honour from the notice of Cobham, Burlington, or Bolingbroke.

273   Of his social qualities, if an estimate be made from his Letters, an opinion too favourable cannot easily be formed; they exhibit a perpetual and unclouded effulgence of general benevolence, and particular fondness. There is nothing but liberality, gratitude, constancy, and tenderness. It has been so long said as to be commonly believed, that the true characters of men may be found in their Letters, and that he who writes to his friend lays his heart open before him. But the truth is, that such were simple friend-ships of the *Golden Age*, and are now the friendships only of children. Very few can boast of hearts which they dare lay open to themselves, and of which, by whatever accident exposed, they do not shun a distinct and continued view; and, certainly, what we hide from ourselves we do not shew to our friends. There is, indeed, no transaction which offers stronger temptations to fallacy and sophistication than epistolary intercourse. In the eagerness of conversation the first emotions of the mind often burst out, before they are considered; in the tumult of business, interest and passion have their genuine effect; but a friendly Letter is a calm and deliberate performance, in the cool of leisure, in the stillness of solitude, and surely no man sits down to depreciate by design his own character.

274   Friendship has no tendency to secure veracity; for by whom can a man so much wish to be thought better than he is, as by him whose kindness he desires to gain or keep? Even in writing to the world there is less constraint; the author is not confronted with his reader, and takes his chance of approbation among the different dispositions of mankind; but a Letter is addressed to a single mind, of which the prejudices and partialities are known; and must therefore please, if not by favouring them, by forbearing to oppose them.

275   To charge those favourable representations, which men give of their own minds, with the guilt of hypocritical falshood, would shew more severity than knowledge. The writer commonly believes himself. Almost every man's thoughts, while they are general, are right; and most hearts are pure, while temptation is away. It is easy to awaken generous sentiments in privacy; to despise death when there is no danger; to glow with benevo-

lence when there is nothing to be given. While such ideas are formed they are felt, and self-love does not suspect the gleam of virtue to be the meteor of fancy.

If the Letters of Pope are considered merely as compositions, they seem 276 to be premeditated and artificial. It is one thing to write because there is something which the mind wishes to discharge, and another, to solicit the imagination because ceremony or vanity requires something to be written. Pope confesses his early Letters to be vitiated with *affectation and ambition*: to know whether he disentangled himself from these perverters of epistolary integrity, his book and his life must be set in comparison.

One of his favourite topicks is contempt of his own poetry. For this, if it 277 had been real, he would deserve no commendation, and in this he was certainly not sincere; for his high value of himself was sufficiently observed, and of what could he be proud but of his poetry? He writes, he says, when *he has just nothing else to do*; yet Swift complains that he was never at leisure for conversation, because he *had always some poetical scheme in his head*. It was punctually required that his writing-box should be set upon his bed before he rose; and Lord Oxford's domestick related, that, in the dreadful winter of Forty, she was called from her bed by him four times in one night, to supply him with paper, lest he should lose a thought.

He pretends insensibility to censure and criticism, though it was ob- 278 served by all who knew him that every pamphlet disturbed his quiet, and that his extreme irritability laid him open to perpetual vexation; but he wished to despise his criticks, and therefore hoped that he did despise them.

As he happened to live in two reigns when the Court paid little attention 279 to poetry, he nursed in his mind a foolish disesteem of Kings, and proclaims that *he never sees Courts*. Yet a little regard shewn him by the Prince of Wales melted his obduracy; and he had not much to say when he was asked by his Royal Highness, *how he could love a Prince while he disliked Kings?*

He very frequently professes contempt of the world, and represents 280 himself as looking on mankind, sometimes with gay indifference, as on emmets of a hillock, below his serious attention; and sometimes with gloomy indignation, as on monsters more worthy of hatred than of pity. These were dispositions apparently counterfeited. How could he despise those whom he lived by pleasing, and on whose approbation his esteem of himself was superstructed? Why should he hate those to whose favour he owed his honour and his ease? Of things that terminate in human life, the world is the proper judge; to despise its sentence, if it were possible, is not just; and if it were just, is not possible. Pope was far enough from this unreasonable temper; he was sufficiently *a fool to Fame*, and his fault was that he pretended to neglect it. His levity and his sullenness were only in his

Letters; he passed through common life, sometimes vexed, and sometimes pleased, with the natural emotions of common men.

281   His scorn of the Great is repeated too often to be real; no man thinks much of that which he despises; and as falsehood is always in danger of inconsistency, he makes it his boast at another time that he lives among them.

282   It is evident that his own importance swells often in his mind. He is afraid of writing, lest the clerks of the Post-office should know his secrets; he has many enemies; he considers himself as surrounded by universal jealousy; *after many deaths, and many dispersions, two or three of us*, says he, *may still be brought together, not to plot, but to divert ourselves, and the world too, if it pleases*; and they can live together, and *shew what friends wits may be, in spite of all the fools in the world*. All this while it was likely that the clerks did not know his hand; he certainly had no more enemies than a publick character like his inevitably excites, and with what degree of friendship the wits might live, very few were so much fools as ever to enquire.

283   Some part of this pretended discontent he learned from Swift, and expresses it, I think, most frequently in his correspondence with him. Swift's resentment was unreasonable, but it was sincere; Pope's was the mere mimickry of his friend, a fictitious part which he began to play before it became him. When he was only twenty-five years old, he related that *a glut of study and retirement had thrown him on the world*, and that there was danger lest *a glut of the world should throw him back upon study and retirement*. To this Swift answered with great propriety, that Pope had not yet either acted or suffered enough in the world to have become weary of it. And, indeed, it must be some very powerful reason that can drive back to solitude him who has once enjoyed the pleasures of society.

284   In the Letters both of Swift and Pope there appears such narrowness of mind, as makes them insensible of any excellence that has not some affinity with their own, and confines their esteem and approbation to so small a number, that whoever should form his opinion of the age from their representation, would suppose them to have lived amidst ignorance and barbarity, unable to find among their contemporaries either virtue or intelligence, and persecuted by those that could not understand them.

285   When Pope murmurs at the world, when he professes contempt of fame, when he speaks of riches and poverty, of success and disappointment, with negligent indifference, he certainly does not express his habitual and settled sentiments, but either wilfully disguises his own character, or, what is more likely, invests himself with temporary qualities, and sallies out in the colours of the present moment. His hopes and fears, his joys and sorrows, acted strongly upon his mind; and if he differed from others, it was not by

carelessness; he was irritable and resentful; his malignity to Philips, whom he had first made ridiculous, and then hated for being angry, continued too long. Of his vain desire to make Bentley contemptible, I never heard any adequate reason. He was sometimes wanton in his attacks; and, before Chandos, Lady Wortley, and Hill, was mean in his retreat.

The virtues which seem to have had most of his affection were liberality   286 and fidelity of friendship, in which it does not appear that he was other than he describes himself. His fortune did not suffer his charity to be splendid and conspicuous; but he assisted Dodsley with a hundred pounds, that he might open a shop; and of the subscription of forty pounds a year that he raised for Savage, twenty were paid by himself. He was accused of loving money, but his love was eagerness to gain, not solicitude to keep it.

In the duties of friendship he was zealous and constant: his early maturity   287 of mind commonly united him with men older than himself, and therefore, without attaining any considerable length of life, he saw many companions of his youth sink into the grave; but it does not appear that he lost a single friend by coldness or by injury; those who loved him once, continued their kindness. His ungrateful mention of Allen in his will, was the effect of his adherence to one whom he had known much longer, and whom he naturally loved with greater fondness. His violation of the trust reposed in him by Bolingbroke could have no motive inconsistent with the warmest affection; he either thought the action so near to indifferent that he forgot it, or so laudable that he expected his friend to approve it.

It was reported, with such confidence as almost to enforce belief, that   288 in the papers intrusted to his executors was found a defamatory Life of Swift, which he had prepared as an instrument of vengeance to be used, if any provocation should be ever given. About this I enquired of the Earl of Marchmont, who assured me that no such piece was among his remains.

The religion in which he lived and died was that of the Church of Rome,   289 to which in his correspondence with Racine he professes himself a sincere adherent. That he was not scrupulously pious in some part of his life, is known by many idle and indecent applications of sentences taken from the Scriptures; a mode of merriment which a good man dreads for its profaneness, and a witty man disdains for its easiness and vulgarity. But to whatever levities he has been betrayed, it does not appear that his principles were ever corrupted, or that he ever lost his belief of Revelation. The positions which he transmitted from Bolingbroke he seems not to have understood, and was pleased with an interpretation that made them orthodox.

A man of such exalted superiority, and so little moderation, would   290 naturally have all his delinquences observed and aggravated: those who could not deny that he was excellent, would rejoice to find that he was not perfect.

291   Perhaps it may be imputed to the unwillingness with which the same man is allowed to possess many advantages, that his learning has been depreciated. He certainly was in his early life a man of great literary curiosity; and when he wrote his *Essay on Criticism* had, for his age, a very wide acquaintance with books. When he entered into the living world, it seems to have happened to him as to many others, that he was less attentive to dead masters; he studied in the academy of Paracelsus, and made the universe his favourite volume. He gathered his notions fresh from reality, not from the copies of authors, but the originals of Nature. Yet there is no reason to believe that literature ever lost his esteem; he always professed to love reading; and Dobson, who spent some time at his house translating his *Essay on Man*, when I asked him what learning he found him to possess, answered, *More than I expected*. His frequent references to history, his allusions to various kinds of knowledge, and his images selected from art and nature, with his observations on the operations of the mind and the modes of life, shew an intelligence perpetually on the wing, excursive, vigorous, and diligent, eager to pursue knowledge, and attentive to retain it.

292   From this curiosity arose the desire of travelling, to which he alludes in his verses to Jervas, and which, though he never found an opportunity to gratify it, did not leave him till his life declined.

293   Of his intellectual character, the constituent and fundamental principle was Good Sense, a prompt and intuitive perception of consonance and propriety. He saw immediately, of his own conceptions, what was to be chosen, and what to be rejected; and, in the works of others, what was to be shunned, and what to be copied.

294   But good sense alone is a sedate and quiescent quality, which manages its possessions well, but does not increase them; it collects few materials for its own operations, and preserves safety, but never gains supremacy. Pope had likewise genius; a mind active, ambitious, and adventurous, always investigating, always aspiring; in its widest searches still longing to go forward, in its highest flights still wishing to be higher; always imagining something greater than it knows, always endeavouring more than it can do.

295   To assist these powers, he is said to have had great strength and exactness of memory. That which he had heard or read was not easily lost; and he had before him not only what his own meditation suggested, but what he had found in other writers, that might be accommodated to his present purpose.

296   These benefits of nature he improved by incessant and unwearied diligence; he had recourse to every source of intelligence, and lost no opportunity of information; he consulted the living as well as the dead; he read his

compositions to his friends, and was never content with mediocrity when excellence could be attained. He considered poetry as the business of his life, and however he might seem to lament his occupation, he followed it with constancy; to make verses was his first labour, and to mend them was his last.

From his attention to poetry he was never diverted. If conversation 297 offered any thing that could be improved, he committed it to paper; if a thought, or perhaps an expression more happy than was common, rose to his mind, he was careful to write it; an independent distich was preserved for an opportunity of insertion, and some little fragments have been found containing lines, or parts of lines, to be wrought upon at some other time.

He was one of those few whose labour is their pleasure: he was never 298 elevated to negligence, nor wearied to impatience; he never passed a fault unamended by indifference, nor quitted it by despair. He laboured his works first to gain reputation, and afterwards to keep it.

Of composition there are different methods. Some employ at once 299 memory and invention, and, with little intermediate use of the pen, form and polish large masses by continued meditation, and write their productions only when, in their own opinion, they have completed them. It is related of Virgil, that his custom was to pour out a great number of verses in the morning, and pass the day in retrenching exuberances and correcting inaccuracies. The method of Pope, as may be collected from his translation, was to write his first thoughts in his first words, and gradually to amplify, decorate, rectify, and refine them.

With such faculties, and such dispositions, he excelled every other writer 300 in *poetical prudence*; he wrote in such a manner as might expose him to few hazards. He used almost always the same fabrick of verse; and, indeed, by those few essays which he made of any other, he did not enlarge his reputation. Of this uniformity the certain consequence was readiness and dexterity. By perpetual practice, language had in his mind a systematical arrangement; having always the same use for words, he had words so selected and combined as to be ready at his call. This increase of facility he confessed himself to have perceived in the progress of his translation.

But what was yet of more importance, his effusions were always volun- 301 tary, and his subjects chosen by himself. His independence secured him from drudging at a task, and labouring upon a barren topick: he never exchanged praise for money, nor opened a shop of condolence or congratulation. His poems, therefore, were scarce ever temporary. He suffered coronations and royal marriages to pass without a song, and derived no opportunities from recent events, nor any popularity from the accidental disposition of his readers. He was never reduced to the necessity of soliciting the sun to shine upon a birth-day, of calling the Graces and Virtues to a wedding, or of saying what multitudes have said before him. When he could produce nothing new, he was at liberty to be silent.

302   His publications were for the same reason never hasty. He is said to have sent nothing to the press till it had lain two years under his inspection: it is at least certain, that he ventured nothing without nice examination. He suffered the tumult of imagination to subside, and the novelties of invention to grow familiar. He knew that the mind is always enamoured of its own productions, and did not trust his first fondness. He consulted his friends, and listened with great willingness to criticism; and, what was of more importance, he consulted himself, and let nothing pass against his own judgement.

303   He professed to have learned his poetry from Dryden, whom, whenever an opportunity was presented, he praised through his whole life with unvaried liberality; and perhaps his character may receive some illustration, if he be compared with his master.

304   Integrity of understanding and nicety of discernment were not allotted in a less proportion to Dryden than to Pope. The rectitude of Dryden's mind was sufficiently shewn by the dismission of his poetical prejudices, and the rejection of unnatural thoughts and rugged numbers. But Dryden never desired to apply all the judgement that he had. He wrote, and professed to write, merely for the people; and when he pleased others, he contented himself. He spent no time in struggles to rouse latent powers; he never attempted to make that better which was already good, nor often to mend what he must have known to be faulty. He wrote, as he tells us, with very little consideration; when occasion or necessity called upon him, he poured out what the present moment happened to supply, and, when once it had passed the press, ejected it from his mind; for when he had no pecuniary interest, he had no further solicitude.

305   Pope was not content to satisfy; he desired to excel, and therefore always endeavoured to do his best: he did not court the candour, but dared the judgement of his reader, and, expecting no indulgence from others, he shewed none to himself. He examined lines and words with minute and punctilious observation, and retouched every part with indefatigable diligence, till he had left nothing to be forgiven.

306   For this reason he kept his pieces very long in his hands, while he considered and reconsidered them. The only poems which can be supposed to have been written with such regard to the times as might hasten their publication, were the two satires of *Thirty-eight*; of which Dodsley told me, that they were brought to him by the author, that they might be fairly copied. "Almost every line," he said, "was then written twice over; I gave

him a clean transcript, which he sent some time afterwards to me for the press, with almost every line written twice over a second time."

His declaration, that his care for his works ceased at their publication, 307 was not strictly true. His parental attention never abandoned them; what he found amiss in the first edition, he silently corrected in those that followed. He appears to have revised the *Iliad*, and freed it from some of its imperfections; and the *Essay on Criticism* received many improvements after its first appearance. It will seldom be found that he altered without adding clearness, elegance, or vigour. Pope had perhaps the judgement of Dryden; but Dryden certainly wanted the diligence of Pope.

In acquired knowledge, the superiority must be allowed to Dryden, 308 whose education was more scholastick, and who before he became an author had been allowed more time for study, with better means of information. His mind has a larger range, and he collects his images and illustrations from a more extensive circumference of science. Dryden knew more of man in his general nature, and Pope in his local manners. The notions of Dryden were formed by comprehensive speculation, and those of Pope by minute attention. There is more dignity in the knowledge of Dryden, and more certainty in that of Pope.

Poetry was not the sole praise of either; for both excelled likewise in 309 prose; but Pope did not borrow his prose from his predecessor. The style of Dryden is capricious and varied, that of Pope is cautious and uniform; Dryden obeys the motions of his own mind, Pope constrains his mind to his own rules of composition. Dryden is sometimes vehement and rapid; Pope is always smooth, uniform, and gentle. Dryden's page is a natural field, rising into inequalities, and diversified by the varied exuberance of abundant vegetation; Pope's is a velvet lawn, shaven by the scythe, and levelled by the roller.

Of genius, that power which constitutes a poet; that quality without 310 which judgement is cold and knowledge is inert; that energy which collects, combines, amplifies, and animates; the superiority must, with some hesitation, be allowed to Dryden. It is not to be inferred that of this poetical vigour Pope had only a little, because Dryden had more; for every other writer since Milton must give place to Pope; and even of Dryden it must be said, that if he has brighter paragraphs, he has not better poems. Dryden's performances were always hasty, either excited by some external occasion, or extorted by domestick necessity; he composed without consideration, and published without correction. What his mind could supply at call, or gather in one excursion, was all that he sought, and all that he gave. The dilatory caution of Pope enabled him to condense his sentiments, to multiply his images, and to accumulate all that study might produce, or chance might supply. If the flights of Dryden therefore are higher, Pope continues longer on the wing. If of Dryden's fire the blaze is brighter, of Pope's the heat is more regular and constant. Dryden often surpasses expectation, and Pope never falls below it. Dryden is read with frequent astonishment, and Pope with perpetual delight.

311 This parallel will, I hope, when it is well considered, be found just; and if the reader should suspect me, as I suspect myself, of some partial fondness for the memory of Dryden, let him not too hastily condemn me; for meditation and enquiry may, perhaps, shew him the reasonableness of my determination.

312 THE Works of Pope are now to be distinctly examined, not so much with attention to slight faults or petty beauties, as to the general character and effect of each performance.

313 It seems natural for a young poet to initiate himself by Pastorals, which, not professing to imitate real life, require no experience, and, exhibiting only the simple operation of unmingled passions, admit no subtle reasoning or deep enquiry. Pope's Pastorals are not however composed but with close thought; they have reference to the times of the day, the seasons of the year, and the periods of human life. The last, that which turns the attention upon age and death, was the author's favourite. To tell of disappointment and misery, to thicken the darkness of futurity, and perplex the labyrinth of uncertainty, has been always a delicious employment of the poets. His preference was probably just. I wish, however, that his fondness had not overlooked a line in which the *Zephyrs* are made *to lament in silence*.

314 To charge these Pastorals with want of invention, is to require what never was intended. The imitations are so ambitiously frequent, that the writer evidently means rather to shew his literature than his wit. It is surely sufficient for an author of sixteen not only to be able to copy the poems of antiquity with judicious selection, but to have obtained sufficient power of language, and skill in metre, to exhibit a series of versification, which had in English poetry no precedent, nor has since had an imitation.

315 The design of *Windsor Forest* is evidently derived from *Cooper's Hill*, with some attention to Waller's poem on *The Park*; but Pope cannot be denied to excel his masters in variety and elegance, and the art of interchanging description, narrative, and morality. The objection made by Dennis is the want of plan, of a regular subordination of parts terminating in the principal and original design. There is this want in most descriptive poems, because as the scenes, which they must exhibit successively, are all subsisting at the same time, the order in which they are shewn must by necessity be arbitrary, and more is not to be expected from the last part than from

the first. The attention, therefore, which cannot be detained by suspense, must be excited by diversity, such as this poem offers to its reader.

But the desire of diversity may be too much indulged; the parts of *Windsor Forest* which deserve least praise, are those which were added to enliven the stillness of the scene, the appearance of Father Thames, and the transformation of *Lodona*. Addison had in his *Campaign* derided the *Rivers* that *rise from their oozy beds* to tell stories of heroes, and it is therefore strange that Pope should adopt a fiction not only unnatural but lately censured. The story of *Lodona* is told with sweetness; but a new metamorphorsis is a ready and puerile expedient; nothing is easier than to tell how a flower was once a blooming virgin, or a rock an obdurate tyrant. 316

The *Temple of Fame* has, as Steele warmly declared, *a thousand beauties*. Every part is splendid; there is great luxuriance of ornaments; the original vision of Chaucer was never denied to be much improved; the allegory is very skilfully continued, the imagery is properly selected, and learnedly displayed: yet, with all this comprehension of excellence, as its scene is laid in remote ages, and its sentiments, if the concluding paragraph be excepted, have little relation to general manners or common life, it never obtained much notice, but is turned silently over, and seldom quoted or mentioned with either praise or blame. 317

That the *Messiah* excels the *Pollio* is no great praise, if it be considered from what original the improvements are derived. 318

The *Verses on the unfortunate Lady* have drawn much attention by the illaudable singularity of treating suicide with respect; and they must be allowed to be written in some parts with vigorous animation, and in others with gentle tenderness; nor has Pope produced any poem in which the sense predominates more over the diction. But the tale is not skilfully told; it is not easy to discover the character of either the Lady or her Guardian. History relates that she was about to disparage herself by a marriage with an inferior; Pope praises her for the dignity of ambition, and yet condemns the unkle to detestation for his pride; the ambitious love of a niece may be opposed by the interest, malice, or envy of an unkle, but never by his pride. On such an occasion a poet may be allowed to be obscure, but inconsistency never can be right. 319

The *Ode for St. Cecilia's Day* was undertaken at the desire of Steele: in this the author is generally confessed to have miscarried, yet he has miscarried only as compared with Dryden; for he has far outgone other competitors. Dryden's plan is better chosen; history will always take stronger hold of the attention than fable: the passions excited by Dryden are the pleasures and pains of real life, the scene of Pope is laid in imaginary 320 existence; Pope is read with calm acquiescence, Dryden with turbulent delight; Pope hangs upon the ear, and Dryden finds the passes of the mind.

321   Both the odes want the essential constituent of metrical compositions, the stated recurrence of settled numbers. It may be alleged, that Pindar is said by Horace to have written *numeris lege solutis*: but as no such lax perform-ances have been transmitted to us, the meaning of that expression cannot be fixed; and perhaps the like return might properly be made to a modern Pindarist, as Mr. Cobb received from Bentley, who, when he found his criticisms upon a Greek Exercise, which Cobb had presented, refuted one after another by Pindar's authority, cried out at last, *Pindar was a bold fellow, but thou art an impudent one.*

322   If Pope's ode be particularly inspected, it will be found that the first stanza consists of sounds well chosen indeed, but only sounds.

323   The second consists of hyperbolical common-places, easily to be found, and perhaps without much difficulty to be as well expressed.

324   In the third, however, there are numbers, images, harmony, and vigour, not unworthy the antagonist of Dryden. Had all been like this—but every part cannot be the best.

325   The next stanzas place and detain us in the dark and dismal regions of mythology, where neither hope nor fear, neither joy nor sorrow can be found: the poet however faithfully attends us; we have all that can be performed by elegance of diction, or sweetness of versification; but what can form avail without better matter?

326   The last stanza recurs again to common-places. The conclusion is too evidently modelled by that of Dryden; and it may be remarked that both end with the same fault, the comparison of each is literal on one side, and metaphorical on the other.

327   Poets do not always express their own thoughts; Pope, with all this labour in the praise of Musick, was ignorant of its principles, and insensible of its effects.

328   One of his greatest though of his earliest works is the *Essay on Criticism*, which, if he had written nothing else, would have placed him among the first criticks and the first poets, as it exhibits every mode of excellence that can embellish or dignify didactick composition, selection of matter, novelty of arrangement, justness of precept, splendour of illustration, and propriety of digression. I know not whether it be pleasing to consider that he produced this piece at twenty, and never afterwards excelled it: he that delights himself with observing that such powers may be so soon attained, cannot but grieve to think that life was ever after at a stand.

329   To mention the particular beauties of the Essay would be unprofitably tedious; but I cannot forbear to observe, that the comparison of a student's

progress in the sciences with the journey of a traveller in the Alps, is perhaps the best that English poetry can shew. A simile, to be perfect, must both illustrate and ennoble the subject; must shew it to the understanding in a clearer view, and display it to the fancy with greater dignity; but either of these qualities may be sufficient to recommend it. In didactick poetry, of which the great purpose is instruction, a simile may be praised which illustrates, though it does not ennoble; in heroicks, that may be admitted which ennobles, though it does not illustrate. That it may be complete, it is required to exhibit, independently of its references, a pleasing image; for a simile is said to be a short episode. To this antiquity was so attentive, that circumstances were sometimes added, which, having no parallels, served only to fill the imagination, and produced what Perrault ludicrously called *comparisons with a long tail*. In their similies the greatest writers have sometimes failed; the ship-race, compared with the chariot-race, is neither illustrated nor aggrandised; land and water make all the difference: when Apollo, running after Daphne, is likened to a greyhound chasing a hare, there is nothing gained; the ideas of pursuit and flight are too plain to be made plainer, and a god and the daughter of a god are not represented much to their advantage, by a hare and dog. The simile of the Alps has no useless parts, yet affords a striking picture by itself; it makes the foregoing position better understood, and enables it to take faster hold on the attention; it assists the apprehension, and elevates the fancy.

Let me likewise dwell a little on the celebrated paragraph, in which it is 330 directed that *the sound should seem an echo to the sense*; a precept which Pope is allowed to have observed beyond any other English poet.

This notion of representative metre, and the desire of discovering fre- 331 quent adaptations of the sound to the sense, have produced, in my opinion, many wild conceits and imaginary beauties. All that can furnish this representation are the sounds of the words considered singly, and the time in which they are pronounced. Every language has some words framed to exhibit the noises which they express, as *thump, rattle, growl, hiss*. These however are but few, and the poet cannot make them more, nor can they be of any use but when sound is to be mentioned. The time of pronunciation was in the dactylick measures of the learned languages capable of considerable variety; but that variety could be accommodated only to motion or duration, and different degrees of motion were perhaps expressed by verses rapid or slow, without much attention of the writer, when the image had full possession of his fancy; but our language having little flexibility, our verses can differ very little in their cadence. The fancied resemblances, I fear, arise sometimes merely from the ambiguity of words; there is supposed to be some relation between a *soft* line and a *soft* couch, or between *hard* syllables and *hard* fortune.

332   Motion, however, may be in some sort exemplified; and yet it may be suspected that even in such resemblances the mind often governs the ear, and the sounds are estimated by their meaning. One of the most successful attempts has been to describe the labour of Sisyphus:

> With many a weary step, and many a groan,
> Up a high hill he heaves a huge round stone;
> The huge round stone, resulting with a bound,
> Thunders impetuous down, and smoaks along the ground.

Who does not perceive the stone to move slowly upward, and roll violently back? But set the same numbers to another sense;

> While many a merry tale, and many a song.
> Chear'd the rough road, we wish'd the rough road long.
> The rough road then, returning in a round,
> Mock'd our impatient steps, for all was fairy ground.

We have now surely lost much of the delay, and much of the rapidity.

333   But to shew how little the greatest master of numbers can fix the principles of representative harmony, it will be sufficient to remark that the poet, who tells us, that

> When Ajax strives—the words move slow.
> Not so when swift Camilla scours the plain,
> Flies o'er th' unbending corn, and skims along the main;

when he had enjoyed for about thirty years the praise of Camilla's lightness of foot, tried another experiment upon *sound* and *time*, and produced this memorable triplet;

> Waller was smooth; but Dryden taught to join ⎫
> The varying verse, the full resounding line, ⎬
> The long majestick march, and energy divine. ⎭

Here are the swiftness of the rapid race, and the march of slow-paced majesty, exhibited by the same poet in the same sequence of syllables, except that the exact prosodist will find the line of *swiftness* by one time longer than that of *tardiness*.

334   Beauties of this kind are commonly fancied; and when real, are technical and nugatory, not to be rejected, and not to be solicited.

335   To the praises which have been accumulated on *The Rape of the Lock* by readers of every class, from the critick to the waiting-maid, it is difficult to make any addition. Of that which is universally allowed to be the most

attractive of all ludicrous compositions, let it rather be now enquired from what sources the power of pleasing is derived.

Dr. Warburton, who excelled in critical perspicacity, has remarked that 336 the preternatural agents are very happily adapted to the purposes of the poem. The heathen deities can no longer gain attention: we should have turned away from a contest between Venus and Diana. The employment of allegorical persons always excites conviction of its own absurdity; they may produce effects, but cannot conduct actions; when the phantom is put in motion, it dissolves; thus *Discord* may raise a mutiny, but *Discord* cannot conduct a march, nor besiege a town. Pope brought into view a new race of Beings, with powers and passions proportionate to their operation. The sylphs and gnomes act at the toilet and the tea-table, what more terrifick and more powerful phantoms perform on the stormy ocean, or the field of battle, they give their proper help, and do their proper mischief.

Pope is said, by an objector, not to have been the inventer of this petty 337 nation; a charge which might with more justice have been brought against the author of the *Iliad*, who doubtless adopted the religious system of his country; for what is there but the names of his agents which Pope has not invented? Has he not assigned them characters and operations never heard of before? Has he not, at least, given them their first poetical existence? If this is not sufficient to denominate his work original, nothing original ever can be written.

In this work are exhibited, in a very high degree, the two most engaging 338 powers of an author. New things are made familiar, and familiar things are made new. A race of aerial people, never heard of before, is presented to us in a manner so clear and easy, that the reader seeks for no further information, but immediately mingles with his new acquaintance, adopts their interests, and attends their pursuits, loves a sylph, and detests a gnome.

That familiar things are made new, every paragraph will prove. The 339 subject of the poem is an event below the common incidents of common life; nothing real is introduced that is not seen so often as to be no longer regarded, yet the whole detail of a female-day is here brought before us invested with so much art of decoration, that, though nothing is disguised, every thing is striking, and we feel all the appetite of curiosity for that from which we have a thousand times turned fastidiously away.

The purpose of the Poet is, as he tells us, to laugh at *the little unguarded* 340 *follies of the female sex*. It is therefore without justice that Dennis charges the *Rape of the Lock* with the want of a moral, and for that reason sets it below the *Lutrin*, which exposes the pride and discord of the clergy. Perhaps neither Pope nor Boileau has made the world much better than he found it; but if they had both succeeded, it were easy to tell who would have deserved most from publick gratitude. The freaks, and humours, and spleen, and vanity of women, as they embroil families in discord, and fill houses with disquiet, do more to obstruct the happiness of life in a year than the ambition of the clergy in many centuries. It has been well observed, that the misery of man proceeds not from any single crush of overwhelming evil, but from small vexations continually repeated.

341 It is remarked by Dennis likewise, that the machinery is superfluous; that, by all the bustle of preternatural operation, the main event is neither hastened nor retarded. To this charge an efficacious answer is not easily made. The sylphs cannot be said to help or to oppose, and it must be allowed to imply some want of art, that their power has not been sufficiently intermingled with the action. Other parts may likewise be charged with want of connection; the game at *ombre* might be spared, but if the Lady had lost her hair while she was intent upon her cards, it might have been inferred that those who are too fond of play will be in danger of neglecting more important interests. Those perhaps are faults; but what are such faults to so much excellence!

342 The Epistle of *Eloise to Abelard* is one of the most happy productions of human wit: the subject is so judiciously chosen, that it would be difficult, in turning over the annals of the world, to find another which so many circumstances concur to recommend. We regularly interest ourselves most in the fortune of those who most deserve our notice. Abelard and Eloise were conspicuous in their days for eminence of merit. The heart naturally loves truth. The adventures and misfortunes of this illustrious pair are known from undisputed history. Their fate does not leave the mind in hopeless dejection; for they both found quiet and consolation in retirement and piety. So new and so affecting is their story, that it supersedes invention, and imagination ranges at full liberty without straggling into scenes of fable.

343 The story, thus skilfully adopted, has been diligently improved. Pope has left nothing behind him, which seems more the effect of studious perseverance and laborious revisal. Here is particularly observable the *curiosa felicitas*, a fruitful soil, and careful cultivation. Here is no crudeness of sense, nor asperity of language.

344 The sources from which sentiments, which have so much vigour and efficacy, have been drawn, are shewn to be the mystick writers by the learned author of the *Essay on the Life and Writings of Pope*; a book which teaches how the brow of Criticism may be smoothed, and how she may be enabled, with all her severity, to attract and to delight.

345 The train of my disquisition has now conducted me to that poetical wonder, the translation of the *Iliad*; a performance which no age or nation

can pretend to equal. To the Greeks translation was almost unknown; it was totally unknown to the inhabitants of Greece. They had no recourse to the Barbarians for poetical beauties, but sought for every thing in Homer, where, indeed, there is but little which they might not find.

The Italians have been very diligent translators; but I can hear of no version, unless perhaps Anguillara's Ovid may be excepted, which is read with eagerness. The *Iliad* of Salvini every reader may discover to be punctiliously exact; but it seems to be the work of a linguist skilfully pedantick, and his countrymen, the proper judges of its power to please, reject it with disgust. 346

Their predecessors the Romans have left some specimens of translation behind them, and that employment must have had some credit in which Tully and Germanicus engaged; but unless we suppose, what is perhaps true, that the plays of Terence were versions of Menander, nothing translated seems ever to have risen to high reputation. The French, in the meridian hour of their learning, were very laudably industrious to enrich their own language with the wisdom of the ancients; but found themselves reduced, by whatever necessity, to turn the Greek and Roman poetry into prose. Whoever could read an author, could translate him. From such rivals little can be feared. 347

The chief help of Pope in this arduous undertaking was drawn from the versions of Dryden. Virgil had borrowed much of his imagery from Homer, and part of the debt was now paid by his translator. Pope searched the pages of Dryden for happy combinations of heroic diction; but it will not be denied that he added much to what he found. He cultivated our language with so much diligence and art, that he has left in his *Homer* a treasure of poetical elegances to posterity. His version may be said to have tuned the English tongue; for since its appearance no writer, however deficient in other powers, has wanted melody. Such a series of lines so elaborately corrected, and so sweetly modulated, took possession of the publick ear; the vulgar was enamoured of the poem, and the learned wondered at the translation. 348

But in the most general applause discordant voices will always be heard. It has been objected by some, who wish to be numbered among the sons of learning, that Pope's version of Homer is not Homerical; that it exhibits no resemblance of the original and characteristick manner of the Father of Poetry, as it wants his awful simplicity, his artless grandeur, his unaffected majesty. This cannot be totally denied; but it must be remembered that *necessitas quod cogit defendit*; that may be lawfully done which cannot be forborn. Time and place will always enforce regard. In estimating this translation, consideration must be had of the nature of our language, the 349 form of our metre, and, above all, of the change which two thousand years have made in the modes of life and the habits of thought. Virgil wrote in a language of the same general fabrick with that of Homer, in verses of the same measure, and in an age nearer to Homer's time by eighteen hundred years; yet he found, even then, the state of the world so much altered, and the demand for elegance so much increased, that mere nature would be endured no longer; and perhaps, in the multitude of borrowed passages, very few can be shewn which he has not embellished.

350 There is a time when nations emerging from barbarity, and falling into regular subordination, gain leisure to grow wise, and feel the shame of ignorance and the craving pain of unsatisfied curiosity. To this hunger of the mind plain sense is grateful; that which fills the void removes uneasiness, and to be free from pain for a while is pleasure; but repletion generates fastidiousness; a saturated intellect soon becomes luxurious, and knowledge finds no willing reception till it is recommended by artificial diction. Thus it will be found, in the progress of learning, that in all nations the first writers are simple, and that every age improves in elegance. One refinement always makes way for another, and what was expedient to Virgil was necessary to Pope.

351 I suppose many readers of the English *Iliad*, when they have been touched with some unexpected beauty of the lighter kind, have tried to enjoy it in the original, where, alas! it was not to be found. Homer doubtless owes to his translator many *Ovidian* graces not exactly suitable to his character; but to have added can be no great crime, if nothing be taken away. Elegance is surely to be desired, if it be not gained at the expence of dignity. A hero would wish to be loved, as well as to be reverenced.

352 To a thousand cavils one answer is sufficient; the purpose of a writer is to be read, and the criticism which would destroy the power of pleasing must be blown aside. Pope wrote for his own age and his own nation: he knew that it was necessary to colour the images and point the sentiments of his author; he therefore made him graceful, but lost him some of his sublimity.

353 The copious notes with which the version is accompanied, and by which it is recommended to many readers, though they were undoubtedly written to swell the volumes, ought not to pass without praise: commentaries which attract the reader by the pleasure of perusal have not often appeared; the notes of others are read to clear difficulties, those of Pope to vary entertainment.

354 It has however been objected, with sufficient reason, that there is in the commentary too much of unseasonable levity and affected gaiety; that too many appeals are made to the Ladies, and the ease which is so carefully preserved is sometimes the ease of a trifler. Every art has its terms, and

every kind of instruction its proper style; the gravity of common criticks may be tedious, but is less despicable than childish merriment.

Of the *Odyssey* nothing remains to be observed: the same general praise   355
may be given to both translations, and a particular examination of either would require a large volume. The notes were written by Broome, who endeavoured not unsuccessfully to imitate his master.

Of the *Dunciad* the hint is confessedly taken from Dryden's *Mac Fleck-*   356
noe; but the plan is so enlarged and diversified as justly to claim the praise of an original, and affords perhaps the best specimen that has yet appeared of personal satire ludicrously pompous.

That the design was moral, whatever the author might tell either his   357
readers or himself, I am not convinced. The first motive was the desire of revenging the contempt with which Theobald had treated his *Shakspeare*, and regaining the honour which he had lost, by crushing his opponent. Theobald was not of bulk enough to fill a poem, and therefore it was necessary to find other enemies with other names, at whose expence he might divert the publick.

In this design there was petulance and malignity enough; but I cannot   358
think it very criminal. An author places himself uncalled before the tribunal of Criticism, and solicits fame at the hazard of disgrace. Dulness or deformity are not culpable in themselves, but may be very justly reproached when they pretend to the honour of wit or the influence of beauty. If bad writers were to pass without reprehension, what should restrain them? *impune diem consumpserit ingens Telephus*; and upon bad writers only will censure have much effect. The satire which brought Theobald and Moore into contempt, dropped impotent from Bentley, like the javelin of Priam.

All truth is valuable, and satirical criticism may be considered as useful   359
when it rectifies error and improves judgement; he that refines the publick taste is a publick benefactor.

The beauties of this poem are well known; its chief fault is the grossness   360
of its images. Pope and Swift had an unnatural delight in ideas physically impure, such as every other tongue utters with unwillingness, and of which every ear shrinks from the mention.

But even this fault, offensive as it is, may be forgiven for the excellence of   361
other passages; such as the formation and dissolution of Moore, the account of the Traveller, the misfortune of the Florist, and the crouded thoughts and stately numbers which dignify the concluding paragraph.

The alterations which have been made in the *Dunciad*, not always for the   362
better, require that it should be published, as in the last collection, with all its variations.

363   The *Essay on Man* was a work of great labour and long consideration, but
certainly not the happiest of Pope's performances. The subject is perhaps
not very proper for poetry, and the poet was not sufficiently master of his
subject; metaphysical morality was to him a new study, he was proud of
his acquisitions, and, supposing himself master of great secrets, was in haste
to teach what he had not learned. Thus he tells us, in the first Epistle, that
from the nature of the Supreme Being may be deduced an order of beings
such as mankind, because Infinite Excellence can do only what is best. He
finds out that these beings must be *somewhere*, and that *all the question is
whether man be in a wrong place*. Surely if, according to the poet's Leibnitian
reasoning, we may infer that man ought to be, only because he is, we may
allow that his place is the right place, because he has it. Supreme Wisdom is
not less infallible in disposing than in creating. But what is meant by
somewhere and *place*, and *wrong place*, it had been vain to ask Pope, who
probably had never asked himself.

364   Having exalted himself into the chair of wisdom, he tells us much
that every man knows, and much that he does not know himself; that
we see but little, and that the order of the universe is beyond our comprehension; an opinion not very uncommon; and that there is a chain of
subordinate beings *from infinite to nothing*, of which himself and his readers
are equally ignorant. But he gives us one comfort, which, without his
help, he supposes unattainable, in the position *that though we are fools, yet
God is wise*.

365   This Essay affords an egregious instance of the predominance of genius,
the dazzling splendour of imagery, and the seductive powers of eloquence.
Never were penury of knowledge and vulgarity of sentiment so happily
disguised. The reader feels his mind full, though he learns nothing; and
when he meets it in its new array, no longer knows the talk of his mother
and his nurse. When these wonder-working sounds sink into sense, and the
doctrine of the Essay, disrobed of its ornaments, is left to the powers of its
naked excellence, what shall we discover? That we are, in comparison with
our Creator, very weak and ignorant; that we do not uphold the chain of
existence, and that we could not make one another with more skill than we
are made. We may learn yet more; that the arts of human life were copied
from the instinctive operations of other animals; that if the world be made
for man, it may be said that man was made for geese. To these profound
principles of natural knowledge are added some moral instructions equally
new; that self-interest, well understood, will produce social concord; that
men are mutual gainers by mutual benefits; that evil is sometimes balanced
by good; that human advantages are unstable and fallacious, of uncertain
duration, and doubtful effect; that our true honour is, not to have a great

part, but to act it well: that virtue only is our own; and that happiness is always in our power.

Surely a man of no very comprehensive search may venture to say that he 366 has heard all this before; but it was never till now recommended by such a blaze of embellishment, or such sweetness of melody. The vigorous contraction of some thoughts, the luxuriant amplification of others, the incidental illustrations, and sometimes the dignity, sometimes the softness of the verses, enchain philosophy, suspend criticism, and oppress judgement by overpowering pleasure.

This is true of many paragraphs; yet if I had undertaken to exemplify 367 Pope's felicity of composition before a rigid critick, I should not select the *Essay on Man*; for it contains more lines unsuccessfully laboured, more harshness of diction, more thoughts imperfectly expressed, more levity without elegance, and more heaviness without strength, than will easily be found in all his other works.

The *Characters of Men and Women* are the product of diligent speculation 368 upon human life; much labour has been bestowed upon them, and Pope very seldom laboured in vain. That his excellence may be properly estimated, I recommend a comparison of his *Characters of Women* with Boileau's Satire; it will then be seen with how much more perspicacity female nature is investigated, and female excellence selected; and he surely is no mean writer to whom Boileau shall be found inferior. The *Characters of Men*, however, are written with more, if not with deeper, thought, and exhibit many passages exquisitely beautiful. The *Gem and the Flower* will not easily be equalled. In the women's part are some defects; the character of *Attossa* is not so neatly finished as that of *Clodio*; and some of the female characters may be found perhaps more frequently among men; what is said of *Philomede* was true of *Prior*.

In the Epistles to Lord Bathurst and Lord Burlington, Dr. Warburton 369 has endeavoured to find a train of thought which was never in the writer's head, and, to support his hypothesis, has printed that first which was published last. In one, the most valuable passage is perhaps the Elogy on *Good Sense*, and the other the *End of the Duke of Buckingham*.

The Epistle to Arbuthnot, now arbitrarily called the *Prologue to the* 370 *Satires*, is a performance consisting, as it seems, of many fragments wrought into one design, which by this union of scattered beauties contains more striking paragraphs than could probably have been brought together into an occasional work. As there is no stronger motive to exertion than self-defence, no part has more elegance, spirit, or dignity, than the poet's vindication of his own character. The meanest passage is the satire upon *Sporus*.

371   Of the two poems which derived their names from the year, and which are called the *Epilogue to the Satires*, it was very justly remarked by Savage, that the second was in the whole more strongly conceived, and more equally supported, but that it had no single passages equal to the contention in the first for the dignity of Vice, and the celebration of the triumph of Corruption.

372   The Imitations of Horace seem to have been written as relaxations of his genius. This employment became his favourite by its facility; the plan was ready to his hand, and nothing was required but to accommodate as he could the sentiments of an old author to recent facts or familiar images; but what is easy is seldom excellent; such imitations cannot give pleasure to common readers; the man of learning may be sometimes surprised and delighted by an unexpected parallel; but the comparison requires knowledge of the original, which will likewise often detect strained applications. Between Roman images and English manners there will be an irreconcileable dissimilitude, and the work will be generally uncouth and partycoloured; neither original nor translated, neither ancient nor modern.

373   Pope had, in proportions very nicely adjusted to each other, all the qualities that constitute genius. He had *Invention*, by which new trains of events are formed, and new scenes of imagery displayed, as in the *Rape of the Lock*; and by which extrinsick and adventitious embellishments and illustrations are connected with a known subject, as in the *Essay on Criticism*. He had *Imagination*, which strongly impresses on the writer's mind, and enables him to convey to the reader, the various forms of nature, incidents of life, and energies of passion, as in his *Eloisa, Windsor Forest*, and the *Ethick Epistles*. He had *Judgement*, which selects from life or nature what the present purpose requires, and, by separating the essence of things from its concomitants, often makes the representation more powerful than the reality: and he had colours of language always before him, ready to decorate his matter with every grace of elegant expression, as when he accommodates his diction to the wonderful multiplicity of Homer's sentiments and descriptions.

374   Poetical expression includes sound as well as meaning; *Musick*, says Dryden, *is inarticulate poetry*; among the excellences of Pope, therefore, must be mentioned the melody of his metre. By perusing the works of Dryden, he discovered the most perfect fabrick of English verse, and habituated himself to that only which he found the best; in consequence of which restraint, his poetry has been censured as too uniformly musical, and as glutting the ear with unvaried sweetness. I suspect this objection to be the cant of those who judge by principles rather than perception: and who would even themselves have less pleasure in his works, if he had tried

to relieve attention by studied discords, or affected to break his lines and vary his pauses.

But though he was thus careful of his versification, he did not oppress his 375 powers with superfluous rigour. He seems to have thought with Boileau, that the practice of writing might be refined till the difficulty should overbalance the advantage. The construction of his language is not always strictly grammatical; with those rhymes which prescription had conjoined he contented himself, without regard to Swift's remonstrances, though there was no striking consonance; nor was he very careful to vary his terminations, or to refuse admission at a small distance to the same rhymes.

To Swift's edict for the exclusion of Alexandrines and Triplets he paid 376 little regard; he admitted them, but, in the opinion of Fenton, too rarely; he uses them more liberally in his translation than his poems.

He has a few double rhymes; and always, I think, unsuccessfully, except 377 once in the *Rape of the Lock*.

Expletives he very early ejected from his verses; but he now and then 378 admits an epithet rather commodious than important. Each of the six first lines of the *Iliad* might lose two syllables with very little diminution of the meaning; and sometimes, after all his art and labour, one verse seems to be made for the sake of another. In his latter productions the diction is sometimes vitiated by French idioms, with which Bolingbroke had perhaps infected him.

I have been told that the couplet by which he declared his own ear to be 379 most gratified was this:

> Lo, where Mœotis sleeps, and hardly flows
> The freezing Tanais through a waste of snows.

But the reason of this preference I cannot discover.

It is remarked by Watts, that there is scarcely a happy combination of 380 words, or a phrase poetically elegant in the English language, which Pope has not inserted into his version of Homer. How he obtained possession of so many beauties of speech, it were desirable to know. That he gleaned from authors, obscure as well as eminent, what he thought brilliant or useful, and preserved it all in a regular collection, is not unlikely. When, in his last years, Hall's Satires were shewn him, he wished that he had seen them sooner.

New sentiments and new images others may produce; but to attempt any 381 further improvement of versification will be dangerous. Art and diligence have now done their best, and what shall be added will be the effort of tedious toil and needless curiosity.

After all this, it is surely superfluous to answer the question that has once 382 been asked, Whether Pope was a poet? otherwise than by asking in return, If

Pope be not a poet, where is poetry to be found? To circumscribe poetry by a definition will only shew the narrowness of the definer, though a definition which shall exclude Pope will not easily be made. Let us look round upon the present time, and back upon the past; let us enquire to whom the voice of mankind has decreed the wreath of poetry; let their productions be examined, and their claims stated, and the pretensions of Pope will be no more disputed. Had he given the world only his version, the name of poet must have been allowed him: if the writer of the *Iliad* were to class his successors, he would assign a very high place to his translator, without requiring any other evidence of Genius.

383   The following Letter, of which the original is in the hands of Lord Hardwicke, was communicated to me by the kindness of Mr. Jodrell.

> "To Mr. BRIDGES, at the Bishop of
> London's at Fulham.

    "SIR,

"The favour of your Letter, with your Remarks, can never be enough acknowledged; and the speed, with which you discharged so troublesome a task, doubles the obligation.

"I must own, you have pleased me very much by the commendations so ill bestowed upon me; but, I assure you, much more by the frankness of your censure, which I ought to take the more kindly of the two, as it is more advantageous to a scribbler to be improved in his judgment than to be soothed in his vanity. The greater part of those deviations from the Greek, which you have observed, I was led into by Chapman and Hobbes; who are (it seems) as much celebrated for their knowledge of the original, as they are decryed for the badness of their translations. Chapman pretends to have restored the genuine sense of the author, from the mistakes of all former explainers, in several hundred places: and the Cambridge editors of the large Homer, in Greek and Latin, attributed so much to Hobbes, that they confess they have corrected the old Latin interpretation very often by his version. For my part, I generally took the author's meaning to be as you have explained it; yet their authority, joined to the knowledge of my own imperfectness in the language, over-ruled me. However, Sir, you may be confident I think you in the right, because you happen to be of my opinion: (for men (let them say what they will) never approve any other's sense, but as it squares with their own.) But you have made me much more proud of, and positive in my judgement, since it is strengthened by yours. I think your criticisms, which regard the expression, very just, and shall make my profit of them: to give you some proof that I am in earnest, I will alter three verses on your bare objection, though I have Mr. Dryden's example for each of them. And this, I hope, you will account no small piece of obedience, from one, who values the authority of one true poet above that of twenty criticks or commentators. But though I speak thus of commentators, I will continue to read carefully all I can procure, to make up, that way, for my own want of critical understanding in the original beauties of Homer. Though the greatest of them are certainly those of the Invention and Design, which are not at all confined to the language: for the distinguishing excellences of Homer are (by the consent of the best criticks of all nations) first in the manners, (which include all the speeches, as being no other than the representations of each person's manners by his words:) and then in that rapture and fire, which carries you away with him, with that wonderful force, that no man who has a true poetical spirit is master of himself, while he reads him. Homer makes you interested and concerned before you are aware, all at once; whereas Virgil does it by soft degrees. This, I believe, is what a translator of Homer ought principally to imitate; and it is very hard for any translator to come up to it, because the chief reason why all translations fall short of their originals is, that the very constraint they are obliged to, renders them heavy and dispirited.

"The great beauty of Homer's language, as I take it, consists in that noble simplicity, which runs through all his works; (and yet his diction, contrary to what one would imagine consistent with simplicity, is at the same time very copious.) I don't know how I have run into this pedantry in a Letter, but I find I have said too much, as well as spoken too inconsiderately; what farther thoughts I have upon this subject, I shall be glad to communicate to you (for my own improvement) when we meet; which is a happiness I very earnestly desire, as I do likewise some opportunity of proving how much I think myself obliged to your friendship, and how truly I am, Sir,

> Your most faithful, humble servant,
> A. POPE."

The Criticism upon Pope's Epitaphs, which was printed in *The Visitor*, is   384 placed here, being too minute and particular to be inserted in the Life.

EVERY Art is best taught by example. Nothing contributes more to the   385 cultivation of propriety than remarks on the works of those who have most excelled. I shall therefore endeavour, at this *visit*, to entertain the young students in poetry, with an examination of Pope's Epitaphs.

To define an epitaph is useless; every one knows that it is an inscription   386 on a tomb. An epitaph, therefore, implies no particular character of writing, but may be composed in verse or prose. It is indeed commonly panegyrical; because we are seldom distinguished with a stone but by our friends; but it has no rule to restrain or modify it, except this, that it ought not to be longer than common beholders may be expected to have leisure and patience to peruse.

I.

387   *On* CHARLES *Earl of* DORSET, *in the Church of Wythyham in Sussex.*

> Dorset, the grace of courts, the Muse's pride,
> Patron of arts, and judge of nature, dy'd.
> The scourge of pride, though sanctify'd or great,
> Of fops in learning, and of knaves in state;
> Yet soft in nature, though severe his lay,
> His anger moral, and his wisdom gay,
> Blest satyrist! who touch'd the mean so true,
> As show'd, Vice had his hate and pity too.
> Blest courtier! who could king and country please,
> Yet sacred keep his friendships, and his ease.
> Blest peer! his great forefathers every grace
> Reflecting, and reflected on his race;
> Where other Buckhursts, other Dorsets shine,
> And patriots still, or poets, deck the line.

388   The first distich of this epitaph contains a kind of information which few would want, that the man, for whom the tomb was erected, *died.* There are indeed some qualities worthy of praise ascribed to the dead, but none that were likely to exempt him from the lot of man, or incline us much to wonder that he should die. What is meant by *judge of nature*, is not easy to say. Nature is not the object of human judgement; for it is vain to judge where we cannot alter. If by nature is meant, what is commonly called *nature* by the criticks, a just representation of things really existing, and actions really performed, nature cannot be properly opposed to *art*; nature being, in this sense, only the best effect of art.

389   *The scourge of pride—*

Of this couplet, the second line is not, what is intended, an illustration of the former. *Pride*, in the *Great*, is indeed well enough connected with knaves in state, though *knaves* is a word rather too ludicrous and light; but the mention of *sanctified* pride will not lead the thoughts to *fops in learning*, but rather to some species of tyranny or oppression, something more gloomy and more formidable than foppery.

390   *Yet soft his nature—*

This is a high compliment, but was not first bestowed on Dorset by Pope. The next verse is extremely beautiful.

Blest satyrist!— 391

In this distich is another line of which Pope was not the author. I do not mean to blame these imitations with much harshness; in long performances they are scarcely to be avoided, and in shorter they may be indulged, because the train of the composition may naturally involve them, or the scantiness of the subject allow little choice. However, what is borrowed is not to be enjoyed as our own, and it is the business of critical justice to give every bird of the Muses his proper feather.

Blest courtier!— 392

Whether a courtier can properly be commended for keeping his *ease* sacred, may perhaps be disputable. To please king and country, without sacrificing friendship to any change of times, was a very uncommon instance of prudence or felicity, and deserved to be kept separate from so poor a commendation as care of his ease. I wish our poets would attend a little more accurately to the use of the word *sacred*, which surely should never be applied in a serious composition, but where some reference may be made to a higher Being, or where some duty is exacted or implied. A man may keep his friendship *sacred*, because promises of friendship are very awful ties; but methinks he cannot, but in a burlesque sense, be said to keep his ease *sacred*.

Blest peer! 393

The blessing ascribed to the *peer* has no connection with his peerage: they might happen to any other man, whose ancestors were remembered, or whose posterity were likely to be regarded.

I know not whether this epitaph be worthy either of the writer or of the 394 man entombed.

II.

On Sir WILLIAM TRUMBUL, *one of the principal Secretaries of State to* 395 *King* WILLIAM III. *who, having resigned his place, died in his retirement at Easthamsted in Berkshire,* 1716.

> A pleasing form, a firm, yet cautious mind,
> Sincere, though prudent; constant, yet resign'd;
> Honour unchang'd, a principle profest,
> Fix'd to one side, but moderate to the rest:
> An honest courtier, yet a patriot too,
> Just to his prince, and to his country true.
> Fill'd with the sense of age, the fire of youth,
> A scorn of wrangling, yet a zeal for truth;

> A generous faith, from superstition free;
> A love to peace, and hate of tyranny;
> Such this man was; who now, from earth remov'd,
> At length enjoys that liberty he lov'd.

396   In this epitaph, as in many others, there appears, at the first view, a fault which I think scarcely any beauty can compensate. The name is omitted. The end of an epitaph is to convey some account of the dead; and to what purpose is anything told of him whose name is concealed? An epitaph, and a history, of a nameless hero, are equally absurd, since the virtues and qualities so recounted in either, are scattered at the mercy of fortune to be appropriated by guess. The name, it is true, may be read upon the stone; but what obligation has it to the poet, whose verses wander over the earth, and leave their subject behind them, and who is forced, like an unskilful painter, to make his purpose known by adventitious help?

397   This epitaph is wholly without elevation, and contains nothing striking or particular; but the poet is not to be blamed for the defects of his subject. He said perhaps the best that could be said. There are, however, some defects which were not made necessary by the character in which he was employed. There is no opposition between an *honest courtier* and a *patriot*; for an *honest courtier* cannot but be a *patriot*.

398   It was unsuitable to the nicety required in short compositions, to close his verse with the word *too*; every rhyme should be a word of emphasis, nor can this rule be safely neglected, except where the length of the poem makes slight inaccuracies excusable, or allows room for beauties sufficient to overpower the effects of petty faults.

399   At the beginning of the seventh line the word *filled* is weak and prosaic, having no particular adaptation to any of the words that follow it.

400   The thought in the last line is impertinent, having no connexion with the foregoing character, nor with the condition of the man described. Had the epitaph been written on the poor conspirator* who died lately in prison, after a confinement of more than forty years, without any crime proved against him, the sentiment had been just and pathetical; but why should Trumbul be congratulated upon his liberty, who had never known restraint?

III.

401   *On the Hon.* SIMON HARCOURT, *only Son of the Lord Chancellor* HARCOURT, at *the Church of Stanton-Harcourt in Oxfordshire*, 1720.

> To this sad shrine, whoe'er thou art, draw near,
> Here lies the friend most lov'd, the son most dear:

---

* Bernardi.

Who ne'er knew joy, but friendship might divide,
Or gave his father grief but when he dy'd.

How vain is reason, eloquence how weak!
If Pope must tell what Harcourt cannot speak.
Oh, let thy once-lov'd friend inscribe thy stone,
And with a father's sorrows mix his own!

This epitaph is principally remarkable for the artful introduction of the   402
name, which is inserted with a peculiar felicity, to which chance must
concur with genius, which no man can hope to attain twice, and which
cannot be copied but with servile imitation.

I cannot but wish that, of this inscription, the two last lines had been   403
omitted, as they take away from the energy what they do not add to the sense.

IV.
On JAMES CRAGGS, *Esq;*   404
in Westminster-Abbey.

JACOBUS CRAGGS,
REGI MAGNAE BRITANNIAE A SECRETIS
ET CONSILIIS SANCTIORIBVS
PRINCIPIS PARITER AC POPULI AMOR ET
DELICIAE:
VIXIT TITULIS ET INVIDIA MAJOR,
ANNOS HEV PAVCOS, XXXV.
OB. FEB. XVI. MDCCXX.

Statesman, yet friend to truth! of soul sincere,
In action faithful, and in honour clear!
Who broke no promise, serv'd no private end,
Who gain'd no title, and who lost no friend;
Ennobled by himself, by all approv'd,
Prais'd, wept, and honour'd, by the Muse he lov'd.

The lines on Craggs were not originally intended for an epitaph; and   405
therefore some faults are to be imputed to the violence with which they are
torn from the poem that first contained them. We may, however, observe
some defects. There is a redundancy of words in the first couplet: it is
superfluous to tell of him, who was *sincere*, *true*, and *faithful*, that he was *in
honour clear*.

There seems to be an opposition intended in the fourth line, which is not   406
very obvious: where is the relation between the two positions, that he *gained
no title* and *lost no friend?*

It may be proper here to remark the absurdity of joining, in the same   407
inscription, Latin and English, or verse and prose. If either language be

preferable to the other, let that only be used; for no reason can be given why part of the information should be given in one tongue, and part in another, on a tomb, more than in any other place, on any other occasion; and to tell all that can be conveniently told in verse, and then to call in the help of prose, has always the appearance of a very artless expedient, or of an attempt unaccomplished. Such an epitaph resembles the conversation of a foreigner, who tells part of his meaning by words, and conveys part by signs.

V.

408   *Intended for Mr.* ROWE.
        In Westminster-Abbey.

> Thy reliques, Rowe, to this fair urn we trust,
> And sacred, place by Dryden's awful dust:
> Beneath a rude and nameless stone he lies,
> To which thy tomb shall guide inquiring eyes.
> Peace to thy gentle shade, and endless rest!
> Blest in thy genius, in thy love too blest!
> One grateful woman to thy fame supplies
> What a whole thankless land to his denies.

409   Of this inscription the chief fault is, that it belongs less to Rowe, for whom it was written, than to Dryden, who was buried near him; and indeed gives very little information concerning either.

410   To wish, *Peace to thy shade*, is too mythological to be admitted into a christian temple: the ancient worship has infected almost all our other compositions, and might therefore be contented to spare our epitaphs. Let fiction, at least, cease with life, and let us be serious over the grave.

VI.

411   *On Mrs.* CORBET,
        who died of a Cancer in her Breast.

> Here rests a woman, good without pretence,
> Blest with plain reason, and with sober sense:
> No conquests she, but o'er herself desir'd;
> No arts essay'd, but not to be admir'd.
> Passion and pride were to her soul unknown,
> Convinc'd that Virtue only is our own.
> So unaffected, so compos'd a mind,
> So firm, yet soft, so strong, yet so refin'd,
> Heaven, as its purest gold, by tortures try'd,
> The saint sustained it, but the woman dy'd.

412   I have always considered this as the most valuable of all Pope's epitaphs; the subject of it is a character not discriminated by any shining or eminent

peculiarities; yet that which really makes, though not the splendor, the felicity of life, and that which every wise man will choose for his final and lasting companion in the languor of age, in the quiet of privacy, when he departs weary and disgusted from the ostentatious, the volatile, and the vain. Of such a character, which the dull overlook, and the gay despise, it was fit that the value should be made known, and the dignity established. Domestick virtue, as it is exerted without great occasions, or conspicuous consequences, in an even unnoted tenor, required the genius of Pope to display it in such a manner as might attract regard, and enforce reverence. Who can forbear to lament that this amiable woman has no name in the verses?

If the particular lines of this inscription be examined, it will appear less 413 faulty than the rest. There is scarce one line taken from common places, unless it be that in which *only Virtue* is said to be *our own*. I once heard a Lady of great beauty and excellence object to the fourth line, that it contained an unnatural and incredible panegyrick. Of this let the Ladies judge.

VII.

On the Monument of the Hon. ROBERT DIGBY, *and of his Sister* MARY, *erected* 414
  by their Father the Lord DIGBY, *in the Church of Sherborne in Dorsetshire,*
  1727.

> Go! fair example of untainted youth,
> Of modest wisdom, and pacifick truth:
> Compos'd in sufferings, and in joy sedate,
> Good without noise, without pretension great.
> Just of thy word, in every thought sincere,
> Who knew no wish but what the world might hear:
> Of softest manners, unaffected mind,
> Lover of peace, and friend of human kind:
> Go, live! for heaven's eternal year is thine,
> Go, and exalt thy moral to divine.
>
> And thou, blest maid! attendant on his doom,
> Pensive hast follow'd to the silent tomb,
> Steer'd the same course to the same quiet shore,
> Not parted long, and now to part no more!
> Go, then, where only bliss sincere is known!
> Go, where to love and to enjoy are one!
>
> Yet take these tears, Mortality's relief,
> And till we share your joys, forgive our grief:
> These little rites, a stone, a verse receive,
> 'Tis all a father, all a friend can give!

415   This epitaph contains of the brother only a general indiscriminate character, and of the sister tells nothing but that she died. The difficulty in
writing epitaphs is to give a particular and appropriate praise. This, however, is not always to be performed, whatever be the diligence or ability of
the writer; for the greater part of mankind *have no characters at all*, have
little that distinguishes them from others equally good or bad, and therefore
nothing can be said of them which may not be applied with equal propriety
to a thousand more. It is indeed no great panegyrick, that there is inclosed in
this tomb one who was born in one year, and died in another; yet many
useful and amiable lives have been spent, which yet leave little materials for
any other memorial. These are however not the proper subjects of poetry;
and whenever friendship, or any other motive, obliges a poet to write on
such subjects, he must be forgiven if he sometimes wanders in generalities,
and utters the same praises over different tombs.

416   The scantiness of human praises can scarcely be made more apparent,
than by remarking how often Pope has, in the few epitaphs which
he composed, found it necessary to borrow from himself. The fourteen
epitaphs, which he has written, comprise about an hundred and forty lines,
in which there are more repetitions than will easily be found in all the rest
of his works. In the eight lines which make the character of Digby, there
is scarce any thought, or word, which may not be found in the other
epitaphs.

417   The ninth line, which is far the strongest and most elegant, is borrowed
from Dryden. The conclusion is the same with that on Harcourt, but is here
more elegant and better connected.

VIII.

418   *On Sir* GODFREY KNELLER.
                    In Westminster-Abbey, 1723.

> Kneller, by heaven, and not a master taught,
> Whose art was nature, and whose pictures thought;
> Now for two ages, having snatch'd from fate
> Whate'er was beauteous, or whate'er was great,
> Lies crown'd with Princes honours, Poets lays,
> Due to his merit, and brave thirst of praise.
>
> Living, great Nature fear'd he might outvie
> Her works; and dying, fears herself may die.

419   Of this epitaph the first couplet is good, the second not bad, the third is
deformed with a broken metaphor, the word *crowned* not being applicable to
the *honours* or the *lays*, and the fourth is not only borrowed from the epitaph
on Raphael, but of very harsh construction.

IX.

On General HENRY WITHERS. 420
In Westminster-Abbey, 1729.

Here, Withers, rest! thou bravest, gentlest mind,
Thy country's friend, but more of human kind,
O! born to arms! O! worth in youth approv'd!
O! soft humanity in age belov'd!
For thee the hardy veteran drops a tear,
And the gay courtier feels the sigh sincere.

Withers, adieu! yet not with thee remove
Thy martial spirit, or thy social love!
Amidst corruption, luxury, and rage,
Still leave some ancient virtues to our age:
Nor let us say (those English glories gone)
The last true Briton lies beneath this stone.

The epitaph on Withers affords another instance of common places, 421
though somewhat diversified, by mingled qualities, and the peculiarity of
a profession.

The second couplet is abrupt, general, and unpleasing; exclamation 422
seldom succeeds in our language; and, I think, it may be observed that
the particle O! used at the beginning of a sentence, always offends.

The third couplet is more happy; the value expressed for him, by different 423
sorts of men, raises him to esteem; there is yet something of the common cant
of superficial satirists, who suppose that the insincerity of a courtier destroys
all his sensations, and that he is equally a dissembler to the living and the dead.

At the third couplet I should wish the epitaph to close, but that I should 424
be unwilling to lose the two next lines, which yet are dearly bought if they
cannot be retained without the four that follow them.

X.

On Mr. ELIJAH FENTON. 425
At Easthamsted in Berkshire, 1730.

This modest stone, what few vain marbles can,
May truly say, Here lies an honest man:
A poet, blest beyond the poet's fate,
Whom Heaven kept sacred from the Proud and Great:
Foe to loud praise, and friend to learned ease,
Content with science in the vale of peace.
Calmly he look'd on either life; and here
Saw nothing to regret, or there to fear;
From Nature's temperate feast rose satisfy'd,
Thank'd heaven that he had liv'd, and that he dy'd.

426   The first couplet of this epitaph is borrowed from *Crashaw*. The four next lines contain a species of praise peculiar, original, and just. Here, therefore, the inscription should have ended, the latter part containing nothing but what is common to every man who is wise and good. The character of Fenton was so amiable, that I cannot forbear to wish for some poet or biographer to display it more fully for the advantage of posterity. If he did not stand in the first rank of genius, he may claim a place in the second; and, whatever criticism may object to his writings, censure could find very little to blame in his life.

XI.

On Mr. GAY.
In Westminster-Abbey, 1732.

427

Of manners gentle, of affections mild;
In wit, a man; simplicity, a child:
With native humour tempering virtuous rage,
Form'd to delight at once and lash the age:
Above temptation, in a low estate,
And uncorrupted, ev'n among the Great:
A safe companion, and an easy friend,
Unblam'd through life, lamented in thy end.
These are thy honours! not that here thy bust
Is mix'd with heroes, or with kings thy dust;
But that the Worthy and the Good shall say,
Striking their pensive bosoms—Here lies GAY.

428   As Gay was the favourite of our author, this epitaph was probably written with an uncommon degree of attention; yet it is not more successfully executed than the rest, for it will not always happen that the success of a poet is proportionate to his labour. The same observation may be extended to all works of imagination, which are often influenced by causes wholly out of the performer's power, by hints of which he perceives not the origin, by sudden elevations of mind which he cannot produce in himself, and which sometimes rise when he expects them least.

429   The two parts of the first line are only echoes of each other; *gentle manners* and *mild affections*, if they mean any thing, must mean the same.

430   That Gay was a *man in wit* is a very frigid commendation; to have the wit of a man is not much for a poet. The *wit of man*, and the *simplicity of a child*, make a poor and vulgar contrast, and raise no ideas of excellence, either intellectual or moral.

431   In the next couplet *rage* is less properly introduced after the mention of *mildness* and *gentleness*, which are made the constituents of his character; for a man so *mild* and *gentle* to *temper* his *rage*, was not difficult.

The next line is unharmonious in its sound, and mean in its conception; 432 the opposition is obvious, and the word *lash* used absolutely, and without any modification, is gross and improper.

To be *above temptation* in poverty, and *free from corruption among the* 433 *Great*, is indeed such a peculiarity as deserved notice. But to be a *safe companion* is praise merely negative, arising not from the possession of virtue, but the absence of vice, and that one of the most odious.

As little can be added to his character, by asserting that he was *lamented in* 434 *his end*. Every man that dies is, at least by the writer of his epitaph, supposed to be lamented, and therefore this general lamentation does no honour to Gay.

The first eight lines have no grammar; the adjectives are without any 435 substantive, and the epithets without a subject.

The thought in the last line, that Gay is buried in the bosoms of the 436 *worthy* and the *good*, who are distinguished only to lengthen the line, is so dark that few understand it; and so harsh, when it is explained, that still fewer approve.

XII.

Intended for Sir ISAAC NEWTON. 437
In Westminster-Abbey.

ISAACUS NEWTONIUS:
Quem Immortalem
Testantur, *Tempus, Natura, Cœlum:*
Mortalem
Hoc marmor fatetur.

Nature, and Nature's laws, lay hid in night,
God said, *Let Newton be!* And all was light.

Of this epitaph, short as it is, the faults seem not to be very few. Why 438 part should be Latin and part English, it is not easy to discover. In the Latin, the opposition of *Immortalis* and *Mortalis*, is a mere sound, or a mere quibble; he is not *immortal* in any sense contrary to that in which he is *mortal*.

In the verses the thought is obvious, and the words *night* and *light* are 439 too nearly allied.

XIII.

On EDMUND *Duke of* BUCKINGHAM, *who died in the 19th Year of his Age,* 440
1735.

If modest youth, with cool reflection crown'd,
And every opening virtue blooming round,

Could save a parent's justest pride from fate,
Or add one patriot to a sinking state;
This weeping marble had not ask'd thy tear,
Or sadly told, how many hopes lie here!
The living virtue now had shone approv'd,
The senate heard him, and his country lov'd.
Yet softer honours, and less noisy fame
Attend the shade of gentle Buckingham:
In whom a race, for courage fam'd and art,
Ends in the milder merit of the heart;
And chiefs or sages long to Britain given,
Pays the last tribute of a saint to heaven.

441   This epitaph Mr. Warburton prefers to the rest, but I know not for what reason. To *crown* with *reflection* is surely a mode of speech approaching to nonsense. *Opening virtues blooming round*, is something like tautology; the six following lines are poor and prosaick. *Art* is in another couplet used for *arts*, that a rhyme may be had to *heart*. The six last lines are the best, but not excellent.

442   The rest of his sepulchral performances hardly deserve the notice of criticism. The contemptible *Dialogue* between HE and SHE should have been suppressed for the author's sake.

443   In his last epitaph on himself, in which he attempts to be jocular upon one of the few things that make wise men serious, he confounds the living man with the dead:

> Under this stone, or under this sill,
> Or under this turf, &c.

444   When a man is once buried, the question, under what he is buried, is easily decided. He forgot that though he wrote the epitaph in a state of uncertainty, yet it could not be laid over him till his grave was made. Such is the folly of wit when it is ill employed.

445   The world has but little new; even this wretchedness seems to have been borrowed from the following tuneless lines:

> Ludovici Areosti humantur ossa
> Sub hoc marmore, vel sub hac humo, seu
> Sub quicquid voluit benignus hæres
> Sive hærede benignior comes, seu
> Opportunius incidens Viator;
> Nam scire haud potuit futura, sed nec
> Tanti erat vacuum sibi cadaver
> Ut urnam cuperet parare vivens,

Vivens ista tamen sibi paravit.
Quæ inscribi voluit suo sepulchro
Olim siquod haberetis sepulchrum.

Surely Ariosto did not venture to expect that his trifle would have ever   446
had such an illustrious imitator.

PITT

1 CHRISTOPHER PITT, of whom whatever I shall relate, more than has been already published, I owe to the kind communication of Dr. Warton, was born in 1699 at Blandford, the son of a physician much esteemed.

2 He was, in 1714, received as a scholar into Winchester College, where he was distinguished by exercises of uncommon elegance; and, at his removal to New College in 1719, presented to the electors, as the product of his private and voluntary studies, a compleat version of Lucan's poem, which he did not then know to have been translated by Rowe.

3 This is an instance of early diligence which well deserves to be recorded. The suppression of such a work, recommended by such uncommon circumstances, is to be regretted. It is indeed culpable, to load libraries with superfluous books; but incitements to early excellence are never superfluous, and from this example the danger is not great of many imitations.

4 When he had resided at his College three years, he was presented to the rectory of Pimpern in Dorsetshire (1722), by his relation, Mr. Pitt of Stratfeildsea in Hampshire; and, resigning his fellowship, continued at Oxford two years longer, till he became Master of Arts (1724).

5 He probably about this time translated *Vida's Art of Poetry*, which Tristram's splendid edition had then made popular. In this translation he distinguished himself, both by its general elegance, and by the skilful adaptation of his numbers, to the images expressed; a beauty which Vida has with great ardour enforced and exemplified.

6 He then retired to his living, a place very pleasing by its situation, and therefore likely to excite the imagination of a poet; where he passed the rest of his life, reverenced for his virtue, and beloved for the softness of his temper and the easiness of his manners. Before strangers he had something of the scholar's timidity or distrust; but when he became familiar he was in a very high degree chearful and entertaining. His general benevolence procured general respect; and he passed a life placid and honourable, neither too great for the kindness of the low, nor too low for the notice of the great.

7 At what time he composed his miscellany, published in 1727, it is not easy nor necessary to know: those which have dates appear to have been very early productions, and I have not observed that any rise above mediocrity.

The success of his *Vida* animated him to a higher undertaking; and in his 8
thirtieth year he published a version of the first book of the Eneid. This
being, I suppose, commended by his friends, he some time afterwards
added three or four more; with an advertisement, in which he represents
himself as translating with great indifference, and with a progress of which
himself was hardly conscious. This can hardly be true, and, if true, is
nothing to the reader.

At last, without any further contention with his modesty, or any awe of 9
the name of Dryden, he gave us a complete English Eneid, which I am sorry
not to see joined in the late publication with his other poems. It would have
been pleasing to have an opportunity of comparing the two best translations
that perhaps were ever produced by one nation of the same author.

Pitt engaging as a rival with Dryden, naturally observed his failures, and 10
avoided them; and, as he wrote after Pope's Iliad, he had an example of an
exact, equable, and splendid versification. With these advantages, seconded
by great diligence, he might successfully labour particular passages, and
escape many errors. If the two versions are compared, perhaps the result
would be, that Dryden leads the reader forward by his general vigour and
sprightliness, and Pitt often stops him to contemplate the excellence of a
single couplet; that Dryden's faults are forgotten in the hurry of delight,
and that Pitt's beauties are neglected in the languor of a cold and listless
perusal; that Pitt pleases the criticks, and Dryden the people; that Pitt is
quoted, and Dryden read.

He did not long enjoy the reputation which this great work deservedly 11
conferred; for he left the world in 1748, and lies buried under a stone at
Blandford, on which is this inscription:

In memory of
Chr. Pitt, clerk, M. A.
Very eminent
for his talents in poetry;
and yet more
for the universal candour of
his mind, and the primitive
simplicity of his manners.
He lived innocent,
and died beloved,
Apr. 13, 1748,
aged 48.

THOMSON

1   JAMES THOMSON, the son of a minister well esteemed for his piety and diligence, was born September 7, 1700, at Ednam, in the shire of Roxburgh, of which his father was pastor. His mother, whose name was Hume, inherited as co-heiress a portion of a small estate. The revenue of a parish in Scotland is seldom large; and it was probably in commiseration of the difficulty with which Mr. Thomson supported his family, having nine children, that Mr. Riccarton, a neighbouring minister, discovering in James uncommon promises of future excellence, undertook to superintend his education, and provide him books.

2   He was taught the common rudiments of learning at the school of Jedburg, a place which he delights to recollect in his poem of *Autumn*; but was not considered by his master as superior to common boys, though in those early days he amused his patron and his friends with poetical compositions; with which however he so little pleased himself, that on every new-year's day he threw into the fire all the productions of the foregoing year.

3   From the school he was removed to Edinburgh, where he had not resided two years when his father died, and left all his children to the care of their mother, who raised upon her little estate what money a mortgage could afford, and, removing with her family to Edinburgh, lived to see her son rising into eminence.

4   The design of Thomson's friends was to breed him a minister. He lived at Edinburgh, as at school, without distinction or expectation, till, at the usual time, he performed a probationary exercise by explaining a psalm. His diction was so poetically splendid, that Mr. Hamilton, the professor of Divinity, reproved him for speaking language unintelligible to a popular audience, and he censured one of his expressions as indecent, if not profane.

5   This rebuke is reported to have repressed his thoughts of an ecclesiastical character, and he probably cultivated with new diligence his blossoms of poetry, which however were in some danger of a blast; for, submitting his productions to some who thought themselves qualified to criticise, he heard of nothing but faults, but, finding other judges more favourable, he did not suffer himself to sink into despondence.

6   He easily discovered that the only stage on which a poet could appear, with any hope of advantage, was London; a place too wide for the operation of petty competition and private malignity, where merit might soon become

conspicuous, and would find friends as soon as it became reputable to befriend it. A lady, who was acquainted with his mother, advised him to the journey, and promised some countenance or assistance, which at last he never received; however, he justified his adventure by her encouragement, and came to seek in London patronage and fame.

At his arrival he found his way to Mr. Mallet, then tutor to the sons of the 7 duke of Montrose. He had recommendations to several persons of consequence, which he had tied up carefully in his handkerchief; but as he passed along the street, with the gaping curiosity of a new-comer, his attention was upon every thing rather than his pocket, and his magazine of credentials was stolen from him.

His first want was of a pair of shoes. For the supply of all his necessities, 8 his whole fund was his *Winter*, which for a time could find no purchaser; till, at last, Mr. Millan was persuaded to buy it at a low price; and this low price he had for some time reason to regret; but, by accident, Mr. Whatley, a man not wholly unknown among authors, happening to turn his eye upon it, was so delighted that he ran from place to place celebrating its excellence. Thomson obtained likewise the notice of Aaron Hill, whom, being friendless and indigent, and glad of kindness, he courted with every expression of servile adulation.

Winter was dedicated to Sir Spencer Compton, but attracted no regard 9 from him to the author; till Aaron Hill awakened his attention by some verses addressed to Thomson, and published in one of the newspapers, which censured the great for their neglect of ingenious men. Thomson then received a present of twenty guineas, of which he gives this account to Mr. Hill:

"I hinted to you in my last, that on Saturday morning I was with Sir 10 Spencer Compton. A certain gentleman, without my desire, spoke to him concerning me; his answer was, that I had never come near him. Then the gentleman put the question, If he desired that I should wait on him? he returned, he did. On this, the gentleman gave me an introductory Letter to him. He received me in what they commonly call a civil manner; asked me some common-place questions, and made me a present of twenty guineas. I am very ready to own that the present was larger than my performance deserved; and shall ascribe it to his generosity, or any other cause, rather than the merit of the address."

The poem, which, being of a new kind, few would venture at first to like, 11 by degrees gained upon the publick; and one edition was very speedily succeeded by another.

Thomson's credit was now high, and every day brought him new friends; 12 among others Dr. Rundle, a man afterwards unfortunately famous, sought his acquaintance, and found his qualities such, that he recommended him to the lord chancellor Talbot.

13   *Winter* was accompanied, in many editions, not only with a preface and a dedication, but with poetical praises by Mr. Hill, Mr. Mallet (then *Mal-loch*), and *Mira*, the fictitious name of a lady once too well known. Why the dedications are, to *Winter* and the other seasons, contrarily to custom, left out in the collected works, the reader may enquire.

14   The next year (1727) he distinguished himself by three publications; of *Summer*, in pursuance of his plan; of *a Poem on the Death of Sir Isaac Newton*, which he was enabled to perform as an exact philosopher by the instruction of Mr. Gray; and of *Britannia*, a kind of poetical invective against the ministry, whom the nation then thought not forward enough in resenting the depredations of the Spaniards. By this piece he declared himself an adherent to the opposition, and had therefore no favour to expect from the Court.

15   Thomson, having been some time entertained in the family of the lord Binning, was desirous of testifying his gratitude by making him the patron of his *Summer*; but the same kindness which had first disposed lord Binning to encourage him, determined him to refuse the dedication, which was by his advice addressed to Mr. Doddington; a man who had more power to advance the reputation and fortune of a poet.

16   *Spring* was published next year, with a dedication to the countess of Hertford; whose practice it was to invite every Summer some poet into the country, to hear her verses, and assist her studies. This honour was one Summer conferred on Thomson, who took more delight in carousing with lord Hertford and his friends than assisting her ladyship's poetical operations, and therefore never received another summons.

17   *Autumn*, the season to which the *Spring* and *Summer* are preparatory, still remained unsung, and was delayed till he published (1730) his works collected.

18   He produced in 1727 the tragedy of *Sophonisba*, which raised such expectation, that every rehearsal was dignified with a splendid audience, collected to anticipate the delight that was preparing for the publick. It was observed however that nobody was much affected, and that the company rose as from a moral lecture.

19   It had upon the stage no unusual degree of success. Slight accidents will operate upon the taste of pleasure. There was a feeble line in the play;

O Sophonisba, Sophonisba, O!

This gave occasion to a waggish parody;

O, Jemmy Thomson, Jemmy Thomson, O!

which for a while was echoed through the town.

I have been told by Savage, that of the Prologue to *Sophonisba* the first 20
part was written by Pope, who could not be persuaded to finish it, and that
the concluding lines were added by Mallet.

Thomson was not long afterwards, by the influence of Dr. Rundle, sent 21
to travel with Mr. Charles Talbot, the eldest son of the Chancellor. He was
yet young enough to receive new impressions, to have his opinions rectified,
and his views enlarged; nor can he be supposed to have wanted that
curiosity which is inseparable from an active and comprehensive mind.
He may therefore now be supposed to have revelled in all the joys of
intellectual luxury; he was every day feasted with instructive novelties; he
lived splendidly without expence, and might expect when he returned
home a certain establishment.

At this time a long course of opposition to Sir Robert Walpole had filled 22
the nation with clamours for liberty, of which no man felt the want, and
with care for liberty, which was not in danger. Thomson, in his travels on
the continent, found or fancied so many evils arising from the tyranny of
other governments, that he resolved to write a very long poem, in five parts,
upon Liberty.

While he was busy on the first book, Mr. Talbot died; and Thomson, 23
who had been rewarded for his attendance by the place of secretary of the
Briefs, pays in the initial lines a decent tribute to his memory.

Upon this great poem two years were spent, and the author congratulated 24
himself upon it as his noblest work; but an author and his reader are not
always of a mind. *Liberty* called in vain upon her votaries to read her praises
and reward her encomiast: her praises were condemned to harbour spiders,
and to gather dust; none of Thomson's performances were so little regarded.

The judgement of the publick was not erroneous; the recurrence of the 25
same images must tire in time; an enumeration of examples to prove a
position which nobody denied, as it was from the beginning superfluous,
must quickly grow disgusting.

The poem of *Liberty* does not now appear in its original state; but when 26
the author's works were collected, after his death, was shortened by Sir
George Lyttelton, with a liberty which, as it has a manifest tendency to
lessen the confidence of society, and to confound the characters of authors,
by making one man write by the judgement of another, cannot be justified
by any supposed propriety of the alteration, or kindness of the friend.—I
wish to see it exhibited as its author left it.

Thomson now lived in ease and plenty, and seems for a while to have 27
suspended his poetry; but he was soon called back to labour by the death of
the Chancellor, for his place then became vacant; and though the lord

Hardwicke delayed for some time to give it away, Thomson's bashfulness, or pride, or some other motive perhaps not more laudable, withheld him from soliciting; and the new Chancellor would not give him what he would not ask.

28   He now relapsed to his former indigence; but the prince of Wales was at that time struggling for popularity, and by the influence of Mr. Lyttelton professed himself the patron of wit: to him Thomson was introduced, and being gaily interrogated about the state of his affairs, said, *that they were in a more poetical posture than formerly*; and had a pension allowed him of one hundred pounds a year.

29   Being now obliged to write, he produced (1738) the tragedy of *Agamemnon*, which was much shortened in the representation. It had the fate which most commonly attends mythological stories, and was only endured, but not favoured. It struggled with such difficulty through the first night, that Thomson, coming late to his friends with whom he was to sup, excused his delay by telling them how the sweat of his distress had so disordered his wig, that he could not come till he had been refitted by a barber.

30   He so interested himself in his own drama, that, if I remember right, as he sat in the upper gallery he accompanied the players by audible recitation, till a friendly hint frighted him to silence. Pope countenanced *Agamemnon*, by coming to it the first night, and was welcomed to the theatre by a general clap; he had much regard for Thomson, and once expressed it in a poetical Epistle sent to Italy, of which however he abated the value, by transplanting some of the lines into his Epistle to *Arbuthnot*.

31   About this time the Act was passed for licensing plays, of which the first operation was the prohibition of *Gustavus Vasa*, a tragedy of Mr. Brooke, whom the publick recompensed by a very liberal subscription; the next was the refusal of *Edward and Eleonora*, offered by Thomson. It is hard to discover why either play should have been obstructed. Thomson likewise endeavoured to repair his loss by a subscription, of which I cannot now tell the success.

32   When the publick murmured at the unkind treatment of Thomson, one of the ministerial writers remarked, that *he had taken a* Liberty *which was not agreeable to* Britannia *in any* Season.

33   He was soon after employed, in conjunction with Mr. Mallet, to write the masque of *Alfred*, which was acted before the Prince at Cliefden-house.

34   His next work (1745) was *Tancred and Sigismunda*, the most successful of all his tragedies; for it still keeps its turn upon the stage. It may be doubted whether he was, either by the bent of nature or habits of study, much qualified for tragedy. It does not appear that he had much sense of the

pathetick, and his diffusive and descriptive style produced declamation rather than dialogue.

His friend Mr. Lyttelton was now in power, and conferred upon him the office of surveyor-general of the Leeward Islands; from which, when his deputy was paid, he received about three hundred pounds a year. 35

The last piece that he lived to publish was the *Castle of Indolence*, which was many years under his hand, but was at last finished with great accuracy. The first canto opens a scene of lazy luxury, that fills the imagination. 36

He was now at ease, but was not long to enjoy it; for, by taking cold on the water between London and Kew, he caught a disorder, which, with some careless exasperation, ended in a fever that put an end to his life, August 27, 1748. He was buried in the church of Richmond, without an inscription; but a monument has been erected to his memory in Westminster-abbey. 37

Thomson was of stature above the middle size, and *more fat than bard beseems*, of a dull countenance, and a gross, unanimated, uninviting appearance; silent in mingled company, but chearful among select friends, and by his friends very tenderly and warmly beloved. 38

He left behind him the tragedy of *Coriolanus*, which was, by the zeal of his patron Sir George Lyttelton, brought upon the stage for the benefit of his family, and recommended by a Prologue, which Quin, who had long lived with Thomson in fond intimacy, spoke in such a manner as shewed him *to be*, on that occasion, *no actor*. The commencement of this benevolence is very honourable to Quin; who is reported to have delivered Thomson, then known to him only for his genius, from an arrest, by a very considerable present; and its continuance is honourable to both; for friendship is not always the sequel of obligation. By this tragedy a considerable sum was raised, of which part discharged his debts, and the rest was remitted to his sisters, whom, however removed from them by place or condition, he regarded with great tenderness, as will appear by the following Letter, which I communicate with much pleasure, as it gives me at once an opportunity of recording the fraternal kindness of Thomson, and reflecting on the friendly assistance of Mr. Boswell, from whom I received it. 39

"Hagley in Worcestershire, 40
October the 4th, 1747.

"My dear Sister,

"I thought you had known me better than to interpret my silence into a decay of affection, especially as your behaviour has always been such as rather to increase than diminish it. Don't imagine, because I am a bad correspondent, that I can ever prove an unkind friend and brother. I must do myself the justice to tell you, that my affections are naturally very fixed and constant; and if I had ever reason of complaint against you (of which by the bye I have not the least shadow), I am conscious of so many defects in myself, as dispose me to be not a little charitable and forgiving.

41 "It gives me the truest heart-felt satisfaction to hear you have a good kind husband, and are in easy contented circumstances; but were they otherwise, that would only awaken and heighten my tenderness towards you. As our good and tender-hearted parents did not live to receive any material testimonies of that highest human gratitude I owed them (than which nothing could have given me equal pleasure), the only return I can make them now is by kindness to those they left behind them: would to God poor Lizy had lived longer, to have been a farther witness of the truth of what I say, and that I might have had the pleasure of seeing once more a sister, who so truly deserved my esteem and love. But she is happy, while we must toil a little longer here below: let us however do it chearfully and gratefully, supported by the pleasing hope of meeting yet again on a safer shore, where to recollect the storms and difficulties of life will not perhaps be inconsistent with that blissful state. You did right to call your daughter by her name; for you must needs have had a particular tender friendship for one another, endeared as you were by nature, by having passed the affectionate years of your youth together; and by that great softner and engager of hearts, mutual hardship. That it was in my power to ease it a little, I account one of the most exquisite pleasures of my life.—But enough of this melancholy though not unpleasing strain.

42 "I esteem you for your sensible and disinterested advice to Mr. Bell, as you will see by my Letter to him: as I approve entirely of his marrying again, you may readily ask me why I don't marry at all. My circumstances have hitherto been so variable and uncertain in this fluctuating world, as induce to keep me from engaging in such a state: and now, though they are more settled, and of late (which you will be glad to hear) considerably improved, I begin to think myself too far advanced in life for such youthful undertakings, not to mention some other petty reasons that are apt to startle the delicacy of difficult old batchelors. I am, however, not a little suspicious that was I to pay a visit to Scotland (which I have some thoughts of doing soon) I might possibly be tempted to think of a thing not easily repaired if done amiss. I have always been of opinion that none make better wives than the ladies of Scotland; and yet, who more forsaken than they, while the gentlemen are continually running abroad all the world over? Some of them, it is true, are wise enough to return for a wife. You see I am beginning to make interest already with the Scots ladies.—But no more of this infectious subject.—Pray let me hear from you now and then; and though

I am not a regular correspondent, yet perhaps I may mend in that respect. Remember me kindly to your husband, and believe me to be.

> "Your most affectionate brother,
> JAMES THOMSON."
> (Addressed) "To Mrs. Thomson in Lanark."

The benevolence of Thomson was fervid, but not active; he would give, 43 on all occasions, what assistance his purse would supply; but the offices of intervention or solicitation he could not conquer his sluggishness sufficiently to perform. The affairs of others, however, were not more neglected than his own. He had often felt the inconveniences of idleness, but he never cured it; and was so conscious of his own character, that he talked of writing an Eastern Tale of *the Man who loved to be in Distress*.

Among his peculiarities was a very unskilful and inarticulate manner of 44 pronouncing any lofty or solemn composition. He was once reading to Doddington, who, being himself a reader eminently elegant, was so much provoked by his odd utterance, that he snatched the paper from his hand, and told him that he did not understand his own verses.

The biographer of Thomson has remarked, that an author's life is best 45 read in his works: his observation was not well-timed. Savage, who lived much with Thomson, once told me, how he heard a lady remarking that she could gather from his works three parts of his character, that he was a *great Lover, a great Swimmer*, and *rigorously abstinent*; but, said Savage, he knows not any love but that of the sex; he was perhaps never in cold water in his life; and he indulges himself in all the luxury that comes within his reach. Yet Savage always spoke with the most eager praise of his social qualities, his warmth and constancy of friendship, and his adherence to his first acquaintance when the advancement of his reputation had left them behind him.

As a writer, he is entitled to one praise of the highest kind: his mode of 46 thinking, and of expressing his thoughts, is original. His blank verse is no more the blank verse of Milton, or of any other poet, than the rhymes of Prior are the rhymes of Cowley. His numbers, his pauses, his diction, are of his own growth, without transcription, without imitation. He thinks in a peculiar train, and he thinks always as a man of genius; he looks round on Nature and on Life, with the eye which Nature bestows only on a poet; the eye that distinguishes, in every thing presented to its view, whatever there is on which imagination can delight to be detained, and with a mind that at once comprehends the vast, and attends to the minute. The reader of the *Seasons* wonders that he never saw before what Thomson shews him, and that he never yet has felt what Thomson impresses.

47   His is one of the works in which blank verse seems properly used; Thomson's wide expansion of general views, and his enumeration of circumstantial varieties, would have been obstructed and embarrassed by the frequent intersections of the sense, which are the necessary effects of rhyme.

48   His descriptions of extended scenes and general effects bring before us the whole magnificence of Nature, whether pleasing or dreadful. The gaiety of *Spring*, the splendour of *Summer*, the tranquillity of *Autumn*, and the horror of *Winter*, take in their turns possession of the mind. The poet leads us through the appearances of things as they are successively varied by the vicissitudes of the year, and imparts to us so much of his own enthusiasm, that our thoughts expand with his imagery, and kindle with his sentiments. Nor is the naturalist without his part in the entertainment; for he is assisted to recollect and to combine, to arrange his discoveries, and to amplify the sphere of his contemplation.

49   The great defect of the *Seasons* is want of method; but for this I know not that there was any remedy. Of many appearances subsisting all at once, no rule can be given why one should be mentioned before another; yet the memory wants the help of order, and the curiosity is not excited by suspense or expectation.

50   His diction is in the highest degree florid and luxuriant, such as may be said to be to his images and thoughts *both their lustre and their shade*; such as invests them with splendour, through which perhaps they are not always easily discerned. It is too exuberant, and sometimes may be charged with filling the ear more than the mind.

51   These Poems, with which I was acquainted at their first appearance, I have since found altered and enlarged by subsequent revisals, as the author supposed his judgement to grow more exact, and as books or conversation extended his knowledge and opened his prospects. They are, I think, improved in general; yet I know not whether they have not lost part of what Temple calls their *race*; a word which, applied to wines, in its primitive sense, means the flavour of the soil.

52   *Liberty*, when it first appeared, I tried to read, and soon desisted. I have never tried again, and therefore will not hazard either praise or censure.

53   The highest praise which he has received ought not to be supprest; it is said by Lord Lyttelton in the Prologue to his posthumous play, that his works contained

> No line which, dying, he could wish to blot.

WATTS

THE Poems of Dr. WATTS were by my recommendation inserted in the late 1
Collection; the readers of which are to impute to me whatever pleasure or
weariness they may find in the perusal of Blackmore, Watts, Pomfret, and
Yalden.

ISAAC WATTS was born July 17, 1674, at Southampton, where his father, 2
of the same name, kept a boarding-school for young gentlemen, though
common report makes him a shoemaker. He appears, from the narrative of
Dr. Gibbons, to have been neither indigent nor illiterate.

Isaac, the eldest of nine children, was given to books from his infancy; 3
and began, we are told, to learn Latin when he was four years old, I suppose,
at home. He was afterwards taught Latin, Greek, and Hebrew, by
Mr. Pinhorne, a clergyman, master of the Free-school at Southampton, to
whom the gratitude of his scholar afterwards inscribed a Latin ode.

His proficiency at school was so conspicuous, that a subscription was 4
proposed for his support at the University; but he declared his resolution to
take his lot with the Dissenters. Such he was as every Christian Church
would rejoice to have adopted.

He therefore repaired in 1690 to an academy taught by Mr. Rowe, where 5
he had for his companions and fellow-students Mr. Hughes the poet, and
Dr. Horte, afterwards Archbishop of Tuam. Some Latin Essays, supposed
to have been written as exercises at this academy, shew a degree of knowledge, both philosophical and theological, such as very few attain by a much
longer course of study.

He was, as he hints in his Miscellanies, a maker of verses from fifteen to 6
fifty, and in his youth he appears to have paid attention to Latin poetry. His
verses to his brother, in the *glyconick* measure, written when he was
seventeen, are remarkably easy and elegant. Some of his other odes are
deformed by the Pindarick folly then prevailing, and are written with such
neglect of all metrical rules as is without example among the ancients; but
his diction, though perhaps not always exactly pure, has such copiousness
and splendour, as shews that he was but at a very little distance from
excellence.

His method of study was to impress the contents of his books upon his 7
memory by abridging them, and by interleaving them to amplify one system
with supplements from another.

8   With the congregation of his tutor Mr. Rowe, who were, I believe, Independents, he communicated in his nineteenth year.

9   At the age of twenty he left the academy, and spent two years in study and devotion at the house of his father, who treated him with great tenderness; and had the happiness, indulged to few parents, of living to see his son eminent for literature and venerable for piety.

10   He was then entertained by Sir John Hartopp five years, as domestick tutor to his son; and in that time particularly devoted himself to the study of the Holy Scriptures; and being chosen assistant to Dr. Chauncey, preached the first time on the birth-day that compleated his twenty-fourth year; probably considering that as the day of a second nativity, by which he entered on a new period of existence.

11   In about three years he succeeded Dr. Chauncey; but, soon after his entrance on his charge, he was seized by a dangerous illness, which sunk him to such weakness, that the congregation thought an assistant necessary, and appointed Mr. Price. His health then returned gradually, and he performed his duty, till (1712) he was seized by a fever of such violence and continuance, that, from the feebleness which it brought upon him, he never perfectly recovered.

12   This calamitous state made the compassion of his friends necessary, and drew upon him the attention of Sir Thomas Abney, who received him into his house; where, with a constancy of friendship and uniformity of conduct not often to be found, he was treated for thirty-six years with all the kindness that friendship could prompt, and all the attention that respect could dictate. Sir Thomas died about eight years afterwards; but he continued with the lady and her daughters to the end of his life. The lady died about a year after him.

13   A coalition like this, a state in which the notions of patronage and dependence were overpowered by the perception of reciprocal benefits, deserves a particular memorial; and I will not withhold from the reader Dr. Gibbons's representation, to which regard is to be paid as to the narrative of one who writes what he knows, and what is known likewise to multitudes besides.

"Our next observation shall be made upon that remarkably kind Providence which brought the Doctor into Sir Thomas Abney's family, and continued him there till his death, a period of no less than thirty-six years. In the midst of his sacred labours for the glory of God, and good of his generation, he is seized with a most violent and threatening fever, which leaves him oppressed with great weakness, and puts a stop at least to his publick services for four years. In this distressing season, doubly so to his active and pious spirit, he is invited to Sir Thomas Abney's family, nor ever removes from it till he had finished his days. Here he enjoyed the uninterrupted demonstrations of the truest friendship. Here, without any care of his own, he had every thing which could contribute to the enjoyment of life, and favour the unwearied pursuit of his studies. Here he dwelt in a family, which, for piety, order, harmony, and every virtue, was an house of God. Here he had the privilege of a country recess, the fragrant bower, the spreading lawn, the flowery garden, and other advantages, to sooth his mind and aid his restoration to health; to yield him, whenever he chose them, most grateful intervals from his laborious studies, and enable him to return to them with redoubled vigour and delight. Had it not been for this most happy event, he might, as to outward view, have feebly, it may be painfully, dragged on through many more years of languor, and inability for publick service, and even for profitable study, or perhaps might have sunk into his grave under the overwhelming load of infirmities in the midst of his days; and thus the church and world would have been deprived of those many excellent sermons and works, which he drew up and published during his long residence in this family. In a few years after his coming hither, Sir Thomas Abney dies; but his amiable consort survives, who shews the Doctor the same respect and friendship as before, and most happily for him and great numbers besides; for, as her riches were great, her generosity and munificence were in full proportion; her thread of life was drawn out to a great age, even beyond that of the Doctor's; and thus this excellent man, through her kindness, and that of her daughter, the present Mrs. Elizabeth Abney, who in a like degree esteemed and honoured him, enjoyed all the benefits and felicities he experienced at his first entrance into this family, till his days were numbered and finished, and, like a shock of corn in its season, he ascended into the regions of perfect and immortal life and joy."

If this quotation has appeared long, let it be considered that it comprises 14 an account of six-and-thirty years, and those the years of Dr. Watts.

From the time of his reception into this family, his life was no otherwise 15 diversified than by successive publications. The series of his works I am not able to deduce; their number, and their variety, shew the intenseness of his industry, and the extent of his capacity.

He was one of the first authors that taught the Dissenters to court 16 attention by the graces of language. Whatever they had among them before, whether of learning or acuteness, was commonly obscured and blunted by coarseness and inelegance of style. He shewed them, that zeal and purity might be expressed and enforced by polished diction.

He continued to the end of his life the teacher of a congregation, and no 17 reader of his works can doubt his fidelity or diligence. In the pulpit, though his low stature, which very little exceeded five feet, graced him with no advantages of appearance, yet the gravity and propriety of his utterance made his discourses very efficacious. I once mentioned the reputation which Mr. Foster had gained by his proper delivery to my friend Dr. Hawkesworth, who told me, that in the art of pronunciation he was far inferior to Dr. Watts.

18 Such was his flow of thoughts, and such his promptitude of language, that in the latter part of his life he did not precompose his cursory sermons; but having adjusted the heads, and sketched out some particulars, trusted for success to his extemporary powers.

19 He did not endeavour to assist his eloquence by any gesticulations; for, as no corporeal actions have any correspondence with theological truth, he did not see how they could enforce it.

20 At the conclusion of weighty sentences he gave time, by a short pause, for the proper impression.

21 To stated and publick instruction he added familiar visits and personal application, and was careful to improve the opportunities which conversation offered of diffusing and increasing the influence of religion.

22 By his natural temper he was quick of resentment; but, by his established and habitual practice, he was gentle, modest, and inoffensive. His tenderness appeared in his attention to children, and to the poor. To the poor, while he lived in the family of his friend, he allowed the third part of his annual revenue, though the whole was not a hundred a year; and for children, he condescended to lay aside the scholar, the philosopher, and the wit, to write little poems of devotion, and systems of instruction, adapted to their wants and capacities, from the dawn of reason through its gradations of advance in the morning of life. Every man, acquainted with the common principles of human action, will look with veneration on the writer who is at one time combating Locke, and at another making a catechism for children in their fourth year. A voluntary descent from the dignity of science is perhaps the hardest lesson that humility can teach.

23 As his mind was capacious, his curiosity excursive, and his industry continual, his writings are very numerous, and his subjects various. With his theological works I am only enough acquainted to admire his meekness of opposition, and his mildness of censure. It was not only in his book but in his mind that *orthodoxy* was *united* with *charity*.

24 Of his philosophical pieces, his Logick has been received into the universities, and therefore wants no private recommendation: if he owes part of it to Le Clerc, it must be considered that no man who undertakes merely to methodise or illustrate a system, pretends to be its author.

25 In his metaphysical disquisitions, it was observed by the late learned Mr. Dyer, that he confounded the idea of *space* with that of *empty space*, and

did not consider that though space might be without matter, yet matter being extended, could not be without space.

Few books have been perused by me with greater pleasure than his 26 *Improvement of the Mind*, of which the radical principles may indeed be found in Locke's *Conduct of the Understanding*, but they are so expanded and ramified by Watts, as to confer upon him the merit of a work in the highest degree useful and pleasing. Whoever has the care of instructing others, may be charged with deficience in his duty if this book is not recommended.

I have mentioned his treatises of Theology as distinct from his other 27 productions; but the truth is, that whatever he took in hand was, by his incessant solicitude for souls, converted to Theology. As piety predomin- ated in his mind, it is diffused over his works: under his direction it may be truly said, *Theologiæ Philosophia ancillatur*, philosophy is subservient to evangelical instruction; it is difficult to read a page without learning, or at least wishing, to be better. The attention is caught by indirect instruction, and he that sat down only to reason is on a sudden compelled to pray.

It was therefore with great propriety that, in 1728, he received from 28 Edinburgh and Aberdeen an unsolicited diploma, by which he became a Doctor of Divinity. Academical honours would have more value, if they were always bestowed with equal judgement.

He continued many years to study and to preach, and to do good by his 29 instruction and example; till at last the infirmities of age disabled him from the more laborious part of his ministerial functions, and, being no longer capable of publick duty, he offered to remit the salary appendant to it; but his congregation would not accept the resignation.

By degrees his weakness increased, and at last confined him to his 30 chamber and his bed; where he was worn gradually away without pain, till he expired Nov. 25, 1748, in the seventy-fifth year of his age.

Few men have left behind such purity of character, or such monuments 31 of laborious piety. He has provided instruction for all ages, from those who are lisping their first lessons, to the enlightened readers of Malbranche and Locke; he has left neither corporeal nor spiritual nature unexamined; he has taught the art of reasoning, and the science of the stars.

His character, therefore, must be formed from the multiplicity and 32 diversity of his attainments, rather than from any single performance; for it would not be safe to claim for him the highest rank in any single denom- ination of literary dignity; yet perhaps there was nothing in which he would not have excelled, if he had not divided his powers to different pursuits.

As a poet, had he been only a poet, he would probably have stood high 33 among the authors with whom he is now associated. For his judgement was exact, and he noted beauties and faults with very nice discernment; his imagination, as the *Dacian Battle* proves, was vigorous and active, and the stores of knowledge were large by which his fancy was to be supplied. His ear was well-tuned, and his diction was elegant and copious. But his devotional poetry is, like that of others, unsatisfactory. The paucity of its topicks enforces perpetual repetition, and the sanctity of the matter rejects the ornaments of figurative diction. It is sufficient for Watts to have done better than others what no man has done well.

34   His poems on other subjects seldom rise higher than might be expected from the amusements of a Man of Letters, and have different degrees of value as they are more or less laboured, or as the occasion was more or less favourable to invention.

35   He writes too often without regular measures, and too often in blank verse; the rhymes are not always sufficiently correspondent. He is particularly unhappy in coining names expressive of characters. His lines are commonly smooth and easy, and his thoughts always religiously pure; but who is there that, to so much piety and innocence, does not wish for a greater measure of spriteliness and vigour? He is at least one of the few poets with whom youth and ignorance may be safely pleased; and happy will be that reader whose mind is disposed by his verses, or his prose, to imitate him in all but his non–conformity, to copy his benevolence to man, and his reverence to God.

A. PHILIPS

Of the birth or early part of the life of AMBROSE PHILIPS I have not been 1
able to find any account. His academical education he received at St. John's
College in Cambridge, where he first solicited the notice of the world by
some English verses, in the Collection published by the University on the
death of queen Mary.

From this time how he was employed, or in what station he passed his 2
life, is not yet discovered. He must have published his Pastorals before the
year 1708, because they are evidently prior to those of Pope.

He afterwards (1709) addressed to the universal patron, the duke of 3
Dorset, a *poetical Letter from Copenhagen*, which was published in the
Tatler, and is by Pope in one of his first Letters mentioned with high praise,
as the production of a man *who could write very nobly*.

Philips was a zealous Whig, and therefore easily found access to Addison 4
and Steele; but his ardour seems not to have procured him any thing more
than kind words; since he was reduced to translate the *Persian Tales* for
Tonson, for which he was afterwards reproached, with this addition of
contempt, that he worked for half-a-crown. The book is divided into many
sections, for each of which if he received half-a-crown, his reward, as
writers then were paid, was very liberal; but half-a-crown had a mean
sound.

He was employed in promoting the principles of his party, by epitomis- 5
ing Hacket's *Life of Archbishop Williams*. The original book is written with
such depravity of genius, such mixture of the fop and pedant, as has not
often appeared. The Epitome is free enough from affectation, but has little
spirit or vigour.

In 1712 he brought upon the stage *The Distrest Mother*, almost a trans- 6
lation of Racine's *Andromaque*. Such a work requires no uncommon powers;
but the friends of Philips exerted every art to promote his interest. Before
the appearance of the play a whole *Spectator*, none indeed of the best, was
devoted to its praise; while it yet continued to be acted, another *Spectator*
was written, to tell what impression it made upon Sir Roger; and on the first
night a select audience, says Pope*, was called together to applaud it.

* Spence.

7   It was concluded with the most successful Epilogue that was ever yet spoken on the English theatre. The three first nights it was recited twice; and not only continued to be demanded through the run, as it is termed, of the play, but whenever it is recalled to the stage, where by peculiar fortune, though a copy from the French, it yet keeps its place, the Epilogue is still expected, and is still spoken.

8   The propriety of epilogues in general, and consequently of this, was questioned by a correspondent of the *Spectator*, whose Letter was undoubtedly admitted for the sake of the Answer, which soon followed, written with much zeal and acrimony. The attack and the defence equally contributed to stimulate curiosity and continue attention. It may be discovered in the defence, that Prior's Epilogue to *Phædra* had a little excited jealousy; and something of Prior's plan may be discovered in the performance of his rival.

9   Of this distinguished Epilogue the reputed author was the wretched Budgel, whom Addison used to denominate* *the man who calls me cousin*; and when he was asked how such a silly fellow could write so well, replied, *The Epilogue was quite another thing when I saw it first*. It was known in Tonson's family, and told to Garrick, that Addison was himself the author of it, and that when it had been at first printed with his name, he came early in the morning, before the copies were distributed, and ordered it to be given to Budgel, that it might add weight to the solicitation which he was then making for a place.

10   Philips was now high in the ranks of literature. His play was applauded; his translations from Sappho had been published in the *Spectator*; he was an important and distinguished associate of clubs witty and political; and nothing was wanting to his happiness, but that he should be sure of its continuance.

11   The work which had procured him the first notice from the publick was his Six Pastorals, which, flattering the imagination with Arcadian scenes, probably found many readers, and might have long passed as a pleasing amusement, had they not been unhappily too much commended.

12   The rustic Poems of Theocritus were so highly valued by the Greeks and Romans, that they attracted the imitation of Virgil, whose Eclogues seem to have been considered as precluding all attempts of the same kind; for no shepherds were taught to sing by any succeeding poet, till Nemesian and Calphurnius ventured their feeble efforts in the lower age of Latin literature.

13   At the revival of learning in Italy, it was soon discovered that a dialogue of imaginary swains might be composed with little difficulty; because the

---

* Spence.

conversation of shepherds excludes profound or refined sentiment; and, for images and descriptions, Satyrs and Fauns, and Naiads and Dryads, were always within call; and woods and meadows, and hills and rivers, supplied variety of matter; which, having a natural power to sooth the mind, did not quickly cloy it.

Petrarch entertained the learned men of his age with the novelty of 14 modern Pastorals in Latin. Being not ignorant of Greek, and finding nothing in the word *Eclogue* of rural meaning, he supposed it to be corrupted by the copiers, and therefore called his own productions *Æglogues*, by which he meant to express the talk of goatherds, though it will mean only the talk of goats. This new name was adopted by subsequent writers, and amongst others by our Spenser.

More than a century afterwards (1498) Mantuan published his *Bucolicks* 15 with such success, that they were soon dignified by Badius with a comment, and, as Scaliger complained, received into schools, and taught as classical; his complaint was vain, and the practice, however injudicious, spread far and continued long. Mantuan was read, at least in some of the inferior schools of this kingdom, to the beginning of the present century. The speakers of Mantuan carried their disquisitions beyond the country, to censure the corruptions of the Church; and from him Spenser learned to employ his swains on topicks of controversy.

The Italians soon transferred Pastoral Poetry into their own language: 16 Sannazaro wrote *Arcadia* in prose and verse; Tasso and Guarini wrote *Favole Boschereccie*, or Sylvan Dramas; and all nations of Europe filled volumes with *Thyrsis* and *Damon*, and *Thestylis* and *Phyllis*.

Philips thinks it *somewhat strange to conceive how, in an age so addicted to* 17 *the Muses, Pastoral Poetry never comes to be so much as thought upon.* His wonder seems very unseasonable; there had never, from the time of Spenser, wanted writers to talk occasionally of *Arcadia* and *Strephon*; and half the book, in which he first tried his powers, consists of dialogues on queen Mary's death, between *Tityrus* and *Corydon*, or *Mopsus* and *Menalcas*. A series or book of Pastorals, however, I know not that any one had then lately published.

Not long afterwards Pope made the first display of his powers in four 18 Pastorals, written in a very different form. Philips had taken Spenser, and Pope took Virgil for his pattern. Philips endeavoured to be natural, Pope laboured to be elegant.

Philips was now favoured by Addison, and by Addison's companions, 19 who were very willing to push him into reputation. The *Guardian* gave an account of Pastoral, partly critical, and partly historical; in which, when the merit of the moderns is compared, Tasso and Guarini are censured for remote thoughts and unnatural refinements; and, upon the whole, the Italians and French are all excluded from rural poetry, and the pipe of the Pastoral Muse is transmitted by lawful inheritance from Theocritus to Virgil, from Virgil to Spenser, and from Spenser to Philips.

20   With this inauguration of Philips, his rival Pope was not much delighted; he therefore drew a comparison of Philips's performance with his own, in which, with an unexampled and unequalled artifice of irony, though he has himself always the advantage, he gives the preference to Philips. The design of aggrandising himself he disguised with such dexterity, that, though Addison discovered it, Steele was deceived, and was afraid of displeasing Pope by publishing his paper. Published however it was (*Guard.* 40), and from that time Pope and Philips lived in a perpetual reciprocation of malevolence.

21   In poetical powers, of either praise or satire, there was no proportion between the combatants; but Philips, though he could not prevail by wit, hoped to hurt Pope with another weapon, and charged him, as Pope thought, with Addison's approbation, as disaffected to the government.

22   Even with this he was not satisfied; for, indeed, there is no appearance that any regard was paid to his clamours. He proceeded to grosser insults, and hung up a rod at Button's, with which he threatened to chastise Pope, who appears to have been extremely exasperated; for in the first edition of his Letters he calls Philips *rascal*, and in the last still charges him with detaining in his hands the subscriptions for Homer delivered to him by the Hanover Club.

23   I suppose it was never suspected that he meant to appropriate the money; he only delayed, and with sufficient meanness, the gratification of him by whose prosperity he was pained.

24   Men sometimes suffer by injudicious kindness; Philips became ridiculous, without his own fault, by the absurd admiration of his friends, who decorated him with honorary garlands which the first breath of contradiction blasted.

25   When upon the succession of the House of Hanover every Whig expected to be happy, Philips seems to have obtained too little notice; he caught few drops of the golden shower, though he did not omit what flattery could perform. He was only made a Commissioner of the Lottery (1717), and, what did not much elevate his character, a Justice of the Peace,

26   The success of his first play must naturally dispose him to turn his hopes towards the stage: he did not however soon commit himself to the mercy of an audience, but contented himself with the fame already acquired, till after nine years he produced (1721) *The Briton*, a tragedy which, whatever was its reception, is now neglected; though one of the scenes, between *Vanoc* the

British Prince and *Valens* the Roman General, is confessed to be written with great dramatick skill, animated by spirit truly poetical.

He had not been idle though he had been silent; for he exhibited another   27
tragedy the same year, on the story of *Humphry Duke of Gloucester*. This tragedy is only remembered by its title.

His happiest undertaking was of a paper called *The Freethinker*, in   28
conjunction with associates, of whom one was Dr. Boulter, who, then only minister of a parish in Southwark, was of so much consequence to the government, that he was made first bishop of Bristol, and afterwards primate of Ireland, where his piety and his charity will be long honoured.

It may easily be imagined that what was printed under the direction of   29
Boulter, would have nothing in it indecent or licentious; its title is to be understood as implying only freedom from unreasonable prejudice. It has been reprinted in volumes, but is little read; not can impartial criticism recommend it as worthy of revival.

Boulter was not well qualified to write diurnal essays; but he knew how to   30
practise the liberality of greatness and the fidelity of friendship. When he was advanced to the height of ecclesiastical dignity, he did not forget the companion of his labours. Knowing Philips to be slenderly supported, he took him to Ireland, as partaker of his fortune; and, making him his secretary, added such preferments, as enabled him to represent the county of Armagh in the Irish Parliament.

In December 1726 he was made secretary to the Lord Chancellor; and in   31
August 1733 became judge of the Prerogative Court.

After the death of his patron he continued some years in Ireland; but at   32
last longing, as it seems, for his native country, he returned (1748) to London, having doubtless survived most of his friends and enemies, and among them his dreaded antagonist Pope. He found however the duke of Newcastle still living, and to him he dedicated his poems collected into a volume.

Having purchased an annuity of four hundred pounds, he now certainly   33
hoped to pass some years of life in plenty and tranquillity; but his hope deceived him: he was struck with a palsy, and died June 18, 1749, in his seventy-eighth year.

Of his personal character all that I have heard is, that he was eminent for   34
bravery and skill in the sword, and that in conversation he was solemn and pompous. He had great sensibility of censure, if judgement may be made by a single story which I heard long ago from Mr. Ing, a gentleman of great eminence in Staffordshire. "Philips," said he, "was once at table, when I asked him, How came thy king of Epirus to drive oxen, and to say *I'm goaded on by love?* After which question he never spoke again,"

35   Of the *Distrest Mother* not much is pretended to be his own, and therefore it is no subject of criticism: his other two tragedies, I believe, are not below mediocrity, nor above it. Among the Poems comprised in the late collection, the *Letter from Denmark* may be justly praised; the Pastorals, which by the writer of the *Guardian* were ranked as one of the four genuine productions of the rustick Muse, cannot surely be despicable. That they exhibit a mode of life which does not exist, nor ever existed, is not to be objected; the supposition of such a state is allowed to Pastoral. In his other poems he cannot be denied the praise of lines sometimes elegant; but he has seldom much force, or much comprehension. The pieces that please best are those which, from Pope and Pope's adherents, procured him the name of *Namby Pamby*, the poems of short lines, by which he paid his court to all ages and characters, from Walpole the *steerer of the realm*, to miss Pulteney in the nursery. The numbers are smooth and spritely, and the diction is seldom faulty. They are not loaded with much thought, yet if they had been written by Addison they would have had admirers: little things are not valued but when they are done by those who can do greater.

36   In his translations from Pindar he found the art of reaching all the obscurity of the Theban bard, however he may fall below his sublimity; he will be allowed, if he has less fire, to have more smoke.

37   He has added nothing to English poetry, yet at least half his book deserves to be read: perhaps he valued most himself that part, which the critick would reject.

WEST

GILBERT WEST is one of the writers of whom I regret my inability to give a 1
sufficient account; the intelligence which my enquiries have obtained is
general and scanty.

He was the son of the reverend Dr. West; perhaps him who published 2
Pindar at Oxford about the beginning of this century. His mother was sister
to Sir Richard Temple, afterwards lord Cobham. His father, purposing to
educate him for the Church, sent him first to Eton, and afterwards to
Oxford; but he was seduced to a more airy mode of life, by a commission
in a troop of horse procured him by his uncle.

He continued some time in the army; though it is reasonable to suppose 3
that he never sunk into a mere soldier, nor ever lost the love or much
neglected the pursuit of learning; and afterwards, finding himself more
inclined to civil employment, he laid down his commission, and engaged in
business under the lord Townshend, then secretary of state, with whom he
attended the king to Hanover.

His adherence to lord Townshend ended in nothing but a nomination 4
(May 1729) to be clerk-extraordinary of the Privy Council, which produced
no immediate profit; for it only placed him in a state of expectation and right
of succession, and it was very long before a vacancy admitted him to profit.

Soon afterwards he married, and settled himself in a very pleasant house 5
at Wickham in Kent, where he devoted himself to learning, and to piety. Of
his learning the late Collection exhibits evidence, which would have been
yet fuller if the dissertations which accompany his version of Pindar had not
been improperly omitted. Of his piety the influence has, I hope, been
extended far by his *Observations on the Resurrection*, published in 1747, for
which the University of Oxford created him a Doctor of Laws by diploma
(March 30, 1748); and would doubtless have reached yet further had he
lived to complete what he had for some time meditated, the Evidences of
the truth of the New Testament. Perhaps it may not be without effect to tell,
that he read the prayers of the publick liturgy every morning to his family,
and that on Sunday evening he called his servants into the parlour, and read
to them first a sermon, and then prayers. Crashaw is now not the only maker
of verses to whom may be given the two venerable names of *Poet and Saint*.

He was very often visited by Lyttelton and Pitt, who, when they were 6
weary of faction and debates, used at Wickham to find books and quiet, a

decent table, and literary conversation. There is at Wickham a walk made by Pitt; and, what is of far more importance, at Wickham Lyttelton received that conviction which produced his *Dissertation on St. Paul.*

7   These two illustrious friends had for a while listened to the blandishments of infidelity, and when West's book was published, it was bought by some who did not know his change of opinion, in expectation of new objections against Christianity; and as Infidels do not want malignity, they revenged the disappointment by calling him a methodist.

8   Mr. West's income was not large; and his friends endeavoured, but without success, to obtain an augmentation. It is reported, that the education of the young prince was offered to him, but that he required a more extensive power of superintendence than it was thought proper to allow him.

9   In time, however, his revenue was improved; he lived to have one of the lucrative clerkships of the Privy Council (1752), and Mr. Pitt at last had it in his power to make him treasurer of Chelsea Hospital.

10   He was now sufficiently rich; but wealth came too late to be long enjoyed: nor could it secure him from the calamities of life; he lost (1755) his only son; and the year after (March 26), a stroke of the palsy brought to the grave one of the few poets to whom the grave might be without its terrors.

11   Of his translations I have only compared the first Olympick Ode with the original, and found my expectation surpassed, both by its elegance and its exactness. He does not confine himself to his author's train of stanzas; for he saw that the difference of the languages required a different mode of versification. The first strophe is eminently happy; in the second he has a little strayed from Pindar's meaning, who says, *if thou, my soul, wishest to speak of games, look not in the desert sky for a planet hotter than the sun, nor shall we tell of nobler games than those of Olympia.* He is sometimes too paraphrastical. Pindar bestows upon Hiero an epithet, which, in one word, signifies *delighting in horses*; a word which, in the translation, generates these lines:

> Hiero's royal brows, whose care
>   Tends the courser's noble breed,
> Pleas'd to nurse the pregnant mare,
>   Pleas'd to train the youthful steed.

Pindar says of Pelops, that *he came alone in the dark to the White Sea*; and West,

> Near the billow-beaten side
> Of the foam-besilver'd main,
> Darkling, and alone, he stood:

which however is less exuberant than the former passage.

A work of this kind must, in a minute examination, discover many   12
imperfections; but West's version, so far as I have considered it, appears
to be the product of great labour and great abilities.

His *Institution of the Garter* (1742) is written with sufficient knowledge of   13
the manners that prevailed in the age to which it is referred, and with great
elegance of diction; but, for want of a process of events, neither knowledge
nor elegance preserve the reader from weariness.

His *Imitations of Spenser* are very successfully performed, both with   14
respect to the metre, the language, and the fiction; and being engaged at
once by the excellence of the sentiments, and the artifice of the copy, the
mind has two amusements together. But such compositions are not to be
reckoned among the great atchievements of intellect, because their effect is
local and temporary; they appeal not to reason or passion, but to memory,
and presuppose an accidental or artificial state of mind. An Imitation of
Spenser is nothing to a reader, however acute, by whom Spenser has never
been perused. Works of this kind may deserve praise, as proofs of great
industry, and great nicety of observation; but the highest praise, the praise
of genius, they cannot claim. The noblest beauties of art are those of which
the effect is co-extended with rational nature, or at least with the whole
circle of polished life; what is less than this can be only pretty, the plaything
of fashion, and the amusement of a day.

THERE is in the *Adventurer* a paper of verses given to one of the authors as   15
Mr. West's, and supposed to have been written by him. It should not be
concealed, however, that it is printed with Mr. Jago's name in Dodsley's
Collection, and is mentioned as his in a Letter of Shenstone's. Perhaps West
gave it without naming the author; and Hawkesworth, receiving it from
him, thought it his; for his he thought it, as he told me, and as he tells the
publick.

COLLINS

1 WILLIAM COLLINS was born at Chichester on the twenty-fifth of December, about 1720. His father was a hatter of good reputation. He was in 1733, as Dr. Warton has kindly informed me, admitted scholar of Winchester College, where he was educated by Dr. Burton. His English exercises were better than his Latin.

2 He first courted the notice of the publick by some verses to a *Lady weeping*, published in *The Gentleman's Magazine* .

3 In 1740, he stood first in the list of the scholars to be received in succession at New College; but unhappily there was no vacancy. This was the original misfortune of his life. He became a Commoner of Queen's College, probably with a scanty maintenance; but was in about half a year elected a *Demy* of Magdalen College, where he continued till he had taken a Bachelor's degree, and then suddenly left the University; for what reason I know not that he told.

4 He now (about 1744) came to London a literary adventurer, with many projects in his head, and very little money in his pocket. He designed many works; but his great fault was irresolution, or the frequent calls of immediate necessity broke his schemes, and suffered him to pursue no settled purpose. A man, doubtful of his dinner, or trembling at a creditor, is not much disposed to abstracted meditation, or remote enquiries. He published proposals for a History of the Revival of Learning; and I have heard him speak with great kindness of Leo the Tenth, and with keen resentment of his tasteless successor. But probably not a page of the History was ever written. He planned several tragedies, but he only planned them. He wrote now-and-then odes and other poems, and did something, however little.

5 About this time I fell into his company. His appearance was decent and manly; his knowledge considerable, his views extensive, his conversation elegant, and his disposition chearful. By degrees I gained his confidence; and one day was admitted to him when he was immured by a bailiff, that was prowling in the street. On this occasion recourse was had to the booksellers, who, on the credit of a translation of Aristotle's Poeticks, which he engaged to write with a large commentary, advanced as much money as enabled him to escape into the country. He shewed me the guineas safe in his hand. Soon afterwards his uncle, Mr. Martin, a lieutenant-colonel, left him about two

thousand pounds; a sum which Collins could scarcely think exhaustible, and which he did not live to exhaust. The guineas were then repaid, and the translation neglected.

But man is not born for happiness. Collins, who, while he *studied to live*, 6 felt no evil but poverty, no sooner *lived to study* than his life was assailed by more dreadful calamities, disease and insanity.

Having formerly written his character, while perhaps it was yet more 7 distinctly impressed upon my memory, I shall insert it here.

"Mr. Collins was a man of extensive literature, and of vigorous faculties. 8 He was acquainted not only with the learned tongues, but with the Italian, French, and Spanish languages. He had employed his mind chiefly upon works of fiction, and subjects of fancy; and, by indulging some peculiar habits of thought, was eminently delighted with those flights of imagination which pass the bounds of nature, and to which the mind is reconciled only by a passive acquiescence in popular traditions. He loved fairies, genii, giants, and monsters; he delighted to rove through the meanders of inchantment, to gaze on the magnificence of golden palaces, to repose by the waterfalls of Elysian gardens.

"This was however the character rather of his inclination than his genius; 9 the grandeur of wildness, and the novelty of extravagance, were always desired by him, but were not always attained. Yet as diligence is never wholly lost; if his efforts sometimes caused harshness and obscurity, they likewise produced in happier moments sublimity and splendour. This idea which he had formed of excellence, led him to oriental fictions and allegorical imagery; and perhaps, while he was intent upon description, he did not sufficiently cultivate sentiment. His poems are the productions of a mind not deficient in fire, nor unfurnished with knowledge either of books or life, but somewhat obstructed in its progress by deviation in quest of mistaken beauties.

"His morals were pure, and his opinions pious: in a long continuance of 10 poverty, and long habits of dissipation, it cannot be expected that any character should be exactly uniform. There is a degree of want by which the freedom of agency is almost destroyed; and long association with fortuitous companions will at last relax the strictness of truth, and abate the fervour of sincerity. That this man, wise and virtuous as he was, passed always unentangled through the snares of life, it would be prejudice and temerity to affirm; but it may be said that at least he preserved the source of action unpolluted, that his principles were never shaken, that his distinctions of right and wrong were never confounded, and that his faults had nothing of malignity or design, but proceeded from some unexpected pressure, or casual temptation.

11   "The latter part of his life cannot be remembered but with pity and sadness. He languished some years under that depression of mind which enchains the faculties without destroying them, and leaves reason the knowledge of right without the power of pursuing it. These clouds which he perceived gathering on his intellects, he endeavoured to disperse by travel, and passed into France; but found himself constrained to yield to his malady, and returned. He was for some time confined in a house of lunaticks, and afterwards retired to the care of his sister in Chichester, where death in 1756 came to his relief.

12   "After his return from France, the writer of this character paid him a visit at Islington, where he was waiting for his sister, whom he had directed to meet him: there was then nothing of disorder discernible in his mind by any but himself; but he had withdrawn from study, and travelled with no other book than an English Testament, such as children carry to the school: when his friend took it into his hand, out of curiosity to see what companion a Man of Letters had chosen, *I have but one book*, said Collins, *but that is the best*."

13   Such was the fate of Collins, with whom I once delighted to converse, and whom I yet remember with tenderness.

14   He was visited at Chichester, in his last illness, by his learned friends Dr. Warton and his brother; to whom he spoke with disapprobation of his Oriental Eclogues, as not sufficiently expressive of Asiatick manners, and called them his Irish Eclogues. He shewed them, at the same time, an ode inscribed to Mr. John Hume, on the superstitions of the Highlands; which they thought superior to his other works, but which no search has yet found.

15   His disorder was not alienation of mind, but general laxity and feebleness, a deficiency rather of his vital than intellectual powers. What he spoke wanted neither judgement nor spirit; but a few minutes exhausted him, so that he was forced to rest upon the couch, till a short cessation restored his powers, and he was again able to talk with his former vigour.

16   The approaches of this dreadful malady he began to feel soon after his uncle's death; and, with the usual weakness of men so diseased, eagerly snatched that temporary relief with which the table and the bottle flatter and seduce. But his health continually declined, and he grew more and more burthensome to himself.

17   To what I have formerly said of his writings may be added, that his diction was often harsh, unskilfully laboured, and injudiciously selected. He affected the obsolete when it was not worthy of revival; and he puts his words out of the common order, seeming to think, with some later candidates for fame, that not to write prose is certainly to write poetry. His lines

commonly are of slow motion, clogged and impeded with clusters of consonants. As men are often esteemed who cannot be loved, so the poetry of Collins may sometimes extort praise when it gives little pleasure.

Mr. Collin's first production is added here from the *Poetical Calendar*: 18

TO MISS AURELIA C—R,
ON HER WEEPING AT HER SISTER'S WEDDING.

Cease, fair Aurelia, cease to mourn;
    Lament not Hannah's happy state;
You may be happy in your turn,
    And seize the treasure you regret.

With Love united Hymen stands,
    And softly whispers to your charms;
"Meet but your lover in my bands,
    You'll find your sister in his arms."

DYER

1 JOHN DYER, of whom I have no other account to give than his own Letters, published with Hughes's correspondence, and the notes added by the editor, have afforded me, was born in 1700, the second son of Robert Dyer of Aberglasney, in Caermarthenshire, a solicitor of great capacity and note.

2 He passed through Westminster-school under the care of Dr. Freind, and was then called home to be instructed in his father's profession. But his father died soon, and he took no delight in the study of the law, but, having always amused himself with drawing, resolved to turn painter, and became pupil to Mr. Richardson, an artist then of high reputation, but now better known by his books than by his pictures.

3 Having studied awhile under his master, he became, as he tells his friend, an itinerant painter, and wandered about South Wales and the parts adjacent; but he mingled poetry with painting, and about 1727 printed *Grongar Hill* in Lewis's Miscellany.

4 Being, probably, unsatisfied with his own proficiency, he, like other painters, travelled to Italy; and coming back in 1740, published the *Ruins of Rome*.

5 If his poem was written soon after his return, he did not make much use of his acquisitions in painting, whatever they might be; for decline of health, and love of study, determined him to the church. He therefore entered into orders; and, it seems, married about the same time a lady of the name of *Ensor*; "whose grand-mother," says he, "was a Shakspeare, descended from a brother of every body's Shakspeare;" by her, in 1756, he had a son and three daughters living.

6 His ecclesiastical provision was a long time but slender. His first patron, Mr. Harper, gave him, in 1741, Calthorp in Leicestershire of eighty pounds a year, on which he lived ten years, and then exchanged it for Belchford in Lincolnshire of seventy-five. His condition now began to mend. In 1751, Sir John Heathcote gave him Coningsby, of one hundred and forty pounds a year; and in 1755 the Chancellor added Kirkby, of one hundred and ten. He complains that the repair of the house at Coningsby, and other expences, took away the profit.

7 In 1757 he published the *Fleece*, his greatest poetical work; of which I will not suppress a ludicrous story. Dodsley the bookseller was one day men-

tioning it to a critical visiter, with more expectation of success than the other could easily admit. In the conversation the author's age was asked; and being represented as advanced in life, *He will*, said the critick, *be buried in woollen.*

He did not indeed long survive that publication, nor long enjoy the   8
increase of his preferments; for in 1758 he died.

Dyer is not a poet of bulk or dignity sufficient to require an elaborate   9
criticism. *Grongar Hill* is the happiest of his productions: it is not indeed
very accurately written; but the scenes which it displays are so pleasing, the
images which they raise so welcome to the mind, and the reflections of the
writer so consonant to the general sense or experience of mankind, that
when it is once read, it will be read again.

The idea of the *Ruins of Rome* strikes more but pleases less, and the title   10
raises greater expectation than the performance gratifies. Some passages,
however, are conceived with the mind of a poet; as when, in the neighbourhood of dilapidating Edifices, he says,

> —At dead of night
> The hermit oft, 'midst his orisons, hears,
> Aghast, the voice of Time disparting towers.

Of *The Fleece*, which never became popular, and is now universally   11
neglected, I can say little that is likely to recall it to attention. The
woolcomber and the poet appear to me such discordant natures, that an
attempt to bring them together is to *couple the serpent with the fowl*. When
Dyer, whose mind was not unpoetical, has done his utmost, by interesting
his reader in our native commodity, by interspersing rural imagery, and
incidental digressions, by cloathing small images in great words, and by all
the writer's arts of delusion, the meanness naturally adhering, and the
irreverence habitually annexed to trade and manufacture, sink him under
insuperable oppression; and the disgust which blank verse, encumbering
and encumbered, superadds to an unpleasing subject, soon repels the
reader, however willing to be pleased.

Let me however honestly report whatever may counterbalance this   12
weight of censure. I have been told that Akenside, who, upon a poetical
question, has a right to be heard, said, "That he would regulate his opinion
of the reigning taste by the fate of Dyer's *Fleece*; for, if that were ill received,
he should not think it any longer reasonable to expect fame from excellence."

SHENSTONE

1   WILLIAM SHENSTONE, the son of Thomas Shenstone and Anne Pen, was born in November 1714, at the Leasowes in Hales-Owen, one of those insulated districts which, in the division of the kingdom, was appended, for some reason not now discoverable, to a distant county; and which, though surrounded by Warwickshire and Worcestershire, belongs to Shropshire, though perhaps thirty miles distant from any other part of it.

2   He learned to read of an old dame, whom his poem of the *School-mistress* has delivered to posterity; and soon received such delight from books, that he was always calling for fresh entertainment, and expected that when any of the family went to market a new book should be brought him, which when it came, was in fondness carried to bed and laid by him. It is said, that when his request had been neglected, his mother wrapped up a piece of wood of the same form, and pacified him for the night.

3   As he grew older, he went for a while to the Grammar-school in Hales-Owen, and was placed afterwards with Mr. Crumpton, an eminent school-master at Solihul, where he distinguished himself by the quickness of his progress.

4   When he was young (June 1724) he was deprived of his father, and soon after (August 1726) of his grandfather; and was, with his brother, who died afterwards unmarried, left to the care of his grandmother, who managed the estate.

5   From school he was sent in 1732 to Pembroke-College in Oxford, a society which for half a century has been eminent for English poetry and elegant literature. Here it appears that he found delight and advantage; for he continued his name in the book ten years, though he took no degree. After the first four years he put on the Civilian's gown, but without shewing any intention to engage in the profession.

6   About the time when he went to Oxford, the death of his grandmother devolved his affairs to the care of the reverend Mr. Dolman of Brome in Staffordshire, whose attention he always mentioned with gratitude.

7   At Oxford he employed himself upon English poetry; and in 1737 published a small Miscellany, without his name.

8   He then for a time wandered about, to acquaint himself with life; and was sometimes at London, sometimes at Bath, or any other place of publick resort; but he did not forget his poetry. He published in 1740 his *Judgement*

of Hercules, addressed to Mr. Lyttelton, whose interest he supported with great warmth at an election: this was two years afterwards followed by the *School-mistress*.

Mr. Dolman, to whose care he was indebted for his ease and leisure, died   9 in 1745, and the care of his own fortune now fell upon him. He tried to escape it a while, and lived at his house with his tenants, who were distantly related; but, finding that imperfect possession inconvenient, he took the whole estate into his own hands, more to the improvement of its beauty than the increase of its produce.

Now was excited his delight in rural pleasures, and his ambition of rural   10 elegance: he began from this time to point his prospects, to diversify his surface, to entangle his walks, and to wind his waters; which he did with such judgement and such fancy, as made his little domain the envy of the great, and the admiration of the skilful; a place to be visited by travellers, and copied by designers. Whether to plant a walk in undulating curves, and to place a bench at every turn where there is an object to catch the view; to make water run where it will be heard, and to stagnate where it will be seen; to leave intervals where the eye will be pleased, and to thicken the plantation where there is something to be hidden, demands any great powers of mind, I will not enquire; perhaps a sullen and surly speculator may think such perform-ances rather the sport than the business of human reason. But it must be at least confessed, that to embellish the form of nature is an innocent amuse-ment; and some praise must be allowed by the most supercilious observer to him, who does best what such multitudes are contending to do well.

This praise was the praise of Shenstone; but, like all other modes of   11 felicity, it was not enjoyed without its abatements. Lyttelton was his neighbour and his rival, whose empire, spacious and opulent, looked with disdain on the *petty State* that *appeared behind it*. For a while the inhabitants of Hagley affected to tell their acquaintance of the little fellow that was trying to make himself admired; but when by degrees the Leasowes forced themselves into notice, they took care to defeat the curiosity which they could not suppress, by conducting their visitants perversely to inconvenient points of view, and introducing them at the wrong end of a walk to detect a deception; injuries of which Shenstone would heavily complain. Where there is emulation there will be vanity, and where there is vanity there will be folly.

The pleasure of Shenstone was all in his eye; he valued what he valued   12 merely for its looks; nothing raised his indignation more than to ask if there were any fishes in his water.

His house was mean, and he did not improve it; his care was of his   13 grounds. When he came home from his walks he might find his floors flooded by a shower through the broken roof; but could spare no money for its reparation.

14   In time his expences brought clamours about him, that overpowered the lamb's bleat and the linnet's song; and his groves were haunted by beings very different from fawns and fairies. He spent his estate in adorning it, and his death was probably hastened by his anxieties. He was a lamp that spent its oil in blazing. It is said, that if he had lived a little longer he would have been assisted by a pension: such bounty could not have been ever more properly bestowed; but that it was ever asked is not certain; it is too certain that it never was enjoyed.

15   He died at the Leasowes, of a putrid fever, about five on Friday morning, February 11, 1763; and was buried by the side of his brother in the church-yard of Hales-Owen.

16   He was never married, though he might have obtained the lady, whoever she was, to whom his *Pastoral Ballad* was addressed. He is represented by his friend Dodsley as a man of great tenderness and generosity, kind to all that were within his influence; but, if once offended, not easily appeased; inattentive to œconomy, and careless of his expences; in his person larger than the middle size, with something clumsy in his form; very negligent of his cloaths, and remarkable for wearing his grey hair in a particular manner; for he held that the fashion was no rule of dress, and that every man was to suit his appearance to his natural form.

17   His mind was not very comprehensive, nor his curiosity active; he had no value for those parts of knowledge which he had not himself cultivated.

18   His life was unstained by any crime; the Elegy on *Jessy*, which has been supposed to relate an unfortunate and criminal amour of his own, was known by his friends to have been suggested by the story of Miss Godfrey in Richardson's *Pamela*.

19   What Gray thought of his character, from the perusal of his Letters, was this:

"I have read too an octavo volume of Shenstone's Letters. Poor man! he was always wishing for money, for fame, and other distinctions; and his whole philosophy consisted in living against his will in retirement, and in a place which his taste had adorned; but which he only enjoyed when people of note came to see and commend it: his correspondence is about nothing else but this place and his own writings, with two or three neighbouring clergymen, who wrote verses too."

20   His poems consist of elegies, odes, and ballads, humorous sallies, and moral pieces.

21   His conception of an Elegy he has in his Preface very judiciously and discriminately explained. It is, according to his account, the effusion of a

contemplative mind, sometimes plaintive, and always serious, and therefore superior to the glitter of slight ornaments. His compositions suit not ill to this description. His topicks of praise are the domestick virtues, and his thoughts are pure and simple; but, wanting combination, they want variety. The peace of solitude, the innocence of inactivity, and the unenvied security of an humble station, can fill but a few pages. That of which the essence is uniformity will be soon described. His Elegies have therefore too much resemblance of each other.

The lines are sometimes, such as Elegy requires, smooth and easy; but to 22 this praise his claim is not constant: his diction is often harsh, improper, and affected; his words ill-coined, or ill-chosen, and his phrase unskilfully inverted.

The Lyrick Poems are almost all of the light and airy kind, such as trip 23 lightly and nimbly along, without the load of any weighty meaning. From these, however, *Rural Elegance* has some right to be excepted. I once heard it praised by a very learned lady; and though the lines are irregular, and the thoughts diffused with too much verbosity, yet it cannot be denied to contain both philosophical argument and poetical spirit.

Of the rest I cannot think any excellent; the *Skylark* pleases me best, 24 which has however more of the epigram than of the ode.

But the four parts of his *Pastoral Ballad* demand particular notice. 25 I cannot but regret that it is pastoral; an intelligent reader, acquainted with the scenes of real life, sickens at the mention of the *crook*, the *pipe*, the *sheep*, and the *kids*, which it is not necessary to bring forward to notice, for the poet's art is selection, and he ought to shew the beauties without the grossness of the country life. His stanza seems to have been chosen in imitation of Rowe's *Despairing Shepherd*.

In the first part are two passages, to which if any mind denies its 26 sympathy, it has no acquaintance with love or nature:

> I priz'd every hour that went by,
>   Beyond all that had pleas'd me before;
> But now they are past, and I sigh,
>   And I grieve that I priz'd them no more.
>
> When forc'd the fair nymph to forego,
>   What anguish I felt in my heart!
> Yet I thought—but it might not be so,
>   'Twas with pain that she saw me depart.
>
> She gaz'd, as I slowly withdrew;
>   My path I could hardly discern;
> So sweetly she bade me adieu,
>   I thought that she bade me return.

27   In the second this passage has its prettiness, though it be not equal to the
former:

> I have found out a gift for my fair;
> I have found where the wood-pigeons breed:
> But let me that plunder forbear,
> She will say 'twas a barbarous deed:
>
> For he ne'er could be true, she averr'd,
> Who could rob a poor bird of its young;
> And I lov'd her the more, when I heard
> Such tenderness fall from her tongue.

28   In the third he mentions the common-places of amorous poetry with
some address:

> 'Tis his with mock passion to glow;
> 'Tis his in smooth tales to unfold,
> How her face is as bright as the snow,
> And her bosom, be sure, is as cold:
>
> How the nightingales labour the strain,
> With the notes of his charmer to vie;
> How they vary their accents in vain,
> Repine at her triumphs, and die.

29   In the fourth I find nothing better than this natural strain of Hope:

> Alas! from the day that we met,
> What hope of an end to my woes?
> When I cannot endure to forget
> The glance that undid my repose.
>
> Yet Time may diminish the pain:
> The flower, and the shrub, and the tree,
> Which I rear'd for her pleasure in vain,
> In time may have comfort for me.

30   His *Levities* are by their title exempted from the severities of criticism;
yet it may be remarked, in a few words, that his humour is sometimes gross,
and seldom spritely.

31   Of the Moral Poems the first is the *Choice of Hercules*, from Xenophon.
The numbers are smooth, the diction elegant, and the thoughts just; but
something of vigour perhaps is still to be wished, which it might have had
by brevity and compression. His *Fate of Delicacy* has an air of gaiety, but not
a very pointed general moral. His blank verses, those that can read them
may probably find to be like the blank verses of his neighbours. *Love and*

Honour is derived from the old ballad, *Did you not hear of a Spanish Lady*—I wish it well enough to wish it were in rhyme.

The *School-mistress*, of which I know not what claim it has to stand 32 among the Moral Works, is surely the most pleasing of Shenstone's performances. The adoption of a particular style, in light and short compositions, contributes much to the increase of pleasure: we are entertained at once with two imitations, of nature in the sentiments, of the original author in the style, and between them the mind is kept in perpetual employment.

The general recommendation of Shenstone is easiness and simplicity; his 33 general defect is want of comprehension and variety. Had his mind been better stored with knowledge, whether he could have been great, I know not; he could certainly have been agreeable.

YOUNG

1   THE following life was written, at my request, by a gentleman who had better information than I could easily have obtained; and the publick will perhaps wish that I had solicited and obtained more such favours from him.

"DEAR SIR,

2   "In consequence of our different conversations about authentick materials for the Life of Young, I send you the following detail. It is not, I confess, immediately in the line of my profession; but hard indeed is our fate at the bar, if we may not call a few hours now-and-then our own.

3   Of great men something must always be said to gratify curiosity. Of the great author of the *Night Thoughts* much has been told of which there never could have been proofs; and little care appears to have been taken to tell that of which proofs, with little trouble, might have been procured.

4   EDWARD YOUNG was born at Upham, near Winchester, in June 1681. He was the son of Edward Young, at that time Fellow of Winchester College and Rector of Upham; who was the son of Jo. Young of Woodhay in Berkshire, styled by Wood *gentleman*. In September 1682 the Poet's father was collated to the prebend of Gillingham Minor, in the church of Sarum, by bishop Ward. When Ward's faculties were impaired by age, his duties were necessarily performed by others. We learn from Wood, that, at a visitation of Sprat, July the 12th, 1686, the Prebendary preached a Latin sermon, afterwards published, with which the Bishop was so pleased, that he told the Chapter he was concerned to find the preacher had one of the worst prebends in their church. Some time after this, in consequence of his merit and reputation, or of the interest of Lord Bradford, to whom, in 1702, he dedicated two volumes of sermons, he was appointed chaplain to King William and Queen Mary, and preferred to the deanery of Sarum. Jacob, who wrote in 1720, says, he was chaplain and clerk of the closet to the late Queen, who honoured him by standing godmother to the Poet. His fellowship of Winchester he resigned in favour of a Mr. Harris, who married his only daughter. The Dean died at Sarum, after a short illness, in 1705, in the sixty-third year of his age. On the Sunday after his decease Bishop Burnet preached at the cathedral, and began his sermon with saying, "Death has been of late walking round us, and making breach upon breach upon us, and has now carried away the head of this body with a stroke; so that he, whom

you saw a week ago distributing the holy mysteries, is now laid in the dust. But he still lives in the many excellent directions he has left us, both how to live and how to die."

The Dean placed his son upon the foundation at Winchester College, 5 where he had himself been educated. At this school Edward Young remained till the election after his eighteenth birth-day, the period at which those upon the foundation are superannuated. Whether he did not betray his abilities early in life, or his masters had not skill enough to discover in their pupil any marks of genius for which he merited reward, or no vacancy at Oxford afforded them an opportunity to bestow upon him the reward provided for merit by William of Wykeham; certain it is, that to an Oxford fellowship our Poet did not succeed. By chance, or by choice, New College does not number among its Fellows him who wrote the *Night Thoughts*.

On the 13th of October, 1703, he was entered an Independent Member of 6 New College, that he might live at little expence in the Warden's lodgings, who was a particular friend of his father, till he should be qualified to stand for a fellowship at All-souls. In a few months the warden of New College died. He then removed to Corpus College. The President of this Society, from regard also for his father, invited him thither, in order to lessen his academical expences. In 1708, he was nominated to a law fellowship at All-souls by Archbishop Tennison, into whose hands it came by devolution.— Such repeated patronage, while it justifies Burnet's praise of the father, reflects credit on the conduct of the son. The manner in which it was exerted seems to prove that the father did not leave behind him much wealth.

On the 23d of April, 1714, Young took his degree of Batchelor of Civil 7 Laws, and his Doctor's degree on the 10th of June, 1719.

Soon after he went to Oxford, he discovered, it is said, an inclination for 8 pupils. Whether he ever commenced tutor is not known. None has hitherto boasted to have received his academical instruction from the author of the *Night Thoughts*.

It is certain that his college was proud of him no less as a scholar than as a 9 poet; for, in 1716, when the foundation of the Codrington Library was laid, two years after he had taken his Batchelor's degree, he was appointed to speak the Latin oration. This is at least particular for being dedicated in English *To the Ladies of the Codrington Family*. To these Ladies he says, "that he was unavoidably flung into a singularity, by being obliged to write an epistle-dedicatory void of common-place, and such an one as was never published before by any author whatever:—that this practice absolved them from any obligation of reading what was presented to them;—and that the bookseller approved of it, because it would make people stare, was absurd enough, and perfectly right."

10   Of this oration there is no appearance in his own edition of his works; and prefixed to an edition by Curll and Tonson, in 1741, is a letter from Young to Curll, if Curll may be credited, dated December the 9th, 1739, wherein he says he has not leisure to review what he formerly wrote, and adds, "I have not the *Epistle to Lord Lansdowne*. If you will take my advice, I would have you omit that, and the oration on *Codrington*. I think the collection will sell better without them."

11   There are who relate, that, when first Young found himself independent, and his own master at All-souls, he was not the ornament to religion and morality which he afterwards became.

12   The authority of his father, indeed, had ceased some time before by his death; and Young was certainly not ashamed to be patronized by the infamous Wharton. But Wharton befriended in Young, perhaps, the poet, and particularly the tragedian. If virtuous authors must be patronized only by virtuous peers, who shall point them out?

13   Yet Pope is said by Ruffhead to have told Warburton, that "Young had much of a sublime genius, though without common sense; so that his genius, having no guide, was perpetually liable to degenerate into bombast. This made him, pass a *foolish youth*, the sport of peers and poets: but his having a very good heart enabled him to support the clerical character when he assumed it, first with decency, and afterwards with honour."

14   They who think ill of Young's morality in the early part of his life, may perhaps be wrong; but Tindal could not err in his opinion of Young's warmth and ability in the cause of religion. Tindal used to spend much of his time at All-souls. "The other boys," said the atheist, "I can always answer, because I always know whence they have their arguments, which I have read an hundred times; but that fellow Young is continually pestering me with something of his own."

15   After all, Tindal and the censurers of Young may be reconcileable. Young might, for two or three years, have tried that kind of life, in which his natural principles would not suffer him to wallow long. If this were so, he has left behind him not only his evidence in favour of virtue, but the potent testimony of experience against vice.

16   We shall soon see that one of his earliest productiöns was more serious than what comes from the generality of unfledged poets.

17   Young perhaps ascribed the good fortune of Addison to the *Poem to his Majesty*, presented, with a copy of verses, to Somers; and hoped that he also might soar to wealth and honours on wings of the same kind. His first poetical flight was when Queen Anne called up to the House of Lords the sons of the Earls of Northampton and Aylesbury, and added, in one day, ten others to the number of peers. In order to reconcile the people to one at least

of the new Lords, he published in 1712 *An Epistle to the Right Honourable George Lord Lansdowne*. In this composition the poet pours out his pane-gyrick with the extravagance of a young man, who thinks his present stock of wealth will never be exhausted.

The poem seems intended also to reconcile the publick to the late peace.   18 This is endeavoured to be done by shewing that men are slain in war, and that in peace *harvests wave, and commerce swells her sail*. If this be humanity, is it politicks? Another purpose of this epistle appears to have been, to prepare the publick for the reception of some tragedy of his own. His Lordship's patronage, he says, will not let him *repent his passion for the stage*;—and the particular praise bestowed on *Othello* and *Oroonoko* looks as if some such character as *Zanga* was even then in contemplation. The affectionate mention of the death of his friend Harrison of New College, at the close of this poem, is an instance of Young's art, which displayed itself so wonderfully some time afterwards in the *Night Thoughts*, of making the publick a party in his private sorrow.

Should justice call upon you to censure this poem, it ought at least to be   19 remembered that he did not insert it into his works; and that in the letter to Curll, as we have seen, he advises its omission. The booksellers, in the late Body of English Poetry, should have distinguished what was deliberately rejected by the respective authors. This I shall be careful to do with regard to Young. "I think, says he, the following pieces in *four* volumes to be the most excuseable of all that I have written; and I wish *less apology* was needful for these. As there is no recalling what is got abroad, the pieces here republished I have revised and corrected, and rendered them as *pardonable* as it was in my power to do."

Shall the gates of repentance be shut only against literary sinners?   20

When Addison published *Cato* in 1713, Young had the honour of pre-   21 fixing to it a recommendatory copy of verses. This is one of the pieces which the author of the *Night Thoughts* did not republish.

On the appearance of his *Poem on the Last Day*, Addison did not return   22 Young's compliment; but *The Englishman* of October 29, 1713, which was probably written by Addison, speaks handsomely of this poem. The *Last Day* was published soon after the peace. The vice-chancellor's *imprimatur*, for it was first printed at Oxford, is dated May the 19th, 1713. From the Exordium Young appears to have spent some time on the composition of it. While other bards *with Britain's hero set their souls on fire*, he draws, he says, a deeper scene. Marlborough *had been* considered by Britain as her *hero*; but, when the *Last Day* was published, female cabal had blasted for a time the laurels of Blenheim. This serious poem was finished by Young as early as 1710, before he was thirty; for part of it is printed in the *Tatler*. It was inscribed to the Queen, in a dedication, which, for some reason, he did not admit into his works. It tells her, that his only title to the great honour he now does himself is the obligation he formerly received from her royal indulgence.

23   Of this obligation nothing is now known, unless he alluded to her being his godmother. He is said indeed to have been engaged at a settled stipend as a writer for the court. In Swift's "Rhapsody on poetry" are these lines, speaking of the court—

> Whence Gay was banish'd in disgrace,
> Where Pope will never show his face,
> Where Y— must torture his invention
> To flatter knaves, or lose his pension.

24   That Y— means Young, is clear from four other lines in the same poem.

> Attend, ye Popes and Youngs and Gays,
> And tune your harps and strew your bays;
> Your panegyrics here provide;
> You cannot err on flattery's side.

25   Yet who shall say with certainty that Young was a pensioner? In all modern periods of this country, have not the writers on one side been regularly called Hirelings, and on the other Patriots?

26   Of the dedication the complexion is clearly political. It speaks in the highest terms of the late peace;—it gives her Majesty praise indeed for her victories, but says that the author is more pleased to see her rise from this lower world, soaring above the clouds, passing the first and second heavens, and leaving the fixed stars behind her;—nor will he lose her there, but keep her still in view through the boundless spaces on the other side of Creation, in her journey towards eternal bliss, till he behold the heaven of heavens open, and angels receiving and conveying her still onward from the stretch of his imagination, which tires in her pursuit, and falls back again to earth.

27   The Queen was soon called away from this lower world, to a place where human praise or human flattery even less general than this are of little consequence. If Young thought the dedication contained only the praise of truth, he should not have omitted it in his works. Was he conscious of the exaggeration of party? Then he should not have written it. The poem itself is not without a glance to politicks, notwithstanding the subject. The cry that the church was in danger, had not yet subsided. The *Last Day*, written by a layman, was much approved by the ministry, and their friends.

28   Before the Queen's death, *The Force of Religion, or Vanquished Love*, was sent into the world. This poem is founded on the execution of Lady Jane

Gray and her husband Lord Guildford in 1554—a story chosen for the subject of a tragedy by Edmund Smith, and wrought into a tragedy by Rowe. The dedication of it to the countess of Salisbury does not appear in his own edition. He hopes it may be some excuse for his presumption that the story could not have been read without thoughts of the Countess of Salisbury, though it had been dedicated to another. "To behold," he proceeds, "a person *only* virtuous, stirs in us a prudent regret; to behold a person *only* amiable to the sight, warms us with a religious indignation; but to turn our eyes on a Countess of Salisbury, gives us pleasure and improvement; it works a sort of miracle, occasions the biass of our nature to fall off from sin, and makes our very senses and affections converts to our religion, and promoters of our duty." His flattery was as ready for the other sex as for ours, and was at least as well adapted.

August the 27th, 1714, Pope writes to his friend Jervas, that he is just 29 arrived from Oxford—that every one is much concerned for the Queen's death, but that no panegyricks are ready yet for the King. Nothing like friendship had yet taken place between Pope and Young; for, soon after the event which Pope mentions, Young published a poem on the Queen's death, and his Majesty's accession to the throne. It is inscribed to Addison, then secretary to the Lords Justices. Whatever was the obligation which he had formerly received from Anne, the poet appears to aim at something of the same sort from George. Of the poem the intention seems to have been, to shew that he had the same extravagant strain of praise for a King as for a Queen. To discover, at the very outset of a foreigner's reign, that the Gods bless his new subjects in such a King, is something more than praise. Neither was this deemed one of his *excuseable pieces*. We do not find it in his works.

Young's father had been well acquainted with Lady Anne Wharton, the 30 first wife of Thomas Wharton, Esq; afterwards Marquis of Wharton—a Lady celebrated for her poetical talents by Burnet and by Waller. To the Dean of Sarum's visitation sermon, already mentioned, were added some verses "by that excellent poetess Mrs. Anne Wharton," upon its being translated into English, at the instance of Waller, by Atwood. Wharton, after he became ennobled, did not drop the son of his old friend. In him, during the short time he lived, Young found a patron, and in his dissolute descendant a friend and a companion. The Marquis died in April 1715. The beginning of the next year the young Marquis set out upon his travels, from which he returned in about a twelvemonth. The beginning of 1717 carried him to Ireland; where, says the Biographia, "on the score of his extraordinary qualities, he had the honour done him of being admitted, though under age, to take his seat in the House of Lords."

31   With this unhappy character it is not unlikely that Young went to
Ireland. From his Letter to Richardson on *Original Composition*, it is clear
he was, at some period of his life, in that country. "I remember," says he, in
that Letter, speaking of Swift, "as I and others were taking with him an
evening walk, about a mile out of *Dublin*, he stopt short; we passed on; but,
perceiving he did not follow us, I went back, and found him fixed as a statue,
and earnestly gazing upward at a noble elm, which in its uppermost
branches was much withered and decayed. Pointing at it, he said, "I shall
be like that tree, I shall die at top."—Is it not probable, that this visit to
Ireland was paid when he had an opportunity of going thither with his
avowed friend and patron?

32   From *The Englishman* it appears that a tragedy by Young was in the theatre
so early as 1713. Yet *Busiris* was not brought upon Drury-Lane Stage till
1719. It was inscribed to the Duke of Newcastle, "because the late instances
he had received of his Grace's undeserved and uncommon favour, in an affair
of some consequence, foreign to the theatre, had taken from him the privilege
of chusing a patron." The Dedication he afterwards suppressed.

33   *Busiris* was followed in the year 1721 by *The Revenge*. Left at liberty now
to chuse his patron, he dedicated this famous tragedy to the Duke of
Wharton. "Your Grace," says the Dedication, "has been pleased to make
yourself accessary to the following scenes, not only by suggesting the most
beautiful incident in them, but by making all possible provision for the
success of the whole."

34   That his Grace should have suggested the incident to which he alludes,
whatever that incident be, is not unlikely. The last mental exertion of the
superannuated young man, in his quarters at Lerida, in Spain, was some
scenes of a tragedy on the story of Mary Queen of Scots.

35   Dryden dedicated *Marriage à la Mode* to Wharton's infamous relation
Rochester; whom he acknowledges not only as the defender of his poetry,
but as the promoter of his fortune. Young concludes his address to Wharton
thus—"My present fortune is his bounty, and my future his care; which
I will venture to say will be always remembered to his honour, since he,
I know, intended his generosity as an encouragement to merit, though,
through his very pardonable partiality to one who bears him so sincere a
duty and respect, I happen to receive the benefit of it." That he ever had
such a patron as Wharton, Young took all the pains in his power to conceal
from the world, by excluding this dedication from his works. He should
have remembered, that he at the same time concealed his obligation to
Wharton for *the most beautiful incident* in what is surely not his least
beautiful composition. The passage just quoted is, in a poem afterwards
addressed to Walpole, literally copied:

Be this thy partial smile from censure free;
'Twas meant for merit, though it fell on me.

While Young, who, in his *Love of Fame*, complains grievously how often 36
dedications wash an Æthiop white, was painting an amiable Duke of Wharton
in perishable prose, Pope was perhaps beginning to describe the *scorn and
wonder of his days* in lasting verse.

To the patronage of such a character, had Young studied men as much as 37
Pope, he would have known how little to have trusted. Young, however, was
certainly indebted to it for something material; and the Duke's regard for
Young, added to his *Lust of Praise*, procured to All-souls College a donation, which was not forgotten by the poet when he dedicated *The Revenge*.

It will surprize you to see me cite second Atkins, Case 136, Stiles *versus* 38
the Attorney General, 14 March 1740; as authority for the Life of a Poet.
But Biographers do not always find such certain guides as the oaths of those
whose lives they write. Chancellor Hardwicke was to determine whether
two annuities, granted by the Duke of Wharton to Young, were for legal
considerations. One was dated the 24th of March 1719, and accounted for
his Grace's bounty in a style princely and commendable, if not legal—
"considering that the publick good is advanced by the encouragement of
learning and the polite arts, and being pleased therein with the attempts of
Dr. Young, in consideration thereof, and of the love he bore him, &c." The
other was dated the 10th of July, 1722.

Young, on his examination, swore that he quitted the Exeter family, and 39
refused an annuity of 100*l.* which had been offered him for his life if he
would continue tutor to Lord Burleigh, upon the pressing solicitations of
the Duke of Wharton, and his Grace's assurances of providing for him in a
much more ample manner. It also appeared that the Duke had given him a
bond for 600*l.* dated the 15th of March 1721, in consideration of his taking
several journies, and being at great expences, in order to be chosen member
of the House of Commons at the Duke's desire, and in consideration of his
not taking two livings of 200*l.* and 400*l.* in the gift of All-souls College, on
his Grace's promises of serving and advancing him in the world.

Of his adventures in the Exeter family I am unable to give any account. 40
The attempt to get into Parliament was at Cirencester, where Young stood a
contested election. His Grace discovered in him talents for oratory as well as
for poetry. Nor was this judgment wrong. Young, after he took orders,
became a very popular preacher, and was much followed for the grace and
animation of his delivery. By his oratorical talents he was once in his life,
according to the Biographia, deserted. As he was preaching in his turn at St.
James's, he plainly perceived it was out of his power to command the

attention of his audience. This so affected the feelings of the preacher, that he sat back in the pulpit, and burst into tears.—But we must pursue his poetical life.

41   In 1719 he lamented the death of Addison, in a Letter addressed to their common friend Tickell. For the secret history of the following lines, if they contain any, it is now vain to seek:

> *In joy once join'd*, in sorrow, now, for years—
> Partner in grief, and brother of my tears,
> Tickell, accept this verse, thy mournful due.

42   From your account of Tickell it appears that he and Young used to "communicate to each other whatever verses they wrote, even to the least things."

43   In 1719 appeared a *Paraphrase on Part of the Book of Job*. Parker, to whom it is dedicated, had not long, by means of the seals, been qualified for a patron. Of this work the author's opinion may be known from his Letter to Curll: "You seem, in the Collection you propose, to have omitted what I think may claim the first place in it; I mean *a Translation from Part of Job*, printed by Mr. Tonson." The Dedication, which was only suffered to appear in Tonson's edition, while it speaks with satisfaction of his present retirement, seems to make an unusual struggle to escape from retirement. But every one who sings in the dark does not sing from joy. It is addressed, in no common strain of flattery, to a Chancellor, of whom he clearly appears to have had no kind of knowledge.

44   Of his Satires it would not have been impossible to fix the dates without the assistance of first editions, which, as you had occasion to observe in your account of Dryden, are with difficulty found. We must then have referred to the Poems, to discover when they were written. For these internal notes of time we should not have referred in vain. The first Satire laments that "Guilt's chief foe in Addison is fled." The second, addressing himself, asks,

> Is thy ambition sweating for a rhyme,
> Thou unambitious fool, at this late time?
> A fool at *forty* is a fool indeed.

The Satires were originally published separately in folio, under the title of *The Universal Passion*. These passages fix the appearance of the first to about 1725, the time at which it came out. As Young seldom suffered his pen to dry, after he had once dipped it in poetry, we may conclude that he began his Satires soon after he had written the *Paraphrase on Job*. The last Satire was certainly finished in the beginning of the year 1726. In December 1725 the King, in his passage from Helvoetsluys, escaped with great difficulty from a storm by landing at Rye; and the conclusion of the Satire turns the escape into a miracle, in such an encomiastick strain of compliment as poetry too often seeks to pay to royalty.

From the sixth of these poems we learn,

> Midst empire's charms, how Carolina's heart
> Glow'd with the love of virtue and of art:

since the grateful poet tells us in the next couplet,

> Her favour is diffus'd to that degree,
> Excess of goodness! it has dawn'd on me.

Her Majesty had stood godmother and given her name to a daughter of the Lady whom Young married in 1731.

The fifth Satire, *on Women*, was not published till 1727; and the sixth not till 1728. 45

To these Poems, when, in 1728, he gathered them into one publication, he prefixed a Preface; in which he observes, that "no man can converse much in the world but, at what he meets with, he must either be insensible or grieve, or be angry or smile. Now to smile at it, and turn it into ridicule," adds he, "I think most eligible, as it hurts ourselves least, and gives vice and folly the greatest offence.—Laughing at the misconduct of the world, will, in a great measure, ease us of any more disagreeable passion about it. One passion is more effectually driven out by another than by reason, whatever some teach." So wrote, and so of course thought, the lively and witty Satirist at the grave age of almost fifty, who, many years earlier in life, wrote the *Last Day*. After all, Swift pronounced of these Satires, that they should either have been more angry, or more merry. 46

Is it not somewhat singular that Young preserved, without any palliation, this Preface, so bluntly decisive in favour of laughing at the world, in the same collection of his works which contains the mournful, angry, gloomy *Night Thoughts?* 47

At the conclusion of the Preface he applies Plato's beautiful fable of the *Birth of Love* to modern poetry, with the addition, "that Poetry, like Love, is a little subject to blindness, which makes her mistake her way to preferments and honours; and that she retains a dutiful admiration of her father's family; but divides her favours, and generally lives with her mother's relations." Poetry, it is true, did not lead Young to preferments or to honours; but was there not something like blindness in the flattery which he sometimes forced her, and her sister Prose, to utter? She was always, indeed, taught by him to entertain a most dutiful admiration of riches; but surely Young, though nearly related to Poetry, had no connexion with her 48 whom Plato makes the mother of Love. That he could not well complain of being related to Poverty appears clearly from the frequent bounties which his gratitude records, and from the wealth which he left behind him. By *The Universal Passion* he acquired no vulgar fortune, more than three thousand pounds. A considerable sum had already been swallowed up in the South-Sea. For this loss he took the vengeance of an author. His Muse makes poetical use more than once of a *South-Sea* Dream.

49   It is related by Mr. Spence, in his Manuscript Anecdotes, on the authority of Mr. *Rawlinson*, that Young, upon the publication of his *Universal Passion*, received from the Duke of Grafton two thousand pounds; and that, when one of his friends exclaimed, *Two thousand pounds for a poem!* he said it was the best bargain he ever made in his life, for the poem was worth four thousand.

50   This story may be true; but it seems to have been raised from the two answers of Lord Burghley and Sir Philip Sidney in Spenser's Life.

51   After inscribing his Satires, not without the hope of preferments and honours, to the Duke of Dorset, Mr. Dodington, Mr. Spencer Compton, Lady Elizabeth Germain, and Sir Robert Walpole, he returns to plain panegyric. In 1726 he addressed a poem to Sir Robert Walpole, of which the title sufficiently explains the intention. If Young was a ready celebrator, he did not endeavour, or did not choose, to be a lasting one. *The Instalment* is among the pieces he did not admit into the number of his *excuseable writings*. Yet it contains a couplet which pretends to pant after the power of bestowing immortality:

> Oh how I long, enkindled by the theme,
> In deep eternity to launch thy name!

52   The bounty of the former reign seems to have been continued, possibly increased, in this. Whatever it was, the poet thought he deserved it;—for he was not ashamed to acknowledge what, without his acknowledgement, would now perhaps never have been known:

> My breast, O Walpole, glows with grateful fire.
> The streams of royal bounty, turn'd by thee,
> Refresh the dry domains of poesy.

If the purity of modern patriotism term Young a pensioner, it must at least be confessed he was a grateful one.

53   The reign of the new monarch was ushered in by Young with *Ocean, an Ode*. The hint of it was taken from the royal speech, which recommended the increase and encouragement of the seamen; that they might be *invited, rather than compelled by force and violence, to enter into the service of their*

country;—a plan which humanity must lament that policy has not even yet been able, or willing, to carry into execution. Prefixed to the original publication were an *Ode to the King, Pater Patriæ*, and an *Essay on Lyrick Poetry*. It is but justice to confess, that he preserved neither of them; and that the ode itself, which in the first edition, and in the last, consists of seventy-three stanzas, in the author's own edition is reduced to forty-nine. Among the omitted passages is *a Wish*, that concluded the poem, which few would have suspected Young of forming; and of which few, after having formed it, would confess something like their shame by suppression.

It stood originally so high in the author's opinion, that he intitled the   54
Poem, "Ocean, an Ode. *Concluding with a Wish.*" This wish consists of thirteen stanzas. The first runs thus:

> O may I *steal*
> Along the *vale*
> Of humble life, secure from foes!
> My friend sincere,
> My judgment clear,
> And gentle business my repose!

The three last stanzas are not more remarkable for just rhymes; but, altogether, they will make rather a curious page in the life of Young.

> Prophetic schemes,
> And golden dreams,
> May I, unsanguine, cast away!
> Have what I *have*,
> And live, not *leave*,
> Enamoured of the present day!
>
> My hours my own!
> My faults unknown!
> My chief revenue in content!
> Then leave one *beam*
> Of honest *fame*!
> And scorn the laboured monument!
>
> Unhurt my urn
> Till that great *turn*
> When mighty nature's self shall die,
> Time cease to glide,
> With human pride,
> Sunk in the ocean of eternity!

It is whimsical that he, who was soon to bid adieu to rhyme, should fix   55
upon a measure in which rhyme abounds even to satiety. Of this he said, in

his *Essay on Lyrick Poetry*, prefixed to the Poem,—"For the more *harmony* likewise I chose the frequent return of rhyme, which laid me under great difficulties. But difficulties, overcome, give grace and pleasure. Nor can I account for the *pleasure of rhyme in general* (of which the moderns are too fond) but from this truth." Yet the moderns surely deserve not much censure for their fondness of what, by his own confession, affords pleasure, and abounds in harmony.

56　　The next paragraph in his *Essay* did not occur to him when he talked of *that great turn* in the stanza just quoted. "But then the writer must take care that the difficulty is overcome. That is, he must make rhyme consistent with as perfect sense and expression, as could be expected if he was perfectly free from that shackle."

57　　Another part of this *Essay* will convict the following stanza of, what every reader will discover in it, "involuntary burlesque."

> The northern blast,
> The shattered mast,
> The syrt, the whirlpool, and the rock,
> The breaking spout,
> The *stars gone out*,
> The boiling streight, the monster's shock.

58　　But would the English poets fill quite so many volumes, if all their productions were to be tried, like this, by an elaborate essay on each particular species of poetry of which they exhibit specimens?

59　　If Young be not a Lyric poet, he is at least a critic in that sort of poetry; and, if his Lyric poetry can be proved bad, it was first proved so by his own criticism. This surely is candid.

60　　Milbourne was styled by Pope *the fairest of Critics*, only because he exhibited his own version of Virgil to be compared with Dryden's which he condemned, and with which every reader had it otherwise in his power to compare it. Young was surely not the most unfair of poets for prefixing to a Lyric composition an essay on Lyric Poetry so just and impartial as to condemn himself.

61　　We shall soon come to a work, before which we find indeed no critical Essay, but which disdains to shrink from the touchstone of the severest critic; and which certainly, as I remember to have heard you say, if it contains some of the worst, contains also some of the best things in the language.

62　　Soon after the appearance of "Ocean," when he was almost fifty, Young entered into Orders. In April 1728, not long after he put on the gown, he was appointed chaplain to George the Second.

The tragedy of *The Brothers*, which was already in rehearsal, he imme- 63
diately withdrew from the stage. The managers resigned it with some
reluctance to the delicacy of the new clergyman. The Epilogue to *The
Brothers*, the only appendage to any of his three plays which he added
himself, is, I believe, the only one of the kind. He calls it an *historical*
Epilogue. Finding that *Guilt's dreadful close his narrow scene denied*, he, in a
manner, continues the tragedy in the Epilogue, and relates how Rome
revenged the shade of Demetrius, and punished Perseus *for this night's
deed.*

Of Young's taking Orders something is told by the biographer of Pope, 64
which places the easiness and simplicity of the poet in a singular light.
When he determined on the Church, he did not address himself to Sherlock, to Atterbury, or to Hare, for the best instructions in Theology, but to
Pope; who, in a youthful frolick, advised the diligent perusal of *Thomas
Aquinas*. With this treasure Young retired from interruption to an obscure
place in the suburbs. His poetical guide to godliness hearing nothing of him
during half a year, and apprehending he might have carried the jest too far,
sought after him, and found him just in time to prevent what Ruffhead calls
an irretrievable derangement.

That attachment to his favourite study which made him think a poet the 65
surest guide in his new profession, left him little doubt whether poetry was
the surest path to its honours and preferments. Not long indeed after he
took Orders, he published in prose, 1728, *A true Estimate of Human Life*,
dedicated, notwithstanding the Latin quotations with which it abounds, to
the Queen; and a sermon preached before the House of Commons, 1729, on
the martyrdom of King Charles, intituled, *An Apology for Princes, or the
Reverence due to Government*. But the "Second Discourse," the counterpart
of his "Estimate," without which it cannot be called "a *true* estimate,"
though in 1728 it was announced as "soon to be published," never
appeared; and his old friends the Muses were not forgotten. In 1730 he
relapsed to poetry, and sent into the world *Imperium Pelagi; a Naval Lyric,
written in Imitation of Pindar's Spirit, occasioned by His Majesty's Return from
Hanover, September 1729, and the succeeding Peace*. It is inscribed to the
Duke of Chandos. In the Preface we are told, that the Ode is the most
spirited kind of Poetry, and that the Pindaric is the most spirited kind of
Ode. "This I speak," he adds, with sufficient candour, "at my own very
great peril. But truth has an eternal title to our confession, though we are
sure to suffer by it." Behold, again, *the fairest of poets*. Young's *Imperium
Pelagi*, as well as his tragedies, was ridiculed in Fielding's *Tom Thumb*; but,
let us not forget that it was one of his pieces which the author of the *Night
Thoughts* deliberately refused to own.

66   Not long after this Pindaric attempt, he published two Epistles to Pope, *concerning the Authors of the Age*, 1730. Of these poems one occasion seems to have been an apprehension lest, from the liveliness of his satires, he should not be deemed sufficiently serious for promotion in the Church.

67   In July 1730 he was presented by his College to the rectory of Welwyn in Hertfordshire. In May 1731 he married Lady Elizabeth Lee, daughter of the Earl of Litchfield, and widow of Colonel Lee. His connexion with this Lady arose from his father's acquaintance, already mentioned, with Lady Anne Wharton, who was coheiress of Sir Henry Lee of Ditchley in Oxfordshire. Poetry had lately been taught by Addison to aspire to the arms of nobility, though not with extraordinary happiness.

68   We may naturally conclude that Young now gave himself up in some measure to the comforts of his new connexion, and to the expectations of that preferment which he thought due to his poetical talents, or, at least, to the manner in which they had so frequently been exerted.

69   The next production of his Muse was *The Sea-piece*, in two odes.

70   Young enjoys the credit of what is called an *Extempore Epigram* on Voltaire; who, when he was in England, ridiculed, in the company of the jealous English poet, Milton's allegory of *Sin and Death*—

> You are so witty, profligate, and thin,
> At once we think thee Milton, Death, and Sin.

From the following passage in the poetical Dedication of his *Sea-piece* to Voltaire, it seems that his extemporaneous reproof, if it must be extemporaneous, for what few will now affirm Voltaire to have deserved any reproof, was something longer than a distich, and something more *gentle* than the distich just quoted.

> No stranger, Sir, though born in foreign climes.
> On *Dorset* downs, when Milton's page,
> With Sin and Death provok'd thy rage,
> Thy rage provok'd, who sooth'd with *gentle* rhymes?

By *Dorset downs* he probably meant Mr. Dodington's seat. In Pitt's Poems is *An Epistle to Dr. Edward Young, at Eastbury in Dorsetshire, on the Review at Sarum*, 1722.

> While with your Dodington retired you sit,
> Charm'd with his flowing Burgundy and wit, &c.

71   Thomson, in his Autumn, addressing Mr. Dodington, calls his seat the seat of the Muses,

> Where, in the secret bower and winding walk,
> For virtuous Young and thee they twine the bay.

The praises Thomson bestows but a few lines before on Philips, the second

> Who nobly durst, in rhyme-unfettered verse,
> With British freedom sing the British song;

added to Thomson's example and success, might perhaps induce Young, as we shall see presently, to write his great work without rhyme.

In 1734 he published *The foreign Address, or the best Argument for Peace; occasioned by the British Fleet and the Posture of Affairs. Written in the Character of a Sailor.* It is not to be found in the author's four volumes.   72

He now appears to have given up all hopes of overtaking Pindar, and perhaps at last resolved to turn his ambition to some original species of poetry. This poem concludes with a formal farewel to Ode, which few of Young's readers will regret: 73

> My shell which Clio gave, which *Kings applaud*,
> Which Europe's bleeding Genius call'd abroad,
> Adieu!

In a species of poetry altogether his own he next tried his skill, and succeeded.

Of his wife he was deprived in 1741. She had lost in her life-time, at seventeen years of age, an amiable daughter, who was just married to Mr. Temple, son of Lord Palmerston. This was one of her three children by Colonel Lee. Mr. Temple did not long remain after his wife*. Mr. and Mrs. Temple have always been considered as Philander and Narcissa. If they were, they did not die long before Lady E. Young. How suddenly and how nearly together the deaths of the three persons whom he laments, happened, none who has read the *Night Thoughts*, and who has not read them? needs to be informed.   74

> Insatiate Archer! could not one suffice?
> Thy shaft flew thrice; and thrice my peace was slain;
> And thrice, ere thrice yon moon had fill'd her horn.

To the sorrow Young felt at his losses we are indebted for these poems. There is a pleasure sure in sadness which mourners only know. Of these poems the two or three first have been perused perhaps more eagerly, and more frequently, than the rest. When he got as far as the fourth or fifth, his

---

* The Irish Peerage, if authentic, in the account of Lord Palmerston's family, somewhat confuses this business; but I take what I have related to be the fact.

grief was naturally either diminished or exhausted. We find the same religion, the same piety; but we hear less of Philander and of Narcissa.

75   Mrs. Temple died *in her bridal hour* at Nice. Young, with the rest of her family, accompanied her to the continent.

> I flew, I snatch'd her from the rigid North,
> And bore her nearer to the sun.

The poet seems to dwell with more melancholy on the deaths of Philander and Narcissa, than of his wife. But it is only for this reason. He who runs and reads may remember, that in the *Night Thoughts* Philander, and Narcissa are often mentioned, and often lamented. To recollect lamentations over the author's wife, the memory must have been charged with distinct passages. This Lady brought him one child, Frederick, now living, to whom the Prince of Wales was godfather.

76   That domestick grief is, in the first instance, to be thanked for these ornaments to our language it is impossible to deny. Nor would it be common hardiness to contend, that worldly discontent had no hand in these joint productions of poetry and piety. Yet am I by no means sure that, at any rate, we should not have had something of the same colour from Young's pencil, notwithstanding the liveliness of his satires. In so long a life, causes for discontent and occasions for grief must have occurred. It is not clear to me that his Muse was not sitting upon the watch for the first which happened. *Night Thoughts* were not uncommon to her, even when first she visited the poet, and at a time when he himself was remarkable neither for gravity nor gloominess. In his *Last Day*, almost his earliest poem, he calls her the *melancholy Maid*,

> —whom dismal scenes delight,
> Frequent at tombs and in the realms of Night.

In the prayer which concludes the second book of the same poem, he says—

> —Oh! permit the gloom of solemn night
> To sacred thought may forcibly invite.
> Oh! how divine to tread the milky way,
> To the bright palace of Eternal Day!

77   When Young was writing a tragedy, Grafton is said by Spence to have sent him a human skull, with a candle in it, as a lamp; and the poet is reported to have used it.

78   What he calls "The *true* estimate of Human Life," which has already been mentioned, exhibits only the wrong side of the tapestry; and being asked why he did not show the right, he is said to have replied he could

not—though by others it has been told me that this was finished, but that a Lady's monkey tore it in pieces before there existed any copy.

Still, is it altogether fair to dress up the poet for the man, and to bring the 79
gloominess of the *Night Thoughts* to prove the gloominess of Young, and to shew that his genius, like the genius of Swift, was in some measure the sullen inspiration of discontent?

From them who answer in the affirmative it should not be concealed that, 80
though *Invisibilia non decipiunt* was inscribed upon a deception in Young's grounds, and *Ambulantes in horto audiêrunt vocem Dei* on a building in his garden, his parish was indebted to the good humour of the author of the *Night Thoughts* for an assembly and a bowling green.

Whether you think with me, I know not; but the famous *De mortuis nil* 81
nisi bonum, always appeared to me to favour more of female weakness than of manly reason. He that has too much feeling to speak ill of the dead, who, if they cannot defend themselves, are at least ignorant of his abuse, will not hesitate by the most wanton calumny to destroy the quiet, the reputation, the fortune of the living. Censure is not heard beneath the tomb any more than praise. *De mortuis nil nisi verum—De vivis nil nisi bonum*—would approach perhaps much nearer to good sense. After all, the few handfuls of remaining dust which once composed the body of the author of the *Night Thoughts*, feel not much concern whether Young passes now for a man of sorrow, or for a *fellow of infinite jest*. To this favour must come the whole family of Yorick.—His immortal part, wherever that now dwells, is still less solicitous on this head.

But to a son of worth and sensibility it is of some little consequence 82
whether contemporaries believe, and posterity be taught to believe, that his debauched and reprobate life cast a Stygian gloom over the evening of his father's days, saved him the trouble of feigning a character completely detestable, and succeeded at last in bringing his *grey hairs with sorrow to the grave*.

The humanity of the world, little satisfied with inventing perhaps a 83
melancholy disposition for the father, proceeds next to invent an argument in support of their invention, and chooses that Lorenzo should be Young's own son. The Biographia and every account of Young pretty roundly assert this to be the fact; of the absolute impossibility of which the Biographia itself, in particular dates, contains undeniable evidence. Readers I know there are of a strange turn of mind, who will hereafter peruse the *Night Thoughts* with less satisfaction; who will wish they had still been deceived; who will quarrel with me for discovering that no such character as their Lorenzo ever yet disgraced human nature, or broke a father's heart. Yet

would these admirers of the sublime and terrible be offended, should you set them down for cruel and for savage.

84   Of this report, inhuman to the surviving son, if it be untrue, in proportion as the character of Lorenzo is diabolical, where are we to find the proofs? Perhaps it is clear from the poems.

85   From the first line to the last of the *Night Thoughts*, no one expression can be discovered which betrays any thing like the father. In the second *Night* I find an expression which betrays something else; that Lorenzo was his friend; one, it is possible, of his former companions; one of the Duke of Wharton's set. The Poet styles him *gay Friend*—an appellation not very natural from a pious incensed father to such a being as he paints Lorenzo, and that being his son.

86   But let us see how he has sketched this dreadful portrait, from the sight of some of whose features the artist himself must have turned away with horror.—A subject more shocking, if his only child really sat to him, than the crucifixion of Michael Angelo; upon the horrid story told of which, Young composed a short Poem of fourteen lines in the early part of life, which he did not think deserved to be republished.

87   In the first *Night*, the address to the Poet's supposed son is,

> Lorenzo, Fortune makes her court to thee.

88   In the fifth *Night*—

> And burns Lorenzo still for the sublime
> Of life? to hang his airy nest on high?

Is this a picture of the son of the rector of Welwyn?

89   Eighth *Night*—

> In foreign realms (for thou hast travelled far)—

which even now does not apply to his son.

90   In *Night* five—

> So wept Lorenzo fair Clarissa's fate,
> Who gave that angel-boy on whom he dotes,
> And died to give him, orphan'd in his birth!

91   At the beginning of the fifth *Night* we find—

> Lorenzo, to recriminate is just.
> I grant the man is vain who writes for praise.

92   But, to cut short all enquiry; if any one of these passages, if any passage in the poems be applicable, my friend shall pass for Lorenzo. The son of the

author of the *Night Thoughts* was not old enough, when they were written, to recriminate, or to be a father. The *Night Thoughts* were begun immediately after the mournful events of 1741. The first *Nights* appear in the books of the company of Stationers, as the property of Robert Dodsley, in 1742. The Preface to *Night* Seven is dated July the 7th, 1744. The marriage, in consequence of which the supposed Lorenzo was born, happened in May 1731. Young's child was not born till June 1733. In 1741 this Lorenzo, this finished infidel, this *father*, to whose education Vice had for some years put the last hand, was only *eight* years old.

An anecdote of this cruel sort, so open to contradiction, so impossible to   93
be true, who could propagate? Thus easily are blasted the reputations of the living and of the dead.

Who then was Lorenzo? exclaim the readers I have mentioned. If he was   94
not his son, which would have been finely terrible, was he not his nephew, his cousin?

These are questions which I do not pretend to answer. For the sake of   95
human nature, I could wish Lorenzo to have been only the creation of the Poet's fancy—no more than the Quintius of Anti Lucretius, *quo nomine*, says Polignac, *quemvis Atheum intellige*. That this was the case, many expressions in the *Night Thoughts* would seem to prove, did not a passage in *Night* Eight appear to shew that he had somebody in his eye for the ground-work at least of the painting. Lovelace or Lorenzo may be feigned characters; but a writer does not feign a name of which he only gives the initial letter.

> Tell not Calista. She will laugh thee dead,
> Or send thee to her hermitage with L—.

The Biographia, not satisfied with pointing out the son of Young, in that   96
son's lifetime, as his father's Lorenzo, travels out of its way into the history of the son, and tells of his having been forbidden his college at Oxford for misbehaviour. How such anecdotes, were they true, tend to illustrate the life of Young, it is not easy to discover. If the son of the author of the *Night Thoughts* was indeed forbidden his college for a time, at one of our Universities, the author of *Paradise Lost* is by some supposed to have been disgracefully ejected from the other. From juvenile follies who is free? But, whatever the Biographia chooses to relate, the son of Young experienced no dismission from his college either lasting or temporary.

Yet, were nature to indulge him with a second youth, and to leave him at   97
the same time the experience of that which is past, he would probably spend it differently—who would not?—he would certainly be the occasion of less uneasiness to his father. But, from the same experience, he would as certainly, in the same case, be treated differently by his father.

98 Young was a poet; poets, with reverence be it spoken, do not make the best parents. Fancy and imagination seldom deign to stoop from their heights; always stoop unwillingly to the low level of common duties. Aloof from vulgar life, they pursue their rapid flight beyond the ken of mortals, and descend not to earth but when obliged by necessity. The prose of ordinary occurrences is beneath the dignity of poetry.

99 He who is connected with the Author of the *Night Thoughts* only by veneration for the Poet and the Christian, may be allowed to observe, that Young is one of those concerning whom, as you remark in your account of Addison, it is proper rather to say "nothing that is false than all that is true."

100 But the son of Young would almost sooner, I know, pass for a Lorenzo, than see himself vindicated, at the expence of his father's memory, from follies which, if it was blameable in a boy to have committed them, it is surely praise-worthy in a man to lament, and certainly not only unnecessary but cruel in a biographer to record.

101 Of the *Night Thoughts*, notwithstanding their author's professed retirement, all are inscribed to great or to growing names. He had not yet weaned himself from Earls and Dukes, from Speakers of the House of Commons, Lords Commissioners of the Treasury, and Chancellors of the Exchequer. In *Night* Eight the politician plainly betrays himself—

> Think no post needful that demands a knave.
> When late our civil helm was shifting hands,
> So P— thought: think better if you can.

Yet it must be confessed, that at the conclusion of *Night* Nine, weary perhaps of courting earthly patrons, he tells his soul,

> Henceforth
> Thy *patron* he, whose diadem has dropt
> Yon gems of heaven; Eternity thy prize;
> And leave the racers of the world their own.

102 The Fourth *Night* was addressed by "a much-indebted Muse" to the Honourable Mr. Yorke, now Lord Hardwicke; who meant to have laid the Muse under still greater obligations, by the living of Shenfield in Essex, if it had become vacant.

103 The First *Night* concludes with this passage—

> Dark, though not blind, like thee, Meonides;
> Or Milton, thee, Ah! could I reach your strain;
> Or his who made Meonides our own!
> Man too he sung. Immortal man I sing.

Oh had he prest his theme, pursued the track
Which opens out of darkness into day!
Oh had he mounted on his wing of fire,
Soar'd, where I sink, and sung immortal man—
How had it blest mankind, and rescued me!

To the author of these lines was dedicated, in 1756, the first volume of an 104
Essay on the Writings and Genius of Pope, which attempted, whether justly or
not, to pluck from Pope his *Wing of Fire*, and to reduce him to a rank at least
one degree lower than the first class of English poets. If Young accepted and
approved the dedication, he countenanced this attack upon the fame of him
whom he invokes as his Muse.

Part of "paper-sparing" Pope's Third Book of the *Odyssey*, deposited in 105
the Museum, is written upon the back of a Letter signed *E. Young*, which is
clearly the handwriting of our Young. The Letter, dated only May the 2d,
seems obscure; but there can be little doubt that the friendship he requests
was a literary one, and that he had the highest literary opinion of Pope. The
request was a prologue, I am told.

"Dear Sir, May the 2d. 106
Having been often from home, I know not if you have done me the favour
of calling on me. But, be that as it will, I much want that instance of your
friendship I mentioned in my last; a friendship I am very sensible I can
receive from no one but yourself. I should not urge this thing so much but
for very particular reasons; nor can you be at a loss to conceive how a *trifle of
this nature* may be of serious moment to me; and while I am in hopes of the
great advantage of your advice about it, I shall not be so absurd as to make
any further step without it. I know you are much engaged, and only hope to
hear of you at your entire leisure.

I am, Sir, your most faithful,
and obedient servant,
E. YOUNG."

Nay, even after Pope's death, he says, in *Night* Seven:

Pope, who could'st make immortals, art thou dead?

Either the *Essay*, then, was dedicated to a patron who disapproved its
doctrine, which I have been told by the author was not the case; or
Young, in his old age, bartered for a dedication an opinion entertained of
his friend through all that part of life when he must have been best able to
form opinions.

From this account of Young, two or three short passages, which stand 107
almost together in *Night* Four, should not be excluded. They afford a

picture, by his own hand, from the study of which my readers may choose to form their own opinion of the features of his mind, and the complexion of his life.

> Ah me! the dire effect
> Of loitering here, of death defrauded long;
> Of old so gracious (and let that suffice),
> *My very master knows me not.*
>
> *
>
> I've been so long remember'd, I'm forgot.
>
> *
>
> When in his courtier's ears I pour my plaint,
> They drink it as the Nectar of the Great;
> And squeeze my hand, and beg me come to-morrow.
>
> *
>
> Twice-told the period spent on stubborn Troy,
> Court-favour, yet untaken, I *besiege.*
>
> *
>
> If this song lives, Posterity shall know,
> One, though in Britain born, with courtiers bred,
> Who thought ev'n gold might come a day too late;
> Nor on his subtle death-bed plann'd his scheme
> For future vacancies in church or state.

Deduct from the writer's age *twice told the period spent on stubborn Troy*, and you will still leave him more than 40 when he sate down to the miserable siege of *court* favour. He has before told us

> "A fool at 40 is a fool indeed."

After all, the siege seems to have been raised only in consequence of what the General thought his *death bed.*

108   By these extraordinary Poems, written after he was sixty, of which I have been led to say so much, I hope, by the wish of doing justice to the living and the dead, it was the desire of Young to be principally known. He entitled the four volumes which he published himself, *The Works of the Author of the Night Thoughts.* While it is remembered that from these he excluded many of his writings, let it not be forgotten that the rejected pieces contained nothing prejudicial to the cause of virtue, or of religion. Were every thing that Young ever wrote to be published, he would only appear perhaps in a less respectable light as a poet, and more despicable as a dedicator: he would not pass for a worse christian, or for a worse man.— This enviable praise is due to Young. Can it be claimed by every writer? His dedications, after all, he had perhaps no right to suppress. They all,

I believe, speak, not a little to the credit of his gratitude, of favours received; and I know not whether the author, who has once solemnly printed an acknowledgement of a favour, should not always print it.

Is it to the credit or to the discredit of Young, as a poet, that of his *Night Thoughts* the *French* are particularly fond?   109

Of the *Epitaph on Lord Aubrey Beauclerk*, dated 1740, all I know is, that I find it in the late body of English Poetry, and that I am sorry to find it there.   110

Notwithstanding the farewell which he seemed to have taken in the *Night Thoughts* of every thing which bore the least resemblance to ambition, he dipped again in politics. In 1745 he wrote *Reflections on the publick Situation of the Kingdom, addressed to the Duke of Newcastle*—indignant, as it appears, to behold   111

> —a pope-bred Princeling crawl ashore,
> And whistle cut-throats, with those swords that scrap'd
> Their barren rocks for wretched sustenance,
> To cut his passage to the British throne.

This political poem might be called a *Night Thought*. Indeed it was originally printed as the conclusion of the *Night Thoughts*, though he did not gather it with his other works.

Prefixed to the second edition of Howe's *Devout Meditations* is a Letter from Young, dated January 19, 1752, addressed to Archibald Macauly, Esq; thanking him for the book, which he says "he shall never lay far out of his reach; for a greater demonstration of a sound head and a sincere heart he never saw."   112

In 1753, when *The Brothers* had lain by him above thirty years, it appeared upon the stage. If any part of his fortune had been acquired by servility of adulation, he now determined to deduct from it no inconsiderable sum, as a gift to the Society for the Propagation of the Gospel. To this sum he hoped the profits of *The Brothers* would amount. In his calculation he was deceived; but by the bad success of his play the Society was not a loser. The author made up the sum he originally intended, which was a thousand pounds, from his own pocket.   113

The next performance which he printed was a prose publication, entitled, *The Centaur not fabulous, in six Letters to a Friend on the Life in Vogue.* The conclusion is dated November 29, 1754. In the third Letter is described the death-bed of the *gay, young, noble, ingenious, accomplished, and most wretched Altamont*. His last words were—"My principles have poisoned my friend, my extravagance has beggared my boy, my unkindness has murdered my wife!" Either Altamont and Lorenzo were the twin   114 production of fancy, or Young was unlucky enough to know two characters who bore no little resemblance to each other in perfection of wickedness. Report has been accustomed to call Altamont Lord Euston.

115   *The Old Man's Relapse*, occasioned by an Epistle to Walpole, if it was written by Young, which I much doubt, must have been written very late in life. It has been seen, I am told, in a Miscellany published thirty years before his death.—In 1758, he exhibited *The Old Man's Relapse* in more than words, by again becoming a dedicator, and publishing a sermon addressed to the King.

116   The lively Letter in prose on *Original Composition*, addressed to Richardson the author of *Clarissa*, appeared in 1759. Though he despairs "of breaking through the frozen obstructions of age and care's incumbent cloud, into that flow of thought and brightness of expression which subjects so polite require;" yet is it more like the production of untamed, unbridled youth, than of jaded fourscore. Some sevenfold volumes put him in mind of Ovid's sevenfold channels of the Nile at the conflagration.

> —ostia septem
> Pulverulenta vocant, septem sine flumine valles.

Such leaden labours are like Lycurgus's iron money, which was so much less in value than in bulk, that it required barns for strong boxes and a yoke of oxen to draw five hundred pounds.

117   If there is a famine of invention in the land, we must travel, he says, like Joseph's brethren, far for food; we must visit the remote and rich antients. But an inventive genius may safely stay at home; that, like the widow's cruse, is divinely replenished from within, and affords us a miraculous delight. He asks why it should seem altogether impossible, that Heaven's latest editions of the human mind may be the most correct and fair? And Jonson, he tells us, was very learned, as Sampson was very strong, to his own hurt. Blind to the nature of tragedy, he pulled down all antiquity on his head, and buried himself under it.

Is this "care's incumbent cloud," or "the frozen obstructions of age?"

118   In this letter Pope is severely censured for his "fall from Homer's numbers, free as air, lofty and harmonious as the spheres, into childish shackles and tinkling sounds; for putting Achilles in petticoats a second time;"—but we are told that the dying swan talked over an Epic plan with Young a few weeks before his decease.

119   Young's chief inducement to write this letter was, as he confesses, that he might erect a monumental marble to the memory of an old friend. He, who employed his pious pen for almost the last time in thus doing justice to the

exemplary death-bed of Addison, might probably, at the close of his own life, afford no unuseful lesson for the deaths of others.

In the postscript he writes to Richardson, that he will see in his next how far Addison is an original. But no other letter appears. 120

The few lines which stand in the last edition, as *sent by Lord Melcombe to Dr. Young, not long before his Lordship's death*, were indeed so sent, but were only an introduction to what was there meant by *The Muse's latest Spark*. The poem is necessary, whatever may be its merit, since the Preface to it is already printed. Lord Melcombe called his *Tusculum La Trappe*. 121

> "Love thy country, wish it well,
>   Not with too intense a care,
> 'Tis enough, that, when it fell,
>   Thou its ruin didst not share.
>
> Envy's censure, Flattery's praise,
>   With unmov'd indifference view;
> Learn to tread Life's dangerous maze,
>   With unerring Virtue's clue.
>
> Void of strong desire and fear,
>   Life's wide ocean trust no more;
> Strive thy little bark to steer
>   With the tide, but near the shore.
>
> Thus prepar'd, thy shorten'd sail
>   Shall, whene'er the winds increase,
> Seizing each propitious gale,
>   Wast thee to the Port of Peace.
>
> Keep thy conscience from offence,
>   And tempestuous passions free,
> So, when thou art call'd from hence,
>   Easy shall thy passage be;
>
> Easy shall thy passage be,
>   Chearful thy allotted stay,
> Short the account 'twixt God and thee;
>   Hope shall meet thee on the way;
>
> Truth shall lead thee to the gate,
>   Mercy's self shall let thee in,
> Where its never-changing state
>   Full perfection shall begin."

The Poem was accompanied by a Letter. 122

"*La Trappe*, the 27th Oct. 1761.

Dear Sir,

You seemed to like the ode I sent you for your amusement; I now send it you as a present. If you please to accept of it, and are willing that our friendship should be known when we are gone, you will be pleased to leave this among those of your own papers that may possibly see the light by a posthumous publication. God send us health while we stay, and an easy journey!

My dear Dr. Young,
Yours, most cordially,
MELCOMBE."

123   In 1762, a short time before his death, Young published *Resignation*. Notwithstanding the manner in which it was really forced from him by the world, criticism has treated it with no common severity. If it shall be thought not to deserve the highest praise, on the other side of fourscore by whom, except by Newton and by Waller, has praise been merited?

124   To Mrs. Montagu, the famous champion of Shakspeare, I am indebted for the history of *Resignation*. Observing that Mrs. Boscawen, in the midst of her grief for the loss of the admiral, derived consolation from the perusal of the *Night Thoughts*, Mrs. Montagu proposed a visit to the author. From conversing with Young Mrs. Boscawen derived still further consolation, and to that visit she and the world were indebted for this poem. It compliments Mrs. Montagu in the following lines:

> Yet, write I must. A Lady sues,
>   How shameful her request!
> My brain in labour with dull rhyme,
>   Her's teeming with the best!

And again—

> A friend you have, and I the same,
>   Whose prudent soft address
> Will bring to life those healing thoughts
>   Which died in your distress.
>
> That friend, the spirit of my theme
>   Extracting for your ease,
> Will leave to me the dreg, in thoughts
>   Too common; such as these.

125   By the same Lady I am enabled to say, in her own words, that Young's unbounded genius appeared to greater advantage in the companion, than even in the author—that the christian was in him a character still more

inspired, more enraptured, more sublime than the poet—and that, in his ordinary conversation,

> —letting down the golden chain from high,
> He drew his audience upward to the sky.

Notwithstanding Young had said, in his *Conjectures on original Compos-* 126 *ition*, that "blank verse is verse unfallen, uncurst; verse reclaimed, reinthroned in the true language of the Gods"—notwithstanding he administered consolation to his own grief in this immortal language— Mrs. Boscawen was comforted in rhyme.

While the poet and the christian were applying this comfort, Young had 127 himself occasion for comfort, in consequence of the sudden death of Richardson, who was printing the former part of the poem. Of Richardson's death he says—

> When heaven would kindly set us free,
>   And earth's enchantment end;
> It takes the most effectual means,
>   And robs us of a friend.

To *Resignation* was prefixed an Apology for its appearance: to which 128 more credit is due than to the generality of such apologies, from Young's unusual anxiety that no more productions of his old age should disgrace his former fame. In his will, dated February 1760, he desires of his executors, *in a particular manner*, that all his manuscript books and writings whatever might be burned, except his book of accounts.

In September 1764 he added a kind of codicil, wherein he made it his 129 dying intreaty to his housekeeper, to whom he left 1000*l.* "that all his manuscripts might be destroyed as soon as he was dead, which would greatly oblige her deceased *friend.*"

It may teach mankind the uncertainty of worldly friendships, to know 130 that Young, either by surviving those he loved, or by outliving their affections, could only recollect the names of two friends, his housekeeper and a hatter, to mention in his will; and it may serve to repress that testamentary pride, which too often seeks for sounding names and titles, to be informed that the author of the *Night Thoughts* did not blush to leave a legacy to his "*friend* Henry Stevens, a hatter at the Temple-gate." Of these two remaining friends, one went before Young. But, at eighty-four "where," as he asks in *The Centaur*, "is that world into which we were born?"

The same humility which marked a hatter and a housekeeper for the 131 *friends* of the author of the *Night Thoughts*, had before bestowed the same title on his footman, in an epitaph in his *Church-yard* upon James Barker, dated 1749; which I am glad to find in the late collection of his works.

132   Young and his housekeeper were ridiculed, with more ill-nature than wit, in a kind of novel published by Kidgell in 1755, called *The Card*, under the names of Dr. Elwes and Mrs. Fusby.

133   In April 1765, at an age to which few attain, a period was put to the life of Young.

134   He had performed no duty for the last three or four years of his life, but he retained his intellects to the last.

135   Much is told in the *Biographia*, which I know not to have been true, of the manner of his burial—of the master and children of a charity-school, which he founded in his parish, who neglected to attend their benefactor's corpse; and of a bell which was not caused to toll so often as upon those occasions bells usually toll. Had that humanity, which is here lavished upon things of little consequence either to the living or to the dead, been shewn in its proper place to the living, I should have had less to say about Lorenzo. They who lament that these misfortunes happened to Young, forget the praise he bestows upon Socrates, in the Preface to *Night* Seven, for resenting his friend's request about his funeral.

136   During some part of his life Young was abroad, but I have not been able to learn any particulars.

137   In his seventh Satire he says,

> When, after battle, I the field have *seen*
> Spread o'er with ghastly shapes which once were *men*.

138   And it is known that from this or from some other *field* he once wandered into the enemy's camp, with a classic in his hand, which he was reading intently; and had some difficulty to prove that he was only an absent poet and not a spy.

139   The curious reader of Young's life will naturally inquire to what it was owing, that, though he lived almost forty years after he took Orders, which included one whole reign uncommonly long, and part of another, he was never thought worthy of the least preferment. The author of the *Night Thoughts* ended his days upon a Living which came to him from his College without any favour, and to which he probably had an eye when he determined on the Church. To satisfy curiosity of this kind is, at this distance of time, far from easy. The parties themselves know not often, at the instant, why they are neglected, nor why they are preferred. The neglect of Young is by some ascribed to his having attached himself to the Prince of Wales, and to his having preached an offensive sermon at St. James's. It has been told me, that he had two hundred a year in the late reign, by the patronage of

Walpole; and that, whenever the King was reminded of Young, the only answer was, *he has a pension*. All the light thrown on this inquiry, by the following Letter from Secker, only serves to shew at what a late period of life the author of the *Night Thoughts* solicited preferment.

"Deanry of St. Paul's, July 8, 1758. 140

"Good Dr. Young,

"I have long wondered, that more suitable notice of your great merit hath not been taken by persons in power. But how to remedy the omission I see not. No encouragement hath ever been given me to mention things of this nature to his Majesty. And therefore, in all likelihood, the only consequence of doing it would be weakening the little influence, which else I may possibly have on some other occasions. Your fortune and your reputation set you above the need of advancement; and your sentiments, above that concern for it, on your own account, which, on that of the Public, is sincerely felt by

Your loving Brother,
THO^s. CANT."

At last, at the age of fourscore, he was appointed, in 1761, Clerk of the Closet to the Princess Dowager.

One obstacle must have stood not a little in the way of that preferment 141 after which his whole life panted. Though he took Orders, he never intirely shook off Politics. He was always the Lion of his master Milton, *pawing to get free his hinder parts*. By this conduct, if he gained some friends, he made many enemies.

Again, Young was a poet; and again, with reverence be it spoken, poets 142 by profession do not always make the best clergymen. If the author of the *Night Thoughts* composed many sermons, he did not oblige the public with many.

Besides, in the latter part of life, Young was fond of holding himself out 143 for a man retired from the world. But he seemed to have forgotten that the same verse which contains *oblitus meorum*, contains also *obliviscendus & illis*. The brittle chain of worldly friendship and patronage is broken as effectually, when one goes beyond the length of it, as when the other does. To the vessel which is sailing from the shore, it only appears that the shore also recedes; in life it is truly thus. He who retires from the world, will find himself, in reality, deserted as fast, if not faster, by the world. The publick is not to be treated as the coxcomb treats his mistress—to be threatened with desertion, in order to increase fondness.

Young seems to have been taken at his word. Notwithstanding his 144 frequent complaints of being neglected, no hand was reached out to pull him from that retirement of which he declared himself enamoured. Alexander assigned no palace for the residence of Diogenes, who boasted his surly satisfaction with his tub.

145   Of the domestick manners and petty habits of the author of the *Night Thoughts*, I hoped to have given you an account from the best authority;—but who shall dare to say, To-morrow I will be wise or virtuous, or to-morrow I will do a particular thing? Upon enquiring for his housekeeper, I learned that she was buried two days before I reached the town of her abode.

146   In a Letter from Tscharner, a noble foreigner, to Count Haller, Tscharner says, he has lately spent four days with Young at Welwyn, where the author tastes all the ease and pleasure mankind can desire. "Every thing about him shews the man, each individual being placed by rule. All is neat without art. He is very pleasant in conversation, and extremely polite."

147   This, and more, may possibly be true; but Tscharner's was a first visit, a visit of curiosity and admiration, and a visit which the author expected.

148   Of Edward Young an anecdote which wanders among readers is not true, that he was Fielding's *Parson Adams*. The original of that famous painting was William Young. He too was a clergyman. He supported an uncomfortable existence by translating for the booksellers from Greek; and, if he was not his own friend, was at least no man's enemy. Yet the facility with which this report has gained belief in the world, argues, were it not sufficiently known, that the author of the *Night Thoughts* bore some resemblance to *Adams*.

149   The attention Young bestowed upon the perusal of books is not unworthy imitation. When any passage pleased him, he appears to have folded down the leaf. On these passages he bestowed a second reading. But the labours of man are too frequently vain. Before he returned, a second time, to much of what he had once approved, he died. Many of his books, which I have seen, are by those notes of approbation so swelled beyond their real bulk, that they will not shut.

> What though we wade in wealth, or soar in fame!
> Earth's highest station ends in *Here he lies!*
> And *dust to dust* concludes her noblest song!

The author of these lines is not without his *hic jacet*.

150   By the good sense of his son, it contains none of that praise which no marble can make the bad or the foolish merit; which, without the direction of a stone or a turf, will find its way, sooner or later, to the deserving.

M. S.
Optimi parentis
EDWARDI YOUNG, LL. D.
Hujus Ecclesiæ rect.

Et Elizabethæ
fæm. prænob.
Conjugis ejus amantissimæ
Pio & gratissimo animo
Hoc marmor posuit
F. Y.
Filius superstes.

Is it not strange that the author of the *Night Thoughts* has inscribed no 151
monument to the memory of his lamented wife? Yet what marble will
endure as long as the poems?

Such, my good friend, is the account I have been able to collect of Young. 152
That it may be long before any thing like what I have just transcribed be
necessary for you, is the sincere with of,

Dear Sir,
Your greatly obliged Friend,
Lincoln's Inn,   HERBERT CROFT, Jun.
Sept. 1780.

P. S. This account of Young was seen by you in manuscript you know, 153
Sir; and, though I could not prevail on you to make any alterations, you
insisted on striking out one passage, only because it said, that, if I did not
wish you to live long for your sake, I did for the sake of myself and of the
world. But this postscript you will not see before it is printed; and I will say
here, in spite of you, how I feel myself honoured and bettered by your
friendship—and that, if I do credit to the church, after which I always
longed, and for which I am now going to give in exchange the bar, though
not at so late a period of life as Young took Orders, it will be owing, in no
small measure, to my having had the happiness of calling the author of
The Rambler my friend.

Oxford,   H. C."
Sept. 1782.

OF Young's Poems it is difficult to give any general character; for he has 154
no uniformity of manner: one of his pieces has no great resemblance to
another. He began to write early, and continued long; and at different times
had different modes of poetical excellence in view. His numbers are sometimes smooth, and sometimes rugged; his style is sometimes concatenated,
and sometimes abrupt; sometimes diffusive; and sometimes concise. His
plan seems to have started in his mind at the present moment, and his
thoughts appear the effects of chance, sometimes adverse, and sometimes
lucky, with very little operation of judgement.

155   He was not one of the writers whom experience improves, and who
observing their own faults become gradually correct. His Poem on the
Last Day, his first great performance, has an equability and propriety,
which he afterwards either never endeavoured or never attained. Many
paragraphs are noble, and few are mean, yet the whole is languid; the plan is
too much extended, and a succession of images divides and weakens the
general conception; but the great reason why the reader is disappointed is,
that the thought of the LAST DAY makes every man more than poetical, by
spreading over his mind a general obscurity of sacred horror, that oppresses
distinction, and disdains expression.

156   His story of *Jane Grey* was never popular. It is written with elegance
enough, but *Jane* is too heroick to be pitied.

157   The *Universal Passion* is indeed a very great performance. It is said to be a
series of Epigrams: but if it be, it is what the author intended: his endeavour
was at the production of striking distichs and pointed sentences; and his
distichs have the weight of solid sentiment, and his points the sharpness of
resistless truth. His characters are often selected with discernment, and
drawn with nicety; his illustrations are often happy, and his reflections often
just. His species of satire is between those of Horace and of Juvenal; he has
the gaiety of Horace; without his laxity of numbers, and the morality of
Juvenal with greater variation of images. He plays, indeed, only on the
surface of life; he never penetrates the recesses of the mind, and therefore
the whole power of his poetry is exhausted by a single perusal; his conceits
please only when they surprise.

158   To translate he never condescended, unless his *Paraphrase on Job* may be
considered as a version; in which he has not, I think, been unsuccessful: he
indeed favoured himself, by chusing those parts which most easily admit
the ornaments of English poetry.

159   He had least success in his lyrick attempts, in which he seems to have
been under some malignant influence: he is always labouring to be great,
and at last is only turgid.

160   In his *Night Thoughts* he has exhibited a very wide display of original
poetry, variegated with deep reflections and striking allusions, a wilderness
of thought, in which the fertility of fancy scatters flowers of every hue and
of every odour. This is one of the few poems in which blank verse could not
be changed for rhyme but with disadvantage. The wild diffusion of the
sentiments, and the digressive sallies of imagination, would have been
compressed and restrained by confinement to rhyme. The excellence of
this work is not exactness, but copiousness; particular lines are not to be
regarded; the power is in the whole, and in the whole there is a magnificence

like that ascribed to Chinese Plantation, the magnificence of vast extent and endless diversity.

His last poem was the *Resignation*; in which he made, as he was accus- 161 tomed, an experiment of a new mode of writing, and succeeded better than in his *Ocean* or his *Merchant*. It was very falsely represented as a proof of decaying faculties. There is Young in every stanza, such as he often was in his highest vigour.

His Tragedies not making part of the Collection, I had forgotten, till 162 Mr. Steevens recalled them to my thoughts by remarking, that he seemed to have one favourite catastrophe, as his three Plays all concluded with lavish suicide; a method by which, as Dryden remarked, a poet easily rids his scene of persons whom he wants not to keep alive. In *Busiris* there are the greatest ebullitions of imagination; but the pride of Busiris is such as no other man can have; and the whole is too remote from known life to raise either grief, terror, or indignation. The *Revenge* approaches much nearer to human practices and manners, and therefore keeps possession of the stage: the first design seems suggested by *Othello*; but the reflections, the incidents, and the diction, are original. The moral observations are so introduced, and so expressed, as to have all the novelty that can be required. Of *The Brothers* I may be allowed to say nothing, since nothing was ever said of it by the Publick.

It must be allowed of Young's poetry, that it abounds in thought, but 163 without much accuracy or selection. When he lays hold of an illustration, he pursues it beyond expectation, sometimes happily, as in his parallel of *Quicksilver* with *Pleasure*, which I have heard repeated with approbation by a Lady, of whose praise he would have been justly proud, and which is very ingenious, very subtle, and almost exact; but sometimes he is less lucky, as when, in his *Night Thoughts*, having it dropped into his mind, that the orbs, floating in space, might be called the *cluster* of Creation, he thinks on a cluster of grapes, and says, that they all hang on the great Vine, drinking the *nectareous juice of immortal Life*.

His conceits are sometimes yet less valuable; in the *Last Day*, he hopes 164 to illustrate the re-assembly of the atoms that compose the human body at the *Trump of Doom*, by the collection of bees into a swarm at the tinkling of a pan.

The Prophet says of Tyre, that *her Merchants are Princes*; Young says of 165 Tyre in his *Merchant*,

> Her merchants Princes, and each *deck a Throne*.

Let burlesque try to go beyond him.

166   He has the trick of joining the turgid and familiar: to buy the alliance of Britain, *Climes were paid down*. Antithesis is his favourite. *They for kindness hate*; and *because she's right, she's ever in the wrong*.

167   His versification is his own, neither his blank nor his rhyming lines have any resemblance to those of former writers: he picks up no hemistichs, he copies no favourite expressions; he seems to have laid up no stores of thought or diction, but to owe all to the fortuitous suggestions of the present moment. Yet I have reason to believe that, when once he had formed a new design, he then laboured it with very patient industry, and that he composed with great labour, and frequent revisions.

168   His verses are formed by no certain model; for he is no more like himself in his different productions than he is like others. He seems never to have studied prosody, nor to have had any direction but from his own ear. But, with all his defects, he was a man of genius and a poet.

MALLET

Of DAVID MALLET, having no written memorial, I am able to give no other 1 account than such as is supplied by the unauthorised loquacity of common fame, and a very slight personal knowledge.

He was by his original one of the Macgregors, a clan that became, about 2 sixty years ago, under the conduct of Robin Roy, so formidable and so infamous for violence and robbery, that the name was annulled by a legal abolition; and when they were all to denominate themselves anew, the father, I suppose, of this author called himself Malloch.

David Malloch was, by the penury of his parents, compelled to be *Janitor* 3 of the High School at Edinburgh; a mean office, of which he did not afterwards delight to hear. But he surmounted the disadvantages of his birth and fortune; for when the Duke of Montrose applied to the College of Edinburgh for a tutor to educate his sons, Malloch was recommended; and I never heard that he dishonoured his credentials.

When his pupils were sent to see the world, they were entrusted to his 4 care; and having conducted them round the common circle of modish travels, he returned with them to London, where, by the influence of the family in which he resided, he naturally gained admission to many persons of the highest rank, and the highest character, to wits, nobles, and statesmen.

Of his works, I know not whether I can trace the series. His first 5 production was *William and Margaret**; of which, though it contains nothing very striking or difficult, he has been envied the reputation; and plagiarism has been boldly charged, but never proved.

Not long afterwards he published the *Excursion* (1728); a desultory and 6 capricious view of such scenes of Nature as his fancy led him, or his knowledge enabled him, to describe. It is not devoid of poetical spirit. Many of the images are striking, and many of the paragraphs are elegant. The cast of diction seems to be copied from Thomson, whose *Seasons* were then in their full blossom of reputation. He has Thomson's beauties and his faults.

His poem on *Verbal Criticism* (1733) was written to pay court to Pope, on 7 a subject which he either did not understand or willingly misrepresented;

---

* Mallet's *William and Margaret* was printed in Aaron Hill's *Plain Dealer*, No. 36, July 24, 1724. In its original state it was very different from what it is in the last edition of his works.

and is little more than an improvement, or rather expansion, of a fragment which Pope printed in a Miscellany long before he engrafted it into a regular poem. There is in this piece more pertness than wit, and more confidence than knowledge. The versification is tolerable, nor can criticism allow it a higher praise.

8   His first tragedy was *Eurydice*, acted at Drury-Lane in 1731; of which I know not the reception nor the merit, but have heard it mentioned as a mean performance. He was not then too high to accept a Prologue and Epilogue from Aaron Hill, neither of which can be much commended.

9   Having cleared his tongue from his native pronunciation so as to be no longer distinguished as a Scot, he seems inclined to disencumber himself from all adherences of his original, and took upon him to change his name from Scotch *Malloch* to English *Mallet*, without any imaginable reason of preference which the eye or ear can discover. What other proofs he gave of disrespect to his native country I know not; but it was remarked of him, that he was the only Scot whom Scotchmen did not commend.

10   About this time Pope, whom he visited familiarly, published his *Essay on Man*, but concealed the author; and when Mallet entered one day, Pope asked him slightly what there was new. Mallet told him, that the newest piece was something called an *Essay on Man*, which he had inspected idly; and seeing the utter inability of the author, who had neither skill in writing nor knowledge of his subject, had tossed it away. Pope, to punish his self-conceit, told him the secret.

11   A new edition of the works of Bacon being prepared (1740) for the press, Mallet was employed to prefix a Life, which he has written with elegance, perhaps with some affectation; but with so much more knowledge of history than of science, that when he afterwards undertook the Life of Marlborough, Warburton remarked, that he might perhaps forget that Marlborough was a general, as he had forgotten that Bacon was a philosopher.

12   When the Prince of Wales was driven from the palace, and, setting himself at the head of the opposition, kept a separate Court, he endeavoured to encrease his popularity by the patronage of literature, and made Mallet his under-secretary, with a salary of two hundred pounds a year: Thomson likewise had a pension; and they were associated in the composition of the Masque of *Alfred*, which in its original state was played at Cliefden in 1740; it was afterwards almost wholly changed by Mallet, and brought upon the stage, at Drury-Lane in 1751, but with no great success.

13   Mallet, in a familiar conversation with Garrick, discoursing of the diligence which he was then exerting upon the Life of *Marlborough*, let him know that in the series of great men, quickly to be exhibited, he should *find a nich* for the hero of the theatre. Garrick professed to wonder by

what artifice he could be introduced; but Mallet let him know, that, by a dexterous anticipation, he should fix him in a conspicuous place. "Mr. Mallet," says Garrick, in his gratitude of exultation, "have you left off to write for the stage?" Mallet then confessed that he had a drama in his hands. Garrick promised to act it; and *Alfred* was produced.

The long retardation of the Life of the duke of Marlborough shews, with 14 strong conviction, how little confidence can be placed in posthumous renown. When he died, it was soon determined that his story should be delivered to posterity; and the papers supposed to contain the necessary information were delivered to the lord Molesworth, who had been his favourite in Flanders. When Molesworth died, the same papers were transferred with the same design to Sir Richard Steele, who in some of his exigences put them in pawn. They then remained with the old dutchess, who in her will assigned the task to Glover and Mallet, with a reward of a thousand pounds, and a prohibition to insert any verses. Glover rejected, I suppose, with disdain the legacy, and devolved the whole work upon Mallet; who had from the late duke of Marlborough a pension to promote his industry, and who talked of the discoveries which he made; but left not, when he died, any historical labours behind him.

While he was in the Prince's service he published *Mustapha*, with a 15 Prologue by Thomson, not mean, but far inferior to that which he had received from Mallet for *Agamemnon*. The Epilogue, said to be written by a friend, was composed in haste by Mallet, in the place of one promised, which was never given. This tragedy was dedicated to the Prince his master. It was acted at Drury-Lane in 1739, and was well received, but was never revived.

In 1740, he produced, as has been already mentioned, the masque of 16 *Alfred*, in conjunction with Thomson.

For some time afterwards he lay at rest. After a long interval, his next work 17 was *Amyntor and Theodora* (1747), a long story in blank verse; in which it cannot be denied that there is copiousness and elegance of language, vigour of sentiment, and imagery well adapted to take possession of the fancy. But it is blank verse. This he sold to Vaillant for one hundred and twenty pounds. The first sale was not great, and it is now lost in forgetfulness.

Mallet, by address or accident, perhaps by his dependance on the Prince, 18 found his way to Bolingbroke; a man whose pride and petulance made his kindness difficult to gain, or keep, and whom Mallet was content to court by an act, which, I hope, was unwillingly performed. When it was found that Pope had clandestinely printed an unauthorised number of the pamphlet called *The Patriot King*, Bolingbroke, in a fit of useless fury, resolved to blast his memory, and employed Mallet (1747) as the executioner of his vengeance. Mallet had not virtue, or had not spirit, to refuse the office; and was rewarded, not long after, with the legacy of lord Bolingbroke's works.

19 Many of the political pieces had been written during the opposition to Walpole, and given to Franklin, as he supposed, in perpetuity. These, among the rest, were claimed by the will. The question was referred to arbitrators; but when they decided against Mallet, he refused to yield to the award; and by the help of Millar the bookseller published all that he could find, but with success very much below his expectation.

20 In 1753, his masque of *Britannia* was acted at Drury-Lane, and his tragedy of *Elvira* in 1763; in which year he was appointed keeper of the book of Entries for ships in the port of London.

21 In the beginning of the last war, when the nation was exasperated by ill success, he was employed to turn the publick vengeance upon Byng, and wrote a letter of accusation under the character of a *Plain Man*. The paper was with great industry circulated and dispersed; and he, for his seasonable intervention, had a considerable pension bestowed upon him, which he retained to his death.

22 Towards the end of his life he went with his wife to France; but after a while, finding his health declining, he returned alone to England, and died in April 1765.

23 He was twice married, and by his first wife had several children. One daughter, who married an Italian of rank named Cilesia, wrote a tragedy called *Almida*, which was acted at Drury-Lane. His second wife was the daughter of a nobleman's steward, who had a considerable fortune, which she took care to retain in her own hands.

24 His stature was diminutive, but he was regularly formed; his appearance, till he grew corpulent, was agreeable, and he suffered it to want no recommendation that dress could give it. His conversation was elegant and easy. The rest of his character may, without injury to his memory, sink into silence.

25 As a writer, he cannot be placed in any high class. There is no species of composition in which he was eminent. His Dramas had their day, a short day, and are forgotten: his blank verse seems to my ear the echo of Thomson. His Life of Bacon is known as it is appended to Bacon's volumes, but is no longer mentioned. His works are such as a writer, bustling in the world, shewing himself in publick, and emerging occasionally from time to time into notice, might keep alive by his personal influence; but which, conveying little information, and giving no great pleasure, must soon give way, as the succession of things produces new topicks of conversation, and other modes of amusement.

AKENSIDE

MARK AKENSIDE was born on the ninth of November, 1721, at Newcastle 1
upon Tyne. His father, Mark, was a butcher of the Presbyterian sect;
his mother's name was Mary Lumsden. He received the first part of his
education at the grammar-school of Newcastle; and was afterwards
instructed by Mr. Wilson, who kept a private academy.

At the age of eighteen he was sent to Edinburgh, that he might qualify 2
himself for the office of a dissenting minister, and received some assistance
from the fund which the Dissenters employ in educating young men of
scanty fortune. But a wider view of the world opened other scenes, and
prompted other hopes: he determined to study physic, and repaid that
contribution, which, being received for a different purpose, he justly
thought it dishonourable to retain.

Whether, when he resolved not to be a dissenting minister, he ceased to be 3
a Dissenter, I know not. He certainly retained an unnecessary and outrageous zeal for what he called and thought liberty; a zeal which sometimes
disguises from the world, and not rarely from the mind which it possesses,
an envious desire of plundering wealth or degrading greatness; and of which
the immediate tendency is innovation and anarchy, an impetuous eagerness
to subvert and confound, with very little care what shall be established.

Akenside was one of those poets who have felt very early the motions of 4
genius, and one of those students who have very early stored their memories
with sentiments and images. Many of his performances were produced in
his youth; and his greatest work, *The Pleasures of Imagination*, appeared
in 1744. I have heard Dodsley, by whom it was published, relate, that when
the copy was offered him, the price demanded for it, which was an hundred
and twenty pounds, being such as he was not inclined to give precipitately,
he carried the work to Pope, who, having looked into it, advised him not to
make a niggardly offer; for *this was no every-day writer*.

In 1741 he went to Leyden, in pursuit of medical knowledge; and three 5
years afterwards (May 16, 1744) became doctor of physick, having, according to the custom of the Dutch Universities, published a thesis, or dissertation. The subject which he chose was *the Original and Growth of the
Human Fœtus*; in which he is said to have departed, with great judgement,
from the opinion then established, and to have delivered that which has
been since confirmed and received.

6   Akenside was a young man, warm with every notion that by nature or accident had been connected with the sound of liberty, and by an excentricity which such dispositions do not easily avoid, a lover of contradiction, and no friend to any thing established. He adopted Shaftesbury's foolish assertion of the efficacy of ridicule for the discovery of truth. For this he was attacked by Warburton, and defended by Dyson: Warburton afterwards reprinted his remarks at the end of his dedication to the Freethinkers.

7   The result of all the arguments which have been produced in a long and eager discussion of this idle question, may easily be collected. If ridicule be applied to any position as the test of truth, it will then become a question whether such ridicule be just; and this can only be decided by the application of truth, as the test of ridicule. Two men, fearing, one a real and the other a fancied danger, will be for a while equally exposed to the inevitable consequences of cowardice, contemptuous censure, and ludicrous representation; and the true state of both cases must be known, before it can be decided whose terror is rational, and whose is ridiculous; who is to be pitied, and who to be despised. Both are for a while equally exposed to laughter, but both are not therefore equally contemptible.

8   In the revisal of his poem, which he died before he had finished, he omitted the lines which had given occasion to Warburton's objections.

9   He published, soon after his return from Leyden (1745), his first collection of odes; and was impelled by his rage of patriotism to write a very acrimonious epistle to Pulteney, whom he stigmatizes, under the name of Curio, as the betrayer of his country.

10   Being now to live by his profession, he first commenced physician at Northampton, where Dr. Stonhouse then practised, with such reputation and success, that a stranger was not likely to gain ground upon him. Akenside tried the contest a while; and, having deafened the place with clamours for liberty, removed to Hampstead, where he resided more than two years, and then fixed himself in London, the proper place for a man of accomplishments like his.

11   At London he was known as a poet, but was still to make his way as a physician; and would perhaps have been reduced to great exigences, but that Mr. Dyson, with an ardour of friendship that has not many examples, allowed him three hundred pounds a year. Thus supported, he advanced gradually in medical reputation, but never attained any great extent of practice, or eminence of popularity. A physician in a great city seems to be the mere play-thing of Fortune; his degree of reputation is, for the most part, totally casual: they that employ him, know not his excellence; they that reject him, know not his deficience. By an acute observer, who had looked

on the transactions of the medical world for half a century, a very curious book might be written on the *Fortune of Physicians*.

Akenside appears not to have been wanting to his own success: he placed 12 himself in view by all the common methods; he became a Fellow of the Royal Society; he obtained a degree at Cambridge, and was admitted into the College of Physicians; he wrote little poetry, but published, from time to time, medical essays and observations; he became physician to St. Thomas's Hospital; he read the Gulstonian Lectures in Anatomy; but began to give, for the Crounian Lecture, a history of the revival of Learning, from which he soon desisted; and, in conversation, he very eagerly forced himself into notice by an ambitious ostentation of elegance and literature.

His Discourse on the Dysentery (1764) was considered as a very con- 13 spicuous specimen of Latinity, which entitled him to the same height of place among the scholars as he possessed before among the wits; and he might perhaps have risen to a greater elevation of character, but that his studies were ended with his life, by a putrid fever, June 23, 1770, in the forty-ninth year of his age.

AKENSIDE is to be considered as a didactick and lyrick poet. His great 14 work is the *Pleasures of Imagination*; a performance which, published, as it was, at the age of twenty-three, raised expectations that were not afterwards very amply satisfied. It has undoubtedly a just claim to very particular notice, as an example of great felicity of genius, and uncommon amplitude of acquisitions, of a young mind stored with images, and much exercised in combining and comparing them.

With the philosophical or religious tenets of the author I have nothing to do; 15 my business is with his poetry. The subject is well-chosen, as it includes all images that can strike or please, and thus comprises every species of poetical delight. The only difficulty is in the choice of examples and illustrations, and it is not easy in such exuberance of matter to find the middle point between penury and satiety. The parts seem artificially disposed, with sufficient coherence, so as that they cannot change their places without injury to the general design.

His images are displayed with such luxuriance of expression, that they 16 are hidden, like Butler's Moon, by a *Veil of Light*; they are forms fantastic-ally lost under superfluity of dress. *Pars minima est ipsa Puella sui.* The words are multiplied till the sense is hardly perceived; attention deserts the mind, and settles in the ear. The reader wanders through the gay diffusion, sometimes amazed, and sometimes delighted; but, after many turnings in the flowery labyrinth, comes out as he went in. He remarked little, and laid hold on nothing.

17   To his versification justice requires that praise should not be denied. In the general fabrication of his lines he is perhaps superior to any other writer of blank verse; his flow is smooth, and his pauses are musical; but the concatenation of his verses is commonly too long continued, and the full close does not recur with sufficient frequency. The sense is carried on through a long intertexture of complicated clauses, and as nothing is distinguished, nothing is remembered.

18   The exemption which blank verse affords from the necessity of closing the sense with the couplet, betrays luxuriant and active minds into such self-indulgence, that they pile image upon image, ornament upon ornament, and are not easily persuaded to close the sense at all. Blank verse will therefore, I fear, be too often found in description exuberant, in argument loquacious, and in narration tiresome.

19   His diction is certainly poetical as it is not prosaick, and elegant as it is not vulgar. He is to be commended as having fewer artifices of disgust than most of his brethren of the blank song. He rarely either recalls old phrases or twists his metre into harsh inversions. The sense however of his words is strained; when *he views the* Ganges *from* Alpine *heights*; that is, from mountains like the Alps. And the pedant surely intrudes, but when was blank verse without pedantry? when he tells how *Planets* absolve *the stated round of Time.*

20   It is generally known to the readers of poetry that he intended to revise and augment this work, but died before he had completed his design. The reformed work as he left it, and the additions which he had made, are very properly retained in the late collection. He seems to have somewhat contracted his diffusion; but I know not whether he has gained in closeness what he has lost in splendor. In the additional book, the *Tale of Solon* is too long.

21   One great defect of his poem is very properly censured by Mr. Walker, unless it may be said in his defence, that what he has omitted was not properly in his plan. "His picture of man is grand and beautiful, but unfinished. The immortality of the soul, which is the natural consequence of the appetites and powers she is invested with, is scarcely once hinted throughout the poem. This deficiency is amply supplied by the masterly pencil of Dr. Young; who, like a good philosopher, has invincibly proved the immortality of man, from the grandeur of his conceptions, and the meanness and misery of his state; for this reason, a few passages are selected from the *Night Thoughts*, which, with those from Akenside, seem to form a complete view of the powers, situation, and end of man." *Exercises for Improvement in Elocution*, p. 66.

22   His other poems are now to be considered; but a short consideration will dispatch them. It is not easy to guess why he addicted himself so diligently

to lyrick poetry, having neither the ease and airiness of the lighter, nor the vehemence and elevation of the grander ode. When he lays his ill-fated hand upon his harp, his former powers seem to desert him; he has no longer his luxuriance of expression, nor variety of images. His thoughts are cold, and his words inelegant. Yet such was his love of lyricks, that, having written with great vigour and poignancy his *Epistle to Curio*, he transformed it afterwards into an ode disgraceful only to its author.

Of his odes nothing favourable can be said; the sentiments commonly 23 want force, nature, or novelty; the diction is sometimes harsh and uncouth, the stanzas ill-constructed and unpleasant, and the rhymes dissonant, or unskilfully disposed, too distant from each other, or arranged with too little regard to established use, and therefore perplexing to the ear, which in a short composition has not time to grow familiar with an innovation.

To examine such compositions singly, cannot be required; they have 24 doubtless brighter and darker parts: but when they are once found to be generally dull, all further labour may be spared; for to what use can the work be criticised that will not be read?

GRAY

1   THOMAS GRAY, the son of Mr. Philip Gray, a scrivener of London, was born in Cornhill, November 26, 1716. His grammatical education he received at Eton under the care of Mr. Antrobus, his mother's brother, then assistant to Dr. George; and when he left school, in 1734, entered a pensioner at Peterhouse in Cambridge.

2   The transition from the school to the college is, to most young scholars, the time from which they date their years of manhood, liberty, and happiness; but Gray seems to have been very little delighted with academical gratifications; he liked at Cambridge neither the mode of life nor the fashion of study, and lived sullenly on to the time when his attendance on lectures was no longer required. As he intended to profess the Common Law, he took no degree.

3   When he had been at Cambridge about five years, Mr. Horace Walpole, whose friendship he had gained at Eton, invited him to travel with him as his companion. They wandered through France into Italy; and Gray's Letters contain a very pleasing account of many parts of their journey. But unequal friendships are easily dissolved: at Florence they quarrelled, and parted; and Mr. Walpole is now content to have it told that it was by his fault. If we look however without prejudice on the world, we shall find that men, whose consciousness of their own merit sets them above the compliances of servility, are apt enough in their association with superiors to watch their own dignity with troublesome and punctilious jealousy, and in the fervour of independance to exact that attention which they refuse to pay. Part they did, whatever was the quarrel, and the rest of their travels was doubtless more unpleasant to them both. Gray continued his journey in a manner suitable to his own little fortune, with only an occasional servant.

4   He returned to England in September 1741, and in about two months afterwards buried his father; who had, by an injudicious waste of money upon a new house, so much lessened his fortune, that Gray thought himself too poor to study the law. He therefore retired to Cambridge, where he soon after became Bachelor of Civil Law; and where, without liking the place or its inhabitants, or professing to like them, he passed, except a short residence at London, the rest of his life.

5   About this time he was deprived of Mr. West, the son of a chancellor of Ireland, a friend on whom he appears to have set a high value, and

who deserved his esteem by the powers which he shews in his Letters, and in the Ode to *May*, which Mr. Mason has preserved, as well as by the sincerity with which, when Gray sent him part of *Agrippina*, a tragedy that he had just begun, he gave an opinion which probably intercepted the progress of the work, and which the judgement of every reader will confirm. It was certainly no loss to the English stage that *Agrippina* was never finished.

In this year (1742) Gray seems first to have applied himself seriously to 6 poetry; for in this year were produced the *Ode to Spring*, his *Prospect of Eton*, and his *Ode to Adversity*. He began likewise a Latin poem, *de Principiis cogitandi*.

It may be collected from the narrative of Mr. Mason, that his first 7 ambition was to have excelled in Latin poetry: perhaps it were reasonable to wish that he had prosecuted his design; for though there is at present some embarrassment in his phrase, and some harshness in his Lyrick numbers, his copiousness of language is such as very few possess; and his lines, even when imperfect, discover a writer whom practice would quickly have made skilful.

He now lived on at Peterhouse, very little solicitous what others did or 8 thought, and cultivated his mind and enlarged his views without any other purpose than of improving and amusing himself; when Mr. Mason, being elected fellow of Pembroke-hall, brought him a companion who was afterwards to be his editor, and whose fondness and fidelity has kindled in him a zeal of admiration, which cannot be reasonably expected from the neutrality of a stranger and the coldness of a critick.

In this retirement he wrote (1747) an ode on the *Death of Mr. Walpole's* 9 *Cat*; and the year afterwards attempted a poem of more importance, on *Government and Education*, of which the fragments which remain have many excellent lines.

His next production (1750) was his far-famed *Elegy in the Church-yard*, 10 which, finding its way into a Magazine, first, I believe, made him known to the publick.

An invitation from lady Cobham about this time gave occasion to an odd 11 composition called *a Long Story*, which adds little to Gray's character.

Several of his pieces were published (1753), with designs, by Mr. Bentley; 12 and, that they might in some form or other make a book, only one side of each leaf was printed. I believe the poems and the plates recommended each other so well, that the whole impression was soon bought. This year he lost his mother.

Some time afterwards (1756) some young men of the college, whose 13 chambers were near his, diverted themselves with disturbing him by frequent and troublesome noises, and, as is said, by pranks yet more offensive and contemptuous. This insolence, having endured it a while, he represented to the governors of the society, among whom perhaps he had no friends; and, finding his complaint little regarded, removed himself to Pembroke-hall.

14   In 1757 he published *The Progress of Poetry* and *The Bard*, two compositions at which the readers of poetry were at first content to gaze in mute amazement. Some that tried them confessed their inability to understand them, though Warburton said that they were understood as well as the works of Milton and Shakspeare, which it is the fashion to admire. Garrick wrote a few lines in their praise. Some hardy champions undertook to rescue them from neglect, and in a short time many were content to be shewn beauties which they could not see.

15   Gray's reputation was now so high, that, after the death of Cibber, he had the honour of refusing the laurel, which was then bestowed on Mr. Whitehead.

16   His curiosity, not long after, drew him away from Cambridge to a lodging near the Museum, where he resided near three years, reading and transcribing; and, so far as can be discovered, very little affected by two odes on *Oblivion* and *Obscurity*, in which his Lyrick performances were ridiculed with much contempt and much ingenuity.

17   When the Professor of Modern History at Cambridge died, he was, as he says, *cockered and spirited up*, till he asked it of lord Bute, who sent him a civil refusal; and the place was given to Mr. Brocket, the tutor of Sir James Lowther.

18   His constitution was weak, and believing that his health was promoted by exercise and change of place, he undertook (1765) a journey into Scotland, of which his account, so far as it extends, is very curious and elegant; for as his comprehension was ample, his curiosity extended to all the works of art, all the appearances of nature, and all the monuments of past events. He naturally contracted a friendship with Dr. Beattie, whom he found a poet, a philosopher, and a good man. The Mareschal College at Aberdeen offered him the degree of Doctor of Laws, which, having omitted to take it at Cambridge, he thought it decent to refuse.

19   What he had formerly solicited in vain, was at last given him without solicitation. The Professorship of History became again vacant, and he received (1768) an offer of it from the duke of Grafton. He accepted, and retained it to his death; always designing lectures, but never reading them; uneasy at his neglect of duty, and appeasing his uneasiness with designs of reformation, and with a resolution which he believed himself to have made of resigning the office, if he found himself unable to discharge it.

Ill health made another journey necessary, and he visited (1769) West- 20
moreland and Cumberland. He that reads his epistolary narration wishes,
that to travel, and to tell his travels, had been more of his employment; but
it is by studying at home that we must obtain the ability of travelling with
intelligence and improvement.

His travels and his studies were now near their end. The gout, of which 21
he had sustained many weak attacks, fell upon his stomach, and, yielding to
no medicines, produced strong convulsions, which (July 30, 1771) terminated in death.

His character I am willing to adopt, as Mr. Mason has done, from a 22
Letter written to my friend Mr. Boswell, by the Rev. Mr. Temple, rector of
St. Gluvias in Cornwall; and am as willing as his warmest well-wisher to
believe it true.

"Perhaps he was the most learned man in Europe. He was equally
acquainted with the elegant and profound parts of science, and that not
superficially but thoroughly. He knew every branch of history, both natural
and civil; had read all the original historians of England, France, and Italy;
and was a great antiquarian. Criticism, metaphysics, morals, politics, made
a principal part of his study; voyages and travels of all sorts were his
favourite amusements; and he had a fine taste in painting, prints, architec-
ture, and gardening. With such a fund of knowledge, his conversation must
have been equally instructing and entertaining; but he was also a good man,
a man of virtue and humanity. There is no character without some speck,
some imperfection; and I think the greatest defect in his was an affectation
in delicacy, or rather effeminacy, and a visible fastidiousness, or contempt
and disdain of his inferiors in science. He also had, in some degree, that
weakness which disgusted Voltaire so much in Mr. Congreve: though he
seemed to value others chiefly according to the progress they had made in
knowledge, yet he could not bear to be considered himself merely as a man
of letters; and though without birth, or fortune, or station, his desire was to
be looked upon as a private independent gentleman, who read for his
amusement. Perhaps it may be said, What signifies so much knowledge,
when it produced so little? Is it worth taking so much pains to leave no
memorial but a few poems? But let it be considered that Mr. Gray was, to
others, at least innocently employed; to himself, certainly beneficially. His
time passed agreeably; he was every day making some new acquisition in
science; his mind was enlarged, his heart softened, his virtue strengthened;
the world and mankind were shewn to him without a mask; and he was
taught to consider every thing as trifling, and unworthy of the attention of a
wise man, except the pursuit of knowledge and practice of virtue, in that
state wherein God hath placed us."

23   To this character Mr. Mason has added a more particular account of
Gray's skill in zoology. He has remarked, that Gray's effeminacy was
affected most *before those whom he did not wish to please*; and that he is
unjustly charged with making knowledge his sole reason of preference, as he
paid his esteem to none whom he did not likewise believe to be good.

24   What has occurred to me, from the slight inspection of his Letters in
which my undertaking has engaged me, is, that his mind had a large grasp;
that his curiosity was unlimited, and his judgement cultivated; that he was a
man likely to love much where he loved at all, but that he was fastidious and
hard to please. His contempt however is often employed, where I hope it
will be approved, upon scepticism and infidelity. His short account of
Shaftesbury I will insert.

"You say you cannot conceive how lord Shaftesbury came to be a
philosopher in vogue; I will tell you: first, he was a lord; secondly, he was
as vain as any of his readers; thirdly, men are very prone to believe what
they do not understand; fourthly, they will believe any thing at all, provided
they are under no obligation to believe it; fifthly, they love to take a new
road, even when that road leads no where; sixthly, he was reckoned a fine
writer, and seems always to mean more than he said. Would you have any
more reasons? An interval of above forty years has pretty well destroyed the
charm. A dead lord ranks with commoners: vanity is no longer interested in
the matter; for a new road is become an old one."

25   Mr. Mason has added, from his own knowledge, that though Gray was
poor, he was not eager of money; and that, out of the little that he had, he
was very willing to help the necessitous.

26   As a writer he had this peculiarity, that he did not write his pieces first
rudely, and then correct them, but laboured every line as it arose in the train
of composition; and he had a notion not very peculiar, that he could not
write but at certain times, or at happy moments; a fantastick foppery, to
which my kindness for a man of learning and of virtue wishes him to have
been superior.

27   GRAY's Poetry is now to be considered; and I hope not to be looked on as
an enemy to his name, if I confess that I contemplate it with less pleasure
than his life.

28   His ode on *Spring* has something poetical, both in the language and the
thought; but the language is too luxuriant, and the thoughts have nothing
new. There has of late arisen a practice of giving to adjectives, derived from
substantives, the termination of participles; such as the *cultured* plain, the
dasied bank; but I was sorry to see, in the lines of a scholar like Gray, the
honied Spring. The morality is natural, but too stale; the conclusion is pretty.

The poem on the *Cat* was doubtless by its author considered as a trifle,   29
but it is not a happy trifle. In the first stanza *the azure flowers* that *blow*, shew
resolutely a rhyme is sometimes made when it cannot easily be found.
Selima, the *Cat*, is called a nymph, with some violence both to language
and sense; but there is good use made of it when it is done; for of the two
lines,

> What female heart can gold despise?
> What cat's averse to fish?

the first relates merely to the nymph, and the second only to the cat. The
sixth stanza contains a melancholy truth, that *a favourite has no friend*; but
the last ends in a pointed sentence of no relation to the purpose; if *what
glistered* had been *gold*, the cat would not have gone into the water; and, if
she had, would not less have been drowned.

The *Prospect of Eton College* suggests nothing to Gray, which every   30
beholder does not equally think and feel. His supplication to father *Thames*,
to tell him who drives the hoop or tosses the ball, is useless and puerile.
Father *Thames* has no better means of knowing than himself. His epithet
buxom health is not elegant; he seems not to understand the word. Gray
thought his language more poetical as it was more remote from common
use: finding in Dryden *honey redolent of Spring*, an expression that reaches
the utmost limits of our language, Gray drove it a little more beyond
common apprehension, by making *gales* to be *redolent of joy and youth*.

Of the *Ode on Adversity*, the hint was at first taken from *O Diva, gratum*   31
quæ regis Antium; but Gray has excelled his original by the variety of his
sentiments, and by their moral application. Of this piece, at once poetical
and rational, I will not by slight objections violate the dignity.

My process has now brought me to the *wonderful Wonder of Wonders*, the   32
two Sister Odes; by which, though either vulgar ignorance or common
sense at first universally rejected them, many have been since persuaded to
think themselves delighted. I am one of those that are willing to be pleased,
and therefore would gladly find the meaning of the first stanza of the
Progress of Poetry.

Gray seems in his rapture to confound the images of *spreading sound* and   33
running water. A *stream of musick* may be allowed; but where does *Musick*,
however *smooth and strong*, after having visited the *verdant vales, rowl down
the steep amain*, so as that *rocks and nodding groves rebellow to the roar*? If this
be said of *Musick*, it is nonsense; if it be said of *Water*, it is nothing to the
purpose.

The second stanza, exhibiting Mars's car and Jove's eagle, is unworthy of   34
further notice. Criticism disdains to chase a schoolboy to his common places.

35   To the third it may likewise be objected, that it is drawn from Myth-ology, though such as may be more easily assimilated to real life. Idalia's *velvet-green* has something of cant. An epithet or metaphor drawn from Nature ennobles Art; an epithet or metaphor drawn from Art degrades Nature. Gray is too fond of words arbitrarily compounded. *Many-twinkling* was formerly censured as not analogical; we may say *many-spotted*, but scarcely *many-spotting*. This stanza, however, has something pleasing.

36   Of the second ternary of stanzas, the first endeavours to tell something, and would have told it, had it not been crossed by Hyperion: the second describes well enough the universal prevalence of Poetry; but I am afraid that the conclusion will not rise from the premises. The caverns of the North and the plains of Chili are not the residences of *Glory* and *generous Shame*. But that Poetry and Virtue go always together is an opinion so pleasing, that I can forgive him who resolves to think it true.

37   The third stanza sounds big with *Delphi*, and *Egean*, and *Ilissus*, and *Meander*, and *hallowed fountain* and *solemn sound*; but in all Gray's odes there is a kind of cumbrous splendor which we wish away. His position is at last false: in the time of Dante and Petrarch, from whom he derives our first school of Poetry, Italy was over-run by *tyrant power* and *coward vice*; nor was our state much better when we first borrowed the Italian arts.

38   Of the third ternary, the first gives a mythological birth of Shakspeare. What is said of that mighty genius is true; but it is not said happily: the real effects of this poetical power are put out of sight by the pomp of machinery. Where truth is sufficient to fill the mind, fiction is worse than useless; the counterfeit debases the genuine.

39   His account of Milton's blindness, if we suppose it caused by study in the formation of his poem, a supposition surely allowable, is poetically true, and happily imagined. But the *car* of Dryden, with his *two coursers*, has nothing in it peculiar; it is a car in which any other rider may be placed.

40   *The Bard* appears, at the first view, to be, as Algarotti and others have remarked, an imitation of the prophecy of Nereus. Algarotti thinks it superior to its original; and, if preference depends only on the imagery and animation of the two poems, his judgement is right. There is in *The Bard* more force, more thought, and more variety. But to copy is less than to invent, and the copy has been unhappily produced at a wrong time. The fiction of Horace was to the Romans credible; but its revival disgusts us with apparent and unconquerable falsehood. *Incredulus odi*.

41   To select a singular event, and swell it to a giant's bulk by fabulous appendages of spectres and predictions, has little difficulty, for he that forsakes the probable may always find the marvellous. And it has little use; we are affected only as we believe; we are improved only as we find

something to be imitated or declined. I do not see that *The Bard* promotes any truth, moral or political.

His stanzas are too long, especially his epodes; the ode is finished before 42 the ear has learned its measures, and consequently before it can receive pleasure from their consonance and recurrence.

Of the first stanza the abrupt beginning has been celebrated; but technical 43 beauties can give praise only to the inventor. It is in the power of any man to rush abruptly upon his subject, that has read the ballad of *Johnny Armstrong*,

Is there ever a man in all Scotland—

The initial resemblances, or alliterations, *ruin, ruthless, helm nor hauberk,* 44 are below the grandeur of a poem that endeavours at sublimity.

In the second stanza the *Bard* is well described; but in the third we have 45 the puerilities of obsolete mythology. When we are told that *Cadwallo hush'd the stormy main,* and that *Modred* made *huge Plinlimmon bow his cloud-top'd head,* attention recoils from the repetition of a tale that, even when it was first heard, was heard with scorn.

The *weaving* of the *winding sheet* he borrowed, as he owns, from the 46 northern Bards; but their texture, however, was very properly the work of female powers, as the art of spinning the thread of life in another mythology. Theft is always dangerous; Gray has made weavers of his slaughtered bards, by a fiction outrageous and incongruous. They are then called upon to *Weave the warp, and weave the woof,* perhaps with no great propriety; for it is by crossing the *woof* with the *warp* that men *weave* the *web* or piece; and the first line was dearly bought by the admission of its wretched correspondent, *Give ample room and verge enough.* He has, however, no other line as bad.

The third stanza of the second ternary is commended, I think, beyond its 47 merit. The personification is indistinct. *Thirst* and *Hunger* are not alike; and their features, to make the imagery perfect, should have been discriminated. We are told, in the same stanza, how *towers* are *fed.* But I will no longer look for particular faults; yet let it be observed that the ode might have been concluded with an action of better example; but suicide is always to be had, without expence of thought.

These odes are marked by glittering accumulations of ungraceful orna- 48 ments; they strike, rather than please; the images are magnified by affectation; the language is laboured into harshness. The mind of the writer seems to work with unnatural violence. *Double, double, toil and trouble.* He has a kind of strutting dignity, and is tall by walking on tiptoe. His art and his struggle are too visible, and there is too little appearance of ease and nature.

49   To say that he has no beauties, would be unjust: a man like him, of great learning and great industry, could not but produce something valuable. When he pleases least, it can only be said that a good design was ill directed.

50   His translations of Northern and Welsh Poetry deserve praise; the imagery is preserved, perhaps often improved; but the language is unlike the language of other poets.

51   In the character of his Elegy I rejoice to concur with the common reader; for by the common sense of readers uncorrupted with literary prejudices, after all the refinements of subtilty and the dogmatism of learning, must be finally decided all claim to poetical honours. The *Church-yard* abounds with images which find a mirrour in every mind, and with sentiments to which every bosom returns an echo. The four stanzas beginning *Yet even these bones*, are to me original: I have never seen the notions in any other place; yet he that reads them here, persuades himself that he has always felt them. Had Gray written often thus, it had been vain to blame, and useless to praise him.

LYTTELTON

GEORGE LYTTELTON, the son of Sir Thomas Lyttelton of Hagley in 1 Worcestershire, was born in 1709. He was educated at Eton, where he was so much distinguished, that his exercises were recommended as models to his school-fellows.

From Eton he went to Christ-church, where he retained the same 2 reputation of superiority, and displayed his abilities to the publick in a poem on *Blenheim*.

He was a very early writer, both in verse and prose. His *Progress of Love*, 3 and his *Persian Letters*, were both written when he was very young; and, indeed, the character of a young man is very visible in both. The Verses cant of shepherds and flocks, and crooks dressed with flowers; and the Letters have something of that indistinct and headstrong ardour for liberty which a man of genius always catches when he enters the world, and always suffers to cool as he passes forward.

He staid not long at Oxford; for in 1728 he began his travels, and saw 4 France and Italy. When he returned, he obtained a seat in parliament, and soon distinguished himself among the most eager opponents of Sir Robert Walpole, though his father, who was Commissioner of the Admiralty, always voted with the Court.

For many years the name of George Lyttelton was seen in every account 5 of every debate in the House of Commons. He opposed the standing army; he opposed the excise; he supported the motion for petitioning the King to remove Walpole. His zeal was considered by the courtiers not only as violent, but as acrimonious and malignant; and when Walpole was at last hunted from his places, every effort was made by his friends, and many friends he had, to exclude Lyttelton from the Secret Committee.

The Prince of Wales, being (1737) driven from St. James's, kept a 6 separate court, and opened his arms to the opponents of the ministry. Mr. Lyttelton became his secretary, and was supposed to have great influence in the direction of his conduct. He persuaded his master, whose business it was now to be popular, that he would advance his character by patronage. Mallet was made under-secretary, with 200*l*. and Thomson had a pension of 100*l*. a year. For Thomson Lyttelton always retained his kindness, and was able at last to place him at ease.

7   Moore courted his favour by an apologetical poem, called *The Trial of Selim*, for which he was paid with kind words, which, as is common, raised great hopes, that at last were disappointed.

8   Lyttelton now stood in the first rank of opposition; and Pope, who was incited, it is not easy to say how, to increase the clamour against the ministry, commended him among the other patriots. This drew upon him the reproaches of Fox, who, in the house, imputed to him as a crime his intimacy with a lampooner so unjust and licentious. Lyttelton supported his friend, and replied, that he thought it an honour to be received into the familiarity of so great a poet.

9   While he was thus conspicuous, he married (1741) Miss Lucy Fortescue of Devonshire, by whom he had a son, the late lord Lyttelton, and two daughters, and with whom he appears to have lived in the highest degree of connubial felicity: but human pleasures are short; she died in childbed about five years afterwards, and he solaced his grief by writing a long poem to her memory.

10   He did not however condemn himself to perpetual solitude and sorrow; for, after a while, he was content to seek happiness again by a second marriage with the daughter of Sir Robert Rich; but the experiment was unsuccessful.

11   At length, after a long struggle, Walpole gave way, and honour and profit were distributed among his conquerors. Lyttelton was made (1744) one of the Lords of the Treasury; and from that time was engaged in supporting the schemes of the ministry.

12   Politicks did not, however, so much engage him as to withhold his thoughts from things of more importance. He had, in the pride of juvenile confidence, with the help of corrupt conversation, entertained doubts of the truth of Christianity; but he thought the time now come when it was no longer fit to doubt or believe by chance, and applied himself seriously to the great question. His studies, being honest, ended in conviction. He found that religion was true, and what he had learned he endeavoured to teach (1747), by *Observations on the Conversion of St. Paul*; a treatise to which infidelity has never been able to fabricate a specious answer. This book his father had the happiness of seeing, and expressed his pleasure in a letter which deserves to be inserted.

"I have read your religious treatise with infinite pleasure and satisfaction. The style is fine and clear, the arguments close, cogent, and irresistible. May the King of kings, whose glorious cause you have so well defended, reward your pious labours, and grant that I may be found worthy, through the merits of Jesus Christ, to be an eye-witness of that happiness which

I don't doubt he will bountifully bestow upon you. In the mean time, I shall never cease glorifying God, for having endowed you with such useful talents, and giving me so good a son.

> Your affectionate father,
> THOMAS LYTTELTON."

A few years afterwards (1751), by the death of his father, he inherited a baronet's title with a large estate, which, though perhaps he did not augment, he was careful to adorn, by a house of great elegance and expence, and by much attention to the decoration of his park,   13

As he continued his activity in parliament, he was gradually advancing his claim to profit and preferment; and accordingly was made in time (1754) cofferer and privy counsellor: this place he exchanged next year for the great office of chancellor of the Exchequer; an office, however, that required some qualifications which he soon perceived himself to want.   14

The year after, his curiosity led him into Wales; of which he has given an account, perhaps rather with too much affectation of delight, to Archibald Bower, a man of whom he had conceived an opinion more favourable than he seems to have deserved, and whom, having once espoused his interest and fame, he never was persuaded to disown. Bower, whatever was his moral character, did not want abilities; attacked as he was by an universal outcry, and that outcry, as it seems, the echo of truth, he kept his ground; at last, when his defences began to fail him, he sallied out upon his adversaries, and his adversaries retreated.   15

About this time Lyttelton published his *Dialogues of the Dead*, which were very eagerly read, though the production rather, as it seems, of leisure than of study, rather effusions than compositions. The names of his persons too often enable the reader to anticipate their conversation; and when they have met, they too often part without any conclusion. He has copied *Fenelon* more than *Fontenelle*.   16

When they were first published, they were kindly commended by the *Critical Reviewers*; and poor Lyttelton, with humble gratitude, returned, in a note which I have read, acknowledgements which can never be proper, since they must be paid either for flattery or for justice.   17

When, in the latter part of the last reign, the inauspicious commencement of the war made the dissolution of the ministry unavoidable, Sir George Lyttelton, losing with the rest his employment, was recompensed with a peerage; and rested from political turbulence in the House of Lords.   18

His last literary production was his *History of Henry the Second*, elaborated by the searches and deliberations of twenty years, and published with such anxiety as only vanity can dictate.   19

20   The story of this publication is remarkable. The whole work was printed twice over, a great part of it three times, and many sheets four or five times. The booksellers paid for the first impression; but the charges and repeated operations of the press were at the expence of the author, whose ambitious accuracy is known to have cost him at least a thousand pounds. He began to print in 1755. Three volumes appeared in 1764, a second edition of them in 1767, a third edition in 1768, and the conclusion in 1771.

21   Andrew Reid, a man not without considerable abilities, and not unacquainted with letters or with life, undertook to persuade Lyttelton, as he had persuaded himself, that he was master of the secret of punctuation; and, as fear begets credulity, he was employed, I know not at what price, to point the pages of *Henry the Second*. The book was at last pointed and printed, and sent into the world. Lyttelton took money for his copy, of which, when he had paid the *Pointer*, he probably gave the rest away; for he was very liberal to the indigent.

22   When time brought the History to a third edition, Reid was either dead or discarded; and the superintendence of typography and punctuation was committed to a man originally a comb-maker, but then known by the style of Doctor. Something uncommon was probably expected, and something uncommon was at last done; for to the Doctor's edition is appended, what the world had hardly seen before, a list of errors in nineteen pages.

23   But to politicks and literature there must be an end. Lord Lyttelton had never the appearance of a strong or of a healthy man; he had a slender uncompacted frame, and a meagre face: he lasted however sixty years, and was then seized with his last illness. Of his death a very affecting and instructive account has been given by his physician, which will spare me the task of his moral character.

24   "On Sunday evening the symptoms of his lordship's disorder, which for a week past had alarmed us, put on a fatal appearance, and his lordship believed himself to be a dying man. From this time he suffered by restlessness rather than pain; and though his nerves were apparently much fluttered, his mental faculties never seemed stronger, when he was thoroughly awake.

25   "His lordship's bilious and hepatic complaints seemed alone not equal to the expected mournful event; his long want of sleep, whether the consequence of the irritation in the bowels, or, which is more probable, of causes of a different kind, accounts for his loss of strength, and for his death, very sufficiently.

26   "Though his lordship wished his approaching dissolution not to be lingering, he waited for it with resignation. He said, 'It is a folly, a keeping me in misery, now to attempt to prolong life;' yet he was easily persuaded,

for the satisfaction of others, to do or take any thing thought proper for him. On Saturday he had been remarkably better, and we were not without some hopes of his recovery.

"On Sunday, about eleven in the forenoon, his lordship sent for me, and   27 said he felt a great hurry, and wished to have a little conversation with me in order to divert it. He then proceeded to open the fountain of that heart, from whence goodness had so long flowed as from a copious spring. 'Doctor,' said he, 'you shall be my confessor: when I first set out in the world, I had friends who endeavoured to shake my belief in the Christian religion. I saw difficulties which staggered me; but I kept my mind open to conviction. The evidences and doctrines of Christianity, studied with attention, made me a most firm and persuaded believer of the Christian religion. I have made it the rule of my life, and it is the ground of my future hopes. I have erred and sinned; but have repented, and never indulged any vicious habit. In politicks, and publick life, I have made publick good the rule of my conduct. I never gave counsels which I did not at the time think the best. I have seen that I was sometimes in the wrong, but I did not err designedly. I have endeavoured, in private life, to do all the good in my power, and never for a moment could indulge malicious or unjust designs upon any person whatsoever.'

"At another time he said, 'I must leave my soul in the same state it was in   28 before this illness; I find this a very inconvenient time for solicitude about any thing.'

"On the evening, when the symptoms of death came on, he said, 'I shall   29 die; but it will not be your fault.' When lord and lady Valentia came to see his lordship, he gave them his solemn benediction, and said, 'Be good, be virtuous, my lord; you must come to this.' Thus he continued giving his dying benediction to all around him. On Monday morning a lucid interval gave some small hopes, but these vanished in the evening; and he continued dying, but with very little uneasiness, till Tuesday morning, August 22, when between seven and eight o'clock he expired, almost without a groan."

His lordship was buried at Hagley; and the following inscription is cut on   30 the side of his lady's monument:

> "This unadorned stone was placed here
> By the particular desire and express
> directions of the Right Honourable
> GEORGE Lord LYTTELTON,
> Who died August 22, 1773, aged 64."

Lord Lyttelton's Poems are the works of a man of literature and judge-   31 ment, devoting part of his time to versification. They have nothing to be despised, and little to be admired. Of his *Progress of Love*, it is sufficient blame to say that it is pastoral. His blank verse in *Blenheim* has neither much force nor much elegance. His little performances, whether Songs or Epigrams, are sometimes spritely, and sometimes insipid. His epistolary pieces have a smooth equability, which cannot much tire, because they are short, but which seldom *elevates* or *surprizes*. But from this censure ought to be excepted his *Advice to Belinda*, which, though for the most part written when he was very young, contains much truth and much prudence, very elegantly and vigorously expressed, and shews a mind attentive to life, and a power of poetry which cultivation might have raised to excellence.

FINIS.

TEXTUAL NOTES

POPE

1. 21 *MS*] 22 *proof, all edns.*

2. this only] no more *rev. in MS*
   is more] has been *rev. in MS*
   was never discovered . . . in the Strand] has never been discovered *P81, L81*

3. mildness] softness *rev. in MS*

4. retained] obtained *rev. in proof*

6. exhibitions] exhibition *proof*
   personated] represented *MS, rev. in proof*

7. under] at *rev. in MS*

8. the style] an age *MS*; use *rev. in proof to* the stile

9. trade] employment *rev. in MS*; trade, whatever it was *proof, P81, L81*

10. few months] short time *rev. in MS*

11. conspicuously] highly *rev. in MS*
    with confused] to know that *rev. in MS*
    completed with little] prosecuted with *rev. in MS*

12. His primary] To be a *rev. in MS*
    correct] polish *rev. in MS*

13. friend *MS*] friends *proof, P81, L81, L83*

14. twelve] thirteen *MS, proof*

16. amused himself] amused *MS*

17. *Insertion from the appended material is called for in the MS*
    much in the hands] consequent *rev. in MS*
    more fashionable] modern *rev. in MS*

18. after Rochester's] in imita[tion] *rev. in MS*
    a small] but a small *MS, proof, P81*

22. shew, with] give *rev. in MS*

23. Pope was] Pope's friendship *rev. in MS*
    with those] *rev. in MS to* with them *queried in proof by Nichols:* Q ose

24. the life] Pope's poetical [?] *rev. in MS*
    pastorals *MS, L83*] Pastorals *P81, L81*
    time; as . . . they were . . . and many] time, and as . . . were . . . and high *MS, rev. in proof*
    both] very *and* equally *rev. in MS*
    five] four *rev. in MS*

25. exertion] appearance *rev. in MS*

26. Wycherley wrote ... to himself] *in the MS SJ began writing this sentence after* one another *but del. it and ins. it in its present position*

27. revision] correction *rev. in MS*
    sufficiently bold] somewhat free *MS, proof*

28. were now-and-then] were *MS, rev. in proof*
    put ... into his hands for] sent him ... for *MS, proof*

29. and she] who *rev. in MS*
    who inserted ... Miscellanies] *ins. in MS, with* one volume *as in proof*

30. Walsh, a name] A Correspondence *rev. in MS*
    counsel *MS, proof, P81, L81*] council *L83*
    recommended to] advised *rev. in MS*

31. Pope had] He had *MS, proof*
    when he] in his life *rev. in MS*

32. period of] interval *rev. in MS*
    curious; wanting] curious, having not *MS, rev. in proof*
    and money] nor money *MS, rev. in proof*
    certainly] probably *MS, rev. in proof*
    seizing] and seized *MS, rev. in proof*
    voracity, and] voracity *MS*
    In a mind] He used [?] *rev. in MS*; For a mind *rev. in proof*
    necessarily] necessary *MS*
    and in the second] in the second *MS*

33. (1709)] 1709 *ins. in MS*; (1609) *proof, corr. by Nichols*
    began] began *with* unhappily *del. above in MS*

34. two years] a year *rev. in MS*
    being praised ... liberality, met] was praised ... liberality; and met *MS, rev. in proof*

35. in whom ... an appetite] who seems willing *MS, rev. in proof*

37. admits ... false opinions] concludes ... corruption of *rev. in MS*
    The 'quotation' from Dennis became a separate para. in proof. The quotation marks were added in L83
    laws *Dennis, MS*] law *proof, P81, L81, L83*

38. passages. In *MS, proof, P81, L81*] passages, in *L83*
    have ... mirth] shew ... wit *MS, rev. in proof*
    forgotten] omitted *rev. in MS*

39. The first edition had] In the first edition was *MS, rev. in proof*
    the scorn] that scorn *MS*

40. (says Dennis)] says Dennis *ins. in proof*
    wantonly] warmly *corr. in proof*
    very often] often *MS, proof, P81, L81*

41. Essay] piece *MS, proof*
    mentioned] mentions *MS, proof, P81*

43. whose version . . . printed] *ins. in MS*; whose version was not printed *rev. in proof*

44. give] find *and* shew *rev. in MS*
    truths at least] truths however *MS, rev. in proof*
    but if this order] and with equal *rev. in MS*
    Fortitude] Courage the *rev. in MS*
    he might . . . placed] if he had put it after *rev. in MS*
    Fortitude is] it is *MS, rev. in proof*

45. As the end . . . that series] The end . . . and that series *MS, rev. in proof*

46. in compliance] according *rev. in MS*

47. the time] 1710 *rev. in MS*

48–52. *Insertion from the appended material is called for in the MS*

49. can rarely] could not *rev. in MS*

50. still greater] greater *MS, rev. in proof*

51. impatient] of a temper *rev. in MS*
    self-murder] suicide *rev. in MS*

52. is it discovered] does there appear (*with* suff *del.) MS, proof*
    amorous fury] suicide *rev. in MS*
    raving] mad *rev. in MS*

53. stealth] fraud *MS, rev. in proof*
    commerce] friendship *rev. in MS*
    who, being secretary . . . had] who had been secretary . . . and had *MS, rev. in proof*
    who being the author] being the author *MS; rev. in proof to* as the author *P81, L81*
    was entitled . . . Wit] had some claim . . . Poet *MS, rev. in proof*
    bring] put *rev. in MS*
    Caryl's] this *MS, rev. in proof*
    though his name . . . C—l] *ins. in MS*

54. said] said by Ruffhead *MS*
    a niece of Mrs. Fermor] the Lady *rev. in MS*
    honour] favour *rev. in MS*
    opinion] opinions *MS, rev. in proof*

55. imparted] told *MS, rev. in proof*
    told him . . . as it] gave him encouragements to ha [?] *rev. in MS*

56. for as] but as *MS, proof*
    guess] know *MS, rev. in proof*
    persuade] advise *rev. in MS*

57. efflorescence] effervescence *corr. in proof*
    or industry] nor industry *MS*; no industry *rev. in proof*

soft] *ins. in MS*

varieties] colours *MS, rev. in proof*

ready . . . embellish it] prepared for its embellishment *MS, rev. in proof*

58. with elegance . . . exhibited] to elegance . . . added *MS, rev. in proof*

59. intertexture *MS, proof, P81, L81*] intermixture *L83*

most successful] highest *rev. in MS*

Those performances] Every great *rev. in MS*

any felicity,] felicity *rev. in MS*

60. published some] *above* the consta [?] *del. in MS*

61. that work] his work *MS, rev. in proof*

62. *An insertion in the MS, after which SJ repeats the information in* **46** *above*: At this time it appears from the same letters he had written the *Messiah* which [*above* though it *del.*] was first communicated to the publick [*above* printed two years afterwards *del.*] in the Spectator.

63. excelled] surpassed *MS*

the imagination] *ins. in MS*

far greater] far more *MS, proof*

grove] grave *corr. in proof*

65. the addition] the latter part *MS, rev. in proof*

boldness] confidence *MS, rev. in proof*

he would not] what statesman could *rev. in MS to* he could not *rev. in proof*

66. having been] he was *rev. in MS*

he introduced] and when it *rev. in MS*

not indeed] not *MS*; not only *rev. in proof*

67. a man on whom . . . impression] a man . . . impression *MS*; a man . . . impression on *rev. in proof*

68. This year] At this time *rev. in MS*

between] of *MS, rev. in proof*

to which nothing equal will] of which another example will not *MS, rev. in proof*

Steele, being deceived,] Steele was deceived, and *MS, rev. in proof*

69. He was] Pope was *MS, proof*

A picture] Lord Mansfield had a *rev. in MS*

life, he] life Pope *MS*

Pope's . . . new art] This desire *MS*

some . . . verses] an . . . poem *rev. in MS*

70. was related by] I have heard from *MS, proof*

the performance of] written by *rev. in MS*

if he would shew] for the pleasure of seeing *MS, rev. in proof*

74. as each faction then] because each faction *MS, rev. in proof*

75. believe . . . before] remember . . . for any other book *rev. in MS*

76. greatness] success *rev. in MS*

77. sold] *after* and the book so printed he *del., MS*

    books so little . . . Quartos] *ins. in MS*

    those Folios] the Folios *MS, rev. in proof*

    being afterwards] were afterwards *MS, proof*

    top and bottom] margin *rev. in MS*

    were sold] and sold *MS, proof*

78. two hundred and fifty] some *MS, proof, P81, L81*

    of the small Folio, . . . a thousand] but of this experiment he repented, and his son sold copies of the first volume with all their extent of margin for two shillings *MS, proof (with* the copies *rev. to* copies), *P81, L81*

79. printed] published *rev. in MS*

    imported . . . for] brought . . . into *rev. in MS*

    advantage] profit *rev. in MS*

    an intermediate] intermediate *MS*

    two thousand . . . afterwards] the sale was doubtless very numerous *MS, proof, P81, L81*

    indeed] very *MS, proof*

81. by degrees] in time *MS*

    termination] limits *rev. in MS*

83. representations] images *rev. in MS*

    mingling] impressing *rev. in MS*

    diction] language *rev. in MS*

    either] ancient *rev. in MS*

    printed] version *rev. in MS*

    lines literally rendered] literal version *rev. in MS to* pages literally rendered

84. easily] always *MS, proof, P81, L81*

    much] any thing *MS*

85. With Chapman, . . . totally] Of Chapman his use was very frequent *rev. in MS*

87. then employed *P81, L81*] them employed *L83*

    a third, that . . . is now] another . . . who has been *MS*; a third . . . who is now *proof, P81, L81*

    see him, . . . which he worked] see him *MS, proof, P81, L81*

    The second sentence from Fenton's letter appears to be a later insertion in MS

    you return *Pope, Corresp., i. 497*] the return *MS, all edns.*

88. *In the proofs Nichols has written at the foot of the page:* Please to send more Copy

    Broome then] Broome afterwards *MS, rev. in proof*

    contributed] wrote *MS, rev. in proof*

found . . . correcting it] however is said to have taken great pains in correcting *MS, proof*

kindness] he could *rev. in MS*

his version] the version *rev. in MS*

89. containing . . . might] contains . . . it would *MS*

an antagonist] no chance in his *rev. in MS*

90. translation] work *MS*

five hundred and seventy-five] *ins. in proof by Nichols*

given] paid *MS*

six hundred and fifty-four] *ins. in proof by Nichols*

and only six . . . printed] *ins. in L83*

including the two hundred . . . shillings] *left blank in MS and proof, with* four thousand one hundred and twenty fo[ur] pounds *ins. in proof by Nichols*

91. his subscription] this work *MS*

with which, . . . struggled] *ins. in MS*

92. product of this] accumulated *rev. in MS*

considerable] purchasing *rev. in MS*

doubtless . . . purchase] he probably purchased by the profits of his translation *MS*

93. *Iliad*. It is certainly] Iliad, as it is probable *MS; Iliad*. It is probably *proof*

seen; and its] seen, of which *MS*

must therefore] must *MS*

94. have skill] know how *MS*

such an] this *MS*

is now by the] was afterwards *rev. in MS*

the late Dr.] Dr *MS, rev. in proof in response to marginal query by Nichols*: Q the late

95. Between] This copy *rev. in MS*

must have been . . . that] was . . . which *MS*

returned] was returned *MS, proof*

96–7. *Pp. 71–4 of the proofs, including part of these paragraphs, are missing*

96. first copy] original *rev. in MS*

cancelled] blotted *rev. in MS*

97–8. *The transcriptions are initially by SJ himself, but later by George Steevens and Hester Thrale. (See commentary to* 97–8)

97. *Only the first sentence appears in the MS, but insertion of the transcriptions is called for. The final sentence of* 97 *is not present*

then low *Pope*] The low *MS, proof, P81, L81, L83*

98. The beginning . . . elaborately displayed] The first lines differ (*after* vary *del.*) so little from the print, that I give (*after* have *del.*) only the Start [?] in the first copy *MS, with the rev. text also at the end of the transcripts for* 97

99. trace] persue *and* follow *rev. in MS*

its first] first *MS, rev. in proof by Nichols*

I am not] he who writes *rev. in MS*

writing] now writing *MS, rev. in proof*

100. four first] first four *MS, P81, L81*

high] great *MS, rev. in proof*

Insertion of the quotation from Spence, transcribed by Hester Thrale, from the appended materials is called for in the MS

passages] passage *MS, corr. in proof*

observations] observation *MS, proof*

101. the great] either the great *MS, rev. in proof*

despised or cheated] cheated *MS, rev. in proof*

Halifax, thinking . . . made] Halifax thought . . . and made *MS, rev. in proof*

All our] All that is *rev. in MS*

must not be] must not *proof, corr. by Nichols (?)*

reason] version *proof, corr. by Nichols (?)*

102. without] in no *rev. in MS*

praise on one side] praise *MS*

and hatred] or hatred *MS, proof, P81*

103. gradual abatement] disgust *rev. in MS*

continued] effected *MS, rev. in proof*

incivilities] reciprocal *rev. in MS*

of pride] pride *MS, rev. in proof*

deduced] defined *corr. in proof*

104. abilities . . . acknowledged] character was high *rev. in MS*

immediate . . . intended] publication was intended and delayed *MS, rev. in proof*

105. Pope saw] Pope found *MS, rev. in proof*

more frequently compared] had more frequently *MS, rev. in proof to* compared more frequently

delight] great delight *MS, rev. in proof*

106. wrote to Pope] told *MS, rev. in proof*

close a] much *rev. in MS*

were . . . in regard] was . . . with regard *MS, rev. in proof*

demanded] obliged him *MS, rev. in proof*

Mr. Addison] Addison *MS, rev. in proof*

in what regards himself] of his own affairs though he *rev. in MS*

to be Pope] to have *MS, proof, all edns. (see commentary to* **106**)

consciousness] conscious *MS*; censure *corr. in proof*

behaviour, . . . deficient] inattentive or careless behaviour *rev. in MS*

107. *The quotation from Kennett is not in the MS but its insertion is called for*

108. and, telling] and told *MS, rev. in proof*

improvements] advantages *rev. in MS*

Steele, said, that] Steele. That *MS, rev. in proof*

nor had any] and that he had no *MS, rev. in proof*

109. is said] made *rev. in MS*

severity, upbraiding] *MS, rev. in proof to* severity; he upbraided

charging] *MS, rev. in proof to* charged

progress] rise *rev. in MS*

110. of the first *Iliad*] *ins. in proof*

with the name] *blotted in MS, left blank by the printer and supplied by SJ in proof*

among] by *rev. to* from *MS, rev. in proof*

111. had ever] ever had *MS, proof, P81, L81*

113. intended] prepared *MS (after* desi *del.), rev. in proof*

publick was *MS, proof, P81, L81*] publick were *L83*

divided] suspended *MS, proof, P81, L81*

114. the other] the rival *MS, rev. in proof*

115. *Insertion of the quotation from Spence, transcribed by Hester Thrale, from the appended materials is called for in the MS*

grossly *Spence*] grosly *MS, proof, all edns.*

that it was] That t'was *MS*

should not *Spence*] should *MS, proof, all edns. (see commentary to* **115***)*

117. having persuaded . . . he] he persuaded . . . and *MS, rev. in proof*

that house] the house *MS, rev. in proof*

118. the road] a road *MS, proof*

119. the wish or] a place of *rev. in MS*

seem frivolous] are frivolous *MS, rev. in proof*

admission] use *MS, rev. in proof*

eagle into] eagle beyond *MS, rev. in proof*

lament . . . ever] imagine . . . never *MS, rev. in proof*

120. one quarto volume] a volume *MS, rev. in proof (where a marginal note by Nichols (?) has been cut away)*

elegance, which] elegance, and which *MS, rev. in proof*

some passages . . . that he] the addition of which *rev. in MS*

other] many *and* some *rev. in MS*

the later] later *MS, rev. in proof*

Pope's . . . taught him] Pope found *rev. in MS*

121. privacy] retirement *MS*

122. raised Pope] procured him *MS*

enemies, that] enemies, who *MS, rev. in proof*

censured him] censured the version *MS, rev. in proof to* censured it

published; Ducket likewise] published, and Ducket *MS, rev. in proof*

him ridiculous. Dennis was] it ridiculous, with Dennis *MS*

123. year (1720)] year *MS*

than Peru can boast] *ins. in MS*

panted] hoped *rev. in MS*

get clear] save himself *MS, rev. in proof*

124. who . . . then lived] who then . . . lived *MS, rev. in proof*

125. entitled] authorised *MS*

annexing] adding *MS, rev. in proof*

printed, he dispersed a great number] printed he sold *with blank space for the figure in MS and proof*

one hundred and forty copies] *left blank in MS and proof*

126. On this] Of this *rev. to* On this *MS;* Of this *proof*

two hundred . . . shillings] five hundred pounds *rev. in MS*

heavy diligence] diligence *MS, rev. in proof*

now high] high *MS, rev. in proof*

from others all] all *MS*

supplied] given *MS, rev. in proof*

127. undertaking] edition *MS*

128. early] first *MS, rev. in proof*

given] drawn *MS, rev. in proof*

his works] those pla[ys] *rev. in MS*

129. appearance] publication *MS*

resolving] he pub *rev. in MS*

general] publick *MS*

was willing] resolved *MS, rev. in proof*

labour] work *MS, rev. in proof*

and liking] he liked *MS*

130. patent] proposals *rev. in MS*

in the proposals . . . said] in the proposals the subscription *rev. to* in the proposals is said *MS;* in the proposals it is said *rev. in proof*

his . . . him] my . . . me *MS, rev. in proof*

131–2. *Insertion from the appended materials is called for in the MS*

131. while he was . . . new version] *ins. in MS with* work *for* version *rev. in proof*

answered in a] returned such an *rev. in MS*

In questions . . . agreed better.] *ins. in MS*

those few] those *MS, rev. in proof*

133. carefully] I believe *MS, rev. in proof*

subjoined] published *MS, rev. in proof*

134. sheet] book *MS*

more facility] less trouble *MS, proof*

found; but Pope] found. Pope *MS, proof*

135. five hundred and seventy-four] *ins. by Nichols in MS*

eight hundred and nineteen] *ins. by Nichols in MS*

The final sentence appears to be a later insertion in the MS

137–8. *Insertion from the appended materials is called for in the MS*

137. whose learning] moderate *rev. in MS*

138. and compiled . . . his conversation] *ins. in MS*

139. Not long after Pope] In the following year he *MS, rev. in proof in response to Nichols's marginal* Q

was returning] escaped *rev. in MS*

windows] glasses *MS, rev. in proof*

being unable . . . open, he] Pope who could not force them *MS, rev. in proof*

snatched him out by] broke the glass and *rev. in MS*

141. Swift] *after* Arbuthnot and *del. in MS*

volumes of Miscellanies, in . . . he inserted] volumes . . . written by Pope contained *MS, rev. in proof*

often committed for] committed for a few *MS*

real] gold *rev. in MS*

treasures; as if] treasures, and *MS, rev. in proof*

wit winded by booksellers] wit *MS*

142. attestation] credit *MS*

Curll, who printed them] Curll *MS, rev. in proof*

143. *Insertion here is called for, but this para. is not in the appended materials in the MS*

passes] pass *rev. in proof*

144. all the] almost all the *MS*

146. was gradual and slow] however was gradual *MS, rev. in proof*

plan] species *rev. in MS*

understood by] known to *MS, rev. in proof*

recollected. The] recollected; and the *MS, proof*

had nothing] was such *rev. in MS*

147. pains, is] pains is *MS*; pains, he is *rev. in proof*

related by himself] published by themselves *MS*

the sorrows of vanity] vanity depressed *MS, proof*

148. *Insertion of the quotation, transcribed by Hester Thrale, from the appended material is called for*

[*Para. 1 of quotation*] relate] *followed in MS by a deletion of 5 ll.*

[*Para. 6 of quotation*] satisfactions *1732, MS, proofs, P81*] satisfaction *L81, L83*

149. *At the foot of p. 129 of the proofs Nichols asked*: Is any thing to be added in p. 136? or in 141 or 142? *A further note at the foot of p. 136, apparently related to* **149**, *has been excised. No changes were made in proof to the text of* **149** *or* **156-8** *(pp. 141-2)*

150. had affected] affected *MS, rev. in proof*

151. telling] explaining *rev. in MS*

delighted . . . effect] delighting in the effect *MS, rev. in proof*

152. fresh] new *MS, rev. in proof*

till then] before *rev. in MS*

154. much] manly *rev. in MS*

155. ad[dressed]] *above* ded *del. in MS*

of the notes . . . written] who had not been publickly *rev. in MS*

156. tranquillity] repose *MS, proof*

published] then published *MS, proof*

the Earl of] Lord *rev. in MS*

said] allowed *and* decla *rev. in MS*

consequently] therefore *MS, proof*

157. for a present . . . pounds] *ins. in MS with* present *after* very lavish *del.*

158. He said, that to] What is said *rev. in MS*

less easily excused] criminal *MS, proof*

159. easily] always *MS, rev. in proof*

revenge . . . the bridge] enforce his demands by threatening to beat his head against the wall *MS, rev. in proof*

talked of laying] threatened to lay *MS, proof*

160. The following] In the next *rev. in MS*

age at] age in *MS*

less easily] not easily *MS, rev. in proof*

to admit new confidence, and] to assimilitate itself to *rev. in MS to* to admit confidence, in

to grow less flexible] or the opinions of others *MS*

departure] loss *MS*

is very] is more *MS*

161. had lasted to] expired at *MS*; lived to *rev. in proof*

quiet] gentle *MS*

162. passages] passages *rev. to* transactions *in MS*

which seems . . . enquiry,] that was most exposed to publick disquisition *MS*

between him and many] by Curl in 1735 *rev. in MS*

falling ... were by him] fell ... by whom they were *MS, rev. in proof*

from noblemen] of Noblemen *MS*

infringed] offended [?] *MS*

163. was, that] of the *rev. in MS*

gown] habit *rev. in MS*

with a lawyer's band] not very regularly dressed *rev. in MS*

164. copies, because] copies, of which *MS*

parcel was ... sent] parcel had ... been sent *MS*

he made] he had made *MS*

165. sent at once] sent *MS*

shewed that ... motive] bore a very small proportion to the cost *MS, rev. in proof*

166. Pope, being] Pope was *MS*

printing ... and] publishing ... but *MS*

contrived] he contrived *MS*

that when] and when *MS, rev. in proof*

he could complain that] *ins. in MS*

were surreptitiously published] published *MS (with* were *om. at turn of page)*

might] could *MS, rev. in proof*

167. impracticable] useless *MS, proof*

168. edition] publication *MS, rev. in proof*

cost] cost of the impression *MS, rev. in proof*

169. in time] again *MS, rev. in proof*

appeared] he published, *MS*

(1737) *MS, L81, L83*] (1737), *proof, P81*

tells that] tells how *MS*

thence stolen ... the press] was stolen, and published *MS*

The story] to which *rev. in MS*

who carried] employed *rev. in MS*

170. persons] characters *MS*

being either] either *MS*

were little ... regarded, they] that mingled with no general interest, nor *MS*; mingled with no general interest, they *rev. in proof*

awakened] excited *rev. in MS*

no popular] any popular *MS*

contemporary] literary *MS*; a literary *proof*

Not much] Little *MS, rev. in proof*

171. continue] continues *MS, rev. in proof*

those of Herbert] A small volume *rev. in MS*

Phillips's *MS, proof, P81, L81*] Phillip's *L83*

as exercises] to be printed *MS, rev. in proof*

Pope's . . . had an] Pope as a writer of letters had *rev. in MS*

172. is seen] appears *MS, rev. in proof*

connected] compared *rev. in MS*

written *MS, proof, P81, L81*] writen *L83*

afterwards selected] selected *MS*

I know not whether] the Reader *rev. in MS*

It is . . . not easy] Pope may be found always *rev. in MS*

Swift perhaps] Swift *MS*

but Arbuthnot] and Arbuthnot *MS*

thoughts] his thoughts *MS, proof, P81*

173. Before . . . appeared,] Soon after *rev. in MS to* About this time (1732) *and rev. again in proof in response to Nichols's marginal* Q

think] call *rev. in MS*

Man; which] *Man;* a work which *MS, rev. in proof*

eight] seven *MS, rev. in proof*

publickly] now publickly *MS, rev. in proof*

the world] many *MS, rev. in proof*

174. poem] work *MS, rev. in proof*

wandered] happened *rev. in MS*

it was] and was *MS*

admired] praised *MS, rev. in proof*

Those friends . . . that] The friends . . . who *MS, rev. in proof*

honours] praises *MS, rev. in proof*

175. whose opinion] whose infl *rev. in MS*

essay] poem *MS, proof*

defeat . . . by] entangle [?] . . . in *rev. in MS*

176. 1733] *blank space in MS;* 17 *proof, with* 33 *ins. in response to Nichols's marginal* Q

had been] had *MS*

thought him] considered him as *MS*

177. free o'er all *Pope, MS*] free o'er *proof, P81 (corr. in Gent. Mag. (1781), 358)*; freely o'er *L81, L83*

it was in vain] he was going *rev. to* it was vain *in MS, proof, P81*

but having] he *rev. in MS*

clear, he] *clear,* and *MS*

178. writing them] writing *MS*

1734] *a later insertion in MS*

179. That those . . . had] Those . . . have *MS*; Those . . . had *rev. in proof*

only] merely [?] *MS*; newly *corr. in proof*

verse . . . reported, but] verse. The report *MS*; *rev. in proof to* verse, is reported, but *P81*, L81

order,] *ins. in proof*

180. but they] as they *corr. in proof*

abounded . . . amplifications] has flourished in the sunshine *rev. in MS*

which were] found many *rev. in MS*

gay foliage] *ins. in proof in space left by printer (see Commentary)*

as innocence is] its innocence was *corr. in proof*

many] they *rev. in MS*

read it for] read it as *MS, rev. in proof*

181. invited] incited *rev. in proof*

French] *del. in MS*

Both] The first *rev. in MS*

Crousaz] Creusaz *proof, corr. by Nichols [?] as in* **182** *and* **189**
censure] condemnation *rev. in MS*

182. Logick] *Cogreli rev. in proof in response to Nichols's* Q

regarded here] regarded *MS, proof, P81, L81*

and perhaps . . . detecting] but seems to have lost some of his benevolence *rev. in MS*

183. Theology] religion *rev. in MS*

it was not] he was not *MS, rev. in proof*

a religious eye] the expression *rev. to* a suspicious eye *in MS, proof*

184. a mind fervid and vehement,] *ins. in MS*

supplied] furnished *rev. in MS*

perspicacity] perspicuity *corr. in proof*

work] composition *MS, rev. in proof*

memory] mind *rev. in MS*

full fraught, together with] replete and *MS*; *rev. to* full fraught with *in proof, P81, L81*

fertile of] crowded with *MS, rev. in proof*

excited] united *MS, rev. in proof*

the advocate] him *MS, proof, P81, L81*

favoured] wished *rev. in MS*

the cause] his cause *MS, proof, P81, L81*

Roman] *ins. in MS*

wished] wishes *MS, rev. in proof*

185. his diction is] to his mind *rev. in MS*

    coarse and impure] unformed *MS, rev. in proof to* impure

186. "Dryden...*out of modesty*."] *that* Milton *borrowed by affectation,* Dryden *by idleness, and* Pope *by necessity. MS, proof, P81, L81*

187. his opinion] his *MS (omission at turn of the page)*

    exaltation] operations *MS, rev. in proof*

188. artifice] practice *MS, rev. in proof*

    union] connexion *rev. in MS*

    hypocritical] criminal *rev. in MS*

    greater] far greater *rev. in MS*

189. talons] valour *corr. in proof*

    by freeing] and free *MS, proof*

    fatality, or] fatality and *MS, rev. in proof*

    continued] published *rev. in MS*

190. mode] note *corr. in proof*

    Insertion of P's letter, transcribed by Hester Thrale, is called for from the appended materials in MS

    all of them] all them *MS, proof, P81 (queried in Gent. Mag. (1781), 358)*

192. He once...related...and was told] When he had once...told...Hooke was told *MS, rev. in proof*

193. Bolingbroke] *del. at the end of* 192 *in MS*

    they parted] both were *rev. in MS*

    aversion] disgust *rev. in MS*

194. lived] *after* and his Commentator *del. in MS*

    with his commentator...his zeal] and the good offices of Warburton were amply rewarded *rev. in MS*

    introduced him] him *ins. by another hand in MS*

    bishoprick. When] Bishoprick, and when *MS, rev. in proof to* bishoprick; when *P81*

194–5. *The end of* 194 *and the whole of* 195 *appear on p. 65 of the MS, which is noticeably neater than the heavily corrected p. 64, occupying less than half the page. SJ may have retranscribed it*

195. by Benson's invitation] *ins. in MS*

    friend] friends [?] *MS*

    scholar] Latinist *rev. in MS*

    Latin prose] Latin *ins. in MS*

196. works] Genius *rev. in MS*

    at his request] *ins. in MS*

197. This may have been] It was perhaps *rev. in MS, with* may *ins. by another hand*

notice] an honour *rev. in MS*

soon] seen *corr. in proof by Nichols [?]*

mouths] months *proof*

if I . . . Savage's account] *ins. in MS*

would not] he should *rev. in MS*

what had never] what never *MS*

198. (1733)] *ins. in MS*

199. some incidents . . . some known] *ins. in MS above* many *del., with* related *for* thrown

with others . . . difficult] of which it is difficult *rev. in MS*

praise] Man *rev. in MS*

the wealthy . . . contributions . . . charitable] the great and wealthy . . . their contributions . . . useful and charitable *MS, rev. in proof*

this influence he obtained] but this influence he could not have obtained but *MS, rev. in proof with* inference *corr. to* influence

and was thus . . . than he had] *ins. in proof*

preserved it] preserved *MS, rev. in proof*

will be read] may be read *MS, rev. in proof*

200–1. *The end of* **200** *and the whole of* **201** *fill only half of p. 68 of the MS, suggesting retranscription by SJ*

200. is the] Epistle *rev. in MS*

a hint] any hint *MS, rev. in proof*

202. afterwards] afterward *MS*

written] a poem written *MS, proof*

The first sentence in the MS is followed by: The character of Clodio was undoubtedly written in emulation *(revising* imitation*)* of Dryden's Zimri, and written with such success that the preference cannot safely be settled. Dryden excels in spriteliness, and Pope in elegance. *(later del.)*

more secretly] secretly *MS, rev. in proof*

203. Human characters are] The characters of *rev. in MS*

indeed who attain . . . spend] who have attained excellence have commonly spent *MS, proof*

directed] divided *corr. in proof by Nichols [?]*

ardour] his ardour *MS, rev. in proof*

204. an object independent] a natural obj *rev. in MS*

acceptation] sense *rev. in MS*

society . . . contradistinguished from] society is named emphatically in opposition to *MS, proof with* so *ins. before* named

any attention] that attention *rev. to* an attention *MS, proof* that coalition . . . which makes] the coalition . . . make, *MS, rev. in proof*

a country, is] country, is *MS*; a country, and is *rev. in proof*

is possible only to] can be expected *rev. in MS*

205. is in itself] the ruling passion is *rev. in MS*

predestination, or] predestination of an *MS, rev. in proof to* predestination, an

admits it] admits *MS*

in obeying] and obeys *MS, rev. in proof*

206. formed his theory] considered his *rev. in MS*

207. edition] Editor *MS. In the proofs Nichols wrote in the margin:* Q Warburton's

which Pope] which he *MS, proof*

telling] informing *MS, rev. in proof*

209. upon moral principles] *ins. in MS*

210. first practised] I think *rev. in MS*

in the reign of] not long after the *rev. in MS*

Oldham] Rochester *rev. in MS*

unexpectedly] *ins. in MS*

211. contending] endeavouring *rev. in MS*

212. seems to be] was *rev. in MS*

published . . . a month before] was not published till (1735) about a year after *MS; rev. in proof by Nichols who had queried SJ's statement in the margin*

inscribed] *followed in MS by* in a melancholy confederation *del.*

life] wit *MS, rev. in proof*

213. *Not a new para. in MS*

who, in . . . retained] with all the orthodoxy of cloistered innocence *rev. in MS, after an earlier revision to* whose religious zeal *del.*

discovered . . . ardour of] professed *MS, rev. in proof*

216. *Insertion from the appended material is called for in MS*

made the first attack] were the aggressor *rev. in MS*

this poem] this poem *MS, rev. in proof to* his poems

but to a] and to a *MS, rev. in proof*

malignity] *followed in MS by* the writer however thought it too wit [?] *del.*

218. which was] and it was *rev. in MS*

softened into] changed, and he now called *MS*; changed, and he now called him *rev. in proof*

220. hung] was *rev. in MS*

221. He was . . . have been] It is not likely that he was *MS, proof*

of opinion] persuaded *rev. in MS*

222–7. *Insertion from the appended material is called for in MS*

222. extend] fill on *rev. in MS*

Scriblerus] Scriblers *corr. in proof*

Life] narrative *rev. in MS*

infatuated] absurd *MS, proof*

dispersed; the] dispersed, and the *MS, proof*

disastrous] desultory *corr. in proof by Nichols*

223. this specimen] the specimen *MS, rev. in proof*

raises] revises *corr. in proof*

drives] throws *corr. in proof*

diseases . . . felt] those that were never sick *rev. in MS*

224. this joint] the joint *MS, proof, P81, L81*

three great] these great *MS, rev. in proof*

little] never *MS, rev. in proof*

225. *Oufle MS*] Ousle *corr. in proof; Ouffle P81, L81, L83*

226. Swift] *after* There may be found in it *del. in MS*

227. not known to] unexplored, no *rev. in MS*

Boileau endeavoured] it is too much *rev. in MS*

To these books] Of this publication *rev. in MS*

228. sink] however *rev. in MS*

has given] gave *MS, rev. in proof*

Insertion of P's letter, not in SJ's hand, from the appended material is called for in the MS

Arts *MS, L83*] Acts *proof, P81, L81 (corr. in Gent. Mag. (1781), 359)*

Science of Pope] Science, of *all edns. (corr. in Gent. Mag. (1781), 359)*

229. being now . . . with] he never finished *rev. in MS*

added] made *rev. in MS*

as either pursue] either pursue *MS*; either to pursue *rev. in proof*

attained *MS, P81, L81*] artained *L83*

230. (1742)] *ins. in MS*

has liberally enough] had added his *rev. in MS*

as more injurious] as more to be resented *MS*; in a manner to be resented *rev. in proof*

231. again] afterwards *rev. in MS*

232. any patience] patient *MS, rev. in proof*

amuse] gratify *MS, rev. in proof*

strength] force *rev. in MS*

233. After the] When the *MS, rev. in proof*

that Cibber] Cibber *MS, rev. in proof*

contempt] their proportiona[ble] contempt *Cibber, MS; left blank in proof by printer. SJ supplied* contempt *in response to Nichols's marginal* Q *(see commentary to* 233)

234. adds] tells *MS, proof*

235. acquainted] conversant *rev. in MS*

but in hope that] but as *MS, proof*

237. published] prepared *MS, rev. in proof*

poem] powers *proof, corr. by Nichols [?]*

the old books] *ins. in MS*

cold pedantry] pedantry *MS, rev. in proof*

238. Pope... enough] Such as it was however *rev. in MS*

change] charge *corr. in proof by Nichols [?]*

introduced] introduce *MS*

was... entirely] who would *rev. in MS*

without... He] who had no... and who *rev. in MS*

till... I saw] but the new *rev. in MS*

himself; by] himself; and by *MS, rev. in proof*

239. father the painter] father *MS, proof, P81, L81*

240. composition] work *rev. in MS*

241. *At the foot of the page in the proofs Nichols wrote:* Pray send more Copy

not... recalled,] easily be recalled, at least *MS, rev. in proof*

I think... consideration] with great ignorance *rev. in MS*

with terminations... places them] according to the terminations of different tongues *(with* tongues *above* Languages *del.) MS; rev. to* sometimes with Greek, and sometimes with Saxon terminations *in proof;* with discordant terminations not known in the same age *P81, L81*

242. himself up] up himself *MS*

a dropsy] dropsy *corr. in proof*

had many enemies] was not popular *rev. in MS*

243. *Insertion from the appended materials is called for in the MS*

favourite] old *rev. in MS*

but Lord] and Lord *MS, rev. in proof*

who, when] when *ins. in another hand in MS*

is said] *after* had neg *del. in MS*

began] had began *MS, corr. in proof to* had begun; begun *P81*

endearing, for when] endearing; when *MS, rev. in proof*

or, though... might] or, if... he might *MS, rev. in proof*

he could have] and must have *rev. in MS*

244. In May 1744... approaching] His end was now near *rev. in MS*

245. this state . . . decay] his state of helplessness *MS, proof*

246. his friend . . . papist,] a friend (I believe by Mr Hooke) *MS, rev. in proof*

die like] call a *rev. in MS*

247. *There are no quotation marks in MS*

248. near] with *MS*

mother, where a] mother. A *MS, rev. in proof to* mother, and a

his commentator] *ins. in MS*

249–54. *Insertion from the appended material is called for in MS*

249. first to Lord Bolingbroke . . . undoubtedly expecting them] the Earl of March-mont and Lord Bolingbroke, whom undoubtedly he expected *MS (with the spelling* Bolinbroke*), proof, P81, L81*

went] attended one of them *MS, proof, P81, L81*

the parcel] Pope's writings *MS, proof*

250. retain in] keep *rev. in MS*

252. incited *MS, proof, P81, L81*] excited *L83*

blast the] intrust [?] *rev. in MS*

proper for him] now a proper time *MS, proof*

avarice; for] avarice, for he could gratify his avarice for *MS*

253. Pope thought] to Pope seemed *rev. in MS*

To this apology . . . *man living.*] *added in L83.*

254. reproach] censure *rev. in MS*

female] posthumous *MS, rev. in proof*

accomptant] accountant *MS*

255. spider . . . described as] spider. He is described as *above* was according to Voltaire *and before* by one that knew him *both del. in MS*; *rev. in proof to* spider, and is described *P81, L81*

is said . . . but he] *ins. in MS*

weak] tender *rev. in MS*

257. Most of] Much of *MS, rev. in proof*

can be told] is known *rev. in MS*

petty] private *MS, rev. in proof*

perhaps . . . middle of] in the latter part of his *rev. in MS*

doublet] doublet next him *rev. in MS*

and neither . . . without help] *ins. in MS, with* he *for* and

258. of ceremony] commonly *corr. in proof*

259–75. *These paras. (pp. 225–40) are missing from the proofs*

259. sickness] sickliness *MS*

taught him] given *MS*

nodded] *slept rev. in MS*

slumbered] went to sleep *MS*

260. constant] *ins. in MS*

261. the table] regular *rev. in MS*

dry conserves] dried sweetmeats *rev. in MS*

revenged] punished *rev. in MS*

heat] stew *MS*

262. too well to eat] to eat too well *rev. in MS*

hastily] too free [?] *rev. in MS*

six and] till two *rev. in MS*

263. was not . . . ask] never asked *rev. in MS*

though,] but *MS*

264. excelled] much excelled *MS*

may be said] seems *MS*

nothing either . . . merry] *ins. in MS*

publisher] *maker rev. in MS*

265. the friend of] related to *MS*

266. be jocular] jest *rev. in MS*

ever seen] seen *MS*

267. This general care must be] To look upon this practice *rev. in MS*

or . . . niggardly] and sometimes *rev. in MS*

268. of which . . . to charity] *ins. in MS with* give *rev. to* assign

269. or some . . . opulence] *ins. in MS*

topick . . . poverty; the] *ins. in MS*

antagonists are] critick is his poverty *and* enemies is their *rev. in MS*

270. very few poets have] scarcely any other poet *rev. in MS*

set his genius to sale *MS (above* sold his praise *del.)*, *P81*, *L81*] set genius to sale *L83*

his Highness's] the Prince's *rev. in MS*

271. admiration] fondness *rev. in MS*

a magnanimity] magnanimity *MS*

Why he] How Congreve *rev. in MS*

intimacy . . . or consequence] intimacy. In his letters there is no mention of Congreve *rev. to* intimacy, nor does the name of Congreve appear in the letters *MS*; intimacy between them; nor does the name of Congreve appear in the Letters *P81*, *L81*

272. *Not a separate para. in MS, P81 and L81*

were such as that a] have left *rev. in MS*

his intimacy with them] *ins. in MS*

273. were simple] friendships were *MS*

dare] *ins. in MS*

by whatever . . . exposed,] when they expose themselves *MS*

transaction] occasion *rev. in MS*

the eagerness] *ins. in MS*

they are considered] no consideration *rev. in MS*

tumult] storm *rev. in MS*

274. whose] whom *rev. in MS*

kindness] friendship *MS*

275. men give . . . minds] every Man gives of himself *MS, P81, L81*

right] virtuous *MS*

awaken] excite *rev. in MS*

the gleam of virtue] them *MS*

276–311. *The surviving proofs (sigg. R–S) are evidently revises with few corrections*

276. vitiated] written *MS*

277. if it had been . . . commendation] he was modestly reproved in his lifetime by Mrs. Cockbourn *MS, proof, with* Cockburne *for* Cockbourn *and a marginal query by Nichols: Q. intended to reprove* Did Pope ever *see* the reproof?

punctually] always *MS*

a thought] his thoughts *MS*

278. observed by] known to *MS*

his criticks . . . did despise] criticks . . . despised *MS*

279. paid] had *MS*

nursed] therefore nursed *MS*

foolish disesteem] contempt *MS*

regard] notice *rev. in MS*

280. world . . . mankind] great; yet whenever he complains of the great shews that *rev. in MS*

neglect] despise *MS*

281. makes it his] values him *rev. in MS*

282. secrets] friends [?] *rev. in MS*

says he] he says *MS*

so much fools] fools enough *rev. in MS*

283. learned] borrowed *rev. in MS*

it must] there must *rev. in MS*

285. riches and] the joys and *rev. in MS*

acted strongly . . . and if] were like those of other mortals, if *MS*

from others] from them *MS*

he was irritable] of his interests *rev. in MS*

286. eagerness] rather *rev. in MS*

287. duties] offices *rev. in MS*

   commonly] naturally *MS*

   coldness] neglect *rev. in MS*

   whom he naturally ... fondness] whose influence was irrestibly prevalent *MS*

288. It was reported] There is a report *rev. in MS*

   his remains] the posthumous papers *MS, proof*

289. is known] appears *MS, proof*

   of Revelation] in Chr *rev. in MS*

290. exalted] conspicuous *rev. in MS*

   all his delinquences] his faults *rev. in MS*

291. with which] with *MS,* *with* which *ins. by another hand*

   literary] *ins. in MS*

   for his age, a] much *rev. in MS*

   reality not] reality, and not *MS*

   when I] told me *and* answered *rev. in MS*

   what learning ... possess] what degree of literature he found *rev. in MS*

   More] greater *rev. in MS*

   retain it] accumulate *MS*

292. From this] From his *MS*

293. consonance] congruity *rev. in MS*

   of his own conceptions] *ins. in MS*

   and, in the works of others] *ins. in MS*

294. active] excursive *MS*

   widest] noblest *MS*

   imagining] *ins. in MS*

295. That which] What *MS, proof*

296. These benefits] Those benefits *proof*

   and however he might ... constancy] *ins. in MS with* however *for* and however

297. some little] many little *MS*

298. he never] never *MS*

299. polish] finish *rev. in MS*

   to write] to put *rev. in MS*

   rectify,] *ins. in MS*

300. expose him] expose *MS*

   those few] the few *MS*

   essays] attempts *rev. in MS*

   Of this] By this *rev. in MS*

301. nor any popularity] or popularity *MS, proof, P81, L81*

 of calling] or calling *MS*

302. its own productions] the bloom [?] of *rev. in MS*

304. nicety] justness *rev. in MS*

 rectitude] force *rev. to* justness *in MS, proof*

 never desired] was far from *rev. in MS*

 He spent no time . . . he never] To make what was good *and* with himself, nor *del. and rev. to* He spent no time in contest with his own powers, he never *MS*

 nor often . . . faulty] *ins. in MS*

 tells us, with very] tells himself *rev. to* writes, with very *MS*; relates, with very *proof*

 poured out] gave *MS*

305. retouched every] left nothing *rev. in MS*

 indefatigable] indefatigatigable *MS*

306. The only poems . . . written with such] and sometimes delayed them till the allusions became obscure *rev. in MS but with* been *om.*

 were brought] were *ins. in MS by another hand*

 Almost every] Every *MS, proof, P81, L81*

 he said] said he *MS, proof, P81, L81*

 almost every] every *MS, proof, P81, L81*

308. before he became] was later *rev. in MS*

 larger] wider *rev. in MS*

 more extensive] wider *rev. in MS*

 science.] Science. Dryden was more acquainted with remote, and Pope with familiar objects. *MS*

 Dryden . . . his local] Dryden knew more of general nature, and Pope of present *rev. (with* present *for* local) *in MS, proof*

 notions of] There was more di *and* know *del. and rev. in MS*

 certainty] convenience *MS, proof*

309. vehement . . . always] vehement and eager, and his sentences are *rev. in MS, with* his language *also del. before* Pope

 by . . . exuberance] with the colours *rev. in MS*

 abundant] spontaneous *MS, proof*

310. *Perhaps a retranscription of an earlier draft*

 it must] it can only *rev. in MS*

 excited] elicited *MS*

 without] with little *rev. (twice) in MS*

 sentiments, to] thoughts, and *rev. in MS*

 If the flights . . . Pope] The flights . . . but Pope *MS*

If of Dryden's] of Dryden's *MS*

more regular] regular *MS*

surpasses] exceeds *rev. in MS*

311. *Not present in MS*

and if] but *proof*

Dryden, let] Dryden. Let *proof*

reasonableness] justice *proof*

312. so much with] with frequent *MS, proof*

as to] but to *MS, proof*

313. exhibiting] admitting *MS, proof*

to thicken] and to diffuse *rev. in MS*

futurity] uncertainty *rev. in MS*

delicious] favourite *MS, proof*

His preference was probably] I will not attempt the *rev. in MS*

314. means] shews *rev. in MS*

poems] poetry *rev. in MS*

sufficient power ... skill ... to exhibit] such power ... such skill ... as to have exhibited *MS, rev. in proof*

which had] such as had *MS, rev. in proof*

in English poetry] *ins. in MS*

315. derived] copied *rev. in MS*

and elegance] of description *rev. in MS*

because as ... the order] because ... and therefore the order *MS, proof, P81, L81*

attention] curiosity *rev. in MS*

this poem *MS, proof, P81*] his poem *L81, L83*

316. those which ... the scene] *ins. in MS*

Lodona] London *corr. in proof (twice)*

derided] divided *corr. in proof*

sweetness] great sweetness *MS, proof, P81, L81*

flower] tree *MS, rev. in proof*

317. the imagery is] and the imagery *MS, proof*

it never] it seems never to have *MS, proof, P81, L81*

and seldom] seldom *MS, rev. in proof*

318. original] author *rev. in MS*

319. vigorous] great *rev. in MS*

produced] written *MS, proof*

poem] thing *rev. in MS*

sense] sentiment *rev. in MS*

marriage] an all[iance?] *rev. in MS*

ambition, and] ambition, *MS, rev. in proof*

the ambitious] but the ambitious *MS, proof*; though the ambitious *P81, L81*

a poet] he *MS, proof*

320. yet he] but he *MS, proof*

stronger . . . attention] hold of the attention better *MS, rev. in proof*

321. It may be] if it *rev. in MS*

but as no such] it must be *and* let it be *rev. in MS*

like return] return *MS*

as Mr. Cobb . . . who,] which Bentley made to Mr. Cobb *rev. in MS*

323. to be as well] as well to be *rev. in MS*

326. common-places. The] common places, and *MS, rev. in proof*

comparison of each is] comparisons of each are *MS*; comparisons of each *rev. in proof*

328. exhibits] contains *rev. in MS*

arrangement] disposition *MS, rev. in proof*

powers] acquisitions *rev. in MS*

329. particular] various *rev. in MS*

English poetry] our language *rev. in MS*

subject] original *rev. in MS*

does not illustrate.] *Followed in MS by* To say that truth is recommended by sweetness of verse, as physick is made alluring to children by honey, though not improper in *del.*

may be] should be *rev. in MS*

required to] *rev. to* necessary that it *in MS, proof*

references] reference *proof, P81*

running after] pursuing *rev. in MS*

represented much] much represented *MS, rev. in proof*

faster] greater *rev. in MS*

330. paragraph, in which] paragraph: in *MS, proof*

331. noises] sounds *MS, proof*

mentioned] exhibited *rev. in MS*

rapid or slow] more or less *rev. in MS*

without much] with very little *MS* (*with* with *above* rapid *del.*), *proof, P81, L81*

having . . . flexibility, our] has . . . flexibility; our *MS, rev. in proof*

cadence] flow *rev. in MS*

I fear] perhaps *MS, rev. in proof*

332. resemblances] representation *rev. in MS*

mind] fancy *MS, rev. in proof*

heaves ... Thunders ... smoaks] heav'd ... Thunder'd ... smoak'd *MS, rev. in proof*

another sense] another *rev. in proof*

road long *MS, proof, P81, L81*] road along *L83*

333. can fix] has fixed *MS, rev. in proof*

334. fancied] fanciful *rev. in MS*

335. Of that which] It *MS, rev. in proof*

let it rather be now] and it is only to be *MS, rev. in proof to* let it be now

the power] its power *MS, rev. in proof*

336. can no longer] are at last *rev. in MS*

tea-table,] teatable *MS*; tea-table; *P81, L81*

phantoms] Beings *MS, proof*

337. this ... nation] these ... Beings *MS, proof*

for what] for of what *MS, rev. in proof*

338. reader] mind *rev. in MS to* Reader

interests] interest *proof*

339. here brought] brought *MS, rev. in proof*

340. *Lutrin*] *Lublin corr. in proof*

has ... than he] have ... than they *MS, proof*

vanity] variety *corr. in proof*

as they embroil] that embroil *MS, rev. in proof*

do more to] far more *MS, rev. in proof*

crush] shake *rev. in MS*

341. their power] this power *corr. in proof*

spared, but if] spared; if *MS, rev. in proof*

it might have been] these occult [?] *rev. in MS*

who are ... will be] who were ... were *MS, rev. in proof*

342. turning over] turning *MS*

regularly] naturally *MS, proof*

heart] mind *MS, proof*

fate] story *MS, rev. in proof*

scenes] fiction *rev. in MS*

343. improved] cultivated *MS, rev. in proof*

344. sentiments] the sentiments *MS, rev. in proof*

mystick] *ins. in MS*

teaches] shews *MS, rev. in proof*

be enabled] learn *MS, rev. in proof*

346. *Not originally a separate para. in MS*

Salvini] Salini *corr. in proof*

a linguist] pedantick *rev. in MS*

347. translation] translations *corr. in proof*

some credit] credit enough among *MS*; credit enough *rev. in proof*

The French, in the] nor do I remember any other name *rev. in MS*

wisdom] learning *MS, proof, P81, L81*

Greek and Roman poetry] poets *rev. in MS*

349. discordant] some discordant *MS, rev. in proof*

Poetry *MS, P81, L81*] Peotry *L83*

our language] English *rev. in MS*

Homer, in] Homer, and in *MS, proof*

Homer's] that *rev. in MS*

mere nature . . . longer; and] *ins. in MS*

very few . . . embellished] it will be difficult to shew [find *del.*] one which he has not embellished with added ornaments *MS, proof*

350. and falling into] begin to *rev. in MS*; following in *corr. in proof*

in the progress of learning] as learning advances *MS, proof, P81, L81*

all nations] every Nation *MS, proof*

One refinement . . . another] till perhaps the [?] of refinement *rev. in MS*

expedient] necessary *rev. in MS*

necessary] still *rev. in MS*

351. many readers . . . English *Iliad*] every reader . . . translation *rev. in MS*

some unexpected] unexpected *MS, rev. in proof*

352. colour] embellish *MS, rev. in proof*

but lost him] though he lost *rev. in MS*; but left him *corr. in proof*

sublimity] own sublimity *MS, proof*

353. readers] writers *corr. in proof*

clear] remove *rev. in MS*

355. remains . . . the same] particular can easily be said *rev. in MS*

356. personal] *ins. in MS*

357. opponent] opponents *corr. in proof*

358. culpable] crim *rev. in MS*

pretend to] claim *rev. in MS*

Priam] Priam thrown at Neoptolemus *MS, proof, P81, L81*

359. useful] more so *MS, rev. in proof*

361. such as the] the *MS, proof*

formation ... account of the] and particularly of the concluding paragraph *and* crowded thoughts *rev. in MS*

which dignify *MS, proof, P81, L81*] with dignify *L83*

362. require] make it necessary *rev. in MS*

the last collection] this edition *MS, proof, P81*

363. to him a new] a new *MS, proof, P81, L81*

tells us,] tells *MS*

that these beings ... that *all the*] that the only *rev. to* that *all the in MS, proof, P81, L81*

whether man] *whether he MS, rev. in proof*

disposing] one case *rev. in MS*

vain] in vain *corr. in proof*

364. much that every man knows] that we see but little *rev. in MS*

an opinion ... uncommon] a position which will easily be granted *rev. in MS*

gives] gives *with* charitably *ins. in MS*

in the position] the position *MS, proof, P81, L81*

365. genius, the] genius, of the *MS, proof*

Never were] Never was *corr. in proof*

When these] If these *rev. in MS;* When those *proof*

Essay, disrobed ... is] Essay is disrobed ... and *corr. in proof*

make one another] have made ourselves *MS, proof*

instinctive] instructive *corr. in proof*

geese] the Goose *MS, proof*

concord] beneficence *rev. in MS*

effect] effects *MS, proof, P81, L81*

that our true ... act it well] *ins. (with* it *om.) in MS, rev. in proof*

366. enchain] enchant [?] *MS;* enrich *corr. in proof*

suspend] and suspend *MS*

overpowering] delusions *rev. in MS*

367. diction, more] diction, and more *MS, proof*

more thoughts] and more thoughts *MS*

more levity ... strength] *ins. in MS*

368. *Men and Women*] *Men* and *Women MS*

diligent] much *MS, rev. in proof*

That his ... properly] To know *(with* estimate *del.)* the height of his excellence *rev. in MS*

perspicacity] discrimination *rev. in MS*

nature] vice *rev. in proof*

more ... deeper,] more enquiry and *rev. in MS*

women's] part *rev. in MS*

are some defects] *ins. in MS*

370. design, which] design, and *MS, rev. in proof*

which by ... beauties] and by ... beauties it *MS*

contains more striking] abounds more with s *rev. to* it contains more striking *MS, rev. in proof*

work. As] work; but as *MS, rev. in proof*

passage ... upon] part ... on *MS, rev. in proof*

371. poems] satires *rev. in MS*

in the first] *ins. in proof*

celebration of the] concluding *rev. in MS*

372. give pleasure ... readers;] often give generall pleasure, *MS, rev. in proof*

the comparison requires] to this pleasure is required *MS, rev. in proof*

strained] forced *rev. in MS*

images] sentiments *MS, rev. in proof*

generally] at last *rev. to* too often *MS, rev. in proof*

373. genius] a Poet *rev. in MS*

trains] scenes *rev. in MS*

and new] or new *MS, rev. in proof*

and by which] or *MS, proof, P81, L81*

which strongly] by which the var *rev. in MS*; by which strength *rev. in proof*

of nature] and nature *MS, rev. in proof*

his *Eloisa*] his *apparently del. in MS*

Judgement, P81, L81] *Judgement L83*

selects] enables *rev. in MS*

essence ... from] active from the *rev. in MS*

374. melody] peculiar *rev. in MS*

habituated] constrained *rev. in MS*

to that] to it. *rev. in MS*

who ... themselves] that even themselves would *MS, rev. in proof*

break his lines] vary his *rev. in MS*

375. superfluous] unremitted *MS, rev. in proof*

thought with] been of *rev. in MS*

The construction ... grammatical; with] *ins. in MS (with* grammatical. With), *rev. in proof*

376. but] but not frequently, and *rev. in MS*

translation *MS, proof, P81, L81*] transtation *L83*

377. a few] ended *rev. in MS*

and always] but, always *MS*; but always *proof, P81, L81*

378. *The final sentence was added in L83*

380. preserved it all] reposited them *rev. to* preserved it *in MS, rev. in proof*

wished *MS, proof, P81, L81*] wish'd *L83*

381. have now done] have done *MS, rev. in proof*

382. will only . . . definer] is the pedantry *[rev. from* pedantick*]* of a narrow mind *MS, rev. in proof*

time] age *rev. in MS*; race *corr. in proof*

must] would *rev. in MS*

a very high place . . . of Genius] no humble seat [seat *rev. from* station*]* to his translator *MS, rev. in proof*

383. *The insertion of P's letter is called for in the MS by* (The Letter). *The text in the proofs is incomplete*

him. Homer *Pope, P81*] him, Homer *L81, L83*

384. was printed in *The Visitor*] has been already printed *MS*

385–444. *Not in the MS or proofs. Variants are noted from 'A Dissertation on the Epitaphs written by Pope' in The Universal Visiter, 5 (May 1756), 205–19 (56), reprinted in the Idler (3rd edn., 1767), 302–24 (67), and Miscellaneous and Fugitive Pieces, ii (1774), 192–207 (74)*

385. endeavour, at this *visit, 56, 74, P81, L81, L83*] endeavour *67*

386. modify *56, 67, 74, P81, L81*] mollify *L83*

387. *(l. 10 of verse):* keep his friendships *Pope, 56, 67, 74*] kept his friendship *P81, L81, L83*

(l. 11 of verse): forefathers *Pope, 56, 67, 74, P81, L81*] forefather's *L83*

391. shorter] slender *56, 67, 74*

392. his ease] this ease *56, 67, 74*

395. TRUMBUL *56, 67, 74, P81*] TRUMBAL *L81, L83*

(l. 6 of verse): country true *56, 67, 74, P81, L81*] country too *L83*

400. Trumbul *56, 67, 74, P81*] Trumbal *L81, L83*

400. note. *The note on Bernardi was added in P81, L81, and L83*

406. relation . . . and *lost*] wonder, that he who *gained no title*, should *lose 56, 67, 74, P81, L81*

410. To wish *74, P81, L81, L83*] The wish *56, 67*

411. *(l. 3 of verse):* conquests *Pope, 56, 67, 74, P81, L81*] conquest *L83*

(l. 10 of verse): sustained it *Pope, 56, 67, 74*] sustained *P81, L81, L83 (corr. in Gent. Mag. (1781), 359)*

413. excellence] elegance *56, 67, 74, P81, L81*

414. *(l. 10 of verse):* moral *Pope, 56, 74, P81, L81 (queried in Gent. Mag. (1781), 359)*] mortal *67, L83*

415. *characters Pope, 56, 67*] *character 74, P81, L81, L83*

417. from Dryden] *added in L83*

419. is not only...construction] wants grammatical construction, the word *dying* being no substantive *56, 67, 74*; is not only borrowed, but of very harsh construction *P81, L81*

426. from *Crashaw*] *added in L83*

428. successfully] happily *56, 67, 74, P81, L81*

will not] does not *56, 67, 74, P81, L81*

433. vice] a vice *56, 67, 74*

435. first eight] eight first *56, 67, 74, P81, L81*

441. This epitaph] XIII. This *epitaph 56*

445–6. *Not in 56, 67, and 74*

445. this wretchedness] this *P81, L81*

(l. 8 of verse): urnam] utnam *P81, L81, L83 (corr. in Gent. Mag. (1781), 359)*

(l. 11 of verse): haberetis] haberet is *P81*; haberet *L81*

446. Ariosto] even the writer of these lines *P81, L81*

his trifle would] he should *P81, L81*

PITT

4. three] five *rev. in proof*

Pimpern] Pimperne *rev. in proof*

(1722)] *ins. in proof*

two] *revision of* two *to* five *in proof cancelled*

(1724)] *ins. in proof, in response to* June 19 1724 *written in the margin by Nichols*

5. splendid] elegant *P81, L81*

7. miscellany] Miscellany *P81, L81*

8. Eneid] Æneid *P81*

This can hardly...the reader.] *added in L83*

9. not to see...other poems] to see excluded from this collection *P81*; to see excluded from the collection of his poems *L81*

11. Blandford] Blandford Forum *rev. in proof*

THOMSON

2. those early days] these early years *proof*

3. the school] school *P81*

4. he censured] censured *proof*

8. Thomson obtained . . . adulation.] *ins. in the proof*

9. *Not a separate para. in the proof*

    Winter] It *rev. in proof*

    then received . . . Mr. Hill:] was then invited and received a present of twenty guineas. *rev. in proof, with a marginal call for the insertion of the passage from T's letter*

11. *Not originally a separate para., which is called for in proof*

12. sought] who sought *proof*

13. once] then *proof*

14. *Summer*, in *P81, L81*] *Summer*, in *L83*

26. to see it exhibited] it had been exhibited in this Collection *P81*

30. night, and was welcomed . . . to *Arbuthnot*] night *P81, L81*

34. It may be . . . he was] He seems not to be *P81, L81*

42. Scotland (which] Scotland (of which *P81*

    JAMES THOMSON."] (Signed) "JAMES THOMSON." *P81*

47. *Added in proof*

    intersections *proof (revising* pauses which*), P81*] intersection *L81, L83*

48. His descriptions] The description *proof*

49. yet the memory . . . suspense or] but the memory is not helped by order, nor the curiosity excited by suspense and *rev. in proof*

50. luxuriant] exuberant *rev. in proof*

    invests *P81, L81*] invest *L83*

51. word which] word *corr. in proof*

52. soon desisted] desisted *rev. in proof*

    Followed in P81 by 'Prologue To Sophonisba, By Pope And Mallet'

53. *Added in L83*

WATTS

1. the late] this *P81*

2. Gibbons] Gibson *corr. in proof*

5. Horte] Hort *P81*

6. *glyconick*] *lyconick corr. in proof*

    at a very] a very *rev. in proof*

7. and by] or by *rev. in proof*

    with supplements from] by the help of *rev. in proof*

8. With the] While *corr. in proof*

9. tenderness] indulgence *rev. in proof*
   his son] him *rev. in proof*
13. notions] thoughts *rev. in proof*
   Gibbons's] Gibbon's *proof*; Gibbons' *P81*
   pursuit *Gibbons, P81*] pursuits *L81, L83*
15. extent] extensiveness *rev. in proof*
17. graced] furnished *rev. in proof*
18. not precompose] precompose *corr. in proof*
22. revenue . . . a year] revenue *P81, L81*
   hardest] best *rev. in proof*
23. his meekness . . . of censure] the meekness of his opposition, and the mildness of his censures *P81, L81*
33. fancy] imagination *P81, L81*
35. He writes] His writes *P81*
   He is at least] But he is at least *P81, L81*

AMBROSE PHILIPS

3. is by Pope] which Pope *rev. in proof*
   could write] *can write rev. in proof*
4. kind words] kindness *rev. in proof*
   since] for he *proof*
   for which] with which *rev. in proof*
   received] was paid *rev. in proof*
5. book] Life *rev. in proof*
6. while] and while *rev. in proof*
8. much zeal] zeal *rev. in proof*
9. reputed] reputative *rev. in proof*
   and when] and who when *rev. in proof*
   when it had . . . his name,] it was at first printed with his name, but that *rev. in proof*
   the copies] copies *rev. in proof*
10. witty and political] political *proof, with* literary and *ins. and rev. to* witty and
11. long passed] passed *rev. in proof*
13. because . . . excludes] for the composition seemed to exclude *proof, with* for *rev. to* because
   variety of matter;] variety, *P81, L81*
14. *Æglogues*] *Eglogues rev. in proof* new
   name] name *rev. in proof*
   our Spenser] Spenser *rev. in proof*

15. (1498) Mantuan] (1598) the Mantuan *corr. in proof*

    vain, and] vain, for *rev. in proof*

    country] county *corr. in proof*

    to censure] and censured *P81, L81*

16. *Boschereccie P81, L81*] *Goschereccie corr. in proof; Boschareccie L83*

17. that any one] any one that *rev. in proof*

18. pattern] patron *corr. in proof*

19. who were very] and they were *proof*

    moderns is] moderns was *proof*

    are censured] *rev. in proof to* were censured

    refinements; and . . . Italians and French] refinements. *[new paragraph]* At last the Italians and the French *proof*

20. aggrandising] justifying *proof*

    (*Guard.* 40)] (17==) *rev. in proof, with* Qu *in margin*

21. hurt Pope] hurt him *rev. in proof*

22. the first . . . Letters] his Letters, printed more than [ ] *rev. in proof (incomplete)*

    for Homer] *ins. in L83*

25. Lottery (1717), *P81*] Lottery, (1717), *L81, L83*

27. exhibited] had *rev. in proof*

28. who, then only . . . was of] then . . . where he was of *rev. in proof*

    honoured] remembered *rev. in proof*

29. printed] *del. in proof*

    It has been] It is *rev. in proof*

31. *Not in proofs*

32. London] England *rev. in proof*

    antagonist] rival *rev. in proof*

33. Having . . . four . . . he now] He . . . five . . . with which he *rev. in proof*

    was struck . . . year] lasted but a short time after his return *rev. in proof*

34. and that . . . pompous] *ins. in proof*

    Mr. Ing] Mr. Jug *corr. in proof*

35. the late] this *P81*

    ranked] placed *rev. in proof*

    please best] please most *rev. in proof*

    nursery. The] nursery: the *P81, L81*

    seldom . . . are not loaded with . . . yet] not often . . . have not often . . . but *rev. in proof*

    can do *P81, L81*] cannot do *L83*

36. found . . . all] will not be denied to have reached *rev. in proof*

WEST

2. sent him] put him *rev. in proof*

3. though] but *proof*

   then secretary . . . with] who was then secretary . . . and with *rev. in proof*

4. ended in] procured him *rev. in proof*

   (May 1729)] *not in proof*

5. the late] this *P81*

   improperly] *ins. in proof*

   published in 1747 . . . New Testament.] *not in proofs*

   1748); and *P81, L81*] 1748) and *L83*

   would doubtless . . . Testament *added in L83*

   Perhaps] and perhaps *P81, L81*

   the prayers . . . sermon, and then prayers] prayers every evening to his family *P81, L81*

6. a decent] and a decent *rev. in proof*

7. *Added in L83*

9. (1752)] *not in proofs*

10. enjoyed: nor could . . . (March 26)] enjoyed. In 1755 *proof*

    might be . . . terrors] needed not to be terrible *P81, L81*

10. *Followed in proof and P81 by:* His poems are in this Collection neither selected nor arranged as I should have directed, had either the choice or the order fallen under my care or notice. His *Institution of the Garter [Installation rev. in proofs]* is improperly omitted; instead of the mock tragedy of Lucian, the version from Euripedes, if both could not *[not ins. in proof]* be inserted, should have been taken. Of the *Imitations of Spenser*, one was published before the version of *Pindar*, and should therefore have had the first place. *The final sentence originally began* The *Imitations of Spenser* were *(rev. in proof, with* had *ins. later in the sentence)*

11. *thou, my soul . . . hotter]* hast any soul . . . better] *corr. in proof*

13. *Garter* (1742)] *Garter*, which is omitted in this Collection, *proof, P81 (with* (1742) *ins.)*

    weariness] impatience *rev. in proof*

14. together] at once *P81, L81*

    intellect] intellects *P81, L81*

    accidental or] accidental and *P81, L81*

    An Imitation . . . been perused.] *ins. in proof*

    circle] will *corr. in proof*

15. verses . . . supposed to have been] verses *proof*

    by him] by him *[Mr. West proof]*, which, having been left out by the compilers, it is proper to insert here *P81*

    it is] this Elegy is *P81*

15. *Followed in proof and P81 by [Richard Jago's] 'Elegy, Occasioned by shooting a BLACKBIRD on Valentine's Day.'*

COLLINS

1. *In the proofs SJ wrote in the margin*: The author is much obliged to Mr Nicol for his help in dates. &c

   At the foot of the page in the proofs Nichols wrote: There is no mention when Mr Collins died. It was in 1756 at Chichester.

4. designed] planned *rev. in proof*

   remote] historical *rev. in proof*

   now-and-then] however *rev. in proof first to* from time to time *and then to* now and then

5. translation] translator *corr. in proof by Nichols*

   Poeticks] poetick works *corr. in proof*

   as much money as] money which *rev. in proof*

   did not live] did nothing *queried by Nichols and rev. in proof*

6. happiness. *P81, L81*] happiness, *L83*

   disease] by disease *proof*

7. while perhaps] when perhaps *rev. in proof*

   insert it here] now insert it *rev. in proof*

8–12. *Variants from The Poetical Calendar (1763) (63) and Miscellaneous and Fugitive Pieces, ii (1774) (74) have been noted. That P81 was set from 74 is indicated by repetition in the proofs of variants in* 11 *and* 12 *unique to 74*

9. Yet as diligence] But diligence *63, 74, rev. in proof*

11. he perceived] he found *63, 74, rev. in proof*

    gathering on] gathering on in *74, proof*

    Chichester] Colchester *63, 74, rev. in proof*

    in 1756] at last *63, 74, proof*

12. waiting] writing *74, rev. in proof*

    withdrawn] then withdrawn *63, 74, rev. in proof*

    said] says *63, 74, proof, P81, L81*

13. *Marked by SJ as a separate para. in the proofs*

14. visited] once visited *rev. in proof*

15. couch, till a] couch: a *proof*

DYER

5. acquisitions in painting] acquisitions *P81, L81*

6. 1751] 1752 *P81, L81*

   forty] twenty *P81, L81*

   in 1755] afterwards *P81, L81*

7. In 1757] About the time of his removal to Coningsby *P81, L81*

SHENSTONE

  2. fresh] new *P81*, *L81*

  5. in the book] there *P81*, *L81*

 10. was excited] began *P81*, *L81*

     heard, and] heard, or *P81*, *L81*

 18. *Jessy P81*, *L81*] *Jesse L83*

 31. air of] airy *P81*

YOUNG

[Herbert Croft wrote paragraphs 2–153 (see headnote). Although Croft's numerous revisions have not been recorded, his more substantial changes to the text in L83 are summarized in the commentary]

  2. Young] Young, and in consequence of your fears lest, for want of proper infor-
     mation, you might say any thing of the father which should hurt the son *P81*

153. *Added by Croft in L83*

160. confinement] regard *P81*, *L81*

162. the Collection] this Collection *P81*

MALLET

  4. to wits] with wits *rev. in proof*

  5 note. *Not in proof*

     the last edition of his works] this Collection *P81*

  6. (1728)] *not in proof*

  7. engrafted] engrossed *rev. in proof*

     poem] form *proof*

  8. *Eurydice*, acted . . . 1731] *Eurydice proof*

  9. original] country *rev. in proof*

 10. secret] author *rev. in proof*

 11. forgotten] forgot *rev. in proof*

 12. under-secretary] secretary *proof*

     Cliefden in 1740; it] Cliefden; but *proof, with* but *rev. to* it

     stage . . . in 1751] publick stage *proof*

 13. anticipation] prolepsis *proof*

 15. It was acted . . . 1739, and was] It was *proof*

 16. *Not in the proofs*

17. adapted] collected *proof*

    This he sold . . . pounds. *ins. in L83*

18. (1747)] *not in proof*

19. award] decision *rev. in proof*

20. *Not in the proofs*

21. he was] Mallet was *rev. in proof*

    and he, for] and, for *rev. in proof*

22. alone to] to *rev. in proof*

    died in April 1765] died *proof*

23. One daughter . . . at Drury-Lane.] *not in proof*

24. formed; his] formed; and his *rev. in proof*

25. Bacon's volumes] other works *rev. in proof*

AKENSIDE

2. a different] another *rev. in proof*

3. an unnecessary] a furious *rev. in proof*

   what he called and thought] something which he called, and which he thought, *proof (with* something *rev. to* what), *rev. in later proof*

   a zeal which] which *rev. in proof*

   not rarely] sometimes *rev. in proof*

   wealth or] wealth and *rev. in proof*

4. those poets] those writers *rev. in proof*

   1744] 17== *proof, with* 44 *ins. by another hand*

6. by an . . . which] such . . . as *rev. in proof*

   lover of contradiction] favourer of innovation *proof, rev. in later proof*

7. easily be] be easily *P81*

   consequences] consequence *rev. in proof*

   contemptuous censure] to contemptuous mimickry *rev. in proof*

   Both are . . . contemptible. *added in L83*

8. objections] censure *rev. in proof*

9. of patriotism] for liberty *rev. in proof*

10. Stonhouse] Stonehouse *P81, L81*

    such reputation and success] so favourable an opinion of his abilities *rev. in proof*

    a while] awhile *proof, P81*

11. an ardour] a zeal *rev. in proof*

    had looked] looks *rev. in proof*

12. he read] having read *P81, L81*

Anatomy; but] Anatomy, and then *rev. to* Anatomy, he *in proof, P81, L81*

give] read *rev. in proof*

Crounian] Cronian *P81, L81 (corr. in Gent. Mag. (1781), 421)*

eagerly] diligently *rev. in later proofs*

13. conspicuous] elegant *rev. in later proof*

Latinity, which] Latinity and *rev. in proof*

14. that were] which were *P81, L81*

young mind] mind *proof*

15. delight] pleasure *rev. in proof*

16. remarked] found *proof*

18. self-indulgence] indulgence *P81, L81*

upon image, ornament upon] on image, or ornament on *rev. in proof*

tiresome] tedious *rev. in proof*

19. poetical as . . . elegant as it is not vulgar] so far poetical that . . . so far valuable that it is not common *proof (with* that *twice rev. to* as), *P81, L81*

fewer artifices of disgust] more artifices of language *proof, with* more *rev. to* fewer

either recalls old phrases or] recalls old words, and rarely *rev. in proof*

surely . . . but] sometimes . . . for *rev. in proof*

20. additions] addition *P81, L81*

in the late collection] by the compilers *rev. to* in this collection *in proof, P81*

too long] surely tiresome *rev. in proof to* wearisome *and then to* too long

21. *Added in L83*

22. dispatch them] dispatch him *rev. in proof*

grander ode] grander *rev. in proof*

his luxuriance] luxuriance *rev. in proof*

into an ode] to an ode *rev. in proof*

23. Of his odes . . . novelty; the] Of this ode the *rev. in proof (with* often want force, or *for* commonly want force,*)*

24. generally dull] dull *rev. in proof*

to what use can the work] why should that *rev. in proof*

GRAY

1. under the care of] under *P81, L81*

brother . . . Dr. George] brother *P81, L81*

4. professing] pretending *P81, L81*

7. may be . . . the narrative] seems to be the opinion *P81, L81*

11. which adds] which, though perhaps it adds *P81, L81*

character] character, I am not pleased to find wanting in this collection. It will therefore be added to this Preface *P81*; character, was inserted at the end of my preface to the late Collection *L81*

13. noises ... contemptuous] noises *P81, L81*

14. admire] praise *P81, L81*

17. History] Languages *P81, L81*

19. History] Languages *P81, L81*

22. a Letter ... in Cornwall] a nameless writer *P81, L81*

well-wisher] friend *P81, L81*

23. To this] In this *corr. in proof*

In the margin of the proofs: Please to return the *MS Cases* [?]. The Printer hopes for *new Copy* when this sheet is returned

24. from the slight] in the slight *rev. in proof*

26. could not write ... or at happy] could write ... but at happy *rev. in proof*

him to have been] him *rev. in proof*

28. giving to ... substantives,] forming from nouns derivative adjectives, with *rev. in proof*

stale; the] stale, and the *rev. in proof*

29. a pointed] pointed *corr. in proof*

31. was at first] seems to have been *proof*

32. would gladly] wish to *rev. in proof*

33. where does] how does *rev. in proof*

34. further] much *proof*

common places] refuge *rev. in proof*

36. *Glory* and *P81, L81*] *Glory* and *L83*

But that] That *rev. in proof*

38. this poetical] his poetical *proof, P81*

counterfeit *P81, L81*] connterfeit *L83*

41. difficulty, for] difficulty, *corr. in proof*

marvellous. And ... use;] marvellous; and ... use, *P81*

42. consonance] confluence *corr. in proof*

43. rush abruptly] break in *rev. in proof*; rush abrutly *P81*

44. *helm nor Gray, proof, P81, L81*] *helm or L83*

45. recoils] recoiled *corr. in proof*

46. owns] says *rev. in proof*

Bards; but their] Barbarians; where *rev. in proof*

the art of spinning] spinning *rev. in proof*

Theft] But theft *rev. in proof*

men *weave* the *web* or piece] they *weave* the piece *rev. in proof*

48. ease and] ease or *P81, L81*

51. *Followed in P81 by 'A Long Story' (pp. 37–48) and 'Ode For Musick' (pp. 49–56).*

LYTTELTON

4. Commissioner] one *P81, L81*

5. hunted] driven *P81, L81*

6. became] was made *P81, L81*

   with 200*l*.] *added in L83*

   of 100*l*. a year] *added in L83*

7. that at] and which at *rev. in proof*

8. Pope, who] Pope *rev. in proof*

   commended] who commended *rev. in proof*

   friend] friends *corr. in MS*

9. Miss] Mrs. *queried and rev. in proof by Nichols*

   his grief] himself *rev. in proof*

10. for, after a while, he] but, after a while *rev. in proof*

11. profit were] profit was *corr. in proof*

12. withhold] withold *corr. in proof*

13. much] great *P81, L81*

14. activity] exertions *P81, L81*

15. Wales; of which] Wales: *rev. in proof*

    at last . . . he sallied] then . . . sallied *rev. in proof*

16. Lyttelton] he *rev. in proof*

    the production . . . compositions] they are the productions of a mind that means
    well, than that thinks vigorously *rev. in proof*

    any conclusion] conclusion *P81, L81*

17. returned, . . . flattery or for] returned his acknowledgements in a note which I have
    read; acknowledgements either for flattery or *P81, L81*

18. with the rest his employment] his employment, with the rest *P81, L81*

19. production] work *rev. in proof*

    published] *in the margin of the proofs Nichols wrote:* 1764, 1767, 1771 *del.*

20. *Not in the proofs, except for* A great part of the work was printed twice. *as the final
    sentence of* **19**

21. *A continuation of* **19** *in proofs*

    undertook] found the way *rev. in proof*

    employed,] employed, but *rev. in proof*

22. *Not in proofs*

    Doctor] Dr. Saunders *P81*, *L81*

    Doctor's edition] edition of Dr. Saunders *P81*, *L81*

    errors in] errors of *P81*, *L81*

23. sixty] to sixty *rev. in proof*

    was then] then was *P81*, *L81*

    his last] the last *proof*

24. and though *Gent. Mag.*, *P81*] though *L81*, *L83*

25. a different] different *P81*

30. Right] late Right *P81*, *L81*

COMMENTARY

ALEXANDER POPE (1688–1744)

Composition. The longest of SJ's biographies was the last to be written. He already had it in mind by early Aug. 1780, when he asked Nichols for 'Ruffhead's life of Pope' and 'Popes Works', although he had still to write about Swift and Lyttelton, whose *Works* he also requested (*Letters*, iii. 295). On 18 Sept. he noted: 'I have not worked diligently. I have Swift and Pope yet to write, Swift is just begun' (*YW*, i. 301). If he had completed 'Swift' by the time he accompanied the Thrales to Brighton on 18 Oct. 1780 (see 'Swift' headnote), the books SJ mentions to Mrs Thrale on 16 Oct. as 'burthening the cart' no doubt included material for 'Pope' (*Letters*, iii. 317). At this stage he seems to have prepared the chronology of P's life, and the notes on his character and works, preserved in his early memoranda for 'Pope' (see below). There is nothing else to document his progress in Brighton, apart from a letter from George Steevens of 27 Oct. about the contributions of Fenton and Broome to P's *Odyssey* (see **129–30**, **133–4** and nn. below).

SJ started writing 'Pope' after returning with the Thrales to Streatham early in Nov., Henry Thrale's latest stroke having foreshortened their stay in Brighton. Thomas Davies told Boswell on 14 Nov. that he had seen SJ 'in perfect health, about two days since', and that he 'is now busy writing the life of Pope which will complete his excellent Biographical & Critical Prefaces' (*Catalogue*, C 906). By 10 Dec. the MS of Pope's translation of the *Iliad* had arrived at Streatham, perhaps through Dr Daniel Solander, assistant librarian at the British Museum and a friend of the Thrales (*Thraliana*, i. 422, 464). Hester Thrale and Steevens helped to transcribe passages from it which SJ quoted in 'Pope' (see **96** n. and cf. **148** n. below for other assistance by Mrs Thrale).

P is mentioned in some of SJ's undated messages to Nichols: one note asking for help with the dates of the *Dunciad* and related works may belong to Dec. 1780 (see below). SJ probably completed 'Pope' during Jan. 1781. At some point he 'entreated' Nichols 'to save the proof sheets of Pope because they are promised to a Lady who desires to have them', presumably Fanny Burney, to whom he duly presented them (now in the Hyde Collection: see below). In Feb. or early Mar. 1781 he asked Nichols to send 'the last leaves of the criticism of Popes Epitaphs, and he will correct them' (*Letters*, iii. 319, 323, 324). This refers to his earlier essay on P's epitaphs (1756), which he had decided to append (see **384–446** and n. below).

On 3 Mar. 1781 the *Public Advertiser* announced the imminent publication of the remaining *Prefaces*, and two of SJ's letters of 5 Mar. confirm that 'the work is at last done' (*Letters*, iii. 324–5, and see also 328). By 14 Apr. 1781 Horace Walpole told Mason that he had borrowed a pre-publication copy of 'Pope' from Reynolds, 'which Sir Joshua holds to be a *chef-d'oeuvre*. It is a most trumpery performance and stuffed with all his crabbed phrases and vulgarisms, and much trash as anecdotes' (*Corresp.*, xxix. 130–1).

Sources. The development of 'Pope' can be traced in an unusual range of surviving materials. The earliest of all are the memoranda he evidently made in Brighton in the autumn of 1780 (British Library Add. MS 5994.2, fos. 159–77; for George Steevens's letter, 14 May 1782, presenting the notes to William Cole, see Add. MS 6401, fo. 175b and *Life*, iv. 499). SJ began by trying to create a chronology based on the account of P's early years in Owen Ruffhead's *Life* (1769) and the letters in Warburton's edition of P's *Works* (1751), vols. vii–ix. Eventually he also began noting significant topics on which he would later enlarge in his biography. Similar notes about P in Alexander Dyce's copy of *Johnsoniana* (1836) (Forster Collection, Victoria and Albert Museum) seem to belong to a later stage of his planning, since they are organized by such headings as 'Poetry', 'Person', and 'Manners domestick' in preparation for his central 'character' of P (255 ff.). SJ later struck through many of these notes as he dealt with the various topics. The surviving memoranda are not, however, complete (*The Rape of the Lock* is unmentioned and there is little on P's Homer) and, given their often cryptic and loosely organized character, it must seem likely that he prepared further notes before actually writing 'Pope'. For a transcript of, and an exhaustive commentary on, the memoranda, see H. Kirkley, *A Biographer at Work* (Lewisburg, Pa., 2002).

At about the same time Isaac Reed compiled for SJ a chronology of P's publications after 1730 (Bodleian, MS Malone 30, fo. 70). His final note gives some idea of his usefulness to SJ: '*Sober Advice from Horace* not being in Dr Warburton's Edition I send for Dr Johnson's perusal. If he desires to see the pieces written by Lord Hervey & Lady M W Montagu after the publication of the 1st Satire of 2 Book of Horace they are in my possession & shall be ready for Dr Johnson whenever they are wanted' (see 209 and n. and 216 below, and, for Reed's asistance more generally, i. 72–6 above). See also SJ's undated note to Nichols (*c*. Dec. 1780): 'Mr. Nicol is desire[d] to procure the dates of Pope's Works upon the Dunciads. Mr. Reed can probably supply them' (*Letters*, iii. 319).

The complete MS of 'Pope' survives in the Pierpont Morgan Library, New York, and most of the revised proofsheets are in the Hyde Collection. F. W. Hilles, 'The Making of *The Life of P*', in F. W. Hilles (ed.), *New Light on Dr J* (New Haven, 1959), 257–84, described the various stages of its composition and printing, and selectively illustrated SJ's original memoranda and later revisions in the MS and proofs. As Hilles showed, SJ's dependence on Ruffhead, whose phrasing he echoes at times (see Hilles, 'Making', 264–6), diminished as he reached P's later career, when he relied more on P's own letters and Warburton's editorial notes, and could also draw on first-hand knowledge and on information from P's contemporaries. SJ only occasionally mentioned Ruffhead (see 48, 129, 241 below), and deleted a reference to him in proof (see 54 n. below).

SJ had one important new source when he began work on 'Pope' in Nov. 1780. This was the four-volume transcript of Joseph Spence's unpublished record of the conversation of P and his contemporaries (now in the British Library), which had been lent to SJ by the Duke of Newcastle by early Feb. 1780, through the good offices of Dr (later Sir) Lucas Pepys, physician to the Thrales (and to George III). SJ had already drawn on Spence in some of the second series of *Prefaces*, notably in 'Addison' (q.v. above). A pencilled list of page numbers, apparently in SJ's hand, is visible at the end of each volume of the MS: see Spence, i. p. lxviii. SJ's 'Advertisement' in *Lives* (1781) is, however, curiously unspecific about Newcastle's important loan: 'great assistance has been given me by Mr. Spence's Collections, of which I consider the communication as a favour worthy of publick acknowledgement.' As Boswell noted, SJ 'made but an awkward return' for the Duke's generosity: 'he has not owned to whom he was obliged;

so that the acknowledgement is unappropriated to his Grace' (*Life*, iv. 63, and cf. 482–3).

In the notes below SJ's sources are often indicated by multiple references to Ruffhead, Warburton, and Spence. As early as 1745 William Warburton, P's friend and editor, announced at the end of an edition of the *Essay on Man* that his 'Life of Mr. Pope, with A Critical Account of his Writings' was 'preparing for the Public'. Although Warburton included many biographical notes in P's *Works* (9 vols., 1751), this work was never to appear, and he eventually passed his materials to Owen Ruffhead (1723–69). Although Ruffhead's *Life* (1769) was a basic source for SJ, he had no high opinion of its author, who 'knew nothing of Pope and nothing of poetry' (*Life*, ii. 166). (SJ was probably unaware of Ruffhead's opinion that he himself had 'evidently misapplied his talents' in *Rasselas*: see *Monthly Review*, 20 (1759), 428–37.) In 1769 Ruffhead inevitably drew on P's letters and Warburton's biographical notes in *Works* (1751), which SJ also consulted, so that particular sources for information or quotations can not always be certain.

Others had, in addition, already had some access to the Spence MSS. While Warburton was still planning his own biography of P, Spence gave him extracts from his MSS, which he either used in *Works* (1751) or passed on to Ruffhead. In 1754 Spence also allowed Joseph Warton to make notes on his MSS, for use in his *Essay on P* (1756). As a result, it is not always clear whether SJ's information derived directly from the Spence MSS, from earlier authors who had seen them, or even from other works, such as the articles on P in Shiels, *Lives*, v. 219–52, and by Philip Nichols in *BB*, v (1760), 3404–17, which used information from Warburton's *Works* (1751) or Warton's *Essay* (1756). After inspecting Spence's MSS in 1794, Edmond Malone later concluded that SJ 'did not take half so much out of them as he might have done' (P. Martin, *Edmond Malone* (Cambridge, 1995), 167). For the early transmission of Spence's anecdotes, which remained unpublished until 1820, see Spence, i, pp. xxviii–xxix, the chart opposite i, p. lvi, and i, pp. lxxxi–xciii.

Although P was still alive in his early years in London, SJ never set eyes on the great poet (*Life*, i. 534). (His friend Joshua Reynolds did so in 1740: see 255 n. below.) He knew, however, that P admired his *London* (1738) and had predicted that its author 'will soon be *déterré*'. (For the story that George Lyttelton brought *London* to P 'in a rapture', believing that P himself was the author, see 'Lyttelton' 8 n. below). Without further knowledge of, or any application from, SJ, in 1738 P tried through Lord Gower to recommend him for a degree at Dublin (see headnote to 'Young' below). Reynolds owned, and later gave to Thomas Percy, a note to Jonathan Richardson in which P referred to 'the Merit' of SJ's imitation of Juvenal and his attempt 'to serve Him'. Although SJ was naturally curious about it, Reynolds was unwilling to show him the letter because P also mentioned SJ's 'Infirmity of the convulsive kind, that attacks him sometimes, so as to make Him a sad Spectacle' (see *Corresp.*, iv. 194 and n., with the suggestion that Savage may have been the common friend who interested P in SJ's situation; *Life*, i. 128–9, 133, 143; and Boswell, *Making of the Life*, 121–2).

Communication of some kind between SJ and P, if only through intermediaries, seems to have occurred in 1743, which may explain the cautious account of Richard Savage's relationship with P, his loyal benefactor in his last years, in SJ's *Life of Savage* (1744) (see 'Savage' headnote above). (For an interpretation of SJ's attitude to P in 1744 as implicitly hostile, see T. Erwin, 'Scribblers, Servants, and J's *Life of Savage*', *Age of J* 14 (2003), 99–130.) In his *Plan of a Dictionary* (1747), 31, SJ later referred to P, 'of whom

I may be justified in affirming, that were he still alive, solicitous as he was for the success of this work, he would not be displeased that I have undertaken it'. P had himself planned a dictionary at the end of his life (Spence, i. 70; see 378 n. below) and, as Boswell suggested, may have conveyed 'hints' about his ideas on lexicography through Robert Dodsley, who first proposed such a work to SJ (*Life*, i. 182–3 and n., iii. 405; Reddick, 17, 22). P had, however, died in May 1744, and even if, as he told Boswell, SJ had 'long thought of' compiling a dictionary, he did not finally commit himself to the great task for another two years.

Without first-hand knowledge of his own, SJ could still draw on a wide range of personal sources, including such friends of P as Richard Savage (63, 197, 270–1 and nn. 371), Walter Harte (70), William Dobson (291), Jonathan Richardson the Younger (239), and Mrs Fermor (54, 260 n.), the niece of P's 'Belinda', whom he met in Paris in 1775. Over the years he had gleaned information about P from booksellers such as Robert Dodsley (244, 249, 306), Henry Lintot (164), and Thomas Osborne (238), and from other acquaintance such as Lord Orrery (263) and Benjamin Victor (199). SJ seems also to have been helped in various ways by his friends Sir John Hawkins (69 n., 254 n.), Thomas Percy (145 n.), R. P. Jodrell (383), and Michael Lort, Professor of Greek at Cambridge and friend of the Thrales (who lent SJ his annotated copies of Warton's *Essay on P* and the *Essay on Man*, which he was still trying to recover in June 1784) (Nichols, *Lit. Anec.*, ii. 596 n.; *Life*, iii. 527).

The assistance of John Nichols, apparent in many of the *Prefaces*, is particularly visible in 'Pope', literally so when SJ left space in the MS or the proofs for information which Nichols was to supply (see e.g. notes to 69, 78–9, 90, 107, 125, 135 below). To the contribution of Isaac Reed may be added the fact that he owned P's annotated copy of Tickell's *Iliad*, mentioned in 113 below.

P's friend Hugh Hume Campbell (1708–94), Earl of Marchmont, is a special case. (For P's admiration of the youthful Marchmont in about 1740, see C. Gerrard, *The Patriot Opposition to Walpole* (Oxford, 1994), 90–1.) On 12 May 1778 Boswell called on Lord Marchmont to request information about P for SJ's biography. When he had earlier proposed that SJ should himself interview Marchmont, SJ had replied, 'Sir, he will tell *me* nothing', but in fact the peer, 'in the most polite and obliging manner, promised to tell all he recollected about Pope', and agreed to call on SJ the next day for this purpose. When the 'elated' Boswell returned to Streatham to report this coup, SJ crushingly told him: 'I don't care to know about Pope . . . If it rained knowledge I'd hold out my hand; but I would not give myself the trouble to go in quest of it' (*Life*, iii. 342–5; *Boswell in Extremes*, 332–8). SJ was presumably irritated not merely by Boswell's 'over-exultation' and officious approach to Marchmont without consulting him, but by a 'suspicion that I had obtruded him on Lord Marchmont, and humbled him too much'. As Boswell later commented, although SJ 'has always shewn great respect to persons of high rank, when he happened to be in their company, yet his pride of character has ever made him guard against any appearance of courting the great' (*Life*, v. 353).

In more practical terms, SJ was preoccupied in May 1778 with 'Dryden', not with 'Pope', and may have felt unprepared to interview Marchmont effectively at short notice. Although he later conceded that 'Lord Marchmont will call on me, and then I shall call on Lord Marchmont', it was left to Boswell to rearrange the interview a year later, his letter to SJ of 29 Apr. 1779 stressing the importance of this engagement. Through Boswell, SJ presented Marchmont with the first set of *Prefaces*, and asked permission to visit him (*Catalogue*, L 670, L 949, C 1943). For the two-hour meeting on

1 May 1779 SJ was 'drest in his best suit and parisian Wig', and he later admitted that 'I would rather have given twenty pounds than not have come' (*Life*, iii. 391–2; Boswell, *Laird of Auchinleck*, 101–2; *J. Misc.*, ii. 4–5). Boswell later (13 Mar. 1780) sent SJ his detailed notes on 'Lord Marchmont's information concerning Pope' (*Life*, iii. 418): for SJ's use of them, see **243, 259** n., **264** n., **288** below.

A 'phantom' source for P's early years cited more than once by Hill (1905) (see iii. 82–3 nn., 86 n.) is Thomas Birch, *The Heads of Illustrious Persons of Great Britain*, ii. 55–6. Although Hill dated the *Heads* 1747, this work in fact appeared in two folio volumes dated 1743 and 1751, and the detailed information about P in vol. ii (1751) clearly derived from Warburton. Hill no doubt used the 2nd edition of vol. i (1747), and failed to notice the later date of vol. ii.

SJ and Joseph Warton. Hilles, 'Making', 268–72, and others have noted SJ's use of earlier critics and biographers, such as Joseph Warton, *Essay on P* (1756) and Ruffhead, *Life of P* (1769), as silent interlocutors in 'Pope', and Warton's criticism is particularly relevant. (For the relationship, see also H. Reid, ' "The Want of a Closer Union" ', *Age of J* 9 (1998), 133–43.)

SJ became friendly with Joseph Warton and his younger brother Thomas, who spent most of his life in Oxford, in the 1750s. On 17 Nov. 1752 Joseph told Thomas: 'I have seen Johnson so very often that we have contracted close friendship & are quite intimate' (British Library, Add. MSS 42560, fos. 24–5). A few months later, he reprinted SJ's *Rambler* 37 on pastoral, and acknowledged other help from his 'learned and ingenious friend', in his *Works of Virgil* (1753), i, pp. xxx, 37–43, and SJ in turn invited Warton to contribute to the *Adventurer* (1753–4). SJ's letters to Warton in these years also refer to the sad fate of their common friend William Collins (q.v. below): see *Letters*, i. 67–8, 77–8, 90–1, 132–4, 255–6, 350–1.

Although Warton's *Essay on P* (1756) expounded P's poetic limitations by comparison with the earlier English tradition of Spenser, Shakespeare, and Milton, SJ's review in the *Literary Mag.* 1 (15 Apr.–15 May 1756) was respectful (*OASJ*, 488–94). On 21 July 1763 he described Warton to Boswell as 'a very agreeable man' and his *Essay* as 'a very pleasing book'. When Boswell asked about the delayed appearance of vol. ii of Warton's *Essay*, however, SJ replied: 'Why, Sir, I suppose he finds himself a little disappointed, in not having been able to persuade the world to be of his opinion as to Pope' (*Life*, i. 448; see ii. 167, for a similar statement on 31 Mar. 1772).

Although social contact between SJ and the Wartons, both eventually members of The Club, continued, his relationships with both brothers cooled in the 1760s, and there was eventually an open quarrel with Joseph (*Life*, i. 270 n., ii. 41 n.). (SJ may have had this in mind in his account of P's rift with Addison and 'the gradual abatement of kindness between friends' in **103** below.) By the 1770s SJ was parodying Thomas Warton's poetry (see **332** n. below) and describing Joseph as 'a rapturist' and 'an enthusiast by rule', whose 'taste is amazement' (*Life*, ii. 41 n.). According to Fanny (Burney) d'Arblay, *Memoirs of Dr. Burney* (1832), ii. 82, 'when in gay spirits', SJ 'would take off Dr. Warton with the strongest humour; describing almost convulsively, the ecstasy with which he would seize upon the person nearest him, to hug in his arms, lest his grasp should be eluded, while he displayed some picture or some prospect'. William Bowles recalled that SJ usually spoke 'with little respect' of the Wartons, describing Joseph as 'a very empty fellow' (*Life*, iv. 523). While writing the *Lives*, SJ did, however, more than once seek Joseph Warton's assistance (see 'Pitt' 1 and 'Collins' 1 and nn. below, and *Letters*, iii. 259–60).

In 'Pope' SJ was clearly intent on replying, politely but firmly, to Warton's views on the limitations of P's poetic genius and other developments in 18th-century poetry. He was not the first to do so. Ruffhead had already challenged Warton's view of P in 1769, and Arthur Murphy had even earlier defended P's genius and 'invention' in the *Works of Fielding* (1762), i. 15–21 (J. Barnard (ed.), *P: The Critical Heritage* (1973), 447–52; see also 464–5, for a favourable review of Ruffhead, which has been attributed to SJ himself, but is probably by Hawkesworth). More recently, Percival Stockdale had replied to Warton in his *Inquiry into the Nature and Genuine Laws of Poetry; including a Particular Defence of the Writings and Genius of Pope* (1778). Stockdale, who also praised the learning, taste, and judgement of SJ, his 'admired, and respected friend' (39), attacked those 'criticks of a vitiated and insatiable taste' who failed to appreciate P's 'delicacy, and refinement': 'Their Gothick souls are only stimulated with the *transcendently* sublime; or, in other words, with the unnatural, the gigantick, and the incoherent' (128–9).

In Stockdale's own account, Tom Davies told him of SJ's 'high praise' of his *Inquiry*, which he had read 'with an evident pleasure, and delight', declaring that he had 'defended the cause of POPE with incontrovertible arguments, and with great eloquence; and ... must be supported in his defence of that great poet'. Face to face with Stockdale, however, SJ was more cautious, expressing reservations about 'your design of reducing my old friend, JO. WARTON, so low, in the field of criticism'. When Stockdale reminded SJ in Oct. 1780 of his promise to mention the *Inquiry* in his own 'Pope', SJ again explained the proprieties of the situation, given that Warton 'was to *him*, a much older acquaintance, and friend, than *I was*' (Stockdale, *Memoirs* (1809), ii. 116–25). Even if the *Inquiry* had reduced the need for SJ himself to confront Warton directly on particular issues, he does not in fact mention Stockdale in 'Pope'. For a reference to Stockdale as biographer of Waller, see 'Waller' **61** and n. above, and see also J. Hardy, 'Stockdale's Defence of P', *RES* 18 (1967), 49–54.

SJ's only direct reference to Warton's *Essay on P* (1756) is in fact decorous and indeed complimentary, describing it as 'a book which teaches how the brow of Criticism may be smoothed, and how she may be enabled, with all her severity, to attract and to delight' (344 below, and cf. 'Addison' **130** above). Yet implicit disagreement with Warton pervades SJ's 'Pope', and SJ's objections are at times fairly explicit (see e.g. notes to **65, 314, 337, 382** below). As Boswell realized, SJ wrote this biography '*con amore*, both from the early possession which that writer had taken of his mind, and from the pleasure which he must have felt, in for ever silencing all attempts to lessen his poetical fame, by demonstrating his excellence, and pronouncing the following triumphant eulogium [quoting **382** below]' (*Life*, iv. 46).

Although the first 260 pages of vol. ii of the *Essay on P* had been printed by the early 1760s, Warton withheld the sequel from publication. The death in 1779 of P's friend and editor, the combative William Warburton, may have removed one inhibition, but it was no doubt the appearance of SJ's 'Pope' in 1781 which prompted Warton belatedly to complete and publish the *Essay*, vol. ii, in 1782. The first version of vol. ii made use of the sheets printed twenty years earlier, but later in 1782 Warton revised the whole *Essay* in two volumes. This revised edition has been cited below, since it was only here that Warton could take full account of SJ's recent defence of P. That the disagreement between the two critics was a matter of public interest is clear from 'A Dream', an elaborate imaginary dialogue between SJ and Warton, in Robert Potter's *The Art of Criticism* (1789), 195–250.

Thomas Warton later replied with some severity to SJ's 'Milton' in Milton's *Poems* (1785; 2nd edn., 1791), and Joseph himself evidently planned a further rejoinder. In Feb. 1792 he referred to 'An Appendix to my Essay on Pope, a pamphlet of about 130 pages ... I find myself obliged frequently to contradict Johnson, as well as Warburton' (W. D. MacClintock, *Joseph Warton's Essay on P* (Chapel Hill, NC, 1933), 24 n.). Although this work seems not to have survived, Warton did retaliate in his *Works of P* (9 vols., 1797) by summarizing his disagreements with 'my old acquaintance' (i, pp. xvi–xviii, 173–4 n.). The occasionally approving but more often acrimonious references to SJ in his notes distressed former friends of both men: e.g. Charles Burney thought Warton's 'bitterness' was 'disgraceful' (to J. C. Walker, 2 Feb. 1801, Osborn Collection, Beinecke Library, Yale). Elsewhere Warton allowed William Hayley in 1796 to make known his disapproval of SJ's views on Milton (see headnote to 'Milton' above).

Even after his death in 1800, Warton continued replying posthumously to SJ in notes he had provided for H. J. Todd's edition of Dryden's *Poetical Works* (1811): see 'Dryden' 268–9 nn., 278 n., 318 n. above, with a final comment on his relationship with SJ: 'I have been censured, I am informed, for contradicting some of Johnson's opinions. As I knew him well, I ever respected his talents; but a love of paradox and contradiction, at the bottom of which was vanity, gave an unpleasant tincture to his manners, and made his conversation boisterous and offensive. I often used to tell the mild and sensible Sir Joshua Reynolds that he and his friends had contributed to spoil Johnson, by constantly and cowardly assenting to all he advanced on any subject. Mr Burke only kept him in order, as did Mr Beauclerc also, sometimes by his playful wit' (ii. 260 n.).

A few years earlier, a facsimile of a letter from Thomas Tyrwhitt to Warton, 22 Jan. 1782, in the *Essay on P* (5th edn., 1806), opp. i, p. 1, tactfully reminded readers of the original purpose of the *Essay*, vol. ii, as a response to SJ's 'Pope'. Tyrwhitt had told Warton:

I confess I must consider the publication of it at the present moment as a fortunate circumstance, for the interests of taste and good letters. I am in hopes that your book may prove a timely antidote to that poison, (*sweet sweet poison*, and suited, I fear too well, *to the ages tooth*), with which we have been lately overflowed. Under the shelter of your authority, one may perhaps venture to avow an opinion, that poetry is not confined to riming couplets, and that its greatest powers are not displayed in prologues and epilogues.

SJ inevitably quoted P frequently in the *Dict.* and DeMaria (1986), 215, has described him as 'the Poet of the *Dictionary*'. Reddick (1990), 223 n., pointed out that SJ in fact quoted Shakespeare, Dryden, and Milton more frequently, adding many quotations from Milton in the 4th edition of 1773.

Publication. In *Prefaces*, vol. vii (15 May 1781).

Pp. 1–336 (sigs. A–x) of the proofs of 'Pope' are in the Hyde Collection, inscribed by Fanny Burney, 'Proof sheets given by Dr. Johnson to F.B.', with a later inscription 'J. H. from Genl. d'Arblay'. She later noted that she had 'secured at once, on the same page, the marginal and second thoughts of that great author, and of his great biographer', referring to P's revisions in the *Iliad* MS as transcribed in 96–9 below, which SJ himself corrected in the proofs: see *Memoirs of Dr. Burney* (1832), ii. 178–9. Proofs of pp. 71–4 and 225–4 (corresponding to 96–7, 259–75 below) are not present, and pp. 145–60 are misbound after 128. Sigg. Q–R (pp. 241–72, i.e. 259–75 below) appear to be from a different and later set of proofs, with little or no correction by SJ. Most other gatherings are inscribed 'Revises' by Nichols, who has written at the foot of p. 208 (**241** below): 'Pray send more Copy'.

The appended discussion of Pope's epitaphs (**384–446** below) is not present in the proofs, presumably because it was reprinted directly from one of the earlier texts in the *Universal Visiter* (1756), *The Idler* (3rd edn., 1767) or, most probably, *Miscellaneous and Fugitive Pieces* (1773–4): see also Fleeman (1962), 229 n. Pp. 333–6 from another, uncorrected set of proofs are in the Bodleian (Percy 74, fos. 57–8). Boswell, *Life*, iv. 52, printed a not entirely reliable selection of 'Various Readings' from 'Pope', presumably from other proofs.

Modern Sources:
(i) Alexander Pope
Correspondence, ed. G. Sherburn (5 vols., Oxford, 1956)
The Dunciad, in Four Books, ed. V. Rumbold (1999)
The Last and Greatest Art: Some Unpublished Poetical Manuscripts of AP, ed. M. Mack (Newark, Del., 1984)
Memoirs of the Extraordinary Life, Works, and Discoveries of Martinus Scriblerus, ed. C. Kerby-Miller (New Haven, 1950)
Prose Works, i: *1711–20*, ed. N. Ault (Oxford, 1936); ii: *1725–1744*, ed. R. Cowler (Oxford, 1986)
The Twickenham Edition of the Poems, ed. J. Butt and others (10 vols., 1938–67)

(ii)
P. K. Alkon, *SJ and Moral Discipline* (Evanston, Ill., 1967)
J. Allison, 'Joseph Warton's Reply to Dr. J's *Lives*', *JEGP* 51 (1952), 186–91
N. Ault, *New Light on P* (1949)
G. Barber, 'Bolingbroke, P and the *Patriot King*', *Library*, 19 (1964), 67–89
J. Barnard (ed.), *P: The Critical Heritage* (1973)
B. Boyce, 'SJ's Criticism of P in the *Life of P*', *RES* 5 (1954), 37–46
M. R. Brownell, *AP and the Arts of Georgian England* (Oxford, 1978)
M. R. Brownell, ' "Like Socrates": P's Art of Dying', *SEL* 20 (1980), 407–23
P. C. Brückmann, *A Manner of Correspondence: A Study of the Scriblerus Club* (Montreal, 1997)
G. J. Clingham and N. Hopkinson, 'J's Copy of *The Iliad* at Felbrigg Hall, Norfolk', *Book Collector*, 37 (1988), 503–21
L. Damrosch, 'P: The Fulfillment of Genius', in *The Uses of J's Criticism* (Charlottesville, Va., 1976), ch. 8
P. Dixon, *The World of P's Satires* (1968)
H. Erskine-Hill, *The Social Milieu of AP* (New Haven, 1975)
H. Erskine-Hill, 'Life into Letters, Death into Art: P's Epitaph on Francis Atterbury', *Yearbook of English Studies*, 18 (1988), 200–20
D. Foxon, *P and the Early Eighteenth-Century Book Trade*, ed. J. McLaverty (Oxford, 1991)
C. Gerrard, *The Patriot Opposition to Walpole: Politics, Poetry, and National Myth, 1725–1742* (Oxford, 1994)
B. A. Goldgar, *Walpole and the Wits: The Relation of Politics to Literature, 1722–1742* (Lincoln, Nebr., 1976)
R. H. Griffith, *AP: A Bibliography* (2 vols., Austin, Tex., 1922–7)
J. V. Guerinot, *Pamphlet Attacks on AP, 1711–1744* (1969)

B. Hammond, *P and Bolingbroke* (Columbia, Mo., 1984)

F. W. Hilles, 'The Making of *The Life of P*', in F. W. Hilles (ed.), *New Light on Dr. J* (New Haven, 1959), 257–84,

M. Hodgart, 'The Subscription List for P's *Iliad*, 1715', in R. B. White (ed.), *The Dress of Words* (Lawrence, Kan., 1978)

C. J. Horne, 'An Emendation to J's *Life of P*', *Library*, 5th ser. 28 (1973), 156–7

C. J. Horne, 'The Biter Bit: J's Strictures on P', *RES* 27 (1976), 310–13

H. Kirkley, 'J's *Life of P*: Fact as Fiction', *Wascana Review*, 15 (1980), 69–80

H. Kirkley, *A Biographer at Work: SJ's Notes for the 'Life of P'* (Lewisburg, Pa., 2002)

I. Kramnick, *Bolingbroke and his Circle* (Cambridge, Mass., 1968)

M. Leranbaum, *AP's 'Opus Magnum' 1729–1744* (Oxford, 1977)

A. McDermott, 'Textual Transformations: *The Memoirs of Martinus Scriblerus* in J's *Dictionary*', *SB* 48 (1995), 133–48

M. Mack, *The Garden and the City* (1969)

M. Mack, *Collected in Himself: Essays Critical, Biographical and Bibliographical on P and Some of his Contemporaries* (Newark, Del., 1982)

M. Mack, *AP: A Life* (1985)

J. McLaverty, 'The First Printing and Publication of P's Letters', *Library*, 6th ser 2 (1980), 264–80

J. McLaverty, 'P and Giles Jacob's *Lives of the Poets*: The *Dunciad* as Alternative History', *MP* 83 (1985–6), 22–32

J. McLaverty, 'The Contract for P's Translation of Homer's *Iliad*', *Library*, 6th ser. 15 (1993), 206–25

J. McLaverty, *P, Print and Meaning* (Oxford, 2001)

M. Maner, *The Philosophical Biographer: Doubt and Dialectic in J's Lives of the Poets* (Athens, Ga., 1988), 121–42

D. W. Nichol (ed.), *P's Literary Legacy: The Book-Trade Correspondence of William Warburton and John Knapton* (Oxford, 1992)

M. Nicolson and G. S. Rousseau, *'This Long Disease, My Life': AP and the Sciences* (Princeton, 1968)

M. J. O'Sullivan, 'Ex Alieno Ingenio Poeta: J's Translation of P's *Messiah*', *PQ* 54 (1975), 579–91

B. Parker, 'P and Mature Augustanism', in *The Triumph of Augustan Poetics: English Literary Culture from Butler to Johnson* (Cambridge, 1998), 96–135

I. Primer, 'Tracking a Source for J's *Life of P*', *Yale University Gazette*, 61 (1986), 55–60)

H. Reid, ' "The Want of a Closer Union . . . ": The Friendship of SJ and Joseph Warton', *Age of J* 9 (1998), 133–43

P. Rogers, 'P and his Subscribers', *Publishing History*, 3 (1978), 7–36

V. Rumbold, *Women's Place in P's World* (Cambridge, 1989)

T. Ruml, 'The Younger J's Texts of P', *RES* 36 (1985), 180–98

S. Shankman, *P's Iliad: Homer in the Age of Passion* (Princeton, 1983)

G. Sherburn, *The Early Career of AP* (Oxford, 1934)

G. Sherburn, 'New Anecdotes about AP', *N & Q* 203 (1958), 343–9

G. Sherburn, 'Letters of AP', *RES* 9 (1958), 388–406

P. J. Smallwood, 'J's Life of P and P's Preface to the *Iliad*', *N & Q* 225 (1980), 50

M. M. Smith and A. Lindsay (eds.), *Index of English Literary Manuscripts*, vol. iii (iii) (1992), 1–78

H. M. Solomon, 'J's Silencing of P: Trivialising *An Essay on Man*', *Age of J* 5 (1992), 247–80

Joseph Spence, *Observations, Anecdotes, and Characters of Books and Men*, ed. J. M. Osborn (2 vols., Oxford, 1966)

F. Stack, *P and Horace: Studies in Imitation* (Cambridge, 1985)

C. Thomas, 'P's *Iliad* and the Contemporary Context of his "Appeals to the Ladies"', *ECL* 14 (1990), 1–17

C. Thomas, *AP and his Eighteenth-Century Women Readers* (Carbondale, Ill., 1994)

D. H. White, *P and the Context of Controversy* (Chicago, 1970)

C. D. Williams, *P, Homer & Manliness: Some Aspects of Eighteenth-Century Classical Learning* (1993)

W. K. Wimsatt, *The Portraits of AP* (New Haven, 1965)

J. A. Winn, *A Window in the Bosom: The Letters of AP* (Hamden, Conn., 1977)

1. Although his first 'Memoranda' and the MS of 'Pope' correctly date P's birth 21 May, SJ failed to notice the printer's error of 'May 22' in proof, which survived in later editions: see Textual Notes.

   For P's parents' 'gentle blood', see *Epistle to Arbuthnot*, l. 388: other information in his note to l. 381 was repeated by Warburton, iv. 42 n. and Ruffhead, *Life*, 10. P believed that his father Alexander Pope (1646–1717) was related to the Oxford-shire family descended from William Pope, Earl of Downe (1573–1631). Joseph Warton noted the error, on the authority of Richard Pottinger, a relative of P, and of John Loveday of Caversham, in *Essay on P*, ii (1782), 262–3 n. His mother was Edith Turner (1643–1733). P no doubt supplied the information about her York-shire family in the obituary in *Grub-Street Journal* (14 June 1733) and *Gent. Mag.* (1733), 326. See also Sherburn, *Early Career*, 27–36.

   Hilles, 'Making', 266, noted the Stuart sympathies revealed in SJ's statement that P's uncles 'had the honour' of dying for Charles I. Ruffhead, *Life*, 10, stated merely that 'one... was killed, another died, in the service of King Charles I'.

2. Cf. *Epistle to Arbuthnot*, l. 381 n.: 'In some of *Curl*'s and other Pamphlets, Mr. *Pope*'s Father was said to be a Mechanic, a Hatter, a Farmer, nay a Bankrupt.' He was in fact an importer and exporter of hollands or linen (Spence, i. 7). For P's efforts to conceal Gay's social origins, see 'Gay' 1 n. above.

   SJ added the information from Thomas Tyers (1726–87) in 1783 (see Textual Notes). Cf. *Gent. Mag.* (Sept. 1781), 432, quoting a correspondent, perhaps Tyers himself: 'Mrs. Racket, the relict of Pope's nephew, could have informed the author, that Pope's father was a linen-draper in the Strand.' (Magdalen Racket was in fact P's half-sister: five of his letters to her between 1719 and 1741 have survived.) Tyers said the same in his *Rhapsody on Mr. Pope* (1781; 2nd edn., 1782), 5, a copy of which he gave to SJ (*Life*, iii. 523, and cf. iii. 307; Fleeman, *Handlist* (1984), 64). 'Tom Restless' in *Idler* 48 (1759) was allegedly based on Tyers (*YW*, ii. 151–2).

3. Spence, i. 5; Ruffhead, *Life*, 10–11. For P's physical weakness, see 255–7 and nn. below.

   The dramatist Thomas Southerne (1659–1746) (see 'Fenton' 7 and n. above) called the young P 'the little nightingale', according to Lord Orrery, *Remarks on Swift* (1752), 225, quoted by Ruffhead, *Life*, 476.

4. Spence, i. 8, 11; Warburton (1751 edn.), iv. 209 n.; Ruffhead, *Life*, 11. P's aunt was probably Elizabeth Turner (1636–1710). For his early 'penmanship', see the MS of his *Pastorals* in Mack, *The Last and Greatest Art* (1984), 24–60.

5–7 and 10–11. The facts about P's education are more complex than Warburton and Ruffhead suggested: see Spence, i. 8–11. SJ eventually admits in 11 below that he has only 'confused, imperfect, and sometimes improbable intelligence' on this subject. SJ had already repeated some of the information in 4–12 in his review of Warton's *Essay* (1756) (*OASJ*, 493–4). P mocked speculation by his enemies about 'his Life, Parentage, and Education' as early as 1729: see *TE*, v. 24, and Mack, *AP*, 47–52.

5. Spence, i. 8–9; Warburton (1751 edn.), iv. 17 n.; Ruffhead, *Life*, 11–12.
    P told Spence in 1742 that teaching Latin and Greek together was 'the way in the schools of the Jesuits . . . which he seemed to think a good way' (i. 8–9). 'Edward Taverner', the alias of John Banister (d. 1745), may at first have been a tutor in the Pope family: see Mack, *AP*, 48.
    For the translations of Homer (1660–5) by John Ogilby and of Ovid (1626) by George Sandys, see also 85 below and 'Dryden' 107, 223, 307 and nn. above. Nichols noted of Ogilby in the proofs (perhaps prompted by Reed): 'On the contrary he [P] speaks very contemptuously of him in the Dunciad Book 1 L 141 & 328' (as a 'great forefather' of Colley Cibber).
    P praised Sandys in a note to *Iliad*, XXII. 196 (*TE*, viii. 463 n.), and Walter Harte told Warton that P also thought highly of 'A Paraphrase of Job' in Sandys's *Paraphrase Upon The Divine Poems* (1638) (*Works of P* (1797), iv. 226 n.). P did, however, use him as a satiric device in 'Sandys Ghost' (*c*.1716), a ballad on contemporary translators of Ovid (*TE*, vi. 170–4).

6. Spence, i. 8–9; Warburton (1751 edn.), iv. 17 n.; Ruffhead, *Life*, 12–13.
    John Banister (see 5 n. above) in fact taught the school at Twyford, near Winchester, Hants., having removed there *c*.1697–8.
    Thomas Deane (1651–1735), who ran the school in London, was a Fellow of University College, Oxford, who converted to Catholicism in the reign of James II. P referred in 1727 to Deane's 'head happy in the highest self opinion' (*Corresp.*, ii. 428 and n.). According to Warburton, the costume of the characters in P's 'kind of play' imitated illustrations in Ogilby's translation.

7. Spence, i. 8, 9, 10; Warburton (1751 edn.), iv. 209 n.; Ruffhead, *Life*, 12.
    P in fact translated Ovid at a later stage of his self-education (Spence, i. 14: see 11 below).

8. Spence, i. 15; Warburton (1751 edn.), iv. 17 n.; Ruffhead, *Life*, 15.
    SJ quotes *Epistle to Arbuthnot*, l. 128: 'I lisp'd in Numbers, for the Numbers came.' The story of the infant Pindar is found in e.g. Pausanias, Aelian, and the *Greek Anthology*. Cf. *Biographia Classica* (2nd edn., 1750), i. 65: 'as he slept one day in the Fields, when he was a little Boy, a Swarm of Bees found him and fed him with their Honey; this Accident determined him, no doubt, to the Study of Poetry.'
    the style of fiction: SJ originally wrote 'the age of fiction' in the MS, which was misprinted as 'the use of fiction', and altered by SJ in proof to the present reading (see Textual Notes).

9. Spence, i. 7 (estimating P's father's fortune as £10,000); Warburton (1751 edn.), iv. 212 n. (£15,000–£20,000); Ruffhead *Life*, 13–14 ('near' £20,000). Although he retired in 1688, he did not in fact move to Binfield in Windsor Forest until *c.*1700.

SJ defines 'Conscientiously' as 'According to the direction of conscience' (*Dict.*), referring here to the elder Pope's Catholicism. He did not keep all his money 'in a chest': P was later anxious about his investments in the French national debt (*Corresp.*, i. 236–7, 242). Martha Blount believed that P eventually inherited only 'about three or four thousand pounds' (Spence, i. 7).

10. Spence, i. 8–10; Warburton (1751 edn.), iv. 209 n.; Ruffhead, *Life*, 13–14.

The priest who taught P Cicero was not Thomas Deane (see **6** n. above), but probably William Mannock (1677–1749). For SJ's error about P's Ovid translations, see **7** n. above.

11. Spence, i. 11–13; Ruffhead, *Life*, 15.

Cf. SJ's reference in his 'Life of Dr. Sydenham' to 'that curiosity which would naturally incline us to watch the first attempts of so vigorous a mind, to persue its childish inquiries' ((2nd edn., 1749), p. v; *Early Biog. Writings* (1973), 189). For another poet who 'resolved to educate himself' at the age of 12, see 'Sheffield' 1 above.

12. Spence, i. 7; Warburton (1751 edn.), iv. 18 n.; Ruffhead, *Life*, 15. SJ had told the story of the elder Pope's concern with correctness when reviewing Warton's *Essay* (1756) (*OASJ*, 494).

13. For P's debt to Dryden, see also **303**, **374** below. Warburton stated that, after reading Waller and Spenser, 'On the first sight of Dryden, he found he had what he wanted. His Poems were never out of his hands; they became his model; and from them alone he learnt the whole magic of his versification' (1751 edn., iv. 18 n.; cf. Spence, i. 7).

Warburton also stated: 'When a very young Boy, he prevailed with a friend to carry him to a Coffee-House which Dryden frequented' (vii. 4 n.). P told Spence: 'I looked upon him with the greatest veneration even then, and observed him very particularly' (i. 25). See also Ruffhead, *Life*, 23, and for Will's Coffee House, 'Dryden' **190** above. For Walter Harte's uncorroborated story that 'Dryden gave Pope a shilling for translating, when a boy, the story of *Pyramus and Thisbe*,' see Warton, *Essay on P*, i (4th edn., 1782), 82 n., and *Works of P* (1797), i, p. xiii n.

SJ followed his sources in stating in the MS that a 'friend' took P to see Dryden, but failed to correct 'friends' in the proofs. For a reverse misprint of 'friends' in the MS as 'friend', see **195** and n. below. SJ did manage to correct 'friends' to 'friend' in 'Lyttelton' 8 below (see Textual Notes). For his printers' difficulties with SJ's plurals, see *Journey* (1985), pp. xlviii–xlix.

14. Dryden in fact died in 1700: for the error, see 'Dryden' **152** and n. above. *Gent. Mag.* (1781), 432, pointed out that P, who was born in 1688, could not have been less than 12 in 1701, but SJ did not correct the mistake in 1783.

15. Warburton (1751 edn.), i. 130 n.; and Ruffhead, *Life*, 22, describing the 'Ode on Solitude' as 'the first fruit now extant of his poetical genius'.

Although Warton, *Essay* (1756), 78, described this 'valuable literary curiosity' as 'a strong instance of that contemplative and moral turn, which was the distinguishing characteristic of our poet's mind', he added that Cowley wrote an ode 'not in the least inferior' to it at the age of 13. See 'Cowley' **6** and n. above and, for SJ's reaction in 1756 to Warton's comments, **18** n. below. P may in fact have revised the 'Ode' in July 1709, the date of the earliest extant MS.

16. See Spence, i. 14–15; Warburton (1751 edn.), ii. 147; Ruffhead, *Life*, 12–13, 179. For P's own belief that his 'application' at this period damaged his health, see **255** below.

    The translation of Statius, *Thebaid*, Bk. I, published in Lintot's *Miscellaneous Poems* (1712), was dated 1703, although P revised it in 1708–9 (see **28** n. below).

17. A later insertion in the MS: see Textual Notes.

    P published his modernizations of Chaucer (*c*.1704) in 1709 and 1713. As he stated in the 'Advertisement' to *Works*, vol. iii (1736): 'Mr. *Dryden*'s Fables came out about that time [1700], which occasion'd the Translations from *Chaucer*' (cf. Warburton (1751 edn.), ii. 48). For later comments on Chaucer, see Spence, i. 178–9. 'Sappho to Phaon' (*c*.1707) appeared in *Ovid's Epistles* (8th edn., 1712), with the explanation that Sir Carr Scrope's earlier translation in *Ovid's Epistles* (1680) had been incomplete (see 'Dryden' **107** above). P later quoted Charles Gildon's preference of his translation to Scrope's in the apparatus to *Dunciad* (1729) (*TE*, v. 40).

18. For P's early imitations of English poets, see *TE*, vi. 7–19. Although revised for publication, 'On Silence, In Imitation of the Earl of Rochester' was said in Lintot's *Miscellaneous Poems* (1712) to have been 'Written Some Years since'. From the mid-1730s P claimed that it was 'done at fourteen years old' (*TE*, vi. 19 n.). Cf. 'Rochester' **20–3** above and, for P's views on Rochester, see Spence, i. 201–2, and P. Baines, 'From "Nothing" to "Silence": Rochester and P', in E. Burns (ed.), *Reading Rochester* (Liverpool, 1995), 137–65.

    In 1756 SJ had reacted to Warton's praise of the 'Ode on Solitude' by claiming that 'On Silence' had 'much greater elegance of diction, music of numbers, extent of observation, and force of thought' (*OASJ*, 491; see **15** n. above). For the importance of 'knowledge' of life, see 'Butler' **37–9** and n. above.

19. See Spence, i. 12–13; Warburton (1751 edn.), iv. 209 n.; Ruffhead, *Life*, 16.

    For P's attempt in 1736 to translate Francesco Maffei's *Merope* (1713), see Spence, i. 236 n.

20. Ruffhead, *Life*, 23–4, 25–6, based on P's 'Preface' to *Works* (1717) in Warburton (1751 edn.), i, p. *xi.

    For the importance of self-confidence, see also 'Milton' **26** and n. above, and for the problems of authorial self-assessment, see **302** below and 'Milton' **146** and n. above. Discussing this stage of P's career, *BB*, v. 3405, also commented on the necessary 'vanity and self-conceit' of a great poet.

21. See Spence, i. 15–19; Warburton (1751 edn.), iv. 17 n.; Ruffhead, *Life*, 25–7, 23–4.

    The subject of 'Alcander', which contained some 4,000 lines, was St Genevieve (*c*.422–512), the patron saint of Paris: Francis Atterbury (see **131** and n. below) mentioned its burning in a letter to P, 18 Feb. 1717 (*Corresp.*, i. 467). Spence later told Warton that some of the anonymous verses ridiculed in *The Art of Sinking in Poetry* (see **143** below) 'were such as our poet remembered from his own ALCANDER' (*Essay* (1756), 83; *Works of P* (1797), vi. 219). For P and the stage, see **70** n. below.

22. Spence, i. 21 (where P states that the MS translation from Cicero was in 'Lord Oxford's library'), 19; Warburton (1751 edn.), vii. 5; Ruffhead, *Life*, 17–18.

For an earlier translation of *De Senectute*, see 'Denham' **33** above, and for Sir William Temple's *Miscellanea* (3 vols., 1680–1701), see 'Swift' **7** ff. above. P at first thought Locke 'quite insipid', but later praised his style and 'close thinking' (Spence, i. 19, 92, 510, 535). For another reference to Locke, see *Imit. Horace, Ep. I. i.* (1737), l. 25, and for P's 'knowledge of books', see also **34** below.

23. See Spence, i. 31; Warburton (1751 edn.), i. 46 n.; Ruffhead, *Life*, 21–2.

P was in fact some forty-nine years younger than Sir William Trumbull (1639–1716), Ambassador to Constantinople 1687–91 and Secretary of State 1695–7. Dryden had stated in the 'Postscript' to the *Aeneid* (1697) that, if Bk. XII 'shine among its fellows, 'tis owing to the commands of Sir William Trumball ... who recommended it, as his favourite, to my care' (Watson, ii. 260). P dedicated the first of his *Pastorals* (1709) to Trumbull, and praised him in *Windsor Forest* (1713), ll. 235–58. For their correspondence, see Sherburn, 'Letters', 388–406; and for P's epitaph on Trumbull, and the spelling of his name (both Warburton and Ruffhead gave 'Trumball'), see **395–400** and n. below.

For P's attitude to 'the great', see **196, 231, 270–2, 279, 281** below. SJ noted earlier that Dryden was 'reproached for boasting of his familiarity with the great' ('Dryden' **168**). For Swift's attitude, and for SJ's own sensitivities, see 'Swift' **52** and n. above.

24. Ruffhead, *Life*, 42, based on P's note (1736) to the *Pastorals* in Warburton (1751 edn.), i. 45 n.

For P's early admirers, see Spence, ii. 616–8. The *Pastorals* first appeared in Tonson's *Poetical Miscellanies*, vi (1709), 723–51 (see **33** and n. below), and the 'Discourse on Pastoral Poetry' in *Works* (1717), where it was dated 1704.

25. See 'Cowley' **6**, and 'Milton' **8, 152** above.

26. Spence, i. 32–41; Warburton (1751 edn.), i. pp. xii–xiv, 62–3 n. (where P describes Wycherley as 'a writer of infinite spirit, satire, and wit'), vii. 38 n.; Ruffhead, *Life*, 46–9.

William Wycherley (1641–1716), author of *The Country Wife* (1675) and *The Plain Dealer* (1676), had long since retired from the theatre. For P's correspondence with him between 1705 and 1710, see *Corresp.*, i. 3–87 *passim*. P dedicated the third of his *Pastorals* to Wycherley, whose poem 'To my friend Mr. Pope, on his Pastorals' appeared in Tonson's *Poetical Miscellanies*, vi (1709), 253–6. In his *Reflections upon An Essay upon Criticism* (1711) (*Works*, i. 417 and cf. ii. 356), John Dennis claimed that P wrote these lines himself. Although P denied this in a note in 1729 (see *Corresp.*, i. 50 n.), he may have revised the poem. For Wycherley's 'obscenity', see 'Granville' **10** above. Thomas Davies, *Dramatic Miscellanies* (1784), iii. 313–14, commented that, for all SJ's 'honest indignation' at the 'impurity' of the 'old scribbler' (see **27** below), Wycherley was no worse in this respect than Dryden and Otway.

SJ noted in his memoranda for 'Pope': 'Cant about criticks and Commentators' (fo. 175^r). Under 'Cant' in the *Dict.* he quotes Addison, *Spectator* 291 (1712): 'A few general Rules extracted out of the *French* Authors, with a certain Cant of Words, has sometimes set up an Illiterate heavy Writer for a most judicious and formidable Critick.' For such 'cant', see P's first surviving letter of 26 Dec. 1704

(*Corresp.*, i. 2), and the letter of 1708 in **383** below, in which P 'values the authority of one true poet above that of twenty criticks or commentators'. SJ also accuses P of 'Cant' in **67, 423** below, and see also 'Addison' **54** and n. above and 'Gray' **35** and n. below.

27. See Spence, i. 35–6, 41 ('He never did an unjust thing to me in his whole life, and I went to see him on his death-bed'); Warburton (1751 edn.), vii. 32–3, 51–4, 93–4 and n.; Ruffhead, *Life*, 46–50.

 Wycherley died on 21 Jan. 1716. P told Swift, 28 Nov. 1729: 'My first friendship at sixteen, was contracted with a man of seventy, and I found him not grave enough or consistent enough for me, tho' we lived well to his death. I speak of old Mr. Wycherley' (*Corresp.*, iii. 80). For Theobald's edition of Wycherley's *Posthumous Works* (1728), and the suppressed 'Volume II' prepared by P in 1729, in response, see Spence i. 35, 36 n., McLaverty, 'First Printing', 264–80, and *Prose Works*, ii (1986), 307–16.

28. Warburton (1751 edn.), vii. 74–152, for P's correspondence (1707–11) with Henry Cromwell (1659?–1728).

 a-hunting in a tye-wig: the point seems to be that the formality of a 'tie-wig', with 'the hair gathered together behind and tied with a knot of ribbon' (*OED*), was inappropriate for riding. Cf. **258** below, 'Addison' **118** above, and Hawkins, *Life* (1787), 238 n. Mrs Thrale-Piozzi later commented, however, that 'Wigs were at first tyed, on purpose that men should ride in them either o' hunting or in battle. The Duke of Marlbro' is represented by painters as winning all his battles in a tye-wig' (Lobban, 152).

 Cromwell's verse appeared in Aphra Behn's *Miscellany: Being a Collection of Poems by Several Hands* (1685), Gildon's *Miscellany Poems* (1692) and *Examen Poeticum* (1693), and P later included it in Lintot's *Miscellaneous Poems and Translations* (1712). P told Gay, 13 Nov. 1712, that Cromwell was 'displeas'd at some or other of my Freedoms' (*Corresp.*, i. 36, 56–7, 68, 153). Several of P's letters in 1708–9 mention Cromwell's correction of his translation of the *Thebaid* (see **16** above).

29. Edmund Curll (1675–1747) published P's early letters to Cromwell, which he obtained from the distressed author Elizabeth Thomas (1677–1731), in *Miscellanea* (1726). This earned her a sordid niche as 'Corinna' in *Dunciad*, ii. 69 ff. See also **141–2** below, 'Dryden' **153** n. above, and *Eighteenth Century Women Poets* (Oxford, 1989), 32–44. P commented in 1735 that these letters 'were not written in sober sadness' (Spence, i. 43).

30. See Spence, i. 31–2; Warburton, i. 45–6 n., iv. 225 n., vii. 57 n.; Ruffhead, *Life*, 43.

 P told Spence in 1743 that Walsh advised him that, 'though we had several great poets, we never had any one great poet that was correct—and he desired me to make that my study and aim'. See also **40** below, 'Walsh' **5** above, and, for 'correctness', 'Roscommon' **24** and n. above.

 Walsh wrote to P about 'pastoral comedy' on 24 June and 2 July 1706 (*Corresp.*, i. 18, 20–2). For SJ's ridicule of such a pastoral drama, see 'Gay' **32** above. For Walsh's comments on the MS of P's *Pastorals*, see *TE*, i. 38–41, and Mack, *Last and Greatest Art*, 62–9.

 Lives (1783) printed 'counsel' in the second sentence as 'council' (see Textual Notes). SJ clearly intended 'counsel' ('1. Advice; direction', *Dict.*).

31. George Granville, 'having learned the art of versifying', had similarly 'declared himself a poet' ('Granville' **26** above).

P mentions Will's Coffee House in a letter to Wycherley, 26 Oct. 1705 (*Corresp.*, i. 11, and cf. i. 288). See **13** above and 'Dryden' **190** and n. above.

32. See the slightly varying accounts in Warburton (1751 edn.), iv. 211 n., and Ruffhead, *Life*, 19–20 n.; and, for SJ's last sentence, Spence, i. 241 (and cf. i. 12, 19).

SJ stated in *Rambler* 103 (1751): 'Curiosity is one of the permanent and certain characteristicks of a vigorous intellect' (*YW*, iv. 104). For P's 'great literary curiosity' as a young man, see also **291** below. SJ comes no closer than this to Shenstone's observation that 'imperfections of one kind have a visible tendency to produce perfections of another. Mr. Pope's bodily disadvantages must incline him to a more laborious cultivation of his talent, without which he foresaw that he must have languished in obscurity.' Such 'unwearied application to poetry' made him 'not only the favourite of the learned, but also of the ladies' (*Works* (1764), ii. 177).

In 'Sermon 8' SJ described the 'patience in enquiry' and 'eagerness of knowledge'—'at the expence of many pleasures and amusements'—required in 'a young man, about to engage in a life of study' (*YW*, xiv. 90). Cf. the student who 'quits his Ease for Fame' in *Vanity of Human Wishes*, ll. 135 ff., perhaps echoing P's own *Temple of Fame*, l. 507: 'Ease, health, and life, for this [i.e. fame] we must resign.' For 'judgement', see **304, 307, 310, 373** below.

For SJ's own reading in the two years before he went to Oxford, see *Life*, i. 57. In July 1763 he stated: 'in my early years I read very hard. It is a sad reflection, but a true one, that I knew almost as much at eighteen as I do now. My judgment, to be sure, was not so good; but I had all the facts.' He told Langton: 'His great period of study was from the age of twelve to that of *eighteen*' (*Life*, i. 445–6 and n., v. 12 n.).

33. For the publication of the *Pastorals*, see **24** and n. above, and 'A. Philips' **18** and n. below.

34. P told Spence that he wrote *An Essay on Criticism* in 1709 (i. 41). Warburton (1751 edn.), i. 133, repeated this, but his omission of the date of publication (1711) may explain SJ's own vagueness.

For the *Essay* as a 'critical synthesis' of 17th-century, mostly French, literary theory, see *TE*, i. 209 ff., and cf. **291** below; for 'comprehension', see 'Cowley' **144** and n. above; and for 'knowledge', 'Butler' **37–9** and n. above.

Addison praised the *Essay* with some reservations in *Spectator* 253 (1711), which P at first believed was by Steele: see his letters to Steele, 30 Dec. 1711, and to Addison, 10 Oct. 1714 (*Corresp.*, i. 139–40, 263–4).

P depicted John Dennis reading the *Essay* in Lintot's shop with 'much Frowning and Gesticulation', and later in 'a terrible Frenzy' ('*By G— he means Me*'), in *The Narrative of Dr. Robert Norris* (1713) (*Prose Works*, i. 166). He quoted Dennis's *Reflections Critical and Satyrical, upon...An Essay upon Criticism* (1711) twice in the 'Testimonies of Authors' prefixed to the *Dunciad* (*TE*, v. 25, 38). For his note (1744) on Dennis's 'perfectly lunatic' reaction to the thinly veiled references to him in *Essay*, ll. 269–70, 584–7, see Warburton (1751 edn.), i. 199 n. Although Ruffhead only briefly mentioned this attack, SJ's early notes for 'Pope' refer to 'Dennis's Remarks' (fo. 162ᵛ).

SJ transposes the quotation from the *Reflections* into the third person (cf. Dennis, *Works*, i. 396–7). For his earlier use of Dennis's criticism, see 'Addison'

138–53 above. E. N. Hooker described SJ's account of *Reflections* in **34–40** as 'woefully inadequate' (Dennis, *Works*, i. 525–6).

35. Dennis presumably described P's jokes about him as 'clandestine' because anonymous, and justifiably thought 'his person...depreciated' by ll. 585–6: 'But *Appius* reddens at each Word you speak, | And *stares, Tremendous!* with a *threatening Eye.*' For P's reaction, see his letters to Caryll and Cromwell of 25 June 1711, the second making clear that Lintot had shown him the *Reflections* before publication (*Corresp.*, i. 121, 125). Lintot paid Dennis £2 12s. 6d. for the pamphlet on 1 June 1712 (Nichols, *Lit. Anec.*, viii. 295).

For P's tendency to 'talk...of his own virtues', see **167, 273** below.

36. See Dennis, *Works*, i. 397.

37. SJ's apparent quotation in fact summarizes Dennis's long discussion (*Works*, i. 398–402). The misleading quotation marks were added in 1783: see Textual Notes.

SJ included 'Dictatorial', but not Dennis's 'dictatorian', in the *Dict.*

38. See *Essay on Criticism*, ll. 80–2, and Dennis, *Works*, i. 404. P revised these lines in 1744 (*TE*, i. 248).

For P's ambiguous use of 'wit' in the *Essay*, and his refusal to follow Locke and others in opposing it to 'judgement', see E. N. Hooker, 'P on Wit: The *Essay on Criticism*', in R. F. Jones (ed.), *The Seventeenth Century* (Stanford, Calif., 1951), 225–46; W. Empson, *The Structure of Complex Words* (1951), 84–100; and *TE*, i. 212–9. For 'Wit', see also 'Cowley' **54–6** and nn. above.

the man who would reform a nation: the opening of Dennis's *Reflections* deplored the national 'Calamity' of the arrival of the Italian opera, and described P's *Essay* as 'A most notorious Instance of this Depravity of Genius and Tast' (*Works*, i. 396).

39. SJ defines 'A Bull' in this sense as '5. A blunder; a contradiction' (*Dict.*), quoting P's letter to Caryll, 25 June 1711, on Dennis's objection to *Essay on Criticism*, ll. 500, 503: ''Tis right Hibernian, and I confess it is what the English call a bull, in the expression, tho' the sense be manifest enough: Mr. Dennis's bulls are seldom in the expression, they are almost always in the sense' (*Corresp.*, i. 121). As P's MS notes indicate, Dennis's mockery of ll. 502–4 prompted his later revisions: see Dennis, *Works*, i. 411, quoted loosely by SJ, and *TE*, i. 295, 483.

40. Dennis, *Works*, i. 416–17, refers to P's tribute to Walsh (see **30** above) in *Essay on Criticism*, ll. 729–34. His references to 'Sunninghill and Oakingham' are explained by the fact that the *Reflections* are addressed 'To Mr. — at Sunning-Hill, Berks', and that Oakingham is near P's home at Binfield.

For Dennis's later attacks on P, see **60, 62, 122, 152** below. P, Gay, and Arbuthnot depicted him as 'Sir Tremendous' in *Three Hours After Marriage* (1717): see **233** below and 'Gay' **10** above. In 1721 P and Dennis exchanged letters regretting the 'State of War' which existed between them, and in 1731 P tried to assist his former enemy in his destitute old age (*Corresp.*, ii. 75–6, iii. 171–2, 174–5; Dennis, *Works*, ii. 322; *Epistle to Arbuthnot*, ll. 370–1). In 1733, three weeks before Dennis died, he wrote a condescending 'Prologue' for a benefit performance for him (*TE*, vi. 355–7, and see **60** n. below).

41. SJ quotes P's statement to Caryll, 19 July 1711, that 1,000 copies of the *Essay* were printed (Warburton (1751 edn.), i. 237–8; *Corresp.*, i. 128). The bookseller William Lewis, a schoolfriend of P, who published the *Essay* on 15 May 1711, told Warton that it 'lay many days in his shop, unnoticed and unread', until P 'packed up and directed twenty copies to several great men' (*Works of P* (1797), i, p. xviii). It had reached a 7th edition by 1722.

For the growth of the reading public in the 17th and 18th centuries, see also 'Milton' **135** and n. above.

42. P's references to monks and to Erasmus in *Essay*, ll. 687–96, offended Catholic readers: see P's letters to Caryll of 18 and 25 June and 19 July 1711 (*Corresp.*, i. 118–19, 122–3, 126–8). P in fact told Caryll: 'I will recant and alter whatever you please in case of a Second Edition' (i. 128).

43. Warburton (1751 edn.), vii. 247–8 n., reprinting P's note (1735) on his translators; and Ruffhead, *Life*, 101. P gave similar information in the *Dunciad*: see *TE*, v. 17–18 n.

The translations were by Anthony Hamilton (1646?–1720), author of *Mémoires de la vie du Comte de Gramont* (1713); John Robethon (d. 1722), secretary to George I, published 1717; and Jean-François Du Bellay Du Resnel (1692–1761), published 1730: see also **181** and n. below and 'Garth' **17** and n. above. P told Hamilton, 10 Oct. 1713: 'In putting me into a *French* dress, you have not only adorned my outside, but mended my shape; and . . . I am now a good figure' (*Corresp.*, i. 192–3, 210).

SJ defines 'To Comment' as '1. To annotate; to write notes upon an author' (*Dict.*). For his elaborate commentary on the *Essay*, see Warburton (1751 edn.), i. 135–211, and, for his tendency to over-interpret P, see also **190** and n., **369** below. Addison in *Spectator* 253 (1711) compared the *Essay*'s lack of 'Methodical Regularity' to Horace's *Ars Poetica*, and Jonathan Richardson the Younger reported that P himself claimed to have imitated Horace's 'irregularity': see *Richardsoniana* (1776), 264.

44–5. See P. K. Alkon, 'Critical and Logical Concepts of Method from Addison to Coleridge', *ECS* 5 (1971–2), 97–121. For 'method' in didactic poetry, see also **328** and n. below.

44. SJ quotes Richard Hooker, *Laws of Ecclesiastical Polity* (1593–7), II. i. 2: 'by long circuit of deduction it may be that even all truth out of any truth may be concluded.' He had quoted versions of this sentence under 'Circumduction' and 'Deduction' in the *Dict.* For SJ's respect for Hooker, see 'Waller' **21–2** and n. above, and for his use of 'concatenation', see 'Akenside' **17** and n. below.

Cf. *Adventurer* 107 (1753): 'As a question becomes more complicated and involved, and extends to a greater number of relations, disagreement of opinion will always be multiplied, not because we are irrational, but because we are finite beings, furnished with different kinds of knowledge, exerting different degrees of attention, one discovering consequences which escape another, none taking in the whole concatenation of causes and effects' (*YW*, ii. 441).

SJ refers finally to Aristotle, *Nicomachean Ethics*, III. vi.

46. P's 'Messiah, A Sacred Eclogue . . . in Imitation of Virgil's Pollio' appeared in *Spectator* 378 (14 May 1712). SJ refers to Steele to P, 1 June 1712 (*Corresp.*, i. 146). Although both these appear in SJ's notes for 'Pope' (fo. 164ʳ), he later omitted them. See also **318** below and, for SJ's own Latin translation of 'Messiah', **195** n. below.

47. There is no evidence that P wrote 'Elegy to the Memory of an Unfortunate Lady' much before its publication in *Works* (1717). The entry in SJ's MS notes for 'Pope' (fo. 163ᵛ), 'Mention made in Lett of an unfortunate Lady', presumably refers to P's letter to Caryll, 28 May 1712, in Warburton (1751 edn.), vii. 241–3, although Kirkley, *Biographer*, 145–6, noted that in the 'Contents' to this volume another letter is described as 'To an unfortunate lady' (vii, p. xxvi). After 'fruitless enquiry', presumably in pursuit of such clues, SJ eventually adopted Ruffhead's account in an insertion to the MS in **48–52** below.

For P's concern in 1711–12 for Elizabeth Weston, who had separated from her husband, and for Anne Cope, another unfortunate lady, see *TE*, ii. 353–5, Rumbold, *Women's Place*, 103–19, and **319** below. Although the 'lady' has not been identified, *Gent. Mag.* (1784), 807, claimed that she belonged to a Catholic family called Scudamore; Hawkins, *J's Works* (1787), iv. 113 n., that her name was Withinbury, and that she committed suicide after her guardian prohibited her marriage to P; and Warton, *Works of P* (1797), i. 336 n., after 'many and wide enquiries', that 'her name was Wainsbury; and that . . . she was as ill-shaped and deformed as our author'.

48–52. In the MS SJ calls for the insertion of these paragraphs from the appended materials: see Textual Notes.

48. SJ follows the account in Ruffhead, *Life*, 133–5, which itself derived from William Ayre, *Memoirs of P* (1745), i. 75–6, as Nichols showed in *Gent. Mag.* (1781), 314–15, and *Lives*, iv (1791), 22 n. It is now considered a fabrication (*TE*, ii. 356). For more cautious speculations, see Warton, *Essay* (1756), 249–50, and, for SJ's views on unequal marriages, see **319** and n. below.

The *Dict.* includes both 'Uncle' and 'Unkle'. SJ had used the spelling 'Unkle' in his notes to Shakespeare (e.g. *YW*, viii. 944, 977, 988), and see *Letters*, i. 401–2, ii. 58, 101, iii. 359.

51. The spelling 'suspense', favoured in the *Dict.*, was revised to 'suspence' in 1783.

52. For the 'false Guardian', see 'Elegy', l. 29.

the amorous fury of a raving girl: SJ first wrote 'the suicide of a mad girl', which he revised in MS (see Textual Notes). For suicide, see also **319** and n. below. SJ's dismissive comments on this admired poem were provocative. Warton, *Essay on P* (1756), 249–54, 333, had praised the 'Elegy' as 'the only instance of the Pathetic' in P's verse apart from 'Eloisa to Abelard', a claim to which SJ did not react in his review in 1756 (*OASJ*, 493). He later complained that SJ had 'too severely censured this elegy' (*Works of P* (1797), i. 336). Ruffhead, *Life*, 135, wrote of the lady's suicide: 'Such a moving catastrophe might have inspired a savage with sensibility; but in Mr. POPE it awakened all the power of the Pathos.' Beattie, *Essays* (Edinburgh, 1776), 361 n., also described the 'Elegy' and 'Eloisa to Abelard' as 'deeply pathetic'.

53. Spence, i. 43–5; Warburton (1751 edn.), i. 217–18 n.; Ruffhead, *Life*, 102–3.

P based the Baron and Belinda in *The Rape of the Lock* on Robert, Lord Petre (1690–1713), and Arabella Fermor (1690?–1738), both members of prominent Catholic families. Lord Petre died shortly afterwards and Miss Fermor married Francis Perkins of Ufton Court, Berks.

SJ follows Warburton and Ruffhead in confusing John Caryll (1667–1736), P's friend and correspondent, with his uncle John Caryll (1625–1711), secretary to

Mary of Modena and the author of *Sir Solomon Single* (1671). Caryll's name was not printed in full in *Rape*, I. 3, in P's lifetime. He told Caryll, 25 Feb. 1714: 'I was strangely tempted to have set your name at length . . . but I remembered your desire you formerly expressed to the contrary' (*Corresp.*, i. 210). SJ inserted his comment on this matter in the MS (see Textual Notes).

P stated in a note (1736) that he wrote the first two-canto version of the poem, published in Lintot's *Miscellaneous Poems and Translations, by Various Hands* (1712), 'in less than a fortnight's time': see also Spence, i. 45. His dedication to the enlarged edition (1714) explained that he had published the first version only because an 'imperfect Copy' had been 'offer'd to a Bookseller' (*TE*, ii. 144 n., 142). In his 'Life of Sir Thomas Browne' (1756), p. vii, SJ described complaints of 'surreptitious editions' as 'a stratagem by which an author panting for fame, and yet afraid of seeming to challenge it, may at once gratify his vanity, and preserve the appearance of modesty'. See **166** below, and 'Dryden' **74** and n. above.

54. Spence, i. 44; Warburton (1751 edn.), i. 252 n.; Ruffhead, *Life*, 103–4. (In the MS SJ made here one of his few direct references to Ruffhead, but later deleted it: cf. **48** above and Textual Notes.)

P based Sir Plume, in *Rape*, IV. 121–30, on Sir George Browne (d. 1730): for his blustering, see *Corresp.*, i. 151, 164 and n.

For SJ's meeting with Mrs Fermor, Abbess of the Austin nuns, in Paris on 16 Oct. 1775, see *YW*, i. 236, *Life*, ii. 392–3 and n., and *Letters*, ii. 272 and n. At the time he noted merely: 'Mrs. Fermor Abbess. She knew Pope, and thought him disagreeable.' Mrs Fermor later told Hester Thrale-Piozzi in Sept. 1784 that 'Mr. Pope's praise made her aunt very troublesome and conceited, while his numberless caprices would have employed ten servants to wait on him' (*Observations and Reflections Made in the Course of a Journey Through France, Italy and Germany* (1789), i. 21: see also **260** n. below).

55. Warburton (1751 edn.), iv. 26 n.; Ruffhead, *Life*, 103, 105, 187.

Addison quoted 'merum sal' ('pure wit') from Lucretius, *De Rerum Natura*, IV. 1162. For his praise of the first version of the poem, see *Spectator* 523 (30 Oct. 1712).

P explained his Rosicrucian 'machinery', supposedly derived from Montfaucon de Villars's *Le Comte de Gabalis* (1670), in the dedication to the revised *Rape of the Lock* (Warburton (1751 edn.), i. 215–16, and cf. i. 210–20 n.; *TE*, ii. 142–3). For earlier poetic use of the Rosicrucian system, see Butler, *Hudibras*, II. iii. 613–22.

For epic 'machinery', see also **336–7** below, and 'Milton' **222** and 'Dryden' **140–1** and nn. above, and cf. P's note to *Iliad*, XXIV. 141: 'It may be thought that so many Interpositions of the Gods, such Messages from Heaven to Earth, and down to the Seas, are needless Machines' (*TE*, viii. 541 n.).

56. Warburton (1751 edn.), iv. 26 n., Warton, *Essay on P* (1756), 159–60, and Ruffhead, *Life*, 187, all attributed Addison's advice to 'jealousy'.

57. For 'imagery', see 'Cowley' **154** and n. above; for 'luxuriance', 'Thomson' **50** and n. below; and for the 'colours' of diction, 'Milton' **193** and n. above.

58. P told Caryll, 12 Mar. 1714, that his poem 'has in four days time sold to the number [of] three thousand, and is already reprinted' (*Corresp.*, i. 214).

Ruffhead, *Life*, 130 n., quoted the letter sent to P from Italy, 1 May 1714, by the philosopher George Berkeley (1685–1753), later Bishop of Cloyne, who was friendly with P and Swift at this time: 'Stile, Painting, Judgment, Spirit, I had already admired in others of your Writings; but in this I am charm'd with the magic of your *Invention*, with all those images, allusions, and inexplicable beauties, which you raise so surprizingly and at the same time so naturally, out of a trifle' (*Corresp.*, i. 221).

The phrase 'powers more truly poetical' is not Berkeley's but SJ's: his emphasis here on P's 'fertility of invention' anticipates his later responses to Warton about 'invention' and 'poetry' in **314, 337, 373, 382** below.

59. Spence, i. 45; Warburton (1751 edn.), i. 218 n.; Ruffhead, *Life*, 107.

P told Spence in 1735 that making the 'machinery' and 'what was published before hit so well together, is I think one of the greatest proofs of judgement of anything I ever did'. SJ's rendering again emphasizes P's 'poetical art'. He had stated in his review of Warton (1756) that the poem 'was always regarded by Pope as the highest production of his genius' (*OASJ*, 492).

In the first sentence 'intertexture', which appears in the MS, was printed in 1783 as 'intermixture': see Textual Notes. SJ defines 'Intermixture' as '1. Mass formed by mingling bodies. 2. Something additional mingled in a mass', and 'Intertexture' as 'Diversification of things mingled or woven one among another' (*Dict.*). For 'intertexture', see 'Akenside' **17** below.

For felicitous combinations of genius and chance, see also **402, 428** below, and 'Denham' **31** and n. above; and for SJ's suspicion of 'wonders', see 'Cowley' **5** and n. above.

By 'casualty' SJ means '1. Accident; a thing happening by chance, not design' rather than '2. Chance that produces unnatural death' (*Dict.*). Cf. the 'favourable casualties' which may affect a new author's reputation in *Rambler* 146 (1751), the 'innumerable casualties' which 'intercept' human happiness in *Rambler* 205 (1752) (*YW*, v. 17, 301), 'extraordinary casualties' in 'Life of Browne' (1756), p. xii, and 'this chaos of mingled purposes and casualties' in the preface to Shakespeare (*YW*, vii. 66). See also **89** below and 'Dryden' **351** above.

60. Ruffhead, *Life*, 129.

Open hostilities between P and Dennis (see **34–40** above) were suspended after 1717. Although 'Letters I–IV' of Dennis's *Remarks on Mr. Pope's Rape of the Lock* (1728) were dated May 1714 (*Works*, ii. 322–52), he withheld this work until the appearance of *The Dunciad* (see **152** below), in which P had behaved 'like a mad *Indian* that runs a muck' (ii. 322). In **340–1** below SJ takes some of Dennis's objections to *The Rape* more seriously than his comments here might lead one to expect. For P's notes on this attack, see *TE*, ii. 249.

61. Ruffhead, *Life*, 172.

P told Steele, 16 Nov. 1712 (Warburton (1751 edn.), vii. 258–9; *Corresp.*, i. 154), that he wrote *The Temple of Fame* (1715) in 1710. A later note to this letter (1735), stating that he wrote it before he was 22, seems to confirm this date, but from 1717 he also described it as 'Written in the Year 1711', which is more likely (*TE*, ii. 249). See also **317** below.

62. Dennis objected to *The Temple of Fame*, ll. 83–92, in his *Remarks upon Mr. Pope's Homer* (1717) that 'Neither Painting, nor Sculpture, can show Local Motion' (*Works*, ii. 143).

63. Ruffhead, *Life*, 171–2.

'Eloisa to Abelard' (written *c*.1716) appeared at the end of *Works* (1717). Savage could not have been SJ's informant before about 1737, but James Ralph's *Sawney* (1728) had already noted P's debt to Prior's 'Henry and Emma', which adapted the much older 'Nut Brown Maid' (see 'Prior' **18, 57** above). For P's prose source, see 'Hughes' **10** n. above. For SJ's later praise of the poem, see **342** below, and for his taste for poetry with gloomy religious settings, see 'Congreve' **34** and n. above.

64. Savage may again have been SJ's informant (cf. **63** above). P's alleged dissatisfaction with 'Eloisa' might have arisen from its original association with Lady Mary Wortley Montagu, with whom he eventually quarrelled bitterly (*TE*, ii. 311–13), or from his dislike of Prior's praise of the poem's eroticism in *Alma* (1718), ii. 287–304, reported by Warton, *Essay* (3rd edn., 1772), 316 n., and *Works of P* (1797), i, p. xxiii. As late as Feb. 1732, however, P referred, with apparent satisfaction, to the poem's 'Descriptive, &, (if I may so say) Enthusiastic Spirit' (*Corresp.*, iii. 269).

65. Both Warburton (1751 edn.), i. 89 n., 105 n., and Ruffhead, *Life*, 50, printed P's notes (1736), which dated the original composition of *Windsor Forest* as 1704, and in fact explained that the 'addition' in 1712 began after l. 290.

Lines 355 ff. refer to the Treaty of Utrecht, for which the preliminaries were signed in Oct. 1711, the main Treaty dating from Apr. 1713, a month after P's poem appeared: see 'Prior' **28** and n. and 'Tickell' **5** and n. above, and 'Young' **17–18** below. For George Granville, Lord Lansdowne, who 'insisted' on the poem's publication, and whose 'moving lays' P had praised in 'Spring', l. 46, see 'Granville' **17** above, Spence, i. 43, Warburton (1751 edn.), vii. 238, and *Corresp.*, i. 172.

SJ replies here to Joseph Warton, who claimed in *Essay* (1756), 29–30, that a person 'of no small rank' had told him that Addison was 'inexpressibly chagrined . . . both as a politician and as a poet' by the ending of *Windsor Forest* (repeated by Ruffhead, *Life*, 57 n.). Addison may have read P's poem as a rejection of the celebration of war in his own 'far-famed' *The Campaign* (1705) ('Addison' **25, 130–4** above); see R. Cummings, 'Addison's "Inexpressible Chagrin" and P's Poem on the Peace', *Yearbook of English Studies*, 18 (1988), 143–58. Addison later deplored the Treaty of Utrecht in *Freeholder* 41 (1716). SJ's discussion of *Windsor Forest* here and in **315–16** below suggests that he took little interest in its political implications.

Discussing youthful authors in June 1779, SJ stated that *Windsor Forest*, 'though so delightful a Poem, by no means required the knowledge of Life & manners, nor the accuracy of observation, nor the skill of penetration' displayed in Fanny Burney's recent *Evelina*: see her *Early Journals*, iii. 329.

66. Spence, i. 64; Warburton (1751 edn.), viii. 264; Ruffhead, *Life*, 139–40, 184.

For SJ's earlier account of these matters, see 'Addison' **54, 58, 63–4, 113–14, 137** above; cf. also **104** below. For P's *Narrative* (1713), see *Prose Works*, i. 155–68.

67. P in fact fabricated the letter supposedly addressed to Addison, 20 July 1713, from a letter to Caryll, 19 Nov. 1712 (*Corresp.*, i. 183–4). See 'Addison' **65** and n. above.

sensibility: '1. Quickness of sensation' and '2. Quickness of perception; delicacy' (*Dict.*; 'delicacy' was added in 1773). In *Rambler* 112 (1751) SJ wrote: 'Sensibility may by an incessant attention to elegance and propriety, be quickened to a tenderness inconsistent with the condition of humanity'; and later referred disapprovingly in *Idler* 50 (1759) to the 'ambition of superior sensibility' (*YW*, iv. 232, ii. 157). While he views it favourably in 'Milton' **264**, 'Dryden' **325**, and 'Congreve' **35** above, and refers to P's 'natural sensibility' in **149** below, his reference to 'cant' (cf. **26** above) makes clear his scepticism about the vogue for 'sensibility' as the basis of taste. In 1769 he said: 'You will find these very feeling people are not very ready to do you good. They *pay* you by *feeling*' (*Life*, ii. 69). See John Mullan, 'Sensibility and Literary Criticism', in H. B. Nisbet and C. Rawson (eds.), *The Cambridge History of Literary Criticism: The Eighteenth Century* (Cambridge, 1997), 419–33.

68. Spence, i. 63, 172; Warburton (1757 edn.), vii. 203 n.; Ruffhead, *Life*, 43–5.

P's ironic *Guardian* 40 (27 Apr. 1713) replied to Tickell's earlier essays on pastoral in the periodical and mocked Ambrose Philips: see *Prose Works*, i. 97–106, and 'Gay' **4** and 'Tickell' **17** n. above and 'A. Philips' **19–20** below. Although Spence, i. 172, stated that Addison did not at first detect the hoax, SJ follows Warburton and Ruffhead. P later triumphantly reprinted *Guardian* 40 in an appendix to the *Dunciad* (*TE*, v. 222–9).

69. Spence, i. 46 (including P's refusal in 1730 to say whether poetry or painting gave him more pleasure); Warburton (1751 edn.), viii. 146; Ruffhead, *Life*, 476–7.

For P's friendship, especially in 1713–14, with the portrait-painter Charles Jervas (1675–1739), later Sir Godfrey Kneller's successor as Principal Painter to George I in 1723 and the translator of *Don Quixote* (1742), see *Corresp.*, i. 174, 177, Brownell, *AP and the Arts*, 10–17, and Mack, *AP*, 226–31. P mentioned his shortsightedness to Cromwell, 11 July 1709; and his portrait of the actor Thomas Betterton (d. 1710) (in fact a copy of Kneller's painting) to Caryll, 31 Aug. 1713 (*Corresp.*, i. 66, 189; Mack, *AP*, 90–1).

Against SJ's statement that P's portrait 'was' in the possession of William Murray (1705–93), Earl of Mansfield, Nichols wrote in the proofs: 'Q. is it not yet there?' SJ replied in the proofs: 'I believe it was burnt in the riots.' He had told Mrs Thrale, 9 June 1780, that Mansfield's possessions had been 'wholly burnt' in the recent Gordon Riots (*Letters*, iii. 268). In his own narrative of the Riots, Nichols also stated in July 1780 that Mansfield's books and paintings had been destroyed, but had learned by Nov. 1780 that P's painting had been moved to Kenwood long before: see *Gent. Mag.* (1780), 313, 330 and n., 515.

Thomas Davies also mentioned Mansfield's ownership of the portrait in *Memoirs of Garrick* (1780), i. 43, and, perhaps because of SJ's uncertainty here, later emphasized that it was safe at Kenwood (*Dramatic Miscellanies* (1784), iii. 400), as did Nichols in *Lives*, iv (1791), 32 n. Hawkins, *J's Works* (1787), iv. 90 n., criticized the 'negligence' of SJ's account of P's 'love of painting, which differs much from the information I gave him on that head', including the fact that the portrait was at Kenwood House. It remains in the possession of the earls of Mansfield at Scone.

Frances Reynolds mentioned SJ's pleasure in reciting P's 'Epistle to Mr. Jervas' (1716), and his praise of ll. 67–8 ('Led by some rule, that guides, but not constrains; | And finish'd more thro' happiness than pains!') as 'a union that constituted the ultimate degree of excellence in the fine arts' (*J. Misc.*, ii. 254). (SJ's first notes for 'Pope', fo. 177ᵛ, in fact refer to 'Forced rhymes in Jervas'.) SJ probably learned of P's 'ignorance of painting' from her brother Sir Joshua Reynolds: Warton, *Works of P* (1797), ll. 314 n., later quoted his objections to ll. 37–8 of the 'Epistle'.

70. See Caryll to P, 23 May 1712, in Warburton (1751 edn.), vii. 239–40, and *Corresp.*, i. 142.

P said in 1739 that he had been 'solicited' to write for the stage by Betterton, 'who (among other things) would have had me turn my early epic poem into a tragedy'. He declined because unwilling to subject himself 'to the players and the town' (Spence, i. 15, 17, 23). Cf. **21** above and 'Dryden' **42** and n. above.

P revised Betterton's versions of Chaucer's 'Prologue' (SJ's 'Prologues' follows Warburton (1751 edn.), vi. 239 n.) and one of the tales, at the request of his widow, before their appearance in Lintot's *Miscellaneous Poems and Translations* (1712) (*Corresp.*, i. 142). Cf. SJ's first notes for 'Pope': 'Betterton's remains suspected to be Pope's—Harte' (fo. 164ʳ). In the MS of 'Pope' he originally wrote 'as I have heard from Mr. Harte', later revised to the impersonal 'was related by': see Textual Notes. Warton, *Works of P* (1797), ii. 166, reported much the same story from Walter Harte (1709–74), the friend of P and Elijah Fenton (q.v. above). Cf. 'Dryden' **264** and n. above, and Nichols's account of Harte in *Sel. Collection*, vii. 302–4 n.: 'He knew many anecdotes of Pope, Swift, Pulteney, Chesterfield, Fenton, &c.' For Harte's relationship with P in the 1730s, see McLaverty, *P, Print and Meaning*, 107–41.

71. P stated in 1744 that he was drawn into the *Iliad* translation by 'the want of money. I had then none—not even to buy books' (Spence, i. 82); see also Ruffhead, *Life*, 180.

Lintot's payments to P in 1712–16 included £7 for the first version of *The Rape of the Lock* (1712) and £15 for the second (1714), and £32 5s. each for *Windsor Forest* (1713) and *The Temple of Fame* (1715) (Nichols, *Lit. Anec.*, viii. 299–300). For his father's financial situation, see **9** and n. above, and, for P's anxiety in Jan. 1714 about an annuity purchased for him by his father, see *Corresp.*, i. 208.

As a Catholic, P was disqualified from the public offices and sinecures enjoyed by Addison, Prior, Congreve, and others. In 1744 he said that he could have accepted a place from Lord Oxford only by 'giving a great deal of pain to my parents', i.e. by renouncing his religion (Spence, i. 98).

72. P issued proposals for the Homer subscription in Oct. 1713.

73. For P's references to the subscriptions to Dryden's *Virgil* (1697) ('Dryden' **147** and n. above) and the collected *Tatler* (4 vols., 1710), see Spence, i. 26–7. Although Dryden's *Virgil* was the first major work by a living author to be published in this way, Nichols (as 'Eugenio') pointed out in *Gent. Mag.* (July 1781), 318, the notable earlier subscription to Milton's *Paradise Lost* in 1688 (see 'Milton' **137** and n. above), emphasized later by Reed in *Lives*, iv (1791), 34 n., and Warton, *Works of P* (1797), i, p. xxvii n. For earlier lists of subscribers or 'recommenders', see F. J. G. Robinson and P. J. Wallis, *Book Subscription Lists* (Newcastle, 1975), 1–2, and *Book Subscription Lists: Extended Supplement* (Newcastle, 1996).

74. P professed political impartiality in the preface to *Works* (1717), in *Imit. Horace, Sat. II. i.* (1733), ll. 67–8 ('In Moderation placing all my Glory, | While Tories call me Whig, and Whigs a Tory'), and often in his letters, e.g. to Swift, 6 Jan. 1734 ('That strict neutrality as to publick parties, which I have constantly observ'd in all my writings') (*Corresp.*, iii. 401). See also **82** and n. and **217** below. For the 'emulation of factious praise' in support of *Cato* in 1713, see 'Addison' **60**–1 above.

75. For P's impressive list of subscribers, see Rogers, 'P and his Subscribers', 7–36, Hodgart, 'Subscription List', 25–34, and Mack, *AP*, 266–8.

George Granville, Lord Lansdowne (see **65** above), told P, 21 Oct. 1713: 'you may therefore depend upon the utmost services I can do you in promoting this work.' A year later P described himself as 'perpetually waiting upon the great . . . to gain their opinion upon my Homer' (*Corresp.*, i. 295, ii. 267).

For the regret of Robert Harley, Lord Oxford, at P's preoccupation with translation, see Spence, i. 98, and **71** n. above; Warburton (1751 edn.), iv. 66–7 n., and Ruffhead, *Life*, 180, 395. Swift told P, 19 July 1725: 'Our Lord Oxford used to curse the Occasions that put you on Translations and if he and the Qu[een] had lived you should entirely have followed your own Genius' (*Corresp.*, ii. 311). See also **91** below.

For Addison's advice, see Spence, i. 61, Warburton (1751 edn.), iv. 25 n., and Addison to P, 2 Nov. 1713 (*Corresp.*, i. 196–7), and cf. **82** below.

76. Spence, i. 85–6; Ruffhead, *Life*, 182 n.

McLaverty, 'Contract', 207, noted that there is no evidence to confirm SJ's claim that there was competitive bidding for the translation. For P's agreement on 23 Mar. 1714 with the bookseller Bernard Lintot (1675–1736), see Foxon, *Book Trade*, 51–63, and cf. **135–6** below.

77. For Thomas Osborne's practice of cropping copies of the folio edition and selling them as the more expensive subscription quartos, see **238** n. below.

78–9. While revising *Lives* (1783), SJ wrote to Nichols, 12 Aug. 1782: 'When the sheet that relates the publication of the English Iliad comes to your hand, be so kind as to keep it, till we can talk together. There is a passage in the life of Bowyer upon which we should confer' (*Letters*, iv. 66). SJ referred to Nichols's account of the printing and sale of the *Iliad* in his recent *Biographical and Literary Anecdotes of William Bowyer* (1782), 502–3 (repeated in *Lit. Anec.*, i. 77–8 n., 109–10 n., viii. 169). For SJ's revision of these paragraphs, see Textual Notes (and cf. **87** n., **90** n. below).

79. For Thomas Johnson (*c*.1677–1735), an assiduous publisher of unauthorized editions of English books at The Hague, see D. W. Nichol, 'A Piracy of P's Homer', *N & Q* 231 (1986), 54–6, and B. J. McMullin, 'T. Johnson. Bookseller in The Hague', in R. Harvey, W. Kirsop, and B. J. McMullin (eds.), *An Index of Civilisation: Studies of Printing and Publishing History in Honour of Keith Maslen* (Melbourne, 1993), 99–112.

Johnson published at The Hague P's *Works* (1718) as well as the *Iliad* (6 vols., 1718–21). Foxon, *Book Trade*, 57–8, doubted SJ's claim that this prompted Lintot's duodecimo edition (6 vols., 1720), pointing out that the Dutch piracy sold mostly in Scotland and Ireland rather than London, and that in 1726 Lintot also produced a duodecimo edition of the *Odyssey* when under no threat of a Dutch piracy: 'The real reason for Lintot's difficulties in making a profit on the folios was not the Dutch piracy, but his own over-optimism when he made his contract with Pope.'

SJ inserted the figures in his final sentence in 1783 (see Textual Notes).

80. Spence, i. 82–3, 84; Ruffhead, *Life*, 181.

81. See Spence, i. 45 (P often wrote 'forty or fifty verses on a morning in bed'), 85–6 ('I fell into the method of translating thirty or forty verses before I got up, and

piddled with it the rest of the morning'); and P to Gay, 23 Sept. 1714 ('the demand . . . to write fifty Verses a day') (Warburton (1751 edn.), viii. 149; *Corresp.*, i. 254). For SJ's later 'computation', based on P's 'fifty Verses a day', see **89** below and cf. **300** below.

82. See P to Caryll, 29 June 1714, about identifying one's friends and enemies through a subscription (*Corresp.*, i. 233). SJ no doubt recalls his own experience of publishing his Shakespeare edition (1765) by subscription (cf. **89** and n. below)

   For P's professed political impartiality and for Addison's 'hint', see **74–5** and nn. above. Ruffhead, *Life*, 186, stated that Addison 'encouraged Philips and others, in their rumours against him as a Tory and Jacobite'. P told Caryll, 12 June 1713, that 'the good people [Jacobites] took it very ill of me that I write with *Steele*', and on 1 May 1714 that some call him 'a Papist and a Tory . . . Others have styled me a Whig, because I have been honoured with Mr Addison's good word, and Mr Jervas's good deeds, and of late with my Lord Halifax's patronage' (*Corresp.*, i. 177, 220, both later printed as letters to Addison, i. 197, 209).

   For the *Guardian*, to which P contributed fourteen essays in 1713, see **68** and n. above and 'Addison' **71–3** above.

83. For attacks on P's Greek, see Dennis, *Remarks on Mr. Pope's Homer* (1717) (*Works*, ii. 123–4), and Guerinot, *Pamphlet Attacks*, 13–14, 100–1, 225–6.

   P admitted his 'imperfectness in the language' in 1708: see **383** below. He told Caryll, 1 May 1714: 'Some have said I am not a master in the Greek' (*Corresp.*, i. 220). See also Broome's letter in **86** n. below, Lord Bathurst's testimony about P's knowledge of Greek quoted in *Life*, iii. 403, and, for a modern assessment, *TE*, vii, pp. lxxxi–cvii. He eventually 'sought assistance' from Parnell, Broome, Jortin, and others (see **87–8** and nn. below, *Corresp.*, i. 496 n., and *TE*, vii, p. xxxix).

   For the inability of later writers to add much to Homer, and for Homer's powers of invention, see e.g *Rambler* 121, *Idler* 66, and the preface to Shakespeare (*YW*, ii. 206, iv. 283, vii. 60, 83, 90) and *Life*, v. 79. SJ did, however, also praise Shakespeare ('above all modern writers, the poet of nature') in similar terms to those used here (*YW*, vii. 62, 69–70). For SJ's earlier comparison of Homer and Virgil, see 'Dryden' **304**, and for Homer's permanence ('the most useful truths are always universal, and unconnected with accidents and customs'), see also *Idler* 66 (1759) (*YW*, ii. 206).

   his positions are general: see 'Cowley' **58** and n. and, for the fate of the merely 'local or temporary' as opposed to 'standing relations and general passions', 'Butler' **41** and n. above. SJ stated his position succinctly in *Rambler* 36 (1750): 'poetry has to do rather with the passions of men, which are uniform, than their customs, which are changeable' (*YW*, iii. 199–200). In 'Cowley' **173** above SJ contrasts the permanent delight offered by the ancients, 'through all the changes of human manners', with Cowley's 'deciduous laurel . . . which time has been continually stealing from his brows'.

   Reynolds had stated the 'presiding principle' of all the arts in similar terms in 1771: 'The works, whether of poets, painters, moralists, or historians, which are built upon general nature, live for ever; while those which depend for their existence on particular customs and habits, a partial view of nature, or the fluctuation of fashion, can only be coeval with that which first raised them from obscurity' (*Discourses*, 134).

No source for SJ's story about the reader of a literal Latin translation of Homer has been traced. Editions of Homer with texts in both Greek and Latin were published from the 16th to the 19th centuries. When the painter Allan Ramsay proposed in Apr. 1778 a translation of the *Iliad* into 'poetical prose' as in the Bible (or, worse, Macpherson's *Fingal*), SJ said, 'Sir, you could not read it without the pleasure of verse' (*Life*, iii. 333).

With SJ's contrast here of 'rude simplicity' and 'laboured elegance', cf. his anxious defence of P's 'elegance' in **349–52** below. For 'simplicity' see also **349** below, and 'Dryden' **325** and n. above.

84. Late in life SJ admitted to Windham that 'he had never read through the "Odyssey" completely in the original': see R. W. Ketton-Cremer, *The Early Life of William Windham* (1930), 263. For a 'very erroneous notion... as to Johnson's deficiency in the knowledge of the Greek language', partly caused by his own modesty, see *Life*, iv. 20, 384–5.

85. SJ refers to translations of Homer by Helius Eobanus Hessus (1540); the Abbé de la Valterie (1681); Anne Lefebvre Dacier (1711); George Chapman (1616) (see 'Waller' **106** and 'Dryden' **207, 344** above); Thomas Hobbes (1676); and John Ogilby (1660–5) (see **5** above). P discussed some of these translations in letters in 1708 (see **383** below on the influence of Chapman and Hobbes), and to Parnell in 1714 (*Corresp.*, i. 225, and cf. i. 492).

Leonard Welsted and James Moore Smythe later accused P of plagiarizing Chapman in *One Epistle to Mr. A. Pope* (1730), 10. Thomas Warton owned P's copy of Chapman, 'in which he has noted many of Chapman's absolute interpolations, extending sometimes to the length of a paragraph of twelve lines. A diligent observer will easily discern, that Pope was no careless reader of his rude predecessor' (*History of English Poetry*, iii (1781), 444). For P's notes on Chapman, see *TE*, x. 474–91, and, for a comparison of their translations, see Shankman, *P's Iliad*, 120–8. SJ included some 120 quotations from Chapman in the *Dict.*, increased to 323 in the 4th edition (1773).

86. SJ states more bluntly in **353** below that the 'copious notes... were undoubtedly written to swell the volumes'. He defines 'A pamphlet' as 'A small book; properly a book sold unbound, and only stitched' (*Dict.*). On 25 Apr. 1778 he dismissed the notion that 'a pamphlet meant a prose piece' (*Life*, iii. 319 and n.).

For P's reluctant dependence on Madame Dacier's notes, see Williams, *P, Homer & Manliness*, 147–53. He later told Broome, 20 Jan. 1726, to acknowledge his 'free use' of Dacier in the notes to the *Odyssey* (*Corresp.*, ii. 363). Dacier criticized P's preface to the *Iliad* in a new edition of her own translation (Paris, 1719). For Curll's mischievous publication of *Madam Dacier's Remarks upon Mr. Pope's Account of Homer* (1724), see Guerinot, *Pamphlet Attacks*, 78, 86–8, and, for P's discomfort, see *Corresp.*, ii. 158, and the long reply in his 'Postscript' to the *Odyssey* (*TE*, x. 391–7).

no man loves to be indebted to his contemporaries: cf. 'Milton' **277** above ('From his contemporaries he neither courted nor received support'). For 'common readers', see 'Cowley' **65** and n. above.

Eustathius, Archbishop of Thessalonica, was a 12th-century commentator on Homer. Broome told Fenton, 15 June 1728, that P 'is no master of Greek... if he can translate ten lines of Eustathius I will own myself unjust and unworthy'

(*Corresp.*, ii. 500). There are several copies of Eustathius in the Sale Catalogue of SJ's library (1785).

87. For Broome's 'Industry as the Annotator in part upon the *Iliad*, and entirely upon the *Odyssey*', see his *Poems on Several Occasions* (1727), 3, and 'Broome' 5 and n. above.

SJ's main source is Fenton to P, Sept. 1718 (*Corresp.*, i. 496–7), which he would find among the Homer MSS, since P wrote some of his translation on the back of it: cf. 95 below. For Broome's work on Eustathius, see *Corresp.*, i. 266, 276, 297, and 'Broome' 4–5 and nn. above.

John Jortin (1698–1770), later well known as a scholar and historian, was recommended to P by Styan Thirlby (1686?–1753) of Jesus College, Cambridge. SJ had used some of Thirlby's MS notes on Shakespeare in 1765 (*YW*, vii, pp. xli, 261, etc.), and later collaborated with Nichols, who published a note about him in *Sel. Collection*, vi. 114–15 n., on an article about Thirlby in *Gent. Mag.* (1784), 260–2, 893. See also *J. Misc.*, ii. 430–1, and *Life*, iv. 161 and n.

For Jortin's account of working for P, and P's lack of curiosity about him, see Nichols, *Anecdotes of Bowyer* (1782), 257–65, and *Lit. Anec.*, ii. 556–7 n., and Jortin's *Tracts, Philological, Critical, and Miscellaneous* (2 vols., 1790), ii. 519–21. SJ inserted 'and who professed to have forgotten the terms on which he worked' in 1783, after reading Jortin's statement in *Anecdotes of Bowyer* (1782), 258 n. (cf. 78–9 n. above): 'I cannot recollect what Mr. *Pope* allowed for each book of *Homer*; I have a notion that it was three or four guineas'. 'Scrutator' (John Loveday) in *Gent. Mag.* (1781), 358, believed that P also employed William Peche (or Peachey) (1704–28) of St John's, Oxford: see *Corresp.*, i. 448 n.

With Fenton's 'mercantile' terms, cf. SJ's comments in 'Blackmore' 8, 18 above.

In the last sentence SJ mistranscribed Fenton's 'you return' as 'the return' in the MS, followed by all later editions: see Textual Notes.

88. SJ's first sentence still draws on Fenton's letter (see 87 n. above). For P's 'pain in the correcting' of Parnell's 'Life' of Homer, see Spence, i. 84, and for 'harsh' language, see 367 below and 'Milton' 177 and n. above.

P told Spence in 1735 that 'I began translating the *Iliad* in the year 1712', but said elsewhere that he started in 1713 and that it took him six years (Spence, i. 26 and n., 68 and n., 82). *The Iliad* appeared in 6 vols. between June 1715 and May 1720 (see 100 and n. below).

89. For P's 'fifty lines a day', see 81 above. For SJ's lifelong interest in such calculations (such as plans for reading so many lines of Greek or biblical verses per day), see also 'Swift' 133 and n. above and *Life*, i. 72 and nn.

the distance . . . between actual performances and speculative possibility: SJ recalls such delayed projects of his own as the *Dict.* and the Shakespeare edition (*Life*, i. 186, 291, 319), quite apart from the *Prefaces* he was still writing. Cf. *Adventurer* 128 (1754): 'We can conceive so much more than we can accomplish, that whoever tries his own actions by his imagination, may appear despicable in his own eyes' (*YW*, ii. 480). He told Charles Burney, 8 Mar. 1758: 'my Shakespeare will not be out so soon as I promised my subscribers; but I did not promise them more than I promised myself' (*Letters*, i. 159). For this recurrent topic, see also *Ramblers* 8, 14, 17 (1750), 122 (1751), 207 (1752), *Adventurers* 45 (1753), 138 (1754), the preface to the *Dict.* ('Such is design, while it is yet at a distance from execution', *OASJ*, 318), *Idler* 88

(1759), and *Letters*, i. 117. Cf. also 'great promises and small performance' in 'Milton' **36** above.

In *Rambler* 127 (1751), SJ described the interruptions and distractions experienced by anyone engaged 'in a great undertaking', who promised himself 'an equal and perpetual progression without impediment or disturbance' (*YW*, iv. 313). A few days after undertaking the *Prefaces*, he noted on 6 Apr. 1777: 'the mornings have been devoured by company, and one intrusion has through the whole week succeeded to another' (*YW*, i. 267). In Apr. 1780, while trying to complete 'Rowe', he told Mrs Thrale: 'I have five or six visitors who hindred me, and I have not been quite well' (*Letters*, iii. 238).

Walpole described SJ's last sentence on 14 Apr. 1781 as 'bombast nonsense' (*Corresp.*, xxix. 130). For 'casualties', see **59** and n. above.

90. The 'report' may be the estimate in Ruffhead, *Life*, 182–3, that the subscription (see **75** n. above) amounted to 'no less than 6000*l*.' and that P later sold the translation to Lintot 'for 1200*l*. in money, besides all the books for his subscribers, as well as those he intended for presents'.

SJ left space in the MS for the figures, which Nichols supplied in the proofs, although one had to be corrected later: see Textual Notes, and cf. **125** n., **135** n. below. SJ added 'and only six hundred and sixty were printed' in 1783 (see Textual Notes), having found this information in Nichols's *Anecdotes of Bowyer*, 502: cf. **78–9** n. above. Dryden's *Virgil* (1697) had attracted 349 subscribers, compared to P's 654.

91. Cf. *Imit. Horace, Ep. II. ii.* (1737), ll. 68–9: 'But (thanks to *Homer*) since I live and thrive, | Indebted to no Prince or Peer alive', and cf. **279** and n. below.

For Robert Harley, Earl of Oxford, see **75** above, Spence, i. 227, Warburton (1751 edn.), iv. 67 n., and Ruffhead, *Life*, 396, and, for his negligence as a literary patron, 'Parnell' **5** and 'Rowe' **19–20** above.

For the younger James Craggs's offer of a pension, see Spence, i. 99–100, Warburton (1751 edn.), iv. 67–8 n., and Ruffhead, *Life*, 398. He succeeded Addison as Secretary of State in 1718, but died in 1721: see **404–7** below, 'Addison' **103** and n., and 'Tickell' **14** above.

92. For all his 'discretion', P did invest in the South Sea Company in 1720: see **123** below. For his annuities, see Spence, i. 7–8 and n., and P to Swift, 9 Oct. 1729 (*Corresp.*, iii. 57). For his annuity with John Sheffield, Duke of Buckingham, see Ruffhead, *Life*, 487 n., and 'Sheffield' **21** n. above: Hawkins owned the deed of an annuity of £200 p.a. P purchased from Buckingham (*J's Works* (1787), iv. 95 n.). P stated that he 'bought an Annual Rent or two' in *Imit. Horace, Ep. I. vii.* (1739), l. 71.

93. SJ echoes P's own description of Dryden's *Virgil* as 'the most noble and spirited translation that I know in any language' (see 'Dryden' **306** above). (SJ was at first less decisive, writing 'probably' in the MS rather than 'certainly': see Textual Notes.) On 9 Apr. 1778, SJ replied to 'the vulgar saying, that Pope's Homer was not a good representation of the original' that 'it is the greatest work of the kind that has ever been produced' (*Life*, iii. 256–7). See also **345–52** below.

version: '3. Translation' (*Dict.*): cf. **382** below.

94. For SJ's interest elsewhere in the origins of works of genius, see **99** below and 'Milton' **91** and n. above.

Ruffhead, *Life*, 181–2 n., stated that the *Iliad* MS 'is yet in being, and is designed for some public library, as of singular curiosity'. It is now in the British Library (Add. MSS 4807–8). For Bolingbroke as P's executor and for Mallet as Bolingbroke's editor, see **249** below and 'Mallet' **18** below.

Dr Matthew Maty (1718–76), a friend of Lord Chesterfield and John Nichols (see 'Hammond' **5** above and *Anecdotes of Bowyer* (1782), 480, 607), was Librarian of the British Museum. When it was proposed to SJ in 1755 that Maty should assist him with a projected learned journal, he allegedly responded: '*He*, . . . the little black dog! I'd throw him into the Thames' (*Life*, i. 284). (William Adams claimed that SJ actually said: 'Damn Maty—little dirty-faced dog', etc.: see Boswell, *Making of the Life*, 24.) SJ probably knew that, in a recent review of the *Dict.* in his *Journal britannique*, Maty had in effect accused him of concealing his obligations to Chesterfield: see J. H. Sledd and G. J. Kolb, *Dr. J's Dictionary* (Chicago, 1955), 103–4.

By 'copy', as in **95, 134, 267** below, SJ means '3. The autograph; the original; the archetype; that from which any thing is copied' (*Dict.*), i.e. P's MS.

SJ defines 'To reposite' as 'To lay up; to lodge in a place of safety' (*Dict.*): see **169** below.

95. For P's habit of drafting his translation on the backs of letters, see **87** n. above and **267** below. Thomas Dancastle of Binfield transcribed much of the printer's copy (*Corresp.*, i. 317 n.), but P's own fair copy of part of the translation has survived, inscribed in an unidentified hand: 'Mr. Pope's own hand writing to send to the Press' (see *TE*, vii, plates 7, 9, between 396 and 397).

96. The Homer MSS arrived at Streatham by 10 Dec. 1780 (*Thraliana*, i. 464). SJ himself started the transcriptions, which are on separate sheets in the MS of 'Pope', and George Steevens and (principally) Mrs Thrale continued them. She reported that when this lengthy task was completed, SJ said: 'And now . . . I fear not Mr. Nichols of a pin' (*J. Misc.*, i. 178): see also Hilles, 'Making', 274, and cf. **148** n. below.

Although the transcriptions are often inaccurate or oversimplified, the attempt by Hill (1905) to emend them according to Pope's MSS (see iii. 459 n.) has not been followed here. Their accuracy can be assessed by comparison of the passage from viii. 687 ff. in **98** below with the much corrected MS as transcribed in *TE*, x. 460–2.

97. See *Iliad*, I. 1–34.

97a. Not numbered as a separate paragraph by Hill (1905). This 'more deformed' MS of *Iliad* Bk. I seems not to have survived.

98. See *Iliad*, II. 1–18, 572–81, V. 1–18, VIII. 687–708.

99. Discussing 'his foul copy of the *Iliad*' in 1742, P told Spence that 'those parts which have been the most corrected read the easiest'. Spence commented: 'What a useful study might it be for a poet . . . to compare what was writ first with the successive alterations' (i. 86–7).

SJ's professed concern for his 'tired' 'readers' (cf. **86** above) may reflect Hester Thrale's reaction to the Homer MSS on 10 Dec. 1780: 'All Wood & Wire behind the Scenes sure enough! . . . how very little effect those glorious Verses at the end of the 8th Book of the Iliad have upon one; when one sees 'em all in their Cradles and Clouts . . . Johnson says 'tis pleasant to see the progress of such a Mind: true; but 'tis a malicious Pleasure, Such as Men feel when they watch a Woman at her Toilet . . . Wood & Wire once more! Wood & Wire!' (*Thraliana*, i. 464).

Although SJ used only about half the transcriptions he and his assistants prepared, reducing those from Bk. VIII in **98** in particular, J. T. Callender objected to the inclusion of so many 'specimens' in *Deformities of J* (1782), 56, and *Critical Review of J* (1783), 25.

100. The *Iliad* appeared as follows: vol. i, June 1715; ii, Mar. 1716; iii, June 1717; iv, June 1718; v and vi, May 1720.

SJ found the anecdote about Lord Halifax, who died shortly before the publication of vol. i, in Spence, i. 87–8. In 1734 P described him as 'rather a pretender to taste than really possessed of it' (Spence, i. 99). For his literary patronage, see 'Halifax' **11–15** and nn. above, and for P's friendship with Sir Samuel Garth, see 'Garth' **15** and n. above.

Argutio, the literary patron in *Rambler* 27 (1750), bears some resemblance to Halifax. See also *Rambler* 23 on the self-important critic who 'considers himself as obliged to shew, by some proof of his abilities, that he is not consulted to no purpose, and looks round for every opportunity to propose some specious alteration' (*YW*, iii. 127).

101. *Iliad*, Bks. I–II, were in Halifax's hands by Oct. 1714 (*Corresp.*, i. 263). P's letter, replying to the offer of a pension (Spence, i. 99), is in fact dated 3 Dec. 1714 (Warburton (1751 edn.), vii. 295–6; *Corresp.*, i. 271). Although *BB*, v. 3412 n., had quoted it, Ruffhead, *Life*, 396, referred only briefly to this episode.

SJ's account in **101–2** of Halifax's 'lucky opportunity of securing immortality' and of P's 'sullen coldness' in response to his offer of patronage inevitably recalls his own letter to Lord Chesterfield in 1755 about the *Dict.* (*Life*, i. 260–5). For another poet who, through pride or indolence, failed to secure Halifax's patronage, see 'Smith' **48** above.

102. For SJ's usual scepticism about authors who aspire to 'the dignity of independence', see 'Milton' **169** and n. above, and cf. the advantages of P's financial independence described in **301** below.

Before his death Halifax subscribed for ten copies of the *Iliad*, and P in fact acknowledged his encouragement in his preface (*TE*, vii. 24), and praised his 'Love of Arts' in his 'Farewell to London. In the Year 1715', ll. 25–8 (*TE*, vi. 129). He later parodied a line from a poem by Halifax in *Dunciad* (1729), II. 148 and n. See also *Epistle to Arbuthnot*, ll. 231–48, where the patron 'Bufo', depicted with 'acrimonious contempt' ('Halifax' **11** above), is at least partly based on him, and *Epilogue to the Satires*, II. 77.

103–6. For P's relationship with Addison, see Spence, i. 68–70, Warburton (1751 edn.), iv. 25–7 n., and Ruffhead, *Life*, 186–93, the last interpreting it entirely in terms of Addison's 'jealousy' and 'treachery'.

103. SJ's final sentence, translating *Iliad*, II. 486, probably alludes to Sir William Blackstone (1723–80), the eminent lawyer, who had 'minutely deduced' the 'abatement of kindness' between P and Addison in *BB*, i (2nd edn., 1778), 56–8 n. Younger than SJ, Blackstone had no more 'personal knowledge' of the matter than SJ himself. Warton, *Essay on P*, ii (1782), 243, later praised Blackstone's account. For the decay of friendship, see *Rambler* 64 (1750).

104. For these matters, see **34** n., **66** above, 'Addison' **58, 64, 108** above, and, for SJ's final sentence, Spence, i. 62.

SJ's comment on 'To Mr. Addison, Occasioned by his Dialogues on Medals' derives from P's note (1735) in Warburton (1751 edn.), iii. 294 n. P probably wrote these lines in 1713, when Addison was intending to publish his 'Dialogues' (see **405** n. below and 'Addison' **20, 110** above), but revised them for publication in 1720.

105. For Addison's 'adherents', see 'Addison' **115** and n. above. and for similar 'instigators' of P's quarrel with Cibber, see **232** below.

106. P said in 1730 that Addison was 'very kind to me at first but my bitter enemy afterwards', and in 1739 that he had originally encouraged the *Iliad* translation (Spence, i. 67–8). P complimented him in his preface in 1715 (*TE*, vii. 23) and Addison in turn praised the translation in *Freeholder* 40 (1716).

SJ refers to Jervas's letter to P, 20 Aug. 1714, P's reply, 27 Aug. 1714, and P to Addison, 10 Oct. 1714 (*Corresp.*, i. 244–5, 263–4 and n.). P's other 'letters' to Addison are fabricated from genuine letters to Caryll, but he may have 'composed' this one as late as the 1730s. For P and Ambrose Philips, see **68** above and **115** and n. below.

A mistranscription in SJ's rather loose quotation from P's letter in the MS has been emended. P in fact wrote 'and has seem'd to be no very just one to me'. In revising a line at the foot of the page in the MS, SJ may have meant to write 'have been' for P's 'be', but omitted 'been' as he turned the page: see Textual Notes and Hilles, 'Making', 281.

107. For White Kennett, see 'King' **13** and n. above, and P's *Imit. Horace, Ep. II. ii.* (1737), ll. 220–1.

Hilles, 'Making', 262, suggested that Steevens provided SJ with this extract from the unpublished diary of White Kennett (1660–1728), Bishop of Peterborough (then owned by the Marquis of Lansdowne, now in the British Library). The passage was more probably pointed out to SJ by Nichols, who felt free to quote it in *Gent. Mag.* (Apr. 1781), 164, shortly before the publication of 'Pope'. He may well have come across it during his recent research on Swift: he reprinted it in 1801, and again in *Lit. Anec.*, i. 399–400 (see Swift, *Corresp.*, v. 228–9).

108–9. From Ruffhead, *Life*, 191, drawing on William Ayre, *Memoirs of P* (1745), i. 100–2.

For Steele's 'political fury' and Addison's 'publick business', see 'Addison' **73, 81** above.

109. P's sarcastic letter to Addison, 10 Oct. 1714, which seems to mark the end of 'civilities' between them, may have been composed much later: see **106** n. above and *Corresp.*, i. 263–4 and n.

110. Spence, i. 68–9, quoted at length in 'Tickell' **10** above; Ruffhead, *Life*, 187; and P to Craggs, 15 July 1715 (*Corresp.*, i. 306), also quoted, with variants, in 'Tickell' **9** above.

Tickell's *The First Book of Homer's Iliad* appeared on 8 June 1715, two days after P's *Iliad*, vol. i, and two days before the Whigs impeached Lords Oxford and Bolingbroke (the latter being mentioned in P's 'Preface'): see *Corresp.*, i. 301–2 (for Swift's comment) and *TE*, vii. 24. Lintot told P on 10 June: 'You have Mr Tickles Book to divert one Hour—It is allready condemn'd here and the malice & juggle at Buttons is the conversation of those who have spare moments from Politicks' (*Corresp.*, i. 294).

Tickell's agreement with Tonson to translate the whole *Iliad* for 100 guineas is dated 31 May 1714 (J. Butt, 'A Study of the Life and Work of Thomas Tickell' (B. Litt. thesis, Oxford, 1929), 25 and 99–100). His prefatory 'To the Reader' was conciliatory towards P, explaining that he had abandoned his plan once 'a much abler Hand' undertook the translation, and that he was offering Bk. I only as a specimen to 'bespeak . . . the Favour of the Publick' towards a translation of the *Odyssey*, on which he was already working. As late as Feb. 1723, P claimed not to know whether Tickell had given up this second plan (*Corresp.*, ii. 158, 159).

111. SJ's source is Gay to P, 8 July 1715 (*Corresp.*, i. 305). For the accusation that P was insufficiently 'Homerical', see **349** and n. below.

112. Jacob Tonson owned the copyright of the translations of *Iliad*, Bk. I, by Dryden (see 'Dryden' **151** above), Arthur Mainwaring (in Tonson's *Poetical Miscellanies*, vol. v, 1704), and Tickell: see Lintot's letter to P, 22 June 1715 in the Homer MSS (*Corresp.*, i. 298). When Tonson said in 1730 that 'Maynwaring, whom we hear nothing of now, was the ruling man in all conversations', P added: 'Indeed what he did write had very little merit in it' (Spence, i. 51: see also 'Congreve' **7** above).

William Melmoth compared P's *Iliad* with translations by Denham, Dryden, Congreve, and Tickell in his *Letters on Several Subjects*, ii (1749), 176–207. John Conington later carried out the comparative scheme P had envisaged in his *Oxford Essays* (1858), 'to enable us to measure Pope's superiority to his predecessors': see R. A. Blanchard (ed.), *Discussions of AP* (Boston, 1960), 48–50.

113. Warburton (1751 edn.), iv. 27 n., mentioned that he owned P's annotated copy of Tickell's translation, later seen by Ruffhead, *Life*, 188–9. It was acquired in Feb. 1776 by Isaac Reed, who no doubt showed it to SJ. In 1784 Reed presented it to Richard Hurd, Bishop of Worcester, at the suggestion of Nichols, and it is still in his library at Hartlebury Castle: see Hurd's *Discourse by Way of General Preface to . . . Warburton's Works* (1794), 58 and n., and Nichols, *Lit. Anec.*, v. 640. Before parting with P's notes, Reed transcribed them into another copy now in the Bodleian (with Nichols's letter to Reed of 7 Jan. 1784). See also F. Rosslyn, 'P's Annotations to Tickell's *Iliad*', *RES* 30 (1979), 49–59.

114. Spence, i. 70; Warburton (1751 edn.), iv. 26–7 n. (for P's accusation in a note of 1735); and Ruffhead, *Life*, 188.

P pointedly attributed quotations from Tickell's *Iliad* to Addison in *The Art of Sinking in Poetry* (1728): see 'Tickell' **11** and n. above, and cf. *TE*, vi. 143, 173. In 'Mr. Pope's Welcome from Greece', ll. 151–2, Gay referred to '*Tickell* whose Skiff (in partnership they say) | Set forth for *Greece*, but founder'd in the way'. Steele and Cibber both believed that Addison was the translator (Spence, i. 70 n., 335), as did Edward Young, William Harte, and Lords Bathurst and Lyttelton, according to Warton, *Essay on P*, ii (1782), 246, and *A New and General Biographical Dictionary*, xi (1762), 166–7, claimed that 'the public are pretty well agreed' on the question.

For Tickell's MS of his translation, heavily corrected by Addison, which the printer John Watts claimed to have seen, see *Gent. Mag.* (1779), 257 and (1784), 112, Nichols, *Sel. Collection*, iv (1780), 317 n., and Warton, *Works of P* (1797), i, p. xxx. Richard Hurd later claimed, however, to have persuaded Warburton that Addison was not involved in it: see *Discourse by Way of General Preface* (1794), 62–3.

115. Spence, i. 71–2 (and, for the identity of Charles Gildon's 'thing about Wycherley', see ii. 625); Warburton (1751 edn.), iv. 26, 27 n.; and Ruffhead, *Life*, 192–3. For P and Ambrose Philips, see **68, 106** above, P to Caryll, 8 June 1714 (*Corresp.*, i. 229), and 'A. Philips' **21–2** below. For Addison's stepson, Edward Henry Rich (1698–1721), Earl of Warwick, see 'Addison' **85, 100–1** above.

P's lines on Addison, first published in 1722 and expanded in *Miscellanies* (1727), evolved into the well-known character of 'Atticus' in *Epistle to Arbuthnot* (1734), ll. 193–214. P always denied that he had dared to write the lines only after Addison's death: see the 'Testimonies' prefixed to the *Dunciad*, and his note to the passage in *Epistle to Arbuthnot* (Warburton (1751 edn.), iv. 29 n.; *TE*, iv. 111 n., v. 32–3). Lady Mary Wortley Montagu, Lord Oxford, and John Dennis were among those who saw the lines in Addison's lifetime.

The passage from Spence was transcribed by Mrs Thrale (see Textual Notes). A small error, which reverses P's meaning, was noted by Horne, 'Emendation', 156–7, and has been emended here. Discussing Horne's note in *The Library*, 29 (1974), 226–7, J. P. Hardy and J. D. Fleeman both assumed that the error was SJ's rather than Mrs Thrale's. According to Spence, P said that, if he spoke severely of Addison, 'it should not be in such a dirty way', etc. Mrs Thrale, and later editions, omitted the crucial 'not'. Sensing a problem, Murphy conjecturally emended 'should be' to 'should be not' in *J's Works* (1792).

Mrs Thrale's spelling of 'grosly' earlier in the passage, which is not in the *Dict.* but survived in 1781–3, has also been emended.

116. See Ruffhead, *Life*, 192 n.; and Atterbury to P, 26 Feb. 1722 (Warburton (1751 edn.), viii. 108–9; *Corresp.*, ii. 104–5).

117. Ruffhead, *Life*, 197, relying on misdated letters (see *Corresp.*, i. 336–7), stated that P and his parents moved to Twickenham by the end of 1715. They in fact moved from Binfield to Chiswick in Apr. 1716, and to Twickenham not before *c.* Mar. 1719.

Ruffhead, *Life*, 199, 407 n., also quoted letters showing that P had only a lifetime lease of the house at Twickenham. He told Hugh Bethel, 9 Aug. 1726: 'I am but a *Lodger* here: this is not an abiding City. I am only to stay out my lease, for what has Perpetuity and mortal man to do with each other?' (*Corresp.*, ii. 387). He referred in *Imit. Horace, Sat. II. ii.* (1734), l. 136, to his 'five acres . . . of rented land': cf. also ll. 161–6. His landlord was the merchant Thomas Vernon of Twickenham Park: when his widow died in 1742, P did not take the opportunity of buying the freehold (*Corresp.*, ii. 82 and n. iv. 387).

118. For P's grotto, and his views on gardening, see Spence, i. 157, 249–57, and Warburton (1751 edn.), v. 38 n.

Cf. *Imit. Horace, Sat. II. i.* (1733), l. 130 ('Now, forms my Quincunx, and now ranks my Vines'), quoted under the long definition of 'Quincunx' as a disposition of five trees in the *Dict.* (cf. **119** n. below); and his earlier couplet (ll. 123–4) on the grotto as a refuge from the din of the world. The *Dict.* does not include the spelling 'fossile', except as the French equivalent of 'fossil'.

Lady Mary Wortley Montagu mentioned the grotto P was creating in the passage to his garden under the London road in Apr. 1722 (*Complete Letters*, ed.

R. Halsband (3 vols., Oxford, 1965–7), ii. 15). He himself did so in July 1723 and later described it to Edward Blount, 2 June 1725 (Warburton (1751 edn.), viii. 37). Swift also referred to it three months later (*Corresp.*, ii. 125, 296–7, 325–6). For a modern account, see Mack, *Garden*, ch. 2 ('The Shadowy Cave').

SJ did not believe that 'cares and passions' could be 'excluded' from any location: cf. 'Cowley' **45** above.

119. SJ had in fact been impressed by a natural 'grotto' or cave in a landscape of 'terrifick grandeur' at Hawkstone in 1774 (*YW*, i. 174–5). For his scepticism about gardening, see also 'Shenstone' **10** and n. below.

For SJ's implicit equation of P's preoccupation with his grotto with his own liking for 'small experiments' such as 'distilling', see *Life*, iv. 9 and cf. iii. 398. P's 'quincunx' (**118** above) would recall Sir Thomas Browne's interest in that topic in *Religio Medici* (mentioned in a quotation under 'Quincunx' in the *Dict.*), which suggested 'that nature and art had no other purpose than to exemplify and imitate a Quincunx': 'Some of the most pleasing performances have been produced by learning and genius exercised upon subjects of little importance. It seems to have been, in all ages, the pride of wit, to shew how it could exalt the low, and amplify the little' ('Life of Browne' (1756), pp. xxiv–xxv). When Reynolds 'observed that a man's real character was betrayed by his amusements, SJ replied: "Yes, Sir; no man is a hypocrite in his pleasures" ' (*Life*, iv. 316).

For 'malicious wonder' at the weaknesses of 'greatness', see **290** below and 'Denham' **11** and n. above, and for comments on 'elevated genius' as observed by those of 'a lower station', in a similarly constructed sentence ('whether it be that . . . or that'), see 'Savage' **1** and n. above. Addison referred in *Spectator* 256 (1711) to those who 'find a Pleasure in . . . spreading abroad the Weaknesses of an exalted Character'.

120. P's *Works* (1717) in fact appeared in both quarto and folio format: for the significance of this collection, published when P was only 29, see McLaverty, *P, Print and Meaning*, 46–81. His 'Preface' stated: 'For what I have publish'd, I can only hope to be pardon'd; but for what I have burn'd, I deserve to be prais'd' (*TE*, i. 8). For passages originally omitted from the 'Preface' itself, see Warburton (1751 edn.), i, pp. x–xii.

P started printing omitted or variant passages in his *Works*, vol. ii (1735), a practice continued by Warburton in 1751 (see *TE*, i, pp. xvi–xvii). Jonathan Richardson the Younger collated several of P's MSS with the printed texts in the poet's lifetime: see *Richardsoniana* (1776), 264, and, for his collations of two MSS of *The Dunciad*, now lost, see Mack, *Last and Greatest Art*, 97–155, and D. L. Vander Meulen, *P's Dunciad of 1728: A History and Facsimile* (Charlottesville, Va., 1991). See also **362** below. P's historical, critical, and autobiographical annotation of his own poetry, especially in the octavo editions of his *Works* from 1735, has been discussed by McLaverty, *P, Print and Meaning*, 209–41, who concludes that his notes 'succeeded in their task of mesmerizing posterity'.

According to Spence, i. 194, P transcribed ll. 41–2 of Waller's 'Upon the Earl of Roscommon's Translation of Horace, "De Arte Poetica" ' in a copy of Denham's *Cooper's Hill*: 'Poets lose half the praise they should have got, | Could it be known what they discreetly blot.' Addison quoted the couplet in *Spectator* 179 (1711), as did SJ under 'Discreetly' in the *Dict.*, and in *Idler* 78 (1759) (*YW*, ii. 245).

Quoting SJ's reference to P's 'voracity of fame', R. Terry, *Poetry and the Making of the English Literary Past* (2001), 73 and n., notes that P was 'also uncommonly prolific in renouncing or deriding it'.

121. P's father was in fact aged 71 when he died on 23 Oct. 1717 at Chiswick, not Twickenham (see **117** n. above). P later erected a monument to both his parents at Twickenham (Warburton (1751 edn.), ix. 367). For P's descriptions of his father, see *Epistle to Arbuthnot*, ll. 388–405, and *Imit. Horace, Ep. II. ii.* (1737), ll. 54–67. On 27 Nov. 1717 he wrote that his father's death 'has left me to the ticklish Management of a narrow Fortune, where every false Step is dangerous' (*Corresp.*, i. 455): cf. **2, 9** above.

122. P completed the *Iliad* in May 1720 (see **100** n. above).

For *Homerides: Or, A Letter to Mr. Pope* (1715) by Thomas Burnet (1694–1753) and George Duckett (see 'Smith' **56–9, 71** above), and a further versified *Homerides* (1716) by the same authors, see *Corresp.*, i. 291, and Guerinot, *Pamphlet Attacks*, 20–3, 35–7. Burnet told Duckett, 19 Feb. 1714, that Addison advised him 'to strike out all the Reflections upon the poor fellow's person', but without dissuading him from publication: see *Letters of Thomas Burnet to George Duckett 1712–1722*, ed. D. Nichol Smith (Oxford, 1914), 81–2.

Dennis (see **40** and n. above) published *Remarks on Mr. Pope's Homer* in 1717, and later dedicated *Remarks on the Rape of the Lock* (1728) to Duckett, as a fellow-victim of P (*Works*, ii. 115–61, 514). For P's revenge for these and other affronts, see **152–3** and nn. below.

123. For the South Sea Bubble of 1720, see also **129** n. below and 'Gay' **14** above. P stated in *Imit. Horace, Sat. II. ii.* (1734), ll. 133–4, that at its height he had been temporarily 'the Lord of Thousands'. He told Atterbury, 23 Sept. 1720, that he was one of those lucky enough 'to remain with half of what they imagined they had' (Warburton (1751 edn.), viii. 89–90; *Corresp.*, ii. 53, and cf. i. 379, ii. 42, 58). Warburton, iv. 91 n., vi. 9 n. (and cf. viii. 53–9), stated that P's subscription had been worth £20,000 or £30,000 before the crash, and that, when James Craggs gave him some South Sea subscriptions, P was 'so indifferent…as to neglect making any benefit of them'. See also *Imit. Horace, Ep. I. vii.* (1739), ll. 65–8.

124. Warburton (1751 edn.), vii. 364–6, and Ruffhead, *Life*, 402.

For P's edition of Parnell's *Poems on Several Occasions* (1722 for Dec. 1721), see 'Parnell' **9** and n. above. In his prefatory 'Epistle to Robert Earl of Oxford', P praised Oxford's 'dauntless Conduct' in the face of 'Princely Power and Popular Hatred' when imprisoned in the Tower in 1715 (*Corresp.*, i. 307). According to Warton, *Essay on P*, ii (1782), 389, Bolingbroke was mortified by P's praise of Oxford. Although P admired Oxford's courage ('He was a steady man and had a great firmness of soul'), he later criticized him as an administrator (Spence, i. 95–7).

125. The misdating of P's edition derives from Ruffhead, *Life*, 203. Although P's contract with Tonson is dated 1721 and the separate title pages of the six volumes are dated 1723, the *Works of Shakespear* in fact appeared on 12 Mar. 1725. Fenton, Gay, and 'a man or two…at Oxford' assisted P with it: see 'Fenton' **10** n. above, *Gent. Mag* (1787), i. 76, and Sherburn, *Early Career*, 234.

SJ left spaces in the MS and proofs for some of the figures. Nichols could supply 'one hundred and forty', but not a precise figure for the total of copies sold:

see Textual Notes. Four hundred and eleven subscribers in fact took 417 copies of the Shakespeare at 5 guineas a set. For Nichols's later version of the figures, see *Gent. Mag.* (1787), 76, referring to the Tonson trade sale in 1767, and *Lit. Anec.*, v. 597.

126. The figure in the first sentence was no doubt supplied by Nichols, who repeated it in *Lit. Anec.*, v. 597.

Lewis Theobald (1688–1744) criticized P's edition in *Shakespeare Restored* (1726). In the preface to his own *Works of Shakespeare* (7 vols., 1733), he thanked Styan Thirlby (see 87 and n. above) and Hawley Bishop for assistance, while acknowledging (i, p. xlvi) that his chief debt was to William Warburton, with whom P himself was later to become so heavily involved (see 184–94 below). Theobald omitted this tribute in the 2nd edition of 1740. See P. Seary, *Lewis Theobald and the Editing of Shakespeare* (Oxford, 1990), esp. 102–30. According to Warburton, Theobald's contract with Tonson brought him 1,100 guineas, making him 'the best paid of all the early editors of Shakespeare' (Seary, *Theobald*, 123–4).

Perhaps because of Theobald's recent death, SJ stated in *Miscellaneous Observations on . . . Macbeth* (1745) that, even when erroneous, his emendations of Shakespeare should be 'treated with indulgence and respect'. In the *Proposals* (1756) for his own edition, he wrote that Theobald 'considered learning only as an instrument of gain', and, in effect, wrote notes merely to fill the page. In 1765 he described him even more bluntly as 'a man of narrow comprehension and small acquisitions . . . but zealous for minute accuracy, and not negligent in pursuing it': 'Theobald, thus weak and ignorant, thus mean and faithless, thus petulant and ostentatious, by the good luck of having Pope for his enemy, has escaped, and escaped alone, with reputation, from this undertaking' (*YW*, vii. 8, 56, 95–6, and cf. viii. 734). See also 145, 237 below, and *Life*, i. 329.

SJ may respond here to Thomas Warton's defence of Theobald's editorial methods in *Observations on the Faerie Queene* (2nd edn., 1762), ii. 264–5, itself an apparent reaction to SJ's *Proposals* (1756). See Seary, *Theobald*, 207–12, and, for the effect of SJ's various dismissive references on Theobald's subsequent reputation, his ch. I, 1–11 ('Theobald and the Johnsonian Shadow'). Joseph Warton, *Essay on P*, ii (1782), 235–6, implicitly supported his brother by claiming that the 'very dull and laborious' Theobald 'discovered the true and rational method of correcting and illustrating his author'.

127. SJ noted in 1765 that P 'past the latter part of his life in a state of hostility with verbal criticism' (*YW*, vii. 95). For his ridicule of editors and commentators, including Theobald and Bentley, see the mock-scholarly apparatus to the *Dunciad Variorum* (1729), *Epistle to Arbuthnot*, ll. 157–72, Spence, i. 242, and 'Mallet' 7 and n. below. Although P professed to be above 'such minute employment', SJ will later emphasize the 'minute and punctilious observation' with which he corrected his own poems (305 below), and contrast the 'minute attention' of his 'notions' with Dryden's 'comprehensive speculation' (308 below).

128. Ruffhead, *Life*, 203–5.

SJ stated in 1765 that P 'collated the old copies, which none had thought to examine before, and restored many lines to their integrity', but 'rejected whatever he disliked, and thought more of amputation than of cure'. Yet P apparently thought collation 'unworthy of his abilities', referring in his preface to 'the dull duty of an editor': as SJ commented, 'He understood but half his undertaking. The duty of a collator is indeed dull, yet, like other tedious tasks, is very necessary' (*YW*, vii. 94). P told Tonson, 3 Sept. 1721, that he had 'got a Man or two at Oxford to ease me of part of the drudgery of Shakespear', and in *c.* May 1722 described collecting 'Parties of my acquaintance ev'ry night, to collate the several Editions of Shakespear's single Plays, 5 of which I have ingaged to this design' (*Corresp.*, ii. 81, 118).

While P may have 'understood but half his undertaking' as an editor, SJ had praised his preface for 'elegance of composition and justness of remark', especially in the 'general criticism on his authour' (*YW*, vii. 94–5). According to Hester Thrale, SJ denied that his own preface (1765) was superior to P's: 'I fear not says he, the little Fellow has done Wonders' (*Thraliana*, i. 164). For Dryden's 'character' of Shakespeare, see 'Dryden' **198** and n. above and *YW*, viii. 112; and, for an earlier editor's contribution to Shakespeare's popularity, see 'Rowe' **18** above.

129. The proposals for the *Odyssey* were in fact dated 10 Jan. 1725 (*TE*, vii, p. xliii). Gay told Swift, 3 Feb. 1723: 'He has engag'd to translate the Odyssey in three years, I believe rather out of a prospect of Gain than inclination, for I am persuaded he bore his part in the loss of the Southsea' (*Letters*, ed. C. F. Burgess (Oxford, 1966), 43; cf. **123** above).

For SJ's earlier accounts of the troubled collaboration on the *Odyssey*, see 'Fenton' **10** and 'Broome' **5–9** above. Although Ruffhead's claim (205–6) that Broome and Fenton were already engaged on a translation of the *Odyssey* has been questioned, this was rumoured as early as 1730 (Spence, i. 89–90), and repeated by Philip Nichols in *BB*, v (1760), 3411 n., as 'Communicated by Mr. Fenton'.

130. Ruffhead, *Life*, 206–7.

The *London Journal* noted the implications of the wording of the patent prefixed to the *Odyssey* as early as 17 July 1725: see Sherburn, *Early Career*, 263, 313 (for the text of the patent), and cf. 'Broome' **6** n. above.

131–2. In the MS the account of the Atterbury trial is marked for insertion from the appended material: see Textual Notes.

131. Spence, i. 102–3.

Francis Atterbury (1663–1732), Bishop of Rochester (1713), wrote to P, 8 Nov. 1717, suggesting that he abandon Roman Catholicism after the death of his father. P replied on 20 Nov.: 'Whether the change would be to my spiritual advantage, God only knows: this I know, that I mean as well in the religion I now profess, as I can possibly ever do in another . . . It is certain, all of the beneficial circumstances of life, and all the shining ones, lie on the part you would invite me to' (Warburton (1751 edn.), viii. 83, 86; Ruffhead, *Life*, 536–40; *Corresp.*, i. 451, 453–4). Warburton also failed to persuade P to change his religion (Spence, i. 156). For P's Catholicism and the effect of anti-Catholic penal laws, see Mack, *AP*, 26–7, 39–44, 61–5, 80–4, 299–301, 326–8, 336–9.

Atterbury was arrested for Jacobite conspiracy on 24 Aug. 1722 and tried for high treason before the House of Lords. At his trial on 10 May 1723, P testified that, having been 'for these Two or Three last Years, the most constant Companion of his Lordship's Hours . . . his Lordship never in the least discover'd any Thoughts or Intentions like those now charged upon him' (William Wynne, *The Defense of Francis, Late Lord Bishop of Rochester* (1723), 41). As he told Spence in

1735, 'though I had but ten words to say . . . I made two or three blunders in it, and that notwithstanding the first row of Lords (which was all I could see) were mostly of my acquaintance' (i. 102–3). P told Atterbury that he was proud to support him in this crisis in a letter of May 1723: for his obvious anxiety as the trial began, see also his letter of 6 May to Lord Harcourt (*Corresp.*, ii. 169, 171–2). Warton, *Essay on P*, ii (1782), 176, claimed that P had 'faltered so much as to be hardly intelligible' at the trial.

Atterbury was found guilty and banished on 15 May. See also **442** n. below, 'Yalden' **11–13** above, and, for the trial and its background, Sherburn, *Early Career*, 228–30, Mack, *AP*, 394–402, and E. Cruickshanks and J. Black (eds.), *The Jacobite Challenge* (Edinburgh, 1987), 92–106. For SJ's own 'slow, deliberate, and distinct' manner as a witness at Baretti's trial in 1769, see *Life*, ii. 98.

132. SJ quotes P to Atterbury, 20 Apr. 1723. Atterbury apparently gave him the folio Bible on 17 June (Warburton (1751 edn.), viii. 131; *Corresp.*, ii. 168, 169 n.). In Atterbury's *Epistolary Corresp.*, ii (1783), 79–82 n., Nichols doubted Lord Chesterfield's claim that P showed him the Bible on the next day (*Miscellaneous Works* (1777), i. 279–80).

For P's epitaph on Atterbury and his daughter, see **442** and n. below.

133. See 'Fenton' **10** and 'Broome' **5–8** and nn. above, for SJ's earlier discussions of 'the several shares' in the *Odyssey*. He had received information on this from Warburton in 1773 and Joseph Warton in May 1780 (*Letters*, iii. 259), as well as from Bennet Langton and George Steevens (see headnote and **134** n. below).

The final note to the *Odyssey*, signed by Broome, implied that he had translated only three books (rather than eight) and Fenton only two (rather than four). Broome also provided the notes (see **355** below and 'Broome' **5** n. above). Unknown to Broome and Fenton, Henry Layng also helped P with parts of Bks. X and XV (Spence, i. 89).

134. P told Spence in 1742 that his own books of the *Odyssey* needed less correction than the earlier *Iliad*, because 'I was got to a greater knack of translating him' (Spence, i. 86). Broome's eight books and one of Fenton's four are not among the Homer MSS (British Library, Add. MS 4809).

Some of this information appears in SJ's early notes for 'Pope' (fo. 172^r), presumably from Steevens's letter of 27 Oct. 1780 (see headnote), replying to SJ's questions about 'a disproportion between the prices paid by Pope to Fenton, and his coadjutor'. Steevens 'was once told (by Spence or Dr [Gloster] Ridley) that Pope complained he had more trouble in the revisal of a single book translated by Broome, than with all that were executed by Fenton. Three of Fenton's books, in his own handwriting, are preserved in the Museum, & countenance, on one part, the observation of Pope; for I do not think that in any one of these he made any more than a dozen corrections.' Steevens commented on P's correction of Broome's books: 'To the weary translator of thirty-six books of Homer, a laborious revision of eight more, was as unwelcome as it might be unexpected' (Pierpont Morgan Library).

P in fact corrected Fenton's Bks. I and IV more heavily than his Bk. XX. He told Broome, 10 Feb. 1722, that he would 'make the whole as finished and spirited as I am able, by giving the last touches'. For his trouble in correcting Broome's translations, see also his letter of 30 Dec. 1725 (*Corresp.*, ii. 102, 356).

135. Spence, i. 86; and Ruffhead, *Life*, 205–6, stating that Broome received £600 and Fenton £300, and defending P's 'candid and disinterested conduct'.

For the implications of P's contract with Lintot for the *Odyssey*, see Foxon, *Book Trade*, 91–101, and for his complaints from 1724 about Lintot as a 'scoundrel', *Corresp.*, ii. 214, 287, 431–2, 470, iii. 294.

SJ left spaces in the MS for the figures, which Nichols supplied in proof: see Textual Notes. Six hundred and ten subscribers in fact took 1,057 sets of the *Odyssey*. For P's solicitation of subscribers, see e.g. *Corresp.*, ii. 156–7, 265, 275–7, 299. P made some £5,000, and his collaborators, who did half the work, some £900.

P told Swift, 14 Sept. 1725: 'I mean no more Translations, but something domestic, fit for my own country, and for my own time' (*Corresp.*, ii. 321–2).

136. Although Ruffhead, *Life*, 207, does not mention Lintot's lawsuit, and *BB*, v. 3411, refers only to his 'loud complaints', P's letter of 18 Mar. 1725 to the lawyer William Fortescue (1687–1749) quotes Fortescue's advice to Lintot: 'whatever you do, don't go to Law!' (*Corresp.*, ii. 290). James McLaverty advises me that it is unlikely that Lintot did so. SJ had conceivably heard more on the subject from Lintot's son (see **164** below). For Bernard Lintot in *The Dunciad*, see i. 40, ii. 53 ff., and for P's later legal dispute with Henry Lintot over *The Dunciad* in Feb. 1743, see Foxon, *Book Trade*, 249–50.

137–8. In the MS SJ calls for the insertion of the account of Joseph Spence (1699–1768) from the appended materials. See also **139** n. below. For his *Essay on Pope's Odyssey* (1726–7) and the origins of his friendship with P, see A. Wright, *Joseph Spence* (Chicago, 1950), 9–41, and Spence, i, pp. xxiii–xxvii.

137. When he published his *Essay*, Spence had in fact not yet succeeded the elder Thomas Warton as Professor of Poetry at Oxford, as Warton, *Works of P* (1797), i, pp. xxxv–xxxvi, noted. For P's efforts to assist Spence's election on 11 July 1728, see Wright, *Spence*, 33.

Fenton told Broome, 10 June 1726, that the *Essay* 'appears to be writ with so much candour that I fancy the world will say that we have employed a friend to fight booty against us, or perhaps that it is one of our own productions' (*Corresp.*, ii. 379). Spence already knew that the translation was a collaboration and that he might at times be discussing as P's the work of his assistants (*Essay*, Pt. i, sig. A4ᵛ).

With SJ's assessment of Spence's learning and intellect, cf. his comment on Addison's poetry in 'Addison' **126** above ('He thinks justly; but he thinks faintly'), and his very different characterization of Warburton in **184–5** below. SJ referred in 1763 to 'That foolish fellow Spence' (*Life*, i. 466), and described him in Oct. 1773 as 'a weak conceited man' and merely 'a pretty scholar'. Having printed these comments in his *Tour to the Hebrides* (1785), Boswell felt bound to add in his 3rd edition (1786) Bennet Langton's objection that he had heard SJ speak respectfully of Spence, and that he had recommended his *Essay* in the preface to Dodsley's *Preceptor* (1748) (*Life*, v. 317 and n.). (For Langton's friendship with Spence in the 1750s, see Boswell, *Members of the Club*, 422–4.) After his only known meeting with Spence, mentioned by Thomas Tyers in Dec. 1784, SJ supposedly said that Spence 'probably may think he visited a bear' (*J. Misc.*, ii. 348).

Joseph Warton described Spence as 'a perfect Master of all Classical Learning, of solid Judgment and refined Taste' in his *Works of Virgil* (1753), i. 19, and in his

Essay on P, ii (1782), 239, paid him a tribute which *Gent. Mag.* (1782), 298, contrasted with SJ's 'frigid' remarks here. Warton objected again in *Works of P* (1797), i, pp. xvii, xxxv–xxxvi: 'I know no critical treatise better calculated to form the taste of young men of genius, than this *Essay on the Odyssey.*' SJ would not necessarily have been persuaded by Warton's citation of similar praise by Akenside and James Harris.

display beauties . . . expose faults: SJ defines 'Critick' as '1. A man skilled in the art of judging of literature; a man able to distinguish the beauties and faults of writing' (*Dict.*). Dennis had noted that 'to find faults requires but common Sense; but to discern rare Beauties, requires a rare Genius' (*Works*, ii. 379). For SJ's complaint that the criticism of Elizabeth Montagu and Joseph Warton failed to discover 'latent' beauties, see *OASJ*, 492, and *Life*, ii. 88, and cf. 'Smith' **62** above. Spence himself wrote: 'it is not enough that Criticism is rational; it shou'd ever be Human and Good-natur'd . . . We ought to shew faults, but we ought never to shew malice' (*Essay*, i. 144, 147).

138. P and Spence met by 1727. According to a MS note by Nichols: 'When Spence had published his first part of the Essay on the Odyssey, Pope immediately introduced himself and interceded for better treatment in the second' (Boswell, *Catalogue*, C 2094). (Like Nichols's preceding note on a couplet omitted from *Windsor Forest*, this may have originated with Spence and been passed on by Dr Gloster Ridley to George Steevens.) Spence acknowledged in *Essay*, ii (1727), 9, that he now had 'the advantage of Mr. *Pope*'s own Observations in several Points'. Through Robert Lowth, Bishop of London, Joseph Warton saw a copy of the *Essay* 'with marginal observations written in Pope's own hand, and generally acknowledging the justness of Spence's observations' (*Essay on P*, ii (1782), 239; *Works of P* (1797), i, p. xxxvi). For P's annotations in the MS of Pt. ii of the *Essay*, see *TE*, x. 594–605. SJ, of course, uses Spence's 'memorials' of P's conversation throughout 'Pope': see headnote.

Spence in fact obtained most of his ecclesiastical preferments after P's death. His patron, Henry Fiennes Clinton (1720–94), Earl of Lincoln, influenced his appointment in 1742 to the Chair of Modern History at Oxford, and to the living of Great Horwood, Bucks.: see Wright, *Spence*, 68.

139. See Spence, i. 4–5; Warburton (1751 edn.), ix. 79 and n.; Ruffhead, *Life*, 211–12. The late insertion of **137–8** in the MS caused SJ to revise his original opening words in the proofs, at Nichols's suggestion: see Textual Notes.

The accident occurred in Sept. 1726, when P was returning from a visit to Bolingbroke: for accounts by Gay, Arbuthnot, and Bolingbroke, see *Corresp.*, ii. 399–403.

140. Ruffhead, *Life*, 212–13; and Voltaire to P, Sept. 1726 (*Corresp.*, ii. 399).

Ruffhead no doubt heard the story of Voltaire's conversation at P's table from Warburton, since Thomas Gray also recorded it as told by Warburton to William Mason (D. C. Tovey, *Gray and his Friends* (Cambridge, 1890), 286 n.). Warburton was probably also the source for the charge that Voltaire spied for Walpole: see Mack, *AP*, 446, 891 n. SJ's criticism of Voltaire's views on Shakespeare in 1765 (*YW*, vii. 65–8) provoked a reply in the *Dictionnaire philosophique* (*Life*, i. 499 and n.).

141. Although Warburton (1751 edn.), ix. 87, printed P's letter to Swift, 8 Mar. 1727, on the subject (*Corresp.*, ii. 426), Ruffhead, *Life*, 207, referred only briefly to their joint *Miscellanies* (4 vols., 1727–32): for their publication after Swift's visit to England in 1727, see 'Swift' **84** above.

In 'Memoirs of P. P. Clerk of this Parish' P and Gay satirized Gilbert Burnet's *History* (1724), although P denied this in the *Dunciad* (*TE*, v. 34). Ruffhead, *Life*, 310 n., noted that in 'Stradling *versus* Stiles' P was assisted by the lawyer William Fortescue (see **136** n. above, and Spence, i. 57), to whom he later addressed *Imit. Horace, Sat. II. i.* (1733). The preface to *Miscellanies*, signed by both P and Swift, was probably by P (*Prose Works*, ii. 101–28, 131–42, 83–98). His 'complaint' alluded to Curll's unauthorized publication of some of his letters in 1726 (see **29** above and **142** and n. below), but was also preparing the ground for an 'authentic' edition of his letters, as SJ notes in **169** below. Cf. Misellus' letter in *Rambler* 16 (1750): 'You must have read in Pope and Swift how men of parts have had their closets rifled, and their cabinets broke open at the instigation of piratical book-sellers, for the profit of their works' (*YW*, iii. 90). In 1777 Mrs Thrale discussed with SJ the inclusion of his own writings, 'without his Knowledge or Consent', in Thomas Davies's *Miscellaneous and Fugitive Pieces* (3 vols., 1773–4): 'what says I would Pope have done had they served him so? we should never have heard the last on't to be sure replied he but then Pope Madam was a narrow Man' (*Thraliana*, i. 164).

SJ defines 'Romantick' as '2. Improbable; false' (cf. **199** below), and 'To wind' (last sentence) as '4. To nose; to follow by the scent' (*Dict.*).

142. P's letters to Henry Cromwell had appeared in Curll's *Miscellanea* (1727 for 1726). For Elizabeth Thomas, see **25** n. above.

143. This paragraph was inserted from materials appended to the MS: see Textual Notes.

Peri Bathous; or, Martinus Scriblerus, his Treatise of the Art of Sinking in Poetry (1728) (*Prose Works*, ii. 186–234) is usually interpreted as P's calculated provoca-tion of his enemies, to justify his forthcoming attack on them in the *Dunciad* (see **148** below). See 'Savage' **108** and 'Broome' **9** above.

144. For Atterbury's 'advice' in 1722, see **116** above. As Hill (1905) noted, Atterbury in fact believed that P had 'engaged himself in a very improper and troublesome scuffle, not worthy of his pen at all' in the *Dunciad*: see his *Epistolary Corresp.*, ed. J. Nichols, iv (1787), 136–7.

P told Spence in 1735 that 'The *Dunciad* cost me as much pains as anything I ever wrote' (i. 147). For his enemies, see his own list appended to the *Dunciad* (1729) (*TE*, v. 207–12), and Guerinot, *Pamphlet Attacks, passim*. SJ said ironically of the *Dunciad* in Oct. 1769: 'It was worth while being a dunce then . . . It is not worth while being a dunce now, when there are no wits' (*Life*, ii. 84). Referring to Ruffhead's account, *Life*, 195, of P's collection of attacks on him (see **278** and n. below), SJ later said on 4 June 1781: 'I wish I had copies of all the pamphlets written against me, as it is said Pope had. Had I known that I should make so much noise in the world, I should have been at pains to collect them' (*Life*, iv. 127).

SJ's use of 'greatest' here is obviously distinct from 'most elaborate': cf. 'Milton' **194** and n. above.

145. For Theobald, see **126** and n. above and **357** below. SJ had referred to him as 'poor Tib.' in conversation in 1758 (*Life*, i. 329): for other authors described by SJ as 'poor', see 'Lyttelton' **17** and n. below. In a note to *Dunciad* (1729), I. 106, P accused Theobald of soliciting favours from him while secretly preparing *Shakespeare Restored* (1726).

SJ defines 'To Blast' as '1. To strike with some sudden plague or calamity. 2. To make to wither. 3. To injure; to invalidate; to make infamous' (*Dict.*). In 1753 Fielding described the effect of an appearance in *The Dunciad*: 'the unhappy Culprit was obliged to lay by his Pen forever; for no Bookseller would venture to print a Word that he wrote' (*The Covent-Garden Journal*, ed. B. A. Goldgar (Oxford, 1988), 153).

According to *Dunciad*, iii. 159 n., the name of James Ralph (1705?–62) was added only after he attacked P in *Sawney. An Heroic Poem* (1728) (*TE*, v. 75, 165). Giles Jacob mentioned the effect of P's mockery on Ralph's reputation in *The Mirrour* (1733), 77–8 (Guerinot, *Pamphlet Attacks*, 232–3), and William Ayre, *Memoirs of P* (1745), i. 329–30, described Ralph as a hireling author who lost all credibility, though without blaming this on the *Dunciad*. SJ says, however, that Ralph 'complained' about P's satire. Since he did not do so in *The Case of Authors by Profession or Trade Stated* (1758), SJ must have learned this from Percy, who owned a transcript of MS notes by P's friend, the painter Jonathan Richardson, one of which reads, 'Ralph complained that he had near being famished by this Line [*Dunciad*, iii. 159]. None of the Booksellers would employ him': see Sherburn, 'New Anecdotes', 348.

146. *prevalence*: 'Superiority; influence; predominance' (*Dict.*). SJ refers to the original anonymous and unannotated *Dunciad* of May 1728.

For 'Common readers', see **151**, **372** below, and 'Cowley' **65** and n. above, and for the wisdom of ignoring attacks, see also **235–6** and n. below, and 'Dryden' **173** and n. above.

147. For the indifference of 'the world' to most individuals, see also **159** and n. below.

148. Ruffhead, *Life*, 352–4, merely summarized the dedication, signed by Richard Savage, of *A Collection of Pieces... Published on Occasion of the Dunciad* (1732), pp. v ff., to Charles Sackville, Earl of Middlesex. For SJ's discussion of it in 1744, see 'Savage' **107–8** above. Although SJ presumably had Savage's authority for attributing it to P, recent scholars have doubted P's authorship: see *Prose Works*, ii, p. xiii and xv n.

Hester Thrale's long transcription of the dedication is in the materials appended to the MS: see Textual Notes. SJ deleted or compressed most of the first paragraph, which in fact begins: 'I will not pretend to display those rising Virtues in your Lordship, which the next Age will certainly know without my Help, but rather relate (what else it will as certainly be ignorant of) the *History* of these *Papers*, and the Occasion which produced the *War of the Dunces*', etc.

149. Fenton told Broome of the 'tumult' over the *Dunciad*, 24 June 1729: 'The war is carried on against him furiously in pictures and libels' (*Corresp.*, iii. 37). For P's pained reactions to later attacks, see **239**, **278** below, and for 'sensibility', **67** and n. above.

150. For P's use of initial 'letters' for the poets mocked in 'Peri Bathous', especially in ch. VI, see also 'Savage' **108** and n. above.

P's note to *Dunciad* (1729), I. i, referred to Walpole's presentation of the *Variorum* edition to the King and Queen on 12 Mar. 1729 (Warburton (1751 edn.), iv. 67 n.; Ruffhead, *Life*, 394–5). P took the precaution of nominally assigning the copyright to Lords Oxford, Burlington, and Bathurst, who as peers were immune from prosecution and who distributed it privately (*TE*, v. pp. xxviii, 461, 463).

151. *The Dunciad, Variorum. With the Prolegomena of Scriblerus* (1729), still in three books, added an elaborate mock-scholarly apparatus of prefaces, notes, and appendices. For its complicated publishing history, see Foxon, *English Verse*, i. 615–16, and Foxon, *Book Trade*, 108–14. For the 'common reader', see **146** and n. above.

Although Swift advised P as early as 26 Nov. 1725 not to transmit the names of bad writers to posterity, he complained, 16 July 1728, about the obscurity of the unannotated *Dunciad* (Warburton (1751 edn.), ix. 117–18). (Curll soon obligingly produced *A Compleat Key to the Dunciad*.) Swift later claimed to have encouraged P to 'hale those Scoundrels out of their Obscurity by telling their Names at length, their Works, their Adventures... not with *A—'s and B—'s* according to the old Way, which would be unknown in a few Years' (*Corresp.*, ii. 343, 504; Swift, *Corresp.*, iv. 53).

152. SJ refers to Dennis's *Remarks on Mr. Pope's Rape of the Lock ... With a Preface, Occasion'd by the Late Treatise on the Profound, and the Dunciad* (1728). His last work was *Remarks upon Several Passages in the Preliminaries to the Dunciad* (1729) (*Works*, ii. 322–76): see **60** above. For other responses, see *Collection of Pieces* (1732) in **148** and n. above, and Guerinot, *Pamphlet Attacks*, 110–15, 123–33, 144–50, 155–74.

153. For Duckett and Burnet, see **122** and n. above. Savage may have told SJ about Duckett's threatened vengeance.

Although Hill (1905) found no edition with the reading 'cordial friendship', it replaced 'pious passion' in *Dunciad*, III. 176, in the 'Third Edition' of 1728 (only) (*TE*, v. 169). P drew attention to the phrase 'pious passion' in long notes in 1729 and 1743, and another damaging note explained the eventual omission of the names of Burnet and Duckett (*TE*, v. 168–70, 329 and n.). Dennis felt called on to confirm Duckett's heterosexuality in *Remarks* (1728) (see **152** and n. above).

154. For Aaron Hill (1685–1750), dramatist, poet, and journalist, see also **285** below and 'Savage' **55** and n. above. Ruffhead, *Life*, 352, 553–65, discussed Hill's supposed 'misapprehension', and appended his correspondence with P.

Having appeared as 'A.H.' in 'Peri Bathous', Hill protested to P about the reference to 'H—' in the diving contest in *Dunciad* (1728), II. 283–6. P omitted it in 1729, but with a note drawing attention to Hill's objections. After further protests from Hill in 1731, P gave a somewhat evasive explanation of his conduct (*Corresp.*, iii. 164–77). By then Hill had criticized P's malice and obscenity in *The Progress of Wit; A Caveat. For the Use of an Eminent Writer* (1730). Malone later suggested that P had not forgiven Hill for addressing *The Fatal Vision* (1716) to Dennis and Gildon as their 'profound admirer' (Bodleian, MS Malone 30, fo. 36). For P's relationship with Hill, see also C. Gerrard, *Aaron Hill: The Muses' Projector* (Oxford, 2003), esp. 124–44, 232–6.

SJ ends by paraphrasing 'Willing to wound, and yet afraid to strike' (*Epistle to Arbuthnot*, l. 203).

155. For the lines to Swift, see *Dunciad* (1729), I. 17–26, and cf. Warburton (1751 edn.), ix. 149, and *Corresp.*, ii. 497–8, 503.

P told Warburton, 27 Nov. 1742, that John Arbuthnot was his collaborator in the notes to *The Dunciad Variorum* (Warburton (1751 edn.), ix. 350; *Corresp.*, iv. 428), but, given Arbuthnot's dislike of personal satire, Savage may be a more likely assistant (see 'Savage' **110–12** above, and *TE*, v. pp. xxiv–xxvii). Arbuthnot probably contributed the Latin appendix, 'Virgilius Restauratus', in *The Dunciad Variorum*, later omitted.

The prefatory letter was signed by William Cleland (1674?–1741), commissioner of taxes and father of John Cleland (1710–89), the author of *Memoirs of a Woman of Pleasure* (1748–9).

156–8. Most of these charges concerning P and the Duke of Chandos have been disproved: see *TE*, ii. (ii), pp. xxvi–xxx, 170–4. Mack, *AP*, 501, criticized SJ's influential 'credulity' about them. See also references to his 'misrepresentations' in *Prose Works*, ii. 405–6, introducing P's prose reply to the accusations, 'A Master Key to Popery', first published in 1949.

156. Spence, i. 140; Ruffhead, *Life*, 306.

'Lord Timon' in P's *Epistle to the Right Honourable Richard Earl of Burlington* (1731), ll. 99–168, was widely identified as referring to James Brydges (1673–1744), Duke of Chandos, and his seat at Cannons, near Edgeware. The only evidence to support SJ's claim that Richard Boyle (1695–1753), Earl of Burlington, believed that Timon was Chandos is P's denial in a letter of 21 Dec. 1731, repeated to Aaron Hill on 22 Dec. (*Corresp.*, iii. 259–61).

Although, as Mack, *AP*, 498–9, noted, P did not know Chandos well and had never visited Cannons, he was embarrassed by the fact that the Duke was a friend of Arbuthnot, Bathurst, Bolingbroke, and Burlington. Timon is now taken to be a composite figure through whom P satirizes contemporary owners of great estates. For a recent panegyric of Chandos and his great house, see Samuel Humphreys, *Cannons. A Poem* (1728).

157. Guerinot, *Pamphlet Attacks*, 204–13, 225–8, 236–8, lists seven attacks on P's alleged ingratitude in 1732–3, including Leonard Welsted's *Of Dulness and Scandal* and the *Verses Address'd to the Imitator of . . . Horace* by Lady Mary Wortley Montagu and Lord Hervey. The sum P allegedly received from Chandos was usually said to be £500 (Guerinot, *Pamphlet Attacks*, 227).

158. P denied receiving £500 (not £1,000) from Chandos in a note to *Epistle to Arbuthnot*, l. 375 (Warburton (1751 edn.), iii. 42 n.). His 'apology' took the form of a letter from William Cleland to Gay, 16 Dec. 1731, in the *Daily Post-Boy* of 22 Dec. 1731 (*Corresp.*, iii. 254–7). His 'exculpatory letter' of the same date to Chandos has not survived, but was mentioned by William Ayre, *Memoirs of P* (1745), ii. 73. For Chandos's reply of 27 Dec. 1731, see *Corresp.*, iii. 262–3, 267, and Spence, i. 140. Warton, *Works of P* (1797), i, p. xliii, claimed to have heard from a later Duke of Chandos that his ancestor was 'not perfectly satisfied' with P's explanation. P took the precaution of complimenting Chandos in *Epistle to Cobham* (1734), l. 113 ('Thus gracious CHANDOS is belov'd at sight').

159. SJ quotes (loosely) P to Burlington, Jan. 1732 (Warburton (1751 edn.), viii. 195; *Corresp.*, iii. 266).

For the unimportance of the individual to 'the world' (see also **147** above), see *Rambler* 146 (1751): 'It is long before we are convinced of the small proportion which every individual bears to the collective body of mankind; or learn how few can be interested in the fortune of any single man' (*YW*, v. 15). See also *Ramblers* 159 (1751), 196 (1752), and *Rasselas*, ch. XLVI: 'keep this thought always prevalent, that you are only one atom of the mass of humanity' (*YW*, v. 84, 261, xvi. 163).

SJ substituted the anecdote about the idiot on London Bridge in the proofs for another about 'an idiot who used to enforce his demands by threatening to beat his head against the wall': see Textual Notes.

SJ translates Juvenal, *Sat.*, IV. 70–1.

160. For the death of John Gay on 4 Dec. 1732, see 'Gay' **24** above, and, for P's epitaph on Gay, **427–36** below, where SJ describes him as P's 'favourite'. SJ has not hitherto mentioned this important friendship over some twenty years, although he had emphasized it in 'Gay' **2–3, 10, 13, 19–20, 26** above.

confidence: '1. Firm belief in another's integrity or veracity; reliance' (*Dict.*): cf. the end of **243** below.

161. Warburton (1751 edn.), iv. 43 n., viii. 233 n.; Ruffhead, *Life*, 484.

Edith Pope (see **1** and n. above) in fact died on 7 June 1733, a week before her 90th birthday (Mack, *AP*, 899 n.), but the obituary notice, no doubt by P himself, in *Grub-Street Journal* (14 June 1733) and *Gent. Mag.* (1733), 326, gave her age as 93. For his letters of 10, 25 June 1733 about her death, see *Corresp.*, iii. 374–5.

Gent. Mag. (Nov. 1775), 528 and n., stated that, in spite of her poor spelling, P 'occasionally indulged his affectionate and amiable mother in transcribing some part of his works for the press ... which she justly thought would confer immortality on her son'. For other parents who lived to enjoy their sons' literary fame, see 'Cowley' **2** above, and 'Thomson' **3**, 'Watts' **9**, and 'Lyttelton' **12** below; and for SJ's reaction to the death of his own mother, see *Idler* 41 (1759) and Clifford (1979), 204–10.

162–6. In a somewhat bemused discussion in *BB*, v (1760), 3413–14 n., Philip Nichols had hoped that Warburton's promised biography of P would clarify the question of P's devious dealings with the publisher Edmund Curll, but Ruffhead, *Life*, preferred to ignore the subject. P in effect duped Curll (see **29, 142** above) into buying unbound sheets of the letters from intermediaries and publishing them in May 1735, ostensibly against P's wishes. This enabled P in due course to publish his own 'authentic' *Letters* (1737) (see **166, 169** below).

For concise modern accounts of P's behaviour, see *Corresp.*, i, pp. xiii–xiv, and Mack, *AP*, 653–7; for a detailed 'Timetable' of these events in 1735, see Winn, *Window*, 203–21; and for a further account of P's tactics, see McLaverty, 'First Printing', 264–80. For P's *Narrative of the Method By Which The Private Letters of Mr. Pope Have been procur'd and publish'd by Edmund Curll, Bookseller* (1735), and his preface to *Letters* (1737), see *Prose Works*, ii. 319–83.

162. P's prosecution in the House of Lords in May 1735 failed, because Curll's edition did not in fact contain any of the letters by or about members of the peerage promised in his newspaper advertisements (*Prose Works*, ii. 341–3).

163. For Curll's account, see *Mr. Pope's Literary Correspondence. Volume the Second* (1735), 14.

164. Henry Lintot (1703–58) was the son of the bookseller Bernard Lintot (see **77–8, 135–6** above). For the possibility that SJ wrote 'some things' for him when he first arrived in London, see *Life*, i. 103. When living in Inner Temple Lane in 1760–5, SJ kept his library in Henry Lintot's former warehouse (*Life*, i. 435).

165. *BB*, v. 3413 n., suggested that profit was P's main motive. According to the *Narrative*, Curll was originally offered 650 copies for £75 (*Prose Works*, ii. 337).

166. For professed fear of surreptitious editions, see also **53** and n. and **141** n. above.

167. For P's self-presentation in *Letters* (1737), see **273–84** below, and cf. his 'appetite to talk too frequently of his own virtues' in **35** above.

168. See Warburton (1751 edn.), ix. 312–13 nn.; Ruffhead, *Life*, 406 n., 464; and P to Allen, 7 Apr. 1736 (*Corresp.*, iv. 9 and n.).

  For Ralph Allen (1694–1764) of Prior Park, Bath, pioneer of postal services and philanthropist, see B. Boyce, *The Benevolent Man* (Cambridge, Mass., 1967), Erskine-Hill, *Social Milieu*, 204–40, and **194, 218, 254** below. Fielding complimented Allen in *Joseph Andrews* (1742), used him as a model for Squire Allworthy in *Tom Jones* (1749), and dedicated *Amelia* (1752) to him: see M. C. Battestin, *Henry Fielding, A Life* (1989), 315–17, 532.

169. Ruffhead, *Life*, 464–70, followed the account in P's preface to *Letters* (1737) (*Prose Works*, ii. 368–72). Like P's earlier *Works* (1717–35), the *Letters* appeared in both quarto and folio format. For 'reposited' see **94** n. above.

  P's preface stated that he had 'caus'd a Copy to be taken to deposite in the Library of a noble Friend' (*Prose Works*, ii. 368), but not that the letters had been stolen from the library of Edward Harley, Earl of Oxford, where he had placed them in 1729 (*Corresp.*, iii. 54, 56; *Prose Works*, ii. 312–13 n.). For P's preface to *Miscellanies* (1727), see **141** and n. above.

  SJ seems to have been the first to identify the 'Richard Smith' (or Smythe) who negotiated with Curll as James Worsdale (1692?–1767), painter and dramatist. The cryptic entry 'Worsdale (James) Lintot (Henry)' in his first MS notes for 'Pope' (fo. 167^v) may indicate his source (see **164** and n. above), but Henry Thrale and Arthur Murphy both knew Worsdale, who was described by Mrs Thrale as their 'pimp and parasite ... in their merry hours', and as 'a sad fellow, but very comical as a buffoon' (*Thraliana*, i. 237 and n.; Lobban, 155). Warton, *Works of P* (1797), ii. 339 n., quoted a note by Thomas Birch, 17 Aug. 1749, which stated that George Faulkner, the Dublin bookseller, confirmed that Worsdale was P's agent. Swift described Worsdale in Mar. 1738 as a former leader of the 'Monsters called Blasters, or Blasphemers, or Bacchanalians' in Dublin (*Corresp.*, v. 97).

170. P's *Letters* appeared on 19 May 1737. SJ's account of its cool reception seems to contradict his earlier comments in **167** above, but he may mean that it added little to the impact of Curll's original publication in 1735. For an angry but unpublished 'Letter to A.P. in answer to the preface of His Letters' by Lady Mary Wortley Montagu, see her *Essays and Poems*, ed. R. Halsband and I. Grundy (Oxford, 1977), 98–9.

  SJ can write 'nor do I remember' in his last sentence because he had arrived in London two months earlier in Mar. 1737 (*Life*, i. 102).

171. Warburton (1751 edn.), i, p. ix, described P's letters as 'the only true models which we, or perhaps any of our neighbours have, of *familiar Epistles*'. For letters, see also 'Cowley' **17** and 'Swift' **135** above and 'Gray' **24** below; for Dennis's attempt to suggest rules for the familiar letter, see 'To the Reader', prefixed to his *Letters upon Several Occasions* (1696) (*Works*, ii. 382); and for P's European predecessors, especially Voiture in France, see Winn, *Window*, ch. 2.

   SJ had discussed the absence of notable letter-writers in English, and referred contemptuously to the 'innumerable' letters of the 'wits of France', in *Rambler* 152 (1751). His projected works, as listed by Hawkins, *Life* (1787), 82–3 n., and *Life*, iv. 381 n., include 'A Collection of Letters, translated from the modern writers, with some account of the several authors', 'A book of Letters upon all kinds of subjects', and 'A Collection of Letters from English authors, with a preface giving some account of the writers, with reasons for selection and criticism upon stiles, remarks on each letter, if needful'. He may have dropped such plans after the appearance of John Duncombe's *Select Collection of Original Letters Written by the most Eminent Persons* (2 vols., 1755).

   SJ refers to James Howell, *Epistolae Ho-Elianae. Familiar Letters Domestic and Forren* (4 vols., 1645–55); Daniel George Morhoff (1639–91), *De Ratione Conscribendarum Epistolarum Libellus* (Lübeck, 1716), 66–7; Robert Loveday, *Letters, Domestick and Forrein* (1659, which in fact reached a 7th edition by 1684); George Herbert in Izaak Walton's *Life* (1670), 123–40; and Sir John Suckling's *Last Remains* (1659). Baptist Noel Turner later recalled that in the library of Trinity College, Cambridge, in 1765 SJ picked up the *Polyhistor* of Morhoff, 'a German genius of great celebrity in the 17th century', and exclaimed: 'Here is the book upon which all my fame was originally founded; when I had read this book I could teach my tutors!' (Nichols, *Lit. Ill.*, vi. 155). For Katherine Philips, *Letters from Orinda* (1705), see 'Roscommon' **36** and n. above: Richardson Pack stated in *Miscellanies* (1719), 102, that 'the best Letters I have met with in our Tongue are those of the celebrated Mrs. PHILIPS'. See also 'Walsh' **10–11** above. William Walsh's published letters were not mere exercises, but revised versions of genuine letters now in the British and Bodleian Libraries.

172. P may have envisaged the publication of his letters as early as 1712: Swift mentioned in 1730 P's youthful 'Schemes... of Epistolary fame' (*Corresp.*, i, p. xi, iii. 92). For their artifice, see also **276** below.

   SJ probably refers to the only letter by Bolingbroke in P's *Letters* (1737), to Swift, 14 Sept. 1725 (Warburton (1751 edn.), ix. 42–6; *Corresp.*, ii. 186–9). Discussing Swift's correspondents, Lord Orrery, *Remarks on Dr. Swift* (3rd edn., 1752), 162, found in Bolingbroke's letters 'an elegance and politeness that distinguish them from all the rest', and observed that P's 'chief aim was to be esteemed a man of virtue'. For Arbuthnot, see **212–13** below and, for prose style elsewhere, 'Cowley' **200** and n. above.

173. Fenton told Broome, 24 June 1729, that in future P intended 'to write nothing but epistles in Horace's manner' (*Corresp.*, iii. 37). For his projected 'system of Ethicks', see P to Swift, 28 Nov. 1729 (*Corresp.*, iii. 81).

   P told Swift, 14 Sept. 1725, that he intended to give up translation and write 'something domestic, fit for my own country, and for my own time' (*Corresp.*,

ii. 321–2). Warburton (1751 edn.), ix. 51 (the 'commentator', as in **207, 221** below), interpreted this as a first reference to the *Essay on Man*.

174. P addressed Bolingbroke as 'Laelius' in the 1st edition of the *Essay on Man*, I. i, IV. 18. According to Warburton (1751 edn.), iv. 34 n., and Ruffhead, *Life*, 261 n., the anonymous *Essay* was variously attributed to Bolingbroke, the scientist J. T. Desaguliers (1683–1744), author of *The Newtonian System of the World…An Allegorical Poem* (1728), and Thomas Catesby, Lord Paget (1689–1742), courtier and author of a versified *Essay on Human Life* (1734). Swift told P, 1 May 1733, that in Dublin it was 'understood to come from Doctor Young', adding that 'It is too Philosophical for me' (*Corresp.*, v. 11–12). P preserved his anonymity when writing to Caryll about the *Essay* on 8 and 20 Mar. 1733, mentioning that it had been attributed to various clergymen.

P later told Swift, 15 Sept. 1734, that 'The design of concealing myself was good, and had its full effect' (Warburton (1751 edn.), ix. 257–8), and William Duncombe, 20 Oct. 1734, that 'truly I had not the least thought of stealing applause by suppressing my name to that "essay": I wanted only to hear truth, and was more afraid of my partial friends than enemies' (*Corresp.*, iii. 354, 358, 433, 438). 'Liberalis' described the advantages of anonymous publication in *Rambler* 163 (1751): 'I knew that no performance is so favourably read as that of a writer who supresses his name, and therefore resolved to remain concealed, till those by whom literary reputation is established had given their suffrages too publickly to retract them' (*YW*, v. 103).

175. P was able to quote praise of the anonymous *Essay on Man* by his enemies Leonard Welsted and Bezaleel Morrice in the 'Testimonies of Authors' prefixed to the *Dunciad* (*TE*, iii (i), pp. xv–xvi, v. 43–4). Although there seems to be no evidence that he actually sent them copies of the *Essay*, he had envisaged such a deception on 3 Oct. 1723: 'I cannot but smile, to think how envy and prejudice will be disappointed, if they find things which they have been willing, or forced, to applaud as belonging to one man, to be the just praise of another whom they have a malignity to' (*Corresp.*, ii. 205).

Mallet fell into a different trap by criticizing the anonymous *Essay* to P's face: see 'Mallet' **10** and n. below. For Swift's detection of P's authorship, see his letter of 1 Nov. 1734 (*Corresp.*, iii. 439), and for Walter Harte's story that, to disguise his authorship, P originally included a 'bad rhyme' in *Essay*, II. 205–6, see Warton, *Essay on P*, ii (1782), 154 n.

176. *An Essay on Man. Part I* was published on 20 Feb. 1733 by John Wilford rather than Lawton Gilliver, P's usual publisher since the *Dunciad Variorum* (1729) (*TE*, iii (i), p. xv and n.; McLaverty, *P, Print and Meaning*, 108–10).

For early reactions to the *Essay*, see *TE*, iii (i), pp. xv–xviii, and Barnard (ed.), *P: Critical Heritage*, 278–84, and for the reception of new authors, 'Stepney' **3** and n. above, and *Ramblers* 16 (1750), 146 (1751).

177. P revised *Essay*, I. 5–6, 293–4, in the 2nd edition (1734).

SJ quoted I. 5 correctly in the MS ('Expatiate free o'er all this scene of man'), but the printer omitted 'all' in the proofs and *Prefaces* (1781), as noted by 'Scrutator' (John Loveday) in *Gent. Mag.* (1781), 358. An emendation (probably not by SJ himself) to 'freely o'er' appeared in *Lives* in 1781 and 1783: see Textual Notes.

P discussed the problem of balancing 'argument and poetry' in his prefatory 'The Design' (*TE*, iii (i). 7–8): cf. 'Dryden' **285** and n. and 'Blackmore' **46** above.

178. 'Epistles II–IV' appeared, still anonymously, on 29 Mar. and 8 May 1733, and 24 Jan. 1734. Although P's authorship was widely known by 1734, he in fact first acknowledged it in *Works*, vol. ii (1735) (*TE*, iii (i), p. xvi n.).

179. P praised Bolingbroke in *Essay*, IV. 373–98. Under the influence of Warburton, Ruffhead, *Life*, 216–22, distinguished P's opinions from Bolingbroke's, but later admitted that the 'extravagance' of P's 'attachment' to Bolingbroke 'bordered even upon imbecility' (531). In his *View of Lord Bolingbroke's Philosophy* (1755), Letter IV, Warburton accused him of mocking P, a charge repeated by Ruffhead, *Life*, 221–2, and Warton, *Essay on P*, ii (1782), 120–1 n. See also **191** below.

Bolingbroke summarized 'the noble work which, att my instigation, [P] has begun' in a letter to Swift, 2 Aug. 1731 (*Corresp.*, iii. 213–14). For his assistance to P in 1730–1, see Spence, i. 138, and *Corresp.*, iii. 139, 163, 183, 249. On 10 Oct. 1779 SJ rejected Lord Bathurst's claim ('reported' by Hugh Blair to Boswell, 21 Sept. 1779) to have seen Bolingbroke's prose MS which P had versified in his *Essay*: P 'may have had from Bolingbroke the philosophick *stamina* of his Essay', but 'we are sure that the poetical imagery, which makes a great part of the poem, was Pope's own'. Edmund Law, Bishop of Carlisle, in his edition of William King's *Essay on the Origins of Evil* (1781), p. xvii, and Warton, *Essay on P*, ii (1782), 62, had also heard Bathurst's claim (*Life*, iii. 402–3 and n.). Cf. SJ's earlier distinction in 'Blackmore' **24** above between what others might have contributed to his *Creation*, and what must be essentially the poet's own.

SJ's later account of the 'philosophy', as opposed to the poetry, of the *Essay on Man* in **191–2**, **363–7** below makes clear his hostility to Bolingbroke's alleged scepticism concerning revealed religion. Walter Churchey later published his own *An Essay on Man, upon Principles Opposite to those of Lord Bolingbroke; in Four Epistles* (1804). For assessments of Bolingbroke's influence on P, see *TE*, iii, pp. xxix–xxxi, and Hammond, *P and Bolingbroke*, 69–91.

180. Before admitting authorship of the *Essay*, P wrote to Caryll, 8 Mar. 1733, about aspects of the poem 'which at first glance may be taken for heathenism' (*Corresp.*, iii. 354). For early anxiety about P's orthodoxy in the *Essay*, see Spence, i. 135–6, and Barnard (ed.), *P: Critical Heritage*, 282–4. Jonathan Richardson, *Richardsoniana* (1776), 265, stated that he and his father had repeatedly warned P about the poem's 'fatalism, and deistical tendency'. P claimed in 1743 that he had not dealt with 'the fall of man' and 'the immortality of the soul' because 'They both lay out of my subject, which was only to consider man as he is, in his present state, not in his past or future' (Spence, i. 1436). For 'amplification', see 'Cowley' **59** and n. above.

what the gay foliage concealed: SJ probably meant to write 'its flowers caught the eye, which did not see what they concealed', but wrote 'the' instead of 'they' in the MS. Assuming that a word or phrase had been omitted after 'the', the printer left a space before 'concealed' in the proofs, which SJ duly supplied with 'gay foliage': see Textual Notes.

181. SJ refers to Étienne de Silhouette, *Essai sur l'homme* (1736), and J. F. Du B. Du Resnel, *Les Principes de la morale* (1737). (For Du Resnel see also **43** above and

'Garth' 17 above. P's *Essay* was later translated into German, Italian, Portuguese, Russian, and Latin.)

Jean Pierre de Crousaz (1663–1750), logician and theologian, Professor at Lausanne, based his *Examen de l'Essai de M. Pope sur l'homme* (1737) on Silhouette's prose translation, and his *Commentaire sur la traduction en vers...de l'Essai...sur l'homme* (1738) on Du Resnel's verse. SJ's friend Elizabeth Carter (1717–1806) translated Crousaz's *Examen* in 1738, possibly with some assistance from SJ, who told Edward Cave in Nov. 1738: 'I think the Examen should be push'd forward with the utmost expedition' (*Letters*, i. 20). SJ's notes to his own translation of Crousaz's *Commentaire* (printed 1739 but not published till 1742) repeatedly point out the effect of Du Resnel's distortions of P's meaning on Crousaz's discussion of the *Essay on Man* (see 1742 edn., 3, 6, 40, 139). For these translations of Crousaz, see also *Bibliography*, i. 43–7.

182. SJ refers to Crousaz's *Système de réflexions...ou nouvel essai de logique* (1712) and *Examen du Pyrrhonisme ancien et moderne* (1733). He praised the first work in the preface to Dodsley's *Preceptor* (1748) (Hazen, 185), and Gibbon also admired it (*Memoirs*, ed. G. Bonnard (New York, 1966), 73, 78).

183. For the complaint that P ignored 'revelation' in the *Essay on Man*, see 180 n. above and 'Young' 103 and n. below, and D. H. White, *P and the Context of Controversy* (Chicago, 1970), 10 ff.

184. The death of William Warburton (1698–1779), Bishop of Gloucester, on ll June 1779 made it easier for SJ to write this frank assessment, which he carefully revised in both the MS and proofs: see Textual Notes. He may have noticed a recent discussion in *Gent. Mag.* (Sept. 1780), 413, of Warburton's 'over-bearing haughtiness' and faded reputation, which stated that it 'would be difficult to point out a single compliment paid to him or his writings, since the time that he ceased to write'.

contemptuous superiority: Charles Churchill, in *The Duellist* (1764), ll. 667–810, wrote that Warburton 'was so proud, that should he meet | The Twelve Apostles in the street, | He'd turn his nose up at them all, | And shove his Saviour from the wall'. Walpole told Mason, 25 Sept. 1781, that SJ's account was 'ten times more like to himself than to the Bishop, and expressed in the same uncouth phrases which he criticises' (*Corresp.*, xxix. 155–6). SJ finally quotes Suetonius, *De Vita Caesarum*, IV. xxx, on Caligula, as earlier in *Rambler* 4 (1750): 'The Roman tyrant was content to be hated, if he was but feared' (*YW*, iii. 24).

SJ usually spoke respectfully about the combative Warburton, who had praised his early *Observations on Macbeth* (1745) as by 'a Man of Parts and Genius' in his edition of Shakespeare in 1747 (i, p. xiii; see *Life*, i. 175–6). As SJ recalled: 'He gave me...his good word when it was of use to me' (*J. Misc.*, ii. 7). In 1765 SJ mentioned his 'veneration' for Warburton's 'genius and learning', but went on to criticize the 'sometimes perverse interpretations, and sometimes improbable conjectures' in his notes on Shakespeare (*YW*, vii. 98–100; see also vii, p. xxxviii, for evidence that SJ in fact softened some of his objections). In private, Warburton reacted angrily to SJ's criticism: 'The remarks he makes in every page on my commentaries are full of insolence and malignant reflections, which had they not in them as much folly as malignity, I should have had reason to be offended with' (*Letters from a Late Eminent Prelate* (2nd edn., 1809), 367–8 n.).

SJ modestly told George III in Feb. 1767 that 'he had not read much, compared with Dr. Warburton. Upon which the King said, that he heard Dr. Warburton was a man of such general knowledge, that you could scarce talk with him on any subject on which he was not qualified to speak' (*Life*, ii. 36–7). For SJ's meeting with Warburton in 1773, see 'Broome' **6** and n. above; and for SJ's dislike of his style and admiration for his fertile genius, and Samuel Parr's assessment of the relationship of the two men, see *Life*, iv. 46–9 and nn. See also *Life*, i. 263, iv. 288, v. 80–1 (quoted in **194** n. below), 92–3, and *J. Misc.*, ii. 7, 140–1, 187, 317–18, 331.

Nichols reprinted most of **184–94** in *Anecdotes of Bowyer* (1782), 598–9 nn., later adding, as 'no bad companion', Bishop Newton's 'delineation' of Warburton (642–4).

185. W. G. Hamilton reported that Warburton said of SJ, 'I admire him, but I cannot bear his style', and that, when told of this, SJ responded, 'That is exactly my case as to him' (*Life*, iv. 48). Mrs Thrale noted in 1776 that she once heard SJ compare Warburton to 'a man who goes to War so much overloaden with Armour that he never has it in his power to fight' (*Thraliana*, i. 2). Soon after Warburton's death, a contributor to *Gent. Mag.* (July 1779), 340, discussed the 'strength, spirit, and high-colouring' of his style, his lack of 'purity and accuracy of language', and his 'chief defect' in '*taste* and *judgement*', but asked: 'who among our literary worthies can boast such a variety of knowledge, more extensive learning, or more extraordinary talents?' For prose style, see also 'Cowley' **200** and n. above.

186. SJ said more bluntly in Aug. 1773 that Warburton 'was first an antagonist to Pope, and helped Theobald to publish his Shakespeare', but turned to P when he became 'the rising man' (*Life*, v. 80).

Thomas Birch quoted Warburton's letter to Matthew Concanen, 2 Jan. 1727, in 1751 (Mack, *AP*, 921 n.), and Akenside mentioned it in a note in his *Ode to Thomas Edwards* in 1766 (see 'Akenside' **6** n. below). Malone finally printed it in his *Supplement to Shakespeare* (1780), i. 223–6 (with the spelling 'leasure'), and presumably prompted SJ to correct his quotation from the letter in 1783: see Textual Notes.

A MS note on a copy of Concanen's anonymous attack on P, *A Supplement to the Profound* (1728), at Queen's College, Oxford, states: 'Dr Warton tells me this 1st Feb. 1797 that he believed Concanen was assisted in this Pamplt by Bishp Warburton' (Guerinot, *Pamphlet Attacks*, 149). He also allegedly attacked P's edition of Shakespeare in the *Daily Journal* of 22 Mar., 8, 22 Apr. 1729 (*Life*, v. 490), and was at first hostile to the *Essay on Man*: see Thomas Tyers, *A Historical Rhapsody on Mr. Pope* (1782), 49, Warton, *Essay*, ii (1782), 121 n., and W. Seward's 'Drossiana' in *European Mag.* (Apr. 1792), 258. For Warburton's contribution to Theobald's Shakespeare, see **126** n. above, and for his own explanation of his earlier conduct, see his letter to Hurd, 12 Jan. 1757, in *Letters from a late Eminent Prelate* (2nd edn., 1809), 218–19, 221–4.

187. Hawkins, *J's Works* (1787), iv. 68 n., stated that P and Warburton first met accidentally in Jacob Robinson's shop in Inner Temple Lane, Fleet St (see also **190** n. below). According to Warton, *Works* (1797), ix. 342 n., 'Their very first interview was in Lord Radnor's garden, just by Mr. Pope's at Twickenham.

Dodsley was present; and was, he told me, astonished at the high compliments paid him [Warburton] by Pope as he approached him.' For P's plans for a meeting with Warburton, see his letter of 16 Apr. 1740 (*Corresp.*, iv. 233 and n.).

188. For 'inconstancy' of opinion, see 'Savage' **103–6** above, and, for the natural tendency to change opinion with experience, see *Rambler* 196 (1752).

189. Warburton's defence of P's *Essay* appeared between Dec. 1738 and Apr. 1739 in *The History of the Works of the Learned* (incorporating the earlier *Present State of the Republic of Letters* mentioned by SJ). Collected as *A Vindication of Mr. Pope's Essay on Man* (1739), it was enlarged as *A Critical and Philosophical Commentary on Mr. Pope's Essay on Man* (1742). See **190** below, and, for an extract, Barnard (ed.), *P: Critical Heritage*, 307–16.

SJ acted as 'Moderator' in the dispute between Warburton and Crousaz in an essay in *Gent. Mag.* (Mar. 1743), 152, but the promised continuation was delayed until Nov. 1743 (587–8) and consisted mostly of quotations from Crousaz, whose piety he obviously respected (see Kaminski, 157–8). SJ may have been trying to stimulate interest in his translation of Crousaz's *Commentary* (see **181** and n. above), which Cave was still advertising as 'proper' to be bound with Warburton's defence of P in *Miscellaneous Correspondence . . . Sent to the . . . Gentleman's Magazine*, iii (1744).

Rousseau commented on the controversy in *Julie ou La Nouvelle Héloïse* (1761) that Crousaz's book 'will never excite the reader to do any one virtuous action, while our zeal for every thing great and good is awakened by that of Pope' (trans. W. Kenrick (1761), ii. 74).

190. P described Warburton in 1742 as 'the greatest general critic I ever knew' (Spence, i. 217). He was often accused of discovering implications of which P himself was unaware. Conyers Middleton told him, 7 Jan. 1740, that he had 'found a meaning for [P], that he himself never dreamt of . . . if you did not *find* him a *philosopher*, you will *make* him one' (Warton, *Essay on P*, ii (1782), 262). Warton also referred to his 'fanciful and groundless' discoveries of 'latent beauties . . . never thought of by the author' (ii. 186 n.). Jonathan Richardson, *Richardsoniana* (1776), 263–5, claimed that Warburton discovered a 'regularity' in the *Essay on Criticism*, and 'a whole scheme' in the *Essay on Man*, unenvisaged by P himself. See also **43** above and **369** below; 'A Conversation in the Shades' between P and Warburton in *Gent. Mag.* (1779), 351; and 'Memoirs of Bishop Warburton', *Gent. Mag.* (1780), 360 and n.

gratuitous: 'Voluntary; granted without claim or merit' (*Dict.*).

In his early notes for 'Pope' (fo. 169^v), SJ reminded himself to 'copy' P's letter from Warburton (1751 edn.), ix. 324–5. The correct date is 11 Apr. 1739, as 'Scrutator' (John Loveday) noted in *Gent. Mag.* (1781), 358: see also *Corresp.*, iv. 171–2.

'Mr. R.' is Jacob Robinson, bookseller and publisher of the *History of the Works of the Learned* (see **187** n., **189** n. above). Étienne de Silhouette (see **181** and n. above) added a translation of Warburton's defence of P to later editions of his version of the *Essay on Man* (Warburton (1751 edn.), ix. 325 n.; *Corresp.*, iv. 172 n., 216 and n.).

191. For Bolingbroke's alleged influence on the *Essay*, see **179–80** and nn. above.

192. Spence, i. 127 (from Warburton in 1756, who dated the incident 1744); Ruffhead, *Life*, 219–20.

Nathaniel Hooke (d. 1763), translator and historian, may have been a schoolfellow of P at Twyford (see **6–7** above and Spence, i. 3 n.). P described him in 1731 as 'my particular friend' (*Corresp.*, iii. 185, iv. 31), and Warburton in 1755 as 'an odd sort of Catholic, in his own (mystic) way' (Spence, i. 362). P supported the subscription to Hooke's *Roman History* (1738), which Hooke dedicated to him as 'a worthy Friend, to whom I have been long and much obliged' (i, sig. A2ᵛ) (SJ read it in the Hebrides in Sept. 1773: see *Life*, v. 166, and cf. 175–6). According to Ruffhead, *Life*, 490 n., P influenced Hooke's remunerative appointment to help the Duchess of Marlborough prepare her *Account of the Conduct of the Dowager Duchess of Marlborough* (1742). He was present at P's deathbed (see **246** and n. below) and was remembered in his will (*Prose Works*, ii. 507).

SJ met Hooke's son, Dr Luke Joseph Hooke (1716–96), at the Mazarin Library in Paris in Oct. 1775 (*Life*, ii. 397). In a marginal note to his comments here Mrs Thrale-Piozzi wrote: '*This* Johnson learn'd of Abbé Hook when we were in France together; yet I have my doubts. The Papists are all eager to save *their poet* from imputation of infidelity, and Johnson was very willing to see so great a poet saved' (Lobban, 155–6).

193. Ruffhead, *Life*, 220, 223.

As late as Mar. 1744 P planned to introduce Warburton to Bolingbroke ('the Only Great Man in Europe who knows as much as He') (*Corresp.*, iv. 505). For Warburton's account of the dispute in a letter to Hurd, 29 Dec. 1751, see *Letters from a Late Eminent Prelate* (2nd edn., 1809), 94–5.

194–5. It is likely that, after heavy revision, SJ retranscribed the pages of the MS containing most of **194–5** (and of **200–1** below), for the sake of the printer: see Textual Notes. Cf. the story of his anger at a proofsheet printed by a Mr Manning, one of Nichols's compositors, who, 'By producing the manuscript . . . at once satisfied Dr. Johnson that he was not to blame. Upon which Johnson candidly and earnestly said to him, "Mr. Compositor, I ask your pardon. Mr. Compositor, I ask your pardon," again and again' (*Life*, iv. 321).

194. 'From this time' refers to *c.*1739. By printing P's letters to him (1739–44) in a continuous sequence, Warburton emphasized P's confidence in, and dependence on, him (see Warburton (1751 edn.), i, p. iii, ix. 324–64).

P's friend William Murray, later Earl of Mansfield (see **69** and n. above), influenced Warburton's appointment at Lincoln's Inn in 1746. In 1741 P introduced Warburton to Ralph Allen (see **168** and n. above and *Corresp.*, iv. 370–1), whose niece he married in 1746, and whose estate he inherited in 1766. He became Bishop of Gloucester in 1760, partly through Allen's influence with William Pitt, the Prime Minister: see D. Griffin, *Literary Patronage in England* (Cambridge, 1996), 8.

After praising Warburton's 'great knowledge', 'great power of mind', and 'variety of learning' in Aug. 1773, SJ said: 'Pope introduced him to Allen, Allen married him to his niece: so, by Allen's interest and his own, he was made a bishop. But then his learning was the *sine qua non*: He knew how to make the most of it; but I do not find by any dishonest means' (*Life*, v. 80–1). *Gent. Mag.* (1777),

9–10 n., attributed Warburton's 'high station' to his alliance with P rather than to his theological works.

P's will made the 'property of his works' dependent on Warburton's willingness to edit them (Warburton (1751 edn.), ix. 369; P to Warburton, 21 Feb. 1744, *Corresp.*, iv. 501). For P's *Works* (1751), and Warburton's other dealings with the book trade after P's death, see D. W. Nichol, *P's Literary Legacy* (Oxford, 1992), who estimates that Warburton made £2,626 from the first five editions of the *Works* (p. xxxiii). Nichol, p. xxxviii, also quotes 'Orator' John Henley's ridicule in the *Daily Advertiser* of P's 'intimacy' with his editor: e.g. 'Alliance of Church and State, i.e. Pope and W—b—n; and Scheme for a Funeral Sermon on the Death of Mr. Pope's reputation' (4 Sept. 1742); and 'Mr. P* and W*b*n married?' (31 Dec. 1743).

This paragraph was originally a single sentence in the MS: see Textual Notes.

195. The Earl of Oxford commissioned a Latin translation of the *Essay on Man* c.1736 (Spence, i. 137), for which William Dobson, who published a Latin translation of Prior's *Solomon* (1734–6), was to receive 100 guineas. Although Dobson seems to have translated Epistles I–II (*Corresp.*, iv. 483), Oxford and P allowed him to accept William Benson's offer of £1,000 to translate *Paradise Lost* into Latin as *Paradisus Amissus* (2 vols., 1750–3). For Benson, see 'Milton' 155 and n. above and *Dunciad*, IV. 110 and n., and for SJ's acquaintance with Dobson, 291 and n. below. P mentioned the plan for a prose translation of the *Essay on Man* to Warburton on 24 June and 27 Oct. 1740 (Warburton, (1751 edn.), ix. 334–6; *Corresp.*, iv. 251–2, 288). See also Spence, i. 260, for P's comment in Dec. 1743 on the translators of his verse.

SJ had himself translated P's *Messiah* at Oxford in 1728, apparently to P's satisfaction (*Poems* (1974), 45–9; *Life*, i. 61 and n.): see 46 above and 318 and n. below, and O'Sullivan, 'Ex Alieno Ingenio Poeta', 579–91. William Whitehead translated *Essay on Man*, Ep. I, as a schoolboy in the 1730s (*Poems*, ed. W. Mason, iii (York, 1788), 7). Christopher Smart, who had already translated P's 'Ode on St. Cecilia's Day', proposed a verse translation of the *Essay on Man* in 1743, but instead translated the *Essay on Criticism* in his *Poems* (1752) (*Corresp.*, iv. 251–2, 288, 478, 483). After P's death, James Kirkpatrick (1745) and Usher Gahagan (1747) both translated the *Essay on Criticism* into Latin, Gahagan also translating other poems by P while awaiting execution in Newgate Prison for coining in 1749: see Foxon, *English Verse*, K 88, G 4, G 6.

SJ possibly wrote 'friends' in the last sentence in the MS, although 'friend' appeared in all editions 1781–3: see Textual Notes (and, for an earlier confusion of 'friend' and 'friends', 13 n. above). Hill (1905) identified the 'friend' as Warburton, on the strength of P's letters to him on this subject in 1740.

196. Spence, i. 30–1; Warburton (1751 edn.), iv. 302 n.; Ruffhead, *Life*, 508–9.

SJ quotes *Imit. Horace, Sat. II. i.* (1733), l. 133: '*Envy* must own, I live among the Great' (translating Horace almost literally). For P's attitude to 'the Great', see 23 and n. above and 231, 270–2, 281 below.

P evidently approached Walpole on behalf of Thomas Southcote or Southcott (1670–1748), a Catholic priest, early in 1728. He told Swift, 28 Nov. 1729: 'I am civilly treated by Sir R. Walpole' (*Corresp.* iii. 81). For P's relations with Walpole, see also 148 above, Goldgar, *Walpole, passim*, and Mack, *AP*, 501–4.

197. Ruffhead's account, *Life*, 535, differs from Savage's.

effusion: '3. The act of pouring out words' (*Dict.*).
SJ ends by quoting Swift, *A Libel on Doctor Delany* (1730), ll. 73–4: 'Contemning Courts, at Courts unseen, | Refus'd the visits of a Queen.' See also Swift to P, 6 Feb 1730, and P's reply, 4 Mar. 1730 (Warburton (1751 edn.), ix. 160; *Corresp.*, iii. 90, 95).

198–208. SJ does not use Warburton's collective term *Moral Essays* for these four epistles, although he does so in 'Blackmore' **46** above. In **373** below he refers to them as '*Ethick Epistles*', P's own title when he still envisaged them, together with the *Essay on Man*, as part of his projected 'Opus Magnum': see **228** and n. below.

198. For P's 'great labour' on *Of the Use of Riches, An Epistle to the Right Honourable Allen Lord Bathurst* (1733), see Spence, i. 139, P to Swift, 16 Feb. 1733 (*Corresp.*, iii. 348), and **372** n. below.
The date was a later insertion in the MS: see Textual Notes.

199. Swift complained in 1733 about the 'obscurity of several passages' in the *Epistle to Bathurst* (1733), caused 'by our ignorance of facts and persons, which make us lose abundance of the Satyr' (*Corresp.*, iii. 343).
For his attempt to obtain information about John Kyrle (1634–1724) of Ross-on-Wye, Herefordshire, see P to Tonson, 14 Nov. 1731, 7 June 1732 (*Corresp.*, iii. 244, 290–1). Kyrle appears as the 'Man of Ross' (ll. 249–80), the final couplet mentioning his 'five hundred pounds a year'. Warburton (1751 edn.), iii. 245 n., explained that P referred to 'the contributions which the *Man of Ross* by his assiduity and interest, collected in the neighbourhood' rather than to Kyrle's own acts of benevolence. For Benjamin Victor (d. 1778), theatrical manager and author, see also 'Addison' **7** and n. above, and *Life*, iv. 53; for Spence's efforts to collect information about Kyrle from Stephen Duck and others, see *TE*, iii (ii). 113–14 n.; and for other anecdotes about him, see *Gent. Mag.* (Dec. 1786), 1026.

romantick and impracticable virtue: for 'Romantick' as '2. Improbable; false' (*Dict.*), see **141** above and 'Dryden' **78** and n. above. SJ describes Swift's 'disinterestedness' as 'a strain of heroism, which would have been in his condition romantick and superfluous' in 'Swift' **53** above. William Seward stated that SJ 'used to advise his friends to be upon their guard against romantic virtue, as being founded upon no settled principle. "A plank," added he, "that is tilted up at one end must of course fall down on the other"' (*J. Misc.*, ii. 306 and cf. i. 208). For SJ's scepticism about 'wonders', see 'Cowley' **5** and n. above.

200. See *Epistle to Bathurst*, ll. 213–14, 339–40. As Hill (1905) noted, P also referred to the restrictions placed on his father as a Roman Catholic in *Imit. Horace, Ep. II. ii.* (1737), ll. 60–7. For objections by 'zealous papists' to passages in *An Essay on Criticism*, see **42** and n. above.

201. Warburton (1751 edn.), iii. 215–49, first printed the *Epistle to Bathurst* as a formal dialogue with 'letters of direction', in 1751, presumably on his own initiative (*TE*, iii (ii). 78–80). Warton, *Essay on P*, ii (1782), 158, had heard Bathurst complain that he 'spoke' only twenty-one of the 402 lines of the 'dialogue'.

202. P addressed his *Epistle . . . Of the Knowledge and Characters of Men* (1734) to Sir Richard Temple, Viscount Cobham (see also **272** n. below, and 'West' **2** and n. and 'Lyttelton' **1** n., **4** n. below).

In the MS SJ deleted two sentences about P's depiction of the Duke of Wharton as 'Clodio' in ll. 178–209 (see **368** below), written, SJ suggested, 'in emulation' of the character of 'Zimri' in Dryden's *Absalom and Achitophel*: see Textual Notes. SJ may have omitted them when he decided to focus his discussion on P's theory of the 'Ruling Passion' (ll. 174 ff.): for the background see White, *Controversy*, ch. VI. As early as 1684 Roscommon, *Essay on Translated Verse*, l. 94, had referred to 'the *Ruling Passion* of your Mind'.

SJ defines 'Affection' as '2. Passion of any kind', and 'Propension' as '1. Moral inclination; disposition to anything good or bad' (*Dict.*).

203–5. SJ had objected to P's theory of the Ruling Passion, and to the 'resistless Power and despotick Authority of this Tyrant of the Soul', as early as 1739, in his translation of Crousaz's *Commentary* (1742 edn.), 109 n. (*OASJ*, 91–2). See also *Ramblers* 43 (1750), 103 (on 'the modern dream of the ruling passion'), 113 (1751), in which the learned Misothea 'endeavoured to demonstrate the folly of attributing choice and self-direction to any human being' (*YW*, iv. 188, 239). In SJ's 'Sermon 16' a 'favourite notion or inclination', which can take 'entire possession of a man's mind' as if by 'insuperable destiny', is to be countered by meditation on 'important and eternal rules' (*YW*, xiv. 173–4). Not long before writing 'Pope', SJ mocked the doctrine that 'every Man has his genius' in a letter to Mrs Thrale, 10 July 1780 (*Letters*, iii. 284).

For SJ's careful revision of **203–4** in the MS, see Textual Notes.

203. With SJ's second sentence, cf. his comment that Waller was 'a hoarder in his first years, and a squanderer in his last' ('Waller' **105** above). With his final sentence, cf. 'Butler' **47** and n. and 'Cowley' **3** and n. above.

205. SJ's objection to 'a kind of moral predestination' is at the heart of his hostility to the 'Ruling Passion'. On 28 Oct. 1773 he referred to 'our free agency, an extinction of which would be a still greater evil than any we experience', and on 3 June 1781 asserted that a man who begins 'to *suppose* that he is not a free agent . . . should not be suffered to live; if he declares he cannot help acting in a particular way, and is irresistibly impelled, there can be no confidence in him, no more than in a tyger' (*Life*, v. 366, iv. 122–3).

206. For P's 'examples' in the form of short character sketches, see *Epistle to Cobham*, ll. 228–65.

Mrs Thrale noted in Mar./Apr. 1778: 'Johnson says that Pope's Ideas of the ruling Passion were not well discriminated at all, but mixed with notions of another Sort; the Courtier's Exit [ll. 252–5] is in the performance of a Ceremony & who can call Ceremony a Passion?' (*Thraliana*, i. 249). Cobham himself made similar objections to P 1, 8 Nov. 1733 (*Corresp.*, iii. 392–3). As Hill (1905) noted, this could explain SJ's suggestion that P might have 'condescended to learn' from Blackmore how to 'reason in verse' ('Blackmore' **46** and n. above).

207. *Of the Characters of Women: An Epistle to a Lady* appeared on 8 Feb. 1735. P told Swift, 16 Feb. 1733, that it was 'thought to be . . . my *Chef d'Oeuvre*: but it cannot be printed perfectly, in an age so sore of satire, and so willing to misapply characters' (Warburton (1751 edn.), ix. 234; *Corresp.*, iii. 349). A note in his octavo *Works*, vol. ii (1735), admitted a 'want of connection' in the text: '*Examples* and *Illustrations* of the Maxims laid down' had been omitted as 'Vice too high', to be reserved for the next age, quoting his own *Imit. Horace, Sat. II. i.*, ll. 59–60 (see **249** and n. below, and *TE*, iii (ii). 41, 66 n.).

The poem was clearly addressed to P's friend Martha Blount (1690–1762), as stated by William Ayre, *Memoirs of P* (1745), ii. 30. SJ is in fact mistaken in believing that the 'last edition' had 'taken [it] from her'. P instructed Warburton in 1744 to add a note claiming that he had used 'no *living Examples* or *real Names*' (*Corresp.*, iv. 516). In 1751 Warburton (the 'commentator', as in **173** above and **221** below), iii. 193 n., merely repeated P's own statement that the 'lady' was imaginary and that the poem contained 'nothing personal'.

208. P's character of 'Atossa' (ll. 115–50), added to the 'deathbed' edition of *Epistle to a Lady* in 1744, was widely taken to refer to Sarah Churchill (1660–1744), Duchess of Marlborough, and she herself believed this, according to Warton, *Essay on P*, ii (1782), 145–6. In an undated letter to the Earl of Marchmont written soon after P's death, Bolingbroke was torn between suppressing this identification and denying it, in view of her 'favor' to P (*A Selection from the Papers of the Earls of Marchmont*, ed. Sir G. H. Rose (1831), ii. 334–5).

Bolingbroke has been suspected of responsibility for the separate publication of 'Atossa' in 1746 as *Verses upon the late D——ss of M——. By Mr. P——* (Foxon, *English Verse*, P 984), with a final note stating that P accepted £1,000 from the Duchess to suppress the lines, 'yet the World sees the Verses; but this is not the first Instance where Mr. P.'s practical Virtue has fallen very short of those pompous Professions of it he makes in his Writings.' For the reason for Bolingbroke's anger with P, see **250–3** below.

'Atossa' in fact arguably depicted Katherine Darnley (1682?–1743), Duchess of Buckingham: see 'Sheffield' **20** and n. above, Spence, i. 166 and n., and *TE*, iii (ii). 159–70. 'Scrutator' (John Loveday) suggested in *Gent. Mag.* (1781), 358, that 'it may perhaps be considered as delineating *both* these illustrious ladies': cf. the comment by McLaverty, *P, Print and Meaning*, 226 n., on the mistake of assuming 'that such portraits are directed at one person . . . The trick was to fuse two targets.' For a flattering prose *Character* of the Duchess (published 1746), which P claimed in July 1743 merely to have revised and which she probably wrote herself, see Warburton (1751 edn.), viii. 246–50, and *Corresp.*, iv. 460.

209. P's *Imitations of Horace* which began as a response to hostility to the *Epistle to Burlington*, in fact appeared between 1733 and 1739 (see **156–9** above and **372** and n. below). For their origins at Bolingbroke's suggestion, while P was ill with a fever *c*. Jan. 1733, see Spence, i. 143–4.

SJ alludes to the anonymous and scurrilous *Sober Advice to Horace* (1734), 'Imitated in the Manner of Mr. Pope', which appeared two weeks before the *Epistle to Arbuthnot*, though not from P's usual publisher. It is clear from Bolingbroke to Swift, 27 June–6 July 1734, that P wrote it (*Corresp.*, iii. 413–14), and he collected it in his *Works* from 1738: see McLaverty, *P, Print and Meaning*, 174–5, 194–202. Its mockery of Dr Richard Bentley provoked *A Letter to Mr. Pope, Occasioned by Sober Advice from Horace* (1735) by Thomas Bentley, the great scholar's nephew (see Guerinot, *Pamphlet Attacks*, 251–4, 265, and **285** n. below). P replied in a long note on this 'small critic' in *Dunciad*, ii. 205 n.

SJ told Malone on 15 Mar. 1782 that he would omit *Sober Advice* from an edition of P, 'tho' undoubtedly Pope's' (Bodleian, MS Malone 30, fo. 64ᵛ). When

Warton included it in *Works of P* (1797), vi. 35–51, the *Monthly Review*, 23 NS (1797), 360–71, was shocked by its grossness, and T. J. Mathias commented in *Pursuits of Literature* (5th edn., 1798), 331–3 n.: 'If Mr. Pope had often written *thus*, his works must have been consigned to the library of a brothel.'

SJ's impatience with minutiae (cf. 'Dryden' 11 and n. above) resurfaces in his assertion that 'it is useless to settle the dates' of P's *Imitations*, with which Isaac Reed could have assisted him. P in fact usually published the *Imitations* soon after writing them, and they often bear a clear 'relation to the times': see P. Dixon, *The World of Pope's Satires* (1968).

210. SJ is implicitly replying to Ruffhead's claim, *Life*, 323, that P 'was the first that struck out this manner'. He refers to P's *Imit. Horace, Ep. II. i.* (1737), ll. 69–72, and to Horace, *Sat.*, II. i. 22 (cf. P's *Sat. II. i.*, ll. 37–40).

SJ defines 'Imitation' in this sense as '3. A method of translating looser than paraphrase, in which modern examples and illustrations are used for ancient, or domestick for foreign' (*Dict.*). John Oldham (1653–83) imitated Horace and Juvenal (1681), and for Rochester's 'Allusion to Horace' (1675–6; published 1680), see 'Rochester' 16 and n. above. For earlier examples of the form, see H. F. Brooks, 'The "Imitation" in English Poetry before the Age of Pope' *RES* 25 (1949), 124–40, and H. D. Weinbrot, *The Formal Strain* (Chicago, 1969), chs. 1, 2. For SJ's later reservations about a form he had used successfully in *London* (1738) and *The Vanity of Human Wishes* (1749), see 372 and n. below; and for the related development of free translation in the 17th century, see 'Denham' 32 and n. above.

211. P's modernizations of Donne's *Fourth Satire*, originally published as *The Impertinent* (1733), and *Second Satire* (written *c*.1713), appeared in *Works*, vol. ii (1735). According to his 'Advertisement', he wrote them at the suggestion of Robert Harley, Earl of Oxford, and Charles Talbot, Duke of Shrewsbury (see 'Prior' 30 and n. above): Donne was 'a proof with what Indignation and Contempt a Christian may treat Vice or Folly, in ever so low, or ever so high, a Station' (*TE*, iv. 3). Warburton (1770 edn.), iv. 239–40, claimed that, during the 'great clamour' against him in the early 1730s, P intended 'to shew that two of the most respectable characters in the modest and virtuous age of Elizabeth, Dr. Donne and Bishop Hall, had arraigned Vice publicly, and shewn it in stronger colours, than he had done'. (For Joseph Hall, see 380 and n. below.) Warburton, iv. 247–53, also printed Parnell's imitation of Donne's *Satire III*.

Dryden had asked in 'A Discourse Concerning Satire': 'Would not Donne's satires, which abound with so much wit, appear more charming if he had taken care of his words, and of his numbers?' (Watson, ii. 144). Hume later described the 'flashes of wit and ingenuity' in Donne's satires as 'totally suffocated by the harshest and most uncouth expression, which is any where to be met with' (*History of Great Britain*, i. (Edinburgh, 1754), 138). Cf. the bathetic anecdote of a confused Mr Crauford, who 'having heard that [SJ] preferred Donne's Satires to Pope's version of them said, "Do you know, Dr. Johnson, that I like Dr. Donne's original Satires better than Pope's." Johnson said, "Well, Sir, I can't help that"' (*J Misc.*, ii. 404).

SJ defines 'Imbecility' as 'Weakness; feebleness of mind or body' (*Dict.*): see 'Addison' 163 and n. above.

212. *An Epistle From Mr. Pope, To Dr. Arbuthnot* appeared on 2 Jan. 1735 (dated 1734) and in a revised text in *Works*, vol. ii, three months later (see also **370** below). John Arbuthnot (1667–1735), P's friend, physician, and collaborator, died on 27 Feb. 1735. Nichols corrected SJ's original error over these dates in the proofs: see Textual Notes. Reed's list of P's works included the correct date of publication (Bodleian, MS Malone 30, fo. 70).

   Although 'Épître X' ('A mes vers') may have been P's model for ll. 368 ff., there are resemblances to other epistles by Boileau: see E. F. Mengel, 'P's Imitation of Boileau in *Arbuthnot*', *Essays in Criticism*, 38 (1988), 295–307. P's sense of Boileau as a precedent is clear in 'A Letter to the Publisher' signed by Cleland and prefixed to the *Dunciad* in 1729 (*TE*, V. 17–18). For Boileau as a source, see also **340**, **368** below, and 'Rochester' **26** and n. above.

213. For 'comprehension', see 'Cowley' **144** and n. above.

   SJ described Arbuthnot in July 1763 as 'the first man' among the writers of Queen Anne's reign: 'He was the most universal genius, being an excellent physician, a man of deep learning, and a man of much humour' (*Life*, i. 425). SJ met his relative Robert Arbuthnot (1735–1803) in Edinburgh in Aug. 1773 (*Life*, v. 29). See L. M. Beattie, *John Arbuthnot: Mathematician and Satirist* (Cambridge, Mass., 1935) and R. C. Steensma, *Dr John Arbuthnot* (Boston, 1979).

214. According to P's 'Advertisement', *Arbuthnot* replied to attacks on 'not only my Writings (of which being publick the Publick judge) but my *Person, Morals*, and *Family*, whereof to those who know me not, a truer Information may be requisite' (*TE*, iv. 95). For a recent personal attack by Lady Mary Wortley Montagu and Lord Hervey, see **216** n. below.

215. P's 'Advertisement' explained that the poem was 'drawn up by snatches, as the several Occasions offer'd'.

   The character of Addison as 'Atticus' was the most notable passage to have been written and published earlier: see **115** and n. above, and *Gent. Mag.* (1779), 338. P also sent the closing lines to Aaron Hill on 3 Sept. 1731 (*Corresp.*, iii. 226), and published a version of ll. 289–304 in 1732. By then he had probably written most of the original 260 lines from which *Arbuthnot* later developed. For the complex MS evidence about its evolution, see Mack, *Last and Greatest Art*, 419–54. SJ's variants of P's couplet (ll. 213–14) do not correspond precisely to those recorded from texts before 1735 in *TE*, iv. 111, vi. 143, 285.

   SJ may have had P's tributes to Gay and Arbuthnot in mind when he wrote in *Rambler* 169 (1751) about 'the tardy emission of Pope's compositions, delayed more than once till the incidents to which they alluded were forgotten, till his enemies were secure from his satire, and what to an honest mind must be more painful, his friends were deaf to his encomiums' (*YW*, v. 134). Cf. **209** and n. above.

216. SJ's account of P's quarrel with Hervey was inserted from materials appended to the MS: see Textual Notes. It derives partly from P's note to *Arbuthnot*, l. 381 (Warburton (1751 edn.), iv. 42), but Isaac Reed's offer to provide SJ with relevant material (Bodleian, MS Malone 30, fo. 70) may have prompted SJ to add it: see headnote, and Reed's note in *Lives*, iv (1791), 119 n.

   John, Lord Hervey (1696–1743), agent of Walpole and confidant of Queen Caroline, is best remembered for his posthumously published *Memoirs* (1848) of the court of George II, and as P's 'Sporus' (see 370 and n. below). His brother, the Hon. and Revd Henry Hervey (1701–48), was an early friend of SJ: 'He was a vicious man, but very kind to me. If you call a dog HERVEY, I shall love him' (*Life*, i. 106, 532).

For Hervey's duel in 1731 with the politician William Pulteney (1684–1764), later Earl of Bath, see R. Halsband, *Lord Hervey* (Oxford, 1973), 113–19. Hervey supported Lady Mary Wortley Montagu in her quarrel with P, who dubbed him 'Lord Fanny' in *Imit. Horace, Sat. II. i.* (1733), l. 6, published on 15 Feb. 1733. SJ quotes *Verses Address'd to the Imitator . . . of Horace*, l. 20, from their acriminious reply on 8 Mar. 1733. For the possibility that P himself was responsible for the publication of one of the two versions of the poem published on that day, 'forcing calumny shrouded by the court out into the public', see McLaverty, *P, Print and Meaning*, 177–81. For a spirited response to Lady Mary on P's behalf, see *A Proper Reply to a Lady, Occasioned by Her Verses* (1733).

The 'hint' about P's father appeared in Hervey's *Epistle from a Nobleman to a Doctor of Divinity* (published 10 Nov. 1733), 7. The famous sketch of 'Sporus' is in *Arbuthnot*, ll. 305–33: for SJ's later comment on it, see 370 and n. below. P told Swift, 6 Jan. 1734, that he was 'ashamed to enter the lists' in 'a Woman's war' with Hervey (Warburton (1751 edn.), ix. 254–5; *Corresp.*, iii. 401).

P did not send Hervey his prose 'Letter to A Noble Lord', dated 30 Nov. 1733, which he circulated privately. It was printed by Warburton, viii. 253–80, who called it a 'masterpiece', and discussed by Ruffhead, *Life*, 316–18. Warton, *Essay on P*, ii (1782), 259–60, also considered it a 'masterpiece of *invective*'. Cowler, *Prose Works*, ii (1986), 436–7, describes SJ's comment on its 'tedious malignity' as 'surprising', since it 'resembles in some important respects his own famous letter to Chesterfield', i.e. as a challenge to aristocratic cultural authority.

Damrosch (1976), 205, noted SJ's recurrent use from this point in 'Pope' of the word 'malignity': see also 233, 236, 285, 358 below.

217. The two parts of *One Thousand Seven Hundred and Thirty Eight. A Dialogue Something like Horace* (May, July 1738) were entitled *Epilogue to the Satires* from 1740. See also 306, 371 below.

For P's association with the 'Patriot' opposition to the court headed by Frederick, Prince of Wales, see Goldgar, *Walpole*, 123–32, 159–60, 166–78, Mack, *AP*, 726–7, 755–9, and Gerrard, *Patriot Opposition*, 68–95. For other 'opposition' poets, see 'Hammond' 3, 'Somervile' 8 n., and 'Savage' 114, 206–7, 216–18 above, and 'Pitt' 9 n., 'Thomson' 28, 'West' 8 n., 'Mallet' 12, and 'Lyttelton' 6, 8 below. SJ's own anti-government views at this time are evident in *London*, published on 13 May 1738, the same day as P's first dialogue.

Although SJ refers to P as 'a follower of the Prince of Wales', P explicitly described himself as 'No Follower, but a Friend' of the Prince in *Epilogue to the Satires*, II. 93. He told Lord Bathurst, 8 Oct. 1735, about 'an unexpected Visit of 4 or 5 Hours' from the Prince (*Corresp.*, iii. 500–1), and cf. 259, 279 and nn. below. For a poem 'On hearing of his Royal Highness's visit to Mr POPE at *Twickenham*', by 'Vatillus', see *Gent. Mag.* (Oct. 1735), 610. In his will P left George Lyttelton (q.v. below), the Prince's secretary, the marble busts of Spenser, Shakespeare, Milton, and Dryden, 'which his Royal Master the Prince, was pleased to give me' (*Prose Works*, ii. 507). By Oct. 1738 Lyttelton was complaining that he had been 'almost forced to compell' P to dine with the Prince at Kew (*Corresp.*, iv. 139).

For P's earlier political 'prudence', see **74** and n., **82** above. In the 'Testimonies of Authors' prefixed to the *Dunciad*, he continued quoting such enemies as Theobald and Dennis as proof that he was 'a terrible imposer upon both parties, or very moderate to either' (*TE*, v. 38–9).

218. For Ralph Allen, see **168** and n. above. His father was variously described as a labourer and an innkeeper in Cornwall: see B. Boyce, *The Benevolent Man* (Cambridge, Mass., 1967), 1–3. P asked him, 28 Apr. 1738, whether he objected to being described as 'no Man of high birth or quality' in the poem. See also his letter of 2 Nov. 1738 (Warburton (1751 edn.), ix. 320; *Corresp.*, iv. 93, 144–5), and Warburton's elaborate explanation at iv. 312–14 n.

P revised 'low-born' to 'humble' in the 2nd edition of *Epilogue to the Satires*, I. 135. P's negative use of 'low-born' elsewhere seems to justify Allen's sensitivity: see *Epistle to Bathurst*, l. 140 ('Spread like a low-born mist, and blot the Sun'), and *Dunciad*, II. 356 ('A low-born, cell-bred, selfish, servile band').

219. See *Epilogue to the Satires*, II. 166–70, referring back to I. 69–72 and n., where P seemed to suggest that in 1738 Lord Hervey had written Henry Fox's address of condolence from the House of Commons on the Queen's death. For the protest in 1740 by the politician Henry Fox (1705–74), later Lord Holland, see 'Lyttelton' 8 and n. below.

220. A contemptuous reference to Thomas Sherlock, Bishop of Salisbury (later of London), in *Manners* (1739), a satire by Paul Whitehead (1710–74), led to a summons before the House of Lords. In his absence, Robert Dodsley, by then the publisher of seven of P's works as well as SJ's *London* (1738), had to appear. He was released on 20 Feb. 1739: see *Gent. Mag.* (Feb. 1739), 104, Warton, *Works* (1797), i, pp. lx–lxi, and Dodsley, *Corresp.*, 5–6.

SJ bargained for 10 guineas for *London* in 1738 because 'Paul Whitehead had a little before got ten guineas for a poem; and I would not take less than Paul Whitehead'. Boswell added that SJ 'appeared to me to undervalue Paul Whitehead upon every occasion when he was mentioned, and, in my opinion, did not do him justice'. In 1773 SJ described *Manners* as 'a poor performance' (*Life*, i. 124–5, v. 116). For Francis Lewis, translator of some of the mottoes in the *Rambler*, as another author who 'hung loose upon society', see *Life*, i. e as 225–6.

The spellings 'Sculk' and 'Skulk' are both in the *Dict*. In the MS 'sculked' is slightly blotted, and SJ may have written 'skulked'.

221. D. Griffin, *Patriotism and Poetry in Eighteenth-Century Britain* (Cambridge, 2002), 56 n., suggests that SJ's first sentence alludes to Lyttelton's *Epistle to Mr. Pope* (1730), l. 82, which urged P to 'join the PATRIOT's to the POET's praise'. For P's 'commentator' (as in **173, 207** above), see Warburton (1751 edn.), iv. 338 n.

P was disillusioned with the Patriot opposition rather than intimidated by 'statesmen', as SJ implies. In 1738–9 he in fact planned a third political dialogue, perhaps the fragmentary *1740*, published by Warton in 1797 (see **249** n. below, and *TE*, iv, pp. xl–xli). The *New Dunciad* (1742) (see **229–32** below) also has some political content.

222–7. SJ's discussion of the *Memoirs of Scriblerus* was inserted from materials appended to the MS: see Textual Notes.

222. Spence, i. 56–7; Warburton (1751 edn.), vi. 111–12 n., ix. 5; Ruffhead, *Life*, 208–9.

Although SJ twice referred to 'Scriblerus' in his early notes for 'Pope' (fos. 164ᵛ, 170ᵛ), he has not previously mentioned the 'Scriblerus Club' of *c.*1712–14. The *Memoirs of Martinus Scriblerus*, a collaboration by P, Swift, Gay, Parnell, and Arbuthnot, appeared in P's *Works in Prose*, vol. ii (1740): see C. Kerby-Miller's edition (1950). Warburton claimed that 'Polite learning never lost more than in the defeat of this scheme'.

223. Kerby-Miller (1950 edn.), 58, concluded that Arbuthnot was the most fertile contributor of ideas, but left it to others to give coherence to the *Memoirs*. He also, 66, suggested that the inadequate text and notes in Warburton (1751 edn.), vi. 105–94, help to explain SJ's 'sweeping and ill-considered judgement' on the *Memoirs*. Ruml, 'Younger J's Texts', 180–98, pointed out that in the *Dict.* (1755) SJ in fact quoted a passage omitted by Warburton. Given his low opinion of the *Memoirs*, SJ quoted the work surprisingly often in the *Dict.* without always attributing the 146 quotations in 1755 (reduced to 143 in 1773) to Arbuthnot: see McDermott, 'Textual Transformations', 133–48. *Gent. Mag.* (1783), 246–7, noted Warburton's omissions in *Works* (1751).

SJ's assessment sits oddly with his eulogy of Arbuthnot in **213** above. In contrast, Warton praised the *Memoirs* for a 'rich vein of humour' and 'variety of learning' in *Essay on P*, ii (1782), 403–4, as did J. T. Callender, *Deformities of Dr. SJ* (Edinburgh, 1782), 9. Lord Hailes also claimed in 1782 that the *Memoirs* contained 'many excellent things': see Carnie (1956), 345. The reputation of the *Memoirs* rose after Warton included the full text in *Works of P* (1797), vi. 61–191.

224. Cf. SJ's assertion in 1757 that 'The only end of writing is to enable the readers better to enjoy life, or better to endure it' (*OASJ*, 536), and in 1765 that it should make its readers 'more useful, happier, or wiser' (*YW*, vii. 108).

225. Warburton (1751 edn.), vi. 111 n., and Ruffhead, *Life*, 208, noted the influence of Cervantes.

See Kerby-Miller (1950 edn.), 69–70, who also discussed the *History of the Ridiculous Extravagances of Mr. Oufle* (1711), from the French (1710) of Laurent Bordelon (1653–1730). Although SJ wrote 'Oufle' in the MS, and corrected the printer's 'Ousle' to 'Oufle' in the proofs, 'Ouffle' appeared in 1781–3: see Textual Notes.

226. Spence, i. 56. Kerby-Miller (1950 edn.), 315–20, discussed the relationship of the *Memoirs* to *Gulliver's Travels* (1726) ('Swift' **85** above).

227. For Boileau's hostility to modern Latin verse, see 'Addison' **10** and n. above. SJ then refers to the *Anthologia* (1684) of Latin verse by Italian poets, which has been attributed to P's friend Francis Atterbury (see **131–2** above), and a copy of which SJ owned as an undergraduate (*Gleanings*, v. 216). In Atterbury's *Epistolary Corresp.*, iv (1787), 492, Nichols quoted Walter Harte's inscription in P's later anthology: 'It is surprizing that Mr. Pope should be *silent* upon this point, when he told me 14 years before the publication of this present edition, that the *Anonymus quidam* was Dr. ATTERBURY, Bishop of Rochester. Perhaps the Bishop did not chuse to acknowledge the slight amusements of his youth, or that others should ascertain the Author's name. W.H.' Reed repeated the attribution in *Lives*, iv (1791), 124 n., but Warton, *Works of P* (1797), i, p. lxi, rejected it, and James

Boswell Jr. later stated that the editor was Thomas Power of Trinity College, Cambridge (*J's Works* (1825), viii. 299 n.).

Ruffhead, *Life*, 409, referred only briefly to P's *Selecta Carmina Italorum Qui Latine Scripserunt* (2 vols., 1740), which omitted the 1684 preface and expanded the collection from eighty-one to 119 poems. In a discussion of SJ's interest in neo-Latin verse, R. DeMaria, *SJ and the Life of Reading* (Baltimore, 1997), 96–104, suggested that the neglect which greeted P's collection would remind SJ of the failure of his own early plan to edit the Latin verse of Politian: see 'Milton' 8 and n. above.

228. See *Corresp.*, iv. 5, and cf. Spence, i. 131–4, Warburton (1751 edn.), iii. 163–5 n., ix. 280, Ruffhead, *Life*, 267–70, and **198** and n. above.

This extract from P's letter was inserted from the appended materials in the MS: see Textual Notes. For a detailed account of P's various schemes for this projected work, sometimes described as the 'Opus Magnum', which was to have included the *Moral Essays*, see Leranbaum, *AP's 'Opus Magnum'*.

229. Spence, i. 134, 151; Warburton (1751 edn.), i, pp. vii–viii; Ruffhead, *Life*, 391, 392 n., citing P to Warburton, 28 Dec. 1742 (*Corresp.*, iv. 434–5). For P's asthma, see also **242** below. He incorporated part of a planned 'Epistle on Education' in *Dunciad*, IV. 135–336.

230. The *New Dunciad* (published 20 Mar. 1742) became Bk. IV of the revised *Dunciad, In Four Books* (Oct. 1743). The date in the first sentence was inserted in the MS: see Textual Notes.

Colley Cibber (1671–1757) became Poet Laureate in 1730 (see 'Savage' **172, 177** above). Although P praised *The Careless Husband* (1704) in *Imit. Horace, Ep. II. i.* (1737), ll. 91–2 (cf. Spence, i. 207), he had mentioned Cibber satirically in the original *Dunciad* (1729), I. 240, III. 134, 262, 289, 320. Cibber complained about this in his *Apology for his Life* (1740), 22–3, while referring to P as 'our most celebrated living Author', 'a great Genius' and 'our most eminent Author'. In *Dunciad* (1743), III. 305 n., Pope even jested about the fact that Cibber had subscribed to his *Iliad* thirty years earlier.

For SJ's personal acquaintance with, and opinion of, Cibber, see 'Dryden' **190** and n. above, and cf. 'Fenton' **11**, 'Savage' **54, 57, 177** above, and *Life*, i. 149, ii. 256–7, 340, iii. 72. Early in his career SJ was conventionally contemptuous of the Laureate, as in his *Compleat Vindication of the Licensers of the Stage* (1739) (*OASJ*, 81). For his epigram ('Great George's acts let tuneful Cibber sing; | For Nature form'd the Poet for the King'), see *Poems* (1974), 92, which also quotes the Revd James Hussey's claim to have heard him 'speak respectfully and with kindness' of Cibber.

On at least three occasions (in 1763, 1769, and 1777), SJ recalled that Cibber had consulted him about one of his royal birthday odes and had lost patience with SJ's objections. The 1777 version ends: ' "When we had done with criticism, we walked over to Richardson's, the authour of 'Clarissa,' and I wondered to find Richardson displeased that I 'did not treat Cibber with more *respect*.' Now, Sir, to talk of *respect* for a *player*!" (smiling disdainfully)' (*Life*, i. 401–2, ii. 92–3, iii. 184). Cibber was still alive when SJ quoted under 'Reading' in the *Dict.* a version of *Dunciad*, I. 281–2, 286: 'Less reading than makes felon's 'scape, | Less human genius than God gives an ape, | Can make a Cibber.'

231. P's references in *Imit. Horace, Sat. II. i.* (1733), l. 34, and *Epistle to Arbuthnot* (1735), l. 373, in fact preceded Cibber's 'submissive gentleness' in his *Apology* (1740). See also *New Dunciad* (1742), l. 20 and n. (before Cibber became the 'hero').

For P's attitude to the 'great', see **23, 196** above, and **270–2, 279, 281** below.

232. For similar 'instigators' of P's quarrel with Addison, see **105** above.

In *A Letter from Mr. Cibber, to Mr. Pope* (July 1742), 8, Cibber compared himself to a boxer, 'who should stand being drubbed for hours together', to exhaust his opponent 'by the repeated labour of laying him on'.

233. For the notorious mummy and crocodile in *Three Hours After Marriage* by P, Gay, and Arbuthnot, see 'Gay' **10** above. The farce was staged at Drury Lane on 16 Jan. 1717 (with Cibber as Plotwell) and had six further performances before the end of Jan. There is no cast list for the six performances of Buckingham's *The Rehearsal* (see 'Dryden' **94–100** above) at Drury Lane between 7 Feb. and 28 Mar. 1717 (*London Stage*).

SJ paraphrases Cibber's *Letter to Mr. Pope*, 18–19: 'the Audience by the Roar of their Applause shew'd their proportionable Contempt of the Play . . . he came behind the Scenes, with his Lips pale and Voice trembling, to call me to account for the Insult: And accordingly fell upon me with all the foul Language, that a Wit out of his Senses could be capable of . . . Mr. *Pope*—You are so particular a Man, that I must be asham'd to return your Language as I ought to do: but since you have attacked me in so monstrous a Manner; This you may depend upon, that as long as the Play continues to be acted, I will never fail to repeat the same Words over and over again.'

For the printer's failure to read 'their proportionable contempt' in the MS, see Textual Notes.

234. In *A Letter to Mr. Pope*, 47–9, Cibber claimed to have discovered P in a 'House of Carnal Recreation . . . perching upon the Mount of Love'. SJ's reticence about the details of this 'idle story' contrasts with the franker account of the incident (in a brothel, not 'a tavern') in *BB*, v. 3414 n.

Although P denied the story (see Spence, i. 110 and n.), it prompted at least three engravings in 1742: 'An Essay on Woman, *by the* Author *of the* Essay on Man' (see Mack, *AP*, opp. 781); 'The Poetical Tom-Titt perch'd upon the Mount of Love'; and '*And has not* Sawney *too his* Lord *and* Whore?' (see N. Ault, *New Light*, 302–3, and Wimsatt, *Portraits*, 364). Shenstone commented in Aug. 1742 that 'poor Pope's history, in Cibber's Letter, and the print of him upon the Mount of Love (the *coarsest* is the most *humorous*), must surely mortify him' (*Letters* (1939), 59). The story was later exploited in *The Age of Dullness. A Satire. By a Natural Son of the late Mr. Pope. With a Preface giving some Account of his Mother, and how he came to the Knowledge of his Birth* (1757).

235–6. For the 'general diversion' caused by the 'quarrels of writers', see *Ramblers* 40 (1750), 83, 176 (1751), the last describing the confrontation of sensitive author and 'furious critick' as among 'the principal of comick calamities' (*YW*, iii. 216–17, iv. 70–1, v. 164–5). Cf. **146–7, 232** above, and 'Prior' **5** above.

For SJ's own unwillingness to reply to enemies, see 'Dryden' **173** and n. above. P in fact claimed that this was his own policy, telling Caryll, 2 Aug. 1711: 'I've ever been of opinion that if a book can't answer for its self to the public, 'tis no sort of purpose for the author to do it'; and Jonathan Richardson, 2 Nov. 1732, of his 'resolve to go on in my quiet, calm, moral course, taking no sort of notice of men's, or women's anger, or scandal, with virtue in my eyes, and truth upon my tongue' (*Corresp.*, i. 132, iii. 327). The verdict of *BB*, v. 3415 n., on the quarrel was that 'the general cry ran in favour of Colley'.

237. P's aim in the *New Dunciad* (1742) was in effect to provoke Cibber sufficiently to justify substituting him for Theobald (see **145** above) as the hero of *The Dunciad, In Four Books* (Oct. 1743). See Spence, i. 143–4, for P's supposed plan of torturing Cibber by delaying its publication.

SJ defines 'To deprave' as 'To vitiate; to corrupt; to contaminate' (*Dict.*). For P's attempt to justify his transfer of Theobald's 'old books' to Cibber, see *Dunciad* (1743), I. 147–54 and n. Warton, *Essay on P*, ii (1782), 370, 376–7, made the same point about this 'gothic library', objecting that P had replaced 'a cold, plodding, and tasteless writer and critic' with one, who, for all his faults, 'had sense, and wit, and humour'.

238. In 1743 the bookseller Thomas Osborne (d. 1767) replaced William Chetwood in the urinating contest with Edmund Curll in *Dunciad*, II. 167–90. P believed that Osborne had advertised cut-down copies of the folio *Iliad* as the more expensive subscription quartos in 1739 (II. 167 n.): see **77** n. above and Foxon, *Book Trade*, 57 and n. SJ is here remembering his own early years in London. For the famous incident in which he knocked Osborne down for impertinence, while working for him on the catalogue of the Harleian Library *c.*1743, see *Life*, i. 154 and *J. Misc.*, i. 304.

SJ's third sentence alludes to Cassandra in Greek mythology, whose prophecies were always true but never believed. For Cibber's 'insolence' and 'brutal petulance', see 'Fenton' **11** above. For another author who was 'not constant to his subject', see 'Savage' **105** above. P's magpie which abuses all passers-by is in *Epistle to Cobham*, ll. 5–8.

239. Cibber continued replying to P in *The Difference between Verbal and Practical Virtue* (1742), *The Egotist: Or, Colley upon Cibber* (1743), and a brief *Second Letter* (1743), but SJ refers here to *Another Occasional Letter from Mr. Cibber to Mr. Pope* (1744).

P told Warburton, 12 Jan. 1744: 'He will be more to me than a dose of Hartshorn' (Warburton (1751 edn.), ix. 360–1; *Corresp.*, iv. 492). In the *Dict.* SJ quoted a long description of 'Hartshorn', a drug made from the horns of male deer, 'used to bring people out of faintings by its pungency'. (See also *Imit. Horace, Sat. II. i.*, l. 19.)

Since the younger Jonathan Richardson was born in 1694, the story SJ heard him tell was not a 'childhood memory', as described by H. Kirkley, *Biographer*, 231. See *Richardsoniana* (1776), 311–12, Thomas Davies's *Memoirs of Garrick* (1780), ii. 202, Hawkins's *Life* (1787), 347, and *J's Works* (1787), iv. 84 n. By 'writhen' (not in the *Dict.*), SJ means 'distorted', as in John Philips, *Cyder* (1708), I. 447 ('a writhen Mouth').

For P's reactions to criticism, see also **149** above and **278** below; and, for authorial sensitivity, see *Ramblers* 31, 40 (1750). Cf. also SJ's 'Sermon 17': 'every man is sufficiently sensible, when his own character is attacked, of the cruelty and injustice of calumny . . . those will animadvert, with all the wantonness of malice, upon the moral irregularities of others, whom the least reflection upon their own lives kindles into fury, and exasperates to the utmost severities of revenge' (*YW*, xiv. 183–4).

240. For P's collaboration with Warburton on 'a perfect edition of my works, and then I shall have nothing to do but to die', see Spence, i. 258 and nn.; Warburton (1751 edn.), i, p. i and nn.; and e.g. P. to Warburton, 28 Dec. 1742, 12 Jan. 1744 (*Corresp.*, iv. 434–5, 491). For early objections to Warburton as a defender of and commentator on P, see William Ayre, *Memoirs of P* (1745), ii. 87.

Ruffhead, *Life*, 423–4, in fact mentions P's plans at this period for two poems on 'Arbitrary Power' and 'Ambition': see Mack, *AP*, 769–71.

241. Forgetting that he has not previously mentioned 'Brutus', the epic P was planning at the end of his life, SJ echoes Ruffhead's reference, *Life*, 409, to his earlier discussion of it. Only eight lines of 'Brutus' survive: see *TE*, vi. 404–5, Spence, i. 134, 153, Warburton (1751, edn.), iii. 164–5 n., iv. 341 n., and Ruffhead, *Life*, 27–8, 409–23. Ruffhead printed P's detailed prose outline of the poem, mentioning that 'Part of the manuscript, in blank verse, now lies before me' (423).

John Hawkesworth in *Gent. Mag.* (1769), 256–9, described Ruffhead's account of 'Brutus' as the 'principal novelty' in his biography of P, and quoted it at length. Warton, *Essay* (1756), 278–82, had mentioned 'Brutus', but mistakenly assumed that it would have been in P's usual couplets, which were inappropriate for epic: he corrected his error in *Essay*, i (4th edn., 1782), 282 n. In *Works of P* (1797), i, pp. lxiii–lxiv, he drew P's late decision to use blank verse to the attention of 'defenders of rhyme'. For Young's reference to 'Brutus' in 1759, see 'Young' 118 and n. below; and for modern discussions, see Leranbaum, *AP's 'Opus Magnum'*, 155–74; V. Rumbold, 'P and the Gothic Past' (Ph.D. thesis, Cambridge, 1983), 215–51; and Mack, *AP*, 771–4.

P's late plan of writing an epic on a 'mythological' subject and in blank verse must have disconcerted SJ more than he admits: for his hostility to both, see 'Butler' 41 and n. and 'Milton' 274 and n. above, and for 'fiction', see 'Cowley' 16 and n. above. P had himself objected to blank verse as recently as June 1739: 'I have nothing to say for rhyme, but that I doubt whether a poem can support itself without it in our language, unless it be stiffened with such strange words as are likely to destroy our language itself.' Milton's 'high style' would be intolerable, 'had not his subject turned so much on such strange out-of-the-world things as it does' (Spence, i. 173). For Atterbury's attempts to persuade P of the superiority of blank verse to rhyme in 1716 and 1718, and P's half-serious 'promise . . . as soon as Homer is translated, to allow it [rhyme] unfit for long works', see *Corresp.*, i. 378, 500, 504, and cf. ii. 97.

P's 'Dramatis Personae' included Orontes, Magog, Hanno, Goffarius, Pisander, and Sagibert (Ruffhead, *Life*, 421–3). For similar objections, see 'Roscommon' 28 and n. above. SJ's repeated revision of this final sentence, beginning in the MS and proofs and continuing to 1783 (see Textual Notes), may reflect his uncertainty about what was truly 'Saxon'.

242. P told Warburton, 21 Feb. 1744: 'I have for some months thought myself going, and that not slowly, down the hill' (*Corresp.*, iv. 501). For the asthma and dropsy which afflicted SJ himself less than three years later, see *Life*, iv. 255–72, 353, 380–1.

For the quack Dr Thomas Thompson (d. 1763), see Spence, i. 63–4 and nn. Mallet told Lord Orrery, 19 May 1744, that, after treatment by Thompson, P's 'strength, as well as his senses, is, I think, irrecoverably impaired' (*Corresp.*, iv. 523; see also iv. 512, 521, 525; Hawkins, *Life* (1787), 337–9; and, for Thompson's dispute with another doctor in P's bedroom, Mack, *AP*, 806–7). Under 'Jalap', a root used as 'an excellent purgative where serous humours are to be evacuated', SJ quotes the account in Hill's *Materia Medica* (*Dict.*).

243. SJ heard this story from the Earl of Marchmont in May 1779 (see headnote above and **249** below). It was inserted from the appended materials in the MS: see Textual Notes.

P had known Martha Blount (1690–1762) and her sister Teresa (1688–1759) since 1707. He told Teresa in Sept. 1714 that 'Even from my infancy I have been in love with one after the other of you, week by week', and described Martha to Gay, 1 Oct. 1730, as 'A Friend, (a Woman-friend, God help me!) with whom I have spent three or four hours a day these fifteen years': see *Corresp.*, i. 258, iii. 135, Spence, i. 42, and **207** and n. above.

Warburton's hostility to Martha Blount influenced Ruffhead's reference to 'the indifference and neglect she shewed to him throughout his whole last illness' (*Life*, 548 n.). Spence, i. 264, reported that her visits to P in his last months in fact 'gave a new turn of spirits or temporary strength to him'. Warton, *Essay on P*, ii (1782), 396, claimed that P was enlivened by a visit from her in his last illness, but that the 'antiquated prude' refused to stay at Twickenham 'because of *her reputation*', and that her affectation and illtemper always gave him 'uneasiness and disgust'. See also **254** and n. below. P left her £1,000 of his estate of about £6,000, of which she was also to have the life-use (Spence, i. 359 and n.; Warburton (1751 edn.), ix. 371). For the relationship, see also Rumbold, *Woman's Place*, *passim*. For 'confidence' in the last sentence, see **160** and n. above.

For two early admirers of this paragraph at Streatham in July 1781, see Burney, *Early Journals*, iv. 99. SJ's reflections on P's psychological dependence on Martha Blount seem to foreshadow his own breach with Hester Thrale in 1784, but also recall the death of his wife in 1752, which he told James Elphinston, 27 July 1778, left 'a dismal vacuity in life, which affords nothing on which the affections can fix, or to which endeavour may be directed' (*Letters*, iii. 121). Cf. also *Idler* 41 (1759): 'The loss of a friend upon whom the heart was fixed, to whom every wish and endeavour tended, is a state of dreary desolation in which the mind looks abroad impatient of itself, and finds nothing but emptiness and horror' (*YW*, ii. 129).

244. See Spence, i. 262–3, 264; and Ruffhead, *Life*, 480, 461, 532–3 n. For P's death, see Brownell, ' "Like Socrates" ', 407–23.

George Lyttelton reported to his father, 5 May 1744: 'Poor Pope is, I am afraid, going to resign all that can die of him to death; his case is a dropsy, and he wants strength of nature to bear the necessary evacuations for the cure of that distemper' (*Works* (3rd edn., 1776), iii. 319). Dodsley himself may have told SJ the story about P's delusions, which Joseph Warton had also heard: see *Works of P* (1797), i, p. lxiv. Ruffhead, *Life*, 532–3 n., reported a story from Mallet of another 'odd kind of a vision' the dying P experienced.

245. Spence, i. 266–8; and Ruffhead, *Life*, 510.

Spence described Bolingbroke 'leaning against Mr. Pope's chair and crying over him, for a considerable time with more concern than can be expressed'; and saying, '"Oh great God! What is man?" (Looking on Mr. Pope, and repeating it several times, interrupted with sobs'. Thomas Gray recorded another version of Spence's story from Horace Walpole: 'When Pope was senseless & dying, Ld Bolingbroke stood by him, & broke into violent Exclamations & blasphemies agst Heaven, for suffering its noblest, divinest Work to be reduced to such a wretched Condition' (D. C. Tovey, *Gray and his Friends* (Cambridge, 1890), 287–8).

246. Spence, i. 260, 265, 268; and Ruffhead, *Life*, 543, 540–1 and n.

For Nathaniel Hooke's friendship with P, see **192** and n. above. Warton, *Essay on P*, ii (1782), 145 n., describing Hooke as 'a Mystic, and a Quietist, and warm disciple of Fenelon', confirmed that, to Bolingbroke's indignation, he brought a Catholic priest to P's deathbed. For P's religion, see **131, 200** above and **289** below.

247. Spence, i. 269; and Ruffhead, *Life*, 497.

The priest was Edward Pigott, a Benedictine. Warton, *Works* (1797), i. pp. lxv–lxvi, had heard that P struggled to 'throw himself out of his bed, that he might receive the last sacraments kneeling on the floor'.

248. Spence, i. 269; and Ruffhead, *Life*, 471.

Although P's father had in fact been buried at Chiswick (see **119** n. above), he was named on the memorial at St Mary's, Twickenham (Mack, *AP*, 875 n.). It is clear from P's will and Spence, i. 259, that he wanted only a simple inscription for himself. For Warburton's inscription (1761), see Warton, *Works of P* (1797), i. p. lxvi.

249–54. These paragraphs were inserted from the appended materials in the MS: see Textual Notes.

249. P's will in fact named Lord Bathurst, Lord Marchmont, William Murray, and George Arbuthnot as his executors, but also stated: 'all the Manuscript and unprinted Papers which I shall leave at my Decease, I desire may be delivered to my Noble Friend, *Henry St. John*, Lord *Bolingbroke*, to whose sole Care and Judgment I commit them, either to be preserved or destroyed; or in the case he shall not survive me, to the abovesaid Earl of *Marchmont*' (Warburton (1751 edn.), ix. 368; *Prose Works*, ii. 506).

SJ originally wrote that P left his papers to 'the Earl of Marchmont and Lord Bolingbroke, whom undoubtedly he expected', etc., but revised this in 1783: see Textual Notes. For Malone's complaint that SJ failed to make clear Marchmont's secondary position, and Boswell's continuing disquiet in 1791, see *Life*, iv. 51. For Marchmont's correspondence with P, Bolingbroke, and others in the 1740s, see *A Selection from the Papers of the Earls of Marchmont*, ed. Sir G. H. Rose (3 vols., 1831), ii. 175–389. Dodsley himself may have told SJ about his visit. P had left the property in his printed works to Warburton (see **194** above). Having published many of P's later poems, Dodsley was aggrieved to be excluded from P's *Works* (1751), and was still unsuccessfully seeking a share in Warburton's edition in the mid-1750s: see Dodsley, *Corresp.*, 212–17.

SJ had mentioned the alleged burning of P's MSS 'by those whom he had perhaps selected from all mankind as most likely to publish them' in *Idler*

65 (1759) (*YW*, ii. 202). When told of Lord Marchmont's statement to Boswell on 12 May 1778 that P had left no MSS, SJ replied, 'He lies, Sir', on the strength of Dodsley's story and P's reference in his will to such MSS. (With SJ's use of 'lies', cf. 'Broome' 6 and n.) Although Boswell suggested that P's will referred merely to the possibility that he might leave such papers (*Boswell in Extremes*, 338–9), Mack, *Collected in Himself*, 325, believed that Bolingbroke could have destroyed the MSS of some of P's major poems, as well as of unpublished works, out of anger at P's printing of *The Patriot King* (see **250–3** below) and hostility to Warburton, who would have benefited from their publication. For 'a boxful of the rubbish and sweepings of Pope's study', including the fragmentary MS of *One Thousand Seven Hundred and Forty*, preserved by Bolingbroke and seen by Malone in Dublin in 1774, see *TE*, iv. 330–1.

SJ finally alludes to *Imit. Horace, Sat. II. i.* (1733), ll. 59–60: 'Publish the present Age, but where my Text | Is Vice too high, reserve it for the next' (cf. **207** above).

250. SJ follows the indignant 'Advertisement' in Bolingbroke's *Letters on the Spirit of Patriotism* (1749), pp. vi–vii, reprinted by Ruffhead, *Life*, 522–32.

Bolingbroke entrusted the MS of *The Patriot King* to P in 1738. P's unauthorized edition, which made matters worse by 'improving' the style, was printed by John Wright: see J. McLaverty, *P's Printer, John Wright: A Preliminary Study* (Oxford, 1977). P may have had the secret edition in mind when claiming in 1744 that 'the proofs' that Bolingbroke, 'if in power, would have made the best of minsters' were 'ready, and the world *will* see them' (Spence, i. 124). Bolingbroke believed that he had burned all copies after P's death in 1744, but was forced into print in 1749 when extracts began appearing in a newspaper. See Barber, 'Bolingbroke', 67–89, Mack, *AP*, 733–4, 748–52, and, for the political context, Gerrard, *Patriot Opposition*, 185–210.

252. For David Mallet's part in the quarrel, see 'Mallet' **18** below, and, for Warburton's 'legacy', **194** above.

Warburton replied to Bolingbroke in *A Letter to the Editor of the Letters on the Spirit of Patriotism* (1749) (in Ruffhead, *Life*, 567–78), and Spence and others also defended P: see A. Wright, *Joseph Spence* (1950), 124–6, and *Gent. Mag.* (1749), 195–6, 240. For P's motives, see also **263, 287** below.

253. Martha Blount and Spence both believed that P acted out of 'excessive esteem for [Bolingbroke] and his abilities' (Spence, i. 125). SJ added the reference to *A Familiar Epistle to the Most Impudent Man Living* (1749), in which Bolingbroke replied to Warburton and complained further about P's betrayal, in 1783 (see Textual Notes). For SJ's comments on the controversy to Charles Burney in 1758, see *Life*, i. 329–30.

254. Spence, i. 158–60; Warburton (1751 edn.), ix. 369–70; Ruffhead, *Life*, 547–8, 576. P's reference to Ralph Allen (see **168, 194** above) in his will, which also left Allen his books, was by no means 'petulant and contemptuous', but SJ follows Ruffhead ('unhappily', according to *Corresp.*, iv. 464 n.). Ruffhead was influenced by Warburton, who had married Allen's niece and heiress in 1745, as is clear from another version of these anecdotes about Martha Blount and the Allens recorded by Thomas Gray, attributed to '[William] M[ason]: from Mr & Mrs W[arburto]n' (D. C. Tovey, *Gray and his Friends* (Cambridge, 1890), 280–2).

SJ's early notes for 'Pope' refer cryptically to 'Mrs. Blounts ill behaviour' (fo. 170ᵛ). For Martha Blount, see **243** and n. above, and, for her account of her visit to the Allens in 1743, see Spence, i. 159–60. Replying to her complaints about her treatment in Aug. 1743, P identified Mrs Elizabeth Allen (1698–1766) as the cause of the trouble ('a Minx, & an impertinent one') (*Corresp.*, iv. 462–4; and see also iv. 510, for later comments on the 'mutual misunderstanding'). Hawkins, *J's Works* (1787), iv. 89–90 n., claimed to have given SJ further information about the quarrel which he was 'too indolent' to use: it turned on Allen's refusal, when Mayor of Bath, to lend Martha Blount his coach when she wished to attend a Catholic chapel.

Martha Blount said in 1749 that, although she had not read his will, P 'mentioned to me the part relating to Mr. Allen, and I desired him to omit it, but could not prevail on him' (Spence, i. 158). P in fact instructed his executors to repay Allen £150 which he had borrowed in 1739, with the suggestion that Allen might prefer to give the money to the Bath hospital. For Richard Polwhele's memories of being told when a schoolboy by Ralph Allen's sister about the uneasiness caused by P and Martha Blount at Prior Park, see his *Biographical Sketches in Cornwall* (3 vols, Truro, 1831), i. 11–12. See also **287** below and Mack, *AP*, 765–8.

For 'To Pollute' as '3. To corrupt by mixtures of ill, either moral or physical' (*Dict.*), see also 'Cowley' **159** and 'Dryden' **173** above, and *Life*, i. 330, iv. 404 n. SJ revised 'posthumous resentment' in the MS to 'female resentment' in the proofs. The MS has the spelling 'accountant' but the printed texts have 'accomptant': see 'Textual Notes' and cf. 'Swift' **100** above. The *Dict.* includes both spellings.

255–68. Charles Burney Jr. noted in *Monthly Review*, 74 (1786), 380, that SJ 'has been much criticised for the minuteness with which he has described Pope's mode of living'. See e.g. the objections in J. T. Callender, *Deformities of Dr. SJ* (Edinburgh, 1782), 11, to the 'tiresome and disgusting trifles' in SJ's account, and R. Potter, *Inquiry* (1783), 4.

255. Spence, i. 5–6 (and cf. **3** above); Warburton (1751 edn.), iv. 16 n.; Ruffhead, *Life*, 475. For a description by SJ's friend Joshua Reynolds of P's appearance in 1740, see Mack, *AP*, 153–4 and cf. 214.

P's account of the 'Little Club' in *Guardians* 91–2 (1713) includes what may be a grotesque description of himself: see 'Addison' **72** above. Voltaire described P as 'bossu par-devant et par-derrière' in 'Parallèle d'Horace, de Boileau et de Pope' (1761): see his *Œuvres*, xliii (1821), 157. (SJ deleted his original reference to Voltaire in the MS: see Textual Notes.)

For P's 'diligent application' as a boy see **16, 19** above, and for its effect on his health, Spence, i. 29–30. SJ could have learned about the raising of P's seat at meals, for which there seems to be no printed source, from Savage or Walter Harte.

256. SJ quotes *Epistle to Arbuthnot*, l. 132, 'To help me thro' this long Disease, my Life'; cf. P to Hill, 14 Mar. 1731, 'my whole Life has been but one long disease' (*Corresp.*, iii. 182). For P's medical history, see Nicolson and Rousseau, '*This Long Disease*', 7–82, and Mack, *Collected in Himself*, 372–92.

the headach: this may derive from the servant's account cited in **257–60** n., but see also **260** n. below. The spelling 'headach' is in the *Dict.*

257–60. SJ's main source here and in **265–6** is the report by 'D.' (John Duncombe?) of an interview with a former servant of P's friend Edward Harley, 2nd Earl of Oxford, in *Gent. Mag.* (Sept. 1775), 435, which had also appeared, without the first paragraph and the conclusion, a month earlier in the *Universal Mag.* 57 (Aug. 1775), 91–2. Although Sherburn, *Early Career*, 13, questioned its reliability, Mack, *AP*, 823 n., 848 n., accepted it at face value.

SJ stated in *Rambler* 60 (1750) that 'more knowledge may be gained of a man's real character, by a short conversation with one of his servants, than from a formal and studied narrative, begun with his pedigree, and ended with his funeral' (*YW*, iii. 322); see also *Rambler* 68 (1750) (quoted in 'Swift' **123** n. above). In *Gent. Mag.* (Nov. 1783), 904, 'Y. Z.' reported a recent meeting at Newport with 'Mrs. Serle, housekeeper, for many years, to Pope', then aged about 90, and wished that SJ 'had known of Mrs. Serle before his Lives were published'. Her husband John Searle had been P's gardener, and they are both mentioned in his will (*Prose Works*, ii. 507, 514 n.).

257. SJ defines 'Bodice' as 'Stays; a waistcoat quilted with whalebone, worn by women' (*Dict.*), originally treated as a plural (from 'bodies'). Hawkins, *J's Works* (1787), iv. 2 n., reported that P's 'weakness was so great, that he constantly wore stays, as I have been assured by a waterman at Twickenham, who, in lifting him into his boat, had often felt them'. Potter, *Inquiry* (1783), 4, asked: 'Can it be of any importance to us to be told how many pair of stockings the author of the Essay on Man wore?'

P described himself as 'half Beau, half Sloven' in *Imit. Horace, Ep. I. i.* (1738), l. 161, and admitted in 'A Letter to a Noble Lord' that 'I am short, not well shap'd, generally ill-dress'd, if not sometimes dirty' (*Prose Writings*, ii. 445).

SJ told John Taylor, 12 May 1781, that, 'till his powers really desert him', an old man should 'resolutely disdain' to 'put himself to nurse' (*Letters*, iii. 345).

258. For a 'tye-wig', see **28** and n. above.

259. Although Ruffhead, *Life*, 480, denied that P was 'hippish', SJ agrees with Democritus and Plato, as cited by James Mackenzie, *The History of Health* (Edinburgh, 1758), 15, 74: 'When the body is in pain . . . the mind has no relish for the exercise of virtue', and 'an infirm constitution is an obstacle to the practice of virtue'. SJ said on 16 Sept. 1777: 'I do not know a more disagreeable character than a valetudinarian, who thinks he may do any thing that is for his ease, and indulges himself in the grossest freedoms' (*Life*, iii. 152, and cf. iii. 1 and n.) While writing 'Pope', he said on 29 Dec. 1780 that 'it is so difficult for a sick Man not *to be a Scoundrel*' (*Thraliana*, i. 465). For his belief that 'health is the basis of all social virtues', and that ill-health produces selfishness, see also *Letters*, i. 321, 359, iv. 94, 200, 305, 316, 334, 376, and *Ramblers* 48, 74 (1750).

SJ had quoted the French lines to Hester Thrale as recently as 4 July 1780 (*Letters*, iii. 282). Found in various earlier sources, they were attributed to Antoine Houdar de La Motte (d. 1731) in Charles Iréné Castel, Abbé de Saint Pierre, *Ouvrages*, xvi (Rotterdam, 1741), 157–65: see Primer, 'Tracking a Source', 55–60.

SJ also quotes *Imit. Horace, Sat. II. i.* (1733), l. 13: 'I nod in Company, I wake at night', echoed in P's letter to Richardson, 21 Nov. 1743 (*Corresp.*, iv. 484). Lord Marchmont confirmed his tendency to fall asleep in company (*Boswell in Extremes*,

333; Hawkins, *J's Works* (1787), xi. 200). For the Prince's visit to Twickenham on 4 Oct. 1735, see *Corresp.*, ii. 500–1, **217** above, and **279** below.

260. *Gent. Mag.* (1775), 435.

P gave a complacent, if partly self-mocking, account of the elaborate medical treatment he received from various aristocratic ladies, while staying with Sir William Codrington near Bath, to Martha Blount, 4 Sept. 1728 (*Corresp.*, ii. 513–14). He apologized to Lord Oxford for causing trouble as a guest in letters of [Nov.?] 1725, 13 Mar., 3 Apr. 1731 (*Corresp.*, ii. 335, iii. 179, 187). It was while he was ill at Lord Oxford's house in Jan. 1733 that Bolingbroke suggested that he write his first imitation of Horace (Spence, i. 143–4; *Corresp.*, iii. 345). Three months before he died, SJ told the Duke and Duchess of Devonshire that 'a Sick Man is not a fit inmate of a great house' (*Letters*, iv. 397).

Cf. SJ's early notes for 'Pope': 'Very troublesome in a house. Fermor. Orrery' (fo. 177ᵛ). For Orrery, see **263** and below. 'Fermor' no doubt refers to the Mrs Fermor SJ met in Paris in 1775 (see **54** and n. above). In Paris in Sept. 1784 she told Mrs Thrale more about P's 'numberless caprices' as a guest and, as SJ no doubt heard in 1775, that P 'only sate dozing all day, when the sweet wine was out, and made his verses chiefly in the night; during which season he kept himself awake by drinking coffee, which it was one of the maids business to make for him, and they took it by turns' (*Observations and Reflections* (1789), i. 21).

261. Although Ruffhead, *Life*, 500, claimed that P was 'extremely temperate, and, in general avoided the delicacies of a sumptuous table', William Kent described P to Burlington, 28 Nov. 1738, as 'the greatest Glutton I know', and other friends made similar comments (see *Corresp.*, iv. 150; for his eating habits see 'Personal Traits' in the index, v. 180–1). SJ's acquaintance Dr William King of Oxford (see 'Dryden' **187** and n. above) believed that P 'certainly hastened his death by feeding much on high-seasoned dishes, and drinking spirits', such as cherry brandy (*Political and Literary Anecdotes* (1818), 12–13). For P's own views on 'luxuriousness', see Spence, i. 145–6, and, for his drinking, Mack, *AP*, 272, 590–1 (concluding that P was generally restrained but had occasional excesses), 864 n. SJ defines 'Dram' as '3. Such a quantity of distilled spirits as is usually drank at once' (*Dict.*).

SJ refers to Juvenal, *Sat.*, X. 164–6, imitated in *The Vanity of Human Wishes* (1749), ll. 219–22, where Charles XII of Sweden replaced Hannibal.

SJ may be the first printed source for P's love of lampreys, but Warton, *Essay on P*, ii (1782), 130, also related that P, after languishing in bed with a headache, would rise with alacrity to eat 'stewed lampreys' for dinner. Henry Thrale was devoted to 'stewed Lampreys' in his last years (*Letters*, iii. 239 and n.).

SJ's own 'dietitic management' was fortified by the knowledge that Addison and P had 'shortened their days' by their excesses: see *J. Misc.*, ii. 336. He admitted to Hester Thrale, 15 Apr. 1784, an 'inclination to luxury' in eating (*Letters*, iv. 316, and cf. 427 and n.).

262. *conformation*: '1. . . . the particular texture and consistence of the parts of a body' (*Dict.*).

263. SJ wrote in 1765: 'Whoever is stigmatised with deformity has a constant source of envy in his mind, and would counterballance by some other superiority these advantages which he feels himself to want' (*YW*, viii. 605, and cf. 613).

SJ adapts Young, *Love of Fame*, VI. 190 ('Nor *take* her *Tea* without a *strata-gem*'), quoted earlier in *Idler* 36 (1758). Lord Orrery himself may have told SJ the story of the screen (see 'Dorset' **6** and n. above).

Lord Marchmont was the source for the saying by Marie-Claire St John (*c.*1675–1750), Bolingbroke's second wife (*Boswell in Extremes*, 333). Boswell later used the French version ('un politique aux choux et aux raves') of SJ's own oblique references to his social engagements (*Life*, iii. 324). It also appeared in an apparently forged letter from SJ to Lord Lucan, 1 Mar. 1781, in a newspaper in June 1792 (*Letters*, ed. Chapman, ii. 410).

For *The Patriot King*, see **252** above and **287** below.

264. Ruffhead, *Life*, 478–9, praised P's easy conversation, merely hinting at its limita-tions. See 'Dryden' **166–8** above and, for the conversation of other poets, see 'Cowley' **200** and n. above.

Lord Hervey, hardly an objective witness, wrote that P's 'poor tortur'd Im-agination, perpetually on the Stretch to act the Wit, the Refiner, and the Humor-ist, yields Maxims, Sentences, Observations and Sentiments, just as poor Wretches upon the Rack make Confessions' (*Letter to Mr. C[ib]b[e]r* (1742), 19–20). Thomas Birch stated more blandly in *The Heads of Illustrious Persons*, ii (1751), 56: 'His conversation was natural, easy, and agreeable, without any affectation of displaying his wit, or obtruding his own judgment, even upon subjects of which he was so eminently a master.'

In July 1778, SJ's 'remark that nobody could ever relate any thing that Pope *said*' prompted Elizabeth Montagu to claim 'that She had never heard him speak indeed, but She once had heard him cough: you heard then Madam says Johnson as much from him as anybody ever did' (*Thraliana*, i. 331–2). Spence's record of P's conversation evidently failed to change SJ's mind in 1780. Lord Marchmont in fact told Boswell in 1778 that P 'was not *un homme à bons mots*. His conversation was something better—more manly. A flow of vivacity' (*Boswell in Extremes*, 333), and SJ himself questioned Marchmont about this in May 1779 (Hawkins, *J's Works* (1787), xi. 200). 'Scrutator' (John Loveday) in *Gent. Mag.* (1781), 359, reported from personal knowledge that P's conversation was 'to the last degree engaging and entertaining', and Warton, *Essay on P*, ii (1782), 176, added that P's friends had assured him of his 'admirable talent for telling a story'.

For 'apophthegm', see 'Blackmore' **38** and n. above. The anecdote about Samuel Patrick (1684–1748), editor of Ainsworth's *Latin Dictionary* (1746) and other reference works, is in Warburton (1751 edn.), vi. 148 n., and Ruffhead, *Life*, 205. For P's Latin inscription (1738) on Shakespeare's monument in Westminster Abbey, see Mack, *AP*, 734; for P's disagreement with Dr Mead about 'amor publicus' in the inscription, see *Gent. Mag.* (1741), 105; and for mock-scholarly banter about the monument, see the opening note to *Dunciad* (1743) (*TE*, v. 267–8).

Boswell later noted another example of P's repartee in Ruffhead, *Life*, 535 n., as did Lord Hailes in 1782: see Carnie (1956), 345 and n. For this *bon mot*, and for another addressed to the Prince of Wales, see **279** n. below.

SJ's self-mocking quotation is from *Aeneid*, II. 204 ('I shudder as I mention it'). SJ revised '*maker*' to '*publisher*' in the MS (see Textual Notes). His definitions of 'Publisher' in the *Dict.* do not include the precise sense of 'author' or 'compiler'.

265. *Gent. Mag.* (1775), 435.

SJ defines 'To Infest' as 'To harass; to disturb; to plague' (*Dict.*). Lady Mary Wortley Montagu's descendants explicitly denied that she and P ever met at Lord Oxford's table: see Mack, *AP*, 882 n., who did not identify SJ's source. Mrs Thrale-Piozzi heard SJ describe Lady Mary's *Letters* (1763) as the only book he had ever voluntarily read through (*J. Misc.*, i. 319).

266. See Spence, i. 6, for the testimony of Mrs Racket, P's half-sister, and *Gent. Mag.* (1775), 435.

The accusation that P never produced more than a monkey-like 'broad Grin' is found as early as *Pope Alexander's Supremacy ... Examin'd* (1729), 18. For the views of SJ and others on laughter, see 'Swift' **122** and n. above.

267. For the Homer MSS, and P's habit of translating on the backs of letters, see **95** and n. above.

SJ's source for P's scanty 'entertainment' is Patrick Delany, *Observations upon ... Swift* (1754), 181, on P's 'manner of living' according to Swift, who told Gay, 19 Mar. 1730: 'you ... who have left off drinking Wine ... would not now think it hard if Mr Pope should tell us towards the bottom of a pint: Gentlemen I will leave you to your wine' (*Corresp.*, iii. 97). For Swift's own frugality, see 'Swift' **103** and n. above. SJ ends by quoting P to Swift, 23 Mar. 1737 (*Corresp.*, iv. 64).

268. See Spence, i. 216–17, for P's failure to make Warburton eat lobster at their first dinner together; and i. 156–8, for the testimony of Mrs Racket and Martha Blount that P did not love money and was generous with it.

P told Swift, 9 Oct. 1729, that he could afford to give away £100 p.a. (Warburton (1751 edn.), ix. 139; *Corresp.*, iii. 57). For his support of Robert Dodsley and Richard Savage, see also **286** and n. below, and for the benevolence of other poets, see 'Savage' **91–3** and n. above.

269. For P as 'too much a lover of money', see 'Broome' **9** above, and, for his grotto and 'quincunx', **118–19** and nn. above.

P ridiculed poor authors in the prefatory letter (signed by William Cleland) in the *Dunciad* (*TE*, v. 14–17) and at II. 270 n., and in *Epistle to Arbuthnot*, ll. 13, 151–6. The Mint was a refuge for insolvent debtors: cf. 'Rowe' **21** and n. above. For SJ's own sympathy with the poor, see his review of Soame Jenyns in 1757 (*OASJ*, 527), 'Sermons' **4**, **11**, **19**, and *YW*, xiv. 207 n.

270. Ruffhead, *Life*, 488–91, described P's relations with 'the great and wealthy ... upon the easy terms of reciprocal amity, and social familiarity ... He courted none on account of their honours or titles; but was a friend to such only whom he thought distinguished by their virtues.' Lady Mary Wortley Montagu claimed in 1754 that P in fact 'courted with the utmost assiduity all the old men from whom he could hope a legacy', including various noblemen, Congreve, and Swift (*Complete Letters*, ed. R. Halsband (3 vols., Oxford, 1965–7), iii. 58).

For P and 'the Great', see **23**, **196**, **231** above and **279**, **281** below, and cf. 'Dryden' **172** and n. and 'Swift' **52**, **134** and nn. above. He described his policy of pleasing but not flattering great men to Swift, Aug. 1723 (*Corresp.*, ii. 185). He denied any servility in the prefatory letter in the *Dunciad* ('He has liv'd with the Great without Flattery') (*TE*, v. 18), in conversation with Spence, i. 160, and in *Epistle to Arbuthnot*, ll. 334–9. (For the line P later omitted, 'who pleased ye

Great but not by servile ways', see Mack, *Last and Greatest Art*, 428–9.) Both Savage and SJ seem to miss the point of the mockery of servility in P's 'Epigram' (1738): 'I am his Highness' Dog at *Kew*; | Pray tell me Sir, whose Dog are you?' (*TE*, vi. 372). For P and the Prince of Wales, see **217** and n. above.

271. P said late in life, 'I now fling off lords by dozens' (Spence, i. 167). For his aristocratic friends, see *Imit. Horace, Sat. II. i.*, l. 133, and *Epistle to Arbuthnot*, ll. 265–6. P in fact named peers and statesmen among his patrons in the preface to the *Iliad*, which also mentions Congreve's 'sincere Criticisms', but he withheld the dedication to Congreve to the end of the translation (*TE*, vii. 23–5, viii. 578–9). See also 'Congreve' **22** (for his lack of 'virtue') and **30** above.

The dedication to Congreve was particularly apt because Dryden had hoped in the 1690s that, while he himself was translating Virgil, Congreve would undertake the *Iliad*: see J. Brady in P. Hammond and D. Hopkins (eds.), *John Dryden: Tercentenary Essays* (Oxford, 2000), 122–3. Near the end of the *Iliad* (XXIV. 934 n.) P gracefully admitted to borrowing a couplet from Congreve, 'whose Translation of this Part was one of his first Essays in Poetry' (*TE*, viii. 575 n., and cf. vii. 23, x. 542–9). The dedication described Congreve as 'one of the most valuable Men as well as finest Writers, of my Age and Countrey: One who has try'd, and knows by his own Experience, how hard an Undertaking it is to do Justice to *Homer*' (*TE*, viii. 578).

Ruffhead, *Life*, 493 n., stated that P esteemed Congreve 'for the manners of a gentleman and a man of honour, and the sagest of the poetic tribe'. See also Spence, i. 208, P to Oxford, 21 Jan. 1729, on their 'long 20 years friendship' (*Corresp.*, iii. 10), and his reference to Congreve as an early encourager of his poetry in *Epistle to Arbuthnot*, l. 137 ('And *Congreve* lov'd ... my Lays'). Lady Mary Wortley Montagu, however, told Arbuthnot, 3 Jan. 1735, that Congreve 'was so far from loveing Popes Rhyme, both that & his Conversation were perpetual jokes to him, exceeding despicable in his Opinion' (*Corresp.*, iii. 449).

For SJ's revision in 1783 of his original assertion in the final sentence that P's letters do not mention Congreve, see 'Textual Notes'.

272. P addressed three of the epistles later collected as the *Moral Essays* to Lords Cobham, Bathurst, and Burlington (see **156, 198, 202** above), and the *Essay on Man* and *Imit. Horace, Ep. I. i.* to Bolingbroke (**174** and n. above).

Cf. SJ's early note for 'Pope': 'not happy in his Selection of Patrons. Cobham, Burlington, Bolingbroke' (fo. 159ʳ). He said on 12 May 1778 that P had been foolish 'to give all his friendship to Lords, who thought they honoured him by being with him; and to choose such Lords as Burlington, and Cobham, and Bolingbroke! Bathurst was negative, a pleasing man; and I have heard no ill of Marchmont' (*Life*, iii. 347). Boswell's journal reveals that SJ in fact described Burlington as 'infamous' (*Boswell in Extremes*, 340; cf. 'Gay' **12** above). The reason for SJ's antipathy is unclear, but see D. Nokes, *John Gay* (Oxford, 1995), 203–6, for 'the prevailing homoerotic atmosphere of Burlington's artistic coterie', and Hogarth's depiction in *Masquerades and Operas* (1724) of Burlington 'presiding over an institutionalised cultural decline'. For Cobham's atheism and 'Patriot' politics, see 'West' **7** and n. and 'Lyttelton' **12, 27** and n. below.

Although Bathurst escapes SJ's censure, Lady Mary Wortley Montagu's 'Epistle' to him (*c.*1725) depicted his passion for 'the Fair' (*Essays and Poems*

(Oxford, 1977), 242–4), P described him as 'Philosopher and Rake' in *Sober Advice from Horace*, l. 158, and William Ayre, *Memoirs of P* (1745), ii. 58, noted drily that he 'has a more than common Regard for the Fair Sex'. Bathurst, who introduced himself to Sterne in 1760 as a survivor of the age of Swift and P (Sterne, *Letters*, ed. L. P. Curtis (Oxford, 1955), 305), died in 1775. For SJ's hostility to Bolingbroke, described by P in Mar. 1736 as 'the greatest man in the world, either in his own time, or with posterity' (*Corresp.*, iv. 6; cf. **193** n. above), see 'Mallet' **18–19** and nn. below.

273. SJ revised this paragraph with particular care in the MS: see Textual Notes. Cf. the similar opening to 'Addison' **122** above.

Ruffhead praised P's letters for 'that frank sincerity, that artless *naiveté*, that unaffected openness, which shews the amiable and virtuous disposition of the writer', and which 'flowed from the heart' (*Life*, 406, 470). For Dennis's earlier attack on P's professions of 'truth, candour, friendship, good-nature, humanity, and magnanimity', and for SJ's comments on his tendency to 'talk too frequently of his own virtues', see **34–5, 167** above. For Mary Jones's praise of the 'Spirit of Benevolence' and the 'noble strains of Generosity' in P's *Letters* (1735), see her *Miscellanies in Prose and Verse* (1750), 313–14. Gray wrote of P to Walpole, Feb. 1746: 'it is not from what he told me about himself that I thought well of him, but from a Humanity & Goodness of Heart, ay, & Greatness of Mind, that runs thro his private Correspondence' (Gray, *Corresp.*, i. 229–30).

P stated in the preface to *Letters* (1737) (see **167–9** above) that, except for the earliest, they were 'by no means Efforts of the Genius but Emanations of the Heart' (quoted under 'Emanation' in the *Dict.*), and contained 'his real Sentiments, as they flow'd warm from the heart, and fresh from the occasion; without the least thought that ever the world should be witness to them' (*Prose Works*, ii. 369–70). He had claimed in 1712 that 'my style, like my soul, appears in its natural undress before my friend' in his letters, and in 1716 that they were 'the most impartial Representations of a free heart' (*Corresp.*, i. 155, 353).

SJ mocked the idea that letters reveal the writer's 'naked' soul when writing to Mrs Thrale, 27 Oct. 1777, but had taken a more positive view in an earlier letter of 2 Aug. 1775 (*Letters*, iii. 89–90, ii. 260–1). For our fear of self-examination, see *Idler* 27 (1758): 'very few can search deep into their own minds without meeting what they wish to hide from themselves, scarce any man persists in cultivating such disagreeable acquaintance, but draws the veil again between his eyes and his heart.' In *Idler* 84 (1759) on autobiography, however, he wrote that 'he that speaks of himself has no motive to falshood or partiality except self-love, by which all have so often been betrayed, that all are on the watch against its artifices' (*YW*, ii. 84, 264). For epistolary writing, see also *Rambler* 152 (1751).

Of his own letters, SJ said that 'he did not choose they should be published in his lifetime; but had no objection to their appearing after his death'; and that 'It is now become so much the fashion to publish letters, that in order to avoid it, I put as little into mine as I can' (*Life*, iii. 276, iv. 102, and cf. ii. 60).

274. SJ asked on 9 Apr. 1778: 'Are we to think Pope was happy, because he says so in his writings? We see in his writings what he wished the state of his mind to appear' (*Life*, iii. 251).

A contributor to *Gent. Mag.* (Mar. 1782), 117, complained about SJ's 'strange abuse of the *sacred name* of friendship' as 'a childish weakness' in **273–5**. SJ wrote in *Rambler* 13 (1750) that 'every man desires to be most esteemed by those whom he loves, or with whom he converses', and in *Rambler* 28 (1750) discussed the impediments to sincerity in friendship (*YW*, iii. 70, 154–5).

275. For similar anti-scepticism, see 'Halifax' **12** above: 'To charge all unmerited praise with the guilt of flattery', etc.

SJ may react again to Ruffhead, who claimed that P's 'morals are the best comment on his writing . . . he felt and practised himself what he recommended to others': 'it hurts our pride to be the dupes of hypocrisy. To be truly useful and entertaining, a good writer should likewise be a good man. Such was Mr. Pope' (*Life*, 483–4). SJ asserted in *Rambler* 76 (1750): 'It is natural to mean well, when only abstracted ideas of virtue are proposed to the mind' (*YW*, iv. 34). Hill (1905) noted SJ's response on 19 Oct. 1769 to Boswell's guilt about 'not feeling for others as sensibly as many say they do': 'Sir, don't be duped by them any more. You will find these very feeling people are not very ready to do you good. They *pay* you by *feeling*' (*Life*, ii. 95). SJ's reference to 'benevolence where there is nothing to be given' recalls the opening of Sterne's *Sentimental Journey* (1768).

276–86. SJ had stated in 1742 that the letters in *Memoirs of the Duchess of Marlborough* gave the reader 'the satisfaction of forming to himself the characters of the actors, and judging how nearly such as have hitherto been given of them agree with those which they now give of themselves' (*OASJ*, 114). His sceptical critique of the self-representation in P's published letters uses precisely this technique of setting 'his book and his life . . . in comparison'. Cf. his early notes for 'Pope': 'Amiable disposition—but he gives his own character . . . Ostentatious benevolence Professions of sincerity—Neglect of fame Indifference about every thing', etc. (fo. 170ʳ).

276. SJ uses 'artificial' in the sense of '1. Made by art; not natural' rather than '3. Artful; contrived with skill' as elsewhere (*Dict.*).

P's preface (1737) admits that his early letters had 'too much of a juvenile ambition of Wit, or affectation of Gayety' (*Prose Works*, ii. 368; quoted under 'Ambition' in the *Dict.*). He told Swift, 28 Nov. 1729: 'it is many years ago since I wrote as a Wit' (*Corresp.*, iii. 79). In 1736 he stated that epistolary style should be adapted to the subject, 'an easy familiar style' not always being appropriate (Spence, i. 177). Writing to Ralph Allen, 5 June 1736, about the proposed edition of his *Letters*, he claimed that 'the Only Use to my own Character *as an author*, of such a publication, would be the Suppression of many things', and that 'to add more & more honest Sentiments . . . when done *to be printed*, would surely be wrong, & weak also' (*Corresp.*, iv. 19). See B. Redford, 'P's Epistolary Theory and Practice', *N & Q* 228 (1983), 500–2, and (for SJ's own practice) *The Converse of the Pen: Acts of Intimacy in the Eighteenth-Century Familiar Letter* (Chicago, 1986), 206–43.

277. SJ states in **296** below that P 'considered poetry as the business of his life'. P described himself as 'writing when I have no other thing in the world to do' to Richardson, Feb. or Mar. 1732 (*Corresp.*, iii. 270), and had written similarly in the preface to *Works* (1717) ('I writ because it amused me', etc., *TE*, i. 6: see **296** n. below). SJ quotes Swift to Mrs Caesar, 30 July 1733 (Swift, *Works* (1764), i. 25; Swift, *Corresp.*, iv. 184).

In the MS and proofs the first sentence is followed by: 'For this he was modestly reproved in his life-time by Mrs. Cockburne.' Nichols's query in the proofs ('Did Pope ever *see* the reproof?': see Textual Notes) may have caused SJ to delete these words. The reproof appeared in a letter to P from Catherine Cockburn (née Trotter) (1679–1749) in her *Works* (2 vols., 1751), i, pp. xliii–xliv, where Thomas Birch noted that it was written 'about the year 1738, but . . . never sent'.

The story from Lord Oxford's 'domestick' is not in the anecdotes in *Gent. Mag.* (1775), 435: SJ either misread his notes, or obtained it from some other source. P spent most of the severe winter of 1740 in Bath, but see 'On the Benefactions in the late Frost, 1740' (*TE*, vi. 389). For P's fear 'lest he should lose a thought', see also **297** below, and for Milton composing poetry in the night, see 'Milton' **123**–4 above.

278. *extreme irritability*: cf. the final entry in SJ's early notes for 'Pope': 'Extreme—Sensibility' (Add. MS 5994.2, fo. 177^v). P told Aaron Hill, 26 Jan. 1731: 'I never was angry at any Criticism, made on my Poetry, by whomsoever' (*Corresp.*, iii. 165). For his actual sensitivity, see **149, 239** above, his collection of attacks on him, and his exhaustive listing of such 'Books, Papers, and Verses' in *Dunciad* (1729): see Warburton (1751 edn.), iv. 335 n., *TE*, v. 207–12, and **144** n. above.

279. SJ adapts P to Swift, 20 Apr. 1733: 'Courts I see not, Courtiers I know not, Kings I adore not, Queens I compliment not' (Warburton (1751 edn.), ix. 238; *Corresp.*, iii. 367, and cf. ii. 469). In the 'Testimonies of Authors' in the *Dunciad*, P stated that 'our Poet never had any Place, Pension, or Gratuity, in any shape' from Queen Anne 'or any of her Ministers': 'All he owed, in the whole course of his life, to any court, was a subscription, for his Homer, of 200 *l.* from King George I, and 100 *l.* from the prince and princess' (*TE*, iv. 45).

For the Prince of Wales's visit in 1735, see Spence, i. 245–6, Ruffhead, *Life*, 535 n., and cf. **217, 259, 264** and n. above. According to Ruffhead, P replied to the Prince: 'I consider royalty under that noble and authorised type of the Lion; while he is young, and before his nails are grown, he may be approached, and caressed with safety and pleasure.' Horace Walpole reported a briefer version in 1742 (*Corresp.*, xvii. 143), and Shenstone claimed in 1759 to have heard 'that anecdote of Pope and the Prince of Wales long ago' from Spence or Dodsley (*Letters* (1939), 525). Boswell printed yet another version of P's reply supplied by Wilkes (*Life*, iv. 50; *Catalogue*, C 3094), apparently unaware that SJ was commenting on Ruffhead's account.

Warton, *Essay on P*, ii (1782), 324, described the professed contempt for kings in P's verse as 'almost a nauseous cant', and at ii. 400–1 n. gave a further example of P's wit to the Prince from Richard Glover. For another poet's witty reply to the Prince, see 'Thomson' **28** below.

280. Cf. SJ's notes for 'Pope': 'cant of despising the world' (fo. 174^v). For 'contempt for the world' in P's circle, see also 'Swift' **135** and n. above, and for examples in P's letters, see *Corresp.*, ii. 109, 302, iv. 156, 429.

The vision from a superior vantage-point of mankind as emmets or ants probably originates in Lucian's satiric *Icaromenippus*. See I. Grundy, *Scale of Greatness* (1986), 168–9, which also compares Isaac Watts, 'True Monarchy' (1701): 'drop down a gentle Look | On the great Mole-hill, and with pitying Eye | Survey the busy Emmets round the Heap.' For SJ's condemnation of those who write 'as beholders rather than partakers of human nature', see 'Cowley' **57** above. He defines 'To superstruct' as 'To build upon any thing' (*Dict.*).

For SJ's usual confidence in public judgement, see 'Smith' **49** and n. above, but see also his criticism of Dryden's willingness to write 'merely for the people' in **304** below. For his ambivalent attitude to writers who live by 'pleasing', see 'Cowley' **38** and n. above. SJ quotes 'a fool to Fame' from *Epistle to Arbuthnot*, l. 127.

SJ said on 23 Mar. 1783: 'All the complaints which are made of the world are unjust. I never knew a man of merit neglected: it was generally by his own fault that he failed of success.' Boswell later wrote of SJ: 'Whether the subject was his own situation, or the state of the publick, or the state of human nature in general, though he saw the evils, his mind was turned to resolution, and never to whining or complaint' (*Life*, iv. 172, ii. 357).

281. See e.g. *Essay on Man*, IV. 205–36, and, for P's variable attitude to 'the Great', see **23, 196** ('I live among the Great'), **231, 270–2** and nn. above, and 'Savage' **258** and n. above.

282. SJ's early notes for 'Pope' contain the basis of this paragraph (fo. 174ʳ). He refers first to P to Swift, 15 Sept. 1734 (Warburton (1751 edn.), ix. 255; *Corresp.*, ii. 432, and cf. iv. 187, 363), and then illustrates P's 'universal jealousy' by quoting (loosely) P to Swift, 14 Sept. 1725, 23 Mar. 1737 (Warburton, ix. 51, 298–9; *Corresp.*, ii. 321, iv. 64).

In his *Life of Richard Nash* (1762) Goldsmith also doubted whether the Post Office would be interested in opening P's letters (*Coll. Works* (1966), iii. 343). Yet Swift reported as early as 9 Oct. 1722 that one of his letters had been opened at the Post Office: 'This hath determined me against writing treason' (Swift, *Corresp.*, ii. 435, and cf. iii. 403, iv. 63); P warned Swift, 28 Nov. 1729, that 'the underlings at the Post-office' might 'take a copy' of his letter (*Corresp.*, iii. 80); and William Pulteney told Swift, 22 Nov. 1735: 'Nothing is more certain than that this letter will be opened there, the rascals of the office have most infamous directions to do it upon all occasions' (Swift, *Corresp.*, iv. 435). Hill (1905) noted Gray's later comment to Wharton, 18 Oct. 1753: 'remember, this election time letters are apt to be open'd at the offices' (*Corresp.*, i. 388).

283. For Swift's 'resentment', see 'Swift' **135** and n. above. SJ refers to P to Swift, Aug. 1723, and Swift to P, 20 Sept. 1723 (Warburton (1751 edn.), ix. 39, 47–8; *Corresp.*, ii. 185, 199), when P was in fact aged 35, not 25.

For SJ's disapproval of anti-social solitude, see 'Cowley' **44–5** above and 'Gray' **8** and n. below, *Rambler* 135 (1751), *Adventurer* 67 (1753), *Rasselas*, ch. XXI, 'Sermons' 1, 3 (*YW*, xiv. 3, 32–3), and his letters to Elizabeth Aston, 17 Nov. 1767, and Mrs Thrale, 21 June 1775 (*Letters*, i. 292, ii. 231–2).

284. Warton, *Essay on P*, ii (1782), 406–7, also described P, Swift, and Bolingbroke as forming 'a kind of haughty *triumvirate*, in order to issue forth *prescriptions* against all who would not adopt their sentiments and opinions'.

Addison wrote in *Spectator* 253 (1711): 'a Man seldom sets up for a Poet, without attacking the Reputation of his Brothers in the Art. The Ignorance of the Moderns, the Scriblers of the Age, the Decay of Poetry are the Topicks of Detraction, with which he makes his Entrance into the World.' In *Rambler* 77 (1750) SJ discussed the 'established custom' among the intelligentsia of complaining of 'the prevalence of false taste, and the encroachment of barbarity' (*YW*, iv. 38).

285. Cf. SJ's cryptic early note for 'Pope': 'In his letters there is—Discontent. Resignation—Gayety—too much of all' (fo. 177ᵛ).

For P and Ambrose Philips, see **68, 115** above. Warburton contributed the mockery of Richard Bentley, the classical scholar, as Richardus Aristarchus, prefixed to *Dunciad* (1743) (*Corresp.*, iv. 434), but P also satirized him in iv. 199–274, as earlier in the apparatus to *Sober Advice from Horace* (1734). His hostility to Bentley, which he shared with Swift (see 'Swift' **28** above), is only partly explained by aversion to textual criticism (see **127** and n. above). According to Thomas Bentley, *A Letter to Mr. Pope* (1735), 14, his uncle told P that his Homer translation was 'miserable stuff...That it might be called *Homer modernised* or something to that effect; but that there were little or no Vestiges at all of the old Grecian' (cf. **209** n. above). In another version, Bentley said: 'the verses are good verses, but the work is not Homer' (*Gent. Mag.* (Oct. 1773), 499). For variants of, and comments, on the story, see *Gent. Mag.* (1781), 271, 359, Warton, *Essay on P*, ii (1782), 234, and Hawkins, *J's Works* (1787), iv. 126 n. SJ presumably referred to Bentley when he wrote in 1743 of an *'English* Critic': 'may no Man presume to insult his Memory who wants his Learning, his Reason, or his Wit' (*Life*, i. 153 n. 7).

For the Duke of Chandos and Aaron Hill, see **154, 157** and nn. above, and for P's relations with Lady Mary Wortley Montagu, **216** n., **265** above. The cryptic entry 'Sneaked to Lady Mary' in SJ's notes for 'Pope' (fo. 177ᵛ) may be relevant: he defines 'To Sneak' as '2. To behave with meanness and servility' (*Dict.*). See Rumbold, *Women's Place*, 132–4, 155–61, and I. Grundy, *Lady Mary Wortley Montagu: Comet of the Enlightenment* (Oxford, 1999), chs. 16, 19.

286. Ruffhead, *Life*, 460 n., described friendship as P's 'ruling passion' (and cf. 484–7, 491–7). In 1771 Fanny Burney was moved by P's letters, especially by the importance he attached to friendship: see *Early Journals*, i. 179. For the importance of friendship to SJ himself ('a friendship of twenty years is interwoven with the texture of life'), see his letter to Mrs Thrale, 13 Nov. 1783 (*Letters*, iv. 238–9), and *Life*, i. 300, on the need to keep friendships in constant repair.

For P's patronage in the 1730s of Robert Dodsley, former footman and later author and bookseller, see *Corresp.*, iii. 346, 454, and Dodsley, *Corresp.*, 5. SJ himself called Dodsley his 'patron', as the publisher of *London* (1738): see *Letters*, i. 173, *Life*, i. 326, ii. 446, and *J. Misc.*, ii. 341. According to Warton, *Works of P* (1797), i, p. lxxi, P's 'private charities were many and great; of which *Dodsley*, whom he honoured with his friendship, and who partook of his beneficence, gave me several instances': see also **268** and n. above. For P's patient support of Richard Savage, see 'Savage' **272** and n., **325** above.

287. By the time he published *Letters* (1737), when he was not yet 50, all P's early literary acquaintance, apart from the ailing Swift, were dead, including Trumbull, Wycherley, Walsh, Garth, Prior, Rowe, Parnell, Addison, Congreve, Gay, Atterbury, and Arbuthnot. For reflections on the loss of friends by death or exile, see *Corresp.*, ii. 72–3, 179–80, 227, iii. 470, 474, iv. 49–50 (replying to Swift's letter of 2 Dec. 1736 on the same subject). SJ himself wrote about the death of early friends as a calamity of middle age in *Rambler* 203 (1752).

P had in fact quarrelled with such friends as Addison and Lady Mary Wortley Montagu. For Ralph Allen and Lord Bolingbroke, see **250-4, 263** above.

288. Cf. SJ's early notes for 'Pope': 'No writings against Swift!' (fo. 177^v). Although no printed source has been found for the story that P prepared a 'defamatory' biography of Swift, there is a version of it in the MS materials about Swift preserved by the Revd John Lyon: 'Notwithstanding the seeming regard Pope had for the Dean, it's certain that after Pope's death, some very severe reflections on the Dean were found amongst his papers, which were destroyd': see A. C. Elias, 'Swift's *Don Quixote*, Dunkin's *Virgil Travesty*, and Other New Intelligence', *Swift Studies*, 13 (1998), 69. SJ's source was presumably Nichols, who had Lyon's MSS in his possession in the 1770s. For SJ's interview with Lord Marchmont on 1 May 1779, see headnote above.

289. On 1 Sept. 1742 P wrote about his religious views to Louis Racine (1692-1763), who had attacked the *Essay on Man* in *La Religion* (1742) (*Corresp.*, iv. 415-16). For their exchange of letters, see *Gent. Mag.* (1754), 177-8. For P's impious allusions to Scripture, see 'Blackmore' **31** and n. above, *Dunciad*, IV. 562, and A. L. Williams, *P's Dunciad* (1955), 142-56. With 'easiness and vulgarity', cf. 'Milton' **181** above.

At the time of the Atterbury trial (**131** above), P stated: 'if to be a Papist be to profess & hold many such Tenets of faith as are ascribed to Papists, I am not a Papist. And if to be a Papist, be to hold any that are averse to, or destructive of, the present Government, King, or Constitution; I am no Papist' (to Lord Harcourt, 6 May 1723, *Corresp.*, ii. 171-2). Marchmont said in May 1778 that P 'had no settled faith . . . kept connected with the Catholicks, but . . . had not for long period gone to mass' (*Boswell in Extremes*, 334). For P's religion, see also **131** and n. above; for his 'confidence of a future state', see **246** and n. above; and for Bolingbroke, Warburton, and the *Essay on Man*, see **179-82** above.

290. For those who enjoy the 'degradation' of greatness, see **119** and n. above.

291. For accusations about P's Greek, see **83** above, and for the *Essay on Criticism* (1711), see **32, 34** above. For the importance of 'knowledge' of both books and the 'living world', see 'Butler' **37-9** and n. 'Dryden' **211** above.

SJ described 'curiosity' in *Rambler* 103 (1751) as 'one of the permanent and certain characteristicks of a vigorous intellect': see 'Milton' **229**, 'Addison' **91**, and 'Savage' **138** above, and 'Thomson' **21** and 'Gray' **18, 24** below.

the academy of Paracelsus: soon after starting work on the *Lives*, SJ told Mrs Thrale, 29 Oct. 1777: 'The Chymists call the world Academia Paracelsi, my ambition is to be his fellow student. To see the works of Nature, and hear the lectures of Truth. To London therefore' (*Letters*, iii. 90-1). Paracelsus (Theophrast Bombast Von Hohenheim) (1493-1541), chemist, physician, and occultist, a critic of traditional medical knowledge and the academic world of his day, influenced the mystical preoccupations of the Rosicrucians, whose system P adopted in *The Rape of the Lock* (see **337** and n. below). His *Opera Omnia* (3 vols., 1658) appeared in the sale catalogue (1785) of SJ's library. His 'Credo' contrasted his academic training with knowledge of the world: see *Paracelsus: Selected Writings*, ed. J. Jacobi (Princeton, 1979), 3-9.

For William Dobson, see also **195** and n. above. James Beattie, who admired Dobson's Latin translation of Milton (1750-3), recalled in 1797 that SJ once 'owned he had known him, but did not seem inclined to speak on the subject. But Johnson hated Milton from his heart . . . All that I could ever hear of Dobson's private life was, that in his old age he was given to drinking' (Sir William Forbes, *Life of Beattie* (Edinburgh, 1806), ii. 316–18). Warton, *Works of P* (1797), v. 239, questioned Dobson's competence to assess P's learning.

With SJ's final sentence, cf. *Rambler* 150 (1751): 'Curiosity is, in great and generous minds, the first passion and the last . . . in proportion as the intellectual eye takes in a wider prospect, it must be gratified with variety by more rapid flights, and bolder excursions' (*YW*, iv. 184, v. 34).

292. See Spence, i. 22, and 'Epistle to Mr. Jervas', ll. 23–8 (**69** above). SJ also relates 'that curiosity which is inseparable from an active and comprehensive mind' to travel in 'Thomson' **21** below. For his own desire to travel, see *Life*, iii. 449.

293. P's preface to *Works* (1717) described 'good sense' as 'a quality that not only renders one capable of being a good writer, but a good man' (see *TE*, i. 5, 7, 9). For 'Good Sense, which only is the gift of Heav'n', see *Epistle to Burlington*, ll. 41–4.

consonance: '1. Accord of sound' (cf. 'Gray' **42** below) and '2. Consistency; congruence; agreeableness' (*Dict.*).

294. *quiescent*: 'Resting; not being in motion; not movent; lying at repose' (*Dict.*).

Cf. SJ's comparison of prudence as an 'intellectual quality' to rules in composition in *Idler* 57 (1759): 'it produces vigilance rather than elevation, rather prevents loss than procures advantages . . . The world is not amazed with prodigies of excellence, but when wit tramples upon rules, and magnanimity breaks the chains of prudence' (*YW*, ii. 178). See also **300** below, and SJ's comments on 'judgement' as a faculty which may secure a poet from 'the ridiculous or absurd', and 'hinder faults, but not produce excellence' in 'Prior' **72** above.

For 'genius', see also **310, 373** and nn. below. In *Rambler* 137 (1751) SJ stated: 'It is the proper ambition of the heroes in literature to enlarge the boundaries of knowledge by discovering and conquering new regions of the intellectual world.' For the image of the aspiring mind in flight, see **291** and n. above and **310** below, and *Rambler* 137 again: 'The widest excursions of the mind are made by short flights frequently repeated' (*YW*, iv. 361–2). Oldisworth's eulogy (1714) of Edmund Smith (see 'Smith' **6** above) described his imagination in similar terms.

In his preface to *Works* (1717), P said that his poems 'have always fallen short not only of what I read of others, but even of my own Idea of Poetry' (*TE*, i. 6). For the pursuit of 'an idea of pure perfection', see 'Dryden' **340** and n. above.

295. For P's excellent memory, see Spence, i. 21, 224. In *Rambler* 41 (1750), and *Idlers* 44, 74 (1759), SJ described memory as the basis of all intellectual and creative operations: the mind must be stored 'copiously with true notions, before the imagination should be suffered to form fictions or collect embellishments; for the works of an ignorant poet can afford nothing higher than pleasing sound, and fiction is of no other use than to display the treasures of memory' (*YW*, ii. 229–30). Cf. also SJ's quotation from Watts's *The Improvement of the Mind* under 'Collect': ''Tis memory alone that enriches the mind, by preserving what our labour and our industry daily *collect*' (*Dict.*). For SJ's own memory, see *Life*, i. 39, 48, iii. 318 n., iv. 103 n., 427.

accommodated: SJ defines 'To Accommodate' as '2. With the particle *to*: to adapt; to fit; to make consistent with' (*Dict.*).

296. Cf. P's preface to *Works* (1717): 'I writ because it amused me; I corrected because it was as pleasant to me to correct as to write ... I fairly confess that I have serv'd my self all I could by reading; that I made use of the judgment of authors dead and living; that I omitted no means in my power to be inform'd of my errors, both by my friends and enemies' (*TE*, i. 6–7; quoted in part under 'Allegation' and 'Correct' in the *Dict.*). P seems 'to lament his occupation' by referring to 'the dangerous fate of authors ... The life of a Wit is a warfare upon earth' (*TE*, i. 6–7).

P told Cromwell, 18 Mar. 1708: 'Every day with me ... has the same Business, which is Poetry' (*Corresp.*, i. 42). Cf. **277** and n. above.

297. See also **277** above. Edmund Smith also 'very diligently' wrote down thoughts and images 'in the warmth of conversation': see 'Smith' **65** above. P's MSS reveal that he often used lines he had rejected elsewhere. For early couplets recycled in the *Dunciad*, see Spence, i. 18–19, and Warburton (1751 edn.), vii. 30 and n.

298. Cf. Addison, *Spectator* 203 (1711): 'it is said of some Men, that they make their Business their Pleasure.' SJ wrote in *Idler* 102 (1759): 'It very seldom happens to man that his business is his pleasure. What is done from necessity, is so often to be done when against the present inclination, and so often fills the mind with anxiety, that an habitual dislike steals upon us' (*YW*, ii. 311–12).

In his first surviving letter, SJ told Gregory Hickman, 30 Oct. 1731: 'versifying against ones inclination is the most disagreable thing in the World' (*Letters*, i. 3). More than fifty years later he said on 1 May 1783: 'It has been said, there is pleasure in writing, particularly in writing verses. I allow you may have pleasure from writing, after it is over, if you have written well; but you don't go willingly to it again' (*Life*, iv. 219, and see also ii. 99).

As in *Rambler* 169 (1751), SJ usually emphasized the necessity of labour for literary excellence, as opposed to the products of 'negligence and hurry' (*YW*, v. 130). The obvious contrast is with 'Dryden' **201, 341** above. See also **198, 296** above and **307, 343, 363, 368** below, and 'Milton' **118** and n. above.

299. For SJ's interest elsewhere in methods of composition, see 'Milton' **123–6** and n. above.

Arthur Murphy believed that SJ's second sentence describes his own method: 'He never took his pen in hand till he had weighed well his subject, and grasped in his mind the sentiments, the train of argument, and the arrangement of the whole. As he often thought aloud, he had, perhaps, talked it over to himself' (*J. Misc.*, i. 426; see also Percy's similar account at ii. 215–16).

SJ has already used the account of Virgil's habits from Donatus in 'Dryden' **230** above. For 'exuberances', see 'Thomson' **50** and n. below.

For the Homer MSS, see **94–9** above, and cf. Spence, i. 45, 85, 86. For P's capacity for painstaking revision of his other MSS, see Mack, *Last and Greatest Art*, *passim*, and **305** below. Jonathan Richardson reported that P (while engaged on the *Dunciad*) would write 'the line only but half written, the rest he readily supplyd by memory as he Read': see Sherburn, 'New Anecdotes', 347. The MS of *The Vanity of Human Wishes* shows that SJ used the same method, composing up to fifty lines in his head and writing down only the first half-lines to retain them (*Life*, ii. 15; *Poems* (1974), 415).

300. SJ defines 'Prudence' as 'Wisdom applied to practice' (*Dict.*). For 'prudence' in life and art, see *Idler* 57 (1759), cited in **294** n. above, and for P's 'great imprudence' in deciding to write his epic 'Brutus' in blank verse, see **241** above.

Cf. SJ's early notes for 'Pope': 'Practised only one form of verse. facility from use' (BL, fo. 159ʳ); 'Only one sort of verse—facility from use...Confined to one mode more than any other writer. facility by habit' (Dyce Collection, fo. 1ʳ). Of P's shorter poems in quatrains and other stanzaic forms, SJ discusses only the 'Ode for Musick, on St. Cecilia's Day' at any length (see **320–7** below). For P's 'increase of facility' while translating Homer, see **81** above and Spence, i. 85–6.

301. SJ's early notes for 'Pope' suggest that this was an important aspect of P's poetry: 'Nothing occasional. no haste. no rivals, no compulsion' (BL, fo. 159); 'Nothing occasional no haste no rivals no compulsion independence Choice of Subject', and 'His poems never occasional' (Dyce Collection, fo. 1).

For P's financial independence, see **91–2** above, and for comments on the 'independence' of other poets, see 'Milton' **169** and n. above. P told Caryll, 18 Feb. 1718, that a 'Heroic Poet' could not write occasional poetry (*Corresp.*, i. 465), and said in 1735: 'there is one thing I value myself upon and which can scarce be said of any of our good poets—and that is, that I have never flattered any man, nor ever received anything of any man for my verses' (Spence, i. 168). See also his mockery of dedications in *Guardian* 4 (1713) and *Epistle to Arbuthnot*, ll. 109–10. For his refusal to write panegyrics, see also *Imit. Horace, Sat. II. i.* (1733), ll. 21–36, and *Ep. II. i.* (1737), ironically addressed to George II. SJ quoted P's description of himself as 'Un-plac'd, un-pension'd, no Man's Heir, or Slave' (*Sat. II. i.*, ll. 111–14) under 'Unpensioned' in the *Dict.*

For the obvious contrast, see 'Dryden' **230–3** and nn. above; for Elkanah Settle as an arch-celebrant of weddings and funerals, see 'Dryden' **115** above; and for 'the herd of encomiasts', and the inevitability of 'treading in the footsteps of those who had gone before' in occasional poetry, see 'Savage' **249** above.

302. Although P said in 1736 that two years was 'as little time as ever I let anything of mine lay by me' (Spence, i. 41; cf. Ruffhead, *Life*, 66), his *Imitations of Horace* (see **209** above and **306** below) were usually published more rapidly in the 1730s. SJ had mentioned 'the tardy emission of Pope's compositions' in *Rambler* 169 (1751), when stating that the ancients, 'considering the impropriety of sending forth inconsiderately that which cannot be recalled, deferred the publication...till their fancy was cooled after the raptures of invention, and the glare of novelty had ceased to dazzle the judgment' (*YW*, v. 133). For the problems of authorial self-judgement, see also 'Milton' **146** and n. above.

For P's early critics, see **24, 30, 33** above. Warburton became his main adviser at the end of his life. Ruffhead repeatedly noted P's willingness to listen to constructive criticism: see e.g. 99, 172, 183–4 n., 275 n. In *Rambler* 23 (1751) SJ had in fact argued against 'a solicitous conformity to advice and criticism...consultation and compliance can conduce little to the perfection of any literary performance' (*YW*, iii. 126). The difference was that P also 'consulted himself'.

303–11. As Hilles, 'Making', 276, noted, the importance SJ attached to this comparison of P and Dryden is reflected in his careful revision of it in the MS (see Textual Notes).

The tradition of such formal literary comparisons goes back to those of Demosthenes and Cicero by Longinus, Plutarch, and Quintilian. Damrosch (1976), 209–10, discussed such later examples as Dryden's comparisons of Juvenal and Horace and of Homer and Virgil (Watson, ii. 125–35, 274–7), and P's own comparison of Homer and Virgil in his preface to the *Iliad* (*TE*, vii. 12). For similar comparisons, including Sir William Temple on Homer and Virgil in 1690, see also **309–10** nn. below.

303. See Spence, i. 24, Ruffhead, *Life*, 23, and **13–14** and nn. above.

In *Iliad*, VI. 462 n., P wrote of Dryden, 'I am unwilling to remark upon an Author to whom every *English* Poet owes so much' (*TE*, vii. 349 n.), but some reservations precede and follow his later praise in *Imit. Horace, Ep. II. i.* (1737), ll. 213, 266–9, 280–1.

P's own 'Parallel of the Characters of Mr. Dryden and Mr. Pope, As Drawn by Certain of their Contemporaries', appended to the *Dunciad Variorum* (*TE*, v. 230–5), is a detailed comparison entirely in terms of the hostility they each aroused.

304. For Dryden's progress in 'correctness', see 'Dryden' **236, 343, 356** above, and, for the rejection of 'unnatural' thoughts and 'rugged' versification, see also 'Denham' **35** and n. above.

SJ defines 'Rectitude' as '2. Rightness; uprightness; freedom from moral curvity or obliquity' (*Dict.*). Dryden 'rectified his notions' of poetry 'by experience perpetually increasing'; and a few earlier English poets, 'the favourites of nature', had possessed 'their own original rectitude . . . in the place of rules' ('Dryden' **201, 219** above). Prior also had 'rectitude of judgement' ('Prior' **72** above). For SJ's 'morality of prosody', see also P. Fussell, *Theory of Prosody in 18th-Century England* (1954; repr. New York, 1966), 41–4.

For writing to 'please', see **280** above and **352** below, and 'Cowley' **38** and n. above, and for his willingness to write hastily for money, see 'Dryden' **201, 227–33, 340–1** above. In *Rambler* 169 (1751), SJ condemned the vanity 'which boasts of negligence and hurry. For who can bear with patience the writer who claims such superiority to the rest of his species, as to imagine that mankind are at leisure for attention to his extemporary trifles.' Yet SJ also noted that the 'tardy emission of Pope's compositions' could mean that 'the incidents to which they alluded were forgotten . . . his enemies were secure from his satire, and . . . his friends were deaf to his encomiums' (*YW*, v. 130, 134).

305. See Spence, i. 171, and Ruffhead's description, *Life*, 460, of P's 'unwearied patience' in correcting his verse.

By 'candour', SJ here means 'kindness' (*Dict.*). SJ's remarks again reflect his examination of the Homer MSS: see **299** and n. above. Cf. P's *Imit. Horace, Ep. II. i*, ll. 278–81: 'But Otway fail'd to polish or refine, | And fluent Shakespear scarce effac'd a line. | Ev'n copious Dryden, wanted, or forgot, | The last and greatest Art, the Art to blot.'

SJ wrote in 1765: 'it is seldom that authours . . . rise much above the standard of their own age; to add a little to what is best will always be sufficient for present praise, and those who find themselves exalted into fame, are willing to credit their encomiasts, and to spare the labour of contending with themselves' (*YW*, vii. 91).

306. See **209, 217–19, 302** and n. above. Warton heard the same story from Dodsley (*Works of P* (1797), iv. 294 n.).

307. SJ may refer to P's ironic *Guardian* 40 (1713), which mentions his reputation as one that 'takes the greatest Care of his Works before they are published, and has the least Concern for them afterwards' (*Prose Works*, i. 97). For his revisions to the *Essay on Criticism* and *Essay on Man*, see **38–9, 177** above, and for changes to the *Iliad*, 'Tickell' **12** above.

P made numerous, if usually minor, revisions in the various editions of his *Works*. Warburton told Hurd, 22 Sept. 1751, that P 'used to tell me, that when he had any thing better than ordinary to say, and yet too bold, he always reserved it for a second or third edition, and then nobody took any notice of it' (*Letters from a Late Eminent Prelate* (2nd edn., 1809), 86). Lord Hervey accused P of 'selling the same Work over and over again under the Pretence of correcting, altering, and adding here and there a Word, in *Folios, Quarto's, Octavo's, Duodecimo's, Loose-Sheets, collected Volumes,* and all the *Proteus-Shapes* which the *Press* can furnish' (*Letter to Mr. C—b-r* (1742), 18-19). The contrast is with 'Dryden' **341** above ('What he had once written he dismissed from his thoughts'), and cf. **304** above and **310** below.

308. SJ elaborates his assessment of Dryden's 'genius' in 'Dryden' **211** above, which followed a somewhat more sceptical account of his 'acquired knowledge' in **208–10** (but see also **321**). Although he is initially concerned with learning and 'science' ('1. Knowledge', *Dict.*), SJ's association of Dryden with 'general nature' and of P with 'local manners' inevitably recalls his praise in 1765 of Shakespeare's 'just representations of general nature' as opposed to 'Particular manners' (*YW*, vii. 61–2), and his contrast in 1768 of Richardson's 'characters of nature' with Fielding's 'characters only of manners' (*Life*, ii. 49 and cf. ii. 173–5).

309. For Dryden's prose, see also 'Dryden' **214–15** above, and for prose style elsewhere, 'Cowley' **200** and n. above. Thomas Birch, *The Heads of Illustrious Persons*, ii (1751), 56, stated blandly of P: 'His prose-style is as perfect in its kind as his poetic, and has all the beauties proper to it join'd to an uncommon force and perspicuity.'

For precedents for the metaphoric contrast of writers in SJ's final sentence, see Addison, *Spectator* 417 (1712), comparing Homer's 'Savage' landscape with Virgil's 'well-ordered Garden', Pope's preface to Shakespeare (*Prose Works*, ii. 25–6), SJ's own preface to Shakespeare (*YW*, vii. 84), and his contrast of Corneille and Shakespeare recorded by Mrs Thrale in 1777 (*Thraliana*, i. 165, and *J. Misc.*, i. 187). When Boswell recorded in Feb. 1766 Voltaire's statement that 'Pope drives a handsome chariot, with a couple of neat trim nags; Dryden a coach, and six stately horses', SJ replied: 'Why, Sir, the truth is that they both drive coaches and six; Dryden's horses are either galloping or stumbling: Pope's go at a steady even trot' (*Life*, ii. 5). (Cf. *Thraliana*, i. 201.) See also SJ's comparison of Young's *Night Thoughts* to a 'Chinese Plantation' in 'Young' **160** below.

SJ may recall Burke: 'being swiftly drawn in an easy coach, on a smooth turf, with gradual ascents and declivities...will give a better idea of the beautiful...than almost any thing else' (*Enquiry* (1958), 155). Warton, *Essay on P*, ii (1782), 403 n., considered P's style 'certainly not so melodious and voluble as that of Dryden's enchanting prose'.

For 'uniformity' as a limitation, see 'Butler' **35** and n. and 'Savage' **342** and n. above; for another author whose prose 'is always on a level', see 'Swift' **113** above.

Although SJ often has reservations about the 'exuberance' of contemporary verse (see 'Thomson' **50** and n. below), he uses the word positively here.

310. For 'the impetuosity of his genius', see 'Dryden' **211** and n., **321** above; for 'genius' elsewhere, see **294** above and **365, 373** below, and 'Milton' **277** and n. above. For 'energy', see 'Milton' **249** and n. above, and for the power of 'combination', 'Butler' **37** and n. above. Cf. also *Rambler* 168 (1751) for 'the force of poetry, that force which calls new powers into being, which embodies sentiment, and animates matter' (*YW*, v. 127).

SJ's second sentence ('It is not to be inferred . . . give place to Pope') recalls P's own comparison of Homer and Virgil in 1715: 'Not that we are to think *Homer* wanted Judgment, because *Virgil* had it in a more eminent degree; or that *Virgil* wanted Invention, because *Homer* possest a larger share of it: Each of these great Authors had more of both than perhaps any Man besides, and are only said to have less in Comparison with one another. *Homer* was the greater Genius, *Virgil* the better Artist' (*TE*, vii. 12). SJ echoed this comparison on 22 Sept. 1777: 'We must consider . . . whether Homer was not the greatest poet, though Virgil may have produced the finest poem' (*Life*, iii. 193; and see also v. 79 n., for an argument with Burke in which SJ 'maintained the superiority of Homer' to Virgil).

Cf. also Sir William Temple's comparison of Homer and Virgil in 'Of Poetry' (1690): '*Homer* had more Fire and Rapture, *Virgil* more Light and Swiftness; or at least the Poetical Fire was more raging in one, but clearer in the other, which makes the first more amazing and the latter more agreeable' (Spingarn, iii. 82–3). SJ also echoes at points Dryden's comparison of Homer and Virgil in the 'Preface' to *Fables* (1700) (Watson, ii. 274–7).

Shiels, *Lives*, v. 252, also anticipated SJ's judgement here: 'We admire Dryden as the greater genius, and Pope as the most pleasing versifier.' Although Ruffhead, *Life*, 464, was incredulous in 1769 that 'in our times, fastidious critics, of true taste, prefer Dryden to Pope', SJ said in the same year that there are passages in Dryden 'drawn from a profundity which Pope could never reach' (*Life*, ii. 85; cf. **320** below).

For the image of flight for poetic genius, see **294** and n. above; and for a perspective on SJ's praise of P and Dryden here, see his question in 'Milton' **261** above: 'what other author ever soared so high or sustained his flight so long?'

SJ responds variously to a 'blaze'. In 'Waller' **16** above, 'There are charms made only for distant admiration. No spectacle is nobler than a blaze'; in 'Addison' **167**, 'His page is always luminous, but never blazes in unexpected splendour'; in 'Fenton' **21** below, 'A blaze first pleases, and then tires the sight'; and, in 1773, Warburton 'blazes, if you will, but that is not always the steadiest light' (*Life*, v. 81). Cf. Sheffield, *An Essay upon Poetry* (1682), ll. 9–12: 'Tis not a Flash of Fancy which sometimes | Dasling our Minds, sets off the slightest Rimes, | Bright as a blaze, but in a moment done; | True Wit is everlasting, like the Sun'; and Reynolds in *Idler* 76 (1759) on 'a servile attention to minute exactness, which is sometimes inconsistent with higher excellency, and is lost in the blaze of expanded genius' (*YW*, ii. 238).

SJ's emphasis on the positive aspect of D's 'negligences' recalls Addison's *Spectator* 160 (1711): 'There appears something nobly wild and extravagant in these great natural Genius's, that is infinitely more beautiful than all the Turn and Polishing of what the *French* call a *Bel Esprit*, by which they would express a

Genius refined by Conversation, Reflection, and the Reading of the most polite Authors'; and Spence, *Essay on Pope's Odyssey*, ii (1727), 4: 'A Noble natural Genius... delights us in a much higher degree, than the most uniform and correct: And the Writer who enjoys this freedom of Soul, amidst all his Starts and Errors, is greatly to be prefer'd to the Justness of one, who is too severe to commit a Fault, and too cool and phlegmatic to be a Poet... The very Negligencies of *Homer* shew the Greatness of his Spirit.'

Like his superior knowledge of 'general nature' (**308** above), Dryden's carelessness, in contrast to P's 'indefatigable diligence' (**305** above), links him with Shakespeare, of whom SJ wrote in 1765: 'I am far from thinking, that his works were wrought to his own ideas of perfection; when they were such as would satisfy the audience, they satisfied the author' (*YW*, vii. 91). The contrast of 'astonishment' with 'delight' in SJ's final sentence may also confer a Miltonic quality on Dryden: Milton 'can please when pleasure is required; but it is his peculiar power to astonish' ('Milton' **230** above).

For another elaborate recent comparison of Dryden and P, see James Beattie, *Essays* (Edinburgh, 1776), 358–62 n. Warton, *Essay on P*, ii (1782), 411, probably had SJ's judgement in mind when ranking P just above Dryden as the 'better artist', though Dryden was the 'greater genius' (primarily on the strength of *Alexander's Feast*). Cowper endorsed SJ's opinion in a letter of 5 Jan. 1782 (*Letters*, ii (1981), 3–4).

311. This paragraph is not in the MS and was obviously added later: see Textual Notes.

SJ echoes Dryden's own statement in *Of Dramatick Poesie* (1668) that Ben Jonson was 'the more correct poet, but Shakespeare the greater wit. Shakespeare was the Homer, or father of our dramatic poets: Jonson was the Virgil, the pattern of elaborate writing; I admire him, but I love Shakespeare'; and his comparison of Ovid and Chaucer in *Fables* (1700): 'the figures of Chaucer are much more lively, and set in a better light; which though I have not time to prove, yet I appeal to the reader, and am sure he will clear me from partiality' (Watson, i. 70, ii. 278).

Mrs Thrale noted SJ's preference for Dryden: 'Of Pope as a writer he had the highest opinion... His superior reverence of Dryden notwithstanding still appeared in his talk as in his writings' (*J. Misc.*, i. 184–5). Cf. also 'Halifax' **12** above: 'In determinations depending not on rules, but on experience and comparison, judgement is always in some degree subject to affection.'

312. In **384** below SJ describes his criticism of P's epitaphs as 'too minute and particular' for inclusion in the main survey of his poetry.

313. See **24–5**, **33** above and, for SJ's dislike of modern pastoral, 'Cowley' **7** and n. above. In *Rambler* 36 (1750) he described pastoral as 'generally the first literary amusement of our minds' (*YW*, iii. 196), and in 'Gay' **32** above as pleasing 'barbarians in the dawn of literature, and children in the dawn of life'.

In Oct. 1769 SJ stated that P's pastorals were 'poor things, though the versification was fine' (*Life*, ii. 84). For his objection to the 'impropriety' of lines in P's 'Autumn', see *Rambler* 37 (*YW*, iii. 203–4). He is more respectful here because of his concern to defend P against Warton (see **314** and n.). The *Monthly Review*, I NS (1790), 225, later referred to 'the old exploded pastoral,—which, we hoped, has long since given way to nature, and common sense. Mr. Pope had much to answer, for having, by his example, countenanced this simple species of writing'.

P's own notes (from 1736) explained the 'plan' of the *Pastorals*, later praised by Ruffhead, *Life*, 31–3. Warburton (1751 edn.), i. 69 n., described 'Winter' as P's favourite. Ruffhead's praise of 'Winter', ll. 49–50, no doubt prompted SJ's final sentence. Cf. his defence of Dryden against a similar objection in 'Dryden' **10** above.

314. In *Adventurer* 92 (1753) SJ had written that Virgil 'can derive... very little claim to the praise of an inventor' from his pastorals (*YW*, ii. 417). Warton, *Essay on P* (1756), 2, expressed surprise that pastorals by a young poet should not contain 'a single rural image that is new'. In his review, SJ wrote that Warton 'very justly censures' P's pastorals, 'considered as representations of any kind of life', because of their 'mixture of Grecian and English, of ancient and modern images'. He apparently accepted the 'justice' of Warton's complaint that they contain 'not a single new thought', and that 'their chief beauty consists in their *correct and musical versification, which has so influenced the English ear as to render every moderate rhymer harmonious*' (*OASJ*, 488, compressing Warton, *Essay*, 10). By 1781 SJ was much more concerned to resist Warton's general claim that P lacked poetic 'invention': see also **58** above and **337, 373** and n. below. Warton in turn replied to SJ in *Works of P* (1797), i, pp. xiv, 45–6 n., 66 n.

P told Spence in 1744: 'There is scarce any work of mine in which the versification was more laboured than in my *Pastorals*' (i. 175). In **348** below SJ describes P's Homer translation as a more crucial influence on English versification.

315. See **65** above and 'Denham' **27** above, and for the influence of *Cooper's Hill* (1642) on P, see *TE*, i. 132–5. Waller's *A Poem on St. James's Park, as Lately Improved by His Majesty* (1661) also blended description and politics. Dennis asserted *Windsor Forest*'s inferiority to *Cooper's Hill* in *Remarks on Mr. Pope's Homer* (1717) (*Works*, ii. 136–7).

In 1756 SJ had expressed only muted disagreement with Warton's emphasis in *Essay*, 30–5, on P's limitations as a descriptive poet by comparison with Thomson: 'he declares, I think without proof, that descriptive poetry was by no means the excellence of Pope' (*OASJ*, 489). Ruffhead, *Life*, 51–8, replied to Warton, while attaching only limited importance to powers of description, no doubt influenced by Warburton's view that 'Descriptive poetry is the lowest work of a Genius' (iv. 189 n.). P himself thought that Thomson's great fault was 'to describe every thing' (Spence, i. 168). For descriptive poetry, see also 'Cowley' **154** and n. above. SJ makes the same point about its inevitable arbitrariness in 'Thomson' **49** below.

In the final sentence, both MS and *Prefaces* read 'this poem', 'his poem' first appearing in *Lives* (1781) (see Textual Notes). The distance of 'his' from SJ's previous reference to P suggests that the change was not authorial.

316. For Father Thames and Lodona, see *Windsor Forest*, ll. 329–54, 171–218.

Addison ridiculed loquacious rivers in *The Campaign* (1705), ll. 467–72, and objected in *Spectator* 523 (1712) to 'the Exploits of a River-God' in a poem. Warton, *Essay* (1756), 25–6, had in fact praised P's lines about 'Father Thames'. For another 'puerile' poetic appearance by Father Thames, see 'Gray' **30** and n. below; and for 'fiction', 'Cowley' **16** and n. above.

Warton, *Works of P* (1797), i. 121 n., later commented that SJ had 'passed too severe a censure on this episode of Lodona. A tale in a descriptive poet has certainly a good effect.'

317. For *The Temple of Fame*, see **61–2** above. SJ quotes Steele to P, 12 Nov. 1712, from Ruffhead, *Life*, 172 (*Corresp.*, i. 152). (Steele wrote 'a thousand thousand beauties'.)

In his octavo *Works* (1735), vol. iii, P tried to clarify his debt to Chaucer's *House of Fame*: 'Wherever any hint is taken from him, the passage itself is set down in the marginal notes'. Thomas Warton, *History of English Poetry*, i (1774), 396, had in fact vigorously 'denied' that P had 'improved' Chaucer's 'romantic and anomalous' poem: 'he has not only misrepresented the story, but marred the character of the poem.' Joseph Warton, however, in a long discussion in *Essay on P*, i (4th edn., 1782), 348–415, claimed that P had 'improved and heightened' Chaucer, introducing his alterations 'with judgment and art' (i. 356, 414).

For 'ornament' in poetry, see also **365** below and 'Cowley' **202** and n. above; for allegory and imagery, see 'Cowley' **151** and **154** and nn. above; and for the superiority of 'real life' to 'imaginary existence', see **320** below.

318. For 'Messiah, A Sacred Eclogue', which reconciles the prophecies of Virgil and Isaiah, see **46** and n., **195** n. above.

Steele told P, 1 June 1712, that 'Your Poem is already better than the *Pollio*', i.e. Virgil's 'Eclogue IV' (*Corresp.*, i. 146). SJ may react here to the use of Steele's words by Warton, *Essay* (1756), 11–12, and Ruffhead, *Life*, 39–40. In 1756 he had commented on Warton's discussion of 'Messiah' that 'he justly observes some deviations from the inspired author, which weaken the imagery, and dispirit the expression' (*OASJ*, 488–9). In 1781, apart from alluding to Isaiah as P's 'original', SJ noticeably refuses to discuss this 'sacred poem'. For the superiority of the sacred to the pagan, see 'Milton' **236** and n. above.

SJ had discussed Virgil's 'Eclogue IV' in *Adventurer* 92 (1753) (*YW*, ii. 419), and memorized it in 1774 and again in 1783 (*Life*, ii. 288, iv. 218). In *Works of P* (1797), i. 105, Warton criticized SJ's own early Latin translation of 'Messiah' (see **195** n. above) with some severity.

319. For the supposed origins of 'Elegy to the Memory of an Unfortunate Lady', see **47** and n. above. SJ quoted ll. 25–7 of the 'Elegy' in a note to Shakespeare in 1765 (*YW*, viii. 998), and did so again with some emotion in a letter to Mrs Thrale, 20 Aug. 1783 (*Letters*, iv. 187). He also once recited the final lines 'with a very faultering voice': see *Letters* (1788), ii. 383–4.

For SJ's objections to literary suicide, see **52** above and 'Young' **162** and 'Gray' **47** below. He may allude here to Thomas Warton's recent 'Ode: The Suicide' in his *Poems* (1777), 42–4. English translations (from 1779) of Goethe's *The Sorrows of Young Werther* also helped to make suicide a topic of morbid interest, and, in some quarters, growing concern, by the 1780s. See e.g. *Gent. Mag.* (1784), 964–5, and also 807, which praised SJ for condemning P's 'Elegy' as 'contrary to the principles of society', and describes the lady's uncle as 'acting as a man of honour and a conscientious guardian should do'. SJ himself may have contributed a passage about the recent 'laxity of principles', which was 'making the dreadful act of self-murder more commonly perpetrated', in Sir Robert Chambers's *Lectures on the English Law* (ed. T. M. Curley (Oxford, 1986), i. 240). For his sensitivity about suggestions that a passage in *The Beauties of Johnson* (1782) encouraged suicide, see *Letters*, iv. 40, and *Life*, iv. 149–50.

With SJ's comment on the predomination of 'sense' (revising 'sentiment' in MS) over 'diction' in the 'Elegy', cf. the opposition of 'matter' and 'sense' to 'sounds' and elegant diction in **322–6, 330–4, 365–6** below, and 'Roscommon' **27** above.

disparage: '1. To marry anyone to another of inferiour condition' (*Dict.*). SJ said on 28 Mar. 1775: 'I would not let a daughter starve who had made a mean marriage; but ... would not put her on a level with my other daughters ... it is our duty to maintain the subordination of civilized society; and when there is a gross and shameful deviation from rank, it should be punished so as to deter others from the same perversion' (*Life*, iii. 328–9). For objections to SJ's claim that there is an 'inconsistency' between the niece's 'ambitious love' and her guardian's 'pride' in insisting on her obedience, see *TE*, ii. 356.

Warton, *Essay* (1756), 249–53, had praised the 'Elegy' as 'tender and pathetic'. Attributing its excellence partly to the fact that 'the occasion of it was real', he quoted an 'indisputable maxim' from SJ's *Adventurer* 92 (1753): that 'we can always feel more than we can imagine, and that the most artful fiction must give way to truth' (*YW*, ii. 424). This may explain why SJ said little about the 'Elegy' in his review of Warton. He applies the 'maxim' instead to 'Eloisa to Abelard' in **342** (and cf. **320**) below.

320. See Steele to P, 26 July 1711, and P to Caryll, 2 Aug. 1711 (*Corresp.*, i. 131–2).

P praised Dryden's *Alexander's Feast* (see 'Dryden' **150, 279, 318** above) in a letter to Walsh, 22 Oct. 1706 (*Corresp.*, i. 23). In 1735 he admitted that 'Many people would like my ode on music better if Dryden had never written on that subject', but denied 'any thought of rivalling that great man, whose memory I do and have always reverenced' (Spence, i. 28). William Ayre, *Memoirs of P* (1745), i. 79, considered P's *Ode for Musick* (1713) his worst poem, much inferior to Dryden's. In 1768 Gray praised Dryden's sublime ode, and added: 'That of Pope is not worthy of so great a man' (*Poems* (1969), 175 and n.). For similar comments, see Barnard (ed.), *P: Critical Heritage*, 156, 236, 371, 456, 521.

Warton may for once echo SJ when later stating that 'The subject of Dryden's ode is superior to ... Pope's, because the former is historical, and the latter merely mythological' (*Works of P* (1797), i. 485). SJ noticeably praises *Alexander's Feast* more forcibly when demoting P's *Ode* here than in his earlier discussion in 'Dryden' **318** above. For odes for St Cecilia by 'other competitors', see 'Addison' **128**, 'Hughes' **6**, and 'Congreve' **39** above; and for SJ's amusement at Bonnell Thornton's burlesque *Ode on St. Cecilia's Day, Adapted to the Antient British Musick* (1763), see *Life*, i. 420. For the opposition of 'history' and 'fable', see also **342** below.

For references to the 'passes of the mind' in 18th-century verse, see T. Mason and A. Rounce in P. Hammond and D. Hopkins (eds.), *John Dryden: Tercentenary Essays* (Oxford, 2000), 154. Cf. also 'those ideas that slumber in the heart' in 'Dryden' **326** above, 'the recesses of the mind' in 'Young' **157** and n. below, and SJ in 1768 on Richardson's 'characters of nature, where a man must dive into the recesses of the human heart' (*Life*, ii. 49). Hawkins, *Life* (1787), 217, also reported

SJ describing Richardson and Shakespeare as 'acquainted with the inmost recesses of the human heart'.

321. For SJ's dislike of irregular metre, see 'Cowley' 140–1 and nn. above. He quotes Horace on Pindar, *Odes*, IV. ii. 11–12 ('in measures free from rule'). For Congreve's demonstration that Pindar's odes were not irregular, see 'Congreve' 44 and n. above.

Samuel Cobb (1675–1713), who published several Pindaric odes between 1694 and 1709, was at Trinity College, Cambridge, early in Richard Bentley's Mastership (see 285 and n. above). Although SJ's source for this anecdote has not been identified, it is worth noting that John Nichols collected anecdotes about Bentley: see *Gent. Mag.* (1779), 545–8.

322–6. There were several precedents for detailed analysis of P's *Ode*: see Warburton (1751 edn.), i. 117–18 n., Warton, *Essay* (1756), 52–62, and Ruffhead, *Life*, 59–64, to whom SJ responds at times. He had discussed possible borrowings in the poem in *Rambler* 143 (1751) (*YW*, iv. 398–9). For his comments on Warton's discussion in 1756, see *OASJ*, 489–90.

323. Ruffhead, *Life*, 60–2, particularly praised stanza II.

For 'common-places' (sometimes 'common places', as in SJ's MS here and in 326) in poetry, see also 326, 421 below, and 'Shenstone' 28 and 'Gray' 34 below. (The *Dict.* does not include the word as a noun.)

324. In his review of Warton in 1756, SJ described l. 8 of stanza III ('And Men grew Heroes at the Sound') as the best in the poem (*OASJ*, 489).

325. For SJ's dislike of mythology, see 'Butler' 41 and n. above.

Whereas SJ refers to P's 'sweetness of versification', both Warton, *Essay*, 56–7, and Ruffhead, *Life*, 68–9, objected to stanzas V–VI on metrical grounds, Warton describing 'the numbers' in ll. 87–92 as 'burlesque and ridiculous'.

SJ's final words recall Aaron Hill's complaint about contemporary poetry, pointedly addressed to P, in his 'Preface' to *The Creation* (1720), pp. vi–xiv: 'The most obvious Defect in our Poetry . . . is, that we study *Form*, and neglect *Matter* . . . Poetry, the most elevated Exertion of human Wit, is no more than a weak and contemptible Amusement, wanting Energy of Thought, or Propriety of Expression.'

326. P's *Ode*, ll. 133–4, refers finally to Orpheus and Cecilia: 'His Numbers rais'd a Shade from Hell, | Hers lift the Soul to Heav'n.' In 1756 SJ had agreed with Warton that the odes of both Dryden and P 'conclude unsuitably and unnaturally with an epigram' (*OASJ*, 490). For confusions of the 'literal' and the 'metaphorical', see 'Dryden' 320 and n. above.

327. Not long before he died, P admitted his technical ignorance of music, but claimed to have 'naturally a very good ear' (Spence, i. 174–5; Ruffhead, *Life*, 476). See Brownell, *AP and the Arts*, 368–71, for 'the Myth of Pope's Insensibility to Music', promoted by John Mainwaring, *Memoirs of Handel* (1760), 93–4, and Hawkins, *History of Music* (1776), v. 328, 414.

Since SJ himself, while often professing his ignorance of music, wrote the dedications to Charles Burney's *General History of Music*, vol. i (1776), and *Commemoration of Handel* (1784), there may be a trace of self-mockery here. For Swift's ignorance of music, see 'Swift' 117 above.

328. For SJ's use of 'greatest' see **144** and n. above, and 'Milton' **194** and n. above.

Warton, *Essay* (1756), 100–2, also emphasized the early age at which P wrote *An Essay on Criticism* (see **34–44** above). Reviewing Warton, SJ described the poem as 'the stupendous performance of a youth not twenty years old', written with 'wonderful prematurity of mind' (*OASJ*, 491). His enthusiasm for it here contrasts with his reductive and hostile account of the *Essay on Man* (**363–7** below).

For didactic poetry, see also **44–5** above and **363** below, 'Roscommon' **30**, 'Dryden' **284–5**, 'J. Philips' **15–16**, 'Blackmore' **24, 45–8**, 'Granville' **30**, 'Somervile' **7**, and 'Savage' **117–24** above, and 'Dyer' **11** and 'Akenside' **14–15** below. For other discussions, see Joseph Trapp's 'Of Didactic or Praeceptive Poetry' in *Lectures on Poetry* (1742), 187–201, and Warton's 'Reflections on Didactic Poetry' in *Works of Virgil* (1753), i. 393–440.

329. SJ is probably reacting to Ruffhead's listing of the *Essay*'s 'particular beauties' (69–97).

For SJ's own allegory about climbing 'the Mountain of Existence', see 'The Vision of Theodore' (1766) (*OASJ*, 165–74). Reviewing Warton's *Essay* (1756), SJ described his criticism (141–2) of P's 'Alps' simile (ll. 219–32) as 'too general and indistinct'. SJ already considered it 'the best simile in our language; that in which the most exact resemblance is traced between things in appearance utterly unrelated to each other' (*OASJ*, 491). Ruffhead, *Life*, 81–2, thought it over-extended.

With SJ's definition of a 'perfect' simile, cf. Warton's *Adventurer* 57 (1753): 'The use of similes in general consists in the illustration or amplification of any subject, or in presenting pleasing pictures to the mind by the suggestion of new images.' SJ's reference to a simile as 'a short episode' echoes Addison's *Spectator* 303 (1712) on epic poets: 'their Episodes are so many short Fables, and their Similes so many short Episodes.' SJ also adopts Addison's citation of Charles Perrault's *Parallèle des anciens et des modernes*, ii (1693), 41, which ridiculed some of Homer's similes as '*Comparaisons a longue queue. Long-tail'd Comparisons*'. For P's own parody of '*A Simile* with a long tail, in the manner of *Homer*', see *Dunciad* (1729), II. 237 ff. (*TE*, v. 129–30 and n.). For the 'ship-race' and 'Apollo and Daphne', see *Aeneid*, V. 129 ff., and Ovid, *Metamorphoses*, I. 533 ff. For similes, see also 'Addison' **132** and n. above, where SJ also argues that 'another like consequence from a like cause, or a like performance by a like agency, is not a simile, but an exemplification'.

After the third sentence in the MS, SJ deleted the opening of another: 'To say that truth is recommended by sweetness of verse, as physick is made alluring to children by honey, though not improper in' (see Textual Notes).

330. SJ refers to *Essay on Criticism*, ll. 364–83, quoting l. 365. For P's preoccupation with 'Sound and Sense', see his letters to Walsh, 22 Oct. 1706, and to Cromwell, 25 Nov. 1710 (*Corresp.*, i. 22–3, 107), Spence, i. 172–3, the preface to the *Iliad* on 'one of the most exquisite Beauties of Poetry, and attainable by very few', and the examples of 'Versification Expressing in the Sound the Thing describ'd' listed in the index (*TE*, vii. 20–1, viii. 608).

For other discussions, see Addison, *Spectator* 253 (1711); Spence, *Essay on Pope's Odyssey* (1726–7), i. 150–5, ii. 196–215; Aaron Hill (1738), Lord Kames (1762), and George Campbell (1776), in Barnard (ed.), *P: Critical Heritage*, 82–5, 440–6, 466–9; and James Beattie, *Essays* (Edinburgh, 1776), 568–71. Thomas

Sheridan's minute discussion of versification in *Lectures on the Art of Reading* (1775) prompted William Enfield in *Monthly Review*, 53 (1775), 204–11, to suggest, like SJ, that the poetic effects claimed for it were usually imaginary. For modern discussions, see D. T. Mace, 'The Doctrine of Sound and Sense in Augustan Poetic Theory', *RES* 2 NS (1951), 121–39, and T. Mason and A. Rounce in P. Hammond and D. Hopkins (eds.), *John Dryden: Tercentenary Essays* (Oxford, 2000), 141–2 and nn.

331–2. SJ revised these paragraphs with particular care in the MS: see Textual Notes.

331. For 'representative metre', see also 'Cowley' **194–5** above. SJ had written sceptically about it, especially as discovered in Milton's verse, in *Ramblers* 92, 94 (1751), which Ruffhead, *Life*, 85–8, described as at times 'rather nice and fastidious'. In *Idler* 60 (1759), Dick Minim delighted in the 'hidden beauties' of poetry and found 'the sound an echo to the sense' in some absurd lines from Butler's *Hudibras*. SJ is less sceptical about a poet's 'skilful adaptation of his numbers to the images expressed' in 'Pitt' **5** below.

Rambler 94 had listed 'growl', 'buzz', 'hiss', and 'jar' as English words which 'exhibit the noises which they express' (*YW*, iv. 138). The 'Grammar' prefixed to the *Dict.* (1755) gave a longer list of such words derived from the grammarian John Wallis, whose explanations SJ considered 'ingenious, but of more subtlety than solidity'. SJ's definitions in the *Dict.* occasionally concede that such words as 'Mum' and 'Shrill' may imitate 'the thing expressed': see DeMaria (1986), 164–5.

332. Lord Kames (see **330** n. above) in his *Elements of Criticism* (1762) showed that versification can convey different kinds of 'successive motion', but concluded, like SJ, that qualities 'belonging to the thought solely' can easily be 'transferred to the words' by the reader.

SJ quotes *Odyssey*, XI. 735–8. Although Broome translated Bk. XI (see **133** and n. above), P either wrote or approved the long note on the correspondence of 'sound and sense' in these lines. Addison had praised this aspect of the original Greek in *Spectator* 253 (1711). For P's letter to him about the passage, 10 Oct. 1714, see *Corresp.*, i. 263–4.

Whether or not SJ's parody proves his point, David Fairer has pointed out to me that its diction resembles that of 'To the River London' (1777), a sonnet by Thomas Warton, whose verse SJ enjoyed parodying at this period (see *Poems* (1974), 206–8): cf. Warton's 'fairy ground . . . traces back the round . . . my evening road'.

333. In his earlier analysis of *Essay on Criticism*, ll. 370–3, in *Rambler* 92 (1751), SJ wrote of l. 373: 'why the verse should be lengthened to express speed, will not be easily discovered . . . the Alexandrine, by its pause in the midst, is a tardy and stately measure; and the word "unbending," one of the most sluggish and slow which our language affords, cannot much accelerate its motion' (*YW*, iv. 129). Although Warton, *Essay* (1756), 153, accepted that SJ had 'exploded' P's lines, Smollett accused SJ of having 'an undistinguishing ear', and defended l. 373 in *Critical Review*, 1 (1756), 231–2: 'it exhibits a fine, gay, fleeting picture; and the length of the line implies the length of space through which *Camilla* passed with such velocity' (see J. G. Basker, 'Minim and the Great Cham', in J. Engell (ed.), *J and his Age* (Cambridge, Mass., 1984), 150–1). An 'Essay on Versification' in the *London Chronicle*, 14 (1763), 44–5, also replied to SJ, but George Campbell, *The*

Philosophy of Rhetoric (1776), ii. 237–41, in a discussion of P's alexandrines, accepted SJ's argument. Aaron Hill had earlier objected to the diction of these lines in a letter to P, 11 May 1738 (*Corresp.*, iv. 96–9).

SJ goes on to quote *Imit. Horace, Ep. II. i.* (1737), ll. 267–9, written in fact some twenty-five years later than the *Essay*. His point is that, while both passages end with alexandrines, the line allegedly evoking swiftness has one more metrical stress than the line evoking 'slow-paced majesty'. (SJ defines 'Time' as '15. Musical measure', *Dict.*)

334. *nugatory*: 'Trifling; futile; insignificant' (*Dict.*).

335. For *The Rape of the Lock* see **53–60** above. There were occasional dissenting voices: Hugh Kelly described the poem as 'a glittering toy; an elevated geegaw', which merely amused the fancy, in *The Babler* (1767), ii. 233–6.

SJ's 'waiting-maid' recalls Gay, *Trivia* (1716), II. 563: 'Pleas'd Sempstresses the *Lock*'s fam'd *Rape* unfold.' Cf. SJ's earlier description of Shakespeare's appeal to 'the ignorant' and 'the learned': 'These are beauties that rise out of nature and truth; the superficial reader cannot miss them, the profound can image nothing beyond them' (*YW*, vii. 90, viii. 591). For the 'readers of every class' taught by Addison to admire Milton, see 'Addison' **162** above.

the power of pleasing: SJ stated in *Rambler* 92 (1751) that 'It is... the task of criticism... to distinguish those means of pleasing which depend upon known causes and rational deduction, from the nameless and inexplicable elegancies which appeal wholly to the fancy' (*YW*, iv. 122).

In 1756 SJ stated that, while Warton, *Essay* (1756), 204–48, gave a long account of the 'history of the comic heroic' from Tassoni to Garth (expanding earlier remarks in *Adventurer* 133, 1754), his discussion of *The Rape of the Lock* included 'no discovery of any latent beauty, nor any thing subtle or striking; he is indeed commonly right, but has discussed no difficult question' (*OASJ*, 492). Although SJ's early notes for 'Pope' include the entry, 'Emulated former pieces—Denham. Dryden Boileau, Garth Fleckno Mac' (Dyce MS, fo. 1ʳ), he here ignores P's mock-heroic precursors, apart from a brief reference to Boileau in **340** below, preferring to emphasize the poem's wide appeal rather than an aspect appreciated only by educated readers. P had described Garth as 'his predecessor in this kind of Satire' in a note to *Dunciad* (1729): see *TE*, v. 114, and, for *The Dispensary*, 'Garth' **10, 17** above. SJ saw Dryden's *Mac Flecknoe* as a precedent for the *Dunciad* rather than *The Rape*: see **356** below.

336. See Warburton (1751 edn.), i. 219–20 n., iv. 2 n., and, for SJ's opinion of Warburton, **184** and n. above.

For SJ's objections to 'heathen deities' and 'allegorical persons', see 'Butler' **41** and n. and 'Cowley' **151** and n. above. Cf. also 'Gay' **28** above: 'The attention naturally retires from a new tale of Venus, Diana, and Minerva.' P defended allegorical poetry against the objections of 'modern Criticks' in a prefatory note to his *Temple of Fame* (see **317** above).

337. For SJ's concern to defend P's 'invention', see also **314** and n. above, and, for 'originality', 'Milton' **277** and n. above.

The 'objector' was Warton, *Essay* (1756), 248: 'he was not the FIRST former and creator of those beautiful machines, the sylphs; on which his claim to imagination is chiefly founded.' For P's debt to the Rosicrucians, see **55** and n. above. Arthur

Murphy, in the prefatory 'Essay' to his *Works of Fielding* (1762), i. 15–21, and Ruffhead, *Life*, 107, 446–7, 451–6, had already replied to this charge. In *Adventurer* 93 (1753) Warton had in fact praised P's 'vast exuberance of fancy', while suggesting that he was indebted to Ariel in *The Tempest*, a point repeated in *Essay* (1756), 227. For SJ's comments on the 'system of enchantment' and the 'fairy empire' in earlier English literature, see his notes in 1765 to *The Tempest*, *A Midsummer Night's Dream*, and *Macbeth*.

338–9. For the important blend of the 'natural' and the 'new', see 'Cowley' **55** and n. above. In 1765 SJ wrote similarly that Shakespeare 'approximates the remote, and familiarizes the wonderful; the event which he represents will not happen, but if it were possible, its effects would probably be such as he has assigned' (*YW*, vii. 65).

339. Cf. Reynolds's later insistence in his 'Discourse XIII' (1786) that 'whatever is familiar, or in any way reminds us of what we see and hear every day, perhaps does not belong to the higher provinces of art, either in poetry or painting' (*Discourses*, 290).

340. SJ quotes P's dedication of *The Rape of the Lock* to Arabella Fermor (*TE*, ii. 142).

Dennis stated that P's poem was inferior to Boileau's anti-clerical mock-heroic satire *Le Lutrin* (1674), in *Remarks on Mr. Pope's Homer* (1717) (*Works*, ii. 330–1). For P's MS notes on the *Remarks*, see *TE*, ii. 392–9. Warburton (1751 edn.), iv. 38 n., quoted Voltaire's preference in 1726 for *Le Lutrin*, also discussed by Warton, *Essay* (1756), 208–16.

The freaks, and humours, and spleen, and vanity of women: with this outburst, cf. SJ's praise of Mrs Corbett's domestic virtues in **412** below, and his comments on 'domestick happiness' in 'Waller' **16** above. He said of his own mother that 'her discourse was composed only of complaint, fear, and suspicion' (*YW*, i. 7). In *Rambler* 85 (1751) he praised female domestic employments for preventing idleness, with 'her attendant train of passions, fancies, and chimeras, fears, sorrows, and desires' (*YW*, iv. 86).

Although Mrs Thrale noted in 1777 that SJ 'was always of the Men's Side when there was a domestick Dispute' (*Thraliana*, i. 178–9), and his letters often mention the quarrelsome female inhabitants of his house, he also told John Ryland, 2 Sept. 1784: 'You are without female attention, and you have my sympathy, I know the misery of that vacuity in domestick life. The loss of Mrs. Williams who had been my inmate for about thirty years is not likely to be repaired' (*Letters*, iv. 389). Posing as 'a kind of neutral being between the sexes', he had written in *Rambler* 18 (1750): 'as the faculty of writing has been chiefly a masculine endowment, the reproach of making the world miserable has been always thrown upon the women ... with declamatory complaints, or satirical censures, of female folly or fickleness, ambition or cruelty, extravagance or lust.' *Rambler* 45 (1750) stated that both 'Wives and husbands are, indeed, incessantly complaining of each other' (*YW*, iii. 98, 245). The 'domestic discord' described by Nekayah in *Rasselas* (1759), ch. XXVI, is not blamed only on women.

small vexations: Hill (1905) compared SJ's statement in *Journey to the Western Islands* (1775) that 'Misery is caused for the most part not by a heavy crush of disaster, but by the corrosion of less visible evils, which canker enjoyment and undermine security ... domestick animosities allow no cessation' (Oxford, 1985, 76). See also *Ramblers* 68, 74 (1750): 'peevishness ... wears out happiness by slow corrosion, and small injuries incessantly repeated'; and 'Sermon 1': 'in private families ... Life may be imbittered with hourly vexation' by 'A thousand methods of torture' (*YW*, iv. 23, xiv. 6). See also 'Addison' **37** and 'Swift' **123** above.

341. P added the 'machinery' of the sylphs (see **55** above), and the game of Ombre at III. 25–104, to *The Rape* in 1714. Dennis objected that the sylphs 'neither prevent the Danger of *Belinda*, nor promote it, nor retard it' (*Works*, ii. 337). For SJ's doubts about 'supernatural interposition' elsewhere, see 'Gay' **30** and n. above. In **59–60** above SJ seems to endorse P's own view that 'the intertexture of the machinery with the action' was 'his most successful exertion of poetical art', stating that Dennis's objections had 'very little force, and ... no effect'. For approval of Dennis's point about the irrelevance of the sylphs, and SJ's concession to it, see Parker, 'P and Mature Augustanism', 99 ff.

342. For 'Eloisa to Abelard', see **63** above. Warton had similarly asserted in *Essay* (1756), 298–334, that 'of all stories, ancient or modern, there is not perhaps a more proper one to furnish out an elegiac epistle', emphasizing like SJ the lovers' final 'retirement and piety', rather than Abelard's castration and Eloisa's sexual frustration. Reviewing Warton, SJ described the poem as 'one of the works on which the reputation of Pope will stand in future times', the beauties of its 'sentiments of nature' appealing to 'the learned and the ignorant ... alike' (*OASJ*, 493). He adapted a line (94) from a particularly impassioned passage in a letter to Mrs Thrale, 15 June 1780 (*Letters*, iii. 277).

SJ's belief in the poem's basis in 'undisputed history' rather than 'fable' is hardly justified. Although the Latin letters of Eloisa and Abelard had been published in Paris in 1616, P's source was the romanticized French version of their story (1697) by Roger de Rabutin, Comte de Bussy, as translated into English in John Hughes's *Letters of Abelard and Heloise* (1713) (see 'Hughes' **10** n. above and *TE*, ii. 296–8). This explains why Ruffhead, *Life*, 171–2, in spite of his praise of 'Eloisa', noted that it 'has done no service to the cause of virtue'. Whatever his intentions, P's depiction of 'licentious passion' had 'made fatal impressions on persons of warm temperament', and assisted 'artful libertines' in their seductions.

Other critics agreed. Mrs Thrale wrote in May 1782: 'I have heard that all the kept Mistresses read Pope's Eloisa with singular delight—'tis a great Testimony to its Ingenuity; they are commonly very ignorant Women, & can only be pleased with it as it expresses the strong Feelings of Nature & Passion' (*Thraliana*, i. 536). Walpole (to William Mason, 14 Apr. 1781) was astonished that, after condemning P's 'Elegy on an Unfortunate Lady' (**47–52** above), SJ should admire a poem on such a subject (*Corresp.*, xxix. 130). Mason himself, in William Whitehead's *Poems*, iii (York, 1788), 35–6, ascribed the 'capital charm' of P's poem to his 'happy use ... of the monastic gloom of the paraclete and of what I will call papistical machinery', which should have appealed to SJ's 'own superstitious turn', but also noted that 'Eloisa' contains passages 'which tend to mislead young minds, actuated usually by strong passions'. By 1797, Warton, *Works of P*, i, p. xxiii, was admitting 'the inherent indelicacy of the story'.

For 'truth', see 'Cowley' **14** and n. above, and cf. SJ's assertion in *Rambler* 20 (1750) that 'every man hates falshood, from the natural congruity of truth to his faculties of reason' (*YW*, iii. 110), and his opposition of 'history' to 'fable' in **320** above. For his statement in *Adventurer* 92 that 'we can always feel more than we can imagine, and . . . the most artful fiction must give way to truth' (*YW*, ii. 424), see **319** and n. above.

For SJ's use of 'Eloisa' in the *Dict.*, see under e.g. 'Deepen', 'Quiver', 'Twilight', and 'Visionary', and Henson, 151–2. Malone noted SJ's objection to P's use of 'you' rather than 'thou' in 'Eloisa', ll. 335–6 (Bodleian, MS Malone 30, fo. 29ᵛ).

343. For 'curiosa felicitas' ('studied felicity') in Petronius, *Satyricon*, 118, see 'Smith' **5** and n. above. Reviewing Warton in 1756, SJ suggested that P had referred to Petronius in *Essay on Criticism*, ll. 667–8, merely 'on the credit of two or three sentences which he had often seen quoted' (*OASJ*, 492).

crudeness: 'Unripeness; indigestion' (*Dict.*).

344. Warton, *Essay* (1756), 320, discussed P's 'judicious and poetical use . . . of the opinions of the mystics and quietists'. In his review, SJ commented that Warton had 'justly remarked that the wish of Eloisa for the happy passage of Abelard into the other world is formed according to the ideas of mystic devotion' (*OASJ*, 493). SJ's compliment here is one of his few direct references to Warton, with whom he is often in running disagreement: see headnote, and cf. 'Addison' **130** above.

345. For the *Iliad* translation, see **72–114** above and, for SJ's views on translation elsewhere, 'Denham' **32** and n. above. (For critics who were less convinced about the importance of translation, see Dennis, *Works*, ii. 433–4 n.) In this context, SJ is prepared to suppress his usual suspicion of 'wonders': see 'Cowley' **5** and n. above, and cf. the final words of **348** below. On 9 Apr. 1778 he had described P's *Iliad* as 'the greatest work of the kind that has ever been produced' (*Life*, iii. 257).

SJ's earlier outline of the history of translation in *Idler* 68–9 (1759) emphasized the lack of interest in it in ancient Greece: 'Greece considered herself as the mistress if not as the parent of arts, her language contained all that was supposed to be known' (*YW*, ii. 212).

346. Giovanni Anguillara's translation of Ovid's *Metamorfosi* (1584) and Antonio Salvini's *Iliade* (1723) are both mentioned in Baretti's *The Italian Library* (1757), 127, 135, with which SJ had assisted him (cf. *Corresp.*, i. 447 and 'Addison' **68** and n. above).

Gent. Mag. (1781), 227, asked whether SJ 'has not heard of *Annibal Caro's Virgil*, generally esteemed, both by natives and foreigners, one of the best translations in any language?' Warton's claim in *Essay*, i (4th edn., 1782), 300, that Caro translated Virgil 'admirably' was a further reminder of his omission, which Warton reinforced with an extended list of earlier Italian and Spanish translators. SJ may have remembered that in 1697, while admitting that Caro was 'a great name among the Italians', Dryden had described his translation (1581) as 'most scandalously mean' (Watson, ii. 240).

347. Cicero translated the *Phaenomena* of Aratus (mentioned in *Idler* 68), and orations by Demosthenes and Aeschines (now lost), as well as fragments of Homer and the Greek tragedians. The Roman general Nero Claudius Germanicus (15 BC–AD 19) also translated Aratus, only fragments surviving. With two exceptions, the Latin plays of Terence were adapted from the Greek of Menander.

For French translations, notably those by Madame Dacier, see **85–6** above, and for the inadequacy of the French language for heroic poetry, see 'Dryden' **223** and n. above. Warton, *Essay*, i (4th edn., 1782), 300, made the same point.

348. For Dryden's translation of Virgil, see 'Dryden' 303–13 above, and for his influence on P, see 13 above and 374 below. SJ discussed Virgil's debt to Homer in *Rambler* 121 (1751).

For poetic diction, see 'Cowley' 181–4 and n. above. SJ has already stated that Dryden 'tuned the numbers of English poetry' and introduced 'Those happy combinations of words which distinguish poetry from prose', but later accepts that 'the mellifluence of Pope's numbers' was still more influential (see 'Dryden' 216, 221, 311, and cf. also 314 and n. above), elsewhere describing the *Iliad* as a model of 'an exact, equable, and splendid versification' ('Pitt' 10 below).

In asserting that no later poet 'has wanted melody' SJ means that no later poet has any excuse for wanting it: for the harsh versification of some recent poets, see 'Hammond' 8 above, and 'Collins' 17 and 'Gray' 48 below. Coleridge later described P's *Iliad* as both an 'astonishing product of matchless talent and ingenuity', and 'the main source of our pseudo-poetic diction': see *Biographia Literaria*, ed. J. Engell and W. J. Bate (Princeton, 1983), i. 18, 39 n.

In the final sentence, 'vulgar' is a singular noun: 'The common people' (*Dict.*).

349–52. There are lingering echoes in this discussion of the *querelle d'Homère* in France 1711–16 about whether a translator should remain faithful to the noble simplicity of heroic times or 'improve' Homer's 'barbarism': see *TE*, vii, pp. lxxviii–lxxix, J. M. Levine, *The Battle of the Books: History and Literature in the Augustan Age* (Ithaca, NY, 1991), chs. IV–VI, and D. L. Patey, 'Ancients and Moderns', in H. B. Nisbet and C. Rawson (eds.), *Cambridge History of Literary Criticism*, iv (Cambridge, 1999), 52–63. Whereas Dacier and others argued for a greater understanding of Homeric times, SJ attaches more importance to the translator's own age and audience: 'Time and place must always enforce regard' (349).

349. For Bentley's dismissive opinion of P's Homer, see 285 and n. above, and for SJ's scepticism about the 'learned' see also 'Cowley' 115 above. For Tickell's *Iliad*, Bk. I, as preserving 'more of Homer', see 111 above. In his third sentence SJ quotes and translates Seneca Rhetor, *Controversiae*, IX. iv. 5.

There were early objections to P's translation as 'not Homerical': see e.g. Dennis, *Remarks upon Mr. Pope's Homer* (1717) (in *Works*, ii. 123–4); Bezaleel Morrice in various works, e.g. *Three Satires* (1719), 8 ('He smoothes him o'er, and gives him grace and ease, | And makes him *fine*—the *Beaus* and *Belles* to please'); and Spence's *Essay on Pope's Odyssey* (1726–7), an extended debate about P's tendency to 'turn the Plainness and Strength of the Original, into the *Fine* and the *Artificial*' (i. 18).

Warton, *Essay* (1756), 280–2, considered P's genius unsuited to heroic simplicity, as SJ no doubt remembered when mocking Dick Minim's enthusiasm for 'the noble simplicity of our ancestors, in opposition to the petty refinements, and ornamental luxuriance' of 'false delicacy', and hopes for 'the revival of the true sublime' (*Idler* 61 (1759); *YW*, ii. 190–1). William Wilkie, in *The Epigoniad* (Edinburgh, 1757), p. xl, complained that 'The quaintness of Mr. Pope's expression...is not at all suitable, either to the antiquity or majestic gravity of his author'; and Young, *Conjectures on Original Composition* (1759), 58, deplored P's preference for couplets to blank verse: 'What a fall is it from *Homer*'s numbers, free as air, lofty and harmonious as the spheres, into childish shackles, and tinkling sounds!'

Thomas Gray, however, thought highly of P's *Iliad*, '& when he heard it criticised as wanting the simplicity of the original, or being rather a paraphrase than a translation, & not giving a just idea of the poet's style, & manner, he always said "there would never be another translation of the same poem equal to it"' (*Corresp.*, iii. 1292). Yet William Hawkins objected to P's 'Boldnesses, and Pretty-nesses', and use of rhyme, in his *Works*, iii (Oxford, 1759), 414–42, and *Anecdotes of Polite Literature* (5 vols., 1764), i. 54, claimed that P had turned Homer's marble into brick and pebbles. Even P's admirer Lord Lyttelton wrote in his *Dialogues of the Dead* (1760): 'Your *Homer* is the most spirited, the most poetical, the most elegant, and the most pleasing translation, that ever was made of any ancient poem; though not so much in the *manner* of the original, or so exactly agreeable to the *sense* in all places, as might perhaps be desired' (*Works* (3rd edn., 1776), ii. 189). Robert Wood, *Essay on the Original Genius and Writings of Homer* (1775), 72–92, claimed that P's 'flowing and musical versification freqently betrays him into a florid profusion of unmeaning ornament'. Vicesimus Knox, *Essays Moral and Literary* (1782), ii. 372, stated that 'The chief beauty of Homer is simplicity, which, in the Translation, is sacrificed to a gaudy glare and artificial embellish-ments.'

Changing taste was also reflected in Joseph Nicoll Scott's *Essay towards a Translation of Homer's Works, In Blank Verse* (1755), and Samuel Langley's *The Iliad of Homer, Translated from the Greek into Blank Verse . . . Being a Specimen of the Whole* (1767). Shenstone said in Oct. 1759 that, 'were Pope's Homer to make it's first appearance now, he would be *greatly* blam'd' for using rhyme (*Letters* (1939), 521). Cowper argued in *Gent. Mag.* (Aug. 1785), 610–13, that rhyme occasions 'an almost unavoidable necessity to depart from the meaning of the original', but that it was no surprise 'that Pope, who managed the bells of rhyme with more dexterity than any man, should have tied them about Homer's neck'. Cowper wrote even more bluntly on this subject to Newton, 10 Dec. 1785, and in the preface to his own translation of Homer (1791) (*Letters*, ii (1981), 420, v (1986), 52–3, 61–9). Boswell believed, however, that 'Mr. Cowper, a man of real genius, has miserably failed in his blank verse translation' (*Life*, iii. 333 n.).

For P's reference to Homer's 'noble simplicity' in 1708, see **383** below. SJ had himself seemed to prefer 'rude simplicity' to 'the laboured elegance of polished versions' in **83** above. For 'simplicity', see also 'Dryden' **325** and n. above, and, for Homer's versification, *Rambler* 92 (1751).

350. For 'subordination', opposed here to 'barbarity', see 'Swift' **52** and n. above.

SJ stated in the preface to the *Dict.* that 'every language has a time of rudeness antecedent to perfection, as well as of false refinement and declension' (*OASJ*, 319). In *Idler* 63 (1759) he described 'The natural progress of the works of men . . . from rudeness to convenience, from convenience to elegance, and from elegance to nicety': 'improvement' in language brings 'the regulation of figures, the selection of words, the modulation of periods, the graces of transition, the complication of clauses, and all the delicacies of style and subtilties of compos-ition, useful while they advance perspicuity', but 'easy to be refined by needless scrupulosity'. English writers have 'studied elegance' since Chaucer's times, but 'the danger is, lest care should too soon pass to affectation' (*YW*, ii. 197–8).

For 'That curiosity which always succeeds ease and plenty', see also *Idler* 37 (1758), and cf. *Rasselas*, ch. X: 'it is commonly observed that the early writers are in possession of nature, and their followers of art: that the first excel in strength and invention, and the latter in elegance and refinement' (*YW*, ii. 117, xvi. 40).

SJ wrote to Mrs Thrale from the Highlands, 30 Sept. 1773: 'They are a Nation just rising from barbarity, long contented with necessaries, now somewhat studious of convenience, but not arived at delicate discriminations' (*Letters*, ii. 96). His dedication to Reynolds's *Discourses* (1777) opens by observing that 'The regular progress of cultivated life is from Necessaries to Accommodations, from Accommodations to Ornament' (sig. [A3]), and his 'Sermon 12' also describes the cycle from 'necessity' to the 'refinements of pleasure' and 'the arts of luxury' (*YW*, xiv. 132). Goldsmith more than once described the same process: 'nothing less than the insinuating address of a fine writer can win its way to an heart already relaxed in all the effeminacy of refinement' (*Coll. Works*, ii. 105, 311).

Although it seems hardly to SJ's purpose, in a defence of P's 'elegant' translation, to emphasize such a stage of eventual over-refinement and 'degeneracy', he acknowledges here the danger of 'fastidiousness' ('saturated . . . luxurious . . . artificial'). Yet his argument that 'artificial diction' is an inevitable 'refinement' also recalls his defence of 'luxury' on 14 Apr. 1778: 'to be merely satisfied is not enough. It is in refinement and elegance that the civilized man differs from the savage' (*Life*, iii. 282). For a distinction between mere 'Refinement' ('A studied Advantage in the Manner, independent on an adequate motive in the Thought') and true genius, and a warning that excessive refinement inevitably degenerates into bad taste, see Daniel Webb, *Literary Amusements in Verse and Prose* (1787), 16–18.

SJ uses 'elegance', 'elegant', and 'elegantly' some 130 times in the *Lives*. In 1755 he defined 'Elegance. Elegancy' as 'Beauty of art; rather soothing than striking; beauty without grandeur' (*Dict.*), revising the definition in 1773 to begin 'Beauty rather soothing', etc., and adding 'the beauty of propriety not of greatness'. He also added in 1773: '2. Any thing that pleases by its nicety. In this sense it has a plural', transferring to this definition a quotation from Addison's *Spectator* 447 which opposed the 'elegancies of art' to 'the beautiful wildness of nature'. SJ also defines 'Elegant' as '1. Pleasing with [by *1773*] minuter beauties. 2. Nice; not coarse; not gross'; and 'Elegantly' as '1. In such a manner as to please without elevation [without elevation *omitted in 1773*]. 2. Neatly; nicely; with minute beauty' ('with pleasing propriety' added in 1773).

By 1755 SJ was thus contrasting 'elegance', a soothing and pleasing kind of beauty, with grandeur, elevation, and the striking, reinforced by 'greatness' in 1773. Addison's association of 'elegance' with art as opposed to wild nature is supported by other definitions of 'elegance' as propriety, nicety, neatness, and minute beauty, as opposed to the coarse and gross. Cf. also SJ's definitions of e.g. 'Neat' ('Elegant, but without dignity'), and 'Pretty' ('1. Neat; elegant; pleasing without surprise or dignity. 2. Beautiful without grandeur or dignity'). For 'pretty', see also 'Cowley' 133 and n. above.

For the argument that SJ associated 'elegant' and 'elegance' specifically with precision and economy of thought and expression, see P. Ingham, 'Dr J's Elegance', *RES* 19 (1968), 271–8. SJ normally uses the words in the *Lives*, however, to convey general approval of diction, versification, and other aspects of poetry, which are pleasingly graceful, polished, and refined, rather than coarse, gross, clumsy, or harsh (cf. 'Milton' 177 and n. and 'Dryden' 219–21 above, and *Life*,

iii. 243). His usage does not in fact differ markedly from that of such contemporaries as Shenstone, for whom elegance 'excludes the glare and multiplicity of ornaments on one side, as much as it does dirt and rusticity on the other' (*Works* (1764), ii. 275), and Beattie, *Essays* (Edinburgh, 1776), 433, for whom 'affectation and rusticity are equally remote from true elegance'.

For examples of 'elegant' and 'elegance', which are not merely routine, see **99** above and **367, 373** below, 'Cowley' **61, 85, 184,** 'Otway' **10,** and 'Waller' **150** above, and 'Watts' **16,** 'A. Philips' **18,** 'West' **11,** and 'Akenside' **19** below. For SJ's occasional opposition of 'elegance' to 'grandeur' and 'sublimity', see 'Milton' **230** and n. above. 'Savage' **120** above suggests that by 1744 SJ had not yet arrived at a clear opposition of 'elegance' to 'grandeur': *The Wanderer* 'strikes rather with the solemn magnificence of a stupendous ruin, than the elegant grandeur of a finished pile'. As late as 1773 he referred to York Minster as 'an Edifice of loftiness, and elegance' (*Letters*, ii. 47).

351. SJ's reference to P's 'Ovidian graces' implies some reservations, given Ovid's reputation in the period. Cf. Dryden's preface to *Ovid's Epistles* (1680): 'he is frequently witty out of season leaving the imitation of nature...for the false applause of fancy'; his dedication to *Examen Poeticum* (1693): 'He is often luxuriant, both in his fancy and expressions; and...not always natural'; and his preference in *Fables* (1700) of Chaucer's 'simplicity' to Ovid's 'conceits' (Watson, i. 265, ii. 163, 278–80).

For Spence, *Essay on Pope's Odyssey*, ii (1727), 160–1, 'little and artificial' ornaments 'of the *Ovidian* kind' are 'more apt to hit the Taste of Schoolboys, than of Men': his '*Boyisms*' sink 'beneath that Simplicity and Nature, which is the distinguishing Character' of Homer. William Melmoth illustrated the 'Ovidian' affectations of P's translation in *Letters on Several Subjects*, ii (1749), 133 ff. In 1782, Warton probably had SJ's defence of P's *Iliad* in mind when stating 'how very inferior and unlike it is to the original, and how much overloaded with improper, unnecessary, and Ovidian ornaments' (*Essay on P*, ii. 27, 406–7 n.). For an earlier translation which preserved the 'wit' at the expence of 'the dignity of the original', see 'Dryden' **300** above.

loved, as well as...reverenced: SJ wrote in *Rambler* 188 (1752) that 'it is always necessary to be loved, but not always necessary to be reverenced' (*YW*, v. 224). For the contrast between admiration/esteem and love/delight, see 'Milton' **276** and n. above, where Milton himself, 'like other heroes...is to be admired rather than imitated', and is 'capable of astonishing' rather than concerned to 'please'. Cf. also 'Collins' **17** below: 'men are often esteemed who cannot be loved.'

352. In *Idler* 3 (1758) SJ condemned the critic who debars 'honest minds...from pleasure, by exciting an artificial fastidiousness, and making them too wise to concur with their own sensations' (*YW*, ii. 12).

Reynolds reported a similar justification by SJ ('a learned critic') of P's translation in his 'Discourse XV' (1790): 'if Pope had not cloathed the naked Majesty of Homer with the graces and elegancies of modern fashions,—though the real dignity of Homer was degraded by such a dress, his translation would not have met with such a favourable reception, and he must have been contented with fewer readers' (*Discourses*, 328; cf. *Life*, ii. 256–7). Similarly, for all his scepticism about the authenticity of 'Ossian', SJ 'did not require Mr. McPherson's Ossian to be more like the original than Pope's Homer' (*Life*, v. 242). For SJ's view that 'he that can accommodate himself to the reigning taste, may always have readers', see *Adventurer* 95 (1753) and *Idler* 85 (1759) (*YW*, ii. 426, 266).

P had acknowledged the influence on a translator of 'the Taste of the Age in which he lives' in *Iliad*, XI. 668 n. (*TE*, viii. 64 n.), but in 1728 ironically depicted modern authors pursuing 'Profit or Gain . . . by administring pleasure to the reader: From whence it follows demonstrably, that their productions must be suited to the *present* taste' (*Prose Works*, ii. 188: for a later echo of the same passage, see **382** n. below). SJ's argument recalls Dryden's reply to Rymer in 'Dryden' **398** above ('the climate, the age, the disposition of the people, to whom a poet writes, may be so different, that what pleased the Greeks would not satisfy an English audience'); and his later claim that the translators of Juvenal 'endeavoured to make him speak that kind of English which he would have spoken had he lived in England, and had written to this age' (Watson, ii. 154). Cf. also the argument of Philypsus in Spence's *Essay on Pope's Odyssey* (1726–7), i. 21: 'You are always blaming the Modern Refinements . . . but will you not allow that this taste of the Age is a sufficient justification at least of Mr. *Pope* . . . We must *write* so as to please the World.'

For the 'modern graces' of P's Homer, see also 'Cowley' **115** above. SJ argues somewhat differently in 'Dryden' **223–6** above that 'rugged magnificence is not to be softened . . . A translator is to be like his author; it is not his business to excel him' (**225**). Reservations may also be implicit in his references to 'the mellifluence' of P's numbers and his 'splendid' diction in 'Dryden' **311** above: see also **378** and n. below, where SJ may allude to his criticism of the opening of the *Iliad* in *Idler* 77. With SJ's defence of P's elegance, cf. also his earlier account of the 'stile' and 'phraseology' which remain 'settled and unaltered' in the language, from which Shakespeare 'gathered his comick dialogue', and which is found 'in the common intercourse of life, among those who speak only to be understood, without ambition of elegance. The polite are always catching modish innovations', etc. (*YW*, vii. 70).

For 'colours', see also **373** below and 'Milton' **193** and n. above, and for 'sublimity', 'Cowley' **58** and n. above.

353. For the notes to the *Iliad*, see **86** and n. above. SJ stated in 1765: 'Notes are often necessary, but they are necessary evils . . . Particular passages are cleared by notes, but the general effect of the work is weakened. The mind is refrigerated by interruption' (*YW*, vii. 111).

354. For P's 'appeals . . . to the ladies', see e.g. his notes to *Iliad*, XIV. 191, 198, 203, 216, 218 (*TE*, viii. 168–72). For modern discussions, see Thomas, 'P's *Iliad*', 1–11, and *Women Readers*, 19–67, and Williams, *P, Homer & Manliness*, 146–69. In contrast, Dryden paid virtually no attention to women readers in his translation of Virgil (1697). For 'ease' in writing, see 'Rochester' **18** and n. above.

In *Rambler* 173 (1751) SJ dismissed the old-fashioned belief that 'all appearance of science is particularly hateful to women', and that, to win their approval, an author 'must consider argument or criticism, as perpetually interdicted; and devote all his attention to trifles, and all his eloquence to compliment' (*YW*, v. 152–3). He himself in fact made some similarly gallant 'appeals' in his notes to Shakespeare: e.g. *YW*, vii. 213, 264 ('I know not how the ladies will approve the facility with which both Rosalind and Celia give away their hearts'), and cf. **413** and n. below (written in 1756).

355. SJ's brief treatment of the *Odyssey* suggests that he attached little significance to the fact that Fenton and Broome translated half of it. For Broome's notes, see **133** and n. above.

356. For *The Dunciad* see **144–55** above and, for the influence of *Mac Flecknoe*, see *Dunciad*, II. 2 n., and 'Dryden' **136** above. For 'the praise of an original', see 'Denham' **28** and n. above.

SJ has already called *The Rape of the Lock* 'the most attractive of all ludicrous compositions' (**355** above): the element of 'personal satire' rather than its 'ludicrously pompous' style is what is distinctive in the *Dunciad*. SJ defines 'Satire' as: 'A poem in which wickedness or folly is censured. Proper *satire* is distinguished, by the generality of the reflections, from a lampoon, which is aimed against a particular person; but they are too frequently confounded' (*Dict.*). In 'Dryden' **273** above, however, he in fact concedes that 'Personal resentment, though no laudable motive to satire, can add great force to general principles.'

357. Cf. SJ's opinion that *The Beggar's Opera* (also 1728) was 'written only to divert, without any moral purpose' ('Gay' **22** and n. above). On 2 Apr. 1775 he said that P's 'primary motive' in the *Dunciad* was 'fame': 'Had it not been for that, the dunces might have railed against him till they were weary, without his troubling himself about them. He delighted to vex them, no doubt; but he had more delight in seeing how well he could vex them' (*Life*, ii. 334). Ruffhead, *Life*, 360, had regretted that 'so much good sense and excellent morality should be intermixed with a transient satire on private characters' in the *Dunciad*.

For Lewis Theobald, see **126, 145** above.

358. For 'the tribunal of criticism', see *Rambler* 93 (1751): 'he that writes may be considered as a kind of general challenger, whom every one has a right to attack; since he quits the common rank of life, steps forward beyond the lists, and offers his merit to the publick judgment. To commence author is to claim praise, and no man can justly aspire to honour, but at the hazard of disgrace'; and *Rambler* 176 (1751): 'The diversion of baiting an author has the sanction of all ages and nations, and is more lawful than the sport of teizing other animals, because, for the most part, he comes voluntarily to the stake' (*YW*, iv. 133–4, v. 165). Under 'Culprit' in the *Dict.* SJ quotes Prior, 'An author is in the condition of a culprit; the publick are his judges': for similar quotations about authors in the *Dict.*, see DeMaria (1986), 208–9. In *Rambler* 145 (1751), however, SJ had argued that 'the common interest of learning requires that her sons should cease from intestine hostilities' (*YW*, v. 12).

With 'Dulness or deformity', cf. the letter signed by William Cleland prefixed to the *Dunciad*: 'Deformity becomes the object of ridicule when a man sets up for being handsome: and so must Dulness when he sets up for a Wit' (*TE*, v. 17). This is a common defence of satire, e.g. in Swift's 'Verses on the Death of Dr. Swift', ll. 467–70 ('He spar'd a Hump or crooked Nose, | Whose Owners set not up for Beaux. | True genuine Dulness mov'd his Pity, | Unless it offer'd to be witty'). Cf. also *Rambler* 179 (1751): 'Ignorance or dulness . . . never give disgust except when they assume the dignity of knowledge, or ape the sprightliness of wit . . . Deformity itself is regarded with tenderness rather than aversion, when it does not attempt to deceive the sight by dress and decoration, and to seize upon fictitious claims the prerogatives of beauty' (*YW*, v. 177).

SJ quotes Juvenal, *Sat.*, I. 4–5 ('Shall I have no revenge on one who has taken up the whole day with an interminable Telephus?'), referring to a tragedy on the mythological Telephus.

For James Moore Smythe (1702–34), see *Dunciad*, II. 35–50, 109–20, and **361** below. As Hill (1905) noted, Moore is described in *Tom Jones* (1749), XII. i, as imprisoned 'in the loathsome Dungeon of the *Dunciad*, where his unhappy Memory now remains, and eternally will remain, as a proper Punishment for such his unjust Dealings in the poetical Trade'.

For Richard Bentley, see **285** and n. above. SJ originally described Priam's javelin (*Aeneid*, II. 544–6) as 'thrown at Neoptolemus', but omitted this in 1783: see Textual Notes.

359. For 'truth', see 'Cowley' **14** and n. above.

SJ said on 2 Apr. 1779 that 'the sense of ridicule is given us, and may be lawfully used' (*Life*, iii. 379–80). For his comments, in a different context, on the 'foolish assertion of the efficacy of ridicule for the discovery of truth', see 'Akenside' **6–7** below.

360. For P's own defence of his coarseness, see *Dunciad* (1729), II. 71 n. (*TE*, v. 106–7). Ruffhead, *Life*, 368–9, was disgusted by 'the grossness, nay the filthiness' of *Dunciad*, Bk. II, and deplored its influence on 'authors of inferior genius'. Beattie, *Essays* (Edinburgh, 1776), 438 n., stated that Swift and P 'have given us descriptions which it turns one's stomach to think of'. For a similar objection, see 'Swift' **137** above. While SJ was completing 'Pope' early in 1781, however, Mrs Thrale admitted: 'I like the Dunciad beyond all Pope's Poems' (*Thraliana*, i. 470).

361. For James Moore Smythe see **358** and n. above. SJ also refers to *Dunciad*, IV. 293–336 ('the Traveller', of which P himself thought highly: see Spence, i. 250), 403–36 ('the Florist'), and 627–56 ('the concluding paragraph'). On reading the *New Dunciad* (1742) Gray immediately told Richard West in Apr. 1742 that 'the pleas of the Virtuosos and Florists, and the yawn of dulness in the end, are as fine as anything he has written' (*Corresp*, i. 189).

SJ recited the closing lines of the *Dunciad* 'in his forcible melodious manner' on 26 Oct. 1769 (*Life*, ii. 84; according to Boswell's journal he also recited 'the character of Moore', *Boswell in Search of a Wife*, ed. F. Brady and F. A. Pottle (New York, 1956), 338). Frances Reynolds also mentioned his pleasure in reciting them (*J. Misc.*, ii. 254).

Although he says little here about these famous lines, or about the gloomy magnificence of the passages on the rise and fall of civilizations in Bk. III, they may already have been in his mind in 1742 in his 'Account' of the Harleian Library, on 'how darkness and light succeed each other, by what accident the most gloomy nights of ignorance have given way to the dawn of science, and how learning has languished and decayed, for want of patronage and regard, or been overborne by the prevalence of fashionable ignorance, or lost amidst the tumults of invasion, and the storms of violence' (*OASJ*, 119). Cf. also Imlac in *Rasselas*, ch. XXX, on 'the Vicissitudes of learning and ignorance, which are the light and darkness of thinking beings, the extinction and resuscitation of arts, and the revolutions of the intellectual world' (*YW*, xvi. 113).

362. See Warburton (1751 edn.), i, pp. vi–vii, and **120** and n. above, for his policy of printing variants, initiated by P himself in 1735. For one of P's 'alterations', see **237** above.

By 'the last collection', SJ means *Eng. Poets* (1779): see Textual Notes.

363. Warton stated in his 'Reflections on Didactic Poetry' (1753) that the *Essay on Man* (see **173–80** above) has 'a sublimity of sentiment, an energy of diction, a spirit unextinguish'd by correctness and rhyme . . . that will ever render it the honour of our nation and language'. He also cited Warburton's claim that the poem 'has a precision, force, and closeness of Connection rarely to be met with, even in the most formal Treatises of Philosophy' (*Works of Virgil* (1753), i. 435–6; Warburton, *A Vindication of Mr. Pope's Essay on Man* (2nd edn., 1740), 149–50). Ruffhead, *Life*, 224, 457, described the *Essay* as 'perhaps the most concise and perfect system of ethics in any language': 'no work was ever more frequently quoted by readers of every class. There is scarce a line which has not been committed to the memory, both of the learned and unlearned. Many have no other system of morality, than what they have collected from this excellent piece.'

Arthur Murphy believed that SJ 'conceived an early prejudice' against the *Essay*, which, 'in a mind like his, was not easily eradicated', that his discussion should be viewed with 'great caution', and that he 'was too easily alarmed in the cause of religion' (*J. Misc.*, i. 374, 480–1). SJ's ridicule of P's 'metaphysical morality' in **365–6** is explained by his belief that 'the doctrine . . . was received from Bolingbroke' (see **179** and n. above). Crousaz (see **181–3**, **189** above) and others had already attributed the *Essay*'s illusory philosophical profundity to its poetic power. For the influence of SJ's dismissal of the poem in these terms, see Solomon, 'J's Silencing of P', esp. 258–72, and **366** n. below. Solomon also suggested that SJ intended his unexpected praise of Blackmore's philosophical *Creation* (1712) (see 'Blackmore' **24–5**, **45–8** above) to contrast with this attack on P's much better-known *Essay*.

SJ discusses *Essay on Man*, I. 43–50. He inserted 'that these beings must be *somewhere*, and' in 1783 (see Textual Notes).

Warton, *Essay*, ii (1782), 61–2, was among those who identified P's ideas with those of Gottfried Wilhelm Leibniz (1646–1716). P himself told Racine, 1 Sept. 1742, that his ideas were in fact diametrically opposed to those of Leibniz (*Corresp.*, iv. 415–16: see **289** above), and his influence is now discounted (*TW*, iii (i), pp. xxvi–xxvii).

364. Cf. *Rambler* 72 (1750) on 'Those who exalt themselves into the chair of instruction, without inquiring whether any will submit to their authority' (*YW*, iv. 12).

SJ refers to *Essay on Man*, I. 17–32, 207–58 (quoting 240–1), II. 294.

365. Before embarking on his reductive account of the *Essay*'s ideas (anticipated in **180** above), SJ reaffirms P's poetic 'genius', no doubt unwilling to play into Warton's hands: see also **373** below. Warton later deplored SJ's 'contemptuous and degrading' discussion: 'This sort of burlesque abstract, which may be so easily but so unjustly made of any composition whatever, is exactly similar to the imperfect and unfair representation which the same critic has given of the beautiful imagery in Il Penseroso of Milton' (*Works of P* (1797), iii. 162–3). For an earlier contrast of 'the elegance of the poetry' with 'the sense of the precepts', see 'Roscommon' **27** above (originally 1748). In 1765 SJ had observed more charitably of a crux in Shake-

speare: 'Both the old and the new reading are philosophical nonsense, but they are both, and both equally poetical sense' (*YW*, viii. 941).

R. DeMaria, *Life of SJ* (1993), 71, noted similar criticism of P's ideas in SJ's translation of Crousaz's *Commentary* (1742) (see **181–3** and nn. above): e.g. 'In this Place Mr *Pope* seems to express a great deal in a few Words, but upon Reflection, we learn nothing from him' (59). See also his explicit attack on the theodicy of the *Essay* as paraphrased in Soame Jenyns's *A Free Inquiry into the Nature and Origin of Evil* (1757), in the *Literary Mag.* 2 (May–July 1757) (*OASJ*, 522–43); and *Idler* 36 on 'the stately son of demonstration, who proves with mathematical formality what no man has yet pretended to doubt', in 'a style by which the most evident truths are so obscured that they can no longer be perceived' (*YW*, ii. 113).

With 'When these wonder-working sounds', etc., cf. P's *Essay on Criticism*, ll. 293–6: 'Poets like Painters, thus, unskill'd to trace | The *naked Nature* and the *living Grace*, | With *Gold* and *Jewels* cover ev'ry Part, | And hide with *Ornaments* their *Want of Art*.'

SJ refers in rapid succession to *Essay on Man*, I. 17–42, III. 169–200, 45–6, 269–82, 317–18, IV. 351–4, 396, II. 249–56, III. 112, IV. 114, 67–76, 167–92, 193–4, 309–26. Cf. his reference in **413** below to 'Virtue only is our own' as a commonplace. He in fact quotes IV. 397 ('That Virtue only makes our Bliss below') under 'Virtue' in the *Dict*.

For another poet from whom the reader 'learns nothing', see 'Akenside' **16–17** below; for 'imagery', see 'Cowley' **154** and n. above; for literature as 'seductive', see **366** and n. below; for 'vulgarity', see 'Milton' **181** and n. above; and for 'wonders', see 'Cowley' **5** and n. above.

366. For poetry's power to captivate or seduce the judgement, see also 'Dryden' **312** and n. above; and for 'luxuriant' language, see **350** above and 'Thomson' **50** and n. below. As DeMaria (1986), 156–7, noted, SJ quotes Robert South on 'bewitchery, or fascination in words', and 'that besotting intoxication which verbal magick brings upon the mind' in the *Dict*. ('Bewitchery', 'Intoxication', and 'Acclamation').

In her *Letters on Education* (1790), 131–2, the Whig historian Catherine Macaulay Graham unexpectedly paraphrased SJ's discussion, when illustrating the 'potent power of numbers' with a 'brilliant passage' from P's *Essay*, which 'will be found to be quite nonsense when stripped of the pomp of verse . . . Yet such are the charms of poetry, that most readers of this famous essay think they have gained a great many solid ideas from the most exceptionable passages; and even the philosopher gives way to the pleasures of sense, and suffers himself to be captivated by the power of harmony.'

For Frances Reynolds's vivid vignette of SJ reading and memorizing a passage from the *Essay*, see *J. Misc.*, ii. 254.

367. Swift told P, 1 Nov. 1734: 'I confess I did never imagine you were so deep in Morals, or that so many new & excellent Rules could be produced so advantageously & agreably in that Science from any one head. I confess in some few places I was forced to read twice' (*Corresp.*, iii. 439).

For 'harsh' diction, see 'Milton' **177** and n. above.

368. For P's *Epistle to Lord Cobham* and *Epistle to a Lady*, see **202, 207** above. SJ said on 16 Oct. 1769: 'his characters of men were admirably drawn, those of women not so well' (*Life*, ii. 84).

For a translation (*c*.1717–18) by Lady Mary Wortley Montagu of Boileau's *Satire X*, see her *Essays and Poems*, ed. R. Halsband and I. Grundy (Oxford, 1977), 210–14. For SJ's respect for Boileau, see 'Rochester' 26, 'Dryden' 141, 150, and 'Addison' 10 and nn. above, and P. H. Houston, *Doctor J: A Study in Eighteenth Century Humanism* (Cambridge, Mass., 1923; repr. New York, 1963), 72–110.

For 'The Gem and the Flower', see *To Cobham*, ll. 87–100; for 'Clodio' (identified from 1743 as the Duke of Wharton), see *To Cobham*, ll. 178–209, and 202 n. above; for 'Atossa', see *To a Lady*, ll. 115–50, and 208 and n. above; and for 'Philomede' ('Proud as a Peeress, prouder as a Punk'), see *To a Lady*, ll. 69–86. For Prior's liking for low life, see 'Prior' 49–50 above.

369. See 198–201, 156 above, and Warburton (1751 edn.), iii. 215 ff., 262 ff. For his discovery of meanings of which P himself was unaware, see 43, 190 and n. above.

   P's epistles were in fact published as follows: I *To Cobham* (Jan. 1734); II *To a Lady* (Feb. 1735); III *To Bathurst* (Jan. 1733); IV *To Burlington* (Dec. 1731). SJ is also mistaken about the later arrangement of the poems, which P himself adopted in *Works*, vol. ii (1735). For Warburton's claim that he persuaded P to reorganize *To Cobham* and *To Bathurst* to improve 'the clearness of method, and force of connected reasoning', see *Works* (1751), iii. 163 n.

   For P's 'elogy' ('Praise; panegyrick', *Dict.*, from French 'éloge') on Good Sense, see *To Burlington*, ll. 39–70; and for his account of the Duke of Buckingham's death in 1687, see *To Bathurst*, ll. 299–314.

370. See 212–16 above and, for the origins of the *Epistle to Arbuthnot* in particular, 215 n. above. Warburton (1751 edn.), iv. 9, had placed it at the head of the *Imitations of Horace* as 'Prologue to the Satires'. While the whole poem is a 'vindication of his own character', SJ refers either to P's account of his early career in ll. 125–92, or, more probably, to the passage at ll. 334–59.

   Although SJ is dismissive about P's famous 'character' of 'Sporus' in ll. 305–33, perhaps because of its references to Lord Hervey's ambiguous sexuality, he had quoted these lines repeatedly in the *Dict.*, under e.g. 'Bug', 'Curd', 'Dimple', 'Emptiness', 'Flap', 'Mumble', 'Prompter', 'Puppet', 'Seesaw', etc. Warton, *Essay on P*, ii (1782), 256–7, replied to SJ by emphasizing the intensity of the passage: 'Language cannot afford more glowing or more forcible terms to express the utmost bitterness of contempt . . . He has armed his muse with a scalping-knife.' Mrs Thrale-Piozzi made a marginal comment on SJ's last sentence: 'Certainly not; but Dr. Johnson loved a Hervey' (Lobban, 159; cf. 216 n. above).

371. For the original title of the dialogues, see 217–19 above. SJ no doubt discussed them with Savage when they were first published in 1738. He refers to *Epilogue to the Satires*, I. 113–30, 141–72.

372. For the origins of the *Imitations of Horace* at Bolingbroke's suggestion and their rapid composition, see Spence, i. 143–4, and 209–20 and nn. above. P described the first imitation (*Sat. II. i.*) on 8 Mar. 1733 as 'a slight thing' by comparison with *To Bathurst*, on which he worked 'two years by intervals' (*Corresp.*, iii. 353). Cf. SJ's assertion that 'What is written without effort . . . is in general read without pleasure' (*J. Misc.*, ii. 309).

   SJ defines 'Imitation' as '2. A method of translating looser than paraphrase, in which modern examples and illustrations are used for ancient, or domestick for foreign', citing Dryden (*Dict.*). Sending *London* to Edward Cave in Apr. 1738,

SJ asked for the original Latin to be quoted at the foot of the page, 'part of the beauty of the performance (if any beauty be allow'd it) consisting in adapting Juvenals Sentiments to modern facts and Persons' (*Letters*, i. 16). A contributor to Dodsley's *The Museum*, ii (1747), 431, claimed that P's *Imitations*, 'by entering into the very Spirit and Purpose of the Author, manifested a Train and Connexion of Thought in him, which was new' to those who had studied Horace in the usual 'broken, piece-meal' manner at school.

Although Goldsmith, discussing SJ's *London* in *The Beauties of English Poesy* (1767), claimed that 'Imitation gives us a much truer idea of the ancients than ever translation could do' (*Coll. Works*, v. 320), SJ came to dislike a form which appeals only to the 'man of learning' and excludes the 'common reader'. Cf. 'West' 14 and n. below: 'An Imitation of Spenser is nothing to a reader, however acute, by whom Spenser has never been perused.' No doubt in response to SJ's remarks here, Warton discussed P's *Imitations* respectfully in *Essay*, ii (1782), 272–352, with detailed comparison with the original Latin. For 'imitation', see also 'Cowley' 125, 'Rochester' 19, 'J. Philips' 10–11, 13, and 'Prior' 76 above, and 'Thomson' 36, 'West' 14, and 'Shenstone' 32 below.

Roman images: SJ originally wrote 'Roman sentiments' in the MS, revised in the proofs (see Textual Notes). In a MS note in a copy of *London* (5th edn., 1750), he commented on his lines about 'Orgilio': 'This was by Hitch a Bookseller justly remarked to be no picture of modern manners, though it might be true at Rome' (*Poems* (1974), 64, 77). He may recall here Dryden on the imitators of Juvenal: 'the manners of nations and ages are not to be confounded: we should either make them English, or leave them Roman' (Watson, ii. 155). SJ wrote in 1765 that in *Julius Caesar* Shakespeare's 'adherence ... to Roman manners, seems to have impeded the natural vigour of his genius' (*YW*, viii. 836).

373. SJ originally wrote 'a Poet' in the first sentence in the MS, but revised it to 'genius' (see Textual Notes), perhaps in view of his discussion of 'Whether Pope was a poet?' in 382 below. For poetic genius, see also 310 above and 'Milton' 277 and n. above. SJ here discusses the poetic faculties invoked by Ruffhead, *Life*, 447–9, in his earlier reply to Joseph Warton: Invention, Imagination, Judgement, and Taste (the last including felicity of expression).

Invention: for earlier responses to Warton's insistence on P's limited 'invention', see 58, 314, 337 above. Arthur Murphy, who had defended P in *Works of Fielding* (1762), i. 15–21, described Warton's charge as something of a commonplace (Barnard (ed.), *P: Critical Heritage*, 447–52). As early as 1736 John Henley said of P: 'there is not one Poem which can be called Invention (the main constituent of a Poem) in his whole Collection' (*The Hyp Doctor*, 24 Feb. 1736). SJ discussed the importance of 'invention' in *Rambler* 154 (1751), and in *Rambler* 168 (1751) emphasized 'the force of poetry, that force which calls new powers into being, which embodies sentiment, and animates matter' (*YW*, v. 59, 127). In his dedication to Charlotte Lennox's *Shakespear Illustrated* (1753), he declared that 'Among the powers that must conduce to constitute a poet, the first and most valuable is invention' (*YW*, vii. 47). He defines 'Poet' as '1. An inventor' (*Dict.*). In 1765 he stated that 'it would not be easy to find any authour, except Homer, who invented as much as Shakespeare' (*YW*, vii. 90). See also 'Waller' 137 above: 'the essence of poetry is invention.' Warton, *Essay on P*, ii (1782), 408–10, continued to insist that '*good sense* and *judgment*', rather than '*fancy* and *invention*', were P's strength and limitation.

Imagination: William Duff, *An Essay on Original Genius* (1767), 58, described 'a vigorous, extensive, and PLASTIC Imagination' as the 'principal qualification' of Genius, whose 'proper office . . . is to INVENT incidents or characters, to CREATE new and uncommon scenery, and to describe every object it contemplates, in the most striking manner, and with the most picturesque circumstances'. For 'imagination' and 'impresses', see 'Cowley' **16** and n. above and 'Thomson' **46** and n. below, and for animating 'energy' as the essence of poetical genius, see **294, 310** above. For the title '*Ethick Epistles*' rather than *Moral Essays*, see **198** n. above.

Judgement: see **32** and n. above and 'Roscommon' **23** and n. above.

colours of language: for 'diction', see 'Cowley' **181–4** and n. above. SJ described 'the colours of varied diction' as essential to the imaginative writer in *Adventurer* 115 (1753) (*YW*, ii. 460): see also **352** and 'Milton' **193** and n. above.

374. SJ quotes Dryden's preface to *Tyrannick Love*: 'our solemn music, which is inarticulate poetry' (Watson, i, 239) (quoted under 'Inarticulate' in the *Dict.*). Cf. *Rambler* 86 (1751) on the poet's 'peculiar superiority, that . . . he adds the faculty of joining musick with reason, and of acting at once upon the senses and the passions. I suppose there are few who do not feel themselves touched by poetical melody' (*YW*, iv. 89). In his dedication to Burney's *History of Music*, vol. i (1776), SJ described music itself as 'the art that unites corporal with intellectual pleasure, by a species of enjoyment which gratifies sense, without weakening reason' (i, p. iv). P himself wrote in *Essay on Criticism*, ll. 143–4: '*Musick* resembles *Poetry*, in each | Are *nameless Graces* which no Methods teach.' Ruffhead, *Life*, 441–2, believed that style mattered more than content in poetry.

For Dryden's influence on P, see **13, 348** above. For P's views on versification, see his letter to Walsh, 22 Oct. 1706, perhaps fabricated from a later letter to Cromwell, 25 Nov. 1710 (*Corresp*, i. 22–5, 105–8); and Spence, i. 173–8 ('The great rule of verse is to be musical'). For complaints about the 'smoothness' which had 'swallow'd up all the more substantial Graces of Poetry', with its '*Sameness* of the Sounds and Quantities, a speedy Satiety', see Charles Gildon, *The Complete Art of Poetry* (1718), i. 83, 292. For criticism of P's 'unvaried sweetness' in particular, see e.g. Dennis, *Works*, ii. 108, 135, 324, 466 n.; Welsted, *Palaemon to Caelia, at Bath* (1717), 11–12, on his 'Sweets of Rhime and easie Measures' as 'a vulgar Art, | Which never wakes the Soul, or warms the Heart'; Gildon, *Memoirs of William Wycherley* (1718), 15–17, on his 'Knack in smooth Vercification'; and the debate in Spence, *Essay on Pope's Odyssey* (1726–7), about the propriety of such 'sweetness' in epic poetry. Some of the 'Testimonies of Authors' prefixed to the *Dunciad* (*TE*, v. 40–3) in fact imply reservations about his versification. See also Barnard (ed.), *P: Critical Heritage*, 53, 91–2, 108, 228–9, 427–8.

Shiels, *Lives*, v. 249, gave a representative view of P's 'minutely correct' poetry, which 'has created a kind of mechanical versification; every line is alike; and though they are sweetly musical, they want diversity . . . we are not quite certain, whether the ear is not apt to be soon cloy'd with this uniformity of elegance, this sameness of harmony'. Dick Minim in *Idler* 60 (1759) predictably thought P's 'numbers rather luscious than sweet' (*YW*, ii. 187). After the mid-century, Warton, Kames, Churchill, Shenstone, Webb, Beattie, and others debated the question of P's excessive smoothness. There was little novelty in Wordsworth's assertion in 1815 that P 'bewitched the nation by his melody, and dazzled it by his polished style, and was himself blinded by his own success' (*Prose Works*, iii. 72). For an earlier reference to the 'mellifluence of Pope's numbers', see 'Dryden' **311** above.

principles rather than perception: by 'principles' SJ means rigid rules or dogmatic preconceptions (cf. 'Dryden' **193** and n. above). In Jan. 1779 he told Fanny Burney that there were three kinds of 'Judges': 'the first, are those who know no rules, but pronounce entirely from their natural Taste + feelings; The 2d are those who *know*, & *judge* by *rules*; & the 3d are those who *know*, but are *above* the rules. These last are those you should wish to satisfy: *next* to them, rate the *natural* judges,—but ever despise those opinions that are formed by the *rules*' (*Early Journals*, iii. 222). For 'perception', see also 'Cowley' **115** and n. above.

vary his pauses: cf. Dick Minim's opinion in *Idler* 61 (1759) that 'rhyme may sometimes be borne, if the lines be often broken, and the pauses judiciously diversified' (*YW*, ii. 191). For admirers of Milton's 'varied pauses', and P's claim that he could translate Homer 'more easily into rhyme' than blank verse, see 'Milton' **273–4** and nn. above.

375. *superfluous rigour*: SJ originally wrote 'unremitted rigour' in the MS, revised in the proofs (see Textual Notes).

SJ defines 'Refine' as '1. To improve in point of accuracy or delicacy. 2. To grow pure. 3. To affect nicety'; and 'Refinement' as '3. Improvement in elegance or purity' and (more reservedly) as '5. Affectation of elegant improvement' (*Dict.*). SJ may allude to Boileau, *L'Art poétique*, I. 64–6 ('Souvent la peur d'un mal nous conduit dans un pire. | Un vers était trop faible, et vous le rendez dur; | J'évite d'être long, et je deviens obscur'). But Boileau also stressed the importance of revision, as at I. 172–3 ('Vingt fois sur le métier remettez votre ouvrage; | Polissez-le sans cesse et le repolissez'), and in the preface to his *Œuvres* (1701). For Boileau, see also 'Dryden' **141** and 'Addison' **38** above.

SJ might equally well have cited Dryden's 'Parallel betwixt Painting and Poetry' (1695) (quoted in the *Dict.* under 'Correctness'): 'A work may be over-wrought as well as under-wrought: too much labour often takes away the spirit by adding to the polishing, so that there remains nothing but a dull correctness, a piece without any considerable faults, but with few beauties' (Watson, ii. 207). Walsh told P in 1706 that 'a Man may correct his Verses till he takes away the true Spirit of them' (*Corresp.*, i. 21). In *Spectator* 209 (1711) Addison complained that ancient 'Simplicity' was now hidden in 'Artifices and Refinements, Polished insensibly out of her original Plainness', and SJ himself wrote in *Idler* 63 (1759) that 'every man now endeavours to excel others in accuracy, or outshine them in splendour of style, and the danger is, lest care should soon pass to affectation' (*YW*, ii. 198).

not . . . strictly grammatical: for objections to the grammar of P's epitaphs, see **419, 435** and below, and cf. **376** n. below. As Hill (1905) noted, Robert Lowth had discussed the grammatical irregularities of P and other poets in his *Short Intro-duction to English Grammar: With Critical Notes* (1762; 1781 edn. cited), e.g. in notes on 51, 52, 64, 74, 82, 111 (and cf. *Life*, iv. 311).

rhymes: Swift told P, 28 June 1715, about some 'unjustifiable Rhymes' in his *Iliad* (Warburton (1751 edn.), ix. 8; *Corresp*, i. 301), which Warton illustrated in *Essay on P*, ii (1782), 322–3. P himself in fact disliked close repetition of the same rhymes: see his letter to Walsh, 22 Oct. 1706 (*Corresp.*, i. 24, and cf. i. 107). SJ's early notes for 'Pope' include: 'Forced rhymes in Jervas' (fo. 177ᵛ), referring to P's 'Epistle to Mr. Jervas' (**69** and n. above). For rhymes, see also 'Cowley' **187** and n. above.

376. *Alexandrines and Triplets*: see 'Cowley' **196, 199** and nn. above. P and Swift discussed them in the letters cited in **375** and n. above. P told him, 20 Apr. 1733: 'these things shall lye by, till you come to carp at 'em, and alter rhymes, and grammar, and triplets, and cacaphonies of all kinds' (*Corresp.*, iii. 366). On 12 Apr. 1735 Swift stated that Dryden 'brought in the Alexandrine verse at the end of triplets', mentioned his own parody of the device in 'Description of a City Shower' (see 'Swift' **39** n. above), and claimed: 'I absolutely did prevail with Mr. Pope, and Gay, and Dr. Young, and one or two more, to reject them. Mr. Pope never used them till he translated Homer, which was too long a work to be very exact in' (Swift, *Corresp.*, iv. 321).

Cf. *Essay on Criticism*, ll. 356–7: 'A *needless Alexandrine* ends the Song, | That like a wounded Snake, drags its slow length along.' For P's alexandrines, see also **332–3** above and *Windsor Forest*, l. 218, and cf. *Iliad*, IV. 177 n.: 'the Author's Design being only to image the streaming of the Blood, it seem'd equivalent to make it trickle thro' the Length of an *Alexandrian* Line' (*TE*, vii. 29 n.). For Fenton's opinion, see 'Dryden' **352** and n. above.

377. SJ's notes for 'Pope' (fo. 174ʳ) include: 'His humorous lines end. Sinner it— Prunella', referring to the rhymes 'sinner it, or saint it / paint it' in *Epistle to a Lady*, ll. 15–16, and 'fellow/prunella' in *Essay on Man*, IV. 203–4. He refers here to 'dissever/for ever' in *Rape of the Lock*, III. 153–4. Double rhymes are in fact quite common in P's lighter verse: e.g. *TE*, vi. 137, 140, 162, 250. For an earlier comment, see 'Waller' **147** above.

378. *Expletives*: see 'Cowley' **189** and n. above. P stressed that they should be avoided to Walsh, 22 Oct. 1706 (*Corresp.*, i. 23, and cf. i. 107), and in *Essay on Criticism*, l. 346 ('While *Expletives* their feeble Aid *do* join'). For his removal of expletives when revising the *Essay*, see *TE*, i. 235.

commodious: '1. Convenient; suitable', etc. (*Dict.*).

For Dennis's criticism of the opening lines of P's *Iliad* in 1717, see *Works*, ii. 127–8, 151–3. SJ also discussed them in *Idler* 77 (1759), objecting to P's inversions, superfluities, harsh metaphors, uncommon usages, and epithets which merely padded out the line. For Goldsmith's attempt to omit a word from every line of Gray's *Elegy*, and SJ's omission of alternate lines while reading Thomson to Shiels, see *Life*, i. 404 n., iii. 37. Reviewing Warton's *Essay* (1756), SJ criticized 'common rhymes', which made the second line of a couplet predictable (*OASJ*, 491). Dryden had objected to 'making any part of verse for the sake of the rhyme, or concluding with a word which is not current English' (Watson, i. 96).

French idioms: SJ added this sentence in 1783 (see Textual Notes). For P's interest in 'whether a word is English or not', and his intention of using Bolingbroke as an authority in the dictionary he planned late in life, see Spence, i. 70. For Gallicisms, see 'Dryden' **339** and n. above, and for SJ's objections to Bolingbroke's diction in particular, see *Life*, iii. 343, the definitions of 'Gallicism' and 'Owe' (omitted in 1773) in the *Dict.*, and W. K. Wimsatt, 'SJ's Treatment of Boling-broke in the Dictionary', *MLR* 43 (1948), 78–80.

379. SJ reminded himself of P's fondness for this mellifluous couplet (*Dunciad*, III. 87–8) three times in his notes for 'Pope' (Add. MS 5994.2, fo. 169^v, and Dyce MS, fos. 4^v, 5^r). He may have learned of it from Savage or Walter Harte. 'Scrutator' (John Loveday) in *Gent. Mag.* (1779), 359, noted that Warton, *Essay on P* (1756), 293, identified a couplet in P's 'Sapho to Phaon', ll. 207–8, as 'the most harmonious verses, in our language, I mean in rhyme'. For SJ's observation that 'poets in general preferred some one couplet they had written to any other', and admission that he thought his own 'best lines' were *Vanity of Human Wishes*, ll. 239–40, see *J. Misc.*, ii. 422. For his 'favourite' line in his translation of P's 'Messiah', see *Life*, i. 272.

380. 'Felicities of language—Watts' appears in SJ's early notes for 'Pope' (fo. 159^r), and twice more in the Dyce memoranda (fos. 2^r, 5^r), referring to Isaac Watts, *The Improvement of the Mind* (1741), 357–8: see 'Watts' 26 below.

Hall's Satires: Ruffhead, *Life*, 357–3 n., mentioned P's regret about his belated knowledge of Joseph Hall's satires (1597–8), but SJ's ulimate source seems to be Hall's *Virgidemiarum*, ed. William Thompson (Oxford, 1753), p. iii. For Hall, see also 'Dryden' 344 above. A copy of *Virgidemiarum* (1602) inscribed by a J. West states that P told him that 'It contains the best poetry & truest Satyr of any of our English poets & that he intended to modernise them as he had done Dr. Donne's' (Harvard University).

Hill (1905) noted a similar statement in Warburton (1770 edn.), iv. 239–40, that, as well as modernizing Donne's satires, P 'intended to have given two or three of Bishop Hall's, whose force and classical elegance he so much admired'. He would have needed 'only to correct a little, and smooth the versification'. In a copy of Hall containing P's revisions, now at Hartlebury Castle, Richard Hurd quoted Warburton's account in a letter of 24 Feb. 1753, of the marginal 'expres-sions of admiration' in the volume, with the last satire 'marked throughout in his own hand'. (Prof. Isabel Rivers has pointed out to me that Warburton's letter is quoted in Francis Kilvert, *Memoirs of . . . Hurd* (1860), 50.) Warburton also told Thomas Warton that 'the whole first satire of [Hall's] sixth book was corrected in the margin, or interlined, in Pope's own hand; and that Pope had written at the head of that satire, OPTIMA SATIRA' (*History of English Poetry*, iv (1790), 50). For the two copies of Hall associated with P, see Mack, *Collected in Himself*, 413–14.

Thomas Gray also admired Hall's satires, describing them in 1752 as 'full of spirit & poetry; as much of the first, as Dr Donne, & far more of the latter' (*Corresp.*, i. 370).

381. William Melmoth stated in *Letters on Several Subjects*, ii (1749), 206–7, that P had 'raised our numbers to the highest possible perfection of strength and harmony'. Writing in 1761 that 'The melody of our verse has been perhaps carried to its utmost perfection', Shenstone predicted a reaction in favour of 'the more striking efforts of wild, original, enthusiastic genius' (*Letters* (1939), 596). Goldsmith stated in 1764 that P had 'carried the language to its highest perfection; and those who have attempted still farther to improve it, instead of ornament, have only caught finery' (*An History of England, In a Series of Letters*, ii. 141).

When told in 1775 of Goldsmith's complaint that 'Pope and other poets had taken up the places in the Temple of Fame; so that as but a few at any period can possess poetical reputation, a man of genius can now hardly acquire it', SJ replied: 'That is one of the most sensible things I have ever heard of Goldsmith.' He also said that 'a thousand years may elapse before there shall appear another man with a power of versification equal to that of Pope' (*Life*, ii. 358, iv. 46).

The 'danger' SJ envisages is over-refinement and subsequent degeneration, according to the cycle expounded by commentators in many spheres (cf. **350** and n., **375** above). Leonard Welsted, *Epistles, Odes, &c.* (2nd edn., 1725), pp. vii–ix, had already suggested that 'the *English* language is not capable of a much greater perfection, than it has already attain'd . . . there is a point of perfection in general, which when once a language is arriv'd to, it cannot exceed, tho' it may degenerate from it . . . it is with languages, as it is with animals, vegetables, and all other things; they have their rise, their progress, their maturity, and their decay'.

effort: it is possible that SJ wrote 'effect' in the MS, which is unclear. For the compositor's occasional problems with 'effect' and 'effort' in the MS, see Textual Notes to 'Cowley' **58** and 'Granville' **27** above.

382. This paragraph concludes not only 'Pope' (disregarding the appended letter and reprinted discussion of P's epitaphs in **383–446**), but, in terms of composition, the *Lives* as a whole.

Boswell commented on the pleasure SJ must have felt 'in for ever silencing all attempts to lessen [P's] poetical fame' in this 'triumphant eulogium' (*Life*, iv. 46). As his repeated invocations of the 'poet' and of 'poetry' indicate, SJ is still replying to Warton's opening distinction in *Essay* (1756), i, p. iv, between the Man of Wit, the Man of Sense, and the True Poet, and to his conclusion in 1782 that P's verse 'lies more level to the general capacities of men, than the higher flights of more genuine poetry' (ii. 409). One of Dick Minim's critical concerns in *Idler* 60 (1759) had been to 'degrade [P] from a poet to a versifier' (*YW*, ii. 187). On 29 Apr. 1778, SJ indignantly dismissed Allan Ramsay's assertion that P's poetry had been 'less admired since his death' (*Life*, iii. 332).

For the problem of 'definition', see *Rambler* 125 (1751): 'Definition is, indeed, not the province of man; every thing is set above or below our faculties . . . Definitions have been no less difficult or uncertain in criticism than in law . . . There is therefore scarcely any species of writing, of which we can tell what is its essence, and what are its constituents' (*YW*, iv. 300). SJ in fact defines 'Poetry' merely as 'Metrical composition; the art or practice of writing poems', quietly including among the illustrative quotations to 'Poetical', 'I do not know what *poetical* is' (*As You Like It*, III. iii. 17) (*Dict.*).

On 12 Apr. 1776, SJ said: 'You may find wit and humour in verse, and yet no poetry.' When Boswell asked, 'Then, Sir, what is poetry?', SJ replied: 'it is much easier to say what it is not. We all *know* what light is; but it is not easy to *tell* what it is' (*Life*, iii. 38). Joseph Trapp's definition of poetry in *Lectures on Poetry* (1742), 13, may seem to justify SJ's scepticism: 'An Art of imitating or illustrating in metrical Numbers every Being in Nature, and every Object of the Imagination, for the Delight and Improvement of Mankind.' For earlier attempts to define it, see Dennis, *Works*, i. 215–16, 484 n.

For some of SJ's less guarded indications of what is or is not 'poetry' or 'poetical', see 58, 179, 294, 310, 365, 373 above, 'Cowley' 51–3, 99, 142, 'Milton' 92, 195, 208, 224, 248–50, 'Roscommon' 30, 'Waller' 137–9, 'Dryden' 143, 220–1, 255, 285, 'Sheffield' 28, 'Congreve' 35, and 'Savage' 101 above, and 'Thomson' 46–8, 'Collins' 17, 'Dyer' 10, 'Young' 155, 168, 'Akenside' 15, 19, and 'Gray' 28, 30–9, 51 below. See also *Ramblers* 86, 88, 168 (1751), *Rasselas*, ch. X ('A dissertation upon poetry'), *YW*, vii. 67, 438, viii. 554, 653, 886, 941, and *J. Misc.*, i. 226, 284–5. For the difference between poetry and mere verse, and between poetry and prose, see 'Dryden' 77 and n., 221 and n. above.

Hazlitt no doubt had this paragraph in mind when commenting: 'The question, whether Pope was a poet, has hardly yet been settled, and is hardly worth settling; for if he was not a poet, he must have been a great prose-writer, that is, he was a great writer of some sort' (*Works*, ed. P. P. Howe v. (1930), 69). Cf. also A. E. Housman's comment: 'When I hear anyone say, with defiant emphasis, that Pope was a poet, I suspect him of calling in ambiguity of language to promote confusion of thought. That Pope was a poet is true; but it is one of those truths which are beloved of liars, because they serve so well the cause of falsehood' (*The Name and Nature of Poetry* (Cambridge, 1933), 30–1).

SJ's third sentence ('Let us look round', etc.) oddly echoes P's satiric *Art of Sinking in Poetry* (1728), ch. II: 'Let us look round among the Admirers of Poetry, we shall find those who have a taste of the Sublime to be very few' (*Prose Works*, ii. 188). For an earlier echo of the same passage, see 352 n. above.

his version: P's translation of Homer, as in 93 above. SJ originally wrote in the MS that Homer 'would assign no humble seat to his translator' (see Textual Notes). In Fielding's *A Journey from This World to the Next* (1743), I. viii, Homer states that he had read P's translation 'with almost as much delight, as he believed he had given others in the Original'. In *Amelia* (1752), VIII. v, however, Capt. Booth describes P's *Iliad* as 'certainly a noble Paraphrase, and of itself a fine Poem, yet, in some Places, it is no Translation at all'.

In apparently resting his case for P's 'genius' on a translation, SJ is defying such proponents of 'originality' as Edward Young, *Conjectures on Original Composition* (1759), 68: 'But supposing *Pope's Iliad* to have been perfect in its kind; yet it is a *Translation* still; which differs as much from an *Original*, as the moon from the sun.' In doing so, SJ in effect bequeaths P's translation as a major battlefield to Romantic critics. See Coleridge, *Biographia Literaria*, ed. J. Engell and W. J. Bate (Princeton, 1983), i. 39–40 n.; Wordsworth, *Prose Works*, iii. 73–4, 95 n.; Southey's review of Chalmers's *Works of the English Poets* in *Quarterly Review*, 11 (1814), 480–504, and *Correspondence*, ed. E. Dowden (Dublin, 1881), 224; Byron to J. L. Hunt, 30 Sept. 1815 (*Letters and Journals*, ed. L. A. Marchand, iv (1975), 324–6); and Matthew Arnold in *On Translating Homer* (1861), Lecture I.

Emphasis on the Homer translation enables SJ to avoid the question of whether P's satiric and topical verse would date in the way that *Hudibras* and some of Dryden's poetry already had ('Butler' 41–2 and 'Dryden' 296 above), and Homer's timeless, 'unadulterated nature' emphatically had not (83 above). SJ's relatively perfunctory discussion of the *Imitations of Horace* in 372 above may implicitly acknowledge this possibility. SJ had complained to Lord Orrery as early as 1751 that some satiric allusions in P's *Essay on Criticism* were 'already impenetrably dark to the greater number of readers' (*Letters*, i. 52–3), and did not disagree in 1756 with Warton's prediction that 'the facts and characters alluded to and exposed in his later writings, will be forgotten and unknown, and their poignancy and propriety little relished. For WIT and SATIRE are transitory and perishable, but NATURE and PASSION are eternal' (*Essay*, i. 334; *OASJ*, 493). As SJ later stated when reviewing James Grainger's *The Sugar-Cane* (1764): 'To pursue the topic of the day, or to prop a declining party, are generally sure of immediate applause; but in proportion as such poets write to the present world, they must forgo their claims to posterity' (*Critical Review*, 18 (1764), 270). In 1765 he wrote: 'It is of the nature of personal invectives to be soon unintelligible' (*YW*, vii. 274–5).

383. In 1781 P's letter to Ralph Bridges, 5 Apr. 1708 (see *Corresp.*, i. 43–5), was owned by Philip Yorke, Earl of Hardwicke (1720–90). (Warton, *Essay on P*, ii. 234 n., claimed in 1782 already to have seen the letter in Cambridge in 1771.) SJ obtained the text through the dramatist Richard Paul Jodrell (1745–1831): see *Life*, iv. 254, 272, 437–8, and for a letter to Jodrell, 15 Apr. 1783, *Letters*, iv. 122. Jodrell later gave an account of SJ's Essex Head Club in a letter of 14 May 1824 (Bodleian MS Don. c.52, fo. 8), and his copy of Gray's *Poems* (Glasgow, 1768), with MS notes objecting to SJ's 'Gray', is in the Osborn Collection in the Beineke Library at Yale.

The Revd Ralph Bridges, chaplain to the Bishop of London, was the nephew of P's early friend Sir William Trumbull (see **23** and n. above). For references to P in the correspondence of Bridges and Trumbull in 1707–14, see Sherburn, 'New Anecdotes', 343–9; and for exchanges between P and Bridges about his early translation of the 'Episode of Sarpedon' from the *Iliad*, published in *Poetical Miscellanies*, vi (1709), see *TE*, i. 353–6.

The letter by the 19-year-old P no doubt interested SJ because it concerns Homer, whom he has just invoked in **382** at the end of the biography proper. For Chapman and Hobbes as translators of Homer, see **85** and n. above. For the inaccuracy of P's description of the complimentary reference to Hobbes in the 'large' quarto edition of Homer (Cambridge, 1689), sig. *a4*, see J. P. Hardy (ed.), *J's Lives of the Poets: A Selection* (Oxford, 1971), 363 n.

384–446. SJ wrote to Nichols (*c.* Mar. 1781) asking for 'the last leaves of the Criticism on Popes Epitaphs, and he will correct them' (*Letters*, iii. 324). References in his notes for 'Pope' to 'Paper on his epitaphs' and 'His epitaphs' (fos. 170ʳ, 174ʳ) indicate that he envisaged appending it from an early stage.

SJ's 'Dissertation on the Epitaphs Written by Pope' appeared in Christopher Smart's *Universal Visiter* (May 1756), 207–19, and was collected, with minor revisions, in the *Idler* (3rd edn., 2 vols., 1767), ii. 287–324, and in *Miscellaneous and Fugitive Pieces*, ii (1774), 192–207. (It was also excerpted without attribution in *Lloyd's Evening Post*, 23 Sept. 1765: see *Bibliography*, i. 663 n.) Smart fell ill soon after he and Richard Rolt contracted with a bookseller to compile the *Universal Visiter*, and SJ was among the contributors who kept the periodical going for a time: see SJ's account in 1775 in *Life*, ii. 345, and *Bibliography*, i. 660–9.

In the circumstances it would be unsurprising if SJ fell back on unpublished earlier work, and it is not impossible that the 'Dissertation' dates from as far back as the late 1730s. One clue is SJ's reference in **400** below to the death of Bernardi in 1736 as having happened 'lately', and another is his comment on biographies of

Fenton in **426** below. His early interest in the subject is clear from his 'Essay on Epitaphs' in *Gent. Mag.* (1740), 593–5, and the letter by 'Pamphilus' about Gay's self-epitaph in Westminster Abbey in *Gent. Mag.* (Oct. 1738), 536–7, which has been attributed to him: see J. Leed, 'Two New Pieces by J in the *Gentleman's Magazine*', *MP* 54 (1957), 221–9. SJ may later have reviewed William Toldervy's *Select Epitaphs* (2 vols., 1755) in *Gent. Mag.* (1755), 45–6; see A. Sherbo in M. Wahba (ed.), *Johnsonian Studies* (Cairo, 1962), 156.

For other internal evidence which might link the 'Dissertation' to the 'Essay' (1740), see the notes to **386, 396, 397, 410, 412, 415, 437–9** below. So early a date could obviously not apply to paragraphs **440–4**, which SJ evidently wrote after the appearance of Warburton's *Works of P* (1751), or to **445–6**, which he added in *Prefaces* (1781).

Whenever written, SJ 'minute and particular' analysis of the defects of P's epitaphs, originally intended to promote 'the cultivation of propriety' for the benefit of 'young students in poetry' (**384–5**), inevitably reads somewhat oddly after his eloquent conclusion to the main body of 'Pope'. Ruffhead, *Life*, 405, had briefly praised P's epitaphs as 'equal, if not superior to any compositions of the same kind'. John Nichols (as 'Eugenio') had published an article on SJ's 'Dissertation' (1756) in *Gent. Mag.* (Dec. 1778), 574–5, when SJ was already writing his biographies, to show how 'That pruriency of finding fault, which is the essential part of the critic, sometimes blunts his understanding, as at other times it sharpens it': see **419** n., **427–36** n. below.

Warton, *Essay*, ii (1782), 402, no doubt had SJ's detailed commentary in mind when stating pointedly that the epitaphs 'do not seem to merit a particular discussion'. In his *Works of P* (1797), ii. 389 n., he wrote that they 'are in general over-run with point and antithesis, and are a kind of panegyrical epigrams', and evidently enjoyed revealing SJ as a censorious critic of a poet he usually championed by quoting the 'Dissertation' in notes to ii. 390, 393, 402, 404, 406. For a detailed rebuttal of some of SJ's objections ('my intention is to hypercriticize his criticism'), see William Jackson of Exeter, *The Four Ages; Together with Essays on Various Subjects* (1798), 258–85. George Hoghton later praised Jackson in *European Mag.* (Oct. 1800), 263, and attributed the 'harshness, asperity, and want of taste, absolutely unpardonable' of SJ's critique to his 'morbid melancholy'. The first version (1810) of Wordsworth's 'Essay on Epitaphs' indicates that he had SJ's discussion in mind: 'I now solicit the Reader's attention to a more comprehensive view of the subject; and shall endeavour to treat it with more precision' (*Prose Works*, ii. 49 n.; see also ii. 56, 76, 78, and **411–13** below).

384. With SJ's comment on 'minute and particular' criticism, cf. also **312** above and 'Milton' **243** and 'Waller' **147** ('more faults might be found, were not the enquiry below attention') above. In *Rambler* 90 (1751) he stated: 'It is very difficult to write on the minuter parts of literature without failing either to please or instruct. Too much nicety of detail disgusts the greatest part of readers.' *Rambler* 176 (1751) described those who 'seem always to read with the microscope of criticism, and employ their whole attention upon minute elegance, or faults scarcely visible to common observation' (*YW*, iv. 109, v. 167).

385. SJ's 'at this *visit*' alludes to the *Universal Visiter* (1756), in which he evidently had in mind a more specific audience ('the young students in poetry') than in his *Prefaces*.

386. *To define an epitaph is useless*: one may wonder whether SJ would have written this after 1755, when he duly defined 'Epitaph' as 'An inscription upon a tomb' (*Dict.*). In 'Essay on Epitaphs' (1740) he stated that, 'as malice has seldom produced monuments of defamation, and the tombs hitherto raised have been the work of friendship and benevolence, custom has contracted the original latitude of the word, so that it signifies in the general acceptation an inscription engraven on a tomb in honour of the person deceased' (*OASJ*, 97). He later told Charles Burney: 'The writer of an epitaph should not be considered as saying nothing but what is strictly true. Allowance must be made for some degree of exaggerated praise. In lapidary inscriptions a man is not upon oath' (*Life*, ii. 407).

387–94. For Charles Sackville, Earl of Dorset, who died in 1706, see 'Dorset' above. Perhaps written as late as 1731, P's epitaph was published in 1735: there is no evidence that it was ever inscribed at Withyham, Sussex (*TE*, vi. 334–6).

387. Dorset's 'great forefathers' (l. 11) included Thomas Sackville (1536–1608), 1st Earl of Dorset, co-author of *Gorboduc* (1561), which P's friend Spence edited in 1736. P described him in 1730 as 'the best English poet between Chaucer's and Spenser's time': see Spence, i. 180–1, *Corresp.*, i. 408, 467, and 'Dryden' **207** and n. above.

In l. 11 'forefathers', as in P's own text, and all SJ's texts to 1781, but printed as 'forefather's' in 1783, has been retained: see Textual Notes. P's text reads 'his Nature' (l. 5) and 'in his Race' (l. 12).

388. *distich*: 'A couplet' (*Dict.*). For 'nature', see 'Cowley' **52** and n. above.

390. SJ refers to Rochester's description of Dorset, in 'An Allusion to Horace' (*c*.1675–6), l. 60, as 'The best good man with the worst-natured muse'.

391. P's editors do not note the borrowing SJ has in mind (*TE*, vi. 334–6). For SJ's views on imitation and plagiarism elsewhere, see *Rambler* 143 (1751) and *Adventurer* 95 (1753), and 'Cowley' **60–1** and n. He alludes to the plagiarist as a crow strutting in peacock feathers, in Horace, *Epist.*, I. iii. 15–20. For 'critical justice', see also *YW*, vii. 75.

392. See 'Dorset' **12** above. With SJ's uneasiness about P's casual use of 'sacred', cf. his own definition of 'Sacred': '1. Immediately relating to God. 2. Devoted to religious uses; holy', etc. (*Dict.*). For 'burlesque', see 'Butler' **52** and n. above.

395–400. For P's early friend Sir William Trumbull, who died in 1716, see **23** and n. above. Although P printed the epitaph in *Works* (1717), he did not attach Trumbull's name to it until 1735, no doubt because he also used ll. 1–6 in an unpublished epitaph on John Caryll (d. 1711): see *TE*, vi. 169–70.

In *Lives* (1781) the spelling of 'Trumbul' reverted to the less common 'Trumbal' in **395, 400** (see Textual Notes), presumably to bring it into line with **23** above (where SJ himself wrote 'Trumbal' in the MS). *Gent. Mag.* (1781), 225, 358, 579, repeatedly recommended the spelling 'Trumbull'.

396. *The name is omitted*: SJ complained in 'Essay on Epitaphs' (1740) that, although 'the first rule for writing epitaphs' is 'that the name of the deceased is not to be omitted', this precept 'has not been sufficiently regarded' (*OASJ*, 100). See also **402, 412** below, and 'Cowley' **103, 107** above.

397. SJ uses 'patriot' here in the common sense of '1. One whose ruling passion is the love of his country', rather than the definition he added in 1773: '2. It is sometimes used for a factious disturber of the government' (*Dict.*). His statement in *The Patriot* (1774) that a true patriot 'is he whose public conduct is regulated by one single motive, the love of his country' (*YW*, x. 390) is less familiar than his assertion on 7 Apr. 1775 that 'Patriotism is the last refuge of a scoundrel', probably alluding to John Wilkes. Boswell explained that SJ was referring not to 'a real and generous love of our country, but that pretended patriotism which so many, in all ages and countries, have made a cloak for self-interest' (*Life*, ii. 348). Cf. SJ's reference to Milton's 'patriotism' in 'Milton' **36** above, and his assertion in 'Waller' **19** above that 'Political truth is equally in danger from the praises of courtiers, and the exclamations of patriots'.

SJ's unironic use of 'patriot' here may in itself point to an early date of composition for the 'Dissertation': cf. **400** and n. below. There was, however, already some scepticism about 'patriotism' in the 1730s, as in James Miller's note to *Harlequin-Horace* (3rd edn., 1735), l. 509: 'whereas in Days of Yore it denoted a *Generous* Disposition in a Man towards *Serving* the *Publick*; now . . . it importeth a more *provident* One towards *Serving Himself*.' Warburton (1751 edn.), iii. 222 n., stated that P himself believed that the 'character of modern Patriots was . . . very equivocal; as the name was undistinguishingly bestowed on every one in opposition to the court'. Gerrard, *Patriot Opposition*, 12, suggests that by 1740 'patriot' for P meant 'primarily, a frustrated Whig politician'. For the running debate about true and false 'patriotism' from the 1730s to the 1780s, and for P's own ambivalent views, see D. Griffin, *Patriotism and Poetry in Eighteenth-Century Britain* (Cambridge, 2002), 7–33, 55–63.

398. For the importance of strong rhymes, see 'Cowley' **187** and n. above.

400. *impertinent*: '1. Of no relation to the matter in hand; of no weight' (*Dict.*). In 1783 'connection' was emended to 'connexion', the spelling favoured in the *Dict.*.

the poor conspirator: SJ's note 'Bernardi', added in *Prefaces* (1781), refers to Major John Bernardi (1657–1736), who was captured while resisting William III at the Battle of the Boyne in 1690 and later arrested on suspicion of involvement in the Asassination Plot of 1696. He was imprisoned without trial for some forty years. See *A Short History of the Life of Major John Bernardi. Written by Himself in Newgate* (1729), and, for his death on 20 Sept. 1736, see *Gent. Mag.* (1736), 553: 'Major *John Bernardi*, in *Newgate*, where he had been a State Prisoner 40 Years, for a Conspiracy, against K. *William* III.'

As already noted, SJ's statement that Bernardi 'died lately in prison' is the clearest sign that he may have written the 'Dissertation' in the late 1730s, when Bernardi's fate was still a matter of topical interest (see **384–446** n. above). By 1756 this allusion would already have been obscure, particularly without the identification SJ added in 1781. *Gent. Mag.* (Mar. 1780), 125, had recently summarized Bernardi's strange career from the article in *BB*, ii (2nd edn., 1780), 267–74, which Hawkins cited when using SJ's cryptic footnote on Bernardi to illustrate his 'unwillingness to furnish information from books not within his reach' (*J's Works* (1787), iv. 145 n.).

For SJ's scepticism about appeals to 'liberty', see 'Milton' **169** and n. above.

401–3. The epitaph on Simon Harcourt (1684–1720) (see 'J. Philips' **8** and n. above) was inscribed at Stanton Harcourt and published in 1724 (*TE*, vi. 242–4). Although Atterbury in Mar. 1721 and Lord Harcourt in Dec. 1722 criticized early versions of it (*Corresp.*, ii. 74, 146–7), Aaron Hill praised it in *Plain Dealer* 68 (13 Nov. 1724). For P's friendship with the younger Harcourt, who contributed a commendatory poem to his *Works* (1717), see *Corresp.*, ii. 161, 175, 193.

402. For use of 'the name', see **396** above; and for the concurrence of 'chance . . . with genius', see **59** above and 'Denham' **31** and n. above.

403. For 'energy', see 'Milton' **249** and n. above.

404–7. For James Craggs the younger, who died of small pox on 16 Feb. 1721 (not 1720), see **91, 123** n. above, and 'Addison' **103**, 'Fenton' **9**, 'Gay' **14**, and 'Tickell' **14** above. The epitaph was inscribed in Westminister Abbey in 1727 with the Latin inscription by Peter Le Neve (1661–1729), and published in the same year. SJ asked Birch on 29 Sept. 1743 for information about 'the Lives and Characters' of Craggs and his father (1657–1721) for a history of Parliament he was contemplating (*Letters*, i. 37 and n.).

405. P's lines originated as an imaginary epitaph on a medal for Craggs, who was still alive, at the end of 'To Mr. Addison, Occasioned by his Dialogue on Medals' (written *c*.1715?; published 1720): see **104** and n. above, and *TE*, vi. 204, 282–3 n.

In accusing P of 'redundancy' in ll. 1–2, SJ overlooks the fact that 'In honour clear' alludes to accusations shortly before Craggs's death that he had been dishonestly involved in the South Sea Bubble.

407. For the mixing of Latin and English, see also **438** below. In Sept. 1773 SJ said of an inscription that it 'should have been in Latin, as every thing intended to be universal and permanent should be' (*Life*, v. 154, and cf. iii 85, v. 366).

408–10. See 'Rowe' **26** above. P wrote the epitaph in 1718 and published it in 1720. A different version was inscribed in Westminster Abbey: see *TE*, vi. 209, 400–1.

409. John Sheffield, Duke of Buckingham (q.v. above), eventually erected a memorial to Dryden in 1721: see 'Dryden' **156** and n. above and *TE*, vi. 237–8.

410. SJ's similar objection in 'Essay on Epitaphs' (1740) to 'Allusions to Heathen Mythology' as 'absurd' and 'too ludicrous for reverence or grief, for Christianity and a temple' (*OASJ*, 98–9), may again suggest an early date for the 'Dissertation'. For SJ's hostility to mythology and suspicion of 'fiction', see also 'Butler' **41** and 'Cowley' **16** and nn. above.

411–3. The epitaph for Elizabeth Corbett (d. 1725), daughter of Sir Uvedale Corbett of Lognor, Shropshire, was inscribed at St Margaret's, Westminster, and published in 1730 (*TE*, vi. 323). SJ's praise provoked Wordsworth's detailed objections in his own 'Essay upon Epitaphs' (*Prose Works*, ii. 76–80).

412. SJ stated similarly in 'Essay on Epitaphs' (1740) that 'the best subject for epitaphs is private virtue; virtue exerted in the same circumstances in which the bulk of mankind are placed, and which, therefore, may admit of many imitators' (*OASJ*, 101). Hester Thrale alluded to this epitaph when telling SJ in July 1781 that 'Virtue alone would not make old Age respectable, for that was insisted on: & that the Quiet Character he commended so, would in very advanced Life sink into a poor Thing' (*Thraliana*, i. 502).

I. Grundy, *Scale of Greatness* (1986), 236, compared SJ's discussion here with his 'On the Death of Dr. Robert Levet' (1782) as a similar 'assertion of the value of unglorified, unmagnified humanity'. See, in contrast, his remarks on 'the spleen, and vanity of women' in **340** above. For names in epitaphs, see **396** and n. above.

413. For 'Virtue only is our own' as one of the commonplaces in the *Essay on Man*, see **365** above.

a Lady of great beauty and excellence: identified by Hester Thrale as SJ's Lichfield friend Mary ('Molly') Aston, later Brodie (1706–65?) (*J. Misc.*, i. 258; *Life*, i. 83 and n.).

Of this let the Ladies judge: cf. SJ's remarks in **354** above on P's 'appeals . . . to the ladies' in his notes to Homer. For SJ's other citations of the critical opinions of women, see 'Gay' **27** above and 'Shenstone' **23** and 'Young' **163** below, and, in 1765, *YW*, viii. 971 and n. In contrast, Fielding explicitly excluded women from the lofty 'Realms of Criticism' in 1751 (*Covent-Garden Journal* (Oxford, 1988), 18).

414–7. Robert Digby, P's friend and correspondent, died in 1726. P published the epitaph in 1730, having added the lines on Mary Digby after her death in 1729 (*TE*, vi. 315–16; *Corresp.*, ii. 375–6, iii. 51, 104–5). Warton, *Works of P* (1797), ii. 398, stated that his father, the elder Thomas Warton, Digby's 'intimate friend and contemporary' at Oxford, 'was always saying that this excellent character was not over-drawn, and had every virtue in it here enumerated'.

415. SJ wrote similarly in 'Essay on Epitaphs' (1740): 'The praise ought not to be general, because the mind is lost in the extent of any indefinite idea . . . When we hear only of a great or good man, we know not in what class to place him, nor have any notion of his character, distinct from that of a thousand others; his example can have no effect upon our conduct' (*OASJ*, 100).

Cf. also his later criticism of Dryden's *Eleonora*: 'the praise being therefore inevitably general, fixes no impression on the reader, nor excites any tendency to love, nor much desire of imitation' ('Dryden' **283** above). Writing to Garrick, 12 Dec. 1771, about his epitaph on Hogarth, SJ objected that stanzas 1 and 3 'together give no discriminative character. If the first alone were to stand, Hogarth would not be distinguished from any other man of intellectual eminence' (*Letters*, i. 383–4). For SJ's use of 'general', see 'Cowley' **58** and n. above.

SJ adapts P's *Epistle to a Lady*, l. 2: 'Most Women have no Characters at all.'

416. SJ eventually discusses fourteen epitaphs, if P's epitaph on himself is excluded (see **443** below).

417. Cf. Dryden, 'To the Pious Memory of Mrs. Anne Killigrew', ll. 14–15: 'Thou wilt have Time enough for Hymns Divine, | Since Heav'n's Eternal Year is thine.' SJ inserted 'from Dryden' in 1783 (see Textual Notes).

418–19. The monument in Westminster Abbey to the painter Sir Godfrey Kneller (1646–1723) was erected in 1730, when P's epitaph was published (*TE*, vi. 312–13).

For Kneller's wish, later pursued by his widow, for a monument in Twickenham Church which would have replaced the monument P had erected there to his father, see *Corresp.*, ii. 306–10, and *Richardsoniana* (1776), 134. When P visited Kneller two days before his death, he was still 'contemplating the plan he had made for his own monument . . . and desired me to write an epitaph for it'. It is hardly surprising that P produced 'the worst thing I ever wrote in my life' (Spence, i. 49 and n.).

P said in 1736 that he once tested Kneller's vanity by suggesting, in effect, that God would have made a more perfect world with the painter's assistance, and that Kneller had concurred (Spence, i. 47). The story, which would have made SJ uneasy, was repeated by Warton in *Essay*, ii (1782), 383 n. and *Works* (1797), ii. 381 n. Hawkins, *Life* (1787), 539, mistakenly claimed that SJ's criticism of P's epitaph led to its 'total erasure' in Westminster Abbey.

419. For 'broken metaphors', see also 326 above, and 'Dryden' 320 and n. above.

P acknowledged his debt to Cardinal Pietro Bembo's epitaph on Raphael in a note in 1735: see Bembo's *Opere* (Venice, 1729), iv. 354. SJ quoted Bembo's epitaph without attribution in 1765 (*YW*, viii. 708), and until 1783 merely described P's fourth couplet as 'borrowed' (see Textual Notes). Nichols had in fact noted P's debt to Bembo in *Gent. Mag.* (Dec. 1778), 574–5, when he also replied to SJ's original objection in 1756 to P's final couplet: 'the fourth wants grammatical construction, the word *dying* being no substantive.' This may have prompted SJ's revision in *Prefaces* (1781) (see Textual Notes).

420–4. P's epitaph on General Henry Withers (1651?–1729) was inscribed in the Abbey and published in 1730 (*TE*, vi. 320–1). Withers's long military career began in the 1670s and he fought under Marlborough at Blenheim, Tournai, and Malplaquet. He was thanked 'for the Service he had done his Country' in *Tatler* 46 (1709). Swift dined with him in 1712–13 (*Jnl. to Stella*, ii. 471, 651–2), and Gay referred to him as 'Withers the good' in 'Mr. Pope's Welcome from Greece' (1720), l. 29.

421. For poetic 'common places', see 323 and n., 326, 413 above.

422. The possibility that SJ alludes here to the much-mocked line with an initial 'particle O!' in Thomson's *Sophonisba* (1730) (see 'Thomson' 19 and n. below) might again suggest that he was originally writing in the late 1730s. For initial 'O' or 'Oh' in his own early verse, see e.g. *Poems* (1974), 20, 32, 39.

423. For 'cant', see 26 above and 'Addison' 54 and n. above.

424. SJ may consider the political implications of ll. 9–12 inappropriate in an epitaph. Cf. *Epilogue to the Satires* (1738), ii. 250: 'Here, Last of *Britons!* let your Names be read.'

425–6. See 'Fenton' 17, 30 above. P told Broome, 29 Aug. 1730, 'I shall . . . draw this Amiable, quiet, deserving, unpretending, Christian & Philosophical character, in his Epitaph', and sent it to him on 14 Dec. 1730 (*Corresp.*, iii. 128–9, 156; and *TE*, vi. 319).

Warton, *Works* (1797), ii. 401 n., commented that Fenton's 'integrity, his learning, and his genius, deserved this character; it is not in any respect over-wrought. His poems are not sufficiently read and admired.'

426. As in 'Fenton' 17 above, SJ refers to Richard Crashaw's 'An Epitaph. Upon Mr. Ashton', ll. 1–4: 'The modest front of this small floor | Believe me, Reader can say more | Than many a braver Marble can; | Here lies a truly honest man.' P's debt was noted as early as 1737 (*TE*, vi. 319), and it was pointed out again by SJ in *Rambler* 143 (1751), Warton, *Essay* (1756), 93, and *Gent. Mag.* (1780), 193. SJ did not in fact identify Crashaw as P's source here until 1783: see Textual Notes.

Although he refers in 'Fenton' **20** above to Shiels's article on him in *Lives*, iv. 164–77, SJ writes here as if no account of Fenton had ever been published, suggesting again that he composed the 'Dissertation' much earlier than 1756.

427–36. P in fact wrote his epitaph on Gay in 1733 (published 1735). It was inscribed on Gay's monument in 1737 (*TE*, vi. 351–2). He also paid tribute to Gay in *Epistle to Arbuthnot*, ll. 255–60. For SJ's dislike of Gay's cynical epitaph on himself in *Gent. Mag.* (Oct. 1738), 536–7, see 'Gay' **24** n. above.

Nichols, *Gent. Mag.* (1778), 374, criticized SJ's objections here: 'Mr. Pope was remarkably delicate in all his praises; he did not lavish out flattery where there was no foundation for it, and therefore tempers his love for his friend with the nicest discrimination and propriety.'

428. For P's friendship with Gay, see **160** above.

Cf. 'Waller' **120** and n. above: 'his success was not always in proportion to his labour.' For the unpredictability of poetic inspiration, see **59**, **402** above, and 'Denham' **31** and n. above.

430. SJ defines 'Simplicity' as '1. Plainness; artlessness; not subtilty; not cunning; not deceit', but also as '5. Weakness; silliness' (*Dict.*). Swift warned P, 31 Mar. 1733, that his reference in l. 2 to Gay's 'simplicity' might be misunderstood by 'the vulgar, who cannot distinguish *Simplicity* & Folly' (*Corresp.*, iii. 361; see also iii. 368–9). 'Scrutator' (John Loveday) suggested in *Gent. Mag.* (1781), 359, that P here echoed Dryden, 'To the Pious Memory of Mrs. Anne Killigrew', l. 70: 'Her Wit was more than Man, her Innocence a Child!'

432. The juxtaposition of 'delight' and 'lash' in l. 4 may have made SJ uneasy. His definitions of 'Lash' include '4. To scourge with satire' (*Dict.*).

435. See **375**, **419** and n. above for P's occasional lapses of grammar. Swift allegedly said of P, 'with his usual roughness', 'I could never get the blockhead to study his grammar': see Warton, *Essay on P*, ii (1782), 54–5 n.

436. According to Warburton (1751 edn.), vi. 97 n., P admitted that the conceit in the last line was 'not generally understood'.

Gent. Mag. (1781), 369, suggested that P was again indebted to Crashaw, 'His Epitaph', ll. 50–2: 'For now (alas) not in this stone | Passenger who'er thou art | Is he entomb'd, but in thy Heart.'

437–9. The epitaph on Sir Isaac Newton, who died in 1727, was published in 1730 (*TE*, vi. 318). The Latin may be translated: 'Isaac Newton, whose immortality is witnessed by Time, Nature and the Heavens, whose mortality is confessed by this marble.' P's more ambiguous praise in *Essay on Man*, II. 31–4, may reflect his suspicion of the adulation of Newton after his death: see M. Nicholson, *Newton Demands the Muse* (Princeton, 1946), 133–44.

In 'Essay on Epitaphs' (1740) SJ stated: 'Had only the name of Sir Isaac Newton been subjoined to the design upon his monument, instead of a long detail of his discoveries, which no philosopher can want, and which none but a philosopher can understand, those by whose direction it was raised had done more honour both to him and to themselves.' He then suggested a 'simple and un-adorned' Latin epitaph, translated as: 'Here rests Isaac Newton, who searched out the laws of nature' (*OASJ*, 97–8, 803 n.). For Newton's 'superiority to the rest of mankind', see *Adventurer* 131 (1754) (*YW*, ii. 481–2).

438. For the mixing of Latin and English, see also **407** above.

440–1. For Edmund Sheffield, Duke of Buckingham (1716–35), third son of P's friend, see 'Sheffield' **20** above. The epitaph was not placed on his tomb but was published in 1738 (*TE*, vi. 362–3). There is a long note on the young Duke in John Lockman's article on his father in *GD*, ix. 209–10 n., mostly repeated in *BB*, vi (i) (1763), 3664–5.

Whether or not SJ wrote the 'Dissertation' to this point as early as the late 1730s, it may be assumed from his reference in **441** to P's *Works* (1751), vi. 85 n. (and cf. **442** and n. below) that **440–4** were written later, with **445–6** a further addition in *Prefaces* (1781). (Since this epitaph was published by 1738, SJ could in theory have discussed it before 1751 and added the reference to Warburton later.)

442. For other poems undeserving of 'the notice of criticism', see 'Milton' **206** and n. above.

SJ refers to 'Epitaph. For Dr. Francis Atterbury, Who died in Exile at Paris, in 1732. [His only Daughter having expired in his arms, immediately after she arrived in France to see him]'. Atterbury (see **131–2** above) told P of the death of his daughter Mary in a letter of 20 Nov. 1729 (*Corresp.*, iii. 76–8). P printed the epitaph, a brief dialogue between 'SHE' and 'HE' (i.e. daughter and father), for inclusion in *Works*, vol. ii (1735), but cancelled it, perhaps because of its similarity to his recent *Epistle to Lord Cobham* (*TE*, vi. 344–5). Erskine-Hill, 'Life into Letters', 200–20, has, however, argued that its Jacobite implications explain both P's suppression of it and SJ's contempt.

Since it was first published in Warburton (1751 edn.), vi. 99–100, SJ could not have discussed it earlier (cf. **440–1** n. above). *BB*, v (1760), 3415 n., later objected to Warburton's sarcastic remarks about Atterbury in his notes. Warton, *Works* (1797), ii. 404 n., saw no reason for SJ's 'harsh sentence' on it.

443. P did not acknowledge the 'Epitaph On Himself' (published 1741), first collected in 1751 by Warburton (1751 edn.), vi. 102.

P's text reads 'Under this Marble' rather than 'Under this stone' (*TE*, vi. 386–7). See also *TE*, vi. 376, for an earlier 'Epitaph For One who would not be buried in Westminster Abbey' (1738), which Warburton, contrary to P's wishes in his will, had inscribed on the monument in Twickenham Church in 1750.

445–6. Although he added these paragraphs in *Prefaces* (1781), SJ did not name Ariosto in **446** until 1783: see Textual Notes.

SJ quotes, with variants, 'Ludovicii Areosti Epit.', ll. 1–11, from his *Opere* (Venice, 1730), ii. 399. On 11 Aug. 1777, a few weeks before starting work on the *Lives*, SJ transcribed the lines in his diary, under the heading 'ARIOSTO = POPE' (*YW*, i. 270–1), apparently foreseeing their use at the end of 'Pope'.

Ariosto's uncertainty about his burial place is more pointed than in P's imitation, rendering SJ's commonsense objections in **444** less persuasive: 'The bones of Ludovico Ariosto are buried under this marble, or under this earth, or under whatever pleases his kind heir, or a kinder friend, or a traveller happening upon him more fittingly; for he could not know the future, nor did his empty corpse matter enough to him to make him prepare an urn while he was alive; but while still alive he prepared these lines he wished to be inscribed on his tomb, if he should ever have such a tomb.'

CHRISTOPHER PITT (1699–1748)

Composition. SJ told Mrs Thrale on 9 May 1780 that 'Pitt' was 'done' (*Letters*, iii. 254). Like Collins (q.v. below), P came much later in *Eng. Poets* (1779) than the other poets he was writing about at this time. The arrival of material about both poets from Joseph Warton (1 below) may have prompted him to move ahead in the sequence.

Sources. There was no article on P in *BB*, and SJ had to rely on Shiels, *Lives*, v. 298–307, and private information from Joseph Warton (see 1 below). Warton evidently did not reveal that he possessed transcripts of P's correspondence with Joseph Spence and Pope (see 1 n. below and 'Pope' 137–8 above), and SJ himself made no use of P's conversation as recorded in the Spence MSS, which were available to him from early Feb. 1780. SJ ignores P's friendship with Edward Young, emphasized by Shiels, *Lives*, v. 298: P 'was particularly distinguished by that great poet Dr. Young, who so much admired the early displays of his genius, that with an engaging familiarity he used to call him his son'. SJ also makes no use of the eight letters by P in John Duncombe's *Letters, By Several Eminent Persons Deceased*, ii (1772), *16–6 and 43–64, which he consulted for 'Hughes' and 'Dyer' (q.v.).

P is one of the eight poets (of fifty-two in *Eng. Poets*) who are not quoted in the *Dict.*: but see 9 n. below.

Publication. In *Prefaces*, vol. viii (15 May 1781). The proofs are in the Forster Collection.

Modern Sources:

Robert Dodsley, *Correspondence 1733–1764*, ed. J. E. Tierney (Cambridge, 1988), esp. 74–80, 108–9, 111, 114–15

Joseph Spence, *Observations, Anecdotes and Characters of Books and Men*, ed. J. M. Osborn (2 vols., Oxford, 1966)

M. Thackeray, 'CP, Joseph Warton, and Virgil', *RES* 43 (1992), 329–46

A. Wright, *Joseph Spence* (Chicago, 1950)

1. P was the son of Dr Christopher Pitt (1662?–1723) and his wife Elizabeth (1674?–1743).

    Like P, Joseph Warton (1722–1800) was educated at Winchester, and became its headmaster in 1766. In spite of their strained relations (see headnote to 'Pope' above), Warton gave SJ information for some of his biographies in early 1780. On 23 May 1780 SJ thanked him for the 'useful memorials', acknowledged here and in 'Collins' 1, 14 below (*Letters*, iii. 227, 259–60). Warton evidently withheld, however, his transcripts of P's correspondence with Pope and Spence, some of which he printed in Pope's *Works* (1797): see Pope, *Corresp.*, ii. 382–3, 507–8, and Spence, i, pp. xxiv–xxv, and cf. 'Thomson' 11 n. below.

2. P in fact entered Winchester in 1713, and matriculated from Wadham College, Oxford, on 3 Apr. 1718, before removing as a scholar to New College on 5 Mar. 1719; Fellow 1721, BA 1722, MA 1724. P would not know of Rowe's *Lucan's Pharsalia* because, though dated 1718 on the title page, it was not published until 10 Mar. 1719, a few days after P's removal to New College: see Foxon, *English Verse*, R 292, and 'Rowe' 22, 35 above.

3. SJ's regret at P's suppression of his schoolboy translation of Lucan, of which no MS seems to have survived, already makes clear the importance he attaches to English verse translation (see **5**, **8–10** below).

For diligence, see **10** below and 'Milton' **118** and n. above. and, for libraries of forgotten books, see *Ramblers* 2, 106, and *Idler* 59 (*YW*, iii. 13, iv. 199, ii. 183).

4. P's cousin George Pitt of Stratfield Saye, Hants., to whom he later dedicated *Poems and Translations* (1727), presented him to the living of Pimperne, near Blandford Forum, Dorset.

5. P published *Vida's Art of Poetry* in 1725 (2nd edn., 1742), three years after the appearance of Thomas Tristram's Oxford edition of the *De Arte Poetica* (Rome, 1527) of Marcus Hieronymus Vida (1485–1566).

He dedicated it to the youthful Philip, Earl Stanhope (1714–86), to whom he had been appointed chaplain. James, Earl Stanhope (1673–1721), had married the daughter of P's cousin Thomas Pitt of Blandford (1653–1726), the young Earl's guardian from 1721 (Cokayne, xii (i). 232–3). Pitt, who had been Governor of Fort St George, Madras, 1699–1709 and owner of the famous 'Pitt diamond', may have been a model for the pious but wealthy Sir Balaam in Pope's *Epistle to Bathurst* (1733), ll. 342 ff.

P evidently told Pope that he was 'the occasion' of the translation, referring to his praise of Vida in *Essay on Criticism* (1711), ll. 703–8. Pope described it as 'correct and spirited' to P, 23 July 1726 (*Corresp.*, ii. 382–3). SJ, who owned a copy of P's *Vida* when he was an undergraduate (*Gleanings*, v. 228), referred to Vida in *Rambler* 176 (1751) as 'a man of considerable skill in the politicks of literature', and in 1756 added a long quotation from P's translation to *Rambler* 92, praising Vida's 'great elegance' (*YW*, v. 166, iv. 125–8). Warton also praised P's *Vida* in his *Essay on Pope* (1756), 194.

For SJ's usual scepticism about 'representative metre', see 'Pope' **330–4** and nn. above.

6. For 'the scholar's timidity or distrust', see 'Broome' **2** and n. above.

7. P told Spence on 18 July 1726 that he was 'entering into proposals with a bookseller for printing a little miscellany of my own performances' (Pope, *Corresp.*, ii. 382). Lintot gave him £21 for the volume on 13 Oct. 1726 (Nichols, *Lit. Anec.*, viii. 299).

P's preface to *Poems and Translations* (1727), p. viii, stated that, since some 'were written several Years since' (dated between 1718 and 1722), he had in effect observed the Horatian precept about withholding compositions till the ninth year (*Ars Poetica*, l.388). The volume opens with an 'Epistle to Dr. Edward Young' (1–6). Perhaps in response to SJ's comments here, Warton, *Essay on Pope*, ii (1782), 331 n., later praised P's imitations of Horace for 'a freedom and a facility of versification truly Horatian'.

8. SJ's earlier emphasis on P's 'uncommon elegance' (**2**) and 'general elegance' (**5**), and on the 'mediocrity' of his original verse (**7**), has prepared for this reaffirmation of his belief in verse translation as a proper application of the new refinement of English versification: cf. 'Rowe' **35** above and 'West' **11–12** below.

P first published *An Essay on Virgil's Aeneid. Being a Translation of the First Book* (1728), praised by Pope by 12 Nov. 1728 (*Corresp.*, ii. 507 n.). In the preface to *Virgil's Aeneid*, vol. i (1736), which contained Bks. I–IV, P wrote that the pleasure of reading Virgil 'led me to divert my self, in trying to translate several Parts of his

ÆNEID; till I was carried farther than I expected; and, at last, fell insensibly into the Thought of translating the whole ... the Desire of some Friends, whom I extremely value, drew me to publish the Books I have already finish'd of it' (pp. vii–viii). For his comments in 1737–8 on his later progress, see *Letters, By Several Eminent Persons Deceased*, ii (1772), 52–64.

SJ added the final sentence in 1783.

9. See 'Dryden' 303–13 above. P wrote of Dryden's translation in his 'Preface' (1736): 'There is no Name that I have a greater and more real Respect for. I look on him with a sort of Veneration; and apprehend, that every one must have a mean Opinion of my Judgment, if they suppos'd I thought of entring the Lists with that great Man ... The very working on the same Subject, with so great a Genius, has often serv'd to show me the Superiority of his Hand the more distinctly' (pp. vii–viii).

P in fact repeated much of this in the preface to *The Aeneid of Virgil* (2 vols., 1740; 2nd edn., 1743), admitting that he had borrowed fifty or sixty lines from Dryden. He dedicated the complete translation to Frederick, Prince of Wales, for whose patronage of 'Patriot' poetry, see 'Pope' 217 and n. above. After P's death, Dodsley paid his sister 50 guineas for the copyright and £62 10s. for 500 unsold copies in 1751 (Dodsley, *Corresp.*, 528). SJ owned a copy of the 1740 edition, which he apparently marked for use in the 1773 revision of the *Dict.* without in the end quoting it: see Fleeman, *Handlist* (1984), 66, and Reddick, 221–2 n.

SJ's regret at the omission of P's translation from *Eng. Poets* (1779) may have prompted its inclusion in the 1790 edition (as Reed noted in *Lives*, iv (1791), 244 n.), and in the later collections of British poetry by Anderson (1792–5) and Chalmers (1810).

10. For the versification of Pope's Homer, see 'Pope' 348 and n. above. SJ defines 'Equable' as 'Equal to itself; even; uniform in respect to form, motion, or temperature' (*Dict.*): see also 'Cowley' 200 and n. above.

Through Young, P showed Pope his translation of *Odyssey*, Bk. XXIII, but told Spence in July 1726 that Pope made little use of it when revising Broome's translation in the collaborative *Odyssey* (Pope, *Corresp.*, ii. 382; 'Pope' 133–4 above). In 'To Mr. Pope' in *Poems* (1727), 172–6, P praised the *Iliad* for having 'nat'ralized' Homer into English. His lines 'To Mr. Spence, On his Essay on Mr. Pope's Odyssey' were later appended to Spence's *Essay on Mr. Pope's Odyssey* (2nd edn., 1737).

For P's diffidence as a 'rival' of Dryden, see 9 and n. above, and further remarks in a letter in June 1738 (*Letters, By Several Eminent Persons Deceased*, ii. 59–61). William Benson praised his translation in *Letters Concerning Poetical Translations* (1739), 3–5, 47, 52, 64–8. SJ's comments on Dryden's *Aeneid* echo his earlier discussion in 'Dryden' 311–14 above, which made clear that 'splendid new attempts' to translate Virgil had lacked the 'allurement and delight' of Dryden's version. Although he takes P seriously, SJ is once more implicitly describing the 'vigour' and 'delight' sacrificed in the pursuit of poetic 'correctness' since the death of Dryden.

Spence's exposition of the 'numerous' and sometimes 'unaccountably gross' mistakes in Dryden's *Aeneid* in *Polymetis* (1747), Dial. XI, 309–20, influenced Joseph Warton's preference for P's translation over Dryden's in his *Works of Virgil* (1753), as he explained in his dedication to Lord Lyttelton (i, pp. xvii–xxvi). Shiels,

Lives, v. 300–2, also compared the two translations, favouring P's and citing Warton's preference. For later comparisons, see Robert Anderson, *British Poets*, viii (1794), 793–4, and Thackeray, 'CP'.

With SJ's appeal to 'the people' against 'the criticks', cf. 'Smith' **49** above and 'Gray' **51** below.

11. P's epitaph is from John Hutchins, *History of Dorset* (2 vols., 1774), i. 82, cited but not quoted by Nichols, *Sel. Collection*, iv. 312. (Bowyer and Nichols had printed the *History*.) Hutchins added P's epitaphs on his parents and brother Robert (d. 1730). For his sister Lucy Baskett see Dodsley, *Corresp.*, 108–9, 528.

Some of P's verse appeared posthumously in Christopher Smart's *The Student* (2 vols., 1750–1) and was later collected as *Poems by the Celebrated Translator of Virgil's Aeneid* (1756). Nichols, *Sel. Collection*, iv. 307–12, made further additions.

JAMES THOMSON (1700–48)

Composition. SJ's only reference to 'Thomson' is in an undated note to Nichols: 'I think I must make some short addition to Thomsons sheet but will send it to day' (*Letters*, iii. 227; cf. **47** and n. below). Although this note has been speculatively dated *c.* Apr. 1780, 'Thomson' is not one of the nine lives SJ told Mrs Thrale on 9 May 1780 he had recently completed or was about to write (*Letters*, iii. 254). Given T's relatively late position in the sequence in *Eng. Poets* (1779) (forty-second of fifty-two), it might seem likely that SJ wrote the biography in June or July 1780.

McCarthy, 58, raised the possibility, however, that 'Thomson' was written several months earlier. Although there is no more precise evidence for this than SJ's failure to make use of Mallet's account of T's early years in London in the Spence MSS (i. 370–1), to which he had access from early Feb. 1780, T had been on SJ's mind from an early stage of his entire project. This fact, and SJ's knowledge that Boswell been pursuing material about T on his behalf since 1777, means that the possibility that he wrote 'Thomson' before resuming work on the rest of the *Prefaces* in 1780 cannot be ruled out.

On 3 May 1777, a few weeks after agreeing to write the *Prefaces*, SJ wrote to Boswell: 'I think I have persuaded the booksellers to insert something of Thomson, and if you could give me some information about him, for the life which we have is very scanty, I should be glad' (*Letters*, iii. 20; cf. 'Watts' **1** and n. below). T was duly named as one of the poets chosen for inclusion in a new advertisement for the *English Poets* in the *Publick Advertiser* four days later (*Life*, iii. 489). Boswell took SJ's request seriously, noting on 25 May that he was reading *BB* and Shiels, *Lives* (1753) (*Boswell in Extremes*, 127), and informing SJ of these sources on 9 June 1777. He also referred to Patrick Murdoch's biography (1762) and the life in a later Edinburgh edition of T's *Works* (see below). He expected to obtain some unpublished letters from T's sister Jean in Lanark, and asked SJ to 'send me such questions as may lead to biographical materials' to put to her. Boswell also mentioned the mathematician George Lewis Scott (1708–80) and the poet and physician Dr John Armstrong (1709–79) as surviving friends of T (*Life*, iii. 116–17).

Boswell's efforts did not end there. On 3 Sept. 1777 he visited Lord Hailes in Edinburgh (*Boswell in Extremes*, 141), and six days later told SJ that Hailes would provide some anecdotes of T, who had been tutor to his cousin, later the Earl of Haddington (see 8 n., **15** n., **44** n. below, and *Life*, iii. 133). On 10 Mar. 1778 Boswell reminded Hailes to forward his notes on T: see Carnie (1956), 74, and *Catalogue*, L 610. Boswell sent SJ the information from T's sister on 18 June 1778, together with the text of T's letter to her of 4 Oct. 1747, which SJ prints in **40–2** below (*Life*, iii. 359–60). While Boswell was making all these enquiries, SJ was in fact preoccupied with earlier poets and, when he later turned his attention to T, he did not always make accurate use of Boswell's conscientious findings: see e.g. **1** n. below.

Sources. As Boswell reported to SJ in June 1777, the unsigned article in *BB*, vi (ii) (1766), Suppl. 168–9, merely summarized the 'Life' by T's friend Patrick Murdoch in T's *Works* (2 vols., 1762). Although Murdoch's narrative was a primary source for SJ, he also made intermittent use of the account of T by Shiels, who had also known T, in *Lives*, v. 190–218. While SJ's reference to T's 'biographer' in **45** below may seem clearly to refer to Murdoch (1762 edn.), Boswell pointed out to SJ on 9 June 1777 that information from Shiels had often been conflated with compressed versions of Murdoch's 'Life' in later editions of T's *Works* (*Life*, iii. 117). Citations of Murdoch (1762 edn.) and Shiels below do not, therefore, exclude the possibility that SJ in fact relied on such a later conflation, in which he definitely found one new anecdote (see **39** and n. below).

In **39** below SJ acknowledges the 'friendly assistance' of Boswell, who, as already noted, provided information from T's sister Jean and from Lord Hailes, but he appears to have ignored Boswell's suggestion that he consult T's surviving friends, such as the poet John Armstrong, who attended T in his last illness (see **37** n. below) and did not himself die until Sept. 1779. SJ relies instead on what Savage had told him about T in the late 1730s, some forty years earlier (see **20**, **45**, and cf. 8 n., **16** n., below), and his own memories of the original appearance of some of T's works (see **51–2** below).

For SJ's use of T in the *Dict.*, see **50** n. below.

Publication. In *Prefaces*, vol. ix (15 May 1781). Pp. 1–16 and 33–8 (of 40) of the proofs are in the Forster Collection.

Modern Sources:
(i) James Thomson
Letters and Documents, ed. A. D. McKillop (Lawrence, Kan., 1958)
The Seasons, ed. J. Sambrook (Oxford, 1981)
Liberty, The Castle of Indolence, and Other Poems, ed. J. Sambrook (Oxford, 1986)
(ii)
A. S. Bell, 'Three New Letters of JT', *N & Q* 217 (1972), 367–9
H. Campbell, 'T and the Countess of Hertford Yet Again', *MP* 67 (1970), 367–9
H. Campbell, 'Shiels and J: Biographers of T', *SEL* 12 (1972), 535–44
H. Campbell, *JT: An Annotated Bibliography* (New York, 1976)
H. Campbell, *JT* (Boston, 1979)
J. Chalker, *The English Georgic: A Study in the Development of a Form* (1969), ch. 4
R. Cohen, 'SJ: Imagination and Unity', in *The Art of Discrimination: T's 'The Seasons' and the Language of Criticism* (1964), 94–104
T. Gilmore, 'Implicit Criticism of T's *Seasons* in J's Dictionary', *MP* 86 (1989), 265–73
D. Grant, *JT, Poet of 'The Seasons'* (1951)
D. Griffin, *Patriotism and Poetry in Eighteenth-Century Britain* (Cambridge, 2002), 74–97

H. S. Hughes, 'T and the Countess of Hertford', *MP* 25 (1927–8), 439–68

R. Inglesfield, 'JT, Aaron Hill and the Poetic "Sublime" ', *BJECS* 13 (1990), 215–21

A. Lindsay (ed.), *Index of English Literary Manuscripts*, iii (iv) (1997), 93–118

A. D. McKillop, *The Background of T's 'Seasons'* (Minneapolis, 1942)

A. D. McKillop, *The Background of T's 'Liberty'* (Houston, 1951)

A. D. McKillop, 'The Reception of T's "Liberty" ', *N & Q* 198 (1953), 112–13

A. D. McKillop, 'T and the Licensers of the Stage', *PQ* 37 (1958), 448–53

A. D. McKillop, 'The Early History of *Alfred*', *PQ* 41 (1962), 311–24

A. D. McKillop, 'Two More T Letters', *MP* 60 (1962), 128–30

A. N. L. Munby, *Sale Catalogues of Libraries of Eminent Persons* (1971), i. 45–66

J. Sambrook, *JT 1700–1748: A Life* (Oxford, 1991)

J. Sambrook, "A Just Balance between Patronage and the Press": The Case of JT', *Studies in the Literary Imagination*, 34 (2001), 135–53

M. J. W. Scott, *JT, Anglo-Scot* (Athens, Ga., 1988)

R. Terry (ed.), *JT: Essays for the Tercentenary* (Liverpool, 2000)

1. Murdoch (1762 edn.), i, pp. ii–iv; Shiels, *Lives*, v. 190–1.

   The fourth of the nine children of the Revd Thomas Thomson of Ednam near Kelso and his wife Beatrix (née Trotter), T was probably born on 11 Sept. 1700 (as stated by Murdoch). Boswell wrote to SJ on 18 June 1778 about Murdoch's erroneous maiden name for T's mother, and later complained that SJ had ignored this information (*Life*, iii. 359–60 and n., iv. 51 n.).

   In Nov. 1700, a few weeks after T's birth, his father moved to Southdean near Jedburgh. Robert Riccaltoun or Riccartoun (1691–1769) of Hobkirk near Southdean was only some nine years older than T, and his influence on T's education came later than SJ assumes. His reasons for helping T appear to be SJ's conjecture. In 1725 T stated that a poem on winter by Riccaltoun, never satisfactorily identified, inspired his own *Winter*: see *T Letters*, 17 and n.

2. Murdoch (1762 edn.), i, p. iii, although Shiels, *Lives*, v. 190, is the source for T's lack of motivation at school.

   T attended Jedburgh Grammar School from *c*.1712. He referred to the River Tweed ('With silvan *Jed*, thy tributary Brook') in *Autumn*, ll. 889–91.

3. Murdoch (1762 edn.), i, pp. iii–iv. T entered Edinburgh University in 1715. After his father's death on 9 Feb. 1716, his mother mortgaged her estate at Wideopen or Widehope and moved to Edinburgh, where she died on 12 May 1725, a few weeks after T left for London (Sambrook, *JT*, 30). For his lines 'On his Mother's death', see *Liberty* (1986), 278–80. For other parents who lived to enjoy a son's eminence, see 'Pope' 161 and n. above.

4. Murdoch (1762 edn.), i, pp. v–vi; Shiels, *Lives*, v. 192–3. SJ defines 'To breed' as '6. To educate; to form by education' (*Dict.*). In 1719 T 'was entered in Divinity Hall, as one of the candidates for the ministry, where the students, before they are permitted to enter on their probation, must yield six years attendance' (Shiels, *Lives*, v. 192).

   The translation criticized by Prof. William Hamilton may have been of Psalm 98 written in 1723, but T also wrote a version of Psalm 104 (Sambrook, *JT*, 19–20). SJ compresses Murdoch's account, in which Hamilton's criticism was more genial. According to Shiels, the exercise revealed T's unexpected genius to his fellow-students, and Hamilton merely objected to his blank verse. Neither source states that he 'censured one of his expressions as indecent, if not profane'. For SJ's own reservations about T's 'poetically splendid' diction, 'unintelligible to a popular audience', see **50** below.

5. Murdoch (1762 edn.), i, p. v. Three poems by T appeared in the *Edinburgh Miscellany* (Edinburgh, 1720), to which his friend David Mallet (see 'Mallet' **3** n. below) also contributed (Alexander Campbell, *Introduction to the History of Poetry in Scotland* (Edinburgh, 1798), 168–74, 216 n.; Sambrook, *JT*, 16–19). For Mallet's later report that T's early verse had been mocked in Edinburgh, see *T Letters*, 34.

6. Murdoch (1762 edn.), i, p. vi; Shiels, *Lives*, v. 194, who stated that T was encouraged to set off for London in Feb. 1725 by William Benson's reported praise of his verse (see 'Milton' **155** and 'Pope' **195** above). SJ had himself no doubt arrived in London twelve years later with similar expectations. See also 'Akenside' **10** below.

   The 'lady' may have been Lady Grizel Baillie (1665–1746), a relative of T's mother (Sambrook, *JT*, 22).

7. For Mallet's earlier arrival in London from Edinburgh, see 'Mallet' **3** below. Shiels, *Lives*, v. 195, told the story of the stolen letters of introduction (cf. Sambrook, *JT*, 25–6; *T Letters*, 6–7, 8 n.).

8. Lord Hailes (see headnote) commented in 1782 on T's supposed 'want' of shoes, 'this is certainly a mistake': see Carnie (1956), 487.

   SJ may have heard about T's early poverty in London from Savage, whom T mentioned in a letter as early as 22 Apr. 1725. T explained his financial problems to William Cranstoun, *c*.1 Oct. 1725 (*T Letters*, 15–16). Later in 1725, he became tutor to the 4-year-old son of Charles Hamilton, Lord Binning, the grandson of Lady Grizel Baillie (see **6** n. above; Spence, i. 370; Sambrook, *JT*, 28–9). Although Boswell conveyed this information from Lord Hailes on 9 Sept. 1777 (*Life*, iii. 133), SJ refers only briefly to T's connection with Binning (**15** below).

   According to Mallet, T at first 'wrote single winter pieces; they at last thought it might make a poem' (Spence, i. 370). Shiels, *Lives*, v. 195 n., also stated that Mallet advised uniting the 'detached pieces' into 'one connected piece'. The Scottish bookseller John Millan published *Winter* on 8 Apr. 1726, allegedly giving T only £3 or 3 guineas for it (Shiels, *Lives*, v. 196; Spence, i. 370; B. Victor, *Original Letters* (1776), iii. 27; Sambrook, *JT*, 37–8). Shiels, *Lives*, v. 196–7, described the enthusiasm of 'Mr. Whatley', identified by Nichols as the Revd Robert Whatley (*Lit. Anec.*, vi. 119), presumably the subject of an anonymous *Criticism on the Verses Addressed to the Rev. Mr. Wh—y, in the Daily Gazetteer* (1738).

   SJ inserted the final sentence in the proofs (see Textual Notes). Nichols or Reed could have pointed out this information, as well as that added in **9–10** below. For Aaron Hill, see 'Savage' **55** and n. above. Hill had printed some anonymous lines apparently by T ('The Works and Wonders of Almighty Power') in his *Plain Dealer* 46 as early as 28 Aug. 1724 (*Liberty*, ed. Sambrook, 406–7). For T's effusive letters to Hill in Apr. and May 1726 ('When *You* approve, my whole Soul is awak'd, and charm'd'), see *T Letters*, 24–30; and for the influence of Hill's ideas on T and other members of his circle, see Inglesfield, 'JT', 215–21, and C. Gerrard, *Aaron Hill* (Oxford, 2003), 106–21.

9. T dedicated *Winter* to Sir Spencer Compton (1674?–1743), Speaker of the House of Commons since 1715, later Earl of Wilmington and Prime Minister (1742): see also 'Young' 51 below.

Poems by Hill and others were prefixed to the 2nd edition of *Winter* in July 1726. T discussed Hill's lines ('To Mr. Thomson, Doubtful to what Patron he should address his Poem, call'd, Winter') in a letter of May 1726, but no newspaper publication has been traced (Hill, *Works* (1753), iii. 77–9; *Letters*, 28–30; *Seasons* (1981), 307–8). SJ's source may be Victor's *Original Letters* (1776), iii. 27–8.

SJ added the second reference to Hill and called for the insertion of the quotation in 10 in the proofs (see Textual Notes).

10. SJ quotes T's letter of 7 June 1726, which goes on to ask Hill to soften his satire of ungrateful patrons (*T Letters*, 32–3 and n.).

11. SJ is closer here to Shiels, *Lives*, v. 196, than to Murdoch (1762 edn.), i, pp. vii–viii, who claimed that *Winter* 'was no sooner read than universally admired', except by those who enjoyed only satiric wit, and 'the few' whose 'poetical creed' was disconcerted by T's original genius.

Warton, *Essay on Pope* (1756), 154, claimed that Joseph Spence's praise of *Winter* in his *Essay on Pope's Odyssey*, ii (1727), 15, crucially affected its reputation, as T 'always acknowledged'. Warton later cited a letter in which Spence asked Christopher Pitt to subscribe to *The Seasons* (1730) (*Works of Pope* (1797), i. 236 n., and see 17 n. below). By the time Spence praised *Winter* in his *Essay*, the poem had in fact already enjoyed four editions (Foxon, *English Verse*, T 211–14).

12. Murdoch (1762 edn.), i, p. viii; Shiels, *Lives*, v. 203.

Dr Thomas Rundle (*c*.1688–1743), chaplain to William Talbot, Bishop of Durham, was later accused of heresy and became a controversial figure in 1734 (see 'Savage' 188 and n. above). For his admiration for T's *Sophonisba* in 1730, see 18 n. below. Charles Talbot (1685–1737), the Solicitor-General (1726), did not in fact become Lord Chancellor until 1733 (see 21, 23, 27 and nn. below).

13. T expanded the 2nd edition of *Winter* (16 July 1726) from 405 to 463 lines. For Hill's prefatory poem, see 9 and n. above. For the spelling 'Malloch', see 'Mallet' 9 and n. below.

'Scrutator' (John Loveday) in *Gent. Mag.* (1781), 420, enquired about the identity of the 'Mira' who had been 'once too well known'. She was Martha Fowke Sansom (1690–1736), a member of Aaron Hill's circle originally known as 'Clio', whose reputation had recently suffered at the hands of Eliza Haywood: see *Eighteenth Century Women Poets* (Oxford, 1989), 84–5, and C. Gerrard, *Aaron Hill* (Oxford, 2003), 71–100. The *British Journal*, 24 Sept. 1726, commented that '*Clio* must be allow'd to be a most compleat Poetess, if she really wrote those Poems that bear the Name, but it has of late been so abus'd and scandaliz'd, that I am informed she has lately changed it for that of *Mira*' (supposedly at Mallet's suggestion). (For another personality who was 'too well known', see 'Fenton' 13 above.)

Mallet wrote the original dedication to *Winter*. In the 2nd edition T added a preface on religious poetry, influenced by Hill, which also praised 'the Lines, with which *Mira* has graced my Poem'. Like the commendatory poems, it was thereafter omitted (*Seasons* (1981), pp. xliv–xlv, 303–7). In his own dedication to *Ferdinand Count Fathom* (1753), Smollett stated that T was 'often put to the blush for the undeserved incense he had offered' in his dedications.

SJ does not mention that at this time T was again employed as 'Tutor to a young Gentleman' at 'Mr. Watts's Academy' (*T Letters*, 30, 33).

14. *Summer* appeared on 16 Feb. 1727, and the *Poem Sacred to the Memory of Sir Isaac Newton* (who died on 20 Mar.) on 8 May 1727, dedicated to Sir Robert Walpole, the Prime Minister. Murdoch (1762 edn.), i, p. ix, mentioned the assistance of John Gray FRS (d. 1769), who subscribed to *The Seasons* (1730).

   Britannia, published in fact on 21 Jan. 1729 (the error was in Murdoch (1762 edn.), i, p. ix), reflects opposition criticism of the Walpole government's failure to retaliate against Spanish attacks on British ships trading in the Spanish American colonies (Sambrook, *JT*, 74–6).

15. Lord Hailes informed SJ of Lord Binning's refusal of the dedication of *Summer*, from Binning's relative Lady Murray (see headnote and 8 n. above, Malone, *Prose Works of Dryden* (1800), i. 518, Sambrook, *JT*, 56).

   Spence, i. 370, reported from Mallet *c*.1730 that the politican and literary patron George Bubb Dodington (1691–1762), later Lord Melcombe, hinted through Edward Young that he would accept the dedication of *Summer*, for which T received £50. In 1730 T inserted a passage about him in ll. 21–31. For Dodington's house at Eastbury in Dorset and his literary circle, see J. Carswell, *The Old Cause* (1954), 131–265, and see also 44 below, and 'Young' 51, 70 and n., 121–2 below, and cf. 'Halifax' 11 n. and 'Savage' 64 n. above. For 'a tender of friendship' from Dodington to SJ himself in the 1750s, see Hawkins, *Life* (1787), 328–9.

16. *Spring* appeared on 5 June 1728, with a dedication (later omitted) to Frances Seymour, Countess of Hertford (1699–1754), who is praised in the opening lines. T had visited the Countess at Marlborough in the summer of 1727. A few months later she helped to obtain a pardon for T's friend Richard Savage, after his trial for murder (see 'Savage' 84 and n. above). Savage (see 20, 45 below) may have been the source for the unreliable story of T's carousing with Lord Hertford. T in fact continued visiting the Countess in the 1730s: see Hughes, 'T and the Countess', 443, Campbell, 'T and the Countess', 367–9, and Sambrook, *JT*, 60–4.

17. *Autumn* first appeared in the collected *The Seasons*, published on 8 June 1730. Three hundred and eighty-eight subscribers ordered 457 copies, Bubb Dodington taking twenty (*The Seasons* (1981), p. xlix).

18. Murdoch (1762 edn.), i, p. ix; Shiels, *Lives*, v. 209–10.

   Sophonisba was in fact first staged on 28 Feb. 1730. (Murdoch (1762 edn.), i, p. ix, dated it 1729, but SJ's eye may have caught '1727' in the same line.) For the 'expectation' aroused by T's tragedy, see *T Letters*, 68–9, and for an anecdote about *Sophonisba* in Shiels, *Lives*, v. 210, applied by SJ instead to *Agamemnon*, see 30 and n. below. Sending the play to Mrs Sandys on 16 Mar. 1730, Thomas Rundle stated: 'the writing is incomparable, though the pleasure it affords is not that popular kind, which can draw crouded audiences' (*Letters*, 71). Cf. 34 below, SJ's earlier objection to *Comus* as a moral 'lecture' in 'Milton' 198 above, and his comments on the 'frigid caution' of recent tragedy in 'Addison' 137 and n. above.

19. *Sophonisba*, which included Anne Oldfield's last new tragic role (see Thomas Davies, *Dramatic Miscellanies* (1784), iii. 436–7), had ten performances but was not revived. Few recent commentators have taken T's tragedies seriously, but see B. S. Hammond in Terry (ed.), *JT*, 15–33.

SJ's source for the 'waggish parody' of 'O Sophonisba, Sophonisba, O!' by 'a smart from the pit' is Shiels, *Lives*, v. 209–10. It originated in *A Criticism on the New Sophonisba. A Tragedy* (1730), 22. Fielding also parodied it in *The Tragedy of Tragedies* (1731), II. v. 1, as 'Oh! *Huncamunca, Huncamunca*, oh!' Hill (1905) stated incorrectly that T's 'feeble line' was omitted from the printed text: it was not until T's *Works* (1750) that Lyttelton revised it to 'O Sophonisba! I am wholly thine' (Sambrook, *JT*, 300 n.). Cf. 'Pope' **422** above: 'the particle O! used at the beginning of a sentence, always offends.'

20. Pope's editors attribute ll. 1–26 of the prologue to Pope and ll. 27–32 to Mallet (*TE*, vi. 310–11). See **52** n. below.

21. Murdoch (1762 edn.), i, p. viii; Shiels, *Lives*, v. 203. Charles Talbot, the Solicitor-General, did not in fact become Lord Chancellor until 1733 (cf. **12** n. above). T set off for France and Italy with Charles Richard Talbot in Nov. 1730, and returned early in 1733, receiving £200 p.a. (*T Letters*, 77). For his subsequent reward, see **23** below.

    T's letters from Rome and Paris do not confirm that his travels were enjoyable and beneficial (*T Letters*, 79–82). SJ's comments no doubt reflect the claim by Murdoch (1762 edn.), i, p. x, that T's views on nature, art, human manners, and politics were 'greatly enlarged'. For a discussion by SJ on 11 Apr. 1776 of the importance of visiting Italy, see *Life*, iii. 36. DeMaria (1986), 148–50, noted that many of SJ's quotations in the *Dict.* relating to travel recommended visiting Italy.

    Writing to Saunders Welch, 3 Feb. 1778, SJ mentioned 'the vast accession of images and observation' gained by travel. On 10 Apr. 1778 he stated 'that the mind was enlarged by it, and that an acquisition of dignity of character was derived from it' (*Letters*, iii. 106, and *Life*, iii. 269, and cf. iii. 455–9). (Cf. also 'Milton' **30** above, and, for the importance of 'curiosity', 'Pope' **291–2** above.) He could, however, take a different view, as on 13 May 1778: 'What I gained by my being in France, was learning to be better satisfied with my own country. Time may be employed to more advantage from nineteen to twenty-four almost in any way than in travelling' (*Life*, iii. 352).

22. Walpole was forced to withdraw his unpopular Excise Bill in Apr. 1733. For SJ's usual scepticism about 'clamours for liberty', see 'Milton' **169–70** and n. above.

    T seems to have shown Pope part of his 'new Poem' in Oct. 1733, and Mrs Conduitt told Swift, 29 Nov. 1733, that he was 'far advanced in a poem of 2000 lines, deducing Liberty from the patriarchs to the present times, which if we may judge from the press, is now in full vigour' (Pope, *Corresp.*, iii. 395; Swift, *Corresp.*, iv. 213). *Liberty*, Pts. I–III, dedicated to Frederick, Prince of Wales, appeared in Jan.–Mar. 1735, and Pts. IV–V in Jan.–Feb. 1736.

23. Murdoch (1762 edn.), i, p. xi; Shiels, *Lives*, v. 205. T commemorated Charles Richard Talbot, who died on 27 Sept. 1733 aged 24, in *Liberty*, I. 1–14: see *T Letters*, 100–1, 207.

    Two months later, on 29 Nov. 1733, his father Charles Talbot became Lord Chancellor, and appointed T Secretary of the Briefs in the Court of Chancery, a sinecure worth £300 p.a. The emoluments of this post were reduced during the three years T held it (*T Letters*, 94–6; Sambrook, *JT*, 125–7, 137–8).

24. Murdoch (1762 edn.), i, p. x. For SJ's use of 'great' to refer to length rather than quality, see 'Milton' **194** and n. above.

Although Aaron Hill praised *Liberty* in a letter to T of 17 Jan. 1735 (*Works* (1753), i. 210–15), and in *The Prompter* 28 (14 Feb. 1735), the print run fell from 3,000 (Pt. I) to 1,000 (Pts. IV–V). T sold the copyright to Andrew Millar for £250 in Dec. 1734, but by May 1736 was planning to buy it back, since Millar 'would else be a considerable Loser, by the Paper, Printing, and Publication' (*T Letters*, 89–91, 105). For SJ's later dismissive comments on *Liberty*, see **52** below, and for authors' difficulty in judging their own works, see also 'Milton' **146** and n. above.

25. For 'the judgement of the publick', see 'Smith' **49** and n. above. Cf. *Idler* 97 (1760): 'he that pleases must offer new images to his reader' (*YW*, ii. 298).

26. For Lyttelton's extensive reduction and revision in 1750, see *Liberty* (1986), 35, 323–37. (SJ's reference to his editorial 'liberty' is unlikely to be conscious word-play.) With SJ's complaint that such editorial interference may 'lessen the confidence of society', cf. his statement that falsehoods contribute to 'the general degradation of human testimony' ('Congreve' **3** and n. above). For Lyttelton's revisions in an interleaved copy of *The Seasons* (1752), intended for an unpublished edition, see *The Seasons* (1981), pp. xiii–xiv.

I wish to see it exhibited as its author left it: SJ had stated more pointedly in *Prefaces* (1781) that 'I wish it had been exhibited in this Collection as its author left it', referring to Nichols's inclusion of Lyttelton's revised text of *Liberty* in *Eng. Poets* (1779) (see Textual Notes). Murdoch had restored T's original text in *Works* (1762) (Sambrook, *JT*, 146).

27. Murdoch (1762 edn.), i, p. xi; Shiels, *Lives*, v. 205.
    The Lord Chancellor died on 14 Feb. 1737: T's *Poem* in his memory (17 June 1737) also contained a tribute to Thomas Rundle (ll. 230–53: see **12, 21** above). For T's failure to solicit the continuance of his place from Talbot's successor, Philip Yorke, Earl of Hardwicke (1690–1764), see Sambrook, *JT*, 161–2, and for similar negligence, see 'Smith' **48** above.

28. For T's 'indigence', see Murdoch (1762 edn.), i, pp. xi–xii, and Sambrook, *JT*, 163–4. For Frederick, Prince of Wales, as a patron of 'opposition' writers in the 1730s under the guidance of George Lyttelton, see 'Pope' **217** and n. above and 'Lyttelton' **6** below. As elsewhere, SJ implies that the Prince's 'professed' interest in literature was largely opportunistic.
    Although T referred to Lyttelton in 1735 (*T Letters*, 95), Murdoch (1762 edn.), i, p. xii, stated that they did not meet until 1737, when George II ordered the Prince to leave St James's. T's pension dates from some time after Aug. 1737, when Lyttelton became the Prince's official secretary, and continued until 1748 (*T Letters*, 195–6). T had already dedicated *Liberty* to the Prince (see **22** and n. above) and his 'Ode to the Prince', published in newspapers in Sept. 1737 (perhaps marking the receipt of his pension), allied him with the opposition to the court (*Liberty* (1986), 301–2; C. Gerrard, *The Patriot Opposition to Walpole* (Oxford, 1994), 63–4; Sambrook, *JT*, 168–70, 279).
    Savage may have told SJ of T's witty reply to the Prince. For another poet's similar wit, see 'Pope' **279** and n. above.

29. SJ implies that T's pension 'obliged' him to write in support of the Prince. *Agamemnon*, dedicated to the Prince, was acted at Drury Lane on 6 Apr 1738, and in fact had nine performances by 25 Apr. Shiels, *Lives*, v. 210, mentioned that

it had to be cut for performance (cf. Sambrook, *JT*, 179–80), and printed a long note by Theophilus Cibber, claiming that T had wished him to play the part of Melisander (v. 211–12 n.). For a description of Mary Porter as Clytemnestra, see Thomas Davies, *Dramatic Miscellanies* (1784), iii. 467–9.

Discussing the influence of Aeschylus on T's play, Joseph Warton later claimed that T 'was well acquainted with the Greek Tragedies, on which I heard him talk learnedly, when I was introduced to him by my friend Mr. W. Collin[s]' (*Works of Pope* (1797), iv. 10 n.). For SJ's dislike of 'mythological stories', see 'Butler' **41** and n. above.

The anecdote about T's wig is in Thomas Davies, *Memoirs of Garrick* (1780), ii. 32–3, but Boswell had heard a similar story from T's friend Andrew Mitchell in Berlin in 1764 (*Boswell on the Grand Tour: Germany and Italy* (1953), 37). For another anecdote about *Agamemnon*, see **44** n. below.

30. Although SJ's 'if I remember right' seems to imply personal recollection, Shiels, *Lives*, v. 210, told the same story of *Sophonisba* (1730), performed long before SJ's arrival in London in 1737 (see **18** and n. above). Shiels could, of course, have heard the story from SJ and applied it to the wrong play. Shiels also mentions Pope's attendance at the theatre. For the first night of SJ's own *Irene* in 1749, see *Life*, i. 196–201.

SJ added all that follows 'the first night' in 1783 (see Textual Notes). His source may have been Joseph Warton, who repeated it in a note in *Works of Pope* (1797), iv. 10 n., already quoted in **29** n. above: see also Sambrook, *JT*, 107–8.

Pope quoted some lines to an unnamed friend, possibly T, in a letter of 3 Sept. 1731, and later adapted them in his *Epistle to Arbuthnot*, ll. 406–19: see Pope, *Corresp.*, iii. 226, and 'Pope' **215** and n. above. For SJ's objections to Pope's recycling of other passages in his poetry, see 'Pope' **237–8** above. Pope quoted T's compliment to him in *Winter*, ll. 554–5, in the 'Testimonies of Authors' prefixed to the *Dunciad*, referring to 'his elegant and philosophical poem of the Seasons' (*TE*, v. 37). For his private opinion of *The Seasons* in 1735, see **48** n. below.

abated the value: cf. SJ's earlier statement that Cowley's timidity as a lover 'cannot but abate' our esteem for his love poetry ('Cowley' **15** above).

31. See Murdoch (1762 edn.), i, pp. xii–xiii; Shiels, *Lives*, v. 214; and, for a modern account, V. J. Liesenfeld, *The Licensing Act of 1737* (Madison, 1984).

SJ had attacked the Licensing Act, intended by the Government to inhibit opposition drama, in his ironic *A Compleat Vindication of the Licensers of the Stage* (1739) (*YW*, x. 52–73), on the banning of Henry Brooke's *Gustavus Vasa* on 16 Mar. 1739: SJ was one of the many subscribers when Brooke's text was published in May 1739. For his later views on censorship, see also 'Milton' **58** and n. above.

T criticized the Act in the preface to an edition of Milton's *Areopagitica* in 1738 (Sambrook, *JT*, 173). When *Edward and Eleonora* was refused at Drury Lane, T offered it to John Rich, and it was about to be acted at Covent Garden when the Lord Chancellor prohibited it in Mar. 1739. Like SJ, both Shiels and Murdoch had failed to see why it had given offence. The inevitable publicity led to the sale by subscription of 4,500 copies of the printed play, supposedly bringing T £1,000. T dedicated it, like *Agamemnon*, to the Princess of Wales, with a reference to the

Prince as 'the Darling of a great and free People' (Pope, *Corresp.*, iv. 166–7; Sambrook, *JT*, 189–98). *Edward and Eleonora* was eventually performed at Covent Garden in an adaptation by Thomas Hull in the 1775–6 season.

32. This *bon mot* appeared in the *Daily Gazetteer* of 12 Apr. 1739 (Sambrook, *JT*, 196–7).

33. Murdoch (1762 edn.), i, p. xiii; Shiels, *Lives*, v. 215. *Alfred, A Masque* was performed at Cliveden House, near Maidenhead, on 1 Aug. 1740. Thomas Arne's music included his setting of T's 'Rule, Britannia'. For the revised versions performed in 1745 and 1751, see 'Mallet' 16 and n. below, McKillop, 'Early History', 311–24, and Sambrook, *JT*, 200–9.

34. Murdoch (1762 edn.), i, p. xiii. T dedicated *Tancred and Sigismunda*, adapted from Le Sage's *Gil Blas*, to the Prince of Wales. It was performed at Drury Lane on 18 Mar. 1745, with Garrick and Mrs Cibber in the leading roles, and was acted to the end of the century. For an account of the rehearsals, attended by William Pitt and Lyttelton, see Davies, *Memoirs of Garrick*, i. 78–80. The 'Advertisement' to the printed text stated that it had been cut for performance.

For T's limitations as a dramatist, see Shiels, *Lives*, v. 216–17. Andrew Mitchell (see 29 n. above) told Boswell in 1764 that drama was not T's 'province', and Francis Gentleman, *The Dramatic Censor* (1770), ii. 463, concluded that T 'wrote more for the closet than the stage' (see also Sambrook, *JT*, 181). For the 'pathetick', see 'Cowley' 57 and n. above, and for SJ's objections elsewhere to 'declamation' rather than 'dialogue' in drama, see 'Milton' 198 and n. and 'Addison' 137 and n. above.

For T's 'diffusive' style, see also 50 below.

35. Murdoch (1762 edn.), i, p. xi.

Lyttelton became a Lord of the Treasury in Henry Pelham's government in Dec. 1744 (see 'Lyttelton' 11 below), and subsequently (probably in 1746) obtained for T the post of Surveyor-General of the Customs for the Leeward Islands at £300 p.a. Apparently at T's request, his friend William Paterson became his joint-patentee at £400 p.a., and, unlike T, actually carried out his duties in Barbados (*T Letters*, 175, 199, 208; Sambrook, *JT*, 252, 315 n.). T duly praised Lyttelton in *The Castle of Indolence*, I. lxv–lxvi, as one 'of Sense refin'd, | Who felt each Worth, for every Worth he had; | Serene yet warm, humane yet firm his Mind, | As little touch'd as any Man's with Bad'.

36. Murdoch (1762 edn.), i, p. xiv; Shiels, *Lives*, v. 205–9. T claimed to have begun *The Castle of Indolence* (published 7 May 1748) in the mid-1730s (*T Letters*, 135–6, 197, 201; *Liberty* (1986), 161–2).

Thomas Birch described the poem to Lord Orrery, 30 Sept. 1748, as 'the most intelligible, correct, regular and spiritted of all his performances' (*The Orrery Papers* (1903), ii. 43). Shiels quoted it at length, discussed the influence of Spenser, and concluded that 'this single performance discovers more genius and poetical judgment, than all his other works put together'. For Shenstone's early comments, see his *Letters* (Oxford, 1939), 170, 174–5, 177. Warton, *Essay*, ii (1782), 36–7, described it as 'that exquisite piece of wild and romantic imagery . . . the first canto of which, in particular, is marvellously pleasing, and the stanzas have a greater flow and freedom than his blank-verse'.

For SJ's dislike of Spenserian imitations, see 'West' 14 and n. below.

37. SJ compresses Murdoch (1762 edn.), i, pp. xiv–xv. For defeated expectations of ease and prosperity, see 'Denham' 19 and n. above.

Shiels, who treats T's death rather briefly (*Lives*, v. 216), had in fact published *Musidorus: A Poem Sacred to the Memory of Mr. James Thomson* in 1748. For William Collins's *Ode* (1748) on this occasion, unmentioned by SJ, see 'Collins' 8 n. below. and, for another memorial poem, see 'Damon: A Night Pastoral' (dedicated to Mallet) in Thomas Hudson, *Poems on Several Occasions* (Newcastle, 1752), 13–22.

There are accounts of T's death in *T Letters*, 204–7, and Sambrook, *JT*, 275–8, who quotes John Armstrong's description of T's last hours. Although Hill (1905) stated that 'exasperation' in this sense is not in the *Dict.*, SJ in fact added the definition '1. Aggravation' in 1773. Lyttelton commented that 'Thomson I hope and believe died a Christian', after benefiting from Lyttelton's recent book on St Paul: see 'Lyttelton' 12 below and Doddridge, *Corresp.*, 288.

T was buried on 29 Aug. 1748 at St Mary's, Richmond, where a commemorative plaque was erected in 1792 by David Steuart Erskine, Earl of Buchan. The monument in Westminster Abbey, between Shakespeare and Rowe, was erected by subscription in 1762. T's household effects, including his books, were sold on 15–17 May 1749: see *Sale Catalogues of Libraries of Eminent Persons*, i (1971), 45–66.

38. SJ follows Murdoch (1762 edn.), i, pp. xvi–xvii, and quotes *The Castle of Indolence*, I. lxviii (l. 604). Lord Hailes commented in 1782 on SJ's statement that T was 'above the middle size', 'I think not': see Carnie (1956), 487. SJ once stated bluntly that 'Addison and Thomson were equally dull till excited by wine' (*Life*, i. 359).

39. Murdoch (1762 edn.), i, p. xvi; Shiels, *Lives*, v. 215–16.

T mentioned *Coriolanus* as early as 1742 and had probably completed it by 1746, but Garrick's reluctance to play a supporting role to James Quin (see below) probably delayed its performance: see *T Letters*, 136–7, and Sambrook, *JT*, 256–7, 263. It was acted at Covent Garden on 13 Jan. 1749 for the benefit of T's sisters Mary and Jean (*T Letters*, 188, 196–7, 200).

James Quin (1693–1766), who had earlier acted in T's *Agamemnon* and *Alfred*, played the title role, and spoke Lyttelton's prologue, which SJ quotes briefly (see also 53 below). Shiels, *Lives*, v. 215–16, did so more fully ('forgive this gushing tear: | Alas! I feel I am no actor here'), adding that Quin 'never appeared a greater actor than at this instant, when he declared himself none: 'twas an exquisite stroke of nature'. For T's friendship with Quin, see *T Letters*, 200–1, and Sambrook, *JT*, 164–6. Although the story of T's arrest is not in Shiels or Murdoch, Boswell had pointed it out to SJ by 9 June 1777 (*Life*, iii. 117). Versions had appeared in *The Tell-Tale* (1756), i. 152–4, *The Life of James Quin, Comedian* (1766), 82–4, and several subsequent accounts of T: e.g. in *The Seasons* (Edinburgh, 1768), pp. xvi–xviii. For 'friendship' and 'obligation', see also 'Gray' 3 and n. below.

T owed several hundred pounds at his death (*T Letters*, 208). Birch told Lord Orrery, 30 Sept. 1748, that T's debts 'through his excessive ill economy and luxury are very considerable', and that Lyttelton was having to discharge bills from thirty tradesmen in Richmond and Kew (*The Orrery Papers* (1903), ii. 43). For the allowance T had paid to his unmarried sisters since 1738, see Sambrook, *JT*, 172.

40. Boswell had sent SJ T's letter to his sister Jean, written while visiting Lyttelton at Hagley, by 18 June 1778 (*Life*, iii. 360; for the original text, see *T Letters*, 190–2). Boswell knew Jean because his wife's nephews had attended her husband's school. For two other letters by T, see *Life*, ii. 64, iii. 116.

41. Jean's husband Robert Thomson had a school at Lanark. For the deaths of T's parents, see 3 and n. above. Elizabeth ('poor Lizy') married the Revd Robert Bell of Strathaven, who, after her death *c.*1746, remarried on 27 Aug. 1747. Mary married William Craig: SJ met their son (T's nephew) James Craig (1740–95), later a prominent Edinburgh architect, in St Andrew's in Aug. 1773 (*Life*, v. 68, 484–5).

42. T, who died some ten months later, did not in fact return to Scotland.

43. *fervid*: '2. Vehement; eager; zealous' (*Dict*). For SJ's interest in the benevolence of poets, see 'Savage' 91–3 and n. above. Boswell had emphasized T's 'humane and benevolent disposition' to SJ on 18 June 1778 (see 40 n. above), and later claimed that, by sending him T's letter, he had helped to soften SJ's characterization of the poet. In 1768 he had heard SJ refer to T's 'gross sensuality and licentiousness of manners' (*Life*, ii. 63–4).

SJ is in fact relatively restrained here and in 45 below about T's notorious indolence and financial negligence: see *T Letters*, 112, 123, 155, 178, and Sambrook, *JT*, 207–11 (including Mrs Thrale's anecdote of T 'lounging round Lord Burlington's garden, with his hands in his waistcoat pockets, biting off the sunny side of the peaches'). According to 'Scrutator' (John Loveday) in *Gent. Mag.* (1781), 420, 'such a lover of conviviality was he, that, when the sun has intruded upon the late hour, he has proposed the nailing up of blankets to obstruct the unwelcome morning'. For SJ's own 'indolence', see *Life*, i. 207, 463, 482, ii. 143, etc.

44. Malone, *Prose Works of Dryden* (1800), i (i). 518, attributed this story to a MS note sent to SJ by Lord Hailes (see headnote), based on information from Lady Murray, a relative of Lord Binning (see 8 n. above). See also J. M. Osborn, *TLS* (23 Apr. 1938), 280, and Carnie (1956), 74.

According to Thomas Davies, *Dramatic Miscellanies*, iii (1784), 467–8 n., T's 'broad Scotch accent' provoked the actors to laughter when he read his *Agamemnon* to them. For other poets who were poor readers, see 'Congreve' 7 and n. above; and for SJ's own accomplishment as a reader, as in a 'grand and affecting' recitation from *Macbeth*, see *Life*, ii. 212 and n., v. 115, and *J. Misc.*, i. 347. For Bubb Dodington, see 15 and n. above.

45. Although SJ may seem to refer directly to the opening of Murdoch's 'Life', i, p. i ('It is commonly said, that the life of a good writer is best read in his works'), this sentence also appeared in later accounts of T derived from Murdoch: e.g. in T's *Works* (4 vols., 1766), i, p. v. Murdoch later explained that T's 'distinguishing qualities of *mind* and *heart* . . . are better represented in his writings, than they can be by the pen of any biographer. There, his love of mankind, of his country and his friends; his devotion to the *Supreme Being*, founded in the most elevated and just conceptions of his operations and providence, shine out in every page' (i, p. xix). SJ uses Savage's somewhat absurd evidence to resist such a confusion of life and art.

T met Savage soon after arriving in London in 1725 (see 8 n. above), and Savage stayed with him at Richmond more than once in the 1730s (see 'Savage' 207 n. above). The lady might have formed her impression of T as a 'great lover' from some of T's songs, or such passages as *Spring*, ll. 867 ff., which differentiate 'feverish, extravagant, and unchastened Passion' from 'the Happiness of pure, mutual Love' ('Argument' in *Seasons* (1981), 3); of his swimming, from *Summer*, ll. 1244–68, and the bathing scene in William Kent's frontispiece to *Summer* in *Works* (1730); and of his abstinence, from *Liberty*, v. 157–69, and such passages in *Seasons* as *Summer*, ll. 677–80 ('Give me to drain the Cocoa's milky Bowl, | And from the Palm to draw its freshening Wine! | More bounteous far than all the frantic Juice | Which *Bacchus* pours'). Other passages, however, celebrate wine (*Autumn*, ll. 683–706). By Sept. 1742 the Countess of Hertford was concerned about T's drinking and taste for low company: 'He turns Day into Night, & Night into Day & is (as I am told) never awake till after Midnight & I doubt has quite drown'd his Genius' (*T Letters*, 153 n.). For T's 'gross sensuality', see also 43 n. above.

By 'love ... of the sex', SJ (or Savage) evidently meant an appetite for 'the (female) sex' in general: cf. SJ's definition of 'Sex' as '2. Womankind, by way of emphasis' (*Dict.*), and his reference to 'unlawful pleasures of the sex' in 1765 (*YW*, vii. 370). A meaning closer to modern usage was emerging at this time, as in 'If ever he felt the passion for sex' in *Gent. Mag.* (Oct. 1781), 470. In the 1740s, after Savage's departure from London, T had an unreciprocated passion for Elizabeth Young, the 'Eliza' of his poems (*T Letters*, 146–61, 164–71; Sambrook, *JT*, 214–29, 249–51).

SJ was sometimes willing to deduce information about an author's character from his works: see 'Addison' 121 above and Folkenflik, 141–5. Elsewhere, however, he was more likely to insist on the disappointment so often experienced when meeting an admired author (see *Rambler* 14 and Introduction, i. 82–3 above). For the disparity between an author's principles and practice, see 'Savage' 341 and n. above.

46–53. Hawkins, *Life* (1787), 535, commented on SJ's 'frigid commendation' of T.

46. For 'originality', see 'Milton' 277 and n. above. Unusually, SJ is willing to recognize 'genius' in T's 'peculiar train' of thought. He had stated of the 'original and unborrowed' cast of Milton's early poems that 'their peculiarity is not excellence' ('Milton' 177 above), and later refers disapprovingly to Collins's 'peculiar habits of thought' ('Collins' 8 below).

In Nov. 1756 he had described T as 'a man of genius, but not very skilful in the art of composition, to whom however much will be forgiven as an original, that will not be forgiven to an imitator, or successor' (*Letters*, i. 149–50). On 28 July 1763 he stated that T 'had as much of the poet about him as most writers. Every thing appeared to him through the medium of his favourite pursuit. He could not have viewed those two candles burning but with a poetical eye' (*Life*, i. 453, and cf. 50 n. below). Whatever his reservations, SJ describes T as a 'poet' here and in 48 below with a conviction absent from his discussions of most English poets since Dryden (he had yet to write 'Pope').

the eye which Nature bestows: SJ had objected in *Rambler* 36 (1750) that the general effects of nature offer little variety, and that description dwelling on 'the minuter discriminations, by which one species differs from another' will depart from 'that simplicity of grandeur which fills the imagination' (*YW*, iii. 197). This objection seems not to apply to T, whose powers have some resemblance to those SJ attributed to Shakespeare in 1765: 'There is a vigilance of observation and accuracy of distinction which books and precepts cannot confer; from this almost all original and native excellence proceeds... Shakespeare, whether life or nature be his subject, shews plainly, that he has seen with his own eyes; he gives the image which he receives, not weakened or distorted by the intervention of any other mind' (*YW*, vii. 88, 89–90). Reviewing Warton's *Essay on Pope* (1756), SJ noted that, when discussing T's poetry (41–9), 'he remarks that writers fail in their copies for want of acquaintance with originals, and justly ridicules those who think they can form just ideas of valleys, mountains, and rivers in a garret of the Strand' (*OASJ*, 489).

the vast, and... the minute: Imlac said in *Rasselas*, ch. X, that the poet 'must be conversant with all that is awfully vast or elegantly little' (*YW*, xvi. 42). In Apr. 1778 SJ observed that 'The true strong and sound mind is the mind that can embrace equally great things and small' (*Life*, iii. 334). See also 'Cowley' **58** and n. and 'Milton' **234** and n. above. The discussion by Shiels, *Lives*, v. 202–3, of T's distinctive ('peculiar') diction and style also referred to his 'perfect inspection' of natural objects 'through a microscope capable of discovering all the minute beauties' (cf. also **50** n. below).

never yet has felt what Thomson impresses: SJ had asserted in *Rambler* 36 that detailed description loses poetry's 'general power of gratifying every mind by recalling its conceptions' (*YW*, iii. 197). In 'Gray' **51** below he praises the *Elegy* precisely because the reader 'persuades himself that he has always felt' the poet's 'notions'. Warton had also praised T in *Essay on Pope* (1756), 47, 'for impressing on our minds the effects, which the scene delineated would have on the present spectator or hearer'. For SJ and Warton 'impress' means '1. To print by pressure; to stamp', '2. To fix deep', '3. To mark, as impressed by a stamp' (*Dict.*): cf. 'Savage' **101** and 'Pope' **373** above, and for similar usage, Joseph Trapp, *Lectures on Poetry* (1742), 7, 26, 46, 5, etc., Wordsworth, 'Tintern Abbey', ll. 6–7, and Hazlitt in 1818 on T's power of conveying to readers 'the vivid impression which the whole [landscape] makes upon his own imagination' (*Works*, ed. P. P. Howe, v (1930), 87).

47. This paragraph, inserted in proof, may be the 'short addition to Thomsons sheet' SJ mentions in his undated note to Nichols (see headnote and *Letters*, iii. 227). The grammar ('which are') requires 'intersections', as in the proofs (where it replaced 'pauses') and *Prefaces* (1781), rather than the singular 'intersection' in *Lives* (1781–3): see Textual Notes.

frequent intersections of the sense: SJ stifles one of his deepest convictions about the importance of rhyme. For his usual hostility to blank verse, see 'Milton' **274** and n. above, and for other concessionary statements about it, see 'Young' **160** and 'Akenside' **17–18** below. Dick Minim had observed in *Idler* 61 (1759) 'how often the best thoughts are mangled by the necessity of confining or extending them to the dimensions of a couplet' (*YW*, ii. 191). See also 'Denham' **37** and n. above, and, for 'the distresses of rhyme', 'Milton' **126** above.

48. SJ had discussed the effect of the different seasons on the mind in *Rambler* 80 (1750).

As in **46** above, SJ's emphasis falls on communication between the 'minds' of poet and reader. Cf. Burke in 1757: 'naked description, though never so exact, conveys so poor and insufficient an idea of the thing described, that it could scarcely have the smallest effect, if the speaker did not call in to his aid those modes of speech that mark a strong and lively feeling in himself. Then, by the contagion of our passions, we catch a fire already kindled in another' (*Enquiry* (1958), 175).

For description elsewhere, see 'Cowley' **154** and n. above, and for the 'pleasing or dreadful', 'Milton' **248** and n. above. Swift wrote in 1732 that he was not 'overfond' of *The Seasons*, 'because they are all Description, and nothing is doing, whereas *Milton* engages me in Actions of the highest Importance' (*Corresp.*, iv. 53). Pope commented on T in 1735: ''Tis a great fault in descriptive poetry to describe everything' (Spence, i. 168).

naturalist: 'A student in physicks, or natural philosophy' (*Dict.*), illustrated from More ('Admirable artifice! wherewith Galen, though a mere *naturalist*, was so taken, that he could not but adjudge the honour of a hymn to the wise Creator').

49. As with other genuine poets about whom he had residual reservations, such as Shakespeare and Milton (see *YW*, vii. 71 ff. and 'Milton' **242–63** above), SJ (briefly) balances T's strengths against his 'defects'. A similar discussion of T's 'want of method' in Shiels, *Lives*, v. 202, was conceivably influenced by SJ himself (see **50** n. below and Campbell, 'Shiels', 540–1): 'There appears no particular design; the parts are not subservient to one another; nor is there any dependance or connection throughout; but this perhaps is a fault almost inseparable from a subject in itself so diversified, as not to admit of such limitation'. For 'design', see also 'Savage' **120** above, and, for the inevitable arbitrariness of sequential description, 'Pope' **315** above. In Thomas Gray's opinion, T 'had one talent beyond all other poets, that of describing the various appearances of nature', but 'failed . . . when he attempted to be moral, in which attempt he always became verbose' (*Corresp.*, iii. 1291).

In his edition of *The Seasons* (1793), Percival Stockdale dismissed SJ's comments on T (one of 'the many futile, absurd, and ungenerous passages' in the *Lives*) as 'absolute nonsense' (unpaginated headnote to 'Summer', after p. 222). For the immediate critical context of SJ's discussion, see John More (or Moir), *Strictures, Critical and Sentimental, on Thomson's Seasons* (1777), John Aikin's prefatory essay in his edition of *The Seasons* (1778), and John Scott, *Critical Essays on . . . Several English Poets* (1785), 295–386 (on T's diction).

50. SJ quotes Butler, *Hudibras*, ii. i. 907–8 ('Mysterious Vail, of brightness made, | That's both her luster, and her shade'), alluded to earlier in *Idler* 31 (1758) (*YW*, ii. 95), and again in 'Akenside' **16** below.

SJ said on 11 Apr. 1776 that T 'had a true poetical genius, the power of viewing every thing in a poetical light. His fault is such a cloud of words sometimes, that the sense can hardly peep through. Shiels, who compiled "Cibber's Lives of the Poets," was one day sitting with me. I took down Thomson, and read aloud a large portion of him, and then asked,—Is not this fine? Shiels having expressed the highest admiration. Well, Sir, (said I,) I have omitted every other line' (*Life*, iii. 37). Warton, *Essay on Pope* (1756), 43, admitted that T's diction 'is sometimes harsh and inharmonious, and sometimes turgid and obscure, and . . . the numbers not sufficiently diversified by different pauses'. Lyttelton wrote in his *Dialogues of the Dead* (1760) that T's diction was 'bold and glowing, but sometimes *obscure* and *affected*. Nor did he always know when to *stop*, or what to *reject*' (*Works* (3rd edn., 1776), ii. 202). In 1767 Goldsmith described T bluntly as 'in general, a verbose and affected poet' (*Coll. Works*, v. 325).

SJ defines 'Luxuriant' as 'Exuberant; superfluously plenteous', quoting Pope, *Imit. Horace, Ep. II. ii.* (1737), ll. 174–5: 'Prune the luxuriant, the uncouth refine, | But show no mercy to an empty line.' Since 'Exuberant' has come to mean 'lively' or 'high-spirited', its horticultural sense in SJ's usage should be noted: '1. Growing with superfluous shoots; overabundant; superfluously plenteous; luxuriant.' This is reinforced by 'Florid': '1. Productive of flowers' and '3. Embellished; splendid; brilliant with decorations' (*Dict.*).

At times SJ associates 'luxuriance' and 'exuberance' of diction or wit with pre-Restoration poetry (cf. 'Dryden' 220–2 above). In 1751 he explained that his criticism of *Samson Agonistes* was not intended to damage 'the everlasting verdure of Milton's laurels' but 'to strengthen their shoots by lopping their luxuriance' (*Rambler* 140; *YW*, iv. 383). In the preface to the *Dict.* he similarly described the task of imposing order and selection on the 'wild exuberance' of the language (*OASJ*, 307). See also *Rambler* 106 (*YW*, iv. 201), 'exuberance' of wit in 'Cowley' **105, 119, 164** and 'Dryden' **177** above, and 'luxuriant' diction in 'Milton' **205** and 'Smith' **49** above. For Pope's occasional 'luxurious amplification', see 'Pope' **350, 366** above.

From the 1740s SJ sensed that some of his contemporaries were wilfully relapsing into self-indulgent 'exuberance'. In *Idler* 36 (1758) he described 'The man of exuberance and copiousness, who diffuses every thought thro' so many diversifications of expression, that it is lost like water in a mist' (*YW*, ii. 113). For similar comments on poetic language, see 'West' **11**, 'Akenside **15–16, 18, 22**, and 'Gray' **28** below.

Although 'exuberance' by definition usually needs to be 'reduced' and pruned, SJ can at times associate it with a 'fertile and copious mind' ('Milton' **125** and 'Pope' **299** above). He refers to Butler's 'exuberance of matter' (by comparison with the less fertile Prior) in 'Prior' **64** above, to Congreve's 'exuberance of wit' in 'Congreve' **11** above, to the 'soft luxurance of . . . fancy' in the *Rape of the Lock* in 'Pope' **57** above, and the 'varied exuberance' of Dryden's prose (in contrast to the more uniform Pope) in 'Pope' **309** above. A proper balance is suggested by his praise of Goldsmith, whose 'language was copious without exuberance' ('Parnell' **1** above).

For SJ's use of T in the *Dict.*, see Gilmore, 'Implicit Criticism', 265–73, and Reddick, 136–40. While he sometimes quotes T to illustrate philosophical or scientific language, SJ on some twenty-three occasions accuses him of innovative singularity without proper precedent. In 1773 he reduced his original 619 quotations from T to 553.

51. *Poems, with which I was acquainted at their first appearance*: T is the earliest poet whose entire career SJ had been able to follow at first hand.

T repeatedly revised and expanded *The Seasons*, particularly in the collected editions of 1730 and 1744 (Sambrook, *JT*, 96–103, 229–35). Lyttelton made further revisions in the posthumous *Works* (1750), explaining to Philip Doddridge, 22 Mar. 1750: 'There is not a line in it which a lady of virtue and modesty may not safely read, which is more than can be said of the works of any other of the English poets, except Milton, Spenser and Addison' (R. Phillimore, *Memoirs and Corresp. of George Lord Lyttelton* (1845), i. 322). For the influence of T's reading on the development of *The Seasons*, see McKillop, *Background of T's 'Seasons'*.

SJ defines 'Race' as '6. A particular strength or taste of wine, applied by *Temple* to any extraordinary force of intellect' (*Dict.*). See the phrase 'more Race, more Spirit, more Force of Wit and Genius' in Sir William Temple's 'Essay upon the Ancient and Modern Learning'; 'some great race of Fancy or Judgement in the Contrivance' in 'Upon the Gardens of Epicurus' (cited in the *Dict.*); and 'the greatest Race of Native Genius' in 'Of Poetry' (*Miscellanea. The Second Part* (3rd edn., 1692), 59, 131, 307). See also 'raciness' in 'Milton' **234** above, and SJ's note on 'race' in Shakespeare (*YW*, viii. 841).

52. For *Liberty*, see **22–6** above. SJ's lack of enthusiasm for a poem in which Pt. IV is 'A *locus classicus* for the conjunction of patriotism, the Muses, Whiggery, and Milton' (Lipking (1970), 329 n.) is predictable. In *The Seasons* (1793), Percival Stockdale defended *Liberty* against SJ's '*contemptible contempt*' (unpaginated endnote to 'Winter' after p. 222). For a revival of interest in the poem among members of the popular reform movement, see J. Barrell and H. Guest, 'T in the 1790s', in Terry (ed.), *JT*, 217–46.

In *Prefaces* (1781) the prologue to T's *Sophonisba* by Pope and Mallet (see **20** and n. above) was appended, but later omitted (see Textual Notes).

53. Added in 1783 (see Textual Notes). Like Shiels, *Lives*, v. 218, SJ now ends by quoting Lyttelton's prologue to *Coriolanus* (cf. **39** above): 'Not one immoral, one corrupted thought, | One line which dying he could wish to blot', alluding to Waller's claim that 'he would blot from his works any line that did not contain some motive to virtue' ('Waller' **106** and n. above). See also Lyttelton's letter to Doddridge in **51** n. above, and his praise of T's morality, piety, and 'most *tender* and *benevolent heart*' in *Dialogues of the Dead* (1760) (*Works* (3rd edn., 1776), ii. 203).

ISAAC WATTS (1674–1748)

Composition. Some three years before writing 'Watts', SJ wrote to a Mr W. Sharp on 7 July 1777: 'To the Collection of English Poets I have recommended the volume of Dr. Watts to be added. His name has been long held by me in *veneration*; and I would not willingly be reduced to tell of him, only, that he was born and died. Yet, of his life I know very little; and therefore must pass him in a manner very unworthy of his character, unless some of his friends will favour me with the necessary information... My plan does not exact much; but I wish to distinguish *Watts*; a man who never wrote but for a good purpose' (*Letters*, iii. 38). (For SJ's recommendation that W be included in *Eng. Poets*, see also **1** and n. below.)

SJ was seeking help from the London surgeon William Sharp (*c.*1730–1810), who 'had the honour of possessing Dr. Watts' correspondence with his great friends' (*Gent. Mag.* (1787), 99). Although there is no evidence that SJ's enquiry bore any fruit, Sharp may have told him of Gibbons's forthcoming biography (see below). SJ remained uneasy, saying on 19 May 1778: 'I shall do what I can for Dr. Watts; but my materials are very scanty' (*Life*, iii. 358). W was one of the five 'Poets whose lives he has to write' about whom Boswell requested 'any communications' from Lord Hailes on 7 July 1779 (*Catalogue*, L 615). SJ's problem was eventually solved by the timely publication of Thomas Gibbons's *Memoirs* of W early in May 1780 (*London Chronicle*, 6–9 May 1780), and he no doubt compiled his own account of W within a few weeks.

Sources. *GD, BB,* and Shiels had ignored W and, as SJ's reference in **2** below indicates (without quite stating), he was almost entirely dependent on the very recent *Memoirs of the Rev. Isaac Watts, D.D.* (1780) by Dr Thomas Gibbons (1720–85), Minister of the Independent Church at Haberdashers' Hall and a tutor of the Dissenting Academy at Mile End. Gibbons had been a friend of W, had published an *Elegiac Poem* (1749) on his death and other poems about him in his *Juvenilia* (1750), 168–98, and had access to family MSS.

According to his diary, Gibbons 'Visited the celebrated Dr. Samuel Johnson' on 14 Aug. 1780, not long after SJ must have written 'Watts'. SJ later said, 'I took to Dr. Gibbons', and invited him to call again to 'dawdle over a dish of tea in an afternoon'. Gibbons and SJ later dined with Charles Dilly on 17 May 1784 (*Life*, iv. 126, 278, 494). There are a few other incidental references to SJ in Gibbons's MS diary: see G. M. Ditchfield, 'Dr J and the Dissenters', *Bulletin of the John Rylands Library*, 68 (1986), 378 and n. Gibbons died on 22 Feb. 1785, a few weeks after SJ himself.

For SJ's usual hostility to religious dissent, see *Life*, ii. 150–1, 249–55, iii. 298–9, *J. Misc.*, i. 429, and 'Akenside' **2–3** below. He had opposed the removal of the requirement that officeholders should subscribe to the Thirty-nine Articles of the Anglican Church, as proposed in a parliamentary bill in Feb. 1774, and eventually rejected by the House of Lords. SJ believed that Dissenters were hoping to exploit 'unsettled times, and a government much enfeebled' (*Letters*, ii. 13 and n.). For the link between religious and political dissent, and the debate about the rights of religious minorities in the 1770s leading to the Dissenters Relief Act of 1779, see J. Stephens, 'The London Ministers and Subscription, 1772–1779', *Enlightenment and Dissent*, 1 (1982), 43–71, and P. Langford, *A Polite and Commercial People* (Oxford, 1989), 530–2.

SJ's reputed hostility helps to explain why a correspondent in *Gent. Mag.* (1784), 601–2, praised his respect for W's piety as evidence of goodness of heart in 'a strict churchman, and even a bigot to the national establishment'. Samuel Palmer (1741–1813) also praised SJ's openmindedness about a Dissenter in his edition of SJ's *Life* of W, 'With Notes Containing Animadversions and Additions' (1785, expanded 1791, 1792). George Dyer later related that, when Richard Farmer objected that SJ had failed to emphasize that W was both 'a dissenter and a Whig', SJ replied: 'Sir, you did not know the man; he was a religious, not a political Dissenter' (*Annual Necrology for 1797–8* (1800), 404–5). SJ's support for W's inclusion in *English Poets* may have been intended to underline this distinction.

Charles Burney explained SJ's attitude when reviewing Robert Anderson's *Life of SJ* (1795) in *Monthly Review*, 20 (1796), 26: SJ 'was so much in earnest in his religious belief and practice, that deviations from the rites and ceremonies of our own church were offensive to him ... Yet there were individuals among the Dissenters whom he highly respected: such as Dr. Watts, Dr. Robertson, Dr. Beattie, Dr. Blair, the late Dr. Rose, and several worthy ministers of the church of Scotland, with whom he made acquaintance in his tour to the Hebrides. Much of his pretended abuse of the Presbyterians and Whigs was more playful than malignant.'

There were 959 quotations from W (mostly from *The Improvement of the Mind* and *Logick*) in the *Dict.* (1755), increased to 965 in 1773. See also **24**n. below. Joseph Towers, in his *Essay on SJ* (1786), suggested that SJ had been 'the more inclined to do justice' to W, 'though a Dissenter, not only from respect for his piety, but also from some grateful remembrance of the assistance which he had received from his works' i.e. in the *Dict.* (*Early Biographies* (1974), 214).

Publication. In *Prefaces*, vol. viii (15 May 1781). Pp. 1–16 (of 24) of the proofs are in the Forster Collection.

Modern Sources:

S. L. Bishop, *IW's Hymns and Spiritual Songs (1707): Publishing History and a Bibliography* (Ann Arbor, 1974)

D. Davie, *A Gathered Church* (1978)

D. Davie, *Dissentient Voice* (Notre Dame, Ind., 1982)

A. P. Davis, *IW: His Life and Works* (New York, 1943)

G. M. Ditchfield, 'Dr. J and the Dissenters', *Bulletin of the John Rylands Library*, 68 (1986), 373–409

Philip Doddridge, *Calendar of the Correspondence*, ed. G. F. Nuttall (1979) (twenty-three letters from W to Doddridge)

D. G. Fountain, *IW Remembered* (Worthing, 1974)

E. P. Hood, *IW: His Life and Writings* (1875)

J. Hoyles, *The Waning of the Renaissance, 1640–1740: Studies in the Thought and Poetry of Henry More, John Norris and IW* (The Hague, 1971)

J. H. Leicester, 'Dr J and IW', *New Rambler* (June 1964), 2–10

A. Lindsay (ed.), *Index of English Literary Manuscripts*, iii (iv) (1997), 511–34

M. F. Marshall, 'IW', in *Dictionary of Literary Biography*, xcv (1990), 333–42

M. F. Marshall and J. Todd, *English Congregational Hymns in the 18th Century* (Lexington, Ky., 1982), 28–59

T. Milner, *The Life, Times, and Correspondence of the Rev. IW* (1834)

J. H. P. Pafford (ed.), *IW:, Divine Songs* (Oxford, 1971) (facsimile of 1715 edn.)

I. Rivers, *Reason, Grace, and Sentiment*, vol. i (Cambridge, 1991), ch. 4

J. R. Watson, *The English Hymn: A Critical and Historical Study* (Oxford, 1997), 133–70

1. See SJ's letter to William Sharp in headnote, and, for another 'recommendation', headnote to 'Thomson' above. Elsewhere SJ stated that he 'recommended only Blackmore on the Creation and Watts' for inclusion in *Eng. Poets* (1779) (*Letters*, v. 32; *Life*, iv. 35 n.). Nichols, *Sel. Collection*, iii. 166–7 n., apparently claimed some responsibility for the inclusion of Yalden (see 'Yalden' headnote above).

2. W's mother was Sarah Taunton or Tanton. The elder Isaac Watts (1650–1737) of 21 French St., Southampton, was more than once described as 'a clothier', but later also ran a flourishing boarding-school, and became deacon of the Independent meeting at Southampton. Samuel Palmer, who annotated SJ's *Life* of W in 1785 (see 35 n. below), claimed never to have heard the 'common report' that he had been a shoemaker. SJ ignores Gibbons's statement (1 n.) that W's father was imprisoned for dissent in 1674 and again in 1683, and later spent two years in hiding in London.

3. W was in fact the eldest of eight children. He was taught from *c*.1680 by John Pinhorne, Rector of All Saints, Southampton. For his Latin ode (1694), with a translation, see Gibbons, *Memoirs*, 7–19.

4. Dr John Speed and other citizens of Southampton offered to support W at university (Gibbons, *Memoirs*, 20), at a time when Dissenters were still debarred from the universities. SJ defines 'Dissenter' as '2. One who, for whatever reasons, refuses the communion of the English church' (*Dict.*). For a later poet who

benefited from 'the fund which the Dissenters employ in educating young men of scanty fortune', see 'Akenside' 2 below.

5. Thomas Rowe (1657–1705), whose Dissenting academy at Newington Green later moved to Little Britain in London, was also pastor of the Independent meeting at Girdlers' Hall, Basinghall St. W's 'To the Much Honoured Mr. Thomas Rowe, The Director of my Youthful Studies. *Free Philosophy*' is in *Horae Lyricae*.

W's fellow-students were John Hughes (see 'Hughes' 1 and n. above), and Josiah Hort (1674?–1751), who later had a successful career in the Irish Church, as Bishop of Ferns, Bishop of Kilmore and Ardagh, and Archbishop of Tuam (1742). (For a stern letter from Swift to Hort, 5 May 1736, see his *Corresp.*, iv. 482–4). Another student was Samuel Say (1676–1743), Nonconformist clergyman and poet: see 'Milton' 274 n. above, and *Letters, By Several Eminent Persons Deceased*, i (1772), 8 n., 202–4, and *Gent. Mag.* (1780), 568.

6. SJ refers to W's *Reliquiae Juveniles: Miscellaneous Thoughts in Prose and Verse* (1734), 289, cited by Gibbons, *Memoirs*, 62–4, who also prints the 'glyconick' verses (in a lyric metre of three trochees and a dactyl). Gibbons had translated some of W's Latin verse in *The Christian Minister [with] Original Pieces, Chiefly in Verse, on Various Occasions* (1772), 126–7.

For SJ's dislike of 'the Pindarick folly', see 'Cowley' 143 n. and 'Congreve' 44 above. W himself claimed in 'Two happy Rivals, Devotion and the Muse', ll. 1–2: 'Wild as the Lightning, various as the Moon, | Roves my *Pindaric* Song.'

For 'diction', see also 16, 33 below, and 'Cowley' 181–4 n. above.

7. For W's method of abridgement, see Gibbons, *Memoirs*, 60–1, and Fountain, *IW*, 29–30.

8. *Independents*: SJ defined 'Independent' as 'One who in religious affairs holds that every congregation is a complete church, subject to no superior authority' (*Dict.*). The Independents (later Congregationalists) were a conservative and usually prosperous sect. W was admitted to communion in Dec. 1693 (Gibbons, *Memoirs*, 20*)*.

9. After leaving Rowe's academy in 1694, W spent more than two years at home (cf. 'Milton' 20 above). His father survived until 1737: for other parents who lived to enjoy a son's eminence, see 'Pope' 161 and n. above.

10. W became tutor to the son of Sir John Hartopp (1637?–1722) at Stoke Newington in Oct. 1696 (Gibbons, *Memoirs*, 92 ff.). He originally wrote his *Logick* (1725) (see 24 below) for his pupil, to whom it was dedicated, and also addressed him in two poems in *Horae Lyricae*.

W became assistant to Dr Isaac Chauncey at the Independent Chapel in Mark Lane in Feb. 1699. His 24th birthday would in fact have been on 17 July 1698 (Gibbons, *Memoirs*, 96).

11. W became pastor at Mark Lane on 8 Mar. 1702 and was ordained ten days later. Samuel Price became his assistant in 1703, and co-pastor in 1713 (Gibbons, *Memoirs*, 98–101), after W's dangerous illness in 1712–13, described vividly in his poem 'Thoughts and Meditations in a long Sickness' in *Reliquiae Juveniles* (1734), 172–83. W could not resume his duties until 1716, but retained his pastorship at the meeting in Bury St. (where the church moved in 1708) until his death.

12. Sir Thomas Abney (1640–1722) of Theobalds near Cheshunt, Herts., a member of
the Bury St. congregation, was a pious businessman who had been Lord Mayor of
London in 1700. After his death in 1722, W continued as chaplain and tutor in the
Abney household (in later years at Abney Park, Stoke Newington), probably, in
total, for thirty-four not thirty-six years (1714–48) (Gibbons, *Memoirs*, 101–8).
Lady Abney died in 1750 and her daughter Elizabeth in 1782 (*Gent. Mag.* (1750),
43 and (1782), 407).

13. Writing in 1780, SJ no doubt has in mind here the 'reciprocal benefits' of his own
relationship with the Thrales at Streatham, where he wrote some of the *Lives*.
    SJ quotes Gibbons, *Memoirs*, 113–14. For the biographical importance of per-
sonal knowledge, see 'Swift' 138 above, and *Life*, ii. 79, 166, 446.

14. *six-and-thirty*: see 12 n. above.

15. SJ does not mention some of W's important friendships, notably with the Countess
of Hertford, to whom he dedicated *Reliquiae Juveniles* (1734), although Gibbons,
Memoirs, 364–402, printed her letters to W (1730–47). See also 'Thomson' 16 and
n. above and H. S. Hughes, *The Gentle Hertford* (New York, 1940).
    SJ has difficulty with the 'series' or chronology of W's works, because Gibbons,
Memoirs, 471–81, listed his numerous publications without dates.

16. SJ had earlier described W as 'a writer who, if he stood not in the first class of
genius, compensated that defect by a ready application of his powers to the
promotion of piety . . . one of the first who taught the Dissenters to write and
speak like other men, by shewing them that elegance might consist with piety'
(*Literary Mag.* 1 (1756), 2820.
    For 'polished diction', see 'Dryden' 216 ff. above; for W's contribution to the
literature of dissent, see Davie, *A Gathered Church* and *Dissentient Voice*; and, for
W's adaptation of his prose style to different audiences, see Rivers, *Reason*, 164–204.

17. SJ refers to the 'congregation' ('3. An assembly met to worship God in publick, and
hear doctrine', *Dict.*) at Bury St. (see 11 n. above).
    W was 'perhaps not above five feet, or at most five feet two inches' (Gibbons,
Memoirs, 322). Cf. David Jennings's funeral *Sermon* for W (1749): 'Though his
Stature was low, and *his bodily Presence but weak*, yet *his Preaching was Weighty and
Powerful*' (32). For another clerical voice, see 'Swift' 119 above.
    Dr James Foster (1697–1753) was a popular Nonconformist preacher. See
'Savage' 188 and n. above, and Pope, *Epilogue to the Satires* (1738), I. 131–2: 'Let
modest *Foster*, if he will, excell | Ten Metropolitans in preaching well.' When
Topham Beauclerk asked SJ, 'Why did Pope say this?', he replied: 'Sir, he hoped it
would vex somebody' (*Life*, iv. 9). Although Hawkins, *Life* (1787), 541, claimed
that SJ read the works of such 'sectaries' as W and Foster, Thomas Campbell
recorded that on 16 Mar. 1775, 'When Mrs. Thrale quoted something from Fosters
Sermons he flew in a passion & said that Foster was a man of mean ability, & no
original thinking' (*Diary* (Cambridge, 1947), 54; cf. *Life*, iv. 9). For John Hawkesworth (1715?–73), see 'Swift' 1 and n. above.

18–21. SJ follows Gibbons, *Memoirs*, 142–4.

18. For SJ's advice to a young clergyman about the 'composition of sermons', see his
letter to Charles Lawrence, 30 Aug. 1780, not long after he wrote 'Watts' (*Letters*,
iii. 311–12).

SJ defines 'Cursory' only as 'Hasty; quick; inattentive; careless' (*Dict.*), but evidently means here 'less formal' (cf. *OED*). Under 'Extemporize' in the *Dict.* he quotes Robert South: 'The *extemporizing* faculty is never more out of its element than in the pulpit; though even here it is much more excusable in a sermon than in a prayer'. See also DeMaria (1986), 223.

19. SJ discussed the relevance of 'grace and energy of action' to oratory in *Idler* 90 (1760), concluding that 'theology has few topicks to which action can be appropriated' (*YW*, ii. 281). For preaching, see also his obituary of Zachariah Mudge in *London Chronicle*, 29 Apr.–2 May 1769 (*Life*, iv. 77, and *Early Biographies*, 519), and *Life* i. 334, ii. 211 ('Action can have no effect upon reasonable minds. It may augment noise, but it never can enforce argument'). For his approval of the plainness of Methodist preaching, *Life*, i. 458–60, ii. 123. See also Goldsmith's 'Some Remarks on the modern manner of Preaching' (1760) in *Coll. Works*, iii. 150–5, and cf. i. 480–3, iii. 49–51.

22. For W's 'natural temper' and benevolence, see Gibbons, *Memoirs*, 165, 145. Davis, *IW*, 219, suggested that W gave as much as a fifth of his income to charity. For the benevolence of other poets, see 'Savage' 91–3 and n. above.

SJ defines 'Condescend' as '1. To depart from the privileges of superiority by a voluntary submission; to sink willingly to equal terms with inferiours; to sooth by familiarity', illustrated from W himself (*Dict.*). Gibbons, *Memoirs*, 335, quotes Dr Caleb Ainsworth's memorial sermon on W: 'Though he was capable of conversing with the greatest men on the most abstruse subjects . . . yet he condescended to be a teacher of babes.' Gibbons himself compiled books for children, including *Select Portions of Scripture . . . Versified for the Instruction of Younger Minds* (1781), mocked for its bloodthirsty content by Samuel Badcock in *Monthly Review*, 64 (1781), 390–1.

W dedicated *Divine Songs Attempted in Easy Language, for the Use of Children* (1715) to 'My Dear Young Friends', Sarah, Mary, and Elizabeth Abney, mentioning his 'many Obligations' to their parents. W's preface explained that he had 'endeavoured to sink the Language to the Level of a Child's Understanding, and yet to keep it (if possible) above Contempt'. He also claimed: 'you will find here nothing that savours of a Party: the Children of high and low Degree, of the Church of *England* or Dissenters, baptized in Infancy or not, may all join together in these Songs.' W later wrote a commendatory letter for Thomas Foxton's *Moral Songs Composed for the Use of Children* (1728).

W is now best remembered for the *Divine Songs*, and for some of his *Hymns and Spiritual Songs* (1707) and *Psalms of David Imitated* (1719). Samuel Palmer, editor of SJ's *Life* of W (1785), 25–8 nn., complained that SJ had ignored the *Hymns* and *Psalms*, presumably because *Eng. Poets* (1779) omitted them. *Horae Lyricae* (1706; enlarged, 1709) and *Divine Songs* were included, a reviewer (John Duncombe?) denying that the latter should be 'deemed too puerile for this collection' (*Gent. Mag.* (1779), 599).

W's *Philosophical Essays on Various Subjects: with Some Remarks on Mr. Locke's Essay Concerning Human Understanding* (1733) replied to Locke's attack on innate ideas, though with generous prefatory praise of his political, educational, and philosophical writings (pp. viii–ix).

A voluntary descent from the dignity of science: SJ wrote in *Rambler* 137 (1751) that 'By this descent from the pinacles of art no honour will be lost; for the condescensions of learning are always overpaid by gratitude', but later warned in *Rambler* 173 that 'learning, when she quits her exaltation' should 'descend with dignity. Nothing is more despicable than the airiness and jocularity of a man bred to severe science, and solitary meditation' (*YW*, iv. 364, v. 153). See also his dedications to George Adams, *Treatise on the Globes* (1766): 'It is the privilege of real greatness not to be afraid of diminution by condescending to the notice of little things' (Hazen, 3); and to Charles Burney's *Account of the Commemoration of Handel* (1784): 'Greatness of mind is never more willingly acknowledged . . . than when it descends into the regions of general life, and . . . shows that it borrows nothing from distance or formality' (*OASJ*, 519). For similar comments, see 'Milton' **106, 147** above. According to Mrs Thrale-Piozzi, 'no man was more struck' than SJ 'with voluntary descent from possible splendour to painful duty' (*J. Misc.*, i. 157). For Boswell's fear that, in the Hebrides, SJ would be unable 'to come down from his elevated state of philosophical dignity; from a superiority of wisdom among the wise, and of learning among the learned', see *Life*, v. 14.

23–7. Some degree of identification with W on SJ's part is apparent here. In Aug. 1773, when he and Boswell played with the notion of the Literary Club setting up a college in St Andrews, SJ assigned to himself the teaching of 'logick, metaphysicks, and scholastick divinity' (*Life*, v. 109).

23. SJ defines 'Excursive' only as 'Rambling; wandering; deviating' (*Dict.*), but the word can carry considerable positive force for him in literary contexts, as in 'Pope' **292** above ('an intelligence perpetually on the wing, excursive, vigorous, and diligent').

Cf. SJ's similar praise of Boerhaave in 1739: 'he took Care never to provoke Enemies by Severity of Censure, for he never dwelt on the Faults or Defects of others' (*Gent. Mag.*, ix. 174). He alludes finally to W's *Orthodoxy and Charity United* (1745).

24. SJ refers to W's *Logick: Or, The Right Use of Reason in the Enquiry after Truth* (1725: see **10** above), and the *Logica: sive Ars Ratiocinandi* (1692) of Jean Le Clerc (1657–1737).

W claimed in a letter: 'Even Oxford and Cambridge break thru their bigotry and hatred of ye Dissenters, and use my Logic, Astronomy, & my Poems' (Davis (1943), 255). For the use of his *Logick* at Oxford, see *The History of the University of Oxford*, vol. v, ed. L. S. Sutherland and L. G. Mitchell (1986), 569, 574–6, 590–1. SJ recommended W and Le Clerc as authors on logic in his preface to Dodsley's *Preceptor* (1748) (Hazen, 185), and later commended W's *Logick* to a student (*Life*, iv. 311). SJ marked a copy of the *Logick* (8th edn., 1745) for use in the *Dict.*, which quotes W's prose liberally: see headnote, Fleeman, *Handlist* (1984), 68, and DeMaria (1986), plate opposite p. 3.

25. For SJ's early friend Samuel Dyer (1725–72), see *Life*, i. 478–80, iv. 10–11 and n. Burke admired 'the Little display he made of his extraordinary parts of learning' (*Corresp.*, ii. 335).

See W's *Philosophical Essays* (1733), 'Essay I': 'A fair Enquiry and Debate concerning Space, whether it be Something or Nothing, God or a Creature.'

26. Hawkins confirmed that W's *The Improvement of the Mind* (1741; Pt. ii published posthumously, 1751) was 'a very favourite book' of SJ, who 'used to recommend it' (*J's Works* (1787), xi. 198). For other references, see 'Pope' **380** above, *Life*, iv. 311

and *Letters*, iii. 367, and for its influence on SJ's view of the mind, see Hagstrum (1952), 13–14.

27. 'Theologia Philosophia ancillatur' was a scholastic commonplace: cf. 'Aliae scientiae dicuntur ancillae huius' (i.e., 'sacrae doctrinae'), Aquinas, *Summa Theologica*, Pt. i, q. 1, art. 5a.

For the importance of holding the reader's 'attention', see 'Dryden' 312 and n. above. SJ's final sentence may echo Goldsmith, *The Deserted Village* (1770), l. 180: 'And fools, who came to scoff, remained to pray.'

28. For W's honorary doctorates, see Gibbons, *Memoirs*, 310, and Davis, *IW*, 41. Although SJ himself received doctorates from Trinity College, Dublin, and from Oxford, he never used the title, but evidently thought it appropriate for a clergyman; cf. 1, 14, 17 above, and 'Lyttelton' 22 below.

29. SJ follows Gibbons, *Memoirs*, 146–7.

30. W was interred at the burying-ground for Dissenters at Bunhill Fields, London, accompanied, at his own request, by two Independent, two Presbyterian, and two Baptist ministers, as 'a lecture of moderation' (Gibbons, *Memoirs*, 331; Doddridge, *Corresp.*, 290, 292). Milton lived in Bunhill Fields while writing *Paradise Lost*: see 'Milton' 108, 130, 154 above, and cf. Thomas Gutteridge, *The Universal Elegy, or A Poem on Bunhill Buriall Ground* [173–?].

Reviewing Samuel Palmer's *Appendix to Dr. Samuel Johnson's Life of Dr. Watts* (1792) in *Monthly Review*, 10 (Feb. 1793), 233 n., Christopher Moody recalled an argument between SJ and 'an ingenious, heterodox lady, now deceased' as to whether W 'died a believer in the Trinity'. The lady claimed that ' "in his latter days, he certainly, *you may depend on the fact*, opened his eyes."—"Did he, Madam?" replied Johnson, eagerly interrupting his fair antagonist,—"did he *open his eyes*? then the first thing he saw was the Devil!" *The writer of this note* was present at the conversation.'

31. Apart from *Divine Songs*, W's works for children include *The Art of Reading and Writing English* (1721), *Catechisms* (1730), and *A Short View of the Whole Scripture History* (1733). SJ also refers to Nicolas Malebranche (1638–1715), best known for his *De la recherche de la verité* (1674–5), and W's *The Knowledge of the Heavens and the Earth Made Easy* (1726). For Locke, see 22 and n. above.

33. SJ said on 19 May 1778 that W's poems are 'by no means his best works; I cannot praise his poetry itself highly; but I can praise its design' (*Life*, iii. 358). Obviously taking W's prose writings more seriously, having recommended W's inclusion in *Eng. Poets* (1779) SJ feels bound to give his verse an openminded reading (cf. 6 above), while implicitly refusing to endorse Gibbons's high opinion of it.

'The Celebrated Victory of the Poles over Osman the Turkish Emperor in the Dacian Battle' imitates a poem by the 17th-century Polish poet Casimir Sarbiewski (*Odes*, IV. 4: cf. 'Cowley' 137 above). For 'knowledge' in poetry, see 'Butler' 37–9 and n. above, and for 'diction' and 'ornament', 'Cowley' 181–4, 202 and nn. above.

For SJ's usual dissatisfaction with 'devotional poetry', see 'Waller' 135–41 and n. above. In his revised preface to *Horae Lyricae* (2nd edn., 1709), W disagreed with such critics as Boileau, who believed that 'the Doctrines of our Holy Faith will not indulge or indure a delightful Dress', and outlined a programme for the spiritual renovation of English poetry. For contemporary demands by Dennis, Blackmore, and others for such a revival, see D. B. Morris, *The Religious Sublime* (Lexington, Ky., 1972), esp. 84–5, 105–7.

In 1718 Blackmore admitted that authors of 'Divine and Moral Poetry' had hitherto 'only writ Indifferent Prose in the poorest Verse', but excepted 'the Ingenious Mr. *Watts*, whose Divine Poetry is very Laudable, and much Superior to All that have gone before him, in the Lyrick Kind' (*A Collection of Poems on Various Subjects*, pp. ix–x). The *Monthly Review*, 10 (1754), 93 ff., noted that W's 'florid diction' and 'diffusive and pathetic style' were now considered unsuitable for religious poetry in some quarters.

Cowper, however, described W in 1781 as 'a man of true poetical ability. Careless indeed for the most part, and inattentive to those niceties which constitute Elegance of expression, but frequently sublime in his conceptions and masterly in his Execution.' Although Cowper thought SJ's observations on W's poetry 'judicious' and 'characteristic of a distinguishing taste', he was 'mistaken in his notion that divine Subjects have never been poetically treated with Success. A little more Christian knowledge and Experience would perhaps enable him to discover excellent poetry upon spiritual themes in the aforesaid little Doctor' (to Newton, 18 Sept., 4 Oct. 1781, in *Letters*, i (1979), 520–1, 525–6). Southey later replied to SJ's 'most contracted and shortsighted view' of 'devotional poetry' in his edition of W's *Horae Lyricae* (1834; 1837 edn. cited): SJ 'had forgotten that of all poetry inspired poetry is the most figurative' (p. li).

34. Invited to judge the *Gent. Mag.*'s competition for poems on astronomy in 1734, W stated that he had 'sported with Rhyme as an Amusement in the younger Years of Life', but that 'The gay Colours of Imagery, and the spritely Relish of Verse die away and vanish in my advancing Age; for I have almost left off to read as well as to write that which once was so much engaging' (*Gent. Mag.* (1734), 746). In *Reliquiae Juveniles* (1734), p. xi, he wrote: 'I Make no Pretences to the Name of a Poet, or a polite Writer, in an Age wherein so many superior Souls shine in their Works through this Nation', mentioning Pope's 'Messiah', Young's biblical paraphrases, and Elizabeth Rowe's pious epistles.

W's compliment to Pope was generous, given that 'W—s' had appeared in the original *Dunciad* (1728), I. 126. Pope removed it in 1729, referring in a note to W as the author of 'some valuable pieces in the lyrick kind on pious subjects' (*TE*, v. 78–9 n.). Nichols stated that this followed 'serious, though gentle, remonstrance' from W himself; in another account, the intermediary between W and Pope was Jonathan Richardson, 'a friend to both' (*Lit. Anec.*, v. 218; *Letters, By Several Eminent Persons Deceased*, i (1772), 86–7 n.).

35. Cf. 6 above and, for SJ's objections to blank verse, 'Milton' 274 n. above. For W's interest in metrics, arguments in favour of blank verse, and praise of Milton, see the preface to *Horae Lyricae* (2nd edn., 1709) and *Reliquiae Juveniles* (1734), 309–23.

For 'rhymes', see 'Cowley' 187 and n. above, and for W's inexact rhymes, Davis, *IW*, 184. SJ presumably refers to W's 'unhappy' coinages of names in his essays in *Reliquiae Juveniles*. Boswell later noted SJ's own awkwardness in this respect in *The Rambler* (*Life*, i. 223). For 'ease' in writing, see 'Rochester' 18 and n. above.

Unusually in the *Lives*, SJ allows respect for W's 'purity of character' and 'laborious piety' (31 above) to influence his final literary assessment. He had, however, ended his early 'Life of Boerhaave' in a similar tone: 'May his Example extend its Influence to his Admirers and Followers! May those who study his Writings imitate his Life, and those who endeavour after his knowledge aspire likewise to his Piety!' (*Gent. Mag.* (1739), 176).

Cf. also SJ's discussion in 1756 of W and Elizabeth Singer Rowe (1674–1737), who had married the nephew of W's schoolmaster (see 5 above), and whose *Devout Exercises of the Heart* (1737) W had edited: 'they would both have done honour to a better society, for they had that charity which might well make their failings forgotten, and with which the whole christian world might wish for communion ... This praise the general interest of mankind requires to be given to writers who please and do not corrupt, who instruct and do not weary. But to them all human eulogies are vain whom I believe applauded by angels and numbered with the just' (*Literary Mag.* 1 (1756), 282).

SJ ignores W's *Posthumous Works* (2 vols., 1779), which Boswell drew to his attention in a letter of 20 Sept. 1779 (Boswell Papers). Although W may have written some of this verse in his youth, most of it was probably by his father (Davis (1943), 239–42). The edition was criticized in *Gent. Mag.* (1779), 387–8, and dismissed by Gibbons as inauthentic in 1780, but prompted a lively article on W by Samuel Badcock in *Monthly Review*, 61 (Dec. 1779), 425–32, a few months before SJ wrote his own more sober assessment. In spite of his fertile poetic imagination, W 'wanted a correct judgement to restrain that *hey-day* of the spirit, which too frequently led him astray into the wilds of fanaticism, to play at *bo peep* with the saints ... Like David, he uncovered his nakedness, when he danced before the Ark', etc.

AMBROSE PHILIPS (1674–1749)

Composition. On 23 May 1780 SJ wrote to his friend Richard Farmer, the University Librarian at Cambridge, asking him 'to procure from College or University registers, all the dates or other information which they can supply relating to Ambrose Philips', and other Cambridge poets. Having received no reply, SJ asked Nichols for 'a few dates for A. Philips' on 16 June, when he was presumably close to finishing his account (*Letters*, iii. 257, 278). When writing 'Pope' a few months later, SJ tended to use the spelling 'Phillips', as in *Prefaces* (1781) (e.g. 'Pope' **68, 106**, though not **115**), which was corrected in *Lives* (1781).

Sources. Jacob, i. 203, ii. 139–40, offered only two brief entries for P, who was ignored by both *GD* and *BB*. SJ had therefore to rely on the account in Shiels, *Lives*, v. 122–42, which, though padded out with long quotations, provided most of his information in **1, 3, 5–6, 10, 19–20, 22, 25–30, 33, 35** below. He would have learned little more from later accounts of P in the *New and General Biographical Dictionary* (1762), ix. 317–18, D. E. Baker, *Companion to the Play-House*, vol. i (1764), Nichols, *Supplement to Swift* (1779), iii. 191–2 n., and *Sel. Collection*, iv. 296–7 n., and Reed, *Biographia Dramatica* (1782), i. 352–4. SJ was, however, able to supplement Shiels by use of the Spence MSS in **6, 9**, the *Spectator* in **6–8**, and Pope's *Works* in **4, 21–2**, and gave more substance to his account by including a dissertation on the history of pastoral in **12–17**.

Publication. In *Prefaces*, vol. viii (15 May 1781). Pp. 1–14 and 17–23 (of 23) of the proofs are in the Forster Collection.

Modern Sources:

R. Blanchard (ed.), *Correspondence of Richard Steele* (Oxford, 1941; revised edn., 1968) (eleven letters to P, 1709–19)

W. J. Cameron, 'Ten New Poems by AP', *N & Q* 202 (1957), 469–70

S. F. Fogle, 'Notes on AP', *MLN* 54 (1939), 354–9

R. Halsband, 'A New Letter by Richard Steele and a Pamphlet (Newly Ascribed) by AP', *Scriblerian*, 10 (1977), 1–3

N. Joost, 'The Authorship of the *Free-Thinker*', in R. P. Bond (ed.), *Studies in the Early English Periodical* (Chapel Hill, NC, 1957), 105–34

G. P. Mander, 'AP's English Background', *TLS* (10 Oct. 1942), 504

M. G. Segar (ed.), *Poems of AP*, with a biographical introduction (Oxford, 1937)

M. M. Smith (ed.), *Index of English Literary Manuscripts*, iii (ii) (1989), 341–5

A. Varney, 'P's "Deluded Peasant" and Addison's "Enchanted Hero"', *N & Q* 246 (2001), 403–5

C. Winton, 'Some Manuscripts by and Concerning AP', *ELN* 5 (1967), 99–101

1. Shiels, SJ's main source, gave no information about P's early years. P was in fact born at Shrewsbury, the fourth son of Ambrose Philips, a draper, and Margaret Brookes of Meifod, Montgomeryshire, and baptized on 9 Oct. 1674. (SJ ignores the claim in Shiels, *Lives*, v. 122, and other early accounts that P belonged to an 'ancient' Leicestershire family, as second cousin to Sir Ambrose Philips of Garendon Park, Leics.) He entered St John's College, Cambridge, from Shrewsbury School on 15 June 1693 as a sizar; Scholar, 6 Nov. 1693; BA, 1696; Fellow, 28 Mar. 1699. He may have been ordained deacon while at Cambridge, but did not take the full orders necessary to retain his Fellowship (Segar (ed.), *Poems*, p. xviii).

   P's poem on Queen Mary appeared in *Lacrymae Cantabrigienses* (1695), sigg. Aa4–Bb1ᵛ (see **17** below and, for other verses on this subject, 'Prior' **8** and n. above). It did not appear in P's 1748 collection (see **32** below) or *Eng. Poets* (1779), but SJ may have recalled Pope's mockery of it in 1728 in *Peri Bathous* (*Prose Works*, ii (1986), 193 and n.). W. J. Cameron, 'Ten New Poems', 469–70, noted that four of P's poems appeared anonymously in *Miscellany Poems; with The Cure of Love* (1697), but he is unlikely to have written the whole volume.

2. See **5** below for a publication by P in 1700. By 1703 he was in Utrecht. Although he was no longer resident, his stipend as a Fellow of St John's continued until 1707. He was commissioned in Col. William Breton's regiment of foot on 25 Mar. 1705, served in Spain in 1706–7, and was captured during the Battle at Almanza. He returned to England in Dec. 1707 and by the summer of 1708 was serving in York (Segar (ed.), *Poems*, pp. xix, 87–9).

   For the publication of four of his *Pastorals* in 1708, see **11**, **18** and nn. below.

3. P was secretary to Daniel Pulteney, the Envoy Extraordinary to Denmark, in Jan.–Aug. 1709 and Jan. 1710–Feb. 1711.

   P's well-known 'Winter Piece' ('To the Earl of Dorset. Copenhagen, March 9, 1709'), which appeared in *Tatler* 12 on 7 May 1709, is not in fact addressed to 'the universal patron', Charles Sackville, 6th Earl of Dorset, who had died in 1706 (see 'Dorset' **12–13** and n. and 'Halifax' **5** above and, for SJ's repeated error over his title, 'Dryden' **27** and n. above). P in fact addressed it to Lionel Cranfield Sackville, 7th Earl of Dorset (1688–1765), who became Duke of Dorset in 1721.

Writing to P on 22 Mar. 1709, Swift referred to 'your versifying in a Sledge' (*Corresp.*, i. 128 and cf. 132), and Addison told P, 5 Apr. 1709, that the poem was 'admirable', while urging him to revise its ending (*Letters* (1941), 131–2). Pope wrote on 28 Oct. 1710 that the 'Winter Piece' showed that P 'is capable of writing very nobly', describing it as 'a very Lively Piece of Poetical Painting', and later praised it as 'what the French call very *picturesque*' (*Corresp.*, i. 101, 167–8). Goldsmith in 1767 thought the poem's opening 'incomparably fine. The latter part is tedious and trifling' (*Coll. Works*, v. 321).

4. P and Swift corresponded in 1708–9. Seeking Swift's support for P, Steele told him on 30 Oct. 1709 that P was 'still a Shepheard, and walks very lonely through this unthinking Crowd in London'. Swift himself told P the same day that in Addison, 'You have the best friend in the World'. After the change of government in 1710, Swift still claimed to be recommending 'the Whig Witts' for preferment and occasionally dined with P. On 8 Sept. 1711 he stated that P 'goes constantly' to Harley's 'Levee', and that he himself had recommended P 'as favorably as I could'. By 27 Dec. 1712, however, he noted that Addison and P had become 'terrible dry and cold': 'Philips I should certainly have provided for if he had not run Party-mad and made me withdraw my Recommendation . . . I am worse used by that Faction than any man' (Swift, *Corresp.*, i. 151, 153, 259; *Jnl. to Stella*, i. 129, 297, 304, 360, ii. 589–90).

For Addison's attempts to solicit posts for P between 1710 and 1714, see his *Letters* (1941), 214–15, 249–50, 302, 306, and cf. 'Addison' 115 above. P contributed to the *Spectator* (ed. Bond, i, pp. lxxxi–lxxxii), the *Guardian* (ed. Stephens, 29), and Steele's *Englishman* (Segar (ed.), *Poems*, p. xxxvii; Steele, *Corresp.* (1968), 69 n., 84–5).

P's translation of *The Persian Tales* (1714; 5th edn., 1738) from the French of Pétis de La Croix was soon followed by *The Persian and the Turkish Tales, Compleat* (2 vols., 1714; 6 edns. by 1750), translated by the late Dr William King and others. SJ refers to Pope's mockery of 'The Bard whom pilfer'd Pastorals renown, | Who turns a *Persian* Tale for half a crown' in *Epistle to Arbuthnot*, ll. 179–80 (for an earlier reference, see Pope, *TE*, vi. 173). Both Hill (1905) and *TE*, iv. 339, note that 'half a crown' was 'the prostitute's customary charge', hence perhaps its 'mean sound' for SJ. Pope reported in Nov. 1716 that Bernard Lintot paid his translators 'ten shillings *per* sheet' (*Corresp.*, i. 373). As Hill (1905) also noted, Lord Gower described SJ himself to Swift, 1 Aug. 1739, with some exaggeration, as 'starved to death in translating for booksellers' (*Life*, i. 133).

For Pope's 'inclination to tell a Fairy tale; the more wild & exotic the better', based on 'the Persian Tales', in 1723, see his *Corresp.*, ii. 202; and for the possible influence of *The Persian Tales* on *Rasselas* (1759), see *YW*, xvi, pp. xxxix–xlii.

5. John Hacket's biography of John Williams (1582–1650), Archbishop of York and benefactor of St John's College, appeared as *Scrinia Reserata* (1693), and had been cited by SJ in his notes to Shakespeare (*YW*, vii. 333). P's epitome had in fact appeared in 1700, while he was still at Cambridge. SJ's vagueness about the date reflects that of Shiels, *Lives*, v. 132, who believed that it was published after his *Pastorals*, perhaps confusing it with a new abridgement by the Whig divine William Stephens in 1715.

the principles of his party: Shiels described the work as a vehicle for P's 'own state principles', John Williams having been 'the great opposer of High-Church measures'. With SJ's dismissive remarks on Hacket's 'depravity' ('Corruption; a vitiated state', *Dict.*) of genius, cf. Coleridge's enthusiasm for 'a delightful and instructive book', from which may be obtained a better 'insight into the times preceding the Civil War than from all the ponderous histories and memoirs now composed about that period' (*Table Talk* (1835), ii. 196).

6. *The Distrest Mother: A Tragedy*, adapted from Racine's *Andromaque* (1667), was acted at Drury Lane on 17 Mar. 1712. As earlier accounts misdate it, Reed may have supplied the correct year, as in *Biographia Dramatica* (1782), i. 352–4, ii. 88. His second entry describes it as 'little more than a translation from the *Andromaque* of Racine... yet it never fails bringing tears into the eyes of a sensible audience; and will, perhaps, ever continue to be a stock play on the lists of the theatres'.

Steele wrote the prologue and praised the play (in advance) in *Spectator* 290 (1 Feb. 1712), as did Addison later in nos. 335, 541. For Pope's claim that 'An audience was layed out for the play', see Spence, i. 66. P told Garrick in Dublin in 1742 that he had been 'like a person out of his mind' while writing *The Distrest Mother* (Thomas Davies, *Dramatic Miscellanies* (1784), iii. 267).

7. The fact that Anne Oldfield, who played Andromaque, spoke the humorous epilogue to *The Distrest Mother* helps to explain its success (see 'Savage' **42** and n. above). Replying in *Spectator* 341 (1 Apr. 1712) to objections to the epilogue in no. 338, Eustace Budgell (see **8–9** below) claimed that it 'had received such Honours as were never before given to any in an *English* Theatre'. He later stated in *The Bee* 20 (July 1733) that it had been so popular that Mrs Oldfield spoke it nine times during the first three performances. By then he was having to defend it against charges of indecency. In a discussion of *The Distrest Mother* in *Pamela*, Pt. ii (1742), Richardson's heroine attacked the epilogue for 'lewd, and even senseless *Double Entendre*' (see Shakespeare Head edn., 1929, iv. 76–8). For the youthful SJ's own epilogue to the play, written for 'Some young ladies at Lichfield', see *Life*, i. 55–6, and *Poems* (1974), 34–6.

Although SJ's reference to 'the run, as it is termed, of the play' seems to imply dislike of the expression, he defines 'Run' as '6. Long reception; continued success', illustrated from Addison (*Dict.*). *The Distrest Mother* was acted at Drury Lane on 27 Mar. 1781, shortly before the publication of *Prefaces* (1781).

8. As SJ suggests, *Spectator* 338 may have been published to enable Budgell to reply in no. 341 (see **7** n. above), which mentions Prior's epilogue to Smith's *Phaedra and Hippolitus* (1707): see 'Smith' **46** and n. and 'Prior' **60** above. As *Gent. Mag.* (1781), 272, noted, *Spectator* 338 in fact complained specifically about humorous epilogues to tragedies, not the 'propriety of epilogues in general'. SJ had mentioned in *Idler* 40 (1759) the objection 'by the severer judges, that the salutary sorrow of tragick scenes is too soon effaced by the merriment of the epilogue' (*YW*, ii. 126). For other protests at 'ludicrous' epilogues, see Theophilus Cibber in *Monthly Review*, 10 (1754), 226–9, and Vicesimus Knox, *Essays Moral and Literary* (new edn., 1782), ii. 165–6.

9. SJ describes Eustace Budgell (1686–1737) as 'wretched' because he committed suicide on 4 May 1737. According to Percy in 1787, SJ 'ascertained the Aera of his coming to London, by recollecting that it happen'd within a Day or two of the Catastrophe of Eustace Budgell... who having loaded his Pocket with Stones,

called for a Boat and in the midst of the Thames leap'd over and was drown'd' (Boswell, *Making of the Life*, 207; cf. *Life*, ii. 229, v. 54). *Gent. Mag.* (1737), 315, described Budgell's financial anxieties, and reported that 'The Coroner's Jury brought him in *Lunatick*'. See also Shiels, *Lives*, v. 3–16.

Pope claimed in 1735 that 'Addison used to speak often very slightingly of Budgel: "One that calls me cousin!", "The man stamped himself into my acquaintance", etc.' (Spence, i. 66). Budgell repeatedly stated that he owed 'my principles and part of my education' to Addison, whose mother was the sister of Budgell's grandfather (Smithers, *Life of Addison* (2nd edn., Oxford, 1968), 171 and n.). Addison may have considered Budgell's use of the term 'cousin' provincial; see also 'Addison' **44, 115** above.

In Apr. 1776, SJ said that Somerset Draper, Jacob Tonson's partner, told his wife of Addison's claim to have written the epilogue (*Life*, iii. 46), and Joseph Warton also heard this from the Tonson family through Garrick (*Essay on Pope*, ii (1782), 240 n.). For a more notorious case in which Addison allegedly wrote under another's name, see 'Tickell' **10–11** above. Budgell eventually obtained several 'places' after the Hanoverian accession in 1714. Cf. Pope's mocking 'To Eustace Budgell, Esq.' (*c*.1714) (*TE*, vi. 123).

10. For P's translations from Sappho, quoted in Shiels, *Lives*, v. 140–2, see *Spectators* 223, 229 (1711). Warton, *Essay on Pope* (1756), 290–1, assumed that Addison had 'himself revised, and altered, for his friend Philips' these 'exquisite' fragments.

11. See **2** n. above. Addison had seen two of P's *Pastorals* by 10 Mar. 1704, with a 'little Essay on Pastoral', which had arrived too late for inclusion in Tonson's *Poetical Miscellanies*, vol. v (1704). He also advised P about imitating Spenser (*Letters* (Oxford, 1941), 48–9). Four of the *Pastorals* appeared in Elijah Fenton's *Oxford and Cambridge Miscellany Poems* [1708], 41–69, and all six in Tonson's *Poetical Miscellanies*, vi (1709), 1–48. For their reception and the subsequent rivalry with Pope, see **18–20** and nn. below.

12–16. SJ here elaborates his earlier historical account of pastoral in *Rambler* 37 (1750). The poets discussed are relatively conventional in such surveys: Fontenelle had mentioned all except Petrarch in his *Discours sur la nature de l'eglogue* (1688), translated by Peter Motteux as 'Of Pastorals' and appended to *Monsieur Bossu's Treatise of the Epick Poem* (1695), 277–95.

12. For SJ's own preference of Virgil's pastorals to those of Theocritus, see *Adventurer* 92 (1753) (*YW*, ii. 418). He later described the 'manners' in Theocritus' poems as 'coarse and gross' (*Life*, iv. 2).

SJ referred to Titus Calpurnius Siculus (fl. AD 50 to 60?) as 'an obscure author of the lower ages' in *Adventurer* 92 (*YW*, ii. 418): in early MSS his pastorals accompanied four attributed to M. Aurelius Olympius Nemesianus, a Latin poet of the 3rd century AD. They were printed at Rome in 1471.

13. For SJ's views on modern pastoral elsewhere, see 'Cowley' **7** and n. above. In his survey here he suppresses his usual contempt.

14. Petrarch's *Bucolicum Carmen* (written 1346–61) appeared at Cologne in 1473.

SJ defines 'Eclogue' as 'A pastoral poem, so called because *Virgil* called his pastorals eclogues'. He also explained that '*Æglogue*' was 'written instead of *eclogue*, from a mistaken etymology', defining it as 'A pastoral, a dialogue in verse between goatherds' (*Dict.*). 'Eclogue' had often been taken to mean 'Goteheards tales' (as in Spenser, *Shepheardes Calender*, 1579), but originally meant only a poem selected from a larger collection of works, without pastoral connotations, as Tickell noted in *Guardian* 28 (1713): see **19** n. below. SJ mentioned Alexander Barclay's 'Certain Eglogues' (1570) in a letter to Thomas Warton, 21 Dec. 1754 (*Letters*, i. 89–90).

15. SJ refers to Baptista Spagnuoli Mantuanus, *Bucolica* (Mantua, 1498); Jodocus Badius Ascensius, who published his commentary in 1503; J. C. Scaliger, *Poetices* (1561), 361; and Spenser, *Shepheardes Calender* (1579). There were many 17th-century English editions of Mantuan, and translators included George Turbeville (1567) and Thomas Harvey (1656).

SJ complained in *Rambler* 37 (1750) that it was 'improper to give the title of a pastoral to verses, in which the speakers, after the slight mention of their flocks, fall to complaints of errors in the church, and corruptions in the government' (*YW*, iii. 204–5). See also his objections to 'Lycidas' in 'Milton' **183** above.

16. SJ stated in *Rambler* 121 (1751) that 'there has prevailed in every age a particular species of fiction', and that 'at one period, all the poets followed sheep, and every event produced a pastoral' (*YW*, iv. 284).

He refers to Giacomo Sannazaro, *Arcadia* (1504), Torquato Tasso, *Aminta* (1573), and Giovanni Battista Guarini, *Il pastor fido* (1583), all discussed by Tickell in *Guardian* 28. For Sannazaro, see also 'Cowley' **121** n. above, and *Rambler* 36 (1750); and for Tasso and Guarini, 'Roscommon' **36**, 'Waller' **153**, and 'Gay' **32** above.

Tasso had described *Aminta* as 'Favola boschereccia': for the printer's (or SJ's) problems with the second word, see Textual Notes.

17. For P's preface on the neglect of pastoral, see Segar (ed.), *Poems*, 3; and for the Cambridge verses on Queen Mary (1695), see **1** and n. above.

18. As SJ notes in 'Pope' **33** above (written later), P's complete set of pastorals opened, and Pope's set of four concluded, Tonson's *Poetical Miscellanies*, vi (1709).

SJ's brief contrast of the 'elegant' and the 'natural' reflects the arguments either for idealization or for greater naturalism in pastoral advanced in France by Rapin and Fontenelle: see J. E. Congleton, *Theories of Pastoral Poetry in England 1684–1798* (Gainesville, Fla., 1952). For Pope's view, see his 'Discourse on Pastoral Poetry' (1717) and 'Pope' **24** above; and for Gay's *The Shepherd's Week* (1714) as a by-product of Pope's quarrel with P, see 'Gay' **4–5** and nn. above.

19. P's *Pastorals* were briefly praised in *Tatler* 12 (1709), and in *Spectators* 223 (1711), 400, 523 (1712), where he was said to have given 'a new Life, and a more natural Beauty to this way of Writing'. In 1735 Pope claimed to have heard Addison speak disparagingly of P (Spence, i. 68).

Thomas Tickell wrote the essays on pastoral in *Guardians* 22–3, 28, 30, 32 (1713), which SJ assumed in 'Gay' **4** above were by Steele. John Duncombe attributed them correctly in *Gent. Mag.* (1780), 176. In *Guardian* 30, Tickell quoted P's *Pastorals* at some length, and praised his 'Pastoral Stile according to the *Doric* of *Theocritus*'. He also quoted Pope's 'January and May', but not his *Pastorals*. For his decisive final praise of P in *Guardian* 32, see **35** n. below.

20. *inauguration*: 'Investiture by solemn rites' (*Dict.*).

Pope discussed P's *Pastorals* in a letter of 28 Oct. 1710, admitting that, 'In the whole, I agree with the Tatler, that we have no better Eclogs in our Language' (*Corresp.*, i. 101). For his anonymous *Guardian* 40 (1713), which purported to demonstrate the superiority of P's *Pastorals* to his own, see 'Pope' 68 and n. above. As Henry Layng recalled in 1726, Pope 'either commends Philips in such points as Mr. Pope exceeds him in evidently, or else commends him falsely... Addison and that party then had a great desire of running Pope down' (Spence, i. 63). It is unclear whether Pope's hoax deceived Steele. SJ follows Warburton, *Works of Pope* (1757 edn.), vii. 203 n., but see also Spence, i. 63–4, 172, and Steele, *Corresp.* (1968), 69 n. Knowing the essay was by Pope, Steele may not have read it carefully enough to notice the irony. Warton, *Essay on Pope*, ii (1782), 240 n., attributed P's 'secret malignity' to Pope to the mockery he received from the Hanover Club, of which he was secretary (see 22 below), for taking Pope's ironic praise at face value.

For Pope's early ridicule of P, see 'The Three Gentle Shepherds' (*c.*1713) ('Of *gentle Philips* will I ever sing, | With *gentle Philips* shall the Vallies ring', etc.) and 'Macer' (*c.*1715) (*TE*, vi. 112, 137–8). There are many dismissive references to P in Pope's letters and verse: see e.g. *Epistle to Dr. Arbuthnot*, ll. 181–2, and 30 n. below. Many years later, Edward Young pointed out that Pope had borrowed a line from P's 'Epistle to Lord Halifax', l. 36, in his *Iliad* (Spence, i. 83).

21. SJ may follow Ruffhead, *Life of Pope* (1769), 186, who wrote that Addison 'encouraged Phillips, and others, in their clamours against [Pope] as a Tory and Jacobite', but Pope himself stated in *Dunciad* (1729), III. 322 n., that P's 'constant cry was, that Mr. *P[ope]* was an Enemy to the government'. On 8 June 1714 he had reported P's claim at Button's that Pope 'was entered into a Cabal with Dean Swift and others to write against the *Whig-Interest*', by lowering the reputations of Addison, Steele, and P himself. Pope added that P 'never open'd his lips to my face, on this or any like occasion, tho' I was almost every night in the same room with him, nor ever offer'd me any indecorum' (*Corresp.*, i. 229).

22. For Button's Coffee House, the meeting-place of the Whig wits, see 'Addison' 116 and n. above. Broome mentioned the 'rod at Button's... which scared away the little bard' to Fenton, 3 May 1728 (Pope, *Corresp.*, ii. 489). The story reached print in *Pope Alexander's Supremacy... Examined* (1729), 16: for later versions, as in Cibber's *A Letter... to Mr. Pope* (1742), 65, see J. V. Guerinot, *Pamphlet Attacks on Pope* (1969), 169, 247, 257, 294.

Pope in fact called P a 'scoundrel' rather than a 'rascal', when accusing him of withholding subscriptions from the Hanover Club to his *Iliad*, in his letter of 8 June 1714 (see 21 n. above).

23. The money eventually reached Pope through an intermediary (*Corresp.*, i. 296).

24. *injudicious kindness*: SJ told Mrs Thrale in Sept. 1778 that 'you often *provoke* me to say severe things, by unseasonable commendation', and on 1 Apr. 1781 that 'whenever there is exaggerated praise, every body is set against a character' (Fanny Burney, *Early Journals*, iii. 165; *Life*, iv. 82, and cf. iii. 225).

Although it is often assumed that Pope's *Guardian* hoax punctured the reputation of P's *Pastorals*, Shiels, *Lives*, v. 133, quoted Gildon's comparison of P to Theocritus and Virgil in *The Complete Art of Poetry* (1718), ii. 153–61, and Jacob stated in 1719 that P 'has equall'd his Contemporaries both *French* and *English*, and gain'd a great Reputation' in pastoral (i. 203, and cf. ii. 140).

25. For poets whose fortunes prospered after the Hanoverian accession, see 'Garth' 13, 'Rowe' 21, and 'Addison' 81 above.

P was in fact briefly tutor to George I's grandchildren (1714), Paymaster of the Lottery and Justice of the Peace for Westminster (1715), and Agent for New York to the Commissioners of Trade and Plantations (1717–19) (Segar (ed.), *Poems*, p. xl; Fogle, 'Notes', 354–9). Steele wrote on 24 Sept. 1716 to P in his capacity as a Justice (*Corresp.* (2nd edn., Oxford, 1968), 116).

P celebrated the arrival of George I in his *Epistle* (1714) to Lord Halifax, and later addressed in verse such potential patrons as James Craggs, William Pulteney, Robert Walpole, and Lord Carteret. In the *London Gazette* of 8 Jan. 1715 he invited contributions to a *Collection of Original Poems and Translations* to be published by Tonson. Although Pope mentioned it to Broome, 10 Feb. 1715 (*Corresp.*, i. 276 and n.), no more was heard of this miscellany. For P's projected *Dictionary*, see 'Addison' 91 n. above.

26. *The Briton: A Tragedy* was in fact acted at Drury Lane on 19 Feb. 1722, and had eight performances.

Shiels, *Lives*, v. 135, who may have led SJ to misdate the play, had praised the scene (III. viii) between Vanoc ('*British* Liberty') and Valens (Roman 'Humanity' and 'Knowledge'). SJ does not normally use the phrase 'truly poetical' lightly.

27. *Humfrey, Duke of Gloucester: A Tragedy*, an adaptation of Shakespeare's *2 Henry VI*, was in fact acted at Drury Lane on 15 Feb. 1723. Shiels, *Lives*, v. 137, had again misdated it. As an undergraduate SJ owned 'Phillips's Tragedies' (*Gleanings*, v. 226), presumably a copy of P's *Three Tragedies* (1725).

28. *The Free-Thinker: Or, Essays on Ignorance, Superstition, Bigotry, Enthusiasm, Craft, &c.*, dedicated in its collected editions to 'The Ladies of Great Britain', appeared in 350 numbers, 24 Mar. 1718–28 July 1721. Dr Hugh Boulter (1672–1742) became Bishop of Bristol in 1719 and Archbishop of Armagh in 1724: see 'Swift' 81 and n. above. (SJ's schoolfellow Charles Congreve became his chaplain: Nichols, *Lit. Ill.*, vi. 311.) For other contributors to *The Free-Thinker*, see Joost, 'Authorship', 105–34. Leonard Welsted praised P's prose for its 'liberty of style' in his *Epistles, Odes, &c.* (2nd edn., 1725), p. xli. P had earlier contributed to a periodical called *The Grumbler* (24 Feb.–15 July 1715).

29. SJ defines 'Freethinker' as 'A libertine; a contemner of religion' (*Dict.*). The first number of *The Free-Thinker*, which reflected Whig principles, admitted that its title might cause it to be 'thrown aside with Indignation by several well-meaning Persons', but explained that 'To think Freely . . . is not to think without the Checks of Reason and Judgment; but without the Incumbrances of Prejudice and Passion'. It was originally more popular than SJ suggests: nos. 1–159 were reprinted in 3 vols. in 1722, 1733, and 1739.

For 'impartial criticism', see 'Milton' 242 above.

30. *diurnal*: '3. Performed in a day; daily; quotidian' (*Dict.*).

P accompanied Boulter to Ireland on his elevation to Armagh in 1724. According to the 'Advertisement' to Boulter's *Letters* (2 vols., Oxford, 1769–70), i, p. vii, they 'were collected by the late *Ambrose Philips*, Esq; who was secretary to his Grace and lived in his house during that space of time in which they bear date [1724–38]'. Through Boulter's influence, P became MP for Armagh in the Irish Parliament from 1727 to his death.

Swift told Pope, 29 Sept. 1725, that he had not yet met P in Dublin, 'tho' formerly we were so intimate', and that P had so far 'got nothing, and by what I can find will get nothing'. On 26 Nov. he reported that P was wondering whether 'to turn Parson', rather than remain 'a domestick humble Retainer to an Irish Prelate. He is neither Secretary nor Gentleman usher yet serves in both Capacities' (*Corresp.*, iii. 104, 117). Pope commented on 15 Oct. 1725 that a line he later used in *Dunciad*, III. 326 ('Lo! Ambrose Philips is prefer'd for Wit!') would be spoiled if P were not promoted (*Corresp.*, ii. 332). Cf. *Epistle to Arbuthnot*, ll. 99–100: 'Does not one table Bavius still admit? | Still to one Bishop Philips seem a wit?'

31. Nichols or Reed may have prompted the insertion of this paragraph, which is not in the proofs.

In 1726 P became 'Purse-Bearer' to Thomas Wyndham (1681–1745), the new Lord Chancellor of Ireland, a remunerative post requiring attendance on court and state occasions. He was appointed Registrar of the Court of Faculties and Registrar of the Prerogative Court on 23 Oct. 1734 (*Gent. Mag.* (1734), 512; Segar (ed.), *Poems*, pp. xlvii–1).

32. Archbishop Boulter died on 28 Sept. 1742. For SJ's correction of Samuel Madden's *Boulter's Monument. A Panegyrical Poem, Sacred to the Memory of that Great and Excellent Prelate and Patriot* (1745), see 'Addison' **134** and n. above and *Bibliography*, i. 127–30. P's 'dreaded antagonist' had died in May 1744 (see 'Pope' **248** above).

P dedicated *Pastorals, Epistles, Odes and Other Original Poems* to Thomas Pelham-Holles, Duke of Newcastle (1693–1768). Published by Tonson in May 1748, the volume was edited by Thomas Cooke (*Gent. Mag.* (1781), 318; Nichols, *Sel. Collection*, viii. 298).

33. For defeated hopes of 'plenty and tranquillity', see 'Denham' **19** and n. above.

Shiels, *Lives*, v. 142, mentioned the annuity but misdated P's death 1748. SJ added his own inaccurate date in proof (see Textual Notes): Nichols or Reed may have pointed it out in *Gent. Mag.* (1749), 284, where P is described as 'the last survivor of the excellent authors of the spectators, tatlers, and guardians'. He was in fact buried on 4 June 1749, having died on 1 or 2 June, aged 74 (Segar (ed.), *Poems*, pp. li–lii). SJ quotes a medical explanation of 'Palsy' in the *Dict.*, giving its Latin etymology as 'Paralysis': see also 'West' **10** below.

Hill (1905) noted Hawkins's story (*Life* (1787), 429) that P was accused of purchasing by a deception an estate from the Duke of Buckingham. If true, this must have happened much earlier, since the Duke died in 1721 (see 'Sheffield' **19** above).

34. SJ added his comment on P's 'solemn and pompous' conversation in proof (see Textual Notes), perhaps prompted by Nichols, who later stated (as 'Eugenio'): 'this observation a friend of mine read some time ago in a MS of Dr. Jortin's' (*Gent. Mag.* (July 1781), 318). For Young's anecdote in 1757 about P's vanity in conversation with Swift and Congreve, including P's description of himself as 'of a lean make, pale complexion, extremely neat in his dress, and five feet seven inches tall', see Spence, i. 340–1. He may have been the pompous tragedian described by Pope to Caryll, 19 Nov. 1712 (*Corresp.*, i. 156). For SJ's interest in poets' conversational powers, see 'Cowley' **200** and n. above.

William Inge (1669–1731) of Thorpe Constantine, 9 miles east of Lichfield, married P's cousin Elizabeth Philips. Hearne described him in 1732 as 'a curious Gentleman in the Saxon Tongue and in our Antiquities'. SJ must have heard this story early in life, since Inge died in 1731. His son Theodore William Inge was SJ's contemporary at Oxford (*Gleanings*, v. 71–2). On 9 Nov. 1777 SJ noted in his diary the address of Theodore Inge's widow Henrietta (*YW*, i. 284), and mentioned her again, referring to this passage, to Mrs Thrale, 13 Aug. 1783, as 'a Baronet's Daughter, of an ancient house in Staffordshire' (*Letters*, iv. 185).

As Hill (1905) noted, Orestes, and not King Pyrrhus, is 'goaded on by love' in *The Distrest Mother*, I. i. The joke puzzled some readers. Lord Hailes enquired in 1782: 'Q. what is ye point of Mr Ing's story?': see Carnie (1956), 486. Hill (1905) also commented: 'There is nothing in the play as printed about driving oxen.' Inge obviously associated 'goading' with oxen and thus an inappropriate image for a tragic lover. SJ himself defines 'Goad': 'A pointed instrument with which oxen are driven forward' (*Dict.*).

35. For Racine as the source of *The Distrest Mother*, see 6 and n. above. Pope called it P's 'borrow'd play' in 'Macer', l. 8 (see 24 n. above). For the 'Letter from Denmark', see 3 above.

Tickell wrote in *Guardian* 32 (1713) that '*Theocritus* . . . left his Dominions to *Virgil*, *Virgil* left his to his son *Spencer*, and *Spencer* was succeeded by his eldest-born *Philips*' (see 19 above). Shiels, *Lives*, v. 133, concluded that, for all Pope's ridicule, P 'was no mean Arcadian: By endeavouring to imitate too servilely the manners and sentiments of vulgar rustics, he has sometimes raised a laugh against him; yet there are in some of his Pastorals a natural simplicity, a true Doric dialect, and very graphical descriptions.' By 1764, however, one critic considered P's pastorals 'beneath criticism' (*Anecdotes of Polite Literature* (5 vols., 1764), ii. 16).

For 'comprehension', see 'Cowley' 144 and n. above. Although P had used the same metre in a poem to Walpole in 1724, shortly before going to Ireland (Segar (ed.), *Poems*, 124–6), his best-known and often engaging 'poems of short lines' were about children, such as 'To Miss Charlotte Pulteney, in her Mother's Arms' and 'To Miss Margaret Pulteney . . . in the Nursery'. Henry Carey influentially parodied them in *Namby Pamby; or, A Panegyrick on the New Versification* (Dublin, 1725): see Segar (ed.), *Poems*, 107, 110–12, 122–3, 126–9. Swift told Pope, 8 July 1726: 'There is not so despised a Creature here as your Friend with the soft Verses on children' (*Corresp.*, iii. 140). Pope himself referred to P's 'infantine style' in *Peri Bathous* (1728), ch. XI, and *Dunciad* (1729), III. 322 and n., and cf. *TE*, vi. 173. Isaac Hawkins Browne also mocked P in his popular *A Pipe of Tobacco: In Imitation of Six Several Authors* (1736).

With SJ's final sentence, cf. *Rambler* 166 (1751): 'the same actions performed by different hands produce different effects, and instead of rating the man by his performances, we rate too frequently the performance by the man' (*YW*, v. 118). For the 'condescensions of learning', see 'Watts' 22 and n. above.

36. For P's translations of Pindar's *Olympic Odes*, one of which had appeared in *The Free-Thinker* 339 (1721), see Segar (ed.), *Poems*, 140–55. For SJ's usual dislike of Pindarics, see 'Cowley' 143 and n. above, and for a translator of Pindar he commends, see 'West' 11–12 below.

mentioned W and described himself as 'while I am alive, warmly His' (Pope, *Corresp.*, iii. 244, 480, iv. 354, 368, 451). In his will he left W £5 for a funeral ring, and a further £200 after the death of Martha Blount (who in fact survived W): see Pope, *Prose Works*, ed. R. Cowler, ii (1986), 507–8. For W's friendship with Elizabeth Montagu (1720–1800) in the 1740s and 1750s, see S. H. Myers, *The Bluestocking Circle* (Oxford, 1990), 179–81.

W was planning to translate Pindar by 1736, when Pope advised him to be selective: 'His Dithyrambics, which were his best things, are lost, and all that is left of his works, being on the same subject, is the more apt to be tiresome. This is what induced me to desire Mr. West not to translate the whole, but only to choose out some of them' (Spence, i. 225). His *Odes of Pindar, With several other Pieces in Prose and Verse* appeared in 1749 (see **11–12** below). Walpole described them, 18 May 1749, as 'very stiff' and thought his dedication to Pitt and Lyttelton 'most affected', but found the elaborate 'Dissertation on the Olympick Games' (pp. i–ccvi) 'very entertaining' (*Corresp.*, ix. 84). Joseph Warton published *An Ode Occasion'd by Reading Mr. West's Translation of Pindar* in July 1749. The 'late Collection', which 'improperly omitted' W's prefatory material, was *Eng. Poets* (1779), and SJ's comment was, as usual, directed at Nichols (cf. **10**, **15** nn. below).

For approving comments among the Dissenters on W's *Observations on the Resurrection* (1747 for Dec. 1746), see the *Corresp.* (1979) of Philip Doddridge. In one of his seven letters to Doddridge in 1748–51, W stated that he had been glad to 'contribute, tho' in ever so small a degree, to the glorious enterprise of promoting catholick Christianity' (277).

For W's doctorate at Oxford, see *Gent. Mag.* (1748), 188, and for the late insertion of this information, which is not in the proofs, see Textual Notes. In Dec. 1748 W talked to Joseph Spence about his recent *Observations* and the forthcoming Pindar translation, adding that Oxford had also wished to bestow a doctorate on George Lyttelton (see **6** below), who, 'as his name was not to his piece, excused himself. West had not the same excuse, so they sent him his diploma for it, signed 31 March 1748' (Spence, i. 372–3).

In 1783 SJ enlarged the account of W's routine of family prayers from the MSS of John Jones (see headnote and Textual Notes). SJ may have expected the reader to recall his earlier comments on Milton's neglect of family prayers in 'Milton' **166** above. For a note by SJ in Aug. 1777 about family prayers in Gilbert Walmesley's household, see *YW*, i. 272.

SJ alludes finally to Cowley, 'On the Death of Mr. Crashaw', ll. 1–2: '*Poet* and *Saint*! to thee alone are given | The two most sacred *Names* of *Earth* and *Heaven*' (cf. 'Cowley' **114** and n. above).

6. W's cousin George Lyttelton, politician and poet, and William Pitt (1708–78), later Earl of Chatham, belonged to the group of young politicians known as 'Cobham's cubs' or the 'Boy Patriots': see Wiggin, *Faction*, and Gerrard, *Patriot Opposition*, 36. W elaborately inscribed his *Odes of Pindar* (1749) to Lyttelton and Pitt.

For Lyttelton's *Observations on the Conversion and Apostleship of St. Paul* (1747), addressed to W, see 'Lyttelton' **12** below. His 'Irregular Ode writ at Wickham, in 1746' appeared in Dodsley's *Collection of Poems*, ii (2nd edn., 1748), 67–8.

7. This paragraph, added in 1783, derives from the MSS of John Jones (see headnote).

The 'blandishments of infidelity' were Lord Cobham's: cf. 'Lyttelton' **12**, **27** and nn. below, and the account of W in the *Annual Register for 1782*, ii. 55–8. One of Doddridge's correspondents, in a letter of 3 Feb. 1747, described the author of *Observations on the Resurrection* as 'a converted deist' (Doddridge, *Corresp.*, 247). Thomas Birch told Lord Orrery, 7 Feb. 1747, that Cobham was 'unhappily prejudiced against the subject' of W's *Observations*, and was angry that a layman had written on it. Bishop Berkeley later praised W's book to Orrery, 11 July 1747, commenting that 'men of the world, courtiers and fine gentlemen, are more easily wrought on by those of their own sort, than by recluse and professed divines' (*Orrery Papers* (1903), i. 309, ii. 4).

a methodist: '2. One of a new kind of puritans lately arisen, so called from their profession to live by rules and in constant method' (*Dict.*). Mrs Thrale told SJ in 1780 that Methodism is 'considered always a term of reproach, I trust, because I never yet did hear that any one person called himself a Methodist' (*Life*, i. 459 n.).

8. Frederick, Prince of Wales, had promised to appoint W tutor to Prince George (the future George III), but in 1743 reluctantly granted him a pension of £100 instead. Like Thomson and Mallet, W had lost the pension by 1748, when the political interests of Lyttelton and the Prince diverged. Lyttelton was by then seeking preferment for W from the Pelham government (Davis, *Lyttelton*, 62; Thomson, *Letters*, 194, 196, 199–200; Gerrard, *Patriot Opposition*, 64).

9. W at last became a Clerk of the Privy Council at £100 p.a. in Apr. 1752 (*Gent. Mag.* (1752), 193); see **4** above. Probably through Pitt's influence, he became Treasurer or Paymaster of Chelsea Hospital on 16 Apr. 1754 (*Gent. Mag.* (1754), 292, where he is mistakenly named 'John').

(1752): not in the proofs: see Textual Notes.

10. For other cases of disappointed expectations, see 'Denham' **19** and n. above.

W's only son Richard died on 1 Jan. 1755 aged 19. (His death is not mentioned in the proofs: see Textual Notes.) W himself died on 26 Mar. 1756: see *Gent. Mag.* (1755), 42, and (1756), 150. For 'palsy', see 'A. Philips' **33** and n. above. W had earlier suffered from gout, finding consolation 'during the paroxysms of the disease' in repeating Scripture, according to William Seward in *European Mag.* 34 (1798), 305.

In *Prefaces* (1781) **10** was followed by a long paragraph, later omitted, in which SJ criticized the arrangement (by Nichols) of W's poems in *Eng. Poets* (1779), from which his *Institution of the Order of the Garter* (1742) had been 'improperly omitted' (see Textual Notes and **13** n. below). By now SJ was clearly distancing himself from what were already known as 'Johnson's *Poets*': 'His poems are in this Collection neither selected nor arranged as I should have directed, had either the choice or the order fallen under my care or notice.' Cf. **5** above and 'Somervile' **5** n. above. W's poems were not reordered in *Eng. Poets* (1790).

11. For SJ's views on translation elsewhere, see 'Denham' **32** and n. above; for 'paraphrastical' translators, see 'Addison' **156** and n. above; and for 'exuberant' language, see 'Thomson' **50** and n. above. SJ takes W, as he had Rowe, Fenton, Broome, and Pitt earlier, more seriously as a translator than as an original poet. His implication here is that a modern poet is better employed in translating Pindar faithfully than in misusing his odes as precedents for irregularity and obscurity,

according to the 'Pindarick infatuation' ('Prior' **77**) perversely revived by Gray and others (see 'Gray' **14, 32–48** below).

SJ quotes W's *Odes of Pindar* (1749), 6, 11–12.

12. For an objection by SJ to a 'faulty' passage in W's translation, reported by Bennet Langton, see *Life*, iv. 28.

13. *The Institution of the Order of the Garter, A Dramatick Poem* (1742), though reprinted in Dodsley, *Collection of Poems*, ii (1748), 89–154, was omitted from *Eng. Poets* (1779). For SJ's complaint in *Prefaces* (1781) about its omission, see **10** n. above and Textual Notes.

For the 'Patriot' political context and implications of W's masque-like poem, which is set in the 14th century and introduces bards, druids, and Arthurian knights, see Gerrard, *Patriot Opposition*, (1994), 224–9. Warton had praised the final 'Chorus of Bards' in his *Essay on Pope* (1756), 69. Garrick later adapted it as *The Institution of the Garter; or, Arthur's Round Table Restored*, a masque with music by Charles Dibdin, performed at Drury Lane on 28 Oct. 1771 (see Garrick, *Letters*, ed. D. M. Little and G. M. Kahrl (1963), ii. 756, 759, 763–4).

Robert Southey had the *Institution* in mind when claiming that W 'began a school half Greek, half Gothick, which was followed by Mason, Gray and Warton, and is to be traced in Akenside and Collins' (*Specimens of the Later English Poets* (1807), i, p. xxxii, and cf. ii. 241). Recalling the fashionable verse of his youth, Coleridge later referred to the 'chaste and manly diction' of W's poems, 'but they were cold, and, if I may so express it, only *dead-coloured*' (*Biographia Literaria*, ed. J. Engell and W. J. Bate (Princeton, 1983), i. 24).

14. *two amusements together*: cf. the similar comment on the double pleasure afforded by an 'imitation' in 'Shenstone' **32** below. Writing only a few weeks later, SJ here emphasizes the 'local and temporary' nature of this pleasure.

W's *A Canto of the Faery Queen. Written by Spenser. Never before Published* (1739) was revised as 'On the Abuse of Travelling' in Dodsley, *Collection of Poems*, ii (1748), 63–88. In Florence on 16 July 1740, Gray described it as an 'imitation of Spencer ... with which we are all enraptured and enmarvailed' (*Corresp.*, i. 170). For the use of Spenser by 'opposition' poets and the *Canto*'s political implications, see Gerrard, *Patriot Opposition*, 177–80. W's later *Education. A Poem* (1751) was reprinted in Dodsley, *Collection of Poems*, iv (1755), 9–49.

SJ may have had W's poems in mind in *Rambler* 121 (1751), when discussing 'the imitation of Spenser, which, by the influence of some men of learning and genius, seems likely to gain upon the age'. He disliked pseudo-Spenserian diction and stanzaic forms: 'life is surely given us for higher purposes than to gather what our ancestors have wisely thrown away, and to learn what is of no value, but because it has been forgotten' (*YW*, iv. 285–6). Dodsley's *Collection* (1748) had, however, also included Spenserian imitations by Shenstone, Ridley, Bedingfield, Lowth, and Mason, and similar recent poems included William Thompson's *Sickness* (1745–6), John Upton's *A New Canto of Spencer's Fairy Queen* (1747), James Thomson's *The Castle of Indolence* (1748), Robert Lloyd's *The Progress of Envy* (1751), and Moses Mendez's *The Seasons* (1751). In *The Minstrel*, i (1771), vii, Beattie later attributed the appeal of the Spenserian stanza's 'Gothic structure' to its blend of the 'diversified cadence and complicated modulation of blank verse' with the sententiousness of the couplet.

Given his attitude to blank verse, it is as well that SJ seems not to have encountered the anonymous *Spencer's Fairy-Queen Attempted in Blank Verse. Canto I* (1774), even if it was meant to appeal to those who dislike 'uncouth plainness and obsolete stile'. In 1781 he politely subscribed to Gloster Ridley's Spenserian *Melampus*, edited by George Steevens for the benefit of the poet's widow. For other Spenserian imitators, see 'Prior' **59, 75–6** and 'Thomson' **36** above, and 'Shenstone' **32** below; and for literary 'imitation' generally, see 'Pope' **372** and n. above.

An Imitation of Spenser . . . never been perused: an insertion in the proofs (see Textual Notes). With SJ's appeal to the experience of a 'common reader' who is ignorant of Spenser, cf. Steele's invocation of the 'learned Reader' in *Guardian* 12 (1713): 'over and above a just Painting of Nature, a learned Reader will find a new Beauty superadded in a happy Imitation of some famous Ancient, as it revives in his Mind the Pleasure he took in his first reading such an Author.'

The spelling 'atchievements' (in SJ's second sentence) is not in the *Dict*. For the fate of the 'merely pretty' (final sentence), see also 'Waller' **109** above.

15. After a version of the first sentence, SJ appended in *Prefaces* (1781) an 'Elegy, Occasioned by Shooting a Blackbird on Valentine's Day', which had been 'left out by the compilers' of *Eng. Poets* (1779): see Textual Notes. This further criticism of 'the compilers' (cf. **5, 10** n. above) can hardly have pleased Nichols.

Although Hawkesworth (see 'Swift' **1** and n. above) had implicitly ascribed this poem to W in *Adventurer* 37 (1753), its author was correctly identified as Richard Jago (1715–81) in Dodsley's *Collection*, iv (1755), 322–5. Shenstone also referred to the poem as Jago's in his posthumous *Works*, vol. iii (1769): see his *Letters* (Oxford, 1939), 122, 402. Although *Gent. Mag.* (1781), 276, corrected SJ's misattribution of the 'Elegy', his reluctance to admit his error when rephrasing this paragraph in 1783 prompted John Scott Hylton to emphasize the correct attribution once again in Jago's posthumous *Poems, Moral and Descriptive* (1784), pp. xvii–xx, as *Gent. Mag.* (1784), 842, noted.

WILLIAM COLLINS (1721–59)

Composition. 'Collins' is one of the recently completed lives listed in SJ's letter to Mrs Thrale of 9 May 1780. His note to Nichols about Joseph Warton's attribution of the poem discussed in **2** and n. below is accordingly dated *c*. Apr. 1780 (*Letters*, iii. 254 and 227). SJ may have moved ahead in the sequence of *Eng. Poets* he was roughly following at this time (C appeared in vol. xlix of the 56 vols.) because he had decided to reprint his earlier account of C (see 'Sources' and **8–12** below), and had already received useful information from Joseph Warton (cf. headnote to 'Pitt' above).

Mrs Thrale had read 'Collins' in a pre-publication volume by Aug. 1780, when SJ asked her why she had not liked it as much as 'Akenside' (*Letters*, iii. 301). SJ's reservations about C's admired lyric poetry (see **7–8, 17** below) no doubt explain her reaction. As 'Philo-Lyristes' complained in the *Gent. Mag.* (Jan. 1782), 22: 'I own that I felt myself hurt by the liberties which he has taken with two of our most celebrated Lyric Poets, viz. *Gray* and *Collins* . . . let Dr. Johnson, with all his erudition, produce me another Lyric ode equal to Collins on the Passions: indeed the frequent public recitals of this last-mentioned poem are a mark of its universally-acknowledged excellence.' SJ had in fact ignored this popular poem. Robert Potter, *Inquiry* (1783), 15, acknowledged SJ's personal tenderness towards C, but also disapproved of the 'coldness' of his criticism of 'genius truly sublime'.

Sources. C appeared in none of SJ's standard sources and there was only sparse information about him elsewhere. One obvious source, however, was 'Some Account of the Life and Writings of Mr. William Collins' by C's contemporary at Winchester and Oxford, James Hampton (1721–78) (see 'Milton' **10** and n. above), in Francis Fawkes's and William Woty's *The Poetical Calendar*, xii (Dec. 1763), 107–9, precisely because it was followed there by SJ's own reminiscences of C, attributed to 'a gentleman, deservedly eminent in the republic of letters, who knew him intimately well' (xii. 110–12). Both these accounts were reprinted in *Gent. Mag.* (Jan. 1764), 33–4.

Yet in **1–5** below SJ does not use all the detail in Hampton's brief 'Account' (e.g. dates for C's year of birth, admission at Winchester, and at Magdalen College) and he may in fact not have looked closely at it, relying instead on similar information from a source such as Joseph Warton. As R. Wendorf, 'The Making of J's "Life of C"', *PBSA* 74 (1980), 95–115, pointed out, the textual evidence indicates that, when he reprinted his own account of C in **8–12** below, SJ did not in fact return to *The Poetical Calendar*, which would have reminded him of Hampton's narrative, but relied instead on the unauthorized reprint in Thomas Davies's *Miscellaneous and Fugitive Pieces*, ii (1773), 237–9 (see Textual Notes). Only at a late stage, apparently, did SJ, or more probably Nichols, consult *The Poetical Calendar*: see **11, 18** and nn. below. There is no sign that SJ made any use of the 'Memoirs' in John Langhorne's influential edition of C's *Poetical Works* (1765), pp. i–xv, which derived mostly from *The Poetical Calendar* (but see **4** n. below).

SJ obviously consulted Joseph Warton, a lifelong friend of C (see **1, 2, 14** and nn. below), who had at times been identified as the author of both the accounts of C in *The Poetical Calendar*: see Wendorf, 'Making', 97–8. SJ overlooked, however, a note about C in Thomas Warton's *History of English Poetry*, ii (1778), 361 n., to which *Gent. Mag.* (1778), 270 n., had drawn attention (see **9** n., **13** n. below). Some interesting reminiscences of C at Oxford by Gilbert White of Selborne in *Gent. Mag.* (Jan. 1781), 11–12, several weeks before the publication of *Prefaces* (1781), presumably came too late for SJ to use, and, in spite of the sparseness of information about C, no use was made of White's memoir in the revised *Lives* (1783).

The only quotation from C in the *Dict.* (1755) (under 'Sod') is adapted from 'Ode, Written in the Beginning of the Year 1746', ll. 5–6.

Publication. In *Prefaces*, vol. ix (15 May 1781). Pp. 1–14 and a second set of pp. 1–6 and 11–14 (of 14) of the proofs are in the Forster Collection. SJ inscribed the incomplete set: 'The author is much obliged to Mr Nicol [*sic*] for his help in dates. &c.': see Textual Notes, Fleeman (1962), 223 n., and Wendorf, 'Making', 104–11.

Modern Sources:
(i) William Collins
Drafts & Fragments of Verse, ed. J. S. Cunningham (Oxford, 1956)
Poems of Gray, C and Goldsmith, ed. R. Lonsdale (1969), 355–566, cited as '*Poems* (1969)' below
Works, ed. R. Wendorf and C. Ryskamp (Oxford, 1979)

(ii)

E. G. Ainsworth, *Poor C: His Life, his Art and his Influence* (Ithaca, NY, 1937)

K. Barry, *Language, Music and the Sign: A Study in Aesthetics, Poetics and Poetic Practice from C to Coleridge* (Cambridge, 1987), 27–55

P. L. Carver, *WC: The Life of a Poet* (1967), elaborating 'Notes on the Life of WC', *N & Q* 177 (Aug.–Oct. 1939)

M. Dussutour-Hammer, *La Rhétorique du silence chez WC* (Lille, 1980)

D. Griffin, 'WC: "Virtue's Patriot Theme"', in *Patriotism and Poetry in Eighteenth-Century Britain* (Cambridge, 2002), 119–48

J. Hagstrum, *The Sister Arts: The Tradition of Literary Pictorialism in English Poetry from Dryden to Gray* (Chicago, 1958), 268–86

A. Johnston, 'The Poetry of WC', *Proceedings of the British Academy*, 59 (1973), 321–40

C. Lamont, 'WC's "Ode on the Popular Superstitions of the Highlands of Scotland"—A Newly Recovered Manuscript', *RES* 19 (1968), 137–47

W. Levine, 'C, Thomson and the Whig Progress of Liberty', *SEL* 34 (1994), 553–78

H. W. Liebert, 'J's Revisions', *JNL* 11/2 (1951), 7–8

A. D. McKillop, 'C's *Ode to Evening*—Background and Structure', *Tennessee Studies in Lit.* 5 (1960), 73–83

P. S. Sherwin, *Precious Bane: C and the Miltonic Legacy* (Austin, Tex., 1977)

O. F. Sigworth, *WC* (New York, 1965)

J. Sitter, 'WC', in *Dictionary of Literary Biography*, cix (1991), 97–110

M. M. Smith (ed.), *Index of English Literary Manuscripts*, iii (i) (1986), 227–31

M. M. Stewart, 'C's Letter to Cooper', *N & Q* 212 (1967), 412–14

M. M. Stewart, 'Further Notes on WC', *SEL* 10 (1970), 569–75

E. R. Wasserman, 'C's "Ode on the Poetical Character"', *ELH* 34 (1967), 92–115

H. D. Weinbrot, 'WC and the Mid-Century Ode', in *Context, Influence, and Mid-Eighteenth-Century Poetry* (Los Angeles, 1990), 3–39

R. Wendorf, 'The Making of J's "Life of C"', *PBSA* 74 (1980), 95–115

R. Wendorf, *WC and Eighteenth-Century Poetry* (Minneapolis, 1981)

H. O. White, 'The Letters of WC', *RES* 3 (1927), 12–21

N. Williams, 'The Discourse of Madness: SJ's "Life of C"', *ECL* 14 (1990), 18–28

A. S. P. Woodhouse, 'The Poetry of C Reconsidered', in F. W. Hilles and H. Bloom (eds.), *From Sensibility to Romanticism* (New York, 1965), 93–137

1. C was in fact born on 25 Dec. 1721, the son of William Collins (Mayor of Chichester in 1714 and 1721) and his wife Elizabeth Martin. (Hampton, 'Account', 107, gave '1721'; Langhorne (1765 edn.), p. v, 'about the year 1721'.) For SJ's visit to Chichester in Oct. 1782, while staying at Brighton, see *Life*, iv. 160 and n., and Boswell, *Making of the Life*, 589 and n.

   C entered Winchester on 23 Feb. 1734. Joseph Warton (1722–1800), his contemporary there, succeeded Dr John Burton (1690–1774) as headmaster in 1766. For Warton's assistance to SJ, see headnote above, and for their sometimes strained relationship, see headnote to 'Pope' above.

2. SJ wrote to Nichols, *c*. Apr. 1780: 'Dr. Warton tells me that Collins's first piece is in the G.M. for August, 1739. In August there is no such thing. *Amasius* was at that time the poetical name of Dr. *Swan* who translated Sydenham [1742]. Where to find Collins I know not' (*Letters*, iii. 227). SJ was understandably puzzled, since he had been working for the *Gent. Mag.* in 1739. Nichols may have directed him to

'To Miss *Aurelia C—r*, on her Weeping at her Sister's Wedding', a poem signed by 'Amasius' in *Gent. Mag.* (Jan. 1739), 41, which Hampton had attributed to C in *Poetical Calendar* (1763), xii. 108. It was duly appended to the biography in 18 below.

In *Poems* (1969), 365, 560–1, I suggested that Warton probably intended to direct SJ to the 'Sonnet' signed 'Delicatulus' in *Gent. Mag.* (Oct. 1739), 545, which also concerns a weeping woman, and which Warton attributed to C elsewhere: see John Wooll, *Memoirs of Joseph Warton* (1806), 107 n. Wooll's further suggestion (109 n.) that SJ himself may have praised the poem's '*Force* mix'd with *tenderness*' and 'uncommon *Elevation*' a month later in *Gent. Mag.* (Nov. 1739), 601, was rejected by Alexander Chalmers in *Works of the English Poets* (1810), xviii. 145. In C's *Works* (1979), 99–101, Wendorf and Ryskamp suggested instead that C and Dr Swan may both have used the pseudonym 'Amasius' in Jan. 1739, and 'cautiously' accepted the attribution of 'To Miss Aurelia C—r' to C.

3. For the connection between Winchester and New College, Oxford, see also 'Somervile' 2 above and 'Young' 5–6 below, and for other poets who failed to obtain a college 'vacancy', see 'Broome' 1 above and Mason's 'Memoirs' in William Whitehead's *Plays and Poems*, iii (York, 1788), 8.

C matriculated from Queen's College on 22 Mar. 1740, and did not in fact transfer to Magdalen College as a Demy (Scholar) until 29 July 1741, as Hampton, 'Account', 107, had stated. In moving from Queen's to Magdalen C followed Addison's precedent half a century earlier (see 'Addison' 8 above). An Oxford contemporary, William Bagshaw Stevens, in his *Journal*, ed. G. Galbraith (Oxford, 1965), p. xv, described C's 'very reserved Disposition . . . in a mixed Company', his 'poetical' friendships with 'the two Wartons, Merrie, etc.', his indolent 'tho' not dissipated' character, his disgust with 'the Triflingness of the University Exercises', and his fondness for 'an old poetical translation of the Book of Job', from which he would repeat 'O perish may the Day, which first gave Birth | To me . . .'. 'Merrie' was presumably the poet James Merrick (1720–69), a contemporary at St John's College. (For Stevens's published account of C as a victim of penury and madness, see his *Poems* (1782), 20.)

Joseph Warton matriculated from Oriel College on 16 Jan. 1740, and his younger brother Thomas (1728–90) from Trinity College on 16 Mar. 1744. By then C had probably already left for London, having taken his BA on 18 Nov. 1743. SJ ignores Hampton's explanation that C was 'weary of the confinement and uniformity of an academical life' and, 'struck by the name of author and poet', 'rashly resolved to live by his pen'. Gilbert White recalled C's 'sovereign contempt for all academic studies and discipline' and for 'the dulness of a college life'. He accordingly 'commenced a man of the town, spending his time in all the dissipation of Ranelagh, Vauxhall, and the playhouses', while awaiting literary fame (*Gent. Mag.* (1781), 11).

4. For SJ's similar arrival in London in 1737, see *Life*, i. 101–3.

C's subscription for a 'History of the Revival of Learning' was mentioned by John Mulso in a letter of 18 July 1744 (*Letters to Gilbert White*, ed. R. Holt-White (1907), 3), and in *A Literary Journal*, i (Dublin, Dec. 1744), i. 226. For later references to it, see Joseph Warton, *Essay on Pope* (1756), 186; *The Poetical Calendar*, xii (Dec. 1763), 209, where Hampton stated that C abandoned it because of a lack of subscribers; Thomas Warton, *History of English Poetry*, ii (1778), 361 n.; and Gilbert White, who described it as a 'History of the darker Ages' (*Gent. Mag.* (1781), 11).

Pope Leo X (1475–1521), the great patron of the arts, was succeeded by Adrian VI (1459–1523). Thomas Warton claimed in 1783 that C had in fact completed a 'Preliminary Dissertation' for his 'History', 'written with great judgement, precision, and knowledge of the subject' (*Corresp.* (1995), 476). For SJ's own projected 'History of the Revival of Learning in Europe', see Hawkins, *Life* (1787), 83 n., and *Life*, iv. 382 n.; and for similar plans by Joseph Warton and Mark Akenside in the 1750s, see J. Wooll, *Memoirs of Joseph Warton* (1806), 29 and n., and 'Akenside' 12 below.

Although Hampton, 'Account', 108–9, and Langhorne (1765 edn.), pp. vii, xi, had listed at least some of C's publications, SJ gives the misleading impression that, for all his plans, C wrote little and published nothing. In addition to *Odes on Several Descriptive and Allegoric Subjects* (1747 for Dec. 1746), C also published *Persian Eclogues* (1742), *Verses Humbly Address'd to Sir Thomas Hanmer. On his Edition of Shakespear's Works* (1743; revised 1744), and an *Ode* (1748) on the death of his friend James Thomson (q.v. above). (For Joseph Warton's recollection of being introduced to Thomson by 'my friend Mr. W. Colling' [*sic*], see Pope, *Works* (1797), iv. 10 n.) C also contributed to Dodsley's *The Museum* (1746) and *Collection of Poems* (1748). For his unpublished verse, see *Drafts and Fragments* (1956) and *Poems* (1969), 521–56; and for a periodical C planned with John Gilbert Cooper, mentioned in a letter in Nov. 1747, and other 'Unfinished Projects' in prose, see *Works* (1979), 87–8, 190–4, 209–15.

Langhorne (1765 edn.), pp. xi–xii, related that Andrew Millar agreed to publish C's *Odes* (originally planned as a joint volume with Joseph Warton) only at the poet's expense, and that C later burned the unsold copies in disappointment at its lack of success. SJ presumably overlooked the story because Langhorne later suppressed it, after protests from the book trade: see *Poems* (1969), 409–10. James Grainger told Percy, 13 May 1758, that Millar 'gives a better price for poetical merchandise than any other in the trade', Nichols described Tonson and Millar as 'the best patrons of literature', and SJ himself once described Millar as 'the Maecenas of the age' (Nichols, *Lit. Ill.*, vii. 255, and *Lit. Anec.*, iii. 448; Hawkins, *J's Works* (1787), xi. 200). Cf. 'Dryden' 187 and n. above.

5. *His appearance was decent*: citing SJ's definition of 'Decent' as 'Becoming; fit; suitable' (*Dict.*), Hill (1905) suggested that he means here that C's appearance, unlike that of SJ himself and 'many of his brother authors', was 'that of a gentleman'. Cf., however, the definitions SJ added in 1773: '2. Grave; not gaudy; not ostentatious', and '3. Not wanton; not immodest'. According to Langhorne (1765 edn.), p. xiv, C 'was, in stature, somewhat above the middle size; of a brown complexion, keen, expressive eyes, and a fixed, sedate aspect, which from intense thinking, had contracted an habitual frown'.

C and SJ met *c*.1745. John Mulso referred to C's arrest in a letter of 28 May 1746 (*Letters to Gilbert White* (1907), 14). For the Aristotle project, see *Poems* (1969), 414–15: SJ appears to refer to its imminent publication in his preface to Dodsley's *Preceptor* (1748) (Hazen, 184).

C's uncle, Lieut.-Col. Edmund Martin of the King's Regt. of Foot, died on 18 Apr. 1749, leaving C a third of his property, about £2,000 (*Gent. Mag.* (1749), 188;

Carver, WC, 150–1, 199–200). SJ ignores Hampton's statement (109) that C had visited his uncle in Flanders in 1745 and 1746, perhaps with military service of some sort in mind, e.g. as a chaplain (Carver, WC, 62–3).

6. *man is not born for happiness*: for this recurrent theme, see e.g. *Rasselas*, ch. XI, and the citations in *YW*, xvi. 50 n.; and for the disappointed hopes of poets in particular, see 'Denham' **19** and n. above.

SJ quotes Bacon's 'Notes for an Interview with the King' (1622): 'I would live to study, and not study to live' (*Works*, ed. J. Spedding et al., xiv (1874), 351). SJ had echoed it in his 'Drury-Lane Prologue', l. 54: 'For we that live to please, must please to live.'

7–12. SJ's 'character' of C originally appeared in the *Poetical Calendar*, xii (Dec. 1763), 110–12 (see headnote), and was immediately reprinted in *Gent. Mag.* (Jan. 1764), 23–4. *Prefaces* (1781) did not follow the 1763 text, relying instead on that in Thomas Davies's unauthorized *Miscellaneous and Fugitive Pieces*, ii (1773), 237–9, which has minor variants: see Textual Notes. John Langhorne's enthusiastic review of *Poetical Calendar*, xii, in *Monthly Review*, 30 (1764), 20–6, and his edition of C's *Poetical Works* (1765), with extended and enthusiastic 'Observations' (103–84), decisively influenced C's posthumous reputation.

8. SJ wrote to Joseph Warton, 8 Mar. 1754, about 'the condition of poor Collins': 'I knew him a few years ago full of hopes and full of projects, versed in many languages, high in fancy, and strong in retention. This busy and forcible mind is now under the government of those who lately would not have been able to comprehend the least and most narrow of its designs' (*Letters*, i. 77–8).

He loved fairies, genii, giants, and monsters: SJ's comments recall Addison's *Spectator* 419 (1712) on what Dryden had called 'the Fairie way of Writing', 'wherein the poet quite loses sight of Nature, and entertains his Reader's Imagination with the Characters and Actions of such Persons as have many of them no Existence, but what he bestows on them. Such are Fairies, Witches, Magicians, Demons, and departed Spirits.' Such a poet needs 'an Imagination naturally fruitful and superstitious', and to be 'very well versed in Legends and Fables, antiquated Romances, and the traditions of Nurses and old Women', which appeal to 'those secret Terrours and Apprehensions to which the Mind of Man is naturally subject'. Sir William Temple had written dismissively of such 'Credulity' in 'Of Poetry' as recently as 1690 (Spingarn, iii. 96–7).

Cf. Edward Young's *Conjectures on Original Composition* (1759): 'In the Fairy-land of Fancy, Genius may wander wild; there it has creative power, and may reign arbitrarily over its own empire of Chimeras . . . so boundless are the bold excursions of the human mind, that in the vast void beyond real existence, it can call forth shadowy beings, and unknown worlds' (37–8). Thomas Warton's *Observations on Spenser* (2nd edn., 1762) also described 'some fairy region . . . highly pleasing to the imagination' (i. 197), the 'Terrible Graces of magic and enchantment', and the 'fictions and fablings', which 'rouse and invigorate all the powers of imagination' in poetry (ii. 268). See also Richard Hurd, *Letters on Chivalry and Romance* (1762).

Although, as Henson, 174–6, has shown, SJ was susceptible to the attractions of chivalric romance, and even of 'the Gothick mythology of fairies' (*YW*, vii. 72), he tended to associate a taste for 'adventures, giants, dragons, and enchantments', and for 'that incredibility, by which maturer knowledge is offended', with children, the 'vulgar', and more primitive ages (*YW*, vii. 82; *Life*, iv. 16–17; *J. Misc.*, i. 156). In 1745, at about the time he met C, he wrote that a modern dramatist who relied on 'enchantment, and . . . supernatural agents, would be censured as transgressing the bounds of probability, he would be banished from the theatre to the nursery, and condemned to write fairy tales instead of tragedies' (*YW*, vii. 3).

For 'fiction', see also 'Cowley' **16** and n. above: 'No man needs to be so burthened with life as to squander it in voluntary dreams of fictitious occurrences.' Cf. also *Rambler* 89 (1751) on the 'dreamer' who 'abandons himself to his own fancy', an 'infatuation' comparable to that induced by opiates; *Rambler* 151 (1751) on the immature judgement's delight in the improbable and impractical, and on the resistance to 'falsehood' and affection for 'truth itself' which comes with acquaintance with 'living nature'; *Idler* 32 (1758), on the arts by which men escape their present condition and duties ('All this is a voluntary dream, a temporary recession from the realities of life to airy fictions; and habitual subjection of reason to fancy'); and the preface to *Shakespeare*: 'The mind, which has feasted on the luxurious wonders of fiction, has no taste of the insipidity of truth' (*YW*, iv. 106, v. 39–40, ii. 101, vii. 82).

See also 'Fantastical' and 'Fantastick' in the *Dict.* ('Irrational; bred only in the imagination', etc.); the account of the astronomer in *Rasselas*, chs. XLII, XLIV ('To indulge the power of fiction, and send imagination out upon the wing, is often the sport of those who delight too much in silent speculation'; 'the mind . . . feasts on the luscious falsehood whenever she is offended with the bitterness of truth') (*YW*, xvi. 151–2); and his account of Don Quixote's subjection of 'his understanding to his imagination' in 'Butler' **23** above. Mrs Thrale stated that SJ 'had given particular attention to the diseases of the imagination, which he watched in himself with a solicitude destructive of his own peace' (*J. Misc.*, i. 199). He asserted in Apr. 1783 that 'madness . . . is occasioned by too much indulgence of imagination' (*Life*, iv. 208).

For the one poet entitled by his sublimity to pass 'the bounds of nature', see 'Milton' **232** above. SJ's description of C's mentality oddly echoes Dick Minim's advice in *Idler* 61 (1759) that a young author should 'take care lest imagination hurry him beyond the bounds of nature' (*YW*, ii. 192). Many of SJ's contemporaries did not share his mistrust of 'flights of imagination'. Cf. Hurd, *Letters on Chivalry and Romance*, 93: 'A poet, they say, must follow *Nature*; and by Nature we are to suppose can only be meant the known and experienced course of affairs in this world. Whereas the poet has a world of his own, where experience has less to do, than consistent imagination. He has, besides, a supernatural world to range in. He has Gods, and Faeries, and Witches at his command.' See also 'On the Praeternatural Beings' in Elizabeth Montagu, *Essay on the Writings and Genius of Shakespear* (1769), 133–69, esp. 137–8.

With C's 'peculiar habits of thought', cf. SJ's statement that Thomson 'thinks in a peculiar train' but 'thinks always as a man of genius' ('Thomson' **46** above).

9. SJ was already sensing in 1763 the appeal that C's 'mistaken beauties' would exert to the end of the century. For 'harshness', see **17** below and 'Milton' **177** and n. above; for 'obscurity', 'Dryden' **244** and n. above; for 'sublimity', 'Cowley' **58** and n. above; for 'allegorical imagery', 'Cowley' **151** and n. above; for 'description', 'Cowley' **154** and n. above (and cf. SJ's reverse objection in 'Dryden' **249, 270**, that

Dryden had more sentiment than description); and for 'knowledge either of books or life', 'Butler' 37–9 and n. above.

SJ does not mention C's admired 'Ode to Evening', which, according to John Gilbert Cooper, 'warms the Breast with a sympathetic Glow of retired thought-fulness': C's 'neglected Genius will hereafter be both an Honour and a Disgrace to our Nation' (*Letters Concerning Taste* (3rd edn., 1757), 47 and n., and cf. 96). By 1765 Langhorne, p. xii, was claiming that the 'higher efforts of imagination' in C's 'allegorical and abstracted poetry' were above the capacity of common readers. Thomas Warton believed that C's *Odes* 'will be remembered while any taste for true poetry remains' (*History of English Poetry*, ii (1778), 361 n.), and Joseph Warton was no doubt replying to SJ when he added a reference to C's 'strong and fruitful imagination' to *Essay on Pope*, i (4th edn., 1782), 69 n. In a discussion of C's poetry, Robert Potter, *Inquiry* (1783), 15, replied openly to SJ, who 'in the coldness of criticism expresses some disapprobation of his allegorical imagery and is unjust to his harmony'.

Hill (1905) and others have identified C as the impotent poet and dreamer in Thomson's *The Castle of Indolence* (1748), I. lvii–lix, but he was more probably Thomson's friend William Paterson: see Thomson, *Liberty*, ed. J. Sambrook (Oxford, 1986), 172 and n., 192–3, 387 n. For C as a 'patriot-poet' rather than a poetic 'solipsist', see Griffin, 'WC', 119–48.

10. For 'dissipation' and the loss of 'freedom of agency' entailed by poverty, see 'Savage' 335 and n. above; and for the relationship between principles and practice, see 'King' 17, 'Prior' 52, and 'Savage' 341 and n. above.

fortuitous: 'Accidental; casual; happening by chance' (*Dict.*).

11. From 1751 C travelled to France and Bath in search of a cure for his depression. Thomas Warton recalled that during a visit to Oxford in 1754, C was 'so weak and low, that he could not bear conversation', and was 'labouring under the most deplorable languor of body, and dejection of mind' (*Corresp.* (1995), 469; *Life*, i. 276 n.). Gilbert White also claimed to have seen C in Oxford, 'struggling, and conveyed by force, in the arms of two or three men, towards the parish of St. Clement, in which was a house that took in such unhappy objects' (*Gent. Mag.* (1781), 11). After confinement in MacDonald's madhouse in Chelsea, he was removed to Chichester by his sister Anne (later Semphill, later Durnford) by Sept. 1754.

C did not in fact die until 12 June 1759. In 1763 SJ wrote merely that 'death came to his relief' with no date. In 1781 he was misled by Nichols's note in the proofs: 'There is no mention when Mr Collins died. It was 1756 at Chichester.' Although Hampton, 'Account', 109, and Langhorne (1765 edn.), p. xiv, had given the same date, Goldsmith had referred to C in 1759 as 'still alive. Happy, if *insensible* of our neglect, not *raging* at our ingratitude' (*Coll. Works* (1966), i. 315, 340). Because of this error, 'Collins' preceded 'Dyer' in the reordered *Lives* (1781).

In the proofs Nichols also corrected SJ's original statement in 1763 (112) that C had died at Colchester. Langhorne (1765 edn.), p. xiv, had repeated this, but in fact emended it to Chichester in an erratum (184).

As Hill (1905) noted, 'Intellects' is not in the *Dict.*, although SJ uses the plural form elsewhere (see *YW*, xvi. 15 n.).

12. SJ probably visited C at Islington in 1754. Cowper later cited this story of C and the Bible as an exception to the impression otherwise given by SJ's *Lives*, 'that Poets are a very worthless, wicked set of people' (*Letters*, ii (1981), 225–6).

Richard Shenton, Vicar of St Andrew's, Chichester, told Thomas Warton, 16 Jan. 1783, that he had heard a servant read the Bible to C in his last illness: he 'had been accustomed to rave much & make great Moanings: but while she was reading ... he was not only silent but attentive likewise, correcting her Mistakes' (Warton, *Corresp.* (1995), 474).

13. SJ wrote of 'Poor dear Collins' to Joseph Warton, 24 Dec. 1754: 'I have often been near his state, and therefore have it in great commiseration' (*Letters*, i. 91; see also i. 88–9 for other enquiries about C in 1754). In another letter about C's condition, 15 Apr. 1756, SJ reflected on the 'dreadful' fact that 'understanding may make its appearance and depart, that it may blaze and expire' (*Letters*, i. 134). In 1765 he referred to C as 'my unhappy friend ... a man of uncommon learning and abilities', in a note to *Cymbeline*, IV. ii. 281, in which he reprinted C's 'Song from Shakespear's *Cymbelyne*' (*YW*, viii. 899). For the scholarly argument provoked by Thomas Warton's reference to C's learning in a note in SJ's *Shakespeare*, see A. Sherbo, *Richard Farmer* (Newark, Del., 1992), 185–6. See also Warton's *History*, ii (1778), 360–1 and n., mentioning the visit described in 14 below, and D. Fairer, 'Introduction' to Warton's *History* (1998), i. 34–5 and nn.

14. Thomas Warton described the visit to Chichester in Sept. 1754 in a letter to William Hymers, c. Jan. 1782 (*Corresp.* (1995), 469–70).

This is SJ's first clear reference to C's *Persian Eclogues* (1742) (cf. 4 n. above). Joseph Warton, his source, enlarged on C's joke in *Works of Pope* (1797), i. 61 n.: 'In his maturer years he used to speak very contemptuously of them, calling them his Irish Eclogues, and saying they had not in them one spark of Orientalism.' The revised edition as *Oriental Eclogues* (1757), apparently superintended by Warton (see *Poems* (1969), 366–7), was the first sign of reviving interest in C's poetry. They were praised for their 'expressive beauty' and 'masterly' descriptions in *Anecdotes of Polite Literature* (1764), ii. 17–23, and for their 'Eastern simplicity' by the author of *Saberna. A Saxon Eclogue* (1778).

SJ refers, on Joseph Warton's authority (confirmed in his brother's account), to C's unpublished and incomplete 'Ode on the Popular Superstitions of the Highlands of Scotland', which he had addressed in 1749/50 to the Scottish dramatist John Home (1722–1808). SJ's reference here led to the discovery of C's lost MS by Dr Alexander Carlyle (1722–1805). The 'Ode' was read before the Royal Society of Edinburgh in Apr. 1784, printed in the Society's *Transactions*, i (ii). 63–75, in Mar. 1788 (Carlyle, *Autobiography* (3rd edn., Edinburgh, 1861), 562–3), and added to C's verse in *Eng. Poets* (2nd edn., 1790), vol. lviii. For the rediscovery of C's MS in Scotland in 1967, see Lamont, 'WC's "Ode" ', 137–47, and *Poems* (1969), 492–501.

15. *alienation*: '4. Applied to the mind, it means disorder of the faculties' (*Dict.*). For C's mental illness, see Wendorf, *WC*, 3–26.

In a note to a poem about C in her *Miscellaneous Poems* (Norwich, 1790), 21 n., Ann Francis (1738–1800) stated: 'Collins was, at times, *quite raving*, and *noisy*; though Dr. Johnson thought otherwise.' Since she grew up in Sussex, she presumably based this assertion on personal knowledge.

16. For Lieut.-Col. Martin's death in 1749, see 5 and n. above. As late as 21 Dec. 1754 SJ told Thomas Warton, 'I have a notion that by very great temperance or more properly abstinence [C] might yet recover' (*Letters*, i. 89). Gilbert White recalled that C was 'as long as I knew him, very temperate in his eating and drinking' (*Gent. Mag.* (1781), 11). For other poets who found 'temporary relief' in 'the bottle', see 'Parnell' 6 and 'Addison' 117 and nn. above.

17. Having concentrated in 1763 on C's 'peculiar habits of thought' (8–9 above), SJ now comments on his diction and versification. For 'harsh' diction, see 9 and n. above; for 'the obsolete', 'Gay' 4 and n. above; and for poetic inversions, 'Cowley' 117 and n. above. In Dec. 1746 Thomas Gray had found in C's *Odes* 'a fine Fancy, model'd upon the Antique, a bad Ear, great Variety of Words, & Images with no Choice at all'. He concluded that C and Joseph Warton, whose *Odes* also appeared in Dec. 1746, 'both deserve to last some Years, but will not' (*Corresp.*, i. 121).

not to write prose is certainly to write poetry: for the difference between poetry and prose, see 'Dryden' 221 and n. above and 'Akenside' 19 and 'Gray' 30 and n. below. William Hawkins, *Works*, iii (Oxford, 1758), 303, similarly stated that William Mason believed that 'He writes *Poetry*, because he does not write *Prose*', and Goldsmith disapproved in 1770 of the 'misguided innovators', who imagine that 'the more their writings are unlike prose, the more they resemble poetry' (*Coll. Works*, iii. 423).

For the importance of 'a proportionate mixture of vowels and consonants' in versification, see *Rambler* 88 (1751) (*YW*, iv. 99). With SJ's final contrast of reluctant praise and genuine pleasure, cf. 'Milton' 276 and n. above.

18. For the attribution of this poem to C, see 2 and n. above.

JOHN DYER (1699–1757)

Composition. Although SJ does not refer directly to 'Dyer', D's late place in the sequence in *Eng. Poets* (forty-sixth of the fifty-two poets) makes it likely that he wrote it in June or July 1780. Only two small and ambiguous details might seem to point to an earlier date. On 7 Jan. 1780 Mrs Thrale recorded a version of an anecdote which SJ also relates in 'Dyer' (see 7 n. below). In an undated letter ascribed to *c.* Feb. 1780, SJ asked Nichols to send him 'Hughes's Letters', which would become an important source for 'Dyer'. SJ also, however, requested material on Blackmore, for whom the *Letters* were also a source, if a less important one (see 'Blackmore' 26 and n. above). The evidence of an undated document inevitably remains inconclusive.

Sources. There was no entry for D in SJ's usual sources, and only brief accounts in the 'Advertisement' prefixed to D's *Poems* (1761), and in the *Supplement* (1767), 146–7, to *A New and General Biographical Dictionary* (12 vols., 1761–2). SJ admits in 1 below his reliance on John Duncombe's *Letters, By Several Eminent Persons Deceased* (3 vols., 1772–3), ii. 239–43, iii. 107–17, which included notes about D, and five of his letters to the editor's father William Duncombe in 1756–7. SJ seems in fact to have made little use of the four letters from 1757 in vol. iii. For editions of the *Letters*, see headnote to 'Hughes' above.

For the single quotation from D in the *Dict.* (1755), see 10 n. below.

Publication. In *Prefaces*, vol. x (15 May 1781). There are no proofs.

Modern Sources:

(i) John Dyer

Grongar Hill, ed. R. C. Boys (Baltimore, 1941)

The Poetical Works of Mark Akenside and JD, ed. R. A. Wilmott (1855) (includes unpublished poems from D's MSS)

Selected Poetry and Prose, ed. J. Goodridge (Nottingham, 2000)

(ii)

D. R. Anderson, 'JD', in *Dictionary of Literary Biography*, xcv (1990), 57–63

J. Barrell, *English Literature in History: An Equal Wide Survey* (1993), 90–109

R. Feingold, *Nature and Society: Later Eighteenth-Century Uses of the Pastoral and Georgic* (Hassocks, 1978), 83–119

L. Goldstein, *Ruins and Empire: The Evolution of a Theme in Augustan and Romantic Literature* (Pittsburg, 1977), 25–58

J. Goodridge, *Rural Life in Eighteenth-Century Poetry* (Cambridge, 1995), 91–180

D. Griffin, 'JD: "Sedulous for the Public Weal"', in *Patriotism and Poetry in Eighteenth-Century Britain* (Cambridge, 2002), 180–204

H. S. Hughes, 'JD and the Countess of Hertford', *MP* 27 (1930), 311–20

B. Humfrey, *JD* (Cardiff, 1980)

A. Johnston, 'Dr. J, JD and The Ruins of Rome', *New Rambler* (Jan. 1964), 11–12

J. P. H. D. Longstaffe, 'JD as a Painter', in *Collections Historical and Archaeological Relating to Montgomeryshire and its Borders* (1878), ii. 400–1

W. H. D. Longstaffe, 'Notes Respecting the Life and Family of JD', in J. B. Burke (ed.), *The Patrician*, iv (1847), 1–12, 264–8, 420–6, v (1848), 75–81, 218–35

E. Parker, 'JD in the Light of Fresh Manuscript Material' (B.Litt. thesis, Oxford, 1938)

M. M. Smith (ed.), *Index of English Literary Manuscripts*, iii (i) (1986), 341–53

O. H. K. Spate, 'The Muse of Mercantilism: Jago, Grainger and D', in R. F. Brissenden (ed.), *Studies in the Eighteenth Century* (Canberra, 1968), 119–31

R. M. Williams, *Poet, Painter and Parson: The Life of JD* (New York, 1956)

1. See 'Sources' above. The son of Robert and Catherine (née Cocks) Dyer, D was in fact born in late July or early Aug. 1699 (baptized on 13 Aug.) at Llanfynnydd, Carmarthenshire, five miles from Grongar Hill. His father moved to Aberglasney several years later.

2. D entered Westminster *c.*1713 and may have stayed until 1716/17. Dr Robert Freind (1667–1751) was headmaster 1711–33 (see 'J. Philips' 8 and n. above). Soon after his father's death on 8 July 1720, D became a pupil of Jonathan Richardson (1667–1745), portrait-painter, theorist of painting, Miltonist, and friend of Pope, whom D later addressed in verse. For D and Richardson, and for D's notebooks on painting, see C. Gibson-Wood, *Jonathan Richardson: Art Theorist of the English Enlightenment* (New Haven, 2000), 67, 241 n., and see also 'Cowley' 3 and n. above. For Savage's poem to D, 'To a Young Gentleman, a Painter' (1724), see his *Poetical Works*, ed. C. Tracy (Cambridge, 1962), 52.

3–4. SJ deduced his compressed and defective chronology from D's letter of 24 Nov. 1756 to William Duncombe (the 'friend' in 3), and an editorial note, in *Letters*, ii (1772), 242–3 and n.

3. It was several years after his return from Italy in 1725 (see 4 and n. below) that D became an itinerant painter in Herefordshire and South Wales 1730–4. SJ seems unaware that in the 1720s D was a member of Aaron Hill's circle (see 'Savage' **55**

and n. above), and a friend of Savage and Thomson, all of whom he addressed in verse. See J. Sambrook, *James Thomson* (Oxford, 1991), 39–40, 43, 62, 65, 144, and Thomson's *Letters* (1958), 36, 41.

'Grongar Hill' was first published as a Pindaric ode in Savage's *Miscellaneous Poems* (Mar. 1726) (see 'Savage' **59–63** above). The more familiar version in octosyllabic couplets appeared almost simultaneously in *A New Miscellany* [1726], and was further revised in David Lewis's *Miscellaneous Poems* (July 1726). For SJ's reference in June 1784 to Lewis's collection and to 'Grongar Hill', see *Life*, iv. 306–7, and, for the poem's complex textual history, see Boys (1941 edn.). The *British Journal* (1 Oct. 1726) suggested that D could not have written it without Aaron Hill's assistance: see Thomson, *Letters* (1958), 56 n.

4. Intent on a career as a painter, D visited Italy in 1724/5. According to *Poems* (1761), p. v, 'he frequently spent whole days in the country about Rome and Florence, sketching those pittoresque prospects with facility and spirit' (p. iii). On his return he lived in modest gentility, unable to 'submit to the assiduity required in his profession: his talent indeed was rather for Sketching than Finishing. So he contentedly sat down in the country with his little fortune, painting now and then a Portrait or a Landscape, as his fancy led him' (p. iv). After some years as an itinerant painter (see 3 n. above), D in fact managed his aunt's farm at Mapleton in 1734–5, and was living at Bromyard, Worcester, and Nuneaton in 1736–8.

D drafted *The Ruins of Rome* in *c.*1729–36, i.e. after his return from Italy in 1725, but did not publish it until 1740. For an anonymous poem on a similar subject, see *The Loss of Liberty: or Fall of Rome* (1729).

5. D had fallen ill in Rome in 1724/5 and was in poor health again not long before his ordination, as deacon 20 Sept. and as priest 18 Oct. 1741. In 1738 he had married Sarah Ensor Hawkins, a widow, the daughter of George Ensor of Boston (Nichols, *Lit. Anec.*, vi. 83 and n.). SJ quotes D's letter to Duncombe, 24 Nov. 1756, from *Letters*, ii (1772), 242. There is no evidence to support his wife's supposed descent from Shakespeare. D's son John died in 1782 (*Gent. Mag.* (1782), 262).

6. Joseph Harper, a mercer in Hinckley, presented D to the living of Catthorpe, near Rugby, in 1742. SJ's source for D's subsequent career is his letter to Duncombe in 1756 (*Letters*, ii. 241–3). From 1750 he enjoyed the patronage of Philip Yorke, son of the Earl of Hardwicke, the Lord Chancellor, who had seen the MS of *The Fleece*, Bk. I, which D began writing in about 1741. Letters from Daniel Wray to Yorke in 1750–2 refer to D's slow progress, but by 27 Aug. 1752 he had completed 'more than 600 Verses of his fourth book' (British Library, Add. MS 35401, fo. 163). For Yorke's patronage of D, see D. Griffin, *Literary Patronage in England, 1660–1800* (Cambridge, 1996), 99–100.

In 1751 D exchanged Catthorpe for the living of Belchford, and in 1752 received that of Coningsby, Lincs., from Sir John Heathcote (complimented in *The Fleece*, I. 43–6, and mistakenly identified by Hill in 1905 as the Heathcote mentioned in one of Pope's satires). In 1751 D also obtained a LL B from Cambridge University, of which Lord Hardwicke was Lord Steward, and in 1755 exchanged Belchford for Kirkby, near Coningsby. For SJ's own refusal at this period of 'a living of considerable value in Lincolnshire' offered to him by Bennet Langton, see *Life*, i. 320.

The figure of £140 for the Coningsby stipend in *Lives* (1783) may be a misprint, since both 1781 editions followed *Letters*, ii (1772), 241, in giving it as £120. There were, however, three other small factual changes to **6–7** in 1783, which seem not to be misprints: see Textual Notes.

7. For SJ's use of 'greatest' to mean longest or most elaborate rather than most excellent, see 'Milton' **194** and n. above.

    In 1756, at the beginning of the Seven Years War, D had doubted 'whether this is a proper time for publishing it', when 'people are so taken up with politics, and have so little inclination to read any thing but satire and news-papers' (*Letters*, ii (1772), 241). *The Fleece* appeared on 15 Mar. 1757, and on 12 May D thanked Robert Dodsley 'for your very handsome publication' of the poem, sent corrections for a future edition, and referred to his 'very ill health' (Dodsley, *Corresp.* (1988), 280). For Akenside's assistance with the completion of *The Fleece*, see **12** n. below. Dodsley later published the posthumous edition of D's *Poems* (1761).

    According to Hester Thrale, 7 Jan. 1780, this 'ludicrous story' was SJ's own, and he himself was Dodsley's 'critical visiter': 'When Dyer published his Poem called the *Fleece*—how old is he says Johnson—very old replies Dodsley, and I fear will die soon—he will then returns Johnson be buried in *Woollen* I fancy' (*Thraliana*, i. 417). SJ alluded to the statute of Charles II (1666) which made it compulsory for the dead to be buried in woollens, as a protection for the wool trade against foreign linen. (Under 'Woollen' in the *Dict.*, SJ quoted Pope, *Epistle to Cobham*, ll. 242, 244–5: 'Odious! in woollen! 'twould a Saint provoke, | . . . No, let a charming Chintz, and Brussels lace | Wrap my cold limbs, and shade my lifeless face'.)

    There were immediate complaints about SJ's use of this joke. Edmund Cartwright in *Monthly Review*, 66 (1782), 117, called it 'as lame an attempt at wit as ever disgraced the vilest pages of the vilest jest book', before deploring the neglect of *The Fleece*. Robert Potter, *Inquiry* (1783), 4, condemned it as an 'idle story', and went on to defend D's poetry.

8. D, who died from consumption, was in fact buried on 15 Dec. 1757. For defeated expectations, see 'Denham' **19** and n. above.

    D's letters to Duncombe in 1757 refer to his poor health, and to his dull life in 'a fenny country, where I have been, for the most part, above these five years, without health, without books, and without proper conversation' (*Letters*, iii [1773], 107–17). SJ seems to make no use of these four letters.

9. For other poets who do not deserve serious criticism, see 'Milton' **206** and n. above.

    With SJ's prediction that the reader will voluntarily return to 'Grongar Hill', cf. the many works which he expected would 'repel' the reader, or be laid down and not picked up again, including *The Fleece*: see **11** below and 'Milton' **252** and n. above.

    Joseph Warton, *Essay on Pope* (1756), 35–6, compared the poem's oblique 'moralities' to 'a statue of some Virtue or Muse' unexpectedly encountered when wandering through 'a wilderness'. Subsequent criticism includes William Gilpin, *Observations on the River Wye* (1782), 59–61, and John Scott, *Critical Essays* (1785), 97–112. 'Grongar Hill' had imitators to the end of the century, e.g. John Bethell, *Llangunnor Hill: A Loco-Descriptive Poem* (Carmarthen, [1795]).

10. *strikes more but pleases less*: for this recurrent opposition, see 'Milton' **276** and n. above. For the attraction of poetic night-scenes, see 'Congreve' **34–5** and nn. above.

    SJ appears to have coined 'dilapidating' (*OED*). As in the *Dict.* (1755) (under 'Orisons'), SJ paraphrases *The Ruins of Rome*, ll. 38–40 ('The pilgrim oft | At dead of night, mid his oraison hears', etc.). Wordsworth later admired this 'noble passage' as 'A beautiful instance of the modifying and *investive* power of imagination' (*Prose Works* (Oxford, 1974), iii. 44 n.).

On the appearance of *The Ruins of Rome* and 'Grongar Hill' in Dodsley's *Collection* (1748), i. 72–100, Gray told Walpole: 'Mr. Dyer (here you will despise me highly) has more of poetry in his imagination, than almost any of our number; but rough and injudicious' (*Corresp.*, i. 295–6). Writing to James Beattie, 29 Aug. 1783, John Scott of Amwell made clear that the chapter on *The Ruins of Rome* in his *Critical Essays* (1785), 113–52, was a response to 'the censure of Dr. Johnson', and to his 'parsimony of praise to his cotemporaries, especially to our author' (Sir William Forbes, *Life and Writings of James Beattie* (Edinburgh, 1806), ii. 123–4; *Critical Essays*, 121). For SJ's reaction to *The Ruins of Rome*, see also Johnston, 'Dr. J', 11–21.

In spite of his reservations, SJ grants D 'the mind of a poet', and admits in 11 below that his 'mind was not unpoetical'. For similar concessions about genuinely 'poetical' aspects of mid-century verse of which he does not fully approve, see 'Savage' 342 and 'Thomson' 46 above, and 'Young' 168, 'Mallet' 6, 'Akenside' 15, and 'Gray' 28, 31, 39 below.

11. SJ had rehearsed these objections when talking 'slightingly' of *The Fleece* on 21 Mar. 1776: 'The subject, Sir, cannot be made poetical. How can a man write poetically of serges and druggets? Yet you will hear many people talk to you gravely of that *excellent* poem, "THE FLEECE" ' (*Life*, ii. 453–5). SJ went on to ridicule James Grainger's *The Sugar-Cane* (1764), which he had earlier praised as an imitation of Virgil's *Georgics*, while noting that, 'on the contrary Dyer, [John] Philips, and some others who have pursued his plan, grow languid as they proceed, as if fatigued with their career' (*Critical Review*, 18 (1764), 273; Hazen, 168–7).

SJ's complaint in 1776 that 'many people' thought *The Fleece* 'excellent' in itself contradicts his claim here that the poem 'never became popular' and was now 'universally neglected'. *Gent. Mag.* (Nov. 1779), 505, had in fact looked forward to SJ's forthcoming life of D, 'who has charmed so large a portion of the world by his delightful "Fleece" ', and in Sept. 1781, 421, 'Scrutator' (John Loveday) flatly denied that it was 'universally neglected'. *The Fleece* had in fact been favourably reviewed (by James Grainger) in the *Monthly Review*, 16 (1757), 328–40, and the *Critical Review*, 3 (1757), 402–15, had anticipated SJ's reference to 'our national commodity' by praising D's '*national*' subject. See also the *Literary Mag.* 2 (1757), 134–6. Horace Walpole had for once agreed with SJ, describing *The Fleece* on 3 Feb. 1760 as 'very insipid', whereas *The Ruins of Rome* 'has great picturesque spirit' and 'Grongar Hill' 'was beautiful' (*Corresp.*, xv. 62–3).

Joseph Warton was no doubt replying to SJ in *Essay on Pope*, i (4th edn., 1782), 36 n., when describing *The Fleece* as 'written in a pure and classical taste', and Robert Potter, *Inquiry* (1783), 5, also called it a 'truly classical' poem. Robert Anderson, *Poets of Great Britain*, ix (Edinburgh, 1794), 549–50, praised passages in *The Fleece* to show that 'genius can almost ennoble any subject, however mean or inconsiderable'. Nathan Drake, *Literary Hours* (1798), 137–72, stated that SJ's 'stern critique' and 'harsh censure' of *The Fleece* had 'intervened to blast' the 'rising fame' of a poem, which would otherwise be 'familiar to every lover and judge of nervous and highly finished description'.

Wordsworth later recommended *The Fleece* to Lady Beaumont, 20 Nov. 1811, when sending her his sonnet, 'To the Poet, Dyer': 'his poem is, in several places, dry and heavy; but its beauties are innumerable, and of a high order. In point of *imagination*, and purity of style, I am not sure that he is not superior to any writer in verse since the time of Milton' (*Letters*, ii, Pt. i (2nd edn., Oxford, 1969), 521). Wordsworth also referred admiringly to D in notes to *The Excursion*, VIII. 111–12, and to *The River Duddon*.

D's celebration of the British wool trade also deplored cruelty to animals and the inhumanity of the slave trade, included early descriptions of the new factories in West Yorkshire, and ended with a survey of international trade extending to China and Russia. SJ's conviction that literary elegance and trade were of 'discordant natures' was consistent. (He translates 'couple the serpent with the fowl' from Horace, *Ars Poetica*, l. 13.) He had asked in the preface to the *Dict.* (1755), 'in what pages eminent for purity can terms of manufacture or agriculture be found?': 'Commerce, however necessary, however lucrative, as it depraves the manners, corrupts the language' (*OASJ*, 319, 325). On 18 Oct. 1773 he said: 'A merchant may, perhaps, be a man of an enlarged mind; but there is nothing in trade connected with an enlarged mind' (*Life*, v. 328). Cf. also his earlier comment on Latin verses on subjects which would have been unacceptable in English: 'When the matter is low or scanty, a dead language, in which nothing is mean because nothing is familiar, affords great conveniences' ('Addison' 11 above).

SJ was by no means hostile to trade itself. Between Dec. 1741 and Jan. 1743, he seems to have contributed to a debate about the wool trade in the *Gent. Mag.*: see Kaminski, 149, 151–3, and *Bibliography*, i. 81–2, 93. (For a wider context, see Griffin, 'JD', 188–92.) He later argued in *Rambler* 145 (1751) that 'vocations and employments of least dignity are of the most apparent use', and praised British commerce in *Adventurer* 67 (1753) (*YW*, v. 8, ii. 383–9). See also J. Middendorf, 'Jon Wealth and Commerce', in M. M. Lascelles et al. (eds.), *J, Boswell and their Circle* (Oxford, 1965), 47–64.

For didactic poetry, see 'Pope' **326** and n. above; for SJ's usual hostility to blank verse, see 'Milton' **274** and n. above; and for other, usually ominous, professions of 'willingness to be pleased', see 'Gray' **22, 32** below.

12. From the mid-1740s Akenside was an adviser to Robert Dodsley, the most important publisher of poetry in this period, from whom SJ may have heard these remarks (see **7** and n. above and 'Akenside' **4** n., **12** n. below). Dodsley included 'Grongar Hill' and *The Ruins of Rome* in his *Collection of Poems*, vol. i (1748), 72 ff., on Akenside's recommendation.

D and Akenside probably first met in London in 1753, and did so again in 1754–5. (See C. T. Houpt, *Mark Akenside* (Philadelphia, 1944), 138–9, who partly confused D with SJ's friend Samuel Dyer: see 'Watts' **25** and n. above. Hawkins, *Life* (1787), 232, noted that Reynolds's portrait of Samuel Dyer was prefixed to D's works in John Bell's *British Poets*.) Although D stated in Nov. 1756 that Akenside helped him to complete *The Fleece*, he did not adopt his more radical suggestions for revision (*Letters*, ii (1772), 241; Williams, *Poet*, 128–9). Joseph Warton also 'had the pleasure of reading it in manuscript with Dr. Akenside' (*Essay on Pope*, i (4th edn., 1782), 36 n.).

Although 'Scrutator' (John Loveday) praised SJ's 'candour' in quoting Akenside's high opinion of *The Fleece* after his own unfavourable remarks (*Gent. Mag.* (1781), 421), SJ's later objections to Akenside's own poetry may in fact imply some doubts about his judgement, however 'honestly' reported here.

WILLIAM SHENSTONE (1714–63)

Composition. SJ was preparing to write 'Shenstone' by late May 1780, when Dr William Adams (1706–89), Master of Pembroke College, Oxford, replied on 27 May to SJ's request for information about S's years at Oxford (Boswell Papers, Yale; *Catalogue*, C 12). As well as answering SJ's queries, Adams suggested new lines of enquiry (see below), but SJ did not pursue these and probably wrote 'Shenstone' in June. (In early Aug. 1780 he told Nichols that he had only 'Pope', 'Swift', and 'Lyttelton' still to write: *Letters*, iii. 295.)

Sources. SJ was aware of the 'Preface' (i, pp. iii–viii) and the account of The Leasowes (ii. 333–71), to which Richard Jago and Percy contributed, in S's *Works* (2 vols., 1764), edited by Robert Dodsley and Richard Graves. He appears, however, to have made little use of S's letters in the later *Works*, vol. iii (1769), or of Thomas Hull's edition of the *Select Letters* (2 vols., 1778) of S and his circle, although he quotes S's letters elsewhere: see 'Somervile' **3** and 'West' **15** above, and cf. **19** below.

As J. H. Leicester, 'J's Life of S', in M. Wahba (ed.), *Johnsonian Studies* (Cairo, 1962), 189–222, pointed out, most of SJ's information about S, especially in **1–9** below, in fact derives from 'Some particulars in the Life of William Shenstone' in Treadway Russell Nash's *History and Antiquities of Worcestershire*, i (1781), 528–31, based on information from 'one or two of his intimate friends' (probably including John Scott Hylton). Although Nash issued proposals for his *History* as early as June 1774, his dedication was dated 1 Jan. 1781 and vol. i was not published until 4 Apr. 1781, a month after SJ had finished writing *Prefaces*, vols. v–x. Conveniently for SJ, Nash's *History* was printed by John Nichols, his own printer and co-adjutant, who reported that vol. i had in fact been 'nearly printed off' by 6 June 1780 (Nichols, *Lit. Ill.*, ii. 732).

There seems little doubt that, at about that time, several months before its publication, Nichols showed SJ Nash's account of S, perhaps with the approval of Richard Gough, who was seeing the work through the press for Nash. Nichols had himself already referred in print to the contents of Nash's forthcoming *History* earlier in 1780: see A. Sherbo, 'Nichols's Scholarly Notes', *SB* 44 (1991), 321.

If Nichols had not already alerted him, SJ would have learned about Nash's forthcoming account of S from William Adams's letter of 27 May 1780, already mentioned above. Adams told SJ that Thomas Percy, by now Dean of Carlisle, had also made enquiries about S's residence at Pembroke College, Oxford (see **5** and n. below), 'for the information of Dr. Nash who is preparing a History of Worcestershire and thinking Shenstone a Native of that County intended to insert some short Account of him' (Boswell Papers, Yale). If Adams's words imply that Nash had thought of omitting his account of S on learning that he was technically a native of Shropshire (see **1** and n. below), SJ would have learned from Nichols that this was not the case. There is no indication that SJ consulted his friend Thomas Percy, mentioned by Adams as Nash's intermediary, although Adams recommended that he do so. For Percy's contribution to Nash's *History*, see B. Davis, *Thomas Percy* (Philadelphia, 1989), 221, 224, 240, 242, 250–1, 269.

SJ's debt to Nash was later hinted at in *Gent. Mag.* (Aug. 1781), 374, almost certainly by Nichols, since he did so again in his *Anecdotes of Bowyer* (1782), 353 n.: 'Of Mr. *Shenstone*, besides the Life by Dr. *Johnson*, a good account has been given, from authentic information, in Dr. *Nash*'s "History of Worcestershire".' SJ's failure to acknowledge Nash's help is surprising, unless (as the late J. D. Fleeman once suggested to me) Nichols passed the information to him without identifying his source, which seems unlikely. SJ did in fact acknowledge Nash's *History* as a source for another biography, when revising 'Butler' (q.v.) for *Lives* (1783).

William Adams also told SJ on 27 May 1780 that 'Mr. Greaves . . . now of *Claverton near Bath* was Executor to Mr. Shenstone and can give you more of his History than any one that I know'. There is no sign that SJ took this advice. S's lifelong friend Richard Graves (1715–1804) in fact later replied to SJ's account of S in *Recollections of Some Particulars in the Life of the late William Shenstone, Esq.* (1788), cited in the notes below. SJ also ignored Adams's information that Graves had recently portrayed S as a poetic recluse in his *Columella* (1779). In Graves's earlier and better known *The Spiritual Quixote* (1773), his protagonist Mr Wildgoose paid a visit to The Leasowes (III. vii).

Although he wrote in 1759 that *Rasselas* contained 'a few refined sentiments thinly scattered', S usually expressed a high opinion of SJ, describing him in Feb. 1760 as 'one of the most *nervous*, most *perspicuous*, most concise, and most harmonious prose-writers I know', adding a few months later: 'I do very unfeignedly respect both the *Writer* & the *Man*; and should be sorry to forfeit . . . any degree of Esteem he discovers for me' (*Life*, ii. 452–3; *S Letters*, 528, 549, 553, 559; *Percy Corresp.*, vii (Shenstone). 6, 53, 63, 66–7, 97–8).

SJ had rather more reservations about S. On 25 Feb. 1765, Richard Farmer wrote to Thomas Percy, a friend of both SJ and S, about SJ's recent visit to Cambridge: 'in plain *English*, he seems to have something to *except* in every man's Character. *Hurd* for instance comes off badly, & *Shenstone* still worse: he pitys you for your opinion of ye latter.' Replying on 26 Mar. 1765, Percy admitted that he had irritated SJ by linking his name with S's in his *Reliques* (1765), i, p. ix: 'I know very well he can never forgive me for mentioning him and Shenstone in the same Page' (*Percy Corresp.*, ii (Farmer). 84–5, 87). For Percy's later objections to SJ's account of S, see *Percy Corresp.*, ix (Anderson). 193–4. For miscellaneous comments by SJ on S as a man and a poet, see notes to **10, 12, 17, 19, 25, 33** below.

S is one of the eight poets (of the fifty-two in the *Lives*) not quoted in the *Dict.*

Publication. In *Prefaces*, vol. ix (15 May 1781). There are no proofs.

Modern Sources:
(i) William Shenstone
Correspondence of Thomas Percy and WS, ed. C. Brooks (New Haven, 1977)
Letters, ed. M. Williams (Oxford, 1939) (contains 313 letters; cited below as '*S Letters*')
Letters, ed. D. Mallam (Minneapolis, 1939) (contains 284 letters)
S's Miscellany 1759–1763, ed. I. A. Gordon (Oxford, 1952)

(ii)
S. Bending, 'Prospects and Trifles: The Views of WS and Richard Jago', *Querty*, 10 (2000), 125–31
F. D. A. Burns, 'WS's Years at Oxford', *N & Q* 243 (1998), 462–4
Robert Dodsley, *Correspondence 1733–1764*, ed. J. E. Tierney (Cambridge, 1988) (many letters to and from S and his circle)
P. De Bolla, 'The Charm'd Eye', in V. Kelly and D. Von Mücke (eds.), *Body and Text in the Eighteenth Century* (Stanford, Calif., 1994), 89–111
J. Fisher, 'S, Gray, and the "Moral Elegy" ', *MP* 34 (1936–7), 273–94
H. Hecht, *Thomas Percy und WS* (Strasbourg, 1909)
A. R. Humphreys, *WS: An Eighteenth-Century Portrait* (Cambridge, 1937)

W. H. Hutton, *Burford Papers* (1905), 153–90

J. H. Leicester, 'Dr J and WS', *New Rambler* (June 1960), 29–42

J. H. Leicester, 'J's Life of S: Some Observations on the Sources', in M. Wahba (ed.), *Johnsonian Studies* (Cairo, 1962), 189–222

E. M. Purkis, *WS* (1931)

J. C. Riely, 'S's Walks: The Genesis of The Leasowes', *Apollo*, 110 (Sept. 1979), 202–9

J. Sambrook, 'Parnell's Garden Tours: Hagley and The Leasowes', *ECL* 14 (1983), 51–64

M. M. Smith and A. Lindsay (eds.), *Index of English Literary Manuscripts*, vol. iii (iii) (1992), 293–316

J. E. Tierney, 'WS', in *Dictionary of Literary Biography*, xcv (1990), 268–74

C. Tracy, *A Portrait of Richard Graves* (Toronto, 1987), esp. 24–9, 105–13

J. G. Turner, 'The Sexual Politics of Landscape', *SEC* 11 (1982), 343–66

M. M. Ward, 'S's Birthplace', *MLN* 51 (1936), 440–1

I. A. Williams, *Seven XVIIIth Century Bibliographies* (1924), 41–71

M. Williams, *WS: A Chapter in Eighteenth-Century Taste* (Birmingham, 1935)

1. Nash, *History*, i. 508, 528–9. Thomas Shenstone (1686–1724) farmed at The Leasowes where S was born on 18 Nov. 1714. SJ omitted a precise date because of Nash's uncertainty ('on or about the 18th'). The confusion in Hill (1905) about S's birthplace arose from an error in the matriculation register at Oxford, revealed by Ward, 'S's Birthplace'. Halesowen was in fact only about 10 miles from the rest of Shropshire: SJ was no doubt confused by Dodsley's statement that it was 30 miles from Shrewsbury, *Works* (1764), ii. 333.

2. Nash, *History*, i. 529. The 'old dame' was Sarah Lloyd (*S Letters*, 46). For *The School-Mistress*, see **8**, **32** below, and for 'Dame Oliver', SJ's own first teacher at a small school in Lichfield, see *Life*, i. 43, 525–6. Robert Potter, *The Art of Criticism* (1789), 172, objected to SJ's use of the 'idle jest' about S's childhood love of books.

3. Nash, *History*, i. 529. The headmaster of Solihull School 1704–35 was the Revd James Crompton (1678?–1751). For SJ's unsuccessful attempt to succeed him in 1735, see *Life*, i. 531.

4. Nash, *History*, i. 529. After his father's death in 1724, S's family lived for a time with his mother's parents at Harborough Hall, Hagley. His grandfather in fact died in 1727 (SJ follows Nash), and his mother managed the estate until her own death in 1732 at the age of 39 (Leicester, 1962, 195). For S's brother Joseph (1722–52), a non-practising attorney, see also **9** n. below.

5. Nash, *History*, i. 529–30. William Adams sent SJ similar information on 27 May 1780 (see headnote).

   S matriculated from Pembroke College, Oxford, as a gentleman-commoner on 24 May 1732. For his friends there, including the poets Richard Graves and Anthony Whistler, see Tracy, *Portrait*, 24–9. College contemporaries included William Hawkins (1722–1801), Professor of Poetry at Oxford 1751–6, Sir William Blackstone (1723–80), the eminent lawyer, and George Whitefield (1714–70), the Calvinist Methodist preacher. Williams Adams mentioned all these names, except for Whitefield.

Pembroke had, of course, been SJ's own college, until the premature end of his Oxford career in 1729. He described it in his 'Life of Sir Thomas Browne' (1756) as a college 'to which the zeal or gratitude of those that love it most, can wish little better, than that it may long proceed as it began' (pp. iii–iv). He enjoyed 'mentioning how many of the sons of Pembroke were poets; adding with a smile of sportive triumph, "Sir, we are a nest of singing birds"'. Revisiting Oxford in 1782, he pointed out S's rooms to Hannah More, and spoke warmly about the college on his deathbed (*Life*, i. 75–6 and n.; Boswell, *Making of the Life*, 83).

Although S remained on the college books until 26 Mar. 1742, he was absent from mid-July 1737 to mid-Apr. 1739, and did not reside after 10 Aug. 1739. For the evidence of the Pembroke Battels Books, see Burns, 'WS's years at Oxford', 462–4. SJ defines 'Civilian' as 'One that professes knowledge of the old Roman law, and of general equity' (*Dict.*), i.e. a student of Civil Law. S evidently changed course early in Apr. 1736. By then he was living at Harborough Hall, having inherited part of the income from it. He would have come of age and into the possession of The Leasowes in 1735.

6. The Revd Thomas Dolman, Rector of Broome near Kidderminster, had married S's aunt Mary Penn in 1726, and probably became S's guardian when his mother died in 1732. In the 1750s S was involved in protracted litigation with the younger Thomas Dolman over their shares in the Harborough estates (*S Letters*, 98 n.; Dodsley, *Corresp.*, 210–12 and n.).

7. *Poems upon Various Occasions. Written for the Entertainment of the Author, and Printed for the Amusement of a Few Friends, Prejudic'd in His Favour* was published in Oxford in Apr. 1737. One of the two issues in fact identifies the author as 'William Shenstone, Gent.' (Foxon, *English Verse*, i. 725). S inscribed the flyleaf of one copy, 'Mem. 50 Copies of this were printed & given away': see Burns, 'WS's years at Oxford', 464. For S's notes and revisions in a copy at Yale, see Smith and Lindsay (eds.), *Index of Literary Manuscripts*, iii (iii). 293.

Poems (1737) contained twenty-two pieces later omitted from S's *Works* (1764) and accordingly from *Eng. Poets* (1779). The reviewer of *Eng. Poets* in *Gent. Mag.* (1779), 600 (John Duncombe?), suggested that more verse 'might not improperly have been selected' from this rare early collection, which reflects the influence of Pope and includes a rhymed version of a passage from *Paradise Lost* (40–1). As Hill (1905) noted, George Steevens stated in a note in his copy (now in the Victoria and Albert Museum) that S later tried to suppress it.

For two unpublished poems dating from *c*.1734–5, 'The Snuff-Box, an Heroi-comical Poem' (845 lines) and 'The Diamond' (340 lines), see Smith and Lindsay (eds.), *Index of Literary Manuscripts*, iii (iii). 308, and *S Letters*, 298–9. Graves described the first poem to Dodsley as 'a juvenile & servile Imitation' of *The Rape of the Lock*, and it was omitted from *Works* (1764): see Dodsley, *Corresp.*, 473. Graves, *Recollections*, 23, later claimed that S in fact had serious academic interests at Oxford, and that poetry was only an amusement.

8. Nash, *History*, i. 530. S visited London and Cheltenham in the early 1740s, but not Bath, according to *Gent. Mag.* (1783), 583–4 (correcting Nash). SJ adds the reference to Lyttelton.

The Judgement of Hercules, published in fact in Apr. 1741 (Foxon, *English Verse*, S 394), expanded a poem in S's 1737 volume (1–7). S dedicated it to George

Lyttelton (see **11** below), whose interest he supported at the Worcestershire election of 1741. According to Graves, *Recollections*, 93, S overheard in a London coffee house 'the judicious remarks of some young people on his poem; who came to a resolution, that it must certainly be either Pope's or Mr. R. Dodsley's'. S himself wrote on 30 Apr. 1741 that 'A person cannot be supposed vain from the approbation of such critics . . . I never enquire how my poem takes, and am *afraid* to do so. However, I find *some do* allow it to be *Mallet's*' (*S Letters*, 24).

An early version of *The School-Mistress* had appeared in *Poems* (1737). S expanded it as *The School-Mistress, A Poem. In Imitation of Spenser* (1742), with an 'Advertisement' discussing its Spenserian features. After its inclusion in Ashley Cowper's *Norfolk Poetical Miscellany* (1744), i. 384–404, S enlarged it further in Dodsley's *Collection*, i (2nd edn., 1748), 247–61.

9. Thomas Dolman died on 9 May 1745. S had been boarding at The Leasowes with his tenants, probably relatives, since 1741, but from 1745 lived there permanently with his brother Joseph. He had announced in 1744, 'I have withdrawn all my views from court-preferment' (*S Letters*, 93). For S's supposed preoccupation with 'beauty' rather than 'produce', see also **12–13** below.

10–14. SJ's style in these paragraphs has been discussed by I. Watt, 'The Ironic Tradition in Augustan Prose', in *Restoration and Augustan Prose* (Los Angeles, 1956), 43, and Folkenflik, 191–4.

10. SJ's account is based on, and at times echoes, 'A Description of The Leasowes' attributed to 'R. Dodsley' in *Works*, ii, esp. 337, 360, 365, also cited by Nash, *History*, i. 530. Percy commented: 'Of this Description, I do not believe Mr. Dodsley wrote a single Line. It was begun by Mr. Jago, myself and another Friend or two of Mr. Shenstone's; who meeting at the Leasowe's in Autumn, 1762, agreed to draw up a short account of its Beauties; but Mr. Shenstone's Death prevented our giving it a more correct finishing' (*Percy Corresp.*, vii (Shenstone). 216).

In the first sentence, SJ uses 'point' in the sense of '3. To direct the eye or notice'; and, in the third sentence, 'speculator' in the sense of '2. An observer; a contemplator' (*Dict.*).

SJ had visited, and made some notes on, The Leasowes on 19 Sept. 1774 (*YW*, i. 218–19; see also **14** below and *Thraliana*, i. 114). In 1773 he described S condescendingly as a 'good layer-out of land', but only by comparison with his limitations as a poet (*Life*, v. 267). For his mockery of S's gardening elsewhere, see *J. Misc.*, i. 323, ii. 210. He was obviously sceptical about the claims being made for landscape gardening, such as the opening sentence of Thomas Whately's *Observations on Modern Gardening, Illustrated by Descriptions* (1770; 4 edns. by 1777), 1: 'Gardening, in the perfection to which it has been lately brought in England, is entitled to a place of considerable rank among the liberal arts.' Whately's descriptions included The Leasowes (162–71), Lord Lyttelton's Hagley, and Tintern Abbey.

For SJ's views on landscape gardening elsewhere, see 'Pope' **119** above and *Rasselas*, ch. XX. For references in his earlier essays to those addicted, sometimes ruinously, to building and improving estates, see *Rambler* 71 (1750), *Adventurers* 53, 102, 119 (1753), and *Idler* 73 (1759). He told Hester Thrale, 11 July 1775, that he would prefer travelling to Cairo, the Red Sea, Bengal, and India to 'building and planting. It would surely give more variety to the eye, and more amplitude to the mind' (*Letters*, ii. 243). In *A Journey to the Western Islands* (1775) he contrasted 'the imaginations excited by the view of an unknown and untravelled wilderness' with those which 'arise in the artificial solitude of parks and gardens, a flattering notion of self-sufficiency, a placid indulgence of voluntary delusions, a secure expansion of the fancy, or a cool concentration of the mental powers' (1985, 31–2).

For S's 'Unconnected Thoughts on Gardening' (i.e. 'landskip, or picturesque-gardening'), see *Works* (1764), ii. 125–47. James Woodhouse, the shoemaker-poet patronized by S, described The Leasowes at length in his *Poems on Several Occasions* (2nd edn., 1766), 42–123, and addressed other poems to S (1–23). For another account of 'The Leasowes', 'Revised and Corrected' by S himself, see Joseph Giles, *Miscellaneous Poems: On Various Subjects, and Occasions* (1771), 1–13. See also Richard Jago's fable *Labour and Genius* (1767), and Goldsmith's reflections on S's estate in 'The History of a Poet's Garden' (1773) in *Coll. Works*, iii. 206–9. For more recent accounts, see E. Malins, *English Landscaping and Literature, 1660–1840* (1966), 65–79, and Riely, 'S's Walks', 202–9. Tim Richardson described plans for the restoration of The Leasowes, part of which has been a public park since 1934, in *Country Life* (4 Mar. 1999), 56–9, with illustrations from S's own watercolours.

11. For the inevitable 'abatements' of 'felicity', see 'Denham' 19 and n. above.

For Lyttelton's more elaborate gardens and neo-Palladian house at Hagley, 4 miles from The Leasowes, see 'Lyttelton' 13 below. SJ's printed sources do not mention such 'emulation' between S and Lyttelton, and his remarks here provoked some outrage, as in *Gent. Mag.* (1781), 275, and Potter, *Inquiry* (1783), 8–9. For SJ's spirited, at times violent, defence of his account of Lyttelton's 'illiberal behaviour' to S in conversation in June 1781, see Fanny Burney, *Early Journals*, iv. 366–9.

In 1746 Lyttelton took Thomson to visit S ('They praised my place extravagantly;—proposed alterations, &c.'), but S later complained that Thomson was the 'only Person of Figure' to whom Lyttelton had ever introduced him (*S Letters*, 106, 175, and cf. 112, 116). Hawkins later stated that Joseph Spence stayed at Hagley 'for a fortnight with the Lytteltons, before they offered to shew him Shenstone's place' (*J's Works* (1787), xi. 198, and cf. *J. Misc.*, ii. 3). There are semi-humorous references in Lady Luxborough's *Letters* (1775), 58, 158, to tension between S and Lyttelton, including the latter's 'envy' of The Leasowes in 1749.

For a respectful and sociable letter from S to Lyttelton, 13 Nov. 1756, see *The Lyttelton Papers* (Sothebys, 12 Dec. 1978), 150. In 1758, however, under the influence of 'fine punch', S told John Home, the Scottish dramatist, that 'it was not so agreeable as he thought to live in the neighbourhood and intimacy of Lord Littleton, for he had defects which the benevolence of his general manners concealed, which made him often wish that he had lived at an hundred miles' distance' (Alexander Carlyle, *Autobiography* (3rd edn., Edinburgh, 1861), 372). On 4 Jan. 1763, not long before he died, S admitted to 'the difficulty of keeping my place in countenance, so near the pompous piles of Hagley' (*S Letters*, 647). He must have had Hagley in mind when describing 'An Humourist', who is consoled that 'there is an intermediate hill, intercepting my view of a nobleman's seat, whose ill-obtained superiority I cannot bear to recollect' (*Works* (1764), ii. 23).

Graves, *Recollections*, 83–5, while ridiculing the idea of so unequal a rivalry, admitted that S had complained that the Lytteltons and their friends, when visiting

The Leasowes, 'often went to the principal points of view, without waiting for any one to conduct them regularly through the whole walks'. Mrs Thrale-Piozzi referred in a letter of 5 Feb. 1787 to 'the Folks who walked over the Leasowe Grounds beginning with the Door they should have come out at' (*Queeney Letters*, 246–7).

the petty State: SJ adapts Dryden, *Conquest of Granada, Pt. II*, 1. i. 13: 'When from behind, there starts some petty State'.

a deception: not in the *Dict*. in this sense, but explained in S's own 'Unconnected Thoughts on Gardening': 'A strait lined avenue that is widened in front, and planted there with ewe trees, then firs, then with trees more and more fady, till they end in the almond-willow, or silver osier; will produce a very remarkable deception', etc. (*Works*, ii. 139–40). Like 'deception', 'fady' is not in the *Dict*., but means 'shading off by degrees into a paler hue' (*OED*, citing this passage). For another 'deception', see 'Young' **80** below.

emulation . . . vanity: cf. Swift, *Verses on the Death of Dr. Swift*, ll. 35–6 ('Her End when Emulation misses, | She turns to Envy, Stings and Hisses'). For SJ's dislike of envy, his admission that he felt it at times, and his occasional approval of 'emulation' in writers (as in 'Pope' **203** above), see I. Grundy, *Scale of Greatness* (1986), 104, 112.

12. SJ had introduced the opposition of 'beauty' and 'produce' in **9** above.

Mrs Thrale recalled that SJ 'used to laugh . . . most unmercifully' at S, 'for not caring whether there was any thing good to *eat* in the streams he was so fond of', as if 'one could fill one's belly with hearing soft murmurs, or looking at rough cascades' (*J. Misc.*, i. 323). S was ruefully amused that visitors, '(hearing my place always termed a *farm*) should come expecting to find all things managed here according to the perfection of *husbandry*!', but in fact referred in Oct. 1761 to 'the Evening when my Fish-Ponds had been robbed, and the Fish destroyed' (*S Letters*, 460, 605, and cf. 473, 506).

Graves, *Recollections*, replied to SJ by claiming that S 'generally had an eye to utility, as well as ornament, in his plans': e.g. his 'ruinated priory' also served as a labourer's dwelling. As for the question about the 'fishes in his water', Graves compared it to a lady coldly asking SJ himself at a literary party 'if he had nothing *entertaining* to read to them' (55, 70).

13. In Aug. 1748 S told Graves that his affairs were 'miserably embroiled, by my own negligence, and the nonpayment of tenants', but later letters regularly refer to work on the house (e.g. *S Letters*, 157, 273, 276, 344, 384, etc.). Graves, *Recollections*, 71–2, denied that S neglected it, as did Percy in 1805, alleging that SJ had 'grossly misrepresented' S's situation and noting that the estate sold for £17,000 at auction in June 1795. Percy attributed SJ's insensitivity to 'picturesque gardening' to his poor eyesight (*Percy Corresp.*, ix (Anderson), 193–4).

14. For S's financial circumstances, see Nash, *History*, i. 530–1.

SJ probably alludes to references to The Leasowes as 'the abode of fairies' and to a 'cast of a piping Faunus' in *Works*, ii. 335–6, 340, 342–3, 376–7. For SJ these were childish pleasures, as described in *Idler* 44 (1759), 'when the noise of a torrent, the rustle of a wood, the song of birds, or the play of lambs, had power to fill the attention, and suspend all perception of the course of time' (*YW*, ii. 138). Cf. also

Savage's pastoral fantasies in 'Savage' **262–3** above. In 1774, as well as visiting The Leasowes (see **10n**. above), SJ in fact took the Thrales to see the 'Garden and Grotto' and 'Dryads and fairies' of his friend John Scott of Amwell in Hertfordshire (*Letters*, ii. 142–3).

Although Graves, *Recollections*, 72, denied that S's 'groves were haunted by duns', SJ had no doubt noticed the title of S's poem 'The Poet and the Dun', and his complaint about occasional lack of ready income in 'The Progress of Taste' (*Works*, i. 226–7, 262–4). In his letter to SJ of 27 May 1780 (see headnote), William Adams described the second poem as lamenting 'his own imprudent Conduct in retiring from the World too soon, and too ill provided. It is certain his Taste was too costly for his Finances.' SJ wrote about those who 'ruin their fortunes by expensive schemes of buildings and gardens, which they carry on with the same vanity that prompted them to begin', in *Rambler* 53 (1750) (*YW*, iii. 285).

Dodsley advised S as early as 30 Dec. 1760: 'Now is *your* Time to make Interest for Preferment...and give the Ministry an Opportunity of doing themselves Credit.' A campaign to obtain a pension for him began in 1761, when Lords Loughborough and Stamford applied to the Earl of Bute on his behalf (Graves, *Recollections*, 165–6; Dodsley, *Corresp.*, 445, 467–70; *S Letters*, 644–5, 649, 650–1). Percy believed that 'He was to have had a Pension from the Crown, of £300: pr ann—' (*Percy Corresp.*, vii (Shenstone). 233); and William Adams in May 1780 that S 'obtained as I have been informed by the Interest of the first Ld Littleton a pension of £200 from the Crown of wch. he lived to receive only one half year. And after his Death his Estate sold for little more than would pay his Debts' (Boswell Papers, Yale).

SJ was justifiably sceptical about this information. After visiting The Leasowes in Sept. 1774, he noted: 'Poor Shenstone never tasted his pension. It is not very well proved that any pension was obtained for him. I am afraid that he died of misery' (*Life*, iv. 457; *YW*, i. 218–19). SJ obtained his own pension in 1762: for his alleged irritation when Thomas Sheridan also received one, see Clifford (1979), 298.

15. Nash, *History*, i. 531. Graves, *Recollections*, 167, denied rumours that S caught cold by spending the night outdoors after a quarrel with his housekeeper: see Sir James Prior, *Life of Malone* (1860), 340.

Under 'Putrid' SJ quotes a medical authority: '*Putrid* fever is that kind of fever, in which the humours, or part of them, have so little circulatory motion, that they fall into an intestine one, and putrefy', etc. (*Dict.*). Akenside also died from a 'putrid' fever seven years later: see 'Akenside' **13** below. For S's brother Joseph, see **4** and n. above.

16. See Nash, *History*, i. 531, and the description of S in *Works*, i, pp. iii–iv. For 'A Pastoral Ballad' see **25–9** below. In a letter to Richard Jago in July 1743, S described a young lady he had met at Cheltenham, later identified by Graves as a Miss C—, for whom he expanded the 'Ballad' he had originally written for a Miss G—: see *Letters*, 43–4, and Graves, *Recollections*, 46–7, 103–5.

Graves described S as 'of a good height, but rather of a robust than an elegant form', with 'a dull heavy look' except when animated. He normally wore 'a plain blue coat, and a scarlet waistcoat with a broad gold lace' (*Recollections*, 178–9). Alexander Carlyle found S in 1758 'a large heavy fat man, dressed in white clothes and silver lace, with his grey hairs tied behind and much powdered, which, added to his shyness and reserve, was not at first prepossessing' (*Autobiography* (3rd edn., Edinburgh, 1861), 370). For S's own reflections 'On External Figure' and 'On Dress', see *Works* (1764), ii. 58–62, 164–9. As a young man, SJ also 'wore his hair' rather than a wig (*Life*, i. 94 and n.).

For a later account of S as a 'Man of Feeling', see Thomas Nicholls, *Shenstone; or, The Force of Benevolence. A Poem* (1776).

17. *comprehensive . . . knowledge*: for the importance of comprehension and knowledge, see **33** below and 'Cowley' **144** and n. above.

On 29 Sept. 1773 in Skye, Boswell 'observed that Shenstone, from his short maxims in prose, appeared to have some power of thinking; but Dr. Johnson would not allow him that merit' (*Life*, v. 267). Graves, *Recollections*, 180–3, replied to SJ by claiming that 'no one had a quicker *comprehension* of any subject to which he applied his *mind*; and no one had a mind more capable of *comprehending* a variety of subjects', even if he had not cultivated it 'with learning and knowledge'. Graves also emphasized S's mental 'curiosity'.

18. For 'Jessy' see S's 'Elegy XXVI' in *Works* (1764), i. 97–101. SJ follows Nash's explanation, *History*, i. 531 n., that, while 'some ignorant readers' believed the poem expressed 'his own remorse' for a similar affair, it was in fact inspired by the account of Sally Godfrey, Mr B.'s former mistress, in Richardson's *Pamela* (1740), which S read in 1741 (*S Letters*, 28–9).

For S's steadfast refusal in 1758 to let Dodsley publish the poem, described by Akenside as 'the most charming Elegy in any Language', see Dodsley, *Corresp.*, 292–3, 332–5, 340, 353–4. Langhorne, in *Monthly Review*, 30 (1764), 378–89, thought it 'possibly, the most affecting and pathetic poem that ever was written'.

19. SJ quotes Gray to Norton Nicholls, June 1769 (Gray, *Corresp.*, iii. 1067), on the letters in S's *Works*, iii (1769). Although he himself makes surprisingly little use of them, he had described S on 29 Sept. 1773 as 'a man whose correspondence was an honour', having himself corresponded with him (*Life*, v. 268). There is no sign that Gray or SJ noticed a reference in S's *Works* (1764) to a 'Mr.—, of manners very delicate, yet possessed of a poetical vein fraught with the noblest and sublimest images', identified by Percy as 'Gray' himself (*Percy Corresp.*, vii (Shenstone). 63, 215).

Gray's friend Horace Walpole reacted similarly to S's letters, telling William Cole, 14 June 1769, that he pitied 'the narrow circumstances of the author, and the passion for fame that he was tormented with; and yet he had much more fame than his talents entitled him to. Poor man, he wanted to have the world talk of him for the pretty place he had made, and which he seems to have made only that it might be talked of' (*Corresp.*, i. 165–6)

Graves, *Recollections*, 132, accused SJ of quoting Gray only to make S appear 'guilty of a restless ambition and a ridiculous vanity', and embarked on an extended comparison of S and Gray (132–43). Referring to SJ's hostility to Gray's own poetry, Robert Potter, *The Art of Criticism* (1789), 172, claimed that he 'introduces Gray with his knotted club to knock down the gentle Shenstone, to be himself knocked down at last by our blind Polypheme in the wantonness of his might'. SJ would presumably have enjoyed Gray's earlier comment on S's poems in Dodsley's *Collection*, v (1758): 'But then there is Mr Shenstone, who trusts to nature and simple sentiment, why does he do no better? he goes hopping along his own gravel-walks, and never deviates from the beaten paths for fear of being lost' (*Corresp.*, ii. 566).

S wrote of The Leasowes in 1755: 'I am now grown dependent upon the Friends it brings me, for the principal Enjoyment it affords … the durable Part of my Pleasure appears to be, at the last, of the social Kind' (*Letters*, 451–2). For his ambivalent attitude to literary fame, see his troubled letters in 1761–2 when Dodsley and Graves pressed him to publish a collection of his poems by subscription (*Letters*, 586–7, 603–4, 615, 639).

20. Apart from the works mentioned in 7–8 above, most of the poems published in S's lifetime appeared in Dodsley's *Collection of Poems by Several Hands*, vols. iv–vi (1755–8), for which S also collected contributions from his friends: for his relations with Dodsley, see the *Collection*, ed. M. Suarez, (6 vols., 1997), i. 32–67. SJ ignores Nash's reference, *History*, i. 530, to S's later professed regret at the publication of so many of his own poems.

21. For the MS circulation of S's 'Elegies', which he had written by 1748, see Fisher, 'S, Gray', 273–94. Although Dodsley repeatedly pressed S to publish them in the mid-1750s (see his *Corresp.*, 209–10, 218, 242, 249, 257, 265, etc.), they appeared posthumously in *Works* (1764), with S's 'Prefatory Essay on Elegy' (written *c*.1744) (i. 3–12). For another discussion of the genre in the 1760s, see Hugh Downman, *An Elegy Wrote under a Gallows. With a Preface concerning the Nature of Elegy* [1768].

SJ defines 'Elegy' as '1. A mournful song. 2. A funeral song. 3. A short poem without points or affected elegancies' (*Dict.*; 'elegancies' replaced 'turns' in 1773). The *Monthly Review*, 25 (1761), 62–4, complained that 'elegy' was being used to refer to metre (influenced by Gray's *Elegy*) rather than its generic 'simplicity of sentiment'. For funeral elegies, see 'Cowley' 108 n. above, and for other comments on the mid-century meditative elegy in quatrains, see 'Hammond' 6–8 above and 'Gray' 51 below. For 'ornaments' in poetry, see 'Cowley' 202 and n. above.

SJ defines 'Combination' as '4. Copulation of ideas in the mind' (*Dict.*): see also 'Butler' 37 and n. above. For the importance of 'variety' and the monotony of 'uniformity', see 33 below and 'Butler' 35 and n. above.

22. For 'harshness', see 'Milton' 177 and n. above; for poetic diction and inversions, see 'Cowley' 181–4, 117 and nn. above.

23. For 'airy' verse, see 'Cowley' 109 and n. above. Walpole told John Pinkerton, 6 Oct. 1784: 'Poor Shenstone was labouring through his whole life to write a perfect song, and, in my opinion at least, never once succeeded' (*Corresp.*, xvi. 257).

'Rural Elegance', written in 1750 in irregular stanzas, opened Dodsley's *Collection*, v (1758), 1–13. For SJ's usual objections to such irregularity, see 'Cowley' 140–1 and n. above.

The 'very learned lady' may be SJ's friend Elizabeth Carter (1717–1806): for other references to the critical opinions of the 'ladies', see 'Pope' 413 and n. above.

24. 'The Skylark' appeared in Dodsley's *Collection*, v. 40.

SJ does not mention S's popular 'Written at an Inn at Henley', although Boswell heard him quote it 'with great emotion' on 21 Mar. 1776, and Frances Reynolds learned the poem by hearing SJ repeat it (*Life*, ii. 452; *J. Misc.*, ii. 253). According to Graves, *Recollections*, 151–2, S wrote it after a temporary quarrel with his friend Anthony Whistler.

25. For the textual history of 'A Pastoral Ballad', dated '1743' in *Works*, i. 189–98, probably first printed in *London Mag.* (Dec. 1751), and revised in Dodsley's *Collection*, vol. iv (1755), see *Percy Corresp.*, vii (Shenstone). 239–306.

Discussing S in Skye on 29 Sept. 1773, SJ 'would not allow him to approach excellence as a poet . . . he had tried to read all his Love Pastorals, but did not get through them.' When Boswell quoted 'A Pastoral Ballad', I. 37–40, SJ said only, 'That seems to be pretty' (*Life*, v. 267). Although Langhorne referred to its reputation for 'elegant simplicity' in *Monthly Review*, 30 (1764), 378, Goldsmith commented in 1767: 'These ballads of Mr. Shenstone are chiefly commended for the natural simplicity of the thoughts, and the harmony of the versification. However, they are not excellent in either' (*Coll. Works*, v. 328). For a heartless parody, featuring a one-legged shepherdess, see *A Pastoral Ballad, In Four Parts* (1774) by SJ's namesake, Samuel Johnson of Shrewsbury. For SJ's dislike of modern pastoral, see 'Cowley' 7 n. above.

the poet's art is selection: cf. SJ's reference in *Rambler* 36 (1750) to 'the established maxim, that the poet has a right to select his images' (*YW*, iii. 198). Pope had asserted in 'A Discourse on Pastoral Poetry' that the 'delightful' illusion 'consists in exposing the best side only of a shepherd's life, and in concealing its miseries' (*TE*, i. 27). See also 'Waller' 138 and n. above.

SJ does not mention Rowe's popular 'Colin's Complaint' in 'Rowe' (see 'Rowe' 30 n. above): Graves, *Recollections*, 103, later acknowledged its influence on S.

26. SJ quotes 'Pastoral Ballad', I. 21–4, 33–40 (cf. 25 n. above). His letter to Langton, 20 Mar. 1782, on the death of Robert Levet, may echo these lines: 'How much soever I valued him, I now wish that I had valued him more' (*Letters*, iv. 23).

27. 'Pastoral Ballad', II. 33–40.

28. 'Pastoral Ballad', III. 25–32.
    For 'common-places', see 'Pope' 323 and n. above, and for 'amorous poetry' elsewhere, see 'Cowley' 14 and n. above.

29. 'Pastoral Ballad', V. 25–32.

30. For other poems 'exempted from the severities of criticism', see 'Milton' 206 and n. above.
    'Levities; or Pieces of Humour' is a section in *Works* (1764), i. 201–40. For an example of S's 'sometimes gross' humour, see 'A Solemn Meditation' in *Works*, i. 225, and *New Oxford Book of 18th Century Verse* (1984), 309–10. According to Percy, S 'sorely regretted' the publication of some of his lighter verse in Dodsley's *Collection* (*Percy Corresp.*, ix (Anderson). 193).

31. 'Moral Pieces' is a section in *Works* (1764), i. 241–345.
    SJ refers first to *The Judgement of Hercules* (1741), based on Xenophon, *Memorabilia*, ii. i (see 8 above), and 'The Progress of Taste: or, The Fate of Delicacy. A Poem on the Temper and Studies of the AUTHOR; and how great a Misfortune it is, for a Man of a small Estate to have much TASTE' (*Works*, i. 262–84; see 14 n. above). As elsewhere (cf. 'Otway' 15 above), SJ shows little interest in a professedly autobiographical poem.
    For SJ's usual hostility to blank verse, see 'Milton' 274 and n. above. S's 'blank verses' are 'Oeconomy, A Rhapsody, addressed to young Poets' and 'The Ruin'd Abbey; or, The Effects of Superstition' (*Works*, i. 285–321). 'Love and Honour'

(*Works*, i. 321–32), also in blank verse, elaborates a ballad, 'The Spanish Lady's Love', mentioned by S to Percy in July 1761 (*Percy Corresp.*, vii (Shenstone). 104). Percy later included it in *Reliques* (1765), ii. 227–31, a project to which S himself made a substantial contribution: see N. Groom, *The Making of Percy's Reliques* (Oxford, 1999), esp. 106–44.

32. For *The School-Mistress*, an affectionate evocation of a village school, see **2**, **8** above. SJ's discussion of S's most popular poem would have been clearer had he explained that it professes to be an imitation of Spenser. He comments similarly on the pleasures of poetic 'imitation' in 'West' **14** above, written a few weeks later, although he there denies such poems 'the highest praise, the praise of genius': see also 'Pope' **372** and n. above.

In May 1742 S told Graves of his 'pains to secure myself from A. Philips's misfortune, of mere *childishness*' in *The School-Mistress*: 'I have added a ludicrous index, purely to shew (fools) that I am in jest' (cf. 'A. Philips' **35** and n. above). In 1748 he explained that he 'meant to skreen ye ridicule wch might fall on so *low* a subject (tho' perhaps a *picturesque* one) by *pretending* to *simper* all ye time I was writing' (*S Letters*, 48, 145; for other comments on the poem and on Spenserian imitation, see 36–7, 40, 54–5, 58, 97, 105, 131, 150).

Although Gray described *The School-Mistress* in 1748 as 'excellent in its kind, and masterly', he and S did not think highly of each other's later verse (Gray, *Corresp.*, i. 295, ii. 523, 526, 566, 568). Goldsmith stated in 1767 that S wrote nothing else 'which any way approaches it in merit; and, though I dislike the imitation of our old English poets in general, yet, on this minute subject, the antiquity of the style produces a very ludicrous solemnity' (*Coll. Works*, v. 320–1). Walpole described S, 18 Apr. 1778, as 'that water-gruel bard . . . who never wrote anything good but his *Schoolmistress*' (*Corresp.*, xxviii. 384). Wordsworth later commented on S's 'timidity' in offering as burlesque what 'the People have since continued to read in seriousness' (*Prose Works*, iii. 76, and cf. iii. 98).

33. For 'easiness', see 'Rochester' **18** and n. above.

S claimed that 'Simplicity can scarce be carried too far', although 'you must remove all appearance of poverty' (*Works* (1764), ii. 166), perhaps echoing Pope's preface to the *Iliad* (1715): 'There is a *graceful* and *dignify'd* Simplicity, as well as a *bald* and *sordid* one, which differ as much from each other as the Air of a *plain* Man from that of a *Sloven* . . . Simplicity is the Mean between Ostentation and Rusticity' (*TE*, vii. 18). S also stated that 'Every thing disgusts, but mere simplicity', and 'My chief endeavour . . . has been to produce *ease* & Simplicity' (*Works*, ii. 194; *S Letters*, 616). For his admiration in 1758 of Allan Ramsay's *The Gentle Shepherd* for 'simplicity both of *Sentiment* & *Language*', see his annotated copy (British Library), especially the final MS note on p. 77. See also 'Dryden' **325** and n. above, and, for 'simplicity' in painting, Reynolds's 'Discourse VIII' (1778) (*Discourses*, 208–12).

For S's limited 'comprehension', 'knowledge', and 'variety', see **17**, **21** and nn. above. Hawkins reported SJ's comparison of S as a poet to an 'Italian greyhound': 'he has not the sagacity of the hound, the docility of the spaniel, nor the courage of the bull-dog, yet he is still a pretty fellow' (*J's Works* (1787), xi. 200–1). Cf. SJ's definition of 'Pretty': '3. It is used in a kind of diminutive contempt in poetry, and in conversation: as *a pretty fellow indeed!*' (*Dict.*). S admitted in 1751: 'my verses in general smell too much of King-cups & Daffodils' (*S Letters*, 299).

Leicester, 'J's Life of S', 207, explained SJ's dampening final verdict on S as a reaction to Dodsley's praise of his poetry as 'distinguished by simplicity with elegance, and genius with correctness', and as capable of both 'sublimity' and 'tenderness': 'Of great sensibility himself, he never failed to engage the hearts of his readers: and amidst the nicest attention to the harmony of his numbers, he always took care to express with propriety the sentiments of an elegant mind' (*Works* (1764), i, p. v).

SJ ends by implying that, lacking 'comprehension', 'variety', and 'knowledge', S's poetry did not even succeed in being 'agreeable'. Graves, *Recollections*, 185, replied by concluding his own account of S with the defiant assertion that 'he is universally allowed to be *agreeable*', a claim endorsed by Robert Anderson, *Poets of Great Britain*, ix (Edinburgh, 1794), 591.

EDWARD YOUNG (1683–1765)

Composition. SJ told Mrs Thrale on 1 Aug., 1780, 'I think I have got a life of Dr. Young', and more confidently, on 8 Aug., 'I shall have Young's life given me to spite you' (alluding to her recent criticism of 'Granville') (*Letters*, iii. 294, 296). The biographical narrative in 'Young' 2–153 was written by Herbert Croft, who dated it 'Lincoln's Inn, Sept. 1780' (152 below). SJ may have received it by 18 Sept., when he noted that he had only 'Swift' and 'Pope' to write (*YW*, i. 301). Forwarding Croft's MS to Nichols, SJ explained in an undated note that 'This life of Dr. Young was written by a friend of his son' (*Letters*, iii. 322), presumably having added by then his own contribution in 1, 154–68.

Herbert (later the Revd Sir Herbert) Croft (1751–1816) was educated at Winchester and University College, Oxford, became a barrister in 1775, and was later a clergyman and miscellaneous author. He had been friendly since 1774 with Y's son Frederick (1732–88), who by then had already run through most of the £12,500 he inherited from his father (H. Forster, *EY* (Aldeburgh, 1986), 377).

Croft later claimed that SJ's good opinion of his novel *Love and Madness: A Story Too True, In a Series of Letters* (1780) had brought them together:

To the opinion, which the late Dr. Johnson entertained of these Letters, and of the good they might do, the author was indebted for the acquaintance and friendship of that great and good man. This trifle, which, it is hoped, has not been without doing its service, is now inscribed to the memory of Samuel Johnson. ('Preface to the Fifth Edition' (1786), 340)

In *Gent. Mag.* (Mar. 1800), 223, he repeated that he owed 'the pleasure and honour of ... Johnson's acquaintance' to his novel. At this stage there is no sign that SJ knew of Croft's anonymous *A Brother's Advice to his Sisters* (1775), which incidentally referred to Richard Savage's 'most unnatural mother' (6). Croft was later 'somewhat hurt' in 1784 to learn that SJ was not 'highly pleased' with this earlier work, written 'in a style somewhat of familiarity', since he 'could not approve of any mixture of levity in religious exercises' (Boswell, *Applause*, 236–7; cf. *Life*, iv. 298).

Croft's immediate purpose in *Love and Madness* was to exploit public interest in the sensational murder of Martha Ray, mistress of the prominent politician John Montagu, Earl of Sandwich, by the Revd James Hackman, who was tried and executed in Apr. 1779. For SJ's interest in the Hackman case, see *Life*, iii. 384–5, and for a detailed account of the affair, see John Brewer, *A Sentimental Murder: Love and Madness in the Eighteenth Century* (2004), esp. ch. 6. Although Croft purported to publish the correspondence between Hackman and Martha Ray, the letters were largely his own invention. Such enterprising 'forgery', in 'this age of literary fraud', came as no surprise to *Gent. Mag.* (June 1780), 287. *Love and Madness* also included an investigation of the career of Thomas Chatterton, whose fate Croft compares to that of Richard Savage ('Johnson has moistened many an eye with the sufferings of Savage', 225).

SJ would also have found in *Love and Madness* a reference to his own 'wonderful' *Dictionary* (72), and a description of the execution in 1777 of the Revd William Dodd (103–7, 336–9), a matter of obvious interest to SJ, on which Croft had more to say in the 1786 edition, 336–9. His attention must also have been caught by Croft's use of a letter dated '1 Aug. 1737' from Lord Gower to a friend of Swift about the possibility of obtaining for SJ himself a degree from Trinity College, Dublin, which Croft claimed to have been shown by a clergyman (70–2). Although a detailed discussion of Gower's letter in Boswell, *Making of the Life* (2001), 137 n., concluded that it was first published in *The Beauties of J* (5th edn., 1782), it had in fact recently appeared in the *Gent. Mag.* (Mar. 1779, 117–18 n.) before Croft made use of it in 1780. It had appeared even earlier in the *St James Chronicle* for 9–11 Dec. 1773, and within a few days in several other newspapers: see McGuffie, 118–19. In 1791 Boswell asked for the letter to be printed from Cooke's *Life* of SJ (1785), and to be dated 1739 rather than 1737 (*Life*, i. 133–4). (For Pope's attempt *c.*1739 to help SJ through Lord Gower, see his *Corresp.*, iv. 194, and headnote to 'Pope' above.)

Love and Madness was published on 11 Mar. 1780, so that if, as Croft claimed, it was his novel which brought him SJ's acquaintance, they had known each other for less than five months when SJ in effect commissioned him in early Aug. to write most of 'Young'. In conversation with Boswell and Frederick Young in June 1781, SJ later expressed some doubts about the propriety of Croft's mingling of fact and fiction in *Love and Madness* (*Boswell, Laird of Auchinleck*, 373), but there is no sign that in the previous year he had hesitated for long about accepting his help. He would have learned that Croft had been working on a biography of Y since 1777 (see **145** n. below), and would soon have realized that Croft 'had better information than I could easily have obtained' (1 below).

Although Y was one of the five poets about whom Boswell asked Lord Hailes on 7 July 1779 for 'any communications' he could pass on to SJ (Boswell Papers, Yale; *Catalogue*, L 615), it is unclear whether this means that SJ was already anxious about sources for Y's life. By the summer of 1780 he was also claiming to be uneasy about offending the living relatives of deceased authors (see 'Addison' **98** and headnote to 'Lyttelton' below). In *Prefaces* (1781) Croft originally referred in **2** below to SJ's 'fears lest, for want of proper information, you might say any thing of the father which should hurt the son' (see Textual Notes). The most likely explanation, however, of SJ's willingness to entrust Y to Croft is simple weariness on his part after several months of continuous work on the later *Prefaces*, with the major challenges of 'Swift' and 'Pope' still ahead. (For his simultaneous but unsuccessful attempts in late July 1780 to delegate other biographies, see headnotes to 'West' and 'Lyttelton'.)

If Croft himself is to be believed, SJ did not hand 'Young' over to him in any casual spirit. Croft refers to 'our different conversations about authentick materials' in **2** below, later implied that he had frequently visited SJ while 'collecting materials for this life and putting it together' (*Lives*, iv (1791), 348 n.), and even later recalled reading his MS aloud to SJ (see **93** n. below). SJ also read, and excised passages from, Croft's

MS before forwarding it to Nichols (see below). If *Love and Madness*, and anything else he knew about Croft, raised any doubts in his mind, they may have been allayed by discovering that Croft was thinking of leaving the Bar for the Church, a subject on which he sought SJ's advice (see **153** and n. and cf. **93** n. below).

Whether or not SJ was unaware of, or indifferent to, the more tendentious aspects of Croft's 'Young' is another question. Croft himself later claimed that its 'chief merit is in defending Young's son from . . . silly calumniators' (*Gent. Mag.* (Apr. 1800), 322). He did not, however, confine himself to proving the chronological impossibility of rumours that Y had depicted his son Frederick as the libertine Lorenzo in his *Night Thoughts* (**83–100**), or trying to exonerate him from the charge that his dissolute behaviour and extravagance had led to estrangement from his father. Croft also portrayed the venerated religious poet as a man who, throughout his career, had relentlessly flattered the powerful in the (mostly unsuccessful) pursuit of preferment, while later trying to suppress the 'despicable' dedications and panegyrics (**108** below) which were the clearest evidence of these worldly ambitions.

It may well be that SJ understood, and did not disapprove of, Croft's intentions. When he first met Y himself through Samuel Richardson in 1757 (see **116** n. below), he already knew of the 'quarrel between Young and his son', which he later discussed in Sept. 1773. SJ also stated that Y had 'pressed him much to come to Welwyn. He always intended it, but never went' (*Life*, v. 270–1; see **132** n. below). He was also well aware of, and disliked, Y's pursuit of preferment (see **139** and n. below). Before meeting Croft, he said on 9 Apr. 1778 that Y, 'who pined for preferment, talks with contempt of it in his writings, and affects to despise every thing that he did not despise' (*Life*, iii. 251). In June 1781, he politely told Frederick Young (whom he thought 'very unknowing' with 'uncouth manners'): 'I had the honour to know that great man, your father.' Yet the visit later prompted him to say of Y to Boswell that 'it is not becoming in a man to have so little acquiescence in the ways of Providence, as to be gloomy because he has not obtained as much preferment as he expected' (*Life*, iv. 120–1; *Laird of Auchinleck*, 370).

SJ may not, however, have foreseen that sections of Croft's tendentious biography would offend descendants of Y's relatives by marriage. For an early attack, and a reply in which Croft sought shelter under 'the enviable praise of Dr. Johnson, whose approbation is fame', see *Gent. Mag.* (1782), 70–2, 112. Such objections help to explain Croft's later extensive revisions, which continued after SJ's death (see **74–5** n. below), and his reference to 'my unhappy life of Young' (*Gent. Mag.* (Mar. 1800), 226). Detached admirers of Y were also disconcerted. Hester Thrale-Piozzi, writing from Milan on 5 Jan. 1785, commented: 'I was always vexed about Dr Johnson's suffering poor Young to be so treated in the Lives you know; but I am more sorry now because of the Foreigners, who all reverenced him before, & called him the Christian Poet' (*Queeney Letters*, 192). Joseph Warton, *Works of Pope* (1797), i, p. lv, noted the disparity between SJ's own respectful discussion of of Y's poetry in **154–68** and 'the unfriendly and uncandid Life' which preceded it. For the writing and reception of Croft's biography, see also H. Pettit, 'The Making of Croft's Life of Y for J's *Lives of the Poets*', *PQ* 54 (1975), 333–41.

The extent to which SJ revised Croft's biography is a vexed question. Unfortunately, Croft's original MS, described as bearing SJ's annotations and corrections, vanished after it was sold at auction by Sotheby's on 3 Aug. 1858: see Fleeman, *Handlist* (1967), 28. SJ forwarded it to Nichols in the autumn of 1780 with a covering note which indicates that he had made or recommended excisions, partly no doubt because of its disproportionate length: 'What is crossed with black, is expunged by the author, what is crossed with red is expunged by me, if you find any thing more that can well be omitted I shall not be sorry to see it yet shorter' (*Letters*, iii. 322). When the Revd John Hussey later told him that 'Young' was thought to be too long and that Y 'was too frequently called the Author of the *Night Thoughts*', SJ replied: 'Nay, I can acquit myself of the first charge and Mr. Croft of the other. I expunged nearly half that was written, and he was called the Author of the *Night Thoughts* by my recommendation' (Hill (1905), iii. 361 n.). (For Y as 'the Author of the *Night Thoughts*', see **3, 5, 8, 21, 80–1, 92, 96, 99, 108, 130–1, 139, 142, 145, 148, 151** below. SJ himself avoids the phrase.)

Croft himself, however, in the postscript (dated Sept. 1782) he added in *Lives* (1783), reminded SJ that, 'though I could not prevail on you to make any alterations, you insisted on striking out one passage only because it said that if I did not wish you to live long for your sake, I did for the sake of myself and of the world' (**153** below). Croft no doubt chose these ambiguous words carefully. He appears to say that SJ did not alter his MS and made a single excision purely out of modesty: it is unclear whether Croft's 'only' relates to the two preceding words (i.e. SJ struck out 'one passage only'), or to the following one ('only because' of his modesty).

Many years later, in *Gent. Mag.* (Feb.–Apr. 1800), Croft addressed to Nichols a heated reply to Robert Southey's accusations that he had exploited Thomas Chatterton's relatives by printing material they had entrusted to him in 1778. Croft also incidentally discussed the disparity between his own claim in 1783 that SJ had hardly interfered with the MS of 'Young' and SJ's own reference (by then printed by Nichols) to the various passages he had deleted. Admitting that SJ had in fact made excisions in his MS, Croft now insisted on the distinction between alterations and excisions: 'You, Mr. Nichols, . . . *know* that Johnson did not make a *single* alteration, or correction, nor even correct the press; and that all he did was to strike out some passages because my life was longer, in proportion to Young's works, than the other lives . . . I certainly should have been glad, if Johnson HAD *revised* it, but you know Mr. N. that he did not; and I know, that, when I asked him to correct the press; his answer was—"No, sir; you shall do it all, yourself. If I touch it, the dogs will say I wrote it for you"' (*Gent. Mag.* (Mar. 1800), i. 225).

Nichols commented on Croft's claim in a footnote: 'If any one wishes to see what the Doctor *did* expunge, he may find the whole (three paragraphs) in vol. LI p. 319.' This cross-reference is at first sight puzzling, since *Gent. Mag.* (July 1781), 319, contains only some miscellaneous observations on SJ's *Lives* by Nichols himself as 'Eugenio'. (Y's biographer, Harold Forster, concluded in *N & Q* 223 (1978), 71, that Nichols simply gave an incorrect page reference.) Nichols's article does, however, include three paragraphs about Y, which are presumably the excisions from Croft's 'Young'. Since they concern a suggestion for a compulsory deposit scheme for printed books, Cowley's plan of retiring to America, and a humorous anecdote about Y which turns on a feeble pun, SJ's decision to 'expunge' them seems entirely reasonable. The fact that Nichols added some corrective editorial notes to these paragraphs seems to confirm that they were by a hand other than his own. Needless to say, they hardly corroborate Hussey's claim quoted above that SJ told him he had expunged 'nearly half' of Croft's MS.

Isaac D'Israeli later reported that SJ had in fact also insisted on the omission of the following passage from Croft's account of Y's treatment of his wife and son:

While the poet's eye was glancing from 'Earth to Heaven,' he totally overlooked the lady whom he married, and who soon became the object of his contempt; and his only son, who when he returned home for the vacation from Winchester school, was only admitted into the presence of his poetical father on the first and on the last day; and whose unhappy life is attributed to this unnatural neglect . . .

D'Israeli explained that 'These facts are drawn from a manuscript of the late Sir Herbert Croft, who regretted that Dr. Johnson would not suffer him to give this account during the doctor's lifetime, in his life of Young, but which it had always been his intention to have added to it' (*The Literary Character, Illustrated by the History of Men of Genius* (3rd edn. enlarged, 2 vols., 1822), ii. 109 and n.

In his own copy of *Lives* (1783) (British Library) Croft wrote:

Just before the appearance of the latter half of the lives, a gentleman said to [SJ]—'So, Dr., a young man at the bar writes Young's Life for you, I find.' 'Yes, Sir,' said Johnson, 'Yes, Sir; tis true; and I thought he wd have done it very well, but the rogue deceived me sadly, Sir. He did it a deal better than I thought he was capable of doing it.' (*Life*, iv. 482; first printed in T. J. Mathias, *The Grove. A Satire* [1798], 63 n.)

While Boswell thought that Croft had achieved 'a pretty successful imitation' of SJ's style, he also reported Burke's memorable disagreement, uttered a few days before its publication: 'No, no, it is *not* a good imitation of Johnson; it has all his pomp without his force; it has all the nodosities of the oak without its strength' (*Life*, iv. 59, and cf. iv. 482). Percy's notes on Boswell's *Life* mention 'Steevens's Censure of Croft's Life of Young: wch tho' shortned by J. had no part written by him, as he assured me' (Bodleian, MS Percy d. 11, fo. 14ᵛ). It is unclear whether Steevens objected to Croft's content or style. Most reviewers of the later *Prefaces* commended his attempted impersonation of SJ.

Some idea of Croft's private opinion of SJ's style is conveyed by the mock-epitaph for SJ in his anonymous *The Abbey of Kilkhampton; or, Monumental Records for the Year 1980*, published not long after he completed 'Young', and often reprinted (*Gent. Mag.* (Nov., Dec. 1780), 533, 573). By comparison with his mockery of other contemporaries, Croft's 'epitaph' on SJ is relatively restrained, describing him as 'an illustrious Genius, yet dark—*irradiantly* dark', and as 'descended from the royal Loins of Minos. Hence we may trace the *Labyrinthian*, and (with Reverence be it asserted) the sovereign-like Mazes, in which he sported with the plain Good-sense of the *pure* English Reader' (*The Abbey of Kilkhampton, Part II* (1780), 122).

Croft's ambivalent attitude is also apparent in his later reports on his progress with an elaborate new edition of SJ's *Dictionary* in *Gent. Mag.* (Aug. 1787), 651–2 and (Feb. 1788), 91–2, and in his *Unfinished Letter to the Right Honourable William Pitt Concerning the New Dictionary* (1788), which refers to SJ as 'my great friend and master', but claims that his *Dictionary* was 'from the beginning to the end, most completely, radically and incurably defective' (3, 26). Although Croft published proposals for this work in 1792, he later abandoned the project.

Two weeks after the publication of 'Young' in *Prefaces* (1781), SJ and Boswell paid the visit to Frederick Young at Welwyn already mentioned (see also notes to 48, 74, 80, 150, 154 below). Boswell based his account in *Life*, iv. 119–21, on more detailed entries in his journal (*Boswell, Laird of Auchinleck*, 370–3).

Sources. Since he did not die until 1765, Y did not appear in *GD* or Shiels, *Lives*. Croft himself cites the entries about Y in Jacob, ii. 241–2, and Wood, ii. 991–2, but it was obviously the anonymous account in *BB*, vi (ii) (1766), Suppl. 256–60, which most irritated Frederick Young, and Croft replies directly to it in 30, 40, 83, 96 and n., 135 below. *BB* itself cites as a source Dr Eyre of Gray's Inn, Y's schoolfellow at Winchester.

Frederick himself was obviously a crucial source for Croft. In a letter of 6 Dec. 1786, Thomas Monkhouse, Provost of Queen's College, Oxford, stated that Croft 'has many of Dr. Young's Papers' (*Corresp.*, 60 n.). For some later anecdotes about Y printed by Nichols, see *Gent. Mag.* (1782), 282–4, and **133** n. below.

SJ increased the fifteen quotations from Y in *Dict.* (1755) to 188 in 1773, drawing particularly on *The Love of Fame*: see Reddick (1990), 107, 130–1, 220 nn.

Publication. In *Prefaces*, vol. x (15 May 1781). Pp. 65–80 (of 113) of the proofs in the Forster Collection were corrected by Croft. Some further errors were pointed out in *Gent. Mag.* (1781), 420–1. Croft made numerous revisions in *Lives* (1783), which he sent SJ by Sept. 1782 (see **153** below), and he continued to annotate his copy of this edition (British Library), making further changes after SJ's death in *J's Works* (1787), and minor revisions in *Lives* (1790–1).

Note. Croft's biography nominally takes the form of a letter addressed to SJ, but the opening and closing quotation marks and the epistolary gestures in **2, 152–3**, and even the occasional remarks addressed directly to SJ himself (see **19, 38, 42, 44, 81, 99, 145**), hardly register in an extended narrative. Although Hill's decision not to annotate Croft's text has not been imitated, notes are restricted to more basic corrective and illustrative information than elsewhere.

The Textual Notes record variants only in the paragraphs written by SJ himself, with the exception of **2**, which Croft addressed directly to SJ, and significantly revised in 1783. Although Croft's many other revisions are mostly somewhat obsessive stylistic 'improvements', significant alterations or additions are briefly indicated in the notes. The extent of Croft's revision of 'Young' even before SJ's death is indicated by Nichols's *Principal Additions and Corrections* (1783), in which Croft was responsible for more than a third of the changes and additions to the text of *Lives* (1783), adding some twenty-eight paragraphs, and making additions or alterations affecting at least a complete sentence in another twenty. In conformity with the rest of this edition, the text is that of *Lives* (1783).

Modern Sources:
(i) Edward Young
Complete Works, ed. J. Nichols with life by J. Doran (2 vols., 1854)
Correspondence, ed. H. Pettit (Oxford, 1971)
Night Thoughts, ed. S. Cornford (Cambridge, 1989)
'The Satires of EY', ed. J. Hay (Ph.D. thesis, Univ. of Western Australia, 1977)
(ii)
I. St J. Bliss, *EY* (New York, 1969)
S. N. Brown, 'EY', in *Dictionary of Literary Biography*, xcv (1990), 353–63
H. Forster, 'EY in Translation', *Book Collector*, 19 (1970), 481–500, and 20 (1971), 47–67, 202–24
H. Forster, 'J's Life of Young', *N & Q* 222 (1977), 308–9
H. Forster, *EY: The Poet of the Night Thoughts* (Aldeburgh, 1986)
A. Lindsay (ed.), *Index of English Literary Manuscripts*, iii (iv) (1997), 573–8
M. E. Novak, 'The Sensibility of Sir Herbert Croft in *Love and Madness* and the "Life of EY"', *Age of J* 8 (1997), 189–207
D. W. Odell, 'Y's *Night Thoughts* as an Answer to Pope's *Essay on Man*', *SEL* 12 (1972), 481–501

B. Parker, *The Triumph of Augustan Poetics: English Literary Culture from Butler to J* (Cambridge, 1998), 219–30

H. Pettit, 'The Making of Croft's Life of Y for J's *Lives of the Poets*', *PQ* 54 (1975), 333–41

H. C. Shelley, *Life and Letters of EY* (1914)

J. Sitter, 'Theodicy at Mid-Century: Y., Akenside, and Hume', *ECS* 12 (1978), 90–106

W. Thomas, *Le Poète EY: Étude sur sa vie et ses œuvres* (Paris, 1901)

H. D. Weinbrot, 'EY's *Love of Fame, The Universal Passion*', in *The Formal Strain* (Chicago, 1969), 95–128

2. In *Prefaces* (1781) 'the Life of Young,' was followed by 'and in consequence of your fears lest, for want of proper information, you might say any thing of the father which should hurt the son' (see Textual Notes).

    my profession: for Herbert Croft's legal career, see headnote.

4. Y was in fact baptized on 3 July 1683, the son of Edward and Judith Young. His father (*c.*1642–1705) was a Fellow of Winchester (1679), Rector of Upham (1680), Dean of Salisbury (1702), chaplain to William III and Queen Mary, and later to Queen Anne (Forster, *EY*, 1–8). Croft refers to Bishop Gilbert Burnet.

5. Y attended Winchester 1695–1702 (Forster, *EY*, 8–16).

6–7. Y in fact matriculated from New College, Oxford, as a Gentleman Commoner, on 3 Oct. 1702, but transferred to Corpus Christi College in 1703. He was nominated a Scholar of All Souls College by Thomas Tenison, Archbishop of Canterbury, on 27 Nov. 1708, and became a Fellow in Law on 2 Dec. 1709; BCL, 1714; DCL, 1719 (Forster, *EY*, 17–18, 23–4).

9. For Y's *Oratio Codringtoniana* (1716), on the foundation of the Codrington Library at All Souls, see Forster, *EY*, 46–7.

10. For Y's letter to Edmund Curll, 4 Aug. 1740, see *Corresp.*, 88–9. Curll used it in a composite letter prefixed to Y's *Poetical Works* (2 vols., 1740), i, p. vi, in which, against Y's wishes, the *Oratio* was appended in vol. ii. For Y's dispute with Curll over the edition, see *Corresp.*, 11–14.

11. For rumours of Y's 'lax morals' in early life, see Reed, *Biographia Dramatica* (1782), i. 478, and Forster, *EY*, 69–70.

12. For Philip, Duke of Wharton, see 30–1, 33–9 below.

13. Croft quotes Owen Ruffhead, *Life of Pope* (1769), 291 n.

14. Dr Matthew Tindal (1657–1733), the deist, was also a Fellow of All Souls. Croft later recalled that, when he visited SJ while writing 'Young', SJ used to bid him farewell with such admonitions as 'Don't forget that rascal Tindal, Sir. Be sure to hang up the Atheist' (*Lives*, iv (1791), 348 n.).

16. Added in 1783.

17. See 'Addison' 17 and, for the twelve new peers created in 1711, 'Granville' 17 and n. above. Y's *Epistle* was in fact published on 10 Mar. 1713, three days after Pope's *Windsor Forest*, also dedicated to George Granville, Lord Lansdowne (see 'Pope' 65 above).

    Croft's last sentence echoes SJ's comments on Dryden's flattery in 'Dryden' 172 above.

18. Croft cites Y's *Epistle*, ll. 45, 95, 314–15, 269, 322, and refers to Zanga in Y's *The Revenge* (1721).

In *Epistle*, ll. 494–531, Y paid tribute to the author William Harrison (1685–1713), his contemporary at Winchester and a Fellow of New College, Oxford: see also 22 n. below, and, for Y's reminscences of Harrison in 1759, Spence, i. 338–40.

19. For the letter to Curll, see 10 and n. above.

Nichols replied in *Lives*, iv (1791), 350 n., to Croft's comment on *Eng. Poets* (1779), claiming that SJ 'in many cases, thought and directed differently, particularly in Young's Works'. See also 53 n. below.

Croft quotes the 'Advertisement' in Y's *Works* (4 vols., 1757), i, sig. A2, from which he omitted his early occasional pieces and dedications. These were later collected in his posthumous *Works*, vols. v–vi (1767–78). Isaac Reed edited vol. vi, and later wrote unsympathetically about Y in *Biographia Dramatica* (1782), i. 477–80. Croft repeatedly refers to Y's attempt to suppress his earlier panegyrics, which were defended in *Gent. Mag.* (1782), 70–1. For a statistical context for Y's assiduity as a dedicator, see P. Rogers, 'Book Dedications in Britain 1700–1799', *BJECS* 16 (1993), 224.

21. For the commendatory verses in *Cato* (7th edn., 1713), see 'Addison' 67 and n. above.

22. *A Poem on the Last Day* (published 14 July 1713), dedicated to Queen Anne, had been quoted and praised in William Harrison's continuation of the *Tatler* as early as 22 Mar. 1711. It was also quoted in an essay on sacred poetry, possibly by Y himself, in *Guardian* 51 (1713), and was praised by Steele in the *Englishman* 11 (1713), by Thomas Warton the Elder in *Poems upon Divine and Moral Subjects* (1719), 40–1, and by Hubert Stogdon in his *Poems and Letters* (1729), 1–8. Croft quotes l. 3 of the poem.

The 'female cabal' refers to Abigail Masham's influence in turning Queen Anne against the Marlboroughs in 1711. For SJ's comments on the poem, see 155 below.

23–4. Croft added the quotations from Swift's *On Poetry: A Rapsody* (1733), ll. 307–10, 467–70, in 1783. Swift also refers to '*Young*'s universal passion, *Pride*' (l. 3).

23. See 4 above and 52 and n. below.

24. Swift probably refers to Y's flattery of Walpole in the 1720s (see 51 below).

26. Most of this paragraph is in fact a quotation from Y's effusive dedication to the Queen.

28. *The Force of Religion* appeared on 25 May 1714, some ten weeks before Queen Anne died. For Lady Jane Grey, see 'Smith' 24, 66, and 'Rowe' 16 above, and for SJ's later comments on the poem, see 156 below.

29. See Pope, *Corresp.*, i. 244. An earlier letter in fact makes clear that he already knew Y by 4 May 1714 (i. 223). *On the Late Queen's Death and His Majesty's Accession to the Throne* appeared on 17 Sept. 1714: Addison was then Secretary to the Regency before the arrival of George I (see 'Addison' 81 above).

30. For the Latin visitation sermon (1686) by Y's father, see 4 above. Wood, ii. 992, noted that William Atwood's translation of the sermon in *The Idea of Christian Love* (1688) was accompanied by verses by Anne Wharton (1659–85) and by poems addressed to her by Waller. For these literary relationships, see Wharton's *Surviving Works*, ed. G. Greer and S. Hastings (Stump Cross, 1997), 77–84, and cf. 67 below.

Croft goes on to refer to her husband, the Whig politician Thomas Wharton, later Marquess of Wharton (1648–1715) (cf. 'Addison' **29–30** above), and his son Philip, Duke of Wharton (1698–1731). He quotes the account of the younger Wharton in *BB*, vi (ii), Suppl. (1766), 187. Goldsmith claimed in 1759 to have heard Y say 'that a dinner with his lordship, has procured him invitations for the whole week following; that an airing in his patron's chariot, has supplied him with a citizen's coach on every future occasion. For who would not be proud to entertain a man who kept so much good company?' (*Coll. Works*, i. 311 and n., 340).

31. There is no evidence that Y accompanied Wharton to Ireland as early as 1717, although he did so in July 1720 (Forster, *EY*, 62, 65–6). The passage about Swift in Y's *Conjectures on Original Composition* (1759), 64–5, must refer to this visit to Dublin.

The last sentence originally began 'A note from Wharton, among Swift's Letters, clearly shews', revised in 1783 to 'Is it not probable', etc.

32. Although Steele's *Englishman* 11 (29 Oct. 1713) referred to Y's tragedy as 'in the theatre' (i.e. in rehearsal), *Busiris* was not acted until 7 Mar. 1719, receiving nine performances by 15 Apr. Thomas Pelham Holles, Duke of Newcastle (1693–1768), was the Lord Chamberlain. SJ discusses the play in **162** below.

33. *The Revenge*, performed 18 Apr. 1721, was acted into the 19th century. See also **162** below.

34. Having become a Jacobite, the younger Wharton died in Catalonia in 1731. His tragedy on Mary Queen of Scots may have been written as early as 1722 (Forster, *EY*, 68 n.).

35. See 'Dryden' **62** above. John Wilmot, Earl of Rochester (q. v. above), was uncle to the elder Wharton's first wife. Croft quotes Y's *The Instalment* (1726), ll. 45–6: see **51** below.

36. See *Love of Fame*, I. 27–8: 'Shall *poesy*, like *law*, turn wrong to right, | And Dedications wash an *Aethiop* white.' Croft also quotes Pope's satiric character of Wharton in *Epistle to Cobham* (1734), l. 180.

37. According to Pope's character (see **36** above), Wharton's 'ruling Passion' was 'Lust of Praise' (l. 181). He failed to make the promised donation to All Souls for the Codrington Library in 1720 (Forster, *EY*, 66–7).

38. Y tutored Wharton in Latin in 1719 (Spence, i. 337–8). In Mar. 1720 Wharton granted him an annuity of £100 for life, and a second annuity in July 1722, but from 1729 Y had difficulty in obtaining payment because of Wharton's numerous other creditors. After a protracted legal battle, Y finally won his case in 1743 (Forster, *EY*, 61, 77, 161, 168–71).

39. Y was tutor to John, Lord Burghley, eldest son of the Earl of Exeter, when he accepted Wharton's offer of an annuity of the same amount in 1719 (Forster, *EY*, 62–5).

40. Croft added the first sentence in 1783. For Y's unsuccessful election campaign at Cirencester, see Forster, *EY*, 75–7. Lord Hailes commented in 1782: 'I have heard that, frightened by some mobbers of ye opposite side, he run off from ye town & abandoned ye contest': see Carnie (1956), 487. By Mar. 1723 Y and other creditors were sueing Wharton for repayment of expenses. Croft refers to

BB, vi (ii), Suppl. (1766), 259–60 n., which itself cited the *Universal Museum* (June 1765).

41. Croft quotes *A Letter to Mr. Tickell. Occasioned by the Death of…Joseph Addison* (1719), ll. 111–13: see 'Addison' **101**–3 above.

42. Added in 1783: 'your account' refers to SJ's quotation from Spence in 'Tickell' **10** above.

43. Y dedicated *A Paraphrase on Part of the Book of Job* (1719) to Thomas Parker, Lord Chancellor since 1718 (see 'Hughes' **14** above). For Y's letter to Curll of 7 Dec. 1739, see **10** above and *Corresp.*, 74–5. The poem was included in *Poetical Works* (1741): SJ discusses it in **158** below.
    Croft inserted the penultimate sentence in 1783.

44–5. The seven epistles of *Love of Fame* were originally published separately as *The Universal Passion*: I (25 Jan. 1725); II (2 Apr. 1725); III (26 Apr. 1725); IV (11 June 1725); the 'Last' (i.e. of the original series), always so called though the fifth to appear (17 Jan. 1726); V (8 Feb. 1727); VI (24 Feb. 1728). SJ discusses Y's satires in **157** below.

44. For 'your account' see 'Dryden' **95** above. Croft quotes *Love of Fame*, I. 38, II. 277–8, 282, and VI. 573–6. He added the final sentence in 1783: for Y's marriage, see **67** and n. below.

46. Y was in fact 44 when he collected the seven poems as *Love of Fame, The Universal Passion* in Mar. 1728. For *The Last Day* (1713), see **22** above.
    Croft refers to Swift to Pope, 1 May 1733. Swift had told Charles Wogan in 1732 that Y 'is the gravest among us, and yet his Satyrs have many Mixtures of sharp Raillery' (*Corresp.*, iv. 153, 53). In 'On Reading Dr. Young's Satires' (written 1726) he had dwelt on Y's inconsistency in satirizing '*British* folly' while praising those in power.

48. The fable about poetry as the child of Poverty and Riches is in Plato's *Symposium*.
    Croft probably learned about the profits of *The Universal Passion* from Frederick Young, who told SJ and Boswell in 1781 that his father received 'several thousand pounds' for it. As SJ realized, Frederick was mistaken in believing that this money had been raised by a subscription (although Y originally hoped for one: see *Corresp.*, 30, 40), and that Y lost it in the South Sea Bubble of 1720, several years earlier (*Life*, iv. 121, 493–4; see also Boswell, *Making of the Life*, 502, for Reed's note on the error in Nov. 1792). Y did, however, lose some £3,500 in the Bubble.

49. Spence, i. 341, in fact stated that the present was from the Duke of Wharton, who was in serious financial difficulties by the mid-1720s. In one MS of his anecdotes Spence wrote against this story 'not true', the denial probably coming from Y himself: cf. **77** n. below.

50. The anecdotes about Sir Philip Sidney are in Spenser's *Works* (1679), sigg. A1–A1ᵛ, John Hughes's edition of Spenser (1715), i, pp. v–vii, and Shiels, *Lives*, i. 92–5. In 1783 Croft transferred the anecdote from Spence which originally followed this paragraph to **77** below.

51. Y inscribed his satires variously to the Duke of Dorset (I), Bubb Dodington (II), Sir Spencer Compton, the Speaker (IV), Lady Elizabeth Germain (VI), and Sir Robert Walpole ('Last').

Croft quotes Y's *The Instalment* (5 July 1726), ll. 79–80, addressed to Walpole when he became a Knight of the Garter. Thomson commented: 'The Dr's very Buckram has run short on this Occasion: his affected Sublimity even fails Him, and down He comes, with no small Velocity' (*Letters* (1958), 41). The poem was ridiculed in *Remarks Critical and Political, upon a Late Poem, Intitled the Instalment* (1726) and *The Craftsman* (13 Feb. 1727), and omitted from *Works* (1757).

52. George I granted Y a pension of £200 p.a. on 13 May 1726 (Forster, *EY*, 97). Croft quotes *The Instalment*, ll. 40–2.

53. George I died on 11 June 1727. As epigraph to *Ocean, An Ode. Occasion'd by His Majesty's Late Royal Encouragement of the Sea-Service* (published 8 June 1728), Y quoted George II's first speech from the throne on 27 Jan. 1728, which opposed naval pressganging. For Y's appointment as a royal chaplain, see **62** below. Most of the material omitted by Y from his *Works* (1757) was included in *Eng. Poets* (1779), perhaps on SJ's advice (see **19** n. above).

54. Added in 1783.

56–61. Added in 1783.

57. Croft quotes stanza 17. For SJ's comment on unintended 'burlesque' in Y's poetry, see **165** below.

59. SJ discusses Y's 'turgid' lyric poems in **159** below.

60. For Luke Milbourne, see 'Dryden' **148, 178, 357** above, and Pope, *Dunciad* (1729), II. 325 n.

62. Y was in fact ordained deacon on 20 Dec. 1724, but not apparently as a priest until 9 June 1728. He told Thomas Tickell, 1 Mar. 1726, that his 'prudential motive for taking orders' was hope of preferment from Lord Carteret, the Lord-Lieutenant of Ireland (*Corresp.*, 46–7), a possibility he had been exploring since 1724. Y became chaplain to the Princess of Wales in 1726, and Chaplain in Ordinary to George II on 30 Apr. 1728 (Forster, *EY*, 86, 98, 120–1). For his continuing solicitation of George II's 'favour' through Mrs Howard *c.*1730, see *Corresp.*, 68–9.

63. *The Brothers* was in fact withdrawn in Feb. 1724 several months before Y's ordination, mainly because of doubts about its likely success. For its long-delayed staging in 1753 see **113** below, and for the offensive epilogue David Mallet originally wrote for it, see 'Mallet' **2** n. below. Y's own 'Historical Epilogue' (85–6) summarized events which followed the action of the play.

64. The story (from Warburton) in Owen Ruffhead, *Life of Pope* (1769), 225 n., is 'clearly apocryphal' (Forster, *EY*, 87 n.), but cf. **105–6** n. below. Lord Hailes commented in 1782 on Croft's reference to this 'youthful frolick', 'how so? Pope was then *forty*': see Carnie (1956), 487. Thomas Sherlock (1678–1761) was Bishop in turn of Bangor, Salisbury, and London; Francis Atterbury, Bishop of Rochester (see 'Pope' **131–2** above); and Francis Hare (1671–1740), Bishop of St Asaph's and later of Chichester.

65. Y's two sermons were *The Vindication of Providence, or A True Estimate of Human Life* (1728 for 1727) on the death of George I (quoted by SJ under 'Serious' in the *Dict.* in 1773); and *An Apology for Princes* (1729) in which, while claiming 'an entire abstinence from *Party*', Y attacked opposition to the government.

Imperium Pelagi. A Naval Lyrick (1730) was originally to have been called *The Merchant*, and the Dublin edition of 1730 appeared with this title. It was reissued as *The Merchant, A Naval Lyric, Written in Imitation of Pindar's Spirit, on the British Trade and Navigation* as late as 1771, when *Monthly Review*, 44 (1771), 490–1, condemned its metre, 'low' conceits, and obscurity. Croft added the reference in the final sentence to Fielding's parody in *The Tragedy of Tragedies; Or The Life and Death of Tom Thumb the Great* (1731), I. v. 31–8 and n., in 1783. For SJ's references to *The Merchant*, see **161**, **165** below.

66. Y published *Two Epistles to Mr. Pope, Concerning the Authors of the Age* on 26 Jan. 1730.

67. All Souls presented Y to the Rectory of Welwyn in July 1730, and he was instituted there on 3 Nov. 1730.

Lady Elizabeth Lee was a granddaughter of Charles II. Her father was Anne Wharton's cousin (see **30** above). Aged 36, she was the widow of Col. Francis Lee, by whom she had three children. Lee had died as recently as Mar. 1730 and, although the marriage in fact took place on 4 Aug. 1730, it was not made public until 27 May 1731 (Forster, *EY*, 136–44).

Croft added the reference to Addison's unhappy marriage to the Countess of Warwick ('Addison' **85** above) in 1783.

69. Y in fact revised *The Foreign Address: or, The Best Argument for Peace* (1735) (see **72** below) as *The Sailor's Song of the South* (1755), and then further revised and enlarged it as *A Sea-Piece: Containing I. The British Sailor's Exultation. II. His Prayer before Engagement* (1755), the text and title included in his *Works* (1757). Croft's confusion about these different versions of the poem is understandable.

70. Voltaire objected to the allegory of Sin and Death in *Paradise Lost*, Bk. II, in his *Essay . . . upon the Epic Poetry* (1727) (see 'Milton' **257**–8 above). Y's epigram was circulating by 1728: see Spence, i. 344–5, ii. 644; *Gent. Mag.* (1779), 363 n., and (1780), 64; Goldsmith, *Coll. Works*, iii. 253; Forster, *EY*, 110–11. Croft quotes from stanza 4 of Y's verse dedication to Voltaire in *A Sea-Piece* (1755).

For Christopher Pitt's 'Epistle' to Y, see his *Poems and Translations* (1727), 1–6, and 'Pitt' **7** above. Y had known the politician and patron George Bubb Dodington at Winchester and Oxford, and introduced Thomson to him: see **51** and n. above and **121**–2 below, and 'Thomson' **15** and n. above. Eastbury was Dodington's ostentatious country seat in Dorset. For his account of Y's encounter with Voltaire, see Warton, *Essay on Pope*, ii (1782), 148. Dodington's *A Poetical Epistle from the Late Lord Melcombe to the Earl of Bute. With Corrections by the Author of the Night Thoughts* (1776) had been written in 1761.

71. Added in 1783. See Thomson, *Autumn* (1744), ll. 666–7, 645–7 (on John Philips).

72. Croft has already unwittingly mentioned Y's *The Foreign Address* (1735) under its later title in **69** above. In *Prefaces* (1781) this paragraph continued: 'and the editors of the present collection of English poetry have, for once, followed the decision of the author. Of all the pieces which Young condemned as inexcuseable, this alone has escaped that posthumous insertion, which, in truth, it little merited.' In *Lives* (1781) Croft revised 'the present collection of English poetry' to 'the two subsequent volumes', i.e. *Works*, vols. v–vi (cf. **19** n. above).

73. Croft quotes from stanza 53.

74–5. Under pressure from Lord Palmerston on behalf of the descendants of Y's wife, Croft revised and expanded these paragraphs in *J's Works* (1787), iv. 248–50, correcting some of the biographical information and qualifying the identifications of Y's relatives with 'the three persons whom he laments' in his poem.

74. Y's wife in fact died on 29 June 1740. Elizabeth, her daughter by Col. Lee, had married Henry Temple, son of Vist. Palmerston, in 1735, but died at Lyons on 8 Oct. 1736, when travelling to Nice with Y and his family. Henry Temple did not in fact die until 18 Aug. 1740 (Forster, *EY*, 149–55, 163).

For the publication of *Night Thoughts* (hereafter *NT*), see **92** n. below. The poem mourns the deaths of Lucia, Narcissa, and Philander, often later identified as Y's wife, his stepdaughter, and her husband. Frederick Young told SJ in 1781 that Y 'was never cheerful after my mother's death' (*Life*, iv. 121).

Croft quotes *NT*, I. 212–14, and silently adapts Dryden, *The Spanish Fryar*, II. ii. 114–15: 'There is a Pleasure sure, | In being Mad, which none but Madmen know.'

75. Croft quotes *NT*, III. 117, 119. Frederick, born 20 June 1732, was named after his godfather, Frederick, Prince of Wales (Forster, *EY*, 146): see headnote above, and **82–100** below.

76. See *The Last Day*, I. 143–4, II. 361–2, 369–7, and **22** above.

77. Spence, i. 341–2, recorded this anecdote (which originally followed **50** above), but later annotated it: 'No such thing. Dr Yg' (presumably after questioning Y). The Duke was in any case more likely to have been Wharton than Grafton: cf. **49** and n. above. Y obviously attracted such stories. Cf. Reed, *Biographia Dramatica* (1782), i. 478–9: 'The late Dr. [Gloster] Ridley remembered a report current at Oxford, that when he was composing, he would shut up his windows, and sit by a lamp even at mid day;—nay, that sculls, bones, and instruments of death, were among the ornaments of his study.'

78. Added in 1783. See **65** above.

79. Cf. SJ's account of Swift's 'discontent', 'neglected pride', and 'unsatisfied desire' in 'Swift' **135** above.

80. Added in 1783.

SJ and Boswell saw such inscriptions when they visited Welwyn on 2 June 1781, two weeks after the publication of *Prefaces* (1781): see *Life*, iv. 119–20, *Boswell, Laird of Auchinleck*, 372, and *Corresp.*, 600. *BB*, vi (ii), Suppl. (1766), 259, translated the first as 'The things unseen do not deceive us' (cf. 2 Corinthians 4: 18, 'for the things which are seen are temporal; but the things which are not seen are eternal', and Hebrews 11: 1, 'Now faith is the substance of things hoped for, the evidence of things not seen'). The second is from Genesis 3: 8 ('they heard the voice of the Lord God walking in the garden'). For other inscriptions at Welwyn, see *Life*, iv. 59–60, and Boswell's account of a 'deception' (cf. 'Shenstone' **11** and n. above) by a stream in Y's garden, suggested by Dodsley: 'It is boards painted like a brick summerhouse, the door open and a chair seen' (*Boswell Laird of Auchinleck*, 371–2). For Y's hopes of making Welwyn a fashionable spa, see Forster, *EY*, 217, 251–3.

81. Croft added the second sentence in 1783. He varies here the familiar Latin saying ('Of the dead speak nothing but good') as 'Of the dead speak nothing but the truth, of the living speak nothing but good'. The 'family of Yorick' alludes to *Hamlet*, v. i.

82. The 'son' is Frederick Young, whom Croft now defends against the charge of leading a 'debauched and reprobate life', quoting Genesis 42: 38.

83. Croft reacts to the tentative identification in *BB*, vi (ii), Suppl. (1766), 258 n., of Frederick as the worldly unbeliever Lorenzo in *NT*: Lorenzo, 'it is insinuated by some, was his own son'. *British Mag.* 6 (1765), 299, had made the same identification. For the 'particular dates', see **92** below. Lorenzo was almost certainly a composite figure (Forster, *EY*, 191–2).

85. Croft cites *NT*, II. 356.

86. Y's 'On M. *Angelo*'s famous Piece of the Crucifixion, who stabb'd a Person, that he might draw it more naturally' appeared in Steele's *Poetical Miscellanies* (1714 for 1713), 236–7.

87–91. Croft quotes *NT*, I. 322, V. 935–6, VIII. 343, V. 586–8, V. 1, 3.

92. For the correct dates of Y's marriage in 1730 and Frederick's birth in 1732, see **67** n., **75** n. above. *NT* originally appeared as *The Complaint: or, Night-Thoughts on Life, Death & Immortality*: Nights I–III in May, Nov., Dec. 1742; IV–V in Mar., Dec. 1743; VI–VII in Mar., July 1744; VIII in Mar. 1745; and IX in Jan. 1746. Shenstone commented on the publication of 'Night V' in Dec. 1743: 'I take his case to be wind in a great measure, and would advise him to take rhubarb in powder' (*Letters* (1939), 80).

93. During his exchanges with Southey in *Gent. Mag.* (Feb. 1800), 101–2 (see headnote), Croft wrote: 'But "thus easily are blasted the reputations of the living and the dead;" as I said, in my *Life of Young*, more than 20 years ago. When I had read to Johnson as far as these words . . . he stopped me with—"Yes, sir—and, if you quit Jones's bar" (the great Sir William) "for the church and literature, as Bishop Lowth advises you, it is probable you will be taught the truth of your own reflexion, by literature, long before you are my age." ' This is the only evidence that Croft read 'Young' aloud to SJ, who refers here to Croft's decision to abandon his legal career for the Church.

95. Croft refers to Cardinal Melchior de Polignac, *Anti-Lucretius* (2 vols., Paris, 1747), and Lovelace, the villain of Samuel Richardson's *Clarissa* (1747–8) (see 'Rowe' **8** above). He also quotes *NT*, VIII. 609–10.

96. Frederick matriculated from Balliol College, Oxford, on 12 Nov. 1751. *BB*, vi (ii), Suppl. (1766), 259, stated that he was expelled for misbehaviour, and that 'this misconduct had so highly displeased his father that the old gentleman would never suffer him to come into his sight afterwards'.

   In spite of Croft's claims, Frederick was in fact absent from Balliol in 1754–5 and, although he returned to Oxford for three further years, repeated absences and increasing debts eventually led to estrangement from his father. Elizabeth Montagu described him in a letter of 8 Mar. 1755 as 'a worthless irreclaimable profligate', and, on Samuel Richardson's word, exonerated Y from any blame (*Corresp.*, 478 n.). For SJ's comments on the quarrel in Sept. 1773, see *Life*, v. 270–1 and 132 n. below. By 1781 Frederick's extravagance had exhausted the £12,500 he inherited from Y (Forster, *EY*, 287–90, 329, 337–8, 375–80).

   For Milton's problems at Cambridge, see 'Milton' **12–13** above. In 1783 Croft removed his original reference to Milton's 'additional indignity of publick corporal correction' at Cambridge (see 'Milton' **11** above), and added the final sentence.

98. For Y's 'unnatural neglect' of Frederick when a schoolboy, as reported by Isaac D'Israeli, and supposedly omitted by Croft at SJ's insistence, see headnote.

99. Added in 1783. Croft refers to 'Addison' 98 above.

100. In 1783 Croft moved an anecdote which originally followed 100 to 148 below.

101. Y inscribed 'Night I' (2nd edn.) to Speaker Onslow; II to Spencer Compton, Lord Wilmington, the Prime Minister; III to the Duchess of Portland; V to the Earl of Litchfield; VI to Henry Pelham, the new Prime Minister; and IX to the Duke of Newcastle. See also 102 n. below.

  Croft quotes *NT*, VIII. 370–2 (referring to William Pulteney), and IX. 2382, 2388–90.

102. See *NT*, IV. 1–3, addressed to the youthful Hon. Philip Yorke (1720–90), son of the Lord Chancellor, whom he succeeded as Earl of Hardwicke in 1764.

  The proofs reveal that Croft originally wrote: 'Of the Fourth *Night* it is *remarkable* that he addressed it to the Honourable Mr. Yorke. The title is, *The Christian Triumph. Containing our only Cure for the Fear of Death, and proper Sentiments of Heart on that inestimable Blessing.*' In *Prefaces*, vol. x, leaf E5 (containing mid-101–103) is a cancel, perhaps caused by late revision of this passage.

103. Croft quotes *NT*, I. 449–52, 455–9. Y addressed these lines to Pope, the translator of Homer (Maeonides), regretting that he had not written about 'immortal man' in his *Essay on Man* (see 'Pope' 180 n. above), the task Y was now undertaking in *NT*.

  According to Walter Harte, Y also wrote to Pope, 'urging him to write something on the side of Revelation' (Warton, *Essay on Pope*, ii (1782), 148 n.; *Works of Pope* (1797), iii. 10–11). For the suggestion that Pope encouraged the impression that Harte's own explicitly Christian *Essay on Reason* (1735) was a compatible companion poem to the *Essay on Man*, see J. McLaverty, *Pope, Print and Meaning* (Oxford, 2001), 107–41.

104. Y was the dedicatee of Joseph Warton's *Essay on Pope* (1756), which set out to assess Pope's achievement by comparison with Spenser, Shakespeare, and Milton. Y accepted the dedication on 9 Nov. 1755: 'You do me an honour. I shall not fail to keep your secret.' Warton did not preserve his anonymity: by 8 Apr. 1756 Dodsley was reporting that SJ, Birch, Akenside, and others had identified him as the author of the *Essay* (*Corresp.*, 428–9 and n.).

  Croft exaggerates the supposed discrepancy in Y's attitude to Pope in 1742 and 1756. As Lord Hailes commented in 1782, 'What does all this tend to? Young might have been proud of a dedication from Warton, although, perhaps, their opinion of Pope did not, in every particular, agree': see Carnie (1956), 487, and cf. 118 below.

  In 1783 Croft's last sentence replaced a longer passage in the earlier editions: 'Though the first edition of this Essay was, for particular reasons, suppressed; another was printed. The Dedication still remained. To suppose therefore that Young approved of Warton's opinion of Pope is not unnatural. Yet the author of the passage just quoted would scarcely countenance, by patronage, such an attack', etc. Croft must have learned, perhaps from Warton himself, that he had been misinformed about the 'suppression' of the *Essay on Pope*.

105–6. For Pope's habit of translating Homer on the covers of letters, see 'Pope' **267** above. Croft quotes 'Paper-sparing *Pope*' from Swift's 'Advice to the Grub-street Verse-Writers. Written in the Year 1726', l. 13.

Y's letter probably dates from 1723. Nichols noted on the proofs, 'It was to request a Prologue to one of his Tragedies', a suggestion adopted by Croft first in a footnote to **105**, and, from 1783, in the text. Pettit, *Corresp.*, 22 and n., believed that the letter in fact referred to Y's wavering about turning from literature to the Church (cf. **64** above).

107. Croft quotes *NT*, IV. 52–5, 57, 60–2, 66–7, 101–5.

Since the siege of Troy lasted ten years and *NT* IV was published in 1743, Y saw himself as having pursued 'Court-favour' since 1723, when he was 40 and when his association with Wharton in effect ended. Croft added the last three sentences in 1783, quoting *Love of Fame*, II. 282.

108. Y had at first been more cautious, telling Sir Thomas Hanmer on 20 Nov. 1742, shortly before the appearance of 'Night II': 'I do not own myself the writer of it' (*Corresp.*, 150). For the two posthumous volumes of pieces omitted by Y from *Works* (4 vols., 1757), see **19** n. above.

Croft inserted 'This enviable praise . . . by every writer?' in 1783.

109. German enthusiasm for Y's poetry in fact preceded the vogue in France, which dates from Pierre Le Tourneur's (reorganized) translation in 1769: see Forster, *EY*, 387–91.

110. Lord Beauclerk, a cousin of Y's wife, died in naval action in 1741. Y wrote the verse epitaph in 1745 for a memorial in Westminster Abbey (Forster, *EY*, 204–5). Croft refers to *Eng. Poets* (1779).

111. Y appended 'Thoughts occasioned by the Present Junction', written in Oct. 1745 during the Jacobite rebellion, to *NT*, IX in Jan. 1746. There is nothing to indicate that SJ felt any unease at Croft's quotation of Y's attack on Charles Edward Stuart, the Young Pretender (ll. 161–5).

112. For Y's letter in Charles Howe's *Devout Meditations* (2nd edn., 1752), published by Archibald MacAulay, see *Corresp.*, 379.

113. For *The Brothers*, see **63** above and for its reception **162** and n. below. It was acted on 3 Mar. 1753 with Garrick as Demetrius, and had eight performances. Y sold the copyright to Dodsley for £147 on 7 Mar. (Dodsley, *Corresp.*, 529).

Y's donation to the Society for the Propagation of the Gospel, including some £535 from his own pocket (*Corresp.*, 382 n., and Forster, *EY*, 275–6), was described by *Gent. Mag.* (1753), 135, D. E. Baker, *Companion to the Play-House* (1764), i, sig. D1, and Thomas Davies, *Memoirs of Garrick* (1780), i. 168–72. According to *Gent. Mag.* (1766), 310–1, and (1781), 274, when Dodsley suggested that the money might more usefully have been donated 'to our poor clergy here at home', Y replied, 'that he knew not of any, and hoped there were none such'.

114. *The Centaur Not Fabulous. In Five Letters to a Friend, On The Life in Vogue* appeared on 4 Mar. 1755.

Croft added the final sentence in 1783, responding to the statement in *Gent. Mag.* (1781), 274, that Altamont 'was always understood to be designed for Lord Euston'. George Fitzroy, styled Lord Euston (1715–47), was the eldest son of the

Duke of Grafton. His wife, whom he married for her fortune and allegedly mistreated, died in 1742 at the age of 17.

115. Y was not in fact the author of *The Old Man's Relapse*. He admitted that his *Argument from Christ's Death* (1758), preached before George II, was intended to remind the King of his long service (Forster, *EY*, 314).

116–20. With the exception of the first sentence of 116 and the second of 119, these paragraphs were added in 1783.

116. Y had corresponded since 1744 with Samuel Richardson (1689–1761), the novelist, who was the printer of *NT*, VII–IX. In 1773 SJ recalled meeting Y at Richardson's house in about Feb. 1757, when Y read from the MS of his *Conjectures on Original Composition in a Letter to the Author of Sir Charles Grandison* (1759). He had been 'surprized to find Young receive as novelties, what he thought very common maxims' (*Life*, v. 269–70).

Croft quotes *Conjectures*, 3, 43–4, Y himself quoting Ovid, *Metamorphoses*, II. 255–6.

117. See *Conjectures*, 44, 80.

118. See *Conjectures*, 58, 69. For Pope's projected blank-verse epic 'Brutus', see 'Pope' 241 and n. above.

119. Croft quotes *Conjectures*, 2–3, 109.

Y's famous description of Addison's pious deathbed (*Conjectures*, 101–2: see 'Addison' 101 above) was a late addition: see Richardson to Y, 11 Oct. 1758 (*Corresp.*, 479–80).

120. See *Conjectures*, 112.

121–2. For George Bubb Dodington, who became Lord Melcombe in Apr. 1761, see 70–1 and n. above. His lines, 'Lord Melcombe to his Friend, Dr. Young', appeared in *Eng. Poets* (1779), and Croft now adds Melcombe's best-known composition. The two poems had been printed in newspapers and magazines in Aug. 1762, after his death on 28 July 1762. 'La Trappe' was the name of his house at Hammersmith, Middlesex: see *Corresp.*, 550–1.

123. Most critics took *Resignation* as evidence of 'the senescence of genius' (Forster, *EY*, 339–41, 347–8), and SJ's later discussion in 161 and n. below is unusually respectful.

Croft alludes to SJ's comments on the writings of Waller and Newton in old age in 'Waller' 132 above.

124–7. Added in 1783.

124. Admiral Edward Boscawen died in Jan. 1761. His widow, Frances Boscawen, was a friend of Elizabeth Montagu, the 'Bluestocking' hostess and the author of an *Essay* (1769) on Shakespeare. For Montagu's letter to Croft, 17 Sept. 1782, about the origins of Y's poem, see Cunningham, *Lives* (1854), iii. 346 n. Croft quotes *Resignation* (1762), 9, 26–7.

125. Croft quotes Dryden, 'Character of a Good Parson', ll. 19–20.

126. Croft quotes *Conjectures* (1759), 60.

127. Richardson (see 116 and n. above) died on 4 July 1761. Cf. *Resignation* (1762), 15 n.: 'Whilst the Author was writing This, he received the News of

Mr. *Richardson*'s Death, who was then printing the former Part of the Poem.'
Croft quotes *Resignation*, 16.

128. Y explained in his 'Advertisement' to *Resignation* (1762), and again at 64 n., that
he was publishing this expanded version of the poem only because extracts from a
privately circulated edition of 1761 had appeared in newspapers.

Y had in fact made his first will on 4 Aug. 1759: Croft's details are otherwise
correct (Forster, *EY*, 326, 328). For the will of 5 Feb. 1760, and the codicil
mentioned in **129**, see *Corresp.*, 601–4.

130. Y left £1,000 to Mary Hallows (*c*.1710–1790), his housekeeper, and 20 guineas to
Henry Stevens, a hatter of Temple Gate, but his will mentioned other names
(Forster, *EY*, 373–4).

SJ stated on 30 Sept. 1773 that Y's quarrel with his son was partly caused by
Frederick's dislike of Mary Hallows, 'who, having acquired great influence over
the father, was saucy to the son'. SJ rejected rumours of an 'improper connection
between them': 'He was past fourscore, and she a very coarse woman. She read to
him, and, I suppose, made his coffee, and frothed his chocolate, and did such
things as an old man wishes to have done for him' (*Life*, v. 270–1, and cf. v. 548). A
barber in Stevenage told Boswell on 17 Mar. 1772 of a rumour that Y 'kept a
mistress' (*Boswell for the Defence*, ed. W. K. Wimsatt and F. A. Pottle (1960), 33–
4). Y was in fact 81 when he made the codicil in 1764.

Croft quotes from a passage Y added to *The Centaur Not Fabulous* (2nd edn.,
1755), 284: 'Where is that world into which you and I were born?', to which Byron
later alluded in *Don Juan*, XI (1826), lxxvi. See R. Lonsdale, 'An Allusion to EY in
Byron's *Don Juan*', *N & Q* 248 (2003), 309.

131. For memorials to Y's servants in the churchyard at Welwyn, see Forster, *EY*, 263:
'my friend James Barker' was in fact a labourer.

132. John Kidgell (*c*.1722–1766) ridiculed Y and Mrs Hallows as Dr Elwes and Mrs
Fusby in his novel *The Card* (1755). Kidgell was probably a local clergyman at the
time (Forster, *EY*, 292–5). In 1783 Croft omitted his earlier statement that he had
been Y's curate.

133. Y died on 5 Apr. 1765. In *Gent. Mag* (1782), 284, Nichols printed a letter from
John Jones, Y's curate, which described his refusal to see Frederick on his
deathbed, although he said, 'I heartily forgive him.' For an 'Elegy' on Y, see
Thomas Russel, *Elegies* (1767), 22–9.

134. Added in 1783.

135. The account of Y's funeral in *BB*, vi (ii), Suppl. (1766), 259, derived from *London
Chronicle*, 13–16 Apr. 1765; see also *Gent. Mag.* (Apr. 1765), 198–9.

For Frederick Young as the supposed 'Lorenzo', see **83–100** above. Croft refers
to Y's prose preface to *NT*, VII (1744).

136–8. In 1783 these paragraphs replaced an erroneous attribution to Y: 'After his
death, Dodsley published a novel called *Eliza*, of which I have been told that
Young was the author.' Croft's informant may have confused Y with Arthur
Young (1741–1820), the agriculturist, who also published fiction in the 1760s, but
not apparently *Eliza* (2 vols., 1766).

136. Y had travelled in France in 1736–7 (see **74** n. above and Forster, *EY*, 149–55).

137. See *Love of Fame*, VII. 59–60.

138. This anecdote in fact concerns the Revd William Young, the supposed original of Parson Adams in Fielding's *Joseph Andrews* (1742) (see **148** and n. below). This had been made clear in the article on Fielding in *BB*, vi (ii), Suppl., 58–9 n. See also Forster, *EY*, 95 n., and, for Hester Thrale's version of the story in 1778, *Thraliana*, i. 247.

139. Y's frustrated pursuit of preferment has been a major theme of Croft's biography. Forster, *EY*, 234–50, while noting George II's apparent dislike of Y, could not explain his lack of success. For SJ's own comments on Y's ambitions in *Life*, iii. 251, iv. 120–1, see headnote above.

　　For Y's pension in 1726, see **53** n. above, and for the poets associated with Frederick, Prince of Wales, see 'Pope' **217** and n. Although Y was usually loyal to Walpole and the court interest, Benjamin Victor, *Original Letters* (1776), i. 267, believed that he was denied a bishopric because he had 'returned enraptured' from a visit to Dawley Farm in the 1720s, when Bolingbroke 'was in a paper war with Walpole'.

140. Thomas Secker (1693–1768) had been Archbishop of Canterbury for less than three months when he wrote this letter (*Corresp.*, 474). Y became Clerk of the Closet to the Princess Dowager of Wales, mother of George III, in Jan. 1761, through the influence of Dodington (see **121–2** above) and the Duke of Newcastle, at the prompting of the Duchess of Portland (Forster, *EY*, 333–4).

141. See *Paradise Lost*, VII. 464–5.

142. Added in 1783.

143. Croft quotes Horace, *Epist.*, I. ii. 9.

145. Croft alludes to SJ's emphasis on the biographical importance of 'domestick privacies, and … the minute details of daily life' in *Rambler* 60 (*YW*, iii. 321) and elsewhere.

　　Mary Hallows, Y's housekeeper from 1749 (see **129–32** and nn. above), in fact survived until 1790, as *Gent. Mag.* (1790), 520–1, pointed out. Pettit, 'Making', 337–8, suggested that Croft in fact narrowly missed the funeral of her mother Ann Hallows on 16 Feb. 1777. If so, Croft was already working on his life of Y by that date.

146. For Vincenz Bernhard Tscharner's letter to Albrecht von Haller, 1 Mar. 1751, describing his visit to Y, see *Corresp.*, 359 n.

148. For the Revd William Young, see **138** and n. above, and M. C. and R. R. Battestin, *Henry Fielding: A Life* (1989), 187–90. Croft originally discussed this 'anecdote' after **100** above.

149. For such 'notes of approbation' in Y's copy of the *Rambler*, see *Life*, i. 214–15. For evidence that SJ himself sometimes folded down pages, see R. DeMaria, *SJ and the Life of Reading* (Baltimore, 1997), 70, and, for his earlier comments on the annotation of books, see *Idler* 74 (1759) (*YW*, ii. 231–2).

　　Croft quotes *NT*, IV. 98–100.

150. SJ saw the monument erected by Frederick in 1766 on 2 June 1781 (*Life*, iv. 121; Forster, *EY*, 375–6).

151. Added in 1783.

153. Croft inserted this postscript in 1783, evidently without SJ's knowledge. For SJ's deletions in Croft's biography, see headnote. Croft was ordained in 1786 and inherited a baronetcy in 1797.

154–68. The critical discussion of Y's works is by SJ himself.

154. SJ sees no significant pattern in Y's development from early 'equability and propriety' (154) through formal verse satire in the 1720s (157) and lyric experiment in the 1730s (159) to the treatment of emotional religious experience in blank verse in the 1740s (160), noting only the absence of any 'uniformity of manner' or improvement in 'correctness' with experience (155). For Y's apparent inconsistency and idiosyncratic versification and diction, see also 167–8 below, and cf. SJ's praise of the 'uniformity' of Pope's style in 'Pope' 300 above.

   With 'concatenated without any abruption', cf. 'Cowley' 126 and n. and 'Swift' 112 above. For 'the fortuitous suggestions of the present moment', see 167 below, and for 'judgement', which should ideally be combined with imagination, see 'Roscommon' 23 and n. above.

155. The implicit contrast is again with Pope: see 'Pope' 296–300 above. SJ assumed that a writer, 'like other mortals', would grow 'wiser as he grew older, could display life better, as he knew it more, and instruct with more efficacy, as he was himself more amply instructed' (YW, vii. 87–8).

   For The Last Day (1713), of which SJ owned a copy as an undergraduate (Gleanings, v. 226–7), see 22 above. For his conviction that such a sacred subject 'makes every man more than poetical', see 'Waller' 135–41 and n. above. In contrast, the reader of SJ's favourite lines from The Mourning Bride 'enjoys for a moment the powers of a poet' ('Congreve' 35 above). He had commented on another projected poem on The Last Day that it was 'a subject on which no mind can hope to equal expectation' ('J. Philips' 7 above).

   For SJ's use of 'great', see 157 below and 'Milton' 194 and n. above; for 'equability', 'Cowley' 200 and n. above; for 'propriety' and 'correctness', 'Roscommon' 24 and n. above; and for the 'general', 'Cowley' 58 and n. above.

156. For The Force of Religion (1714), see 28 above, and for other literary treatments of Lady Jane Grey, 'Smith' 54–5 (where SJ mentions the subject's potential 'for moving the passions') and 'Rowe' 16, 31 above.

   SJ praised Shakespeare in 1765 for having 'no heroes; his scenes are occupied only by men, who act and speak as the reader thinks that he should himself have spoken or acted on the same occasion' (YW, vii. 64).

157. For The Universal Passion (1725–8), retitled Love of Fame in 1728, see 44–9, 154 n. above. Aaron Hill's Plain Dealer 92 (5 Feb. 1725) hailed it as 'the Work of some considerable Genius', with 'the most shining Marks, of a Spirit, that is truely poeticaP'. SJ's 'very great' here evidently refers to quality as well as length: cf. 155 and n. above.

   SJ predictably found Y's couplet satires, which may have influenced Pope's poetry in the 1730s, more congenial than his later blank verse on sacred subjects. He used a line from Love of Fame, VI. 206, as epigraph to Rambler 126 (1751) (YW, iv. 306), and quoted it again in a letter in June 1771 (Letters, i. 364). In Sept. 1773 Boswell heard him recite two passages from Love of Fame, VI. 201 ff., V. 145 ff., 'which he praised highly' (Life, v. 269–70, and cf. ii. 96). In contrast, Warton told Y in the dedication of his Essay on Pope (1756), p. vi: 'Had you written only these satires, you would indeed have gained the title of a man of wit, and a man of sense; but, I am confident, would not insist on being denominated a POET, MERELY on their account'.

said to be a series of Epigrams: *BB*, vi (ii) (1766), suppl. 260 n., cited from the *Universal Museum* (followed by *Annual Register for 1765*, ii. 33) the statement that Y's satires 'consist of a string of epigrams, written upon one subject'. Goldsmith wrote in 1767 that Y 'seems fonder of dazzling than pleasing; of raising our admiration for his wit, than our dislike of the follies he ridicules' (*Coll. Works*, v. 328).

Y contrasted Horace's insinuating satire with Juvenal's moral indignation in the preface to *Love of Fame* (1728), sigg. A4–A4ᵛ.

the recesses of the mind: cf. 'the recesses of his heart' in *Rambler* 8 (1750) (*YW*, iii. 46), 'the recesses of the human heart' (of Richardson) in conversation in 1768 (*Life*, ii. 49), 'those ideas that slumber in the heart' in 'Dryden' 326 above, and 'the passes of the mind' in 'Pope' 320 and n. above.

a single perusal: cf. SJ's evocation in 'Dryden' 312 above of the great author, 'whose pages are perused with eagerness, and in hopes of new pleasure are perused again'. For 'conceits', see 'Cowley' 58 and n. above.

158. For *A Paraphrase on Job* (1719), see 43 above. Isaac Watts praised 'its lovely and dreadful Scenes in Lines of such Sweetness and Terror' in *Reliquiae Juveniles* (1734), pp. xi–xii.

To translate he never condescended: this statement must be mildly ironic, given the importance SJ has attached to translations not merely by Dryden and Pope, but by Rowe, Pitt, and West. The Earl of Oxford had in fact lamented that Pope's 'genius should be wasted upon a work not original' (see 'Pope' 75 above). Y himself wrote in *Conjectures* (1759), 68–71: 'supposing *Pope's Iliad* to have been perfect in its kind; yet it is a *Translation* still; which differs as much from an *Original*, as the moon from the sun ... *Originals* shine, like comets; have no peer in their path; are rival'd by none, and the gaze of all', etc.

For 'ornaments' in poetry, see 'Cowley' 202 and n. above. Under 'To Chuse' in the *Dict.* SJ merely cross-refers to 'To Choose'.

159. For Y's odes, see 53–60 above. It is clear from *Rambler* 158 (*YW*, v. 75–8) that SJ would feel little sympathy for Y's argument in 'On Lyrick Poetry', prefixed to *Ocean. An Ode* (1728), that the true ode should be 'rapturous, somewhat abrupt, and immethodical to a vulgar eye', rejecting 'order and connection'. For other unsuccessful 'lyrick attempts', see 'Congreve' 44 and 'Fenton' 21 above and 'Akenside' 22 below.

SJ defines 'Turgid' (see also 166) as '2. Pompous; tumid; fastuous; vainly magnificent', and 'Fastuous' in turn as 'Proud; haughty' (*Dict.*).

160. For originality, see 162 below and 'Milton' 277 and n. above. Although he does not comment on it here, SJ was well aware of Y's *Conjectures on Original Composition* (1759) (see 116–20 and nn. above).

SJ often expressed reservations about Y's poetry in conversation. Croft himself heard SJ say that, 'if it contains some of the worst, [it] contains also some of the best things in the language' (61 above). In Sept. 1773, SJ stated that Y 'was not a great scholar, nor had studied regularly the art of writing; that there were very fine things in his *Night-Thoughts*, though you could not find twenty lines together without some extravagance' (*Life*, v. 269–70, and cf. ii. 96, for an earlier admission in 1769 that it contained 'fine things').

In Nov. 1777 SJ compared Y's works to 'a miry Road, with here & there a Stepping Stone or so; but you must always so dirty your feet before another clean Place appears, that nobody will often walk that way'. Y 'bubbles & froths in his Descriptions' in contrast to the genuine sea-storm found in Dryden's poetry (*Thraliana*, i. 174; cf. *J. Misc.*, i. 187). In Jan. 1777, however, Mrs Thrale had made him 'confess' that Y's description of night in *NT*, I. 18–25, 'is superior to that of either Dryden or Shakespear' (*Thraliana*, i. 362; cf. *J. Misc.*, i. 186, and see 'Dryden' 19 and n. above). Such assertions explain Boswell's anxiety in advance about what SJ would say about *NT*, 'which I esteem as a mass of the grandest and richest poetry that human genius has ever produced', with 'a power of the *Pathetick* beyond almost any example that I have seen', see *Life*, iv. 60–1.

For SJ's usual dislike of blank verse, see 'Milton' 274 and n. above; and for other concessionary statements about it, and about the 'confinement of rhyme', see 'Thomson' 46–7 above and 'Akenside' 17–18 below.

With SJ's image of Y's *NT* as a fertile 'wilderness', cf. the 'Preface to Shakespeare' (1765): 'The work of a correct and regular writer is a garden accurately formed and diligently planted, varied with shades, and scented with flowers; the composition of Shakespeare is a forest, in which oaks extend their branches, and pines tower in the air, interspersed sometimes with weeds and brambles, and sometimes giving shelter to myrtles and to roses; filling the eye with awful pomp, and gratifying the mind with endless diversity' (*YW*, vii. 84). For similar metaphors, see 'Pope' 309 and n. above. Cf. also Collins's 'meanders of inchantment' ('Collins' 8 above) and Akenside's 'flowery labyrinth' ('Akenside' 16 below).

Interest in the aesthetics of Chinese gardening goes back at least to Sir William Temple in the late 17th century and Addison, *Spectator* 414 (1712): see A. O. Lovejoy, 'The Chinese Origin of a Romanticism', in *Essays in the History of Ideas* (Baltimore, 1948), 99–135. Hill (1905) suggested that SJ has in mind here the *Dissertation on Oriental Gardening* (1772) by his friend Sir William Chambers (1726–96), in which, according to Boswell, 'we are told all odd, strange, ugly, and even terrible objects, are introduced, for the sake of variety; a wild extravagance of taste which is so well ridiculed in the celebrated Epistle to him' (*Life*, v. 186). Boswell referred to Mason's *Heroick Epistle to Sir William Chambers* (1773), which SJ enjoyed (in spite of its mockery of his pension) (*Life*, iv. 113). SJ would in fact already have met Chambers's ideas in 'Of the Art of laying out Gardens among the Chinese' in his *Designs of Chinese Buildings* (1757), which Percy believed SJ had 'drawn up' from materials supplied by Chambers. Extracts had appeared in the *Literary Mag.* 2 (1757), 199 and *Gent. Mag.* (1757), 216–19 (*Bibliography*, i. 714–19).

Boswell felt that SJ's account of *NT* overlooks 'a power of the *Pathetick* beyond almost any example that I have seen. He who does not feel his nerves shaken, and his heart pierced by many passages in this extraordinary work . . . must be of a hard and obstinate frame' (*Life*, iv. 61). As Goldsmith noted in 1767, the *NT* 'are spoken of differently, either with exaggerated applause or contempt, as the reader's disposition is either turned to mirth or melancholy' (*Coll. Works*, v. 328).

Still more striking than SJ's refusal to react to the subjectivism of 'the mournful, angry, gloomy' *NT* (Croft in 47 above) is the fact that a reader unfamiliar with the work could hardly deduce from SJ's discussion its intensely emotional religious preoccupations, in the cause of refuting deism and free-thinking. If pressed, SJ might have resorted to the explanation in 'Akenside' 15 below: 'With the philosophical or religious tenets of the author I have nothing to do; my business is with his poetry.' Having made clear his reservations about sacred poetry when discussing *The Last Day* in 155 above, he may have felt entitled to remain tactfully silent on this aspect of Y's most admired poetry, and to concentrate instead on its 'fertility' and 'copiousness'. As if aware of his earlier omission, SJ in fact delegated the subject to another hand in 1783 by adding in 'Akenside' 21 below a passage about *NT* from John Walker's *Exercises for Improvement in Elocution* (1777), 67, in praise of the 'masterly' Y, who 'has invincibly proved the immortality of man'.

For some readers, such as Charles Graham, *Miscellaneous Pieces in Prose and Verse* (Kendal, 1778), 170, Y had written the noblest poem in English or any other language. For an account of the 'distinguishing excellencies' and 'principal faults' of 'the grandest and richest poetry which human genius has ever produced', and which 'irresistibly seizes the mind of the reader', see Robert Anderson, *Poets of Great Britain*, x (Edinburgh, 1794), p. xviii. Robert Southey, *Specimens of the Later English Poets* (1807), ii. 333, observed more reservedly that 'No English Poem has ever been so popular on the Continent. It pleases all readers, for there is genius enough for the few, and folly enough for the many.' For the many translations of *NT*, see Forster, 'EY in Translation; and for SJ's interest in nocturnal settings, see 'Dryden' 19 and n. and 'Congreve' 34–5 and nn. above.

161. For *Resignation* (1762), see 123–8 above and, for Y's earlier 'experiments', 53–61, 65, 69–70 above.

SJ's praise of *Resignation*, if not ironic, is puzzling. *BB*, vi. (ii), Suppl., 259, described it as 'the last and worst' of Y's works, echoing *British Mag.* 6 (1765), 300. Langhorne, in *Monthly Review*, 26 (1762), 462–6, noted Y's continuing fondness for antithesis, pointed expression, hunting down of figures, and 'lowness of metaphors', and Lord Hailes commented in 1782 that 'in Resignation he often copies from himself, & turns ye Night thoughts into *staves*': see Carnie (1956), 487–8. Having ignored Y's claim in 1759 that 'blank verse is verse unfallen, uncurst; verse reclaimed, reinthroned in the true language of the Gods' (126 above), SJ may in fact be insinuating a preference for the simple, even banal, stanzas of *Resignation*.

SJ is also reacting to assumptions about the 'decaying faculties' of old age: see 'Waller' 132 and n. above. He himself was about to be 71, and Y was nearly 80 when he published *Resignation*.

162. For Y's tragedies, see 32–3, 63, 113 above. By 'the Collection' SJ means *Eng. Poets* (1779), which included only a few verse-dramas.

In his article on *Busiris* (1719) in Reed's *Biographia Dramatica* (1782), ii. 39, George Steevens in effect reclaimed his remark on Y's reliance on 'the most hackneyed incident . . . in modern tragedy', citing Dryden's comment on tragic denouements that "'tis more difficult to save than 'tis to kill. The dagger and the cup are always in a readiness' (Watson, i. 279). For literary suicide, see also 'Pope' 52 and 319 and n. above and 'Gray' 47 below. With the remoteness of *Busiris* from 'known life', cf. SJ's approval of 'domestic' tragedy in 'Otway' 10 and n. above.

The Revenge (1721) had been acted in London as recently as the 1776–7 and 1777–8 seasons. D. E. Baker, *Companion to the Play-House* (1764), i, sigg. 3ᵛ–4, suggested that Y borrowed its 'Design' 'partly from *Shakespeare's Othello*, and partly from Mrs. *Behn's Abdelazar*', and compared it in detail with Shakespeare's tragedy, placing it 'in the very first Rank of our Dramatic Writings'. SJ quoted it ironically on 6 Oct. 1777: 'Let me hear the whole series of misery, for as Dr. Young says, *I love horrour*' (*Letters*, iii. 81).

For the reception of *The Brothers* (1753), see **113** n. above. SJ's claim that 'nothing was ever said' of the play is an exaggeration. It has even been suggested that he himself wrote 'Some Account of The Brothers, a New Tragedy' in *Gent. Mag.* (Mar. 1753), 135–7 (see *Bibliography*, i. 403). Shenstone, in a letter of 1753 (published 1778), thought it 'noble' and 'full of refind & elevated Sentiments': 'I am not blind to many of it's Faults; Dr. Young must be Dr. Young; but I have read no Tragedy of late years that has affected me so much' (*Letters* (Oxford, 1939), 355, 357). Richardson, while regretting that it had been 'acted to thin houses', praised Y's 'great action' in donating the proceeds to charity (*Select Letters*, ed. J. Carroll (1964), 224–5).

D. E. Baker, *Companion to the Play-House* (1764), i. sig. D1, praised the contest between Demetrius and Persius in Act III as 'perhaps the finest Piece of Oratory in the *Eng.* Language'. Thomas Davies, *Memoirs of Garrick* (1780), i. 168–72, reported that 'it is thought by some to be his masterpiece'. Steevens, in *Biographica Dramatica* (1782), ii. 37–8, claimed, however, that the speeches in Act III were mostly translated from Livy and that the play was 'coldly received, being undramatical in its conduct, and imperfect in its catastrophe'.

163. *it abounds in thought*: cf. SJ's complaint that Prior 'never made any effort of invention: his greater pieces are only tissues of common thoughts' ('Prior' **70** above).

BB, vi (ii), Suppl., 260, had emphasized Y's unevenness, citing the *Universal Museum* (May 1765): 'there are flights of thinking almost super-human . . . yet all these noble flights are often allay'd by paltry witticisims, and a vile jingle of words.' (These comments were repeated almost *verbatim* in the *British Mag.* 6 (June 1765), 299.) Samuel Jackson Pratt ('Courtney Melmoth') later gave a detailed account of the merits and defects of Y's poetry in *Observations on the Night Thoughts of Dr. Young* (1776).

Ruffhead, *Life of Pope* (1769), 287 n., had praised the 'parallel of *Quicksilver* with *Pleasure*' in *Love of Fame*, V. 291–6. Mrs Thrale-Piozzi claimed to be the 'lady' whose approbation of it would have pleased Y (*J. Misc.*, i. 258), and may have intended her later discussion of Y's epigrammatic wit in *British Synonomy* (1794), ii. 371–2, to confirm this: 'all evince FERTILITY OF IMAGERY springing from the richest soil—as Johnson told me little cultivated.'

SJ refers finally to *NT*, IX. 1910–7.

164. See *The Last Day*, II. 49–52.

165. For the 'Prophet', see Isaiah 23: 8, adapted in Y's *Imperium Pelagi* (1730), II, st. 3. (For its alernative title as *The Merchant*, see **65** and n. above.) For 'burlesque', see 'Butler' **52** and n. above, and cf. Croft's comment on Y's 'involuntary burlesque' in **57** above.

166. For 'turgid' see **159** and n. above, and for the 'familiar', 'Cowley' **138** and n. above. SJ quotes *Imperium Pelagi*, I, st. 12, and *Love of Fame*, V. 551, VI. 200.

SJ defines 'Antithesis' as 'Opposition of words or sentiments; contrast' (*Dict.*), but, as noted by Wimsatt, *Prose Style of SJ* (1963), 90 n., seems here to mean something closer to 'paradox' or 'oxymoron'.

167. Cf. SJ's similar comment on Thomson's blank verse in 'Thomson' **46** above. For other poets who borrowed little, for SJ's views on versification, and for 'hemistichs', see 'Cowley' **172, 185–99** n., **198** and n. above.

SJ implicitly contrasts Y's lack of 'stores of thought or diction' with Pope, who 'gleaned' a 'regular collection' of 'beauties of speech' from other authors ('Pope' **380** above, and cf. 'Dryden' **220–1** above). For the 'suggestions of the present moment', see also **154** above.

Y's will ordered his MSS to be destroyed (see **128–9**), and the few which survive are unrevised: see Lindsay (ed.), *Index of English Literary Manuscripts*, iii (iv), 573–8. He had recommended unhurried composition in *Two Epistles to Mr. Pope* (1730), II. 119–36. SJ's account of his working habits may derive from the report in *British Mag.* 6 (1765), 297, that he 'took very great pains to polish and correct the harshness of his numbers: so that, we are told, he has been for weeks together endeavouring to turn a few lines into mellifluous modulation, and often without success'. For habits of composition, see also 'Milton' **123–6** and n. above.

168. Cf. SJ's earlier statement in **154** above that 'one of his pieces has no great resemblance to another'. In 1765 he wrote that 'some painters have differed as much from themselves as from any other . . . The same variation may be expected in writers' (*YW*, vii. 162). In Sept. 1773 he said that Y had not 'studied regularly the art of writing' (see **160** n. above). According to Mrs Thrale-Piozzi, *British Synonymy* (1794), ii. 371–2, he 'despised Young's quantity of common knowledge as comparatively small . . . because speaking once upon the subject of metrical composition, our courtier seemed totally ignorant of what are called rhepalick or rhopalick verses'. (Successive words in a line of rhopalic verse contain an additional syllable.)

Pope said bluntly that Y 'had much of a sublime genius, though without common sense; so that his genius, having no guide, was perpetually liable to degenerate into bombast' (Ruffhead, *Life of Pope* (1769), 291). For early parodies or disapproval of Y's late style, see William Whitehead's 'New Night Thoughts on Death' in *Gent. Mag.* (Sept. 1747), 444, Henry Jones's 'The Relief: or, Day Thoughts' in *Poems* (Dublin, 1756), 1 ff., and William Kenrick, *Epistles, Philosophical and Moral* (1759), 110–16. Warton, *Essay on Pope*, ii (1782), 149 and n., admitted that Y was 'too often turgid and hyperbolical', and noted: 'So little sensible are we of our own imperfections, that the very last time I saw Dr. Young, he was severely censuring and ridiculing the false pomp of fustian writers, and the nauseousness of *bombast*.' See also his *Works of Pope* (1797), iv. 235 n.

with all his defects, he was a man of genius and a poet: SJ oddly echoes Croft's emphatic assertions in **98, 142** above that 'Young was a poet' to explain his deficiencies as a parent and priest. For poetic genius, see 'Milton' **277** and n. above. As well as remaining silent about the religious dimension of *NT*, SJ has in fact quoted nothing to illustrate the 'genius' he claims for Y. For earlier unspecific statements that there are 'very fine things' in Y's poetry, see **160** n. above. Southey echoed SJ's conclusion when stating that Y's 'manner was unique; it is a compound of wit and religious madness; but that madness was the madness of a man of genius' (*Specimens of the Later English Poets* (1807), i, p. xxxii).

DAVID MALLET (1702?–1765)

Composition. Although SJ does not refer to 'Mallet', it is likely that he wrote it in June or July 1780. This is suggested not merely by M's late place in the sequence in *Eng. Poets* (forty-seventh of fifty-two), but by the similarity of 'Mallet' to the longer account of M in Thomas Davies's *Memoirs of the Life of David Garrick*, published on 6 May 1780 (*Bibliography*, ii. 1524). SJ's involvement with Davies's *Memoirs* before its publication, however, means that his apparent use of this 'source' does not provide unambiguous evidence for a date of composition.

SJ referred in Aug. 1780 to Davies's 'great success as an authour generated by the corruption of a Bookseller' (*Letters*, iii. 302). After his bankruptcy in 1778, SJ helped him with the *Memoirs of Garrick*: Davies's 'Advertisement' thanked him for encouragement, information about Garrick's early life, and 'several diverting anecdotes', and SJ also wrote the book's opening paragraph. While some at least of SJ's information seems certainly to derive from Davies, it is possible that he himself was at times Davies's source, and he may in any case have read Davies's chapter on M in MS or in proof before the *Memoirs* appeared in May 1780.

For these reasons, an earlier date of composition than May 1780 remains a theoretical possibility. SJ's reference to M in conversation on 16 Apr. 1779 (see **14** n. below) has no obvious bearing on his biography, and although Boswell wrote to Lord Hailes on 7 July 1779, requesting 'any communications' about M, he also enquired about four other poets to whom SJ did not turn his attention until 1780. On 15 Sept. 1779, Boswell reminded Hailes that 'I wrote to Dr. Johnson that I hoped by your Lordships means to get him some anecdotes of Mallet particularly the copy of a religious letter written by him in his early years' (Boswell, *Catalogue*, L 615–16). While this does not indicate that SJ himself was already eager to start work on 'Mallet', McCarthy, 57, suggested that 'Mallet' might date from Oct. 1779, when, instead of joining the Thrales in Brighton, SJ 'stays at home & writes, & is diligent' (*Thraliana*, i. 409). The fact that he ignored material deriving from M in the Spence MSS, which became available to him early in Feb. 1780 (see **6, 8** n. below), conceivably strengthens the possibility that he had already written 'Mallet' by then. (For the likelihood that he wrote it before 'Thomson', see **6** n. below.) The fact remains, however, that there is no firm evidence that SJ started work on the later *Prefaces* before Feb. 1780.

Sources. SJ's statement in **1** below that he had 'no written memorial' to rely on probably refers to M's absence from his usual biographical sources, but may indicate that he and Davies had in effect conflated what they knew about M, or even that he did not regard Davies's garrulous *Memoirs* as an authoritative biographical source deserving formal citation. (George Steevens, in Reed's *Biographia Dramatica* (1782), i. 295–6, acknowledged that his article on M was 'chiefly collected' from SJ's 'Mallet', without reference to Davies.) SJ's reliance instead on 'the loquacity of common fame, and a very slight personal knowledge' is illustrated by the frequency with which M had been a topic of SJ's conversation (see notes to **9, 14, 19, 21, 24–5** below), although this also reflects Boswell's own hostile interest in his fellow-Scotsman.

The 'loquacity of common fame' no doubt also fed into the account of M in Davies's *Memoirs of the Life of David Garrick* (2 vols., 1780), ii. 27–60. Thomas Davies (1712?–85) had attended the University of Edinburgh in 1728–9, a few years after M. His long career as an actor and bookseller gave him first-hand knowledge of M's theatrical career and his dealings with the book trade (see **19** and n. below), and

Davies treated both these subjects in more detail than SJ. Of paragraphs 2–25 in SJ's account, seventeen have an obvious equivalent in Davies. In nine of these Davies wrote more fully, if more wordily, than SJ, and in only five paragraphs does SJ add significant detail of his own.

Isaac Reed, who apparently wrote the entries on M's individual plays in *Biographia Dramatica* (1782), and Nichols may well have assisted SJ with the dating of M's various works, about which Davies was often vague. Most such dates, with some other information (see e.g. **5** n., **6, 8, 12, 15, 16, 18, 20, 22–3** below), are absent from the proofs and were probably added later. Nichols later reprinted most of SJ's 'Mallet' in his *Anecdotes of Bowyer* (1782), 328–9 n., combining with it information from Steevens's account of M in the *Biographia Dramatica* (1782): see **25** n. below. As in similar cases (see headnotes to 'West' above and 'Lyttelton' below), Nichols may have felt proprietorial about 'Mallet' because he had himself contributed to it.

Boswell, who gleaned information for SJ about M's friend Thomson (q.v.), may also have been a source for SJ's account of M's early life in Scotland: for his letters to Lord Hailes about M in 1779, see above. Although SJ had subscribed to the work, there is no sign that he made any use of the numerous letters from Aaron Hill to M in Hill's *Works* (4 vols., 1753), vols. i–ii, in which Hill's account of *Irene* in 1749 refers to 'the *Anamalous* (*sic*) Mr. *Johnson*' (ii. 354). For SJ's 'very slight personal knowledge' of M (**1** below), see **9** n., **24** and n. below.

M is one of the eight poets (of fifty-two in *Eng. Poets*) not quoted in the *Dict.*

Publication. In *Prefaces*, vol. x (15 May 1781). The complete proofs are in the Forster Collection.

Modern Sources:
(i) David Mallet
Ballads and Songs, ed. F. Dinsdale (1857)
'The Letters of an Eighteenth-Century Scotsman', ed. D. M. Little (Ph.D. thesis, Harvard University, 1935)
A Poem in Imitation of Donaides (1725), ed. I. S. Lustig (Augustan Reprint Soc. 188, Los Angeles, 1978)
(ii)
R. C. Boys, 'David Malloch and *The Edinburgh Miscellany*', *MLN* 54 (1939), 468–9
I. S. Lustig, 'DM's Published Letters to John Ker Redated', *PBSA* 72 (1978), 228–33
I. S. Lustig, ' "Donaus", *Donaides*, and DM: A Reply to Dr. J', *MP* 76 (1978), 149–62
J. C. Riely, 'Chesterfield, M, and the Publication of Bolingbroke's *Works*', *RES* 25 (1974), 61–5
J. Sambrook, *James Thomson 1700–1748: A Life* (Oxford, 1991)
G. F. Sleigh, 'DM' (B.Litt. thesis, Oxford, 1952)
G. F. Sleigh, 'The Authorship of *William and Margaret*', *Library*, 5th ser. 8 (1953), 121–3
H. W. Starr, 'Notes on DM', *N & Q* 178 (1940), 277–8

1. See headnote.

2. Cf. Davies, *Memoirs*, ii. 28: 'His real name was Macgregor, a member of a Scotch clan, which rendered themselves so notorious, as well as obnoxious to the laws, for acts of violence and robbery, that they were obliged by an act of parliament, to change the name of Macgregor for another.'

The Privy Council proclaimed the Macgregors rebels and abolished the name as early as 1603. The penal laws were lifted at the Restoration but reimposed some thirty years later. The Macgregors were excluded from the Act of Grace of 1717, after the Jacobite Rebellion of 1715 and during the exploits of Robert or Rob Roy Macgregor (1671–1734). For a long account of 'the clan Macgregor' and 'the most severe laws, executed with unheard-of rigour against those who bore this forbidden name', see Sir Walter Scott's 'Introduction' to *Rob Roy* in *Waverley Novels*, vii (1829).

Lord Hailes commented in 1782: 'I suppose that Dr J. has long ago met with some Scottish freind to advise him to strike out ye legend of Rob Roy & ye McGregors, communicated by some ill-informed or malevolent person': see Carnie (1956), 488. In *Biographia Dramatica* (1782), ii. 37–8, Steevens alluded to the story when discussing M's epilogue for Young's *The Brothers* (1753) (see 'Young' 113 and n. above): its tasteless humour 'might have set the whole clan of *MacGregors* on a roar', but so offended Young that he refused to print it with his play. (See A. Sherbo, *The Achievement of George Steevens* (New York, 1990), 123–4.)

3. Davies, *Memoirs*, ii. 28–9.

SJ gives no date for M's birth. Most modern sources, e.g. Sleigh, 'DM', 1–2, accept '1705?', because of the attribution of M's poems in the *Edinburgh Miscellany* (Edinburgh, 1720), 223–33, to 'A Youth in his fifteenth year', although this was not necessarily his age in 1720. M himself gave his age as 28 when matriculating at Oxford in 1733 (see **10** n. below). It must, however, seem unlikely that M became the janitor of Edinburgh High School at the age of 12 or 13, and tutor to the sons of George Home, one of whom was 16, when he himself was only 15. More convincing is the statement in *Scots Mag.* (1765), 224, that he was 63 when he died in 1765, and would therefore have been born *c*.1702. (Cunningham, *Lives* (1854), iii. 361, suggested a date of '1698?' without discussion.)

His father James Malloch (d. 1723) was a farmer or innkeeper near Crieff, Perthshire. M was probably educated at the parish-school in Crieff by John Ker, who was later a teacher at Edinburgh High School (1713), and Professor at Aberdeen (1717) and Edinburgh (1734). Robert Anderson published M's letters to Ker in 1720–7 in the *Edinburgh Mag.* (Jan.–Nov. 1793): they are cited here from 'Original Letters of David Mallet, Esq.', as reprinted in *European Mag.* 23 (1793), 338–40, 412–15; 24 (1793), 22–5, 87–8, 174–6, 257–8, 341–3; 25 (1794), 6–7, 99–101.

M became janitor of Edinburgh High School in 1717, at £10 p.a. (Davies, *Memoirs*, ii. 28; Dinsdale, *Ballads and Songs*, 14–19). The youthful Boswell, and his friends Andrew Erskine and George Dempster, taunted him about this post in *Critical Strictures on the New Tragedy of Elvira, written by Mr. David Mallock* (1763) (see **20** below). As Boswell told Hume, 1 Mar. 1763: 'We have vast satisfaction in making him smart by the rod of criticism, as much as many a tender bum has smarted by his barbarous birch when he was janitor of the High School at Edinburgh' (*London Journal* (1950), 209).

M entered Edinburgh University in Oct. 1720, and while still a student became tutor to the four sons of George Home of Dreghorn: 'He allows me my learning, clothes, and diet, but no fixed salary' (*European Mag.* (1793), 338). He met James Thomson at this time and contributed to the *Edinburgh Miscellany* (1720) (see **3** n. above and 'Thomson' **5** n. above).

M left Edinburgh without a degree in Aug. 1723, on being appointed tutor to the sons of James Graham, Duke of Montrose, at £30 p.a. (see 'Thomson' 7 above), a post he retained until 1731, living with the family either in Hanover Square, London, or at Shawford House, near Winchester. Aberdeen University conferred a MA on him on 11 Jan. 1726, in recognition of his imitation of John Ker's *Donaides*, a Latin poem celebrating the rebuilding of the Library at King's College (*Life*, iv. 216–17; Lustig, 'Donaus', 149–62). For SJ's copy of *Donaides*, see Fleeman, *Handlist* (1984), 48.

4. Davies, *Memoirs*, ii. 29. M travelled with his pupils on the Continent in 1727 (Thomson, *Letters*, 21–2, 29–30). For his quarrel with a General Flobert in Florence over a 'romantic girl', which almost led to a duel, see Walpole, *Corresp.*, xxi. 377, 386.

5. Davies, *Memoirs*, ii. 28–9. For similar uncertainty about 'the series' of an author's works, see 'Watts' 15 above.

   William and Margaret first appeared in 1723 (for the early printings, see Foxon, *English Verse*, M 59–62). After Aaron Hill reprinted it as a genuine old ballad in *Plain Dealer* 36 (24 July 1724), M admitted his authorship in a letter in no. 46 (28 Aug. 1724). (For Hill's *Plain Dealer*, see 'Savage' 59 above.) SJ's footnote about its publication is not in the proofs, and may have been added by Nichols or Reed. The ballad was reprinted in *A Collection of Old Ballads*, vol. iii (1725) (sometimes attributed to Ambrose Philips), and in Allan Ramsay's *The Tea-Table Miscellany*, vol. ii (1726). Ramsay also referred to it in '*To Mr.* DAVID MALLOCH, *On his Departure from* Scotland' (*Poems* (Edinburgh, 1728), 257–9).

   M admitted privately that a 'Stanza in one of Fletcher's Plays gave him the hint' for *William and Margaret*: see *The Knight of the Burning Pestle* (*c*.1607–8), II. viii, now attributed to Francis Beaumont (Spence, ii. 620). He was accused of plagiarizing his most popular poem from an old MS in *The Friends; or, Original Letters of a Person Deceased* (2 vols., 1773), i. 67–76, and by Edward Thompson in Andrew Marvell's *Works* (3 vols., 1776), i, pp. xx–xxiv, a copy of which SJ owned. The charge was rejected in *Gent. Mag.* (1776), 355, 401, 559–60, and (1777), 73, and later by Dinsdale in *Ballads and Songs* 75–8. Davies discussed this matter at much greater length than SJ.

   Writing to Hester Thrale, 20 Aug. 1783, SJ humorously used the phrase 'grimly ghost' from M's ballad in a discussion of Frances Reynolds's recent portrait of him (*Letters*, iv. 188). He was later depicted as a ghost appearing to an alarmed Boswell in 'Dr. Johnson's Ghost' (1786), a parody of *William and Margaret*, by Elizabeth Moody (1737–1814): see Lonsdale, *Eighteenth Century Women Poets* (1989), 402–4.

6. *The Excursion* (ignored by Davies) appeared on 21 Mar. 1728. The date is not in the proofs. M's letters to Ker (see 3 n. above) show that Aaron Hill, Young, and Dennis, as well as Thomson, saw *The Excursion* before publication. With SJ's comment that it is 'not devoid of poetical spirit', cf. 'Dyer' 10 and n. above.

   In Feb. 1725 James Thomson followed M from Scotland to London, where M introduced him to Hill's circle, including Savage and Dyer (see 'Savage' 55 and n. and 'Thomson' 7–8 and nn. above). Shiels, *Lives*, v. 194–5, and Murdoch (Thomson, *Works*, 1762 edn.), i, p. vii, both emphasized the friendship with M in their accounts of Thomson (see 'Thomson' headnote above). Shiels, for example, described their 'early intimacy, which improved with their years, nor was it ever once disturbed by any casual mistake, envy, or jealousy on either side' (v. 194 n.). The fact that SJ virtually ignores the friendship here suggests that he may have written 'Mallet' before 'Thomson', as may his spelling of 'Thompson' in **6, 12, 15–16, 25** in the proofs of 'Mallet'. SJ makes no use of M's account of Thomson's early years in London, recorded in about 1730 by Spence, i. 370 (see headnote).

M and Thomson corresponded about poetry in the mid-1720s, and M had some influence on *The Seasons* (1726–30), which in turn influenced his own *Excursion* (Thomson, *Letters* (1958), 9–12, 20–1, 35–7, 40–54, 64–7). According to Shiels, *Lives*, v. 195 n., M advised Thomson to assemble *Winter* (1726) from 'detached pieces, or occasional descriptions', and later to write the other three *Seasons*. M also wrote the dedication of *Winter* (1726) to Spencer Compton (see 'Thomson' **9** and n. above). See Sambrook, *Thomson*, esp. chs. 2, 3, 8. For Thomson's 'beauties' and 'faults', see 'Thomson' **46–50** above; for a later comment on the similarity of M's blank verse to Thomson's, see **25** below; and for 'images' and 'diction', see 'Cowley' **154, 181–4** and nn. above.

7. Davies, *Memoirs*, ii. 30–1.

On 21 Nov. 1729 Pope mentioned some verses by M, 'relating either to myself, or my Brother Dunces, (which Savage told me obscurely of)', and on 1 Sept. 1731 praised M's epitaph on the painter William Aikman (*Corresp.*, iii. 66, 222). He later claimed that M addressed *Of Verbal Criticism: An Epistle to Mr. Pope* (1733) to him 'before I knew anything of it'. M's preface also stated that he wrote it without Pope's knowledge, although he corrected it before publication (*Corresp.*, iii. 327, 329–30, 357–8, 511). Lawton Gilliver told Thomas Cooke that he had published it (paying M 20 guineas) only at Pope's insistence, and sold a mere hundred copies (*Gent. Mag.* (1791), 1181).

Davies did not refer to Pope's 'Fragment of a Satire' in *Miscellanies. The Third Volume* (1727), which ridiculed textual critics and contained the character of 'Atticus' later included in the *Epistle to Arbuthnot* (1734): see *TE*, vi. 283–6. In 1765 SJ stated that, after Theobald's attack on his edition of Shakespeare in 1726, Pope 'past the latter part of his life in a state of hostility with verbal criticism' (*YW*, vii. 95): see 'Pope' **126–7** and n. above.

M's *Of Verbal Criticism* censured, among others, Richard Bentley and Theobald himself, who replied in the preface to his *Works of Shakespeare* (7 vols., 1734), i, p. lii: 'to pay a servile Compliment to Mr. *Pope*, an *Anonymous* Writer has, like a *Scotch* Pedlar in Wit, unbraced his Pack on the Subject'. Pope quoted M's poem in the 'Testimonies of Authors' in later editions of the *Dunciad*. Warton, *Essay on Pope*, ii (1782), 231 n., was even sterner than SJ about M's 'very feeble and flimsy poem ... stuffed with illiberal cant about pedantry, and collators of manuscripts'. It has been reprinted in D. Womersley (ed.), *Augustan Critical Writing* (1997), 332–9.

8. Davies, *Memoirs*, ii. 29–30.

Eurydice was acted at Drury Lane on 22 Feb. 1731 and in fact received thirteen further performances by 16 Apr. (*London Stage*). (The date is not in the proofs.) For Pope's influence in getting it staged, see his *Corresp.*, iii. 65–6, 82–3, 86–7, 157–8, and Thomson, *Letters*, 64, 67. M admitted to Spence that the tragedy was 'rather *too full* of plot', and that he gave it 'against his own judgement to the taste of the town' (i. 370).

Hill's prologue and epilogue were printed in *Gent. Mag.* (Apr. 1731), 168, and later (with a letter to M, 23 Feb. 1731, criticizing the first performance) in his *Works* (1753), i. 45–8, iii. 334–6, iv. 74–6 (cf. **6** n. above). For an anecdote about M 'chatting among the players in the Green Room' during an early performance, see *Thraliana*, i. 132. M dedicated the printed text to the Duke of Montrose (see **3** above).

Although Aaron Hill hailed *Eurydice* as 'the Dawning of one of those *Lights* . . . bright enough to *give Lustre to a Kingdom!*' (*Advice to the Poets* (1731), p. xv), it provoked some anonymous *Remarks on the Tragedy of Euridice. In which it is endeavoured to prove that the said Tragedy is wrote in favour of the Pretender* (1731). A revised version was staged at Drury Lane on 3 Mar. 1759 with a cast included Garrick and Mrs Cibber, but had only four performances. According to Reed, *Biographia Dramatica* (1782), ii. 110, M blamed its 'cold reception' on the actors, who 'displayed no *pathos* in their performance. This same *pathos* was a thing which Mallet conceived to be . . . the characteristic of his own poetry.'

9. Davies, *Memoirs*, ii. 28.

original: '4. Derivation; descent' (*Dict.*). The word is a revision of 'country' in the proofs (see Textual Notes). SJ said on 28 Mar. 1772: 'I never catched Mallet in a Scotch accent' (*Life*, ii. 159).

According to Davies, M changed his name because 'it sounded so unpolitely and was so unharmonious'. Both forms appear in the mid-1720s. He told John Ker, 15 Sept. 1724 (*European Mag.* 24 (1793), 175), that the English could not pronounce his name, but signed his letters to Ker (to 1727) 'Malloch', the form also used on his *Poem in Imitation of Donaides* (1725). Although Thomson addressed him as Mallet by 1725 (*Letters*, 9), and 'Mallet' subscribed to Savage's *Miscellaneous Poems* (1726), his commendatory verses in Thomson's *Winter* (2nd edn., 1726) were signed 'Malloch', and he is listed as 'Mallock' in the subscribers to Dennis's *Miscellaneous Tracts* (1727). The Register of the University of Edinburgh in 1734 recorded him as 'Malloch alias Mallet' (*N & Q*, 7th ser. 12 (1891), 265).

M was taunted about his change of name to the end of his life. SJ defined 'Alias' in the *Dict.* (1755) merely as 'A Latin word, signifying otherwise', but mischievously added in the abridged 1756 edn.: 'as, Mallet, *alias* Malloch; that is *otherwise* Malloch'. Sir David Dalrymple, later Lord Hailes, referred to 'Malloch' in his *Memorials and Letters* (1762), but corrected the name to 'Mallet' in an erratum, explaining in 1763 that 'I confess I gave him his own name because I thought he did not like it', but that this had confused his printers (Walpole, *Corresp.*, xv. 78 and n.). He later commented in 1782 that 'an Englishman cannot pronounce *Malloch* . . . besides, *Malloch* is not ye name of a Gentleman': see Carnie (1956), 488 and n.

The 'Advertisement' of *Critical Strictures* (1763) on M's *Elvira* by Boswell and others (see **3** n. above and **20** below) claimed that the authority of SJ and Dalrymple for the spelling 'Malloch' carried more weight than 'even that of the said Malloch himself'. Reed used both forms in *Biographia Dramatica* (1782), ii. 295–6. For an anecdote by Thomas Cooke about Thomson's defence of M's change of name, see *Gent. Mag.* (1791), 1183.

SJ's last sentence may derive from Steevens, who reportedly described M in a MS note as 'the only Scotchman who died in my memory unlamented by an individual of his own nation' (Cunningham, *Lives* (1854), iii. 365–6 n.). Scotsmen who 'did not commend' M included Thomson's friend William Robertson, who said that M 'made a cat's-paw of Thomson' (*The Bee*, vi (1792), 284).

For M's 'correction' of Scotticisms in David Hume's *History*, see **14** n. below; and for Scottish and English accents, and the Scottish 'conspiracy to cheat the world by false representations of the merits of their countrymen', see *Life*, ii. 158–9, 307, and cf. iv. 186. See also J. Basker, 'Scotticisms and the Problem of Cultural Identity in 18th-Century Britain', *ECL* 15 (1991), 81–95, and P. Rogers, 'James Boswell and the "Scotticism"', in G. Clingham (ed.), *New Light on Boswell* (Cambridge, 1991), 56–71.

10. The story of M's *faux pas* about the *Essay on Man* (1733–4: see 'Pope' **176** above) is in William Ayre, *Memoirs of Pope* (1745), ii. 215–17, and Owen Ruffhead, *Life of Pope* (1769), 261 n. Although neither source names M, Ayre's allusion to the recent performance of *Alfred* at Cliveden (see **12** below) left his identity in little doubt. In Ayre's version, M told Pope that the *Essay* was 'a most abominable Piece of Stuff, shocking Poetry, insufferable Philosophy, no Coherence, no Connection at all'. (Ayre mistakenly added that M never dared to see Pope again.) The story was later told of a 'Mr. Morris' in *The Tell-Tale* (2 vols., 1756), ii. 331–2.

SJ does not mention that in 1731 M became tutor to James Newsham (1715–69), son (by her first marriage) of Pope's friend Mrs Knight of Gosfield, Essex, daughter of James Craggs. M and his pupil both matriculated as gentlemen-commoners from St Mary Hall, Oxford, on 2 Nov. 1733, M taking BA and MA degrees in Apr. 1734. (To expedite this, he obtained his MA from the University of Edinburgh in Mar. 1734: see Sleigh 'DM', 37–40, and **9** n. above.)

Walter Harte, the poet and friend of Pope, was a tutor at St Mary Hall (see 'Pope' **70** and n. above), and the Principal was the Jacobite William King (1685–1763) (see 'Dryden' **187** and n. above). 'To his Highness the Prince of Orange, on his coming to Oxford' by '*David Mallet* B.A. of St. Mary Hall', appeared in *Epithalamia Oxoniensia* (1734), sigg. O–O2^r, and was also published separately (Foxon, *English Verse*, M 58). Although Nichols referred to M's period in Oxford in *Anecdotes of Bowyer* (1782), 328–9 n., SJ continued to ignore it in *Lives* (1783). M and Newsham travelled on the Continent in 1735–7 (Pope, *Corresp.*, iii. 457–8, 484–5).

11. SJ's friend Thomas Birch edited Francis Bacon's *Works* (4 vols., 1740). SJ's copy, with vol. iii marked for use in the *Dict.*, is at Yale: see Fleeman, *Handlist* (1984), 2.

William Seward later stated that SJ had himself once planned an edition and biography of Bacon, who was 'a favourite author' (*Life*, iii. 194; cf. *J. Misc.*, ii. 302, and 'Cowley' **97** and 'Collins' **6** and n. above). For SJ's early praise of Bacon in the *Harleian Catalogue*, see R. DeMaria, *Life of SJ* (1993), 101. In *Adventurer* 85 (1753) he stated that 'Bacon attained to degrees of knowledge scarcely ever reached by any other man'. See also ch. III ('The Baconian Legacy)' in R. B. Schwarz, *SJ and the New Science* (Madison, 1971), 59–93.

For Warburton's hostility to M in 1749, see 'Pope' **249** and n. above. His remark appeared on a cancelled leaf of Pope's *Works* (1751), in a note to a couplet omitted from the *Epistle to Arbuthnot*: 'Yet worse—vile Poets rise before ye Light | And walk like Margrets Ghost at dead of night' (for the MS, see M. Mack, *The Last and Greatest Art* (Newark, Del., 1984), 430–1). Warburton explained that 'William and

Margaret' (see 5 above) was 'Written by one MALLOCK. Since risen, by due degrees, from a maker of Ballads, to a maker of Lives. He made L. B's life, and by ill hap forgot he was a *Philosopher*; he is now about making the D. of M[arlborough]'s. Be not surprized, therefore, gentle reader, if he should forget that his Grace was a *General*' (see Pope, *Works*, ed. W. Elwin and W. J. Courthope (1871–86), iii. 534–5, and **13–14** below).

Although Warburton cancelled the note, it evidently enjoyed 'common fame' (cf. **1** above and *Life*, iii. 194). A version of it, naming neither Warburton nor M, is in Mason's *Memoirs of Mr. Gray* (2nd edn., 1775), **2**. (For Mason's effort to verify the *bon mot* through Hurd in 1773, see *The Corresp. of Richard Hurd and William Mason*, ed. E. H. Pearce and L. Whibley (Cambridge, 1932), 87, 89.) Malone refers to M's 'florid and empty Life' of Bacon in *Prose Works of Dryden* (1800), i (ii). 81 n.

12. Davies, *Memoirs*, ii. 31–2, 36, 37–40.

For the departure of Frederick, Prince of Wales, from St James's after his breach with George II in 1737, and for his literary patronage, see 'Pope' **217** and n. above. M became Frederick's under-secretary at £200 p.a. in May 1742, retaining the post until 1748 (see *Gent. Mag.* (1742), 33, and 'Thomson' **28** n. above). For an anecdote of the Prince conversing 'with great freedom and familiarity' with M and Thomson by the Thames at Cliveden, see Richard Graves, *Recollections of William Shenstone* (1788), 93–4. M dedicated his *Poems on Several Occasions* (1743) to the Prince.

Alfred, performed for the Prince and Princess of Wales at Cliveden on 1 Aug. 1740, was revised for public performance with Thomas Arne's music in 1745. M adapted it again for Garrick in 1751, with additional music by Charles Burney (see 'Thomson' **33** and n. above). Walpole mentioned the 'fulsome loyalties' of yet another revision by Garrick in 1773 (*Corresp.*, xxviii. 110 and n.).

The dates in this paragraph are not present in the proofs.

13. Davies, *Memoirs*, ii. 55–7, told the same story, but of M's *Elvira* (see **20** below) rather than *Alfred*, as he admitted in his 3rd edn. (1781), ii. 58 n. The spelling 'nich' is not in the *Dict.*

14. Cf. Davies, *Memoirs*, ii. 37, 55 (a shorter account than SJ's), and Nichols, *Supplement to Swift* (1779), i. 157 n. SJ evidently confuses Robert Molesworth, 1st Vis. Molesworth (1656–1725) (see 'King' **4** above), and his son Richard, the 3rd Viscount, who fought under Marlborough but did not die until 1758. It was widely believed at first that Richard Steele had agreed to write the biography (see Steele, *Corresp.*, ed. R. Blanchard, 2nd edn. (Oxford, 1968), 466–7).

In 1744 the Duchess of Marlborough's will directed that 'all such Letters and Papers relating to the said History, as shall be found at any of my Houses after my Decease' should be made available to Richard Glover, author of the once admired epic *Leonidas* (1737) (cf. *Life*, v. 116), and to M ('recommended to me by the late Duke of *Montrose*': see **3–4** above). Once Lord Chesterfield had approved the biography, Glover and M were each to receive £500 and to have 'the Advantage of printing the said History'. The fact that both biographers were poets no doubt explains the Duchess's provision that 'no Part of the said History may be in Verse', a precaution which delighted Horace Walpole in Nov. 1744: 'There is a great deal of humour in the thought' (*Authentick Memoirs of . . . her Grace, Sarah, Late Dutchess of Marlborough* (1744), 62–4; Walpole, *Corresp.*, xxviii. 528, and cf. xx. 62).

Glover declined the task because of the Duchess's 'capricious restrictions' (see his *Memoirs* (1816), 57). M had recently issued proposals (1 Mar. 1742) for a *History of the Reigns of Charles II. and James II.*, expanding a projected *History of the Exclusion-Bill* for which he had already received subscriptions. He evidently abandoned this project, promised for 1 Mar. 1743, and started work on Marlborough, receiving an annual pension from the current Duke.

M's slow progress became notorious. In his 'Advertisement' to *Alfred* (1751) (see 12 n. above), he claimed that he had revised it only while awaiting materials about Marlborough from abroad. In Mar. 1759 Walpole reported that M was planning to have a French translation of his biography ready for the end of the war with France (*Corresp.*, xv. 54). Dedicating his *Poems* (1762) to the Duke of Marlborough, M described it as almost complete. Although Hume, who employed M to remove 'Scottisms' from his *History of England*, vols. ii–iv (1757–62), gathered from M in 1762 that it was 'ready for the Press', and would fill two quarto volumes, no sign of it was found after M's death in 1765, when Hume declined to take over the project (see Hume, *Letters*, ed. J. Y. T. Greig, 2 vols. (Oxford, 1932), i. 233, 236, 368–70 and nn., 385–7, ii. 6).

SJ said on 10 Sept. 1773 that he had always assumed, from M's 'way of talking' about it, that he had 'not written any part of the Life', but had not been 'culpable in taking the pension' as long as he intended to write it. On 16 Apr. 1779 he repeated that M 'never wrote a single line of his projected life ... He groped for materials; and thought of it, till he had exhausted his mind' (*Life*, v. 175, iii. 386). For the treatment of Marlborough by other writers, see 'J. Philips' 12 and n. above.

15. Davies, *Memoirs*, ii. 33–6 gives a fuller account than SJ.

Not yet strictly in 'the Prince's service', M was already associated with the literary opposition to Walpole and the court. *Mustapha* was performed at Drury Lane on 13 Feb. 1739, with a prologue by Thomson. (For *Agamemnon* (1738), see 'Thomson' 29–30 above.) It duly featured an evil minister conspiring against a noble heir to the throne. M dedicated it to the Prince, who, in Aaron Hill's words, was 'so just, as to insist on Mr. *Mallet*'s Tragedy, as the first to be brought on, this season' (*Works* (1753), i. 328). According to Davies, *Memoirs*, ii. 34, 'all the chiefs in opposition to the court' attended the opening night. Pope, who declined to write the prologue, 'at the end of the play went behind the scenes, a place which he had not visited for some years'. Although he congratulated M, Pope told Hill that he thought it 'vilely acted' (*Corresp.*, iv. 132, 166–7).

The date is not present in the proofs. Within a year (Jan. 1740) SJ was hoping that his own *Irene* would be performed at Drury Lane (*Letters*, i. 23).

16. For *Alfred* see 12 and n. above. This paragraph is not in the proofs. By about 1740 M was living at Strand-on-the-Green, near the site of Kew Bridge, where Thomson often visited him (Sambrook, *Thomson*, 210). During 1745 he travelled in Holland (Hill, *Works* (1753), ii. 249), presumably 'researching' Marlborough's life.

17. Davies, *Memoirs*, ii. 41–3, gives a fuller account than SJ.

Amyntor and Theodora, or The Hermit, dedicated to Chesterfield (see 14 n. above) and, according to M's preface, originally conceived as a tragedy, appeared on 27 Apr. 1747. As Hill (1905) noted, an advertisement in *Gent. Mag.* (May 1747), 252 (where it was followed by one for SJ's *Miscellaneous Observations on ... Macbeth* and *Life of Savage*) warned: 'This poem is enter'd in the hall-book of the company of stationers, and whoever pirates it will be prosecuted.' There were in fact three piracies of *Amyntor and Theodora* in 1747, as well as two further authorized editions in 1748 (see Foxon, *English Verse*, M 44–9). Nichols or Reed may have supplied the information about the sale to Paul Vaillant, which was added in 1783: see Textual Notes. Warton, *Works of Pope* (1797), ix. 134, later named the sum as 120 guineas.

The *Museum*, iii (1747), 285–6, particularly praised M's descriptions of St Kilda: 'there is not only Elegance and Variety, fine Sentiments and lofty Expression, but the essential Qualities of a Poet indisputably appear.' Warton's criticism in *Essay on Pope* (1756), 149, of M's 'nauseous affectation of expressing everything pompously and poetically' was quoted by Davies, who instead praised his moral and descriptive power, 'with all the images natural to the tremendous scene'. In spite of his dislike of blank verse (see 'Milton' 274 and n. above), SJ for once grants M both 'elegance' and 'vigour', perhaps in reaction to Warton's attack.

18. Davies, *Memoirs*, ii. 40–1.
   M may have met Bolingbroke through Pope as early as 1733 (Pope, *Corresp.*, iii. 177, 330, 358, 408). It emerged after Pope's death that in 1738 he had surreptitiously printed 1,500 copies of Bolingbroke's *The Idea of a Patriot King*, which had been entrusted to him (see 'Pope' 250–3 above). Although M told Lord Orrery that he would aways cherish Pope's memory 'with all the Regard of Esteem, with all the Tenderness of Friendship' (Pope, *Corresp.*, iv. 523), he accepted Bolingbroke's commission to edit the work as *Letters on the Spirit of Patriotism* (1749), with a preface attacking Pope's conduct. (The erroneous '1747' is not in the proofs.) Like Thomson, M had lost his post with the Prince of Wales (see 12 above) by 1748, when Chesterfield was seeking other preferment for him (*Letters*, iii. 1119).
   In May 1749 Walpole reported that M's preface to the *Letters* 'makes more noise than the work itself' (*Corresp.*, xx. 61). Reprinting it, *Gent. Mag.* (May 1749) referred to M as 'a fellow who, while Mr. *P.* lived, was as diligent in licking his feet, as he is now in licking Ld *B*. 's' (196). Influenced by Warburton, Ruffhead, *Life of Pope* (1769), 523–4, described M as 'an editor, worthy of so dark an office— One who, though he courted Mr. POPE, while living, with a degree of abject servility, yet had not scrupled to mention him, after his death, in the grossest terms of rudeness. But this editor, or to use his own language, this MAN, was never remarkable for the delicacy of his moral feelings.'
   At his death in 1752 Bolingbroke left the editing of his works to M. William Mason later described 'Mallock' as 'Sunk in his St. John's philosophic breast' in his *Heroic Epistle to Sir William Chambers* (1773), ll. 31–2. Hume asked Adam Smith, 3 May 1776: 'Was Mallet any wise hurt by his Publication of Lord Bolingbroke? He received an Office afterwards from the present King and Lord Bute, the most prudish Men in the World; and he always justify'd himself by his sacred Regard to the Will of a dead Friend' (*Letters* (Oxford, 1932), ii. 316; cf. 20 and n. below). For M and Bolingbroke, see also 'Pope' 94 above.

19. Davies, *Memoirs*, ii. 43–8, gives more detail than SJ about this dispute, summarized in *Gent. Mag.* (1754), 247.
   Richard Francklin, formerly publisher of *The Craftsman*, claimed the copyright of some of Bolingbroke's political tracts in his *Short State of the Case with Relation to a Claim . . . on David Mallet* (1754). Undeterred, M published the *Works* (5 vols.,

1754), from which, in Davies's words, he 'dreamt of getting golden mountains', refusing to sell the copyright for £3,000. As Warton, *Essay on Pope*, ii (1782), 120 n., later recalled: 'No writings that raised so mighty an expectation in the public as those of Bolingbroke, ever perished so soon and sunk into oblivion.' The edition had been reprinted as recently as 1777. See also Riely, 'Chesteheld', 61–5. For Andrew Millar, praised elsewhere by SJ for liberality, see *Life*, i. 287–8 and 'Collins' 4 n. above. Hume referred on 20 May 1757 to Millar's expectation that complaints about Bolingbroke's 'irreligion' would in fact help sales of the *Works* (*Letters* (Oxford, 1932), i. 250). George Anderson attacked M in *A Remonstrance against Lord Viscount Bolingbroke's Philosophical Religion. Addressed to David Mallet, Esq; the Publisher* (Glasgow, 1756).

Boswell later reported SJ's 'just indignation' at 'the noble author and his editor': Bolingbroke 'was a scoundrel and a coward: a scoundrel, for charging a blunderbuss against religion and morality; a coward because he had not resolution to fire it off himself, but left half a crown to a beggarly Scotchman, to draw the trigger after his death!' (*Life*, i. 268; cf. *Thraliana*, i. 167, *J. Misc.*, ii. 315, and Hawkins, *J's Works* (1787), xi. 213). Boswell may have learned of SJ's outburst from Arthur Murphy, who claimed in his *Essay on J* (1792), 80, to have heard it in 1754.

SJ's defines 'Irony' as 'A mode of speech in which the meaning is contrary to the words: as, *Bolingbroke was a holy man*' (*Dict.*). Reviewing Soame Jenyns in 1757, he referred to 'the contemptible arrogance, or the impious licentiousness of Bolingbroke' (*OASJ*, 522). He was more restrained when Charles Burney questioned him in 1758 about the recent controversy: 'I have never read Bolingbroke's impiety, and therefore am not interested about its refutation' (*Life*, i. 329–30). In 1773 he reduced the original eight quotations from Bolingbroke in the *Dict.* to three. See also 'Pope' 272 above.

20. Davies, *Memoirs*, ii. 53–4, 55, 57–8, gives a fuller account than SJ. This paragraph is not in the proofs.

M's patriotic *Britannia: A Masque*, with music by Thomas Arne, was in fact performed at Drury Lane on 9 May 1755. (Although 'Scrutator' noted the error in *Gent. Mag.* (1781), 421, it survived in 1783.) In spite of M's 'dreary' libretto and Arne's 'dull' music, there were a dozen performances over four seasons during the Seven Years War (R. Fiske, *English Theatre Music* (2nd edn., Oxford, 1986), 242). For its popular prologue by M and Garrick, spoken by Garrick as 'a drunken sailor reading a play-bill', see Reed, *Biographia Dramatica* (1782), ii. 36.

Elvira: A Tragedy, dedicated to Lord Bute, was performed at Drury Lane on 19 Jan. 1763. M's appointment as 'Keeper of the book of entries for ships in the Port of London' (*Gent. Mag.* (Feb. 1763), 98) was believed to be a reward for his support of Bute, who had in fact said of M in Sept. 1755, 'I have not that great opinion of his taste': see H. Mackenzie, *Account of the Life of John Home* (1822), 143–5. For Bute as a literary patron, see also 'Gray' 17 and n. below, and *Life*, i. 372.

Reed, *Biographia Dramatica* (1782), i. 296, ii. 102, mentioned the hostility to *Elvira* as 'a ministerial play' at the time of 'the Scotch peace' with France. Churchill, who had already attacked M as a follower of Bute in *The Ghost*, III (1762), 499–502, did so again in *The Prophecy of Famine* (1763), ll. 131–4, and for other attacks see *North Briton* 34 (22 Jan. 1763) and Cuthbert Shaw's *The Race* (1765). For the *Critical Strictures* (1763) on *Elvira* by Boswell and others, who also tried to 'damn' the play on the first night, see **3**, **9** and nn. above, *Life*, i. 408–9, ii. 495, and Boswell, *London Journal*, ed. F. A. Pottle (1950), 152–5. M's own supporters in the theatre included the young Edward Gibbon: see Sleigh, 'DM', 130–5.

M also published *Tyburn to the Marine Society* by 'Butler Swift' (1759), the ballad *Edwin and Emma* (printed by John Baskerville, 1760), over which M consulted Horace Walpole (Walpole, *Corresp.*, xl. 151–2), and *Truth in Rhyme* (1761), which complimented Bute.

21. Davies, *Memoirs*, ii. 55–6.

SJ reviewed some of the numerous pamphlets in the controversy over Admiral John Byng, executed on 14 Mar. 1757 for alleged cowardice during the war with France, in the *Literary Mag.* in 1756 (see *YW*, x. 213–60, esp. 238–9 n.). Although the attribution to M by Hill (1905) of *Observations on the Twelfth Article of War. By a Plain Man* (1757), a defence of Byng's execution, has been challenged, he certainly wrote *The Conduct of the Ministry Impartially Examined* (1756), one of the pamphlets for which the Duke of Newcastle paid him £300 out of secret service funds in Nov. 1756 (*YW*, x. 252). A few years earlier M had declined an invitation to edit an opposition periodical, but offered his services to the government on 10 June 1756 (British Library), and continued doing so until 1762, suggesting in 1759 that he should undertake secret work in France: see Sleigh, 'DM', 96–102.

Edmund Cartwright, *Monthly Review*, 66 (1782), 118, was amazed that SJ 'should coolly pass over so atrocious an instance of unprincipled depravity' as M's attack on the victimized Byng. According to Dr Maxwell, SJ was less restrained in private: M was 'ready for any dirty job ... he had written against Byng at the instigation of the ministry, and was equally ready to write for him, provided he found his account in it' (*Life*, ii. 128). In *Rambler* 27 (1750) he had described the pangs of conscience suffered by a political writer who received 'the reward of wickedness' (*YW*, iii. 150). Southey, *Specimens of the Later English Poets* (1807), ii. 342, later described M as 'A man of more talents than honesty, who was always ready to perform any dirty work for interest', and as ' "first assassin" in the Tragedy of Admiral Byng's murder'.

22. M's wife (see **23** below) in fact went to France in Apr. 1764, 'upon a strange Project of living alone in a Hermitage, in the midst of the Forrest of Fontainebleau' (Hume, *Letters*, i. 434). M was in Paris in Dec. 1764, but returned to London and died on 21 Apr. 1765, supposedly of diarrhoea: see *Gent. Mag.* (1765), 199 (describing him as 'well known in the republic of letters'), and Chesterfield, *Letters*, vi. 2651–2. The date of M's death is not in the proofs. M's library was auctioned on 10–15 Mar. 1766: see *Sale Catalogues of Eminent Persons*, vol. vii, ed. H. Amory (1973), 81–122.

23. See Davies, *Memoirs*, ii. 47 (for M's second wife).

M's first wife Susanna, whom he married *c.*1734, died in Jan. 1742. The sentence about their daughter Dorothea (*c.*1738–1790), who married Pietro Paulo Celesia, a Genoese diplomat, in 1758, is not in the proofs. Her *Almida, A Tragedy* from Voltaire, performed on 13 Jan. 1771, was criticized in *Gent. Mag.* (Mar. 1771), 127–8, and Reed, *Biographia Dramatica* (1782), ii. 11, described it as 'very poor', attributing its 'considerable run' to Mrs Barry's acting. She also published *Indolence, A Poem* (1772).

Gent. Mag. (1742), 546, reported the marriage on 7 Oct. 1742 of *'David Mallet* Esq; Under Secretary to the Pr. of *Wales*,—to Miss *Lucy Elstob* with 10,000*l.*' The daughter of a steward of Lord Carlisle and a cousin of Elizabeth Elstob the Anglo-Saxon scholar, she died in 1795 aged 79. M prefixed some emotional lines to her to *Amyntor and Theodora* (1747) (see **17** above). She was disliked for her arrogance and garrulity: see Sleigh 'DM', 64, 67, 124–7.

Between 1758 and 1763 Edward Gibbon (1737–94) saw much of M and his wife, who were his father's neighbours, and mentioned them and their free-thinking frequently in his journal and *Memoirs of my Life*, ed. G. A. Bonnard (New York, 1966): see also **24** n. below. In Paris in 1777, Gibbon 'found her exactly the same talkative, positive, passionate, conceited creature as we knew her twenty years ago . . . She raved with her usual indiscretion of Gods Kings and Ministers, the perfection of her favourites and the vice or folly of every person she disliked' (*Letters*, ed. J. E. Norton (1956), ii. 155).

24. SJ said on 10 Sept. 1773 that M 'was the prettiest drest puppet about town, and always kept good company' (*Life*, v. 174: for 'poppet' in Boswell's MS, see *Tour to the Hebrides*, ed. F. A. Pottle (1963), 140 and n.). According to Davies, *Memoirs*, ii. 47 and n., M's wife bought his clothes to ensure that he 'should appear like a gentleman of distinction', and his 'favourite dress was a suit of black velvet'.

D. E. Baker, *Companion to the Play-House* (1764), vol. ii, stated that M 'has always lived, and been respected as a gentleman'. For his social life among the aristocracy and 'men of letters and *beaux esprits*', see Walpole, *Corresp.*, xxxi. 416. Sir Joseph Mawbey (1730–98) remembered M as 'a distant, formal, precise man, affecting the manners of an old courtier' (*Gent. Mag.* (1791), 1183). By 1764 Andrew Millar (see **19** above) described him as 'grown to an enormous size, exactly the shape of a barrel', living like 'a most thorough courtier' with a French cook (*Ballads and Songs*, 49 n.).

SJ once said: 'I have seldom met with a man whose colloquial ability exceeded that of Mallet' (*J's Works* (1787), xi. 214). Gibbon commented on his praise here of M's conversation that SJ was usually M's 'unforgiving enemy' (*Memoirs* (1966), 94). SJ's final ostentatious 'silence' about M's character no doubt alludes to the free-thinking for which he and his wife were well known (see Davies, *Memoirs*, ii. 58 and **23** n. above). For the 'pert and conceited' Mrs M, who 'was either an infidel, or was ashamed to be thought a Christian', telling Hume that 'We Deists ought to know each other', see Reed, *Biographia Dramatica* (1782), ii. 111, and E. C. Mossner, *Life of David Hume* (2nd edn., Oxford, 1980), 395.

25. *Critical Review*, 7 (1759), 276, respectfully described M as 'an elegant writer, who has so justly succeeded in all his literary enterprizes; and who is so generally admired as a dramatic poet, a lyrist and a biographer'; and later stated of his *Poems on Several Occasions* (1762) that his 'genius is well known and universally admired' (13 (1762), 362). (Boswell, *Life*, i. 409 n., believed that M had himself contributed to the *Critical Review*.)

When Goldsmith spoke 'slightingly' of M on 29 Apr. 1773, SJ stated that he 'had talents enough to keep his literary reputation alive as long as he lived; and that, let me tell you, is a good deal'. Goldsmith believed that in fact M's 'literary reputation was dead long before his natural death' (*Life*, ii. 233). In *Biographia Dramatica* (1782), i. 295–6, Steevens stated of M: 'The news of his death was followed by no encomiums on his writings or virtues. A less display of sorrow, and more scanty marks of respect, have not attended the memory of Warburton, whose various merits might at least have entitled him to such praise as his numerous sacerdotal parasites could bestow.' In *Anecdotes of Bowyer* (1782), 328–9 n., Nichols suggested that SJ had treated M 'perhaps a little too contemptuously'.

For an abusive critique of M by his contemporary Thomas Cooke (1703–56), see *Gent. Mag.* (1791), 1180–3. Cooke concluded that M was 'a whiffler in poetry', and that 'there never was a fellow of more disagreeable manners, a more lying, vain, and hateful fellow. He told me, about eighteen years ago, that he had read all the metaphysical writers who had wrote; and, some years afterwards, that he had lain with a Sovereign Princess in *Italy*.'

MARK AKENSIDE (1721–70)

Composition. SJ does not refer to 'Akenside' but presumably wrote it in the summer of 1780. Mrs Thrale had read it in a pre-publication volume by 18 Aug. 1780, when SJ asked her: 'Why did not You like Collins, and Gay and Blackmore, as well as Akensyde?' (*Letters*, iii. 301). SJ seems to refer to a letter from her, which she dated 20 Aug. 1780 in his *Letters* (1788), ii. 182. Whether or not she redated, or even fabricated, it later, her reaction is of interest: 'I like all the Whig lives prodigiously: Akenside's best of the little one's, for the sake of a pretty disquisition upon ridicule [6–7] that pleased me particularly, and that elegant stricture on the Pleasures of Imagination [14–21]; which will probably be much read and admired by every one.'

Sources. A was one of the five 'Poets whose lives he has to write' about whom Boswell asked Lord Hailes for 'any communications' on 7 July 1779 (Boswell Papers, Yale). SJ in fact followed closely Andrew Kippis's recent article about A in *BB*, i (2nd edn., 1778), 103–7. Only the information in **10** is from another source.

SJ obviously disliked A's religious and political views, but personal experience may lie behind his observation that he 'very eagerly forced himself into notice by an ambitious ostentation of elegance and literature' in conversation (see **12** below). There is, however, little evidence of personal contact between SJ and A, although they had such common friends as Robert Dodsley, whose bookshop SJ frequented from the 1740s, Samuel Richardson (see **12** n. below), and Hawkins, who 'knew [A] well' and gave an account of him in *Life* (1787), 242–8.

Publication. In *Prefaces*, vol. x (15 May 1781). There are three sets of proofs (pp. 1–11, 1–11, 1–18 of 18 pp.) in the Forster Collection.

Modern Sources:
(i) Mark Akenside
The Poetical Manuscripts... in the Ralph M. Williams Collection, Amherst College Library, ed. R. C. Dix (Amherst, Mass., 1988)
Poetical Works, ed. R. C. Dix (1996)
(ii)
R. C. Allen, 'A Philosophical Essay by MA', *N & Q* 243 (1998), 464–5
C. C. Barfoot, 'A Patriot's Boast: A and Goldsmith in Leiden', in J. van Dorsten (ed.), *Ten Studies in Anglo-Dutch Relations* (Leiden, 1974), 197–215

R. C. Dix, 'A's University Career: The Manuscript Evidence', *N & Q* 230 (1985), 212–15

R. C. Dix, 'A's *Odes on Several Subjects*', *Library*, 6th ser. 14 (1992), 51–9

R. C. Dix, 'MA: Unpublished Manuscripts', *Durham Univ. Journal*, 55 (1994), 219–26

R. C. Dix, 'Relations between A and Sir James Stonhouse in Northampton, 1744', *N & Q* 240 (1995), 68–70

R. C. Dix, 'The Pleasures of Speculation: Scholarly Methodology in Eighteenth-Century Literary Studies', *BJECS* 23 (2000), 85–103

R. C. Dix (ed.), *MA: A Reassessment* (2000)

D. Griffin, 'MA: "great citizen of Albion"', in *Patriotism and Poetry in Eighteenth-Century Britain* (Cambridge, 2002), 98–118

J. Hart, 'A's Revision of *The Pleasures of Imagination*', *PMLA* 74 (1959), 67–74

C. T. Houpt, *MA: A Biographical and Critical Study* (Philadelphia, 1944)

H. D. Jump, 'A's Other Epistle', *N & Q* 231 (1986), 508–12

H. D. Jump, 'High Sentiments of Liberty: Coleridge's Unacknowledged Debt to A', *Studies in Romanticism*, 28 (1989), 207–24

R. Mahony, 'MA', in *Dictionary of Literary Biography*, cix (1991), 3–11

J. Sitter, *Literary Loneliness in Mid-Eighteenth-Century England* (Ithaca, NY, 1982), 112–36, 159–79

I. A. Williams, *Seven XVIIIth Century Bibliographies* (1924), 75–97

1. A's parents married on 10 Aug. 1710 (Cunningham, *Lives* (1854), iii. 375 n.). John Brand, *Observations on Popular Antiquities* (Newcastle, 1777), 113–14 n., criticized A's 'False shame' about his father's trade: 'A Halt in his Gait, occasioned when a Boy, by the falling of a *Cleaver* from his *Father's Stall*, must have been a perpetual *Remembrance* of his humble Origin.' (Kippis in *BB* and SJ both ignored Brand's report, quoted in *Gent. Mag.* (1777), 384, and by Nichols in *Anecdotes of Bowyer* (1782), 353–4 n.) According to Alexander Carlyle, 'As he was of low descent, his father being a butcher, he stole through his native town *incog.* as often as he had occasion to pass, and never acknowledged his relation to it' (*Autobiography* (3rd edn., Edinburgh, 1861), 475–6). For such claims, often echoed by later biographers, see Dix, 'Pleasures', 88–92.

   After a period at the Royal Free Grammar School at Newcastle under Richard Dawes (1708–66), A was educated at a private academy run by William Wilson, a minister at the Unitarian chapel attended by A's family (*Poetical Works*, ed. Dix, 14).

2. Dix, 'A's University Career', 212–15, and *Poetical Works*, 14–15, showed that A was admitted as a reader to Edinburgh University Library on 24 Nov. 1738, and was listed in the matriculation register on 23 Mar. 1739. He later changed to the study of medicine, and was remembered as an eloquent speaker in debates at the University's Medical Society, with, at that time, parliamentary ambitions. Dix also quotes a letter of 24 May 1742, when A was working as a surgeon in Newcastle, in which he offered to repay his grant from the Dissenters' Society.

3. For SJ's careful revision of this paragraph in the proofs, in which 'furious . . . zeal' became 'unnecessary . . . zeal', see Textual Notes.

   SJ's outburst about 'liberty' may be a reaction to Andrew Kippis's recent praise of A's attachment to 'the cause of civil and religious liberty', with a cautious reference to his 'republican ideas', in *BB* (2nd edn., 1778), i. 105 n. Lord Hailes commented in 1782 on SJ's reference to A's dissenting background: 'if Akenside was bred in yt line he quickly left it. some of his sarcasms aimed at Religion are yet remembered, but it is fair to observe that, in riper years, he wishes to have these sallies forgotten. this I learnt from ye late Sr Gilbert Elliot, it would be wrong for me to mention ye particulars of an offence which ye offender wishes to have no longer mentioned': see Carnie (1956), 488.

This paragraph and **6** below recall SJ's political pamphlets in the 1770s. Usually, though not invariably (see 'Watts' **35** and n. above), he associated religious dissent with demands for 'liberty'. In *The False Alarm* (1770) he described Dissenters as 'sectaries, the constant fomenters of sedition, and never-failing confederates of the rabble, of whose religion little now remains but hatred of establishments' (*YW*, x. 344). For his hostility to 'liberty' as a slogan elsewhere, see **6, 9** and n., **10** below, 'Thomson' **22** above and 'Lyttelton' **3** below, and his account of the 'envious hatred of greatness' and 'repugnance to authority' underlying Milton's 'love of liberty' in 'Milton' **169–70** and n. above. For 'innovation', see 'Milton' **58** and n. above, and cf. literary 'innovation' in **23** below.

The disputatious 'Pertinax' in *Rambler* 95 (1751) had harangued both the 'zealots of liberty... with great copiousness upon the advantages of absolute monarchy', and 'the assertors of regal authority... with republican warmth' on 'the folly of voluntary submission to those whom nature has levelled with ourselves' (*YW*, iv. 146). SJ was less evenhanded in the 1770s, when he attacked Wilkes's followers as a faction whose 'original principle is the desire of levelling; it is only animated under the name of zeal, by the natural malignity of the mean against the great' (*YW*, x. 342). He had recently experienced the 'anarchy' of the anti-Catholic Gordon Riots in early June 1780, when he described 'a weeks defiance of government' to Mrs Thrale (*Letters*, iii. 267–70).

After the French Revolution, Robert Anderson, *Poets of Great Britain*, ix (Edinburgh, 1794), 725, thought that this paragraph, though 'inapplicable' to A himself, 'may be deemed prophetic by the best friends of rational and regulated freedom, who lament the excesses of what is called and thought liberty in the present day'.

4. As a teenager A contributed poems signed 'Marcus' or 'Britannicus', or dated from Newcastle, to the *Gent. Mag.* in 1737–9, a period when SJ was himself working for it (Houpt, *MA*, 9–29; Dix, *Poetical Works*, 389–408, 513–20). For Edward Cave's separate publication of A's anti-Walpole *A British Philippic, A Poem, in Miltonic Verse* (1738), with a second issue entitled *The Voice of Liberty; Or, A British Philippic*, see Foxon, *English Verse*, A 133–4 and Dix, *Poetical Works*, 57–64.

A had started work on *The Pleasures of Imagination* by 1742. Allen, 'Essay', 464–5, noted that a passage in *Pleasures*, II. 350–63, appeared in a theological article by 'MA' on 'The Principles of a Theory of the Immaterial World', dated 'Edinburgh, 14 December 1742', in *The History of the Works of the Learned* (Dec. 1742), 443–50. A went to London in Aug. 1743, no doubt to negotiate the poem's publication on 16 Jan. 1744: see, Dix *Poetical Works*, 15.

By 'greatest' SJ here means both 'most elaborate' and 'most excellent': cf. 'Milton' **194** and n. above. For A's youthful 'genius', see also **14** below.

SJ appears to be the earliest source for the story of Pope's advice, which he heard from Robert Dodsley himself. In the mid-1740s A became one of the publisher's chief literary advisers: see Dodsley, *Corresp.*, 121 n., and cf. 'Dyer' 12 and n. above.

5. Edinburgh University had a traditional link with Leiden, which enjoyed a high reputation for medicine. (A decade later Goldsmith moved on from Edinburgh to study medicine at Leiden, though without taking a degree.) A was in fact admitted there on 7 Apr. 1744, and obtained his diploma as a Doctor of Physic on 16 May 1744 for his thesis *De Ortu et Incremento Foetus Humani* (Leiden, 1744). (According to the English calendar, the dates would have been 27 Mar. and 5 May.) A may have returned briefly to Leiden in 1745 and 1746 to re-register. For connections between A's thesis and *The Pleasures of Imagination*, see R. C. Dix, 'Organic Theories of Art: The Importance of Embryology', *N & Q* 230 (1985), 215–18; and for A's visits to Holland, see 'On Leaving Holland' in his *Odes* (1745), and Barfoot, 'A Patriot's Boast'.

6. For 'liberty' and hostility to 'any thing established', see 3 and n. above.

Anthony Ashley Cooper (1671–1713), Earl of Shaftesbury, advanced his theory of ridicule as a test of imposture in *A Letter Concerning Enthusiasm* (1708) and *Characteristicks* (1711): see R. A. Voitle, *The Third Earl of Shaftesbury* (Baton Rouge, La., 1984), 325–33, and R. Terry, '"The Mirthful Sting": A and the Eigheenth-Century Controversy over Ridicule', in Dix (ed.), *MA*. SJ refers disapprovingly to the theory in 'Sermon 20' (*YW*, xiv. 220). Hawkins, *Life* (1787), 255–7, later described SJ's dislike of 'the cant of the Shaftesburian school', as well as his 'disputations' with Samuel Dyer at the Ivy Lane Club in the late 1740s about 'that fanciful notion, that ridicule is the test of truth'. For Shaftesbury, see also 'Gray' 24 and n. below.

Warburton attacked the doctrine of ridicule in the 'Dedication to the Freethinkers', prefixed to *The Divine Legation of Moses* (2 vols., 1738–41). A wrote to David Fordyce about it on 30 July 1743 (Houpt, *MA*, 54–5), and defended Shaftesbury ('the noble restorer of ancient philosophy') in *The Pleasures of Imagination* (1744), I. 374 n., III. 73–277 and nn. Warburton replied scathingly in the preface to his *Remarks on Several Occasional Reflections* (1744), pp. iii–xvi, and A responded in turn with *An Epistle to the Rev. Mr. Warburton, Occasioned by his Treatment of the Author of The Pleasures of Imagination* (1744), under the name of Jeremiah Dyson (see 10 n. below).

John Brown joined in the argument in his *Essay on Satire* (1745), 15 and n. For John Gilbert Cooper's support of A against Warburton, see R. C. Dix in *Age of J* 13 (2002), 261–7. When Warburton reprinted his 1744 preface as 'Postscript to the Dedication to the Freethinkers' in *The Divine Legation* (5th edn., 1766), A's parting shot was a note to his *Ode to Thomas Edwards* (1766), 5 n. As well as criticizing Warburton's edition of Pope, A described a letter he owned in which Warburton had referred contemptuously in 1727 to Pope, whose friend and champion he later became (see 'Pope' 186 and n. above). For A's willingness to show the letter to Warburton's friends, see Nichols, *Anecdotes of Bowyer* (1782), 432. Malone had recently printed it in his *Supplement to Shakespeare* (1780), i. 223–6.

7. Cf. 'Butler' 48 ('Cheats can seldom stand long against laughter'), and 'Pope' 359 above ('All truth is valuable, and satirical criticism may be considered as useful when it rectifies error and improves judgement'). Arthur Murphy commented on

SJ's own powers of 'argumentation': 'When he chose by apt illustration to place the argument of his adversary in a ludicrous light, one was almost inclined to think *ridicule the test of truth*' (*Essay on ... SJ* (1792), 139; *J. Misc.*, i. 452).

SJ added the final sentence in 1783.

8. For A's revision of *The Pleasures of Imagination*, see **20** below.

SJ's statement that A omitted the passage which offended Warburton follows *BB*, i. 106 n. Although he reduced the original 181 lines on ridicule to forty-seven, and redeployed them in the revised Bk. II, the key passage in fact survived: cf. *Pleasures* (1744), III. 259–77 and (1772), II. 523–41, and Hart, 'A's Revision'.

which he died before he had finished: although this is the text in the proofs and all SJ's editions, Hill (1905) emended it to 'though he died before he had finished it'. SJ repeats the gist of this sentence less awkwardly in **20** below.

9. A in fact returned from Leiden in May 1744 (see **5** above). His *Odes on Several Subjects* appeared on 26 Mar. 1745 (Foxon, *English Verse*, i. 13). He published a revised edition in 1760, and his posthumous *Poems* (1772) included twenty-three additional odes: see Dix, 'A's *Odes*', 51–9.

of patriotism: see 'Pope' **397** and n. above. SJ originally wrote 'for liberty' (see Textual Notes).

A's *An Epistle to Curio* (published in Nov. 1744) attacked William Pulteney (1684–1764), a prominent opponent of Walpole, whose political reputation suffered when he accepted a peerage as Earl of Bath in July 1742. SJ said on 21 Oct. 1773: 'Pulteney was as paltry a fellow as could be. He was a Whig, who pretended to be honest; and you know it is ridiculous for a Whig to pretend to be honest. He cannot hold it out' (*Life*, v. 339). SJ noticeably attributes 'great vigour and poignancy' rather than mere acrimony to the original *Epistle* when condemning A's later revision of the poem in **22** below. For the possibility that A wrote an even earlier *Epistle to Pulteney* (1742), see Jump, 'A's Other Epistle', 508–12.

10. A was in Northampton by 20 June 1744. Although Kippis had been a pupil in Philip Doddridge's academy in Northampton in the 1740s, his article in *BB* does not refer to A's medical rivalry with Dr (later Sir) James Stonhouse (1716–95), who became a clergyman in 1749. SJ's source may have been Hawkins, a friend of A (see **12** n. below), or Thomas Percy, a clergyman at Easton Maudit near Northampton from 1756, who was a friend of Stonhouse: see B. Davis, *Thomas Percy* (Philadelphia, 1989), 94–6. Stonhouse also knew Garrick, Hannah More, and Mrs Thrale (Garrick, *Letters* (1963), iii. 937 n., 1121, 1316, 1355–8; *Thraliana*, i. 94).

There are many references to Stonhouse, with whom he founded what became Northampton County Infirmary, in Philip Doddridge's *Corresp.* (1979). For Doddridge's attempt to dissuade A from settling in Northampton, see his letters to A and Stonhouse of 20 June 1744 (*Corresp.*, 198–9, and cf. Dix, 'Relations', 68–70). Writing to his wife on 21 June, he hoped that A's 'character is too great to lay him under any temptation of staying at Northampton with so little encouragement' (Ximenes Rare Books, List 98–2, #59). In spite, or because, of the rivalry, Stonhouse wrote a letter of introduction for A when he left Northampton later in 1745. 'Indigator' in *Gent. Mag.* (1793), ii. 885–6 and (1794), i. 206, later accused A of trying to steal Stonhouse's patients, and mentioned 'his outrageous and interested clamours for licentious innovation, with which he unhinged the harmony of his neighbourhood'.

11. By late 1745 A was living at North End, Hampstead, the estate of Jeremiah Dyson (1722?–76), whom he had met by 1742, probably in Edinburgh. Originally a Dissenter and republican like A, Dyson became a lawyer and civil servant, Clerk to the House of Commons 1748–62, MP 1762–76, Secretary to the Treasury 1762–4, Lord of Trade 1764–8, Lord of Treasury 1768–74, and Cofferer to the Royal Household 1774–6: see *The House of Commons 1754–90* (1964), ii. 371–3. In an effusive letter to Dyson from Leiden in Apr. 1744, A told him: 'I look upon my connection with you as the most fortunate circumstance of my life' (Houpt, *MA*, 61–2).

According to Hawkins, *Life* (1787), 243–4, A's social life in the 'opulent neighbourhood' of Hampstead deteriorated because of his own disputatious behaviour, and the contempt of those who discovered that 'he was a man of low birth, and a dependant on Mr. Dyson'. By 1748 he had moved to a small house in Bloomsbury Square, apparently assisted by an allowance from Dyson (Houpt, *MA*, 107, 118). In his will of 6 Dec. 1767 A left Dyson his estate, including his literary MSS: see Dix, 'MA', 219–26. For an interpretation of A's friendship with Dyson, see G. S. Rousseau, 'In the House of Madam Vander Tasse', *Journal of Homosexuality*, 11 (1986), 311–47, reprinted in *Perilous Enlightenment* (Manchester, 1991); and for a sceptical response, see Dix, 'Pleasures', 88–103.

George Hardinge (1743–1816), a lawyer and friend of A, doubted that 'he had much depth of medical science, or much acuteness of medical sagacity; he certainly had no business or fame in that line' (Nichols, *Lit. Anec.*, viii. 522). For SJ's personal interest in 1777 and 1784 in A's proposed remedy for 'angustia pectoris', see *Letters*, iii. 52, iv. 365. For other medical poets, see 'Garth' and 'Blackmore' above, and cf. 'Cowley' 31 above.

a very curious book... on the Fortune of Physicians: SJ may have written the proposals (1741) for Robert James's *Medicinal Dictionary* (3 vols., 1743–5), which claim that 'the *History of Physicians*, being an Account of the Lives, Writings, and Characters of the principal Authors in Physic', was 'not only the Consequence of a natural Curiosity, but of a laudable Gratitude' (Hazen, 70). Although as many as eleven medical biographies in the *Dictionary* have been ascribed to SJ (see Hazen, 70, and *Early Biog. Writings* (1973), 99–158), most of these were questioned by O M Brack and T. Kaminski, 'J, James, and the *Medicinal Dictionary*', *MP* 81 (1983–4), 378–400, as conceded in *Bibliography*, i. 66.

12. A became a Fellow of the Royal Society, and a Doctor of Physic from Emmanuel College, Cambridge, in 1753; and Licentiate of the Royal College of Physicians in 1751, and Fellow, 1754. SJ follows *BB*, i. 104–5, 107 n., in listing A's appointments as principal physician at St Thomas's Hospital (1759), Goulstonian Lecturer to the College of Physicians (1755) (cf. 'Garth' 11 n. above), and Croonian Lecturer (1756). SJ also repeats *BB*'s incorrect statement that A did not complete the Croonian lectures (Houpt, *MA*, 134 n.). For A's other appointments as lecturer to the Royal Society and to the Royal College of Physicians, see Dix, *Poetical Works*, 15–16; and for other projected histories of 'the revival of Learning', including SJ's own, see 'Collins' 4 and n. above.

BB and SJ do not mention that the alleged republicanism or radical Whiggism of A and Dyson had evaporated by the time George III ascended the throne, when A was appointed one of the Queen's physicians (*St James's Chronicle*, 5 Sept. 1761; *Gent. Mag.* (Sept. 1761), 431). George Hardinge described them as by then 'bigoted adherents to Lord Bute and the Tories, having at every earlier period been, as it were, the High Priests of the opposite Creed'; and, although he admired A's poetry, told Walpole in July 1772: 'His apostasy in *politics*, from Cato and Aristides, to the Earl of Bute, was most *unpoetical*, and admits of no palliation' (Nichols, *Lit. Anec.*, viii. 523; Walpole, *Corresp.*, xxxv. 566).

Walpole described Dyson as 'a most usefull Tool of Lord Bute... bred a Republican... but was converted to the service of Prerogative by Lord Bute, & converted his friend Dr Akenside to the same cause' (William Mason, *Satirical Poems... With Notes by Horace Walpole*, ed. P. Toynbee (Oxford, 1926), 63). SJ's friend William Seward recorded in 'Drossiana' in *European Mag.* 34 (1798), 97–8, that A, 'in early life, was distinguished by that roar for general Liberty which too often disgraces the mouths of the ardent and the ingenious; in later life, he was angry with a celebrated Bookseller for having one copy of [Wilkes's] "The North Briton" in his shop'.

SJ may have avoided the subject because he himself accepted a pension from the new government a few months after A's appointment. He also ignores Smollett's depiction of A in *Peregrine Pickle* (1751), chs. 46–7, as a conceited physician and pretentious classicist, who was also 'the greatest poet of the age', an admirer of Pindar and Shaftesbury, and 'a rank republican' ('no country could flourish, but under the administration of the mob') (cf. **3**, **6** above and **22** below).

Griffin, 'MA', 98–118, has argued that the evidence for A's alleged republican principles or sympathies 'is in fact very thin', noting that SJ himself does not refer to them.

BB, i. 107, lists A's medical writings. SJ's assertion that A by now 'wrote little poetry' ignores his *Ode to the Earl of Huntingdon* (1748), *Ode to the Country Gentlemen of England* (1758), and *Ode to Thomas Edwards* (1766). A also edited Dodsley's *The Museum* (29 Mar. 1746–12 Sept. 1747: for the contract, dated 20 Jan. 1746, which brought A £100 p.a., see Dodsley, *Corresp.*, 508); and contributed to his *Collection of Poems*, vi (1758), 1–36. He began revising *The Pleasures of Imagination* in about 1754 (see **20** below).

Relatively silent in the 1760s, A did not respond poetically to the republican Thomas Hollis's unusual gift in 1761 of the bed in which Milton died (see headnote to 'Milton' above), with the message that, if it should 'prompt him to write an Ode to the memory of John Milton, and the assertor of British liberty, that gentleman would think himself abundantly recompensed' (Francis Blackburne, *Memoirs of the late Thomas Hollis* (1780), ii. 111–12).

Hawkins, *Life* (1787), 244–7, described A's 'haughtiness and self-conceit' in argument, but claimed that in private his 'conversation was of the most delightful kind, learned, instructive, and without any affectation of wit, chearful, and entertaining'. Hardinge mentioned A's 'pomp and stiffness of *manner*', his 'altogether unpromising, if not grotesque' primness of appearance, and his humourlessness (Nichols, *Lit. Anec.*, viii. 523). For an account of A monopolizing the conversation for an entire evening at Samuel Richardson's in 1756, see T. C. D. Eaves and B. D. Kimpel, *Samuel Richardson* (Oxford, 1971), 459. The extent of SJ's first-hand knowledge of A's conversation is unclear. For his interest elsewhere in the conversation of poets, see 'Cowley' **200** and n. above.

13. A's *De Dysenteria Commentarius* (1764) was praised in the *Monthly Review*, 35 (1766), 373, and translated into English by Dr. J. Ryan in the same year.

A was buried in St James's, Piccadilly. For Shenstone's death from 'putrid fever' in 1763, see 'Shenstone' **15** and n. above.

14–20. With SJ's account of A's best-known poem, cf. Joseph Warton's praise, with extensive quotations, of his 'glowing and animated style, his lively and picturesque images; the graceful and harmonious flow of his numbers; or the noble spirit of poetical enthusiasm, which breathes thro' his whole work', in *Works of Virgil* (1753), i. 436–40. For other admirers, down to the Romantics, see Dix, *Poetical Works*, 26–31. A's 'The Design' in *Pleasures* (1744), 7, explained that his subject, 'tending almost constantly to admiration and enthusiasm, seem'd rather to demand a more open, pathetic, and figur'd stile' than Pope's 'familiar epistolary' Horatian manner. For his admiration of Young's recent poetry, see 'To the Author of the *Complaint*' in *Gent. Mag.* (June 1744), 329.

14. For SJ's use of 'great' and 'greatest', see **4** and n. above. A was in fact 22 when he published *The Pleasures of Imagination* in Jan. 1744. For Addison's *Spectators* (1712) on the same subject, see 'Addison' **80** and n. above.

For SJ's earlier reference to A's youthful 'genius', see **4** above, and for 'genius', see 'Milton' **277** and n. above. John Gilbert Cooper described A as 'a Poet of as genuine a Genius as this Kingdom has ever produced, SHAKESPEAR alone excepted', and his *Pleasures* as 'the most beautiful *didactic* Poem that ever adorned the English Language' (*Letters Concerning Taste* (3rd edn., 1757), 95). SJ said bluntly of A's poem on 28 Mar. 1772: 'I could not read it through' (*Life*, ii. 164).

SJ once told Boswell that the author Richard Rolt (1725?–70) had published A's poem as his own in Dublin (*Life*, i. 359; see also Reed, *Biographia Dramatica* (1782), i. 372). For Boswell's misgivings about the story, Percy's advice that he suppress it, and notes about it in later editions of the *Life*, see *Life of J: An Edition of the Original Manuscript*, ed. M. Waingrow, i (1994), 251 n. Rolt's name does not appear on the Dublin editions of the *Pleasures* in 1744 and 1748.

15. For SJ's similar statements about his 'business' in the *Lives*, see 'Sprat' **22** and n. above; for didactic poetry, see 'Pope' **328** and n. above; and for 'design' in descriptive poetry, see 'Savage' **120** and 'Thomson' **49** above.

SJ defines 'Exuberance' as 'Overgrowth; superfluous shoots; useless abundance; luxuriance' (cf. **16** n., **18** below and 'Thomson' **50** and n. above), and 'Artificially' as '1. Artfully; with skill' (*Dict.*)

16. For 'images', see also **14–15** above and **18, 22** below, and 'Cowley' **154** and n. above, and for 'luxuriance', **18, 22** below and 'Thomson' **50** and n. above, where SJ also alludes to Butler, *Hudibras*, II. i. 905–8. He goes on to quote Ovid, *Remedia Amoris*, l. 344 ('The real woman is the least part of herself').

attention deserts the mind, and settles in the ear: for the importance of holding the reader's attention, see 'Dryden' **312** and n. above. Thomson is also 'charged with filling the ear more than the mind' in 'Thomson' **50** above.

the flowery labyrinth: cf. Collins's 'meanders of inchantment' ('Collins' **8** above) and Young's 'wilderness' with its 'flowers of every hue and every odour' ('Young' **160** above). See also *Rambler* 122 (1751) on writers 'clouding the facts which they intended to illustrate, and losing themselves and the auditors in wilds and mazes, in digression and confusion'; and *Idler* 36 (1758), on 'authors whose labours counteract themselves. The man of exuberance and copiousness, who diffuses every thought thro' so many diversities of expression, that it is lost like water in a mist' (*YW*, iv. 287, ii. 113).

laid hold on nothing: for another poem from which the reader 'learns nothing', see 'Pope' 365 above, and cf. 'nothing . . . nothing' at the end of 17 below.

In an early response to the *Pleasures*, Thomas Gray wrote on 26 Apr. 1744: 'it seems to me above the middleing, & now & then (but for a little while) rises even to the best, particularly in Description. it is often obscure, & even unintelligible.' According to Norton Nicholls, Gray 'disliked Akenside, & in general all poetry in blank verse except Milton' (*Corresp.*, i. 224, iii. 1291).

17. For SJ's hostility to blank verse elsewhere, see 'Milton' 274 n. above, and for his occasional concessions about it, see 'Thomson' 47 and 'Young' 160 above. A may be 'superior to any other writer of blank verse' because of his relative smoothness and musicality, but SJ's reservations immediately follow.

For 'concatenation', see 'Cowley' 126 and n. above, and for 'intertexture', 'Pope' 59 and n. above. By the 'full close' SJ means the completion of the sense at the end of a line of verse.

18. Cf. Dryden's preface to *The Rival Ladies* (1664): 'The great easiness of blank verse renders the poet too luxuriant; he is tempted to say many things which might better be omitted, or at least shut up in fewer words'; and Crites in *Of Dramatick Poesie* (1668): 'verse, you say, circumscribes a quick and luxuriant fancy, which would extend itself too far on every subject, did not the labour which is required to well turned and polished rhyme set bounds to it. Yet . . . he who wants judgment to confine his fancy in blank verse, may want it as much in rhyme' (Watson, i. 8, 80 and cf. 91).

For 'ornaments', see 'Cowley' 202 n. above, and for 'exuberance', see 15 and n. above.

19. For SJ's careful revision of this paragraph in the proofs, see Textual Notes. Collins similarly believed that 'not to write prose is certainly to write poetry' in 'Collins' 17 above, and cf. also 'Gray' 30 below.

artifices of disgust: distasteful affectations such as those of Collins, who 'affected the obsolete' and 'puts his words out of the common order' ('Collins' 17 above). For 'inversions', see also 'Cowley' 117 and n. above. Archibald Campbell's satiric *Lexiphanes* (1767) had in fact linked A with SJ himself as 'Dealers in *hard words*, and *absurd phrases*', who 'persuade themselves and the publick, that they are the only authors worth regard, and that their uncouth trash is the sole standard of perfection in the English tongue' (p. xvii).

SJ 'quotes' compressed versions of *Pleasures*, I. 177–9, 194–5 (with 'stated' for 'fated'). A later revised both passages (see 20 below). For poetic 'pedantry', see also 23 n. below. SJ defines 'To absolve' as '4. To finish, to complete. This use is not common', with an illustration from Milton (*Dict.*).

20. Jeremiah Dyson included both the original *The Pleasures of Imagination* and A's extensive revision (1757–70) as *The Pleasures of the Imagination* in *Poems* (1772), with an 'Advertisement' (pp. iii–vi) describing A's work on the poem after 1744. A had privately circulated printed revisions of Bks. I (1757) and II (1765).

Poems (1772) was 'Printed by W. Bowyer and J. Nichols', and Nichols included both versions in *Eng. Poets* (1779) ('the late collection'). John Pinkerton, *Letters of*

Literature (1785), 21–32, printed MS revisions of the *Pleasures* by A, which may have preceded his later more drastic recasting of the poem: see Dix, 'MA', 42–3.

The unfinished 'Tale of Solon', the Athenian poet and lawgiver, occupies most of the revised Bk. III. A completed only ll. 1–130 of what he envisaged as Bk. V, in which his 'Wordsworthian' anticipations have often been noted. As Hill (1905) pointed out, Wordsworth himself used a line from it as epigraph to *Yarrow Revisited* (1835). Kippis compared the two versions of the poem in *Monthly Review*, 47 (1772), 428–37, and at greater length in *BB*, i. 106 n. For other contemporary reactions, see Dix, 'MA', 24–5, and for modern assessments, Hart, 'A's Revision', 67–74, M. Meehan in *Liberty and Poetics in Eighteenth Century England* (1986), 52–63, and Dix, *Poetical Works*, 18–25.

21. SJ added this paragraph in 1783.

John Walker (1732–1807), lexicographer, educationist, and a 'celebrated master of elocution' (*Life*, iv. 206), dedicated his *Exercises for Improvement in Elocution* (1777) to Garrick, two other books to SJ himself, and mentioned his friendship with SJ in his *Critical Pronouncing Dictionary* (1791). He visited SJ on 9 Dec. 1782 (*YW*, i. 355; *Letters*, iv. 100), not long before the revised *Lives* (1783) were published.

SJ quotes a passage from Walker's *Exercises*, 67 (not 66), introducing extracts from A's *Pleasures* and Young's *Night Thoughts*. SJ noticeably omits the opening of the first sentence ('This Author is remarkable for his elevation of thought, his dignity of expression, and harmony of numbers'), and concentrates on Walker's exposition of A's theological 'deficiency'. On the other hand, having ignored the religious content of the *Night Thoughts* in his own discussion of Young's poetry, SJ in 1783 allows Walker to emphasize it here: see 'Young' **160** and n. above.

22. For SJ's reservations about modern 'lyric poetry', see *Rambler* 158 (1751), and for other unsuccessful lyric poets, see 'Congreve' **44** (who lacked 'the fire requisite for the higher species of lyrick poetry') and 'Young' **159** above (who is 'always labouring to be great, and at last is only turgid'). For 'ease' see 'Rochester' **18** and n. above, for 'luxuriance', 'Thomson' **50** and n. above, and for 'images' **16** and n. above.

A's revised *Epistle to Curio* (see **9** above) was entitled 'Ode to Curio' in *Poems* (1772). Both versions appeared in *Eng. Poets* (1779), lv. 212–18, 333–45, with an explanatory note by Nichols (333 n.). SJ's objection to the revision of an epistle in couplets into a 'disgraceful' stanzaic 'Ode' is predictable. For the claim that A's reworking of the epistle marks a shift from a notion of poetry 'as possessing moral agency within society' to a 'rhapsodical ideal of liberty . . . outside history', see W. C. Dowling, *The Epistolary Moment* (Princeton, 1991), 121–4. Griffin, 'MA', 118, has argued instead that A sought to 'transcend the world of politics' only in his last years.

23. This paragraph originally continued the discussion of the 'Ode to Curio' in **22**, beginning, 'Of this ode the diction', etc. SJ's revision in the proofs extended his objections to all of A's odes (see Textual Notes).

SJ said on 28 Mar. 1772 of A's posthumous *Poems* (1772): 'One bad ode may be suffered; but a number of them together makes one sick.' On 10 Apr. 1776, however, reacting to Mason's recent *Memoirs* of Gray, he claimed that A 'was a superiour poet to Gray and Mason' (*Life*, ii. 164, iii. 32). For his objections to the influential odes of the 1740s and 1750s, see 'Collins' 8–9, 17 above and 'Gray' 28–48 below.

Although Warton praised two of A's odes in *Essay on Pope* (1756), 69, he had stated of A's *Odes* in Mar. 1745 that 'The thoughts to me are generally trite & common', and his brother agreed 'that they have a vast deal of the *frigid*' (Thomas Warton, *Corresp.* (1995), 7–8). After reading A's odes in Dodsley's *Collection*, vi (1758), Gray described him as 'in a deplorable way' and as a 'sad fellow' (*Corresp.*, ii. 566, 568). The *Monthly Review*, 18 (1758), 335–8, however, discovered in a recent ode by A the 'sacred fire of liberty', and suggested that he should be styled 'the Poet of the Community'.

SJ would have thought no better of A's odes if he knew that the Whig Thomas Hollis (see 12 n. above) used a quotation from A's 'On Leaving Holland' as a motto on books, etchings, medals, bindings, and even bells: see W. H. Bond, *Thomas Hollis of Lincoln's Inn: A Whig and his Books* (Cambridge, 1990), 17–18, 39 n., and 46. A's odes had other admirers. Edward Burnaby Greene in *Anacreon and Sappho, with Pieces from Ancient Authors* (1768), p. xviii, claimed that 'When *polish'd Akenside* commands the string, | Enthusiast fancy soars on judgment's wing', John Scott, *Poetical Works* (1782), 241–4, praised his 'Grecian Muse, severely fair', and John Pinkerton wrote that, 'Tho Akenside, considered as a lyric writer, wants richness of images and melody, his style will ever render what he has done in this way valuable' (*Letters of Literature* (1785), 131). There is a protest at SJ's treatment of A's odes in the 'Corrigenda and Addenda' (sub. 'Akenside') in *BB*, iii (2nd edn., 1784).

For 'diction', see 'Cowley' 181–4 and n. above; for 'harshness', 'Milton' 177 and n. above; for 'rhymes', 'Cowley' 187 and n., and 'Dryden' 279 and n. above; and for another poet whose stanzaic odes were 'perplexing to the ear', see 'Gray' 42 below.

Under 'Innovate' in the *Dict.* SJ quotes Dryden's dedication to the *Aeneid* (1697): 'But every man cannot distinguish between pedantry and poetry: every man, therefore, is not fit to innovate' (Watson, ii. 252; for A's 'pedantry', see 19 above). For political rather than poetic 'innovation and anarchy', see 3 and n. above.

24. For other poems undeserving of serious criticism, see 'Milton' 206 and n. above; for tediousness, see 'Prior' 66–8 above; and for unreadability, see 'Milton' 252 and n. above.

THOMAS GRAY (1716–71)

Composition. On 23 May 1780 SJ wrote to Richard Farmer, the University Librarian at Cambridge, requesting information from the University Registers about G and other Cambridge poets, but on 16 June told Nichols that he had received no reply. Although he did not refer again to 'Gray', he had evidently completed it by early Aug. 1780, when only 'Lyttelton', 'Swift', and 'Pope' remained to be written (*Letters*, iii. 257, 278, 295).

Whether or not 'Gray' was included in the pre-publication volume SJ hoped on 8 Aug. soon to send to Mrs Thrale, it was circulating by 5 Oct. 1780, when she noted that SJ's 'Criticism of Gray displeases many people; Sir Joshua Reynolds in particular'. She believed that, like G, Reynolds was himself a tame, quiet character 'forced into Fire by

Artifice & Effort' (*Letters*, iii. 297; *Thraliana*, i. 459). For Horace Walpole's pursuit of a pre-publication text of 'Gray' early in 1781, see below.

Sources. Although G had died in 1771, too recently to appear in SJ's usual sources, he could find unusually ample information in William Mason's *Poems of Mr. Gray. To Which Are Prefix'd Memoirs of His Life and Writings* (York, 1775). (The revised 2nd edn., 1775, is cited below as 'Mason (1775 edn.)': references are to the 'Memoirs', unless the separately paginated 'Poems' are indicated.) Although SJ refers to it in **5, 7– 8, 22–3, 25** below, he hardly admits the full extent of his factual dependence on Mason's biography, of which he always professed a low opinion.

When told in Mar. 1772 that Mason had undertaken it, SJ had remarked ominously: 'I think we have had enough of Gray' (*Life*, ii. 164). On 2 Apr. 1775 (shortly before it appeared) he asserted: 'I hate Gray and Mason, though I do not know them' (Boswell, *Ominous Years*, 116). Whereas Walpole told Mason on 7 May 1775 that 'You have fixed the method of biography, and whoever will write a life well must imitate you' (*Corresp.*, xxviii. 195), Boswell reported to W. J. Temple three days later that SJ 'does not like the book' (*Letters*, ed. C. B. Tinker, i. 222–3). On 12 May SJ described it to Mrs Thrale as 'but dull . . . I can hardly recommend the purchase' (*Letters*, ii. 206). On 10 Apr. 1776 he 'acquiesced' in Murphy's opinion that Mason's biography set G 'much higher in his estimation than his poems did; for you there saw a man constantly at work in literature', but then 'depreciated the book', as Boswell thought, 'very unreasonably. For he said, "I forced myself to read it, only because it was a common topick of conversation. I found it mighty dull; and, as to the style, it is fit for the second table." Why he thought so, I was at a loss to conceive' (*Life*, iii. 31–2). There is inevitable irony in the fact that in 1791 Boswell would announce that Mason's biography, especially in its use of G's letters, had provided 'the excellent plan' of his own *Life* of SJ (i. 29).

It is worth noting that Mason prevented the reprinting of material from G's MSS he had first published in 1775. He in fact sued John Murray for printing some of the posthumous material in an edition of G's *Poems* in 1776, Murray defending his 'piracy' in his *Letter to W. Mason, A. M. . . . Concerning his Edition of Mr. Gray's Poems and the Practices of Booksellers* (1777). On 15 Apr. 1778 SJ 'signified his displeasure at Mr. Mason's conduct very strongly; but added, by way of shewing that he was not surprized at it, "Mason's a Whig" ' (*Life*, iii. 294). The reviewer of *Eng. Poets* in *Gent. Mag.* (1779), 601, was surprised to find it contained 'so small a part of his poetical writings. If literary property was in the way (and, from a chancery-suit, which happened two years ago, we suppose this to have been the case; see our Magazine for 1777, p. 331,) it reflects no great credit on the undertakers, not to have asked permission to have used them for a work which could in no respect have hurt the separate sale of Gray's Poems. If they asked it, and were refused, it argues illiberality in a mind we should have expected to have been exempt from such frailty.' See also B. Barr and J. Ingamells, *A Candidate for Praise* (York, 1973), 60.

Despite his low opinion of Mason's 'dull' volume, SJ seems not to have felt the need for additional information. G was one of the five poets about whom Boswell asked Lord Hailes for information as early as 7 July 1779 (Boswell Papers, Yale), but there is no sign that this enquiry bore any fruit, or indeed that Boswell, an enthusiastic admirer of G, tried to guide SJ to other possible sources, such as his friend the Revd Norton Nicholls (1741?– 1809), who had known G well at Cambridge in the 1760s and later recorded detailed reminscences of him (*Corresp.*, iii. 1288–304; see Boswell, *Catalogue*, C 2093, for a letter from Nicholls to Boswell, 18 Nov. 1780). Boswell was, however, able to tell both Mason and SJ that the author of an anonymous 'character' of G, reprinted first by Mason in 1775 and then by SJ in 22 below, was his friend William Johnson Temple, although SJ did not add this attribution until 1783.

Horace Walpole, a lifelong friend of G who helped Mason with his biography, claimed in 1791 that Boswell had in fact visited him to request information for SJ's 'Gray' and that he had refused to cooperate. It is unlikely that Boswell did so with SJ's blessing, and Walpole may have been misremembering another visit, apparently to learn his opinion of SJ's still unpublished 'Gray', which he described to Mason on 22 Mar. 1781 (*Corresp.*, xi. 275–7, xxix. 144–5). SJ's unreceptiveness to further information was described by William Cole (1714–82), the Cambridge antiquary, who recalled that, when he 'was publishing his life of Gray, I gave him several anecdotes, but he was very anxious as soon as possible to get to the end of his labours' and made no use of them (*Works of G*, ed. John Mitford, i (1835), p. civ, quoting Cole's MSS in the British Library). (For Cole's account of G and his relations with Richard Farmer, dated 31 Oct. 1780, see *Corresp.*, iii. 1119–20 n., and cf. 23 n. below.)

SJ needed no other source than Mason (1775 edn.) because in a sense he had been composing sections of 'Gray' in his mind for some thirty years. The two men never apparently met, e.g. during the extended period when G was working at the newly opened British Museum (see 16 below), or when SJ visited Cambridge in 1765 (*Life*, i. 517–18). G had at first been impressed by SJ's poetry in Dodsley's *Collection*, telling Walpole in 1748 that *London* (1738) 'is to me one of those few imitations, that have all the ease and spirit of an original', and that his 'Drury-Lane Prologue' (1747) was 'far from bad' (*Corresp.*, i. 295). Norton Nicholls, a close friend in the 1760s, noted, however, that G 'disliked Doctor Johnson, & declined his acquaintance; he disapproved his style, & thought it turgid, & vicious' (*Corresp.*, iii. 1290). G did at least once set eyes on SJ (probably in Dec. 1769), pointing him out to his young Swiss friend Bonstetten in a London street as 'the great bear!—There goes *Ursa Major*!' (Sir Egerton Brydges, *Autobiography* (1834), ii. 111). SJ in turn believed that G's admired *Odes* (1757) had had a malign influence on English poetry, and despised his attempted retreat from the real world in a Cambridge college. (The best that can be said is that each spoke respectfully of the other's benevolence to the poor: see 25 and n. below.)

SJ's conversation makes clear that his attack on G in 1781 merely elaborated long-held convictions about the man and his poetry (see notes to 16, 40–7, 43, 48, 51 below). In contrast, Boswell had always been an passionate admirer of both G and Mason. A few months before meeting SJ himself, Boswell told Goldsmith in Dec. 1762: 'I admire Gray prodigiously. I have read his odes till I was almost mad' (*London Journal*, ed. F. A. Pottle (1950), 106). He later admitted that SJ's opinion of G's poetry 'was widely different from mine, and I believe from that of most men of taste, by whom it is with justice highly admired', but that it was 'what in private and in publick he uniformly expressed, regardless of what others might think' (*Life*, i. 404).

Other sources confirm this claim. Hester Thrale noted that on 18 July 1773 SJ said of 'Mason Gray &c.': 'they seem to have attained that which themselves consider as the Summit of Excellence, and Man can do no more: yet such unmeaning & verbose Language if in the Morning it appears to be in bloom, must fade before Sunset like Cloe's Wreath' (*Thraliana*, i. 172). From 1775 SJ began almost obsessively insisting on the 'dullness' of G and his biographer, claiming on 28 Mar. that G was 'a dull fellow':

'dull in company, dull in his closet, dull every where. He was dull in a new way, and that made many people think him GREAT. He was a mechanical poet' (*Life*, ii. 327).

Few of SJ's friends shared his views on G. Charles Burney claimed in Oct. 1781 to have had 'battles' with SJ at Streatham about his forthcoming 'Gray', and to have joined Mrs Thrale in trying to soften his 'mischievous' severity ('he is only teaching the tasteless & unfeeling to be more dainty & difficult to please'), 'but his opinion was rockey' (*Letters*, ed. A. Ribeiro, SJ, i (1994), 325–6). Reynolds's displeasure when he read SJ's attack on G in Oct. 1780 has been noted above (and cf. **27** n. below). Boswell told SJ on 25 Mar. 1781, a few weeks before the new *Prefaces* appeared, that 'he might have been kinder to Gray. He very justly said that he could not be kind. He was entrusted with so much truth. He was to tell what he thought; and if people differed from him, they were to tell him so' (Boswell, *Laird of Auchinleck*, 295). For the hostile private reaction of R. P. Jodrell, another friend of SJ, see also 'Pope' **383** n. above.

Dissatisfaction with SJ's treatment of G may explain the behaviour of another former friend. *Gent. Mag.* (Feb. 1783), i. 100–1, printed the important letter to Thomas Warton of 15 Apr. 1770, in which G described his own earlier plans for a 'History of English Poetry' (*Corresp.*, iii. 1122–5; Warton, *Corresp.*, 280–3). The letter, 'Communicated by a gentleman of Oxford', can only have been sent by Warton himself or with his permission. Its publication in the month in which the revised *Lives* (1783) appeared can hardly have been coincidental, and it must be assumed that Warton had chosen not to inform SJ of its existence.

SJ added a quotation from the *Elegy*, ll. 125–8, under 'Bosom' ('6. The breast, as the seat of tenderness') to the *Dict.* (4th edn., 1773).

Reception. Perhaps the most controversial of SJ's biographies, 'Gray' was circulating among his friends several months before its official publication. By 27 Jan. 1781 Horace Walpole had heard that it was 'a most wretched, dull, tasteless, *verbal* criticism, yet timid too', and began pursuing a copy of the pre-publication text. By 9 Feb. he was inciting Mason to revenge, having heard from Gibbon that, when asked whether he feared Mason's resentment at his treatment of G, SJ had replied, 'No, no Sir. Mr Mason does not like rough handling' (*Corresp.*, xxix. 120, 106). By 9 Mar. Walpole had obtained a transcript (originating in Oxford) of SJ's critical discussion of G's poetry, which Mason described on 29 Mar. 1781 as 'the meanest business that ever disgraced literature'. (For Walpole's letters to Mason, see *Corresp.*, xxix. 97, 100, 104, 106, 110, 113, 117, 120, xxxv. 272.) Although Mason promised to reply, it was only after SJ's death that he attacked 'Gray' as 'those acid eructations of vituperative criticism, which are generated by unconcocted taste and intellectual indigestion', in William Whitehead's *Works*, iii (1788), 129.

For the early reception of 'Gray', see W. Powell Jones, 'J and G', *MP* 56 (1958–9), 243–53, and R. Lonsdale, 'G and J', in J. Downey and B. Jones (eds.), *Fearful Joy* (Montreal, 1974), 66–84: some of this plentiful material is quoted in the notes below. In spite of his 'veneration for our late Prefatory Biographer', Vicesimus Knox deplored SJ's 'uncandid, not to say injudicious, criticism' of G, his 'wanton malignity' towards the odes, and the 'envy and jealousy' behind such 'singular harshness' (*Essays Moral and Literary* (new edn., 1782), ii. 188, a notable revision of Knox's earlier reservations about the 'gaudy style' promoted by G and Mason). A contributor to *Gent. Mag.* (Nov. 1781), 516, complained that SJ's 'cruel assault' on G 'has given infinite disgust to many who, like myself, feel themselves wounded through the sides of their favourites', and other periodicals printed pained reactions to SJ's unaccountable attack on 'the first and greatest of modern lyric writers ... uniting the perfections of every lyric poet, both of present and former times' (John Pinkerton, *Letters of Literature* (1785), 131).

More extended responses included W. W. FitzThomas's *A Cursory Examination of Dr. J's Strictures on the Lyric Performances of G* (1781) (described by *Monthly Review*, 66.238, in Mar. 1782 as certain to please admirers of 'our modern Pindar'); William Tindal's *Remarks on Dr. J's Life, and Critical Observations on the Works of Mr. G* (1782); sections in J. T. Callender's *Deformities of Dr. SJ* (1782), and Robert Potter's *Inquiry* (1783); and John Young's *Criticism on the Elegy in a Country Church-yard. Being a Continuation of Dr. J's Criticism on the Poems of G* (1783). For SJ's own comments on Young's *Criticism* in a letter of 5 July 1783, see *Letters*, iv. 168–9, and, for Boswell's opinion that it is 'the most perfect imitation' of SJ, see *Life*, iv. 392 and n.

Many notes in Gilbert Wakefield's edition of G's *Poems* (1786) replied to SJ's critique, which threatened to 'operate with malignant influence upon the public taste, and become ultimately injurious to the cause of polite literature' (see pp. iii, 17–19, 27–8, 51–4, 64, 93–4, 120–1). Replies to SJ continued to the end of the century, as in Edward Gardner's *Miscellanies, in Prose and Verse* (2 vols., Bristol, 1798), i. 29–45. In James Gillray's print *Apollo and the Muses, inflicting Penance on Dr. Pomposo, round Parnassus* (July 1783), SJ wears a dunce's hat bearing the names of Milton, Otway, Waller, Shenstone, Lyttelton, and G, and carries a placard which relates his crimes: 'For defaming that Genius I could never emulate, by criticism without judgment;—and endeavouring to cast the beauties of British Poetry into the hideous state of oblivion—.' SJ himself says penitently: 'I acknowledge my transgressions, and my sins are ever before me.' (Cf. *J. Misc.*, ii. 419–20.) G also featured in an epigram about SJ quoted in Robert Potter's *Inquiry* (1783), 12 n.:

> Yon Ass in vain the flow'ry lawns invite;
> To mumble thistles his supreme delight.
> Such is the Critic, who with wayward pride
> To Blackmore gives the praise to Pope denied;
> Wakes Yalden's embers, joys in Pomfret's lay,
> But sickens at the heav'n-strung lyre of Gray.

Explanations of SJ's motives ranged from the political (the Tory SJ v. the Whigs G and Mason) to the merely personal. Boswell referred in 1791 to 'the clamour which has been raised, as if Johnson had been culpably injurious to the merit of that bard, and had been actuated by envy' (*Life*, i. 404). Others explained the attack in terms of traditional rivalry between Oxford and Cambridge: G's 'excellence as a poet will be confessed by all who are entitled to judge of it, except now and then by a jealous critic educated at Oxford, and assiduous at depreciating the merit of every author who flourished at the rival university' (Reed, *Biographia Dramatica* (1782), i. 197). Hawkins, *Life*, (1787), 537, reported that SJ's 'supposed injury ... to the memory of Gray, is resented by the whole university of Cambridge'.

Although SJ no doubt also felt some professional contempt for the consciously gentlemanly authors of the Walpole–Gray–Mason circle (see **22** n. below), Joseph Warton came close to the heart of the matter when suggesting to Boswell in 1791 that SJ's 'strange aversion' to G can be explained by the limitation of his taste to 'that sort of poetry, that deals chiefly, in nervous, pointed, sentimental, didactic Lines' (*Making of the Life*, 311–12). Sir James Mackintosh summarized several of these explanations in 1811: 'His insensibility to the higher poetry, his dislike of a Whig university, and his scorn of a fantastic character, combined to produce that monstrous example of critical injustice which he entitles the *Life of Gray*' (J. T. Boulton (ed.), *J: The Critical Heritage* (1971), 354).

As earlier in 'Milton', SJ's hostility was directed as much at the poet's uncritical admirers as at G himself (see **14, 32** and nn. below). The lesson he was trying to teach is clear from the fact that he follows his scathing attack on G's *Odes* (1757) and the false taste they had fostered with a final paragraph of eloquent and generous praise of the earlier *Elegy in a Country Churchyard* (**51**), which he must have originally assumed would also conclude his entire survey of English poetry. G was the last poet in both *Eng. Poets* (1779) and *Prefaces* (1781). It was only in the rearrangement by date of death in *Lives* (1781) that Lyttelton replaced him at the end of the sequence.

Publication. In *Prefaces*, vol. x (15 May 1781). Pp. 17–32 (of 56) of the proofs are in the Forster Collection.

Modern Sources:
(i) Thomas Gray
Complete Poems, ed. H. W. Starr and J. R. Hendrickson (Oxford, 1966)
Correspondence, ed. P. Toynbee and L. Whibley (3 vols., Oxford, 1935; revised by H. W. Starr, 1971)
Poems of G, Collins and Goldsmith, ed. R. Lonsdale (1969), cited below as '*Poems* (1969)'
(ii)
B. Barr and J. Ingamells, *A Candidate for Praise: William Mason 1725–97* (York, 1973)
M. Golden, *TG* (New York, 1964)
D. Griffin, 'TG: "some great and singular service to his country" ', in *Patriotism and Poetry in Eighteenth-Century Britain* (Cambridge, 2002), 149–79
W. Hutchings and W. Ruddick (eds.), *TG: Contemporary Essays* (Liverpool, 1993)
L. Jestin, *The Answer to the Lyre: Richard Bentley's Illustrations for TG's Poems* (Philadelphia, 1990)
W. P. Jones, 'The Contemporary Readers of G's *Odes*', *MP* 28 (1930–1), 61–82
W. P. Jones, *TG, Scholar* (Cambridge, Mass., 1937)
W. P. Jones, 'J and G: A Study in Literary Antagonism', *MP* 56 (1958–9), 243–53
S. Kaul, *TG and Literary Authority: Ideology and Poetics in Eighteenth-Century Poetry* (Delhi, 1992)
R. W. Ketton-Cremer, *TG* (Cambridge, 1955)
R. Lonsdale, 'The Poetry of TG: Versions of the Self', *Proc. of the British Academy*, 59 (1973), 105–23
R. Lonsdale, 'G and J: The Biographical Problem', in J. Downey and B. Jones (eds.), *Fearful Joy: Papers from the Bicentenary Conference at Carleton University* (Montreal, 1974), 66–84
R. Mack, *TG: A Life* (New Haven, 2000)
A. T. McKenzie, *TG: A Reference Guide* (Boston, 1982)
R. Martin, *Essai sur TG* (Paris, 1934)
C. S. Northup, *A Bibliography of TG* (New Haven, 1917)
M. M. Smith (ed.), *Index of English Literary Manuscripts*, iii (ii) (1989), 71–116
H. W. Starr, *A Bibliography of TG 1917–51* (Philadelphia, 1953)
H. Weinfield, *The Poet Without a Name: G's Elegy and the Problem of History* (Carbondale, Ill., 1991)
L. Zionkowski, 'G, the Marketplace, and the Masculine Poet', in *Men's Work: Gender, Class, and the Professionalization of Poetry, 1660–1784* (New York, 2001), 129–70

1. The fifth son of Philip and Dorothy Gray, G was in fact born on 26 Dec. 1716 (Mason (1775 edn.), 3), in a house in Cornhill, London (see **13** n. below). Milton's father (see 'Milton' **4** above) had also been a scrivener, defined by SJ as '1. One who draws contracts. 2. One whose business is to place money at interest.' At his death in 1741 newspaper reports described Philip Gray as 'an Exchange Broker of Reputation and Fortune' (Mack, *TG*, 72). G's mother and aunt had a milliner's business. For her legal action in 1735 accusing her husband of brutality and failure to support his children, see *Corresp.*, iii. 1195–7, and Mack, *TG*, 79–81.

   G entered Eton, where his uncles Robert and William Antrobus were both Assistants, in 1725. Mason does not mention Dr William George (1697–1756), later Provost of King's College, Cambridge, and Dean of Lincoln. SJ no doubt added his name in 1783 (see Textual Notes) because of a comment in 1782 by Lord Hailes, himself an Etonian: 'Antrobus was only an usher. *r*. Dr. Wm George': see Carnie (1956), 488. G entered Peterhouse, Cambridge, on 4 July 1734.

   In 1783 SJ emended 'Eaton' to 'Eton' here and in **3**, **6**, **30** below, and in 'Lyttelton' **1**, **2** below. 'Eton' had already appeared in 'West' **2** above in *Lives* (1781).

2. SJ may imply that 'manhood, liberty, and happiness' would always elude G, who told Richard West in Dec. 1736 that he expected soon to be free of 'College impertinences' (Mason (1775 edn.), 12–14; *Corresp.*, i. 56–7). He had been admitted to the Inner Temple on 22 Nov. 1735 and was still envisaging a legal career when he left Cambridge in Sept. 1738. For his Latin ode on the subject, see *Poems* (1969), 306–8.

3. Horace Walpole (1717–97), son of Sir Robert Walpole, had been one of the 'Quadruple Alliance' of close friends at Eton, with G, Richard West, and Thomas Ashton. He entered King's College, Cambridge, on 11 Mar. 1735.

   Walpole and G set off for France and Italy on 29 Mar. 1739. For G's travel-letters, see Mason (1775 edn.), 40–118. Mason consulted Walpole before briefly referring to the quarrel at Reggio in about May 1741, for which Walpole was now prepared to take 'the chief blame' (40–1). Walpole admitted to Mason, 2 Mar. 1773, that he had been 'too much intoxicated by indulgence, vanity, and the insolence of my situation, as a prime minister's son . . . I treated him insolently: he loved me, and I did not think he did . . . his temper was not conciliating' (*Corresp.*, xviii. 68–9). G himself told Norton Nicholls that 'Walpole was son of the first minister, & you may easily conceive that on this account he might assume an air of superiority . . . or do or say something which perhaps I did not bear as well as I ought'. Nicholls also referred to G's 'independent, & lofty spirit' (*Corresp.*, iii. 1299).

   association with superiors: SJ wrote in *Rambler* 64 (1750) that 'Friendship is seldom lasting but between equals . . . Benefits which cannot be repaid, and obligations which cannot be discharged, are not commonly found to increase affection' (*YW*, iii. 344). SJ may echo Hobbes: 'benefits oblige; and obligation is thraldome' (*Leviathan*, ed. A. R. Waller (Cambridge, 1904), 64). Cf. also 'Thomson' **39** above ('friendship is not always the sequel of obligation'). Reynolds said of SJ that 'if any man drew him into a state of obligation without his own consent, that man was the first he would affront, by way of clearing off the account' (*Life*, iii. 345 n.).

   For SJ's usual scepticism about authors who aspired to 'independence', see 'Milton' **169** and n. above.

4. G returned to England via Milan, Lyons, and Paris in July–Sept. 1741. His father died on 6 Nov. 1741, having expended much of his wealth on a country house at Wanstead. For G's financial circumstances, see Mason (1775 edn.), 199, and Mack *TG*, 281.

G marked his return to Cambridge on 15 Oct. 1742 by writing his ironic and unfinished 'Hymn to Ignorance' (*Poems* (1969), 74–7). He took his LL B in Oct. 1743. Hill (1905) noted that G later told Wharton, 15 Mar. 1768, that 'I am so totally uninform'd, indeed so helpless, in matters of law, that there is no one perhaps in the kingdom you could apply to for advice with less effect', but not that G went on to give him detailed legal counsel (*Corresp.*, iii. 1027–30).

For his 'residence at London' in 1759–61, see 16 and n. below. SJ follows Mason (1775 edn.), 170–1: G in fact often left Cambridge for shorter periods, especially in the summer (see 18, 20 below).

5. Richard West, G's close friend at Eton, died on 1 June 1742 aged 25. His father Richard West (*c.*1691–1726) became Lord Chancellor of Ireland in 1725 and published *Hecuba* (1726), a tragedy. His mother was Bishop Gilbert Burnet's daughter. Many of his letters to G are in Mason (1775 edn.). Norton Nicholls later noted: 'Whenever I mentioned Mr West he looked serious, & seemed to feel the affliction of a recent loss' (*Corresp.*, iii. 1300).

West sent G his 'Ode to May' on 5 May 1742, a month before his death (Mason (1775 edn.), 147–8). He had criticized the opening scene of 'Agrippina, A Tragedy' on 4 Apr. 1742. G's reply on 8 Apr. included his notorious assertion that 'the language of the age is never the language of poetry', but he soon abandoned the tragedy (Mason (1775 edn.), 136–7, 139–41; *Corresp.*, i. 192–3).

no loss to the English stage: Reed, *Biographia Dramatica* (1782), ii. 5, stated that 'The loss of the reader . . . may have been considerable'. Thomas Twining regretted 'that a work of genius, should have been smothered in its birth, by a little cold and trifling criticism!', noting that SJ's opinion of 'Agrippina' came from one who had dismissed Gray's 'The Bard' and Milton's early poetry, and had 'admitted, with seeming complacence, into the catalogue of English POETS, such names as *Blackmore, Yalden,* and *Pomfret*' (*Aristotle's Treatise on Poetry, Translated* (1789), 385–6).

6. G wrote these poems between June and Aug. 1742. 'Ode on the Spring' (28 below) appeared in Dodsley's *Collection* (1748), the *Eton Ode*, his first published poem in English, in May 1747 (30 below), and 'Ode to Adversity' (31 below) in *Six Poems* (1753) (*Poems* (1969), 47–74).

G sent West 'Ode on the Spring' (see 28 below) in early June 1742, but his letter was returned unopened and he learned of West's death from a newspaper. SJ does not connect G's sudden burst of creativity with West's death, also commemorated in a 'Sonnet' and in lines added to 'De Principiis Cogitandi', which he began writing in 1740. He had told West, 12 Apr. 1741: 'A metaphysical poem is a contradiction in terms. It is true, but I will go on. It is Latin too to increase the absurdity.' Mason published the unfinished poem and the 'Sonnet' in 1775 (*Corresp.*, i. 183; *Poems* (1969), 321–2, 328).

7. G wrote most of his poetry before 1742 in Latin (Mason (1775 edn.), 157–8; *Poems* (1969), 285–332), using English only for humorous verse and translations.

embarrassment: 'Perplexity; entanglement' (*Dict.*). For earlier writers of Latin verse, see 'Cowley' 32–4, 'Milton' 10, and 'Addison' 9–11 above.

8. Walpole described G, 3 Sept. 1748, as 'the worst company in the world—from a melancholy turn, from living reclusely, and from a little too much dignity, he never converses easily . . . his writings are admirable; he himself is not agreeable' (*Corresp.*, ix. 76). G's reserve is partly attributable to the fact that he had only recently renewed his friendship with Walpole.

Mason noted that 'the greatest part of Mr. Gray's life was spent in that kind of learned leisure, which has only self-improvement and self-gratification for its object' (Mason (1775 edn.), 335). SJ usually emphasized the selfish aspect of such academic seclusion. In *Rambler* 24 (1750) he described the 'great fault of men of learning' as their inability 'to perform those offices by which the concatenation of society is preserved, and mutual tenderness excited and maintained' (*YW*, iii. 132). *Adventurer* 67 (1753), on the 'universal hurry' of London, may echo G's 'Ode on the Spring', ll. 41–50, in condemning the man who is willing to 'please himself with the happiness of a drone, while the active swarms are buzzing about him' (*YW*, ii. 386). See also *Adventurers* 85 (1753) and 126 (1754), the second seeming to echo G's *Elegy*, ll. 55–61: 'Piety practised in solitude, like the flower that blooms in the desert, may give its fragrance to the winds of heaven . . . but it bestows no assistance upon earthly beings' (*YW*, ii. 475). *Idler* 19 (1758) also discusses the dangers of a reclusive scholarly life. In 1755 SJ contrasted the circumstances in which he had compiled his *Dictionary* with 'the soft obscurities of retirement' and 'the shelter of academic bowers' (*OASJ*, 328).

SJ believed that 'It is our first duty to serve society' (*Life*, ii. 10). In 'Sermon 3' he wrote that 'it cannot be allowed, that . . . he fills his place in the creation laudably, who does no ill, *only* because he does *nothing*'; and in 'Sermon 8' condemned 'those, who have secluded themselves from the world, in pursuit of petty enquiries, and trivial studies', such as 'the idle amusements' of 'the pedant' in 'his college' (*YW*, xiv. 32–3, 95). SJ wrote on 24 July 1783: 'Retreat from the world is flight rather than conquest, and in those who have any power of benefiting others, may be consider[ed] as a kind of *moral suicide*' (*Letters*, iv. 177–8).

Mrs Thrale later recalled SJ's remarks on the scholar Jeremiah Markland: 'remember that he would run from the world, and that it is not the world's business to run after him. I hate a fellow whom pride, or cowardice, or laziness drives into a corner, and who does nothing when he is there but sit and *growl*; let him come out as I do, and *bark*' (*J. Misc.*, i. 315, and cf. i. 219–20). For anti-social solitude, see also 'Cowley' **24, 44** and 'Pope' **283** and n. above, and for SJ's opinion of the inhabitants of colleges, 'Milton' **182** and n. above.

William Mason (1725–97) took his BA at St John's College, Cambridge, in 1746, and became a Fellow of Pembroke College in Mar. 1749. After winning a considerable reputation as a poet in the 1750s, he became Precentor of York in 1762. In adopting the stance of a neutral 'stranger' and cold 'critick', SJ is already hinting that he found Mason's *Memoirs of G* (Apr. 1775) effusive and uncritical.

9. G's 'Ode on the Death of a Favourite Cat' appeared in Dodsley's *Collection of Poems*, ii (Jan. 1748), 267–9. Walpole wrote of G, 25 Apr. 1775: 'Humour was his natural and original turn—and though from childhood he was grave and reserved, his genius led him to see things ludicrously and satirically; and though his health and dissatisfaction gave him low spirits, his melancholy turn was much more affected than his pleasantry in writing' (*Corresp.*, i. 367; and cf. xxviii. 217).

'The Alliance of Education and Government. A Fragment', written in 1748/9, was published by Mason (1775 edn.), 193–200. Richard Payne Knight, *The Progress of Civil Society. A Didactic Poem* (1796), 111 n., claimed to have imitated and continued G's 'splendid' fragment. For Walpole's indignation at Knight's 'audacity in polluting Gray's *champagne* and Heliconian element with his hog-wash', and Mason's sonnet on the subject, see his *Corresp.*, xxix. 334–6, 338–9.

10. G sent Walpole the recently completed *Elegy Written in a Country Churchyard*, probably begun in 1746, on 12 June 1750. (The title of the Eton MS is 'Stanza's Wrote in a Country Church-Yard'.) The poem circulated in MS (see 11 n. below), and G eventually asked Walpole to arrange its hurried publication by Dodsley on 15 Feb. 1751, ahead of its unauthorized appearance in Feb. 1751 in the *Magazine of Magazines*, which revealed G's authorship: see *Poems* (1969), 103–12. The *Elegy* was reprinted in other periodicals, and Dodsley had published eight quarto editions by 1753.

11. 'A Long Story' reflects G's uneasiness while the *Elegy* was circulating in MS in 1750. It wryly depicts the poet coping with an invitation from Anne Temple, Viscountess Cobham, the widow of Pope's friend ('Pope' 202 and n. above), who lived in the Manor House at Stoke Poges, where G often visited relatives (*Poems* (1969), 142–52). G tried to suppress it after its appearance in *Six Poems* (1753), and in 1775 Mason included it in the *Memoirs* rather the main body of G's poetry, adding that it had 'proved the least popular of all his productions' (211–20, 227).

In *Prefaces* (1781) SJ complained at this point that 'A Long Story' had been omitted from *Eng. Poets* (1779), and it was accordingly appended, together with G's *Installation Ode*, after 51 below. Although it was dropped thereafter, SJ still pointed out in *Lives* (1781) that it had been 'inserted at the end of my preface to the late Collection': see Textual Notes. For notable satirical poems by G omitted by Mason in 1775, see *Poems* (1969), 243–52, 259–64.

12. In spite of SJ's obvious scepticism, *Designs by Mr. R. Bentley for Six Poems by Mr. T. Gray* (1753) is a notable example of 18th-century English book-production and book-illustration: see Jestin, *Answer*.

Richard Bentley (1708–81), son of the classical scholar, was helping to plan 'Gothic' alterations to Strawberry Hill when Walpole commissioned his illustrations to G's poetry in 1751. By 28 Aug. 1752 Walpole could report that the 'Poemata Grayo-Bentleiana' were 'in great forwardness' (*Corresp.*, ix. 143). G asked Dodsley, 12 Feb. 1753, to make clear that 'the Verses are only subordinate, & explanatory to the Drawings, & suffer'd by me to come out thus only for that reason' (*Corresp.*, i. 371). For his 'Stanzas to Mr. Bentley' (published 1775), see *Poems* (1969), 152–5. William Tindal, *Remarks* (1782), 18, believed that SJ implies here that G hoped to profit from the book, and that he 'ought to have added, that the writer had no advantage in the sale of them'.

Dorothy Gray, G's mother, died on 11 Mar. 1753.

13. Mason only briefly mentioned G's removal from Peterhouse to Pembroke College on 5 Mar. 1756 (242 n.). SJ added the reference to 'pranks yet more offensive and contemptuous' in 1783 (see Textual Notes). Although the story about G's undignified descent from his room in Peterhouse by rope after a hoax fire-alarm had appeared in Archibald Campbell's *The Sale of Authors* (1767), Thomas Percy, who heard the story from Cambridge friends, may have been SJ's informant. For

other contemporary accounts, see Nichols, *Lit. Ill.*, vi. 805, and *Corresp.*, ii. 458, iii. 1216–20. G's alarm is understandable: the house in which he was born, still owned by his mother, had been destroyed in a notable fire in Cornhill, London, in Mar. 1748 (see Mack, *TG*, 364–7).

14. G's two *Odes* were printed by Walpole at Strawberry Hill and published by Dodsley on 8 Aug. 1757. Some 1,200 or 1,300 copies were sold within a month (*Corresp.*, ii. 524). Dodsley also used them to conclude his *Collection of Poems*, vi (1758), 321–32, with an engraving of the Bard's final suicidal leap.

Walpole wrote of G's 'amazing odes' that 'they are Greek, they are Pindaric, they are sublime—consequently I fear a little obscure' (4 Aug. 1757). Three weeks later he told Lyttelton that he did not believe G's readers had 'ever admired him except in his *Churchyard* . . . Yet not to admire [the *Odes*] is total want of taste. I have an aversion to tame poetry' (*Corresp.*, xxi. 120, xl. 103). G had himself predicted in Aug. 1756 that the *Odes* would appear 'a wild obscure unedifying jumble' to most readers, and later referred ruefully to the incomprehension which duly greeted them ('the great objection is obscurity'): see *Corresp.*, ii. 478, 518, 519, 522–4, 532, 538, and *Poems* (1969), 157–8, 180. Goldsmith complained in Dec. 1762 that G's *Odes* (1757) were 'terribly obscure. We must be historians and learned men before we can understand them' (Boswell, *London Journal*, ed. F. A. Pottle (1950), 106). For G's 'obscurity' see also **16, 32** and nn. below.

On 7 Oct. 1757 G mentioned both Warburton's praise and Garrick's lines 'To Mr. Gray' in the *London Chronicle* of 1 Oct., later reprinted by Walpole at Strawberry Hill (Mason (1775 edn.), 250 n.; *Corresp.*, ii. 532, 535–6 n.). For the 'fashion' of admiring Shakespeare and Milton, see *YW*, vii. 59–61, and headnote to 'Milton' above. One of G's 'hardy champions' was Arthur Murphy in the *Literary Mag.* 2 (Oct.–Nov. 1757), 422–6, 466–8, who found in the *Odes* 'Sublimity of conception, a nobleness in his diction, daring figures, quick transition, harmony of numbers, and an enthusiasm that hurries the reader along with him', and none of 'that unintelligible obscure which has been in every body's mouth'. For other admirers, see Jones, 'Contemporary Readers', 61–82, and Lonsdale, 'G and J', 66–84.

SJ had told Thomas Warton, 25 Mar. 1755, that his own *Dict.* 'must stand the censures of the *great vulgar and the small*, of those that understand it and that understand it not, but in all this I suffer not alone, every writer has the same difficulties, and perhaps every writer talks of them more than he thinks' (*Letters*, i. 101). Reviewing William Tytler's *Historical Enquiry into Mary, Queen of Scots* in 1760, he wrote: 'When an opinion has once become popular, very few are willing to oppose it. Idleness is more willing to credit than enquire; cowardice is afraid of controversy, and vanity of answer' (*OASJ*, 551).

15. G refused the Laureateship, offered to him through Mason, on the death of Colley Cibber in 1757 (see 'Savage' **172** and n. above). Writing to Mason, 19 Dec. 1757, he compared the appointment to being '*Rat-Catcher* to his Majesty' and claimed that he 'would rather be Serjeant-Trumpeter, or Pin-Maker to the Palace' (*Corresp.*, ii. 543–5; for a modified text, see Mason (1775 edn.), 258–9). G's letter provided the epigraph and some of the content of Tony Harrison's 'Laureate's Block for Queen Elizabeth', on his own unwillingness to be considered for the post after the death of Ted Hughes (*The Guardian*, 9 Feb. 1999).

William Whitehead (1715–85) became Laureate. Although G politely approved of his official odes (*Corresp.*, ii. 602, 604), SJ thought them '*Grand* nonsense' (*Life*, i. 402).

16. G lived in Southampton Row, London, July 1759–Nov. 1761, while reading at the new British Museum, 'with all its manuscripts and rarities by the cart-load' (Mason (1775 edn.), 274, and *Corresp.*, ii. 629–30).

Two Odes (1760) by George Colman (1732–94) and Robert Lloyd (1733–64) in fact parodied Mason's odes as well as G's, as *Gent. Mag.* (1781), 276, noted. G told Mason in June 1760 that the parody 'makes very tolerable fun with me', and later that a bookseller had recommended the *Two Odes* to him 'as a very pretty thing' (Mason (1775 edn.), 283–4; *Corresp.*, ii. 673–5, 681).

A letter in *Lloyd's Evening Post* (2–4 June 1760) explained that the target of the first parody was 'a wilful obscurity, a species of false sublime, and a pedantic imitation of Pindar. This Comic Ode therefore abounds with sudden transitions, and forced reflections.' On 11 Aug. 1760 Shenstone recommended to Percy, 'if you love *mischief*, the two Odes yt ridicule Grays & Masons manner' (*Letters*, 560). James Grainger also told Percy he had read the parodies 'with uncommon satisfaction' and hoped that they would 'produce a proper change in the future compositions of Mason and Gray' (Nichols, *Lit. Ill.*, vii. 275).

SJ praised the parodies on 2 Apr. 1775 ('they are both good. They exposed a very bad kind of writing'), leading Boswell to ponder once again SJ's 'low estimation of the writings of Gray and Mason' (*Life*, ii. 334–5). Steevens heard SJ say that 'Colman never produced a luckier thing than his first Ode in ridicule of Gray; a considerable part of it may be numbered among those felicities which no man has twice attained' (*J. Misc.*, ii. 320–1; see also Hawkins, *J's Works* (1787), xi. 214). Colman himself later described the *Two Odes* as 'a piece of boys' play with my schoolfellow Lloyd' (*Prose on Several Occasions* (1787), i, p. xi), and Warton, *Works of Pope* (1797), i. 236 n., claimed that they had eventually regretted publishing them. William Tindal, *Remarks* (1782), 22, pointed out that SJ was himself ridiculed by Charles Churchill and Archibald Campbell in the 1760s: 'I know not what feeling the Lexiphanes or the Ghost excited in the breast of that great critic.' For *Lexiphanes* (1767), see 'Akenside' 19 n. above.

Adam Smith, for whom G combined Milton's 'sublimity' with Pope's 'elegance and harmony', and could have been 'the first poet in the English language' if he had 'written a little more', believed that G was 'so much hurt, by a foolish and impertinent parody of two of his finest odes, that he never afterwards attempted any considerable work' (*The Theory of Moral Sentiments* (6th edn., 1790); ed. D. D. Raphael and A. L. Macfie (Oxford, 1976), 123–4 and n.). Richard Payne Knight, *The Progress of Civil Society* (1796), 65 n., also claimed that the 'burlesque parodies...added to some coarse sarcasms of Dr. Johnson, prevented him from writing any more'. It is unclear which of SJ's 'sarcasms' would have reached G in the 1760s.

17. G told Mason, 4 Dec. 1762, that he had been 'cockered and spirited up by some friends' into applying to John Stuart, Earl of Bute (1713–92), the Prime Minister, for the Chair of Modern History at Cambridge (see Mason (1775 edn.), 293; *Corresp.*, ii. 787–8; and, for Bute, 'Mallet' 20 n. above). The Chair went instead to Lawrence Brockett (1724–68), Fellow of Trinity College, Cambridge. Brockett

was the tutor of Bute's son-in-law, Sir James Lowther, later the powerful Earl of Lonsdale and an alarming patron of Boswell, who recorded in 1786 that Lonsdale 'Told us that Gray lived over him at Cambridge, and abused him for effeminate priggery' (*The English Experiment* (1986), 107).

Here, and in **19** below, SJ originally wrote 'Modern Languages' instead of 'Modern History': see Textual Notes. Lord Hailes noted the error in 1782: see Carnie (1956), 488–9.

18. G's letters about his journey to Scotland in 1765 are in Mason (1775 edn.), 308–20, and *Corresp.*, ii. 887–95. For G as a travel-writer, see also **20** below, for 'comprehension', see 'Cowley' **144** and n. above, and for 'curiosity', see also **24** below and 'Pope' **291** and n. above.

For James Beattie (1733–1803), Professor of Moral Philosophy at Aberdeen University, see e.g. *Life*, ii. 148. G wrote to Beattie, 2 Oct. 1765, to decline the doctorate (Mason (1775 edn.), 318–19; *Corresp.*, ii. 895). Beattie later supervised the Foulis edition of G's *Poems* (Glasgow, 1768). While regretting SJ's severity 'on my poor friend, Gray', Beattie was gratified on 16 May 1781 by his 'very great compliment' here: see Sir William Forbes, *Life and Writings of James Beattie* (Edinburgh, 1806), ii. 91.

19. G accepted the Duke of Grafton's offer of the Chair of Modern History, worth £400 p.a, on 28 July 1768 (Mason (1775 edn.), 331–4), after the death of Lawrence Brockett ('of a fall from his horse, drunk, I believe', *Corresp.*, iii. 1039). Partly because of ill-health, G planned but never delivered any lectures, more than once admitting to a troubled conscience over this failure (see Mason (1775 edn.), 395–8, and *Corresp.*, iii. 1114, 1188, 1253–9). (Edward Burnaby Greene, in *Cam, An Elegy* (1764), 10–12, had earlier accused G of taking refuge in poetry from the melancholy condition of Cambridge.)

G did, however, reluctantly compose an elaborate *Ode* on the installation of his benefactor, Augustus Henry Fitzroy, Duke of Grafton (1735–1811), the Prime Minister, as Chancellor of the University in July 1769, with a musical setting by Professor John Randall. SJ ignores the *Ode*, which had not been included in *Eng. Poets* (1779), although it was appended to **51** below in *Prefaces* (1781) (see Textual Notes).

G was predictably abused by Grafton's political opponents (see *Poems* (1969), 264–7). One such attack in fact linked G with SJ himself as recent flatterers of the government: in Wilkes's brave new world, 'No *pension'd* Johnson's prostituted pen | Shall varnish crimes, and praise the worst of men— | No softly-warbling, sweetly-pensive Gray, | Attempting ode, shall blunder in his way, | Mistake his talent, see his laurels fade | In madrigals of praise to villains paid' (*Verses Addressed to John Wilkes, Esq; On his Arrival at Lynn* (Lynn, 1771), 4–7).

20. G travelled in the Lake District in late Sept. and Oct. 1769, after an earlier visit in 1766. For the journal on which he drew in his letters from the Lakes, see Mason (1775 edn.), 350–79, *Corresp.*, iii. 1074–80, 1087–91, 1094–110, and *TG's Journal of his Visit to the Lake District in October 1769*, ed. W. Roberts (Liverpool, 2001). For G as travel-writer see also **18** above.

SJ said on 17 Apr. 1778: 'books of travel will be good in proportion to what a man has previously in his mind; his knowing what to observe; his power of contrasting one mode of life with another . . . a man must carry knowledge with him, if he would bring home knowledge' (*Life*, iii. 301–02). For earlier scepticism about 'the narrations of travellers', see *Idler* 97 (1760).

21. Although he declared, 'travel I must, or cease to exist', G had to abandon a plan of visiting Switzerland in the summer of 1771 (*Corresp.*, iii. 1189; cf. **24** n. below).

For G's final illness, see Mason (1775 edn.), 399–400, who in fact misdated his death as 31 July. For his will, see *Corresp.*, iii. 1283–6, and for an 'Ode Written upon the Death of Mr. Gray', see Frederick Howard, Earl of Carlisle, *Poems* (1773), 3–8.

22. William Johnson Temple (1739–96) knew G in Cambridge in 1763–5, when Boswell, a former fellow-student at Edinburgh, envied his friend's familiarity with the poet: see Lonsdale, 'G and J', 68–70, and *Corresp.*, iii. 928–9 and n., 1137–8, 1174, etc. He sent his account of G on 3–4 Sept. 1771 to Boswell, who arranged its publication without Temple's knowledge as 'A Sketch of the Character of the Celebrated Mr. Gray' by 'a gentleman of Cambridge' in the *London Mag.* 41 (Mar. 1772), 140. In 1775 Boswell was elated to find it 'placed as the top stone of [G's] monument' at the end of Mason's biography (*Omninous Years*, 120, 122). For Boswell's letter to Mason in May 1775 informing him of Temple's authorship, Mason's dismissive comments to Walpole on this news, and Temple's surprise at the use of his letter, see *Catalogue* L 956, C 1978, 2727, 2760, 2764, and Walpole, *Corresp.*, xxviii. 209. Although Boswell named Temple as author of the 'character' of G in a review of Mason in *London Mag.* 44 (1775), 217, SJ ascribed it to 'a nameless author' in *Prefaces* and *Lives* (1781). On 24 Aug. 1782 he asked Boswell for the author's name for insertion in *Lives* (1783): see *Letters*, iv. 70, and Textual Notes.

SJ begins by implicitly dissociating himself from G's 'warmest well-wishers', and conveying some scepticism about Temple's account of G. For other ominous professions of willingness to be pleased by, or to believe, something, see **32** below and 'Dyer' **11** above. Mason's quotation omitted Temple's opening statement that G's 'poetry was in so superior a stile, that it could be relished only by the few', whose minds are 'cultivated to a high degree'. G told Algarotti, 9 Sept. 1763, that he had 'no relish for any other fame than what is confer'd by the few real Judges, that are so thinly scatter'd over the face of the earth' (*Corresp.*, ii. 813).

For G's 'learning', see Jones, *TG*. Norton Nicholls recalled: 'When I expressed my astonishment at the extent of his reading he said, "Why should you be surprised, for I do nothing else." He said he knew from experience how much might be done by a person who did not fling away his time on middling or inferiour, authors, & read with method' (*Corresp.*, iii. 1296). R. DeMaria, *SJ and the Life of Reading* (Baltimore, 1997), 106–7, suggested that SJ envied G's ability to devote himself to methodical reading of a kind his own circumstances and temperament prevented.

SJ would notice Temple's reference to G's desire 'to be looked upon as a private independent gentleman, who read for amusement', and to Congreve's similar 'weakness', as reported by Voltaire, which SJ had earlier described as a 'despicable foppery' ('Congreve' **31** and n. above). Mason (1775 edn.), 335, also mentioned, as one of G's 'foibles', 'a certain degree of pride, which led him, of all other things, to despise the idea of being thought an author professed', i.e. a professional author who wrote for profit. For Walpole's assessments of G's personality, see **8–9** nn. above.

23. For G's interest in zoology, see Mason (1775 edn.), 341.

    For G's 'effeminacy' (mentioned by Temple in 22 above), see Mason (1775 edn.), 402–3 nn. William Cole described G in 1780 as 'of a most fastidious & recluse Distance of Carriage, rather averse to all Sociability, but of the graver Turn: nice & elegant in his Person, Dress & Behaviour, even to a Degree of Finicalness & Effeminacy' (*Corresp.*, iii. 1119–20 n.). William Hayley, *Philosophical, Historical and Moral Essay on Old Maids* (1785), i. 9, referred to G as 'a justly-admired poet, who might himself be called . . . an Old Maid in breeches'.

24. SJ's reference to his 'slight inspection' of G's letters in Mason (1775 edn.), which he has praised in 3, 20 above, seems gratuitous; cf. the extended assessment of the evidence of letters in his 'character' of Pope ('Pope' 273 ff. above). He had earlier used a letter by G in 'Shenstone' 19 above. Cowper wrote, 20 Apr. 1777, that he preferred G's letters to Swift's: 'his Humour or his Wit, or whatever it is to be called is never illnatur'd or offensive, & yet I think equally poignant with the Dean's' (*Letters*, i (Oxford, 1979), 268).

    a man likely to love much where he loved at all: SJ's comment is perceptive, given that he would be unaware of G's ardent letters in 1770 to Charles Victor von Bonstetten (1745–1832), a young Swiss visitor to Cambridge (*Corresp.*, iii. 1117–19, 1127–8, 1132). For the dangers of fastidiousness, see *Rambler* 112 (1751).

    For G's contempt for French atheism, see his letters to Walpole, 13 Dec. 1765, 7 Mar. 1771 (*Corresp.*, ii. 907, iii. 1175). SJ disapproved of the writings of Anthony Ashley Cooper, Earl of Shaftesbury (1671–1713), the author of *Characteristicks* (1711). In May 1777 he told Mrs Thrale that 'he would never give Shaftesbury Chubb or any wicked Writer's Authority for a Word [in the *Dict.*], lest it should send People to look in a Book that might injure them for ever' (*Thraliana*, i. 34). See also 'Akenside' 6 and n. above, and, for SJ's dislike of 'the cant of the Shaftesburian school', Hawkins, *Life* (1787), 253–5.

    SJ quotes G's comments from Mason (1775 edn.), 263–4, perhaps implying some similarity between Shaftesbury's once inflated reputation and that of G himself. For temporary fame based on rank and power, see 'Halifax' 15, 'Sheffield' 22, and 'Granville' 25 above.

25. Mason (1775 edn.), 335, wrote that, 'when his circumstances were at the lowest, he gave away such sums in private charity as would have done credit to an ampler purse'. Norton Nicholls noted that G in turn respected SJ's 'understanding, & still more his goodness of heart;—I have heard him say that Johnson would go out in London with his pockets full of silver & give it all away in the streets before he returned home' (*Corr.*, iii. 1290). For the benevolence of other poets, see 'Savage' 91–3 and n. above.

26. On 13 Jan. 1758 G criticized Mason's method 'of casting down your first Ideas carelessly & at large, and then clipping them here & there and forming them at leisure', which 'will leave behind it in some places a *laxity*, a diffuseness' (Mason (1775 edn.), 233–4; *Corresp.*, ii. 551–2). Nicholls also heard G complain that Mason 'never gave himself time to think but imagined that he should do best by writing hastily in the first fervour of his imagination, & therefore never waited for epithets if they did not occur readily but left spaces for them & put them in afterwards. This . . . enervated his poetry' (*Corresp.*, iii. 1293–4). For habits of composition see also 'Milton' 117–18, 123–6 and nn. above.

For 'happy moments' and 'inspiration', see 'Denham' 31 and n. above. G told Wharton, 18 June 1758: 'I by no means pretend to inspiration, but yet I affirm, that the faculty in question is by no means voluntary. it is the result (I suppose) of a certain disposition of mind, wch does not depend on oneself, & wch I have not felt this long time' (Mason (1775 edn.), 270–1; *Corresp.*, ii. 571). Hill (1905) compared G's 'Education and Government', ll. 72–3: 'Unmanly thought! what season can control, | What fancied zone can circumscribe the Soul.'

SJ usually insisted that 'a man may write at any time, if he will set himself doggedly to it' (*Life*, i. 203), sharing William Wycherley's scepticism about 'a Sect of Writers, who . . . would be thought to go to Work by *Inspiration*; as the Quakers, lay the Nonsense they preach on the *Spirit*, and make their Fustian pass for *Illumination*' (*Posthumous Works* (1728), ii. 5–6). Isaac Watts, an author SJ respected, believed, however, that 'Poesy is not always under the Command of the Will. As there have been Occasions heretofore when I have wished to write, but the Imagination has refused to attend the Wish; so there are Seasons when Verse comes almost without a Call, and the Will might resist in vain' (*Reliquiae Juveniles* (1734), 223).

foppery: '1. Folly; impertinence. 2. Affectation of show or importance; showy folly. 3. Foolery; vain or idle practice; idle affectation' (*Dict.*). SJ's reference to 'fantastic foppery' links his (and Temple's) comments on G's fastidiousness in 22–4 above to the poetry he is about to discuss.

27. SJ is well aware that his survey of G's poetry will reveal him as an 'enemy to his name'. W. W. FitzThomas, *Cursory Examination* (1781), 13, believed that SJ adopts a special method here: 'more verbal, logical, and minute, where these critical niceties ought, in reason, least of all to be practised.' When discussing *The Progress of Poesy* in particular (32–9 below), SJ seemed 'to interdict the use of all figurative decoration' in poetry (2–5), and G's technique of 'uniting the subject and the simile' proved 'an eternal *stumbling block* to his critical sagacity' (8). Reynolds later suggested that, 'in order to depreciate [G's poems], the method he seems to have taken is to take up those higher excellencies which are on the verge of defects and condemning them as such' (*Portraits*, 72).

With SJ's dissection of G's odes, cf. his account of those who 'read with the microscope of criticism, and employ their whole attention upon minute elegance, or faults scarcely visible to common observation' in *Rambler* 176 (1751) (*YW*, v. 167); his assertion that 'It is not by comparing line with line that the merit of great works is to be estimated, but by their general effects and ultimate result' ('Dryden' 312 above); and his admission that his criticism of Pope's epitaphs was 'too minute and particular to be inserted in the Life' ('Pope' 384 above).

28. For SJ's concessionary use of 'poetical' and 'poetically' for verse about which he has obvious reservations, see 31, 39 below and 'Dyer' 10–11 and n. above. For 'luxuriant' language, see 'Thomson' 50 and n. above.

adjectives, derived from substantives: Thomson has 'Countries cultur'd high' in *Liberty*, II (1735), 163, Shenstone 'cultur'd vales' in 'Elegy XXV', l. 18, and Goldsmith 'life's more cultured walks' in *The Traveller* (1764), l. 236. *Gent. Mag.* (1783), 929, noted that 'To culture' appears in the *Dict.*, although SJ comments that it 'is used by *Thomson*, but without authority'. SJ cites 'Dazied' in the *Dict.* from Shakespeare's *Cymbeline*, IV. ii. 398. Cf. 'daisy'd lawns' in Gay, *Dione*, I. iv. 4.

SJ quotes 'the honeyed spring' from 'Ode on the Spring', l. 26. 'Scrutator' (John Loveday) in *Gent. Mag.* (1781), 421, noted that SJ illustrates 'Honeyed' in the *Dict.* from both Shakespeare and Milton (who uses the epithet three times): see also *Poems* (1969), 51.

In terms of SJ's demand for an ideal blend of the 'natural' and the 'new' (see 'Cowley' 55 and n. above), G's 'thoughts have nothing new', and his 'morality is natural, but too stale'.

29. SJ refers to the 'Ode on the Death of a Favourite Cat' (1748), ll. 3, 19, 36, 42, and quotes 23–4 (see 9 above). Mason (1775 edn.), ii. 74, had described it as a 'little piece, in which comic humour is so happily blended with lyrical fancy'. G wrote it not long after his reconciliation with Walpole (cf. 3 and n. above), and there is a rueful personal element beneath its humour. Cf. SJ's definition of 'Favourite': '2. One chosen as a companion by a superiour; a mean wretch, whose whole business is by any means to please' (*Dict.*).

For 'rhyme', see 'Cowley' 187 and n. above. Although 'shew resolutely' appears in all editions, SJ may have intended 'shew how resolutely'. For 'broken' metaphors, see 'Dryden' 320 and n. above, and for SJ's capacity for stubbornly literal analysis elsewhere, see 'Addison' 129 and n. above. SJ wrote to Reynolds, 2 Oct. 1784: 'All is not gold that glitters, as we have often been told' (*Letters*, iv. 413).

30. With SJ's suggestion that the *Ode on a Distant Prospect of Eton College* (1747) offers only commonplaces, cf. his earlier statement that 'The reader of *The Seasons* wonders that he never saw before what Thomson shews him, and that he never yet has felt what Thomson impresses' ('Thomson' 46 above). Yet he later praises the *Elegy* for 'images which find a mirrour in every mind, and . . . sentiments to which every bosom returns an echo' (51 below).

For Father Thames, see *Eton Ode*, ll. 21–30. Warton, *Works of Pope* (1797), i. 134 n., described SJ's remarks here as 'disgraceful and impotent'. For 'Old Father Thames' in Dryden's *Annus Mirabilis*, l. 925, see 'Dryden' 61 above. SJ considers 'the appearance of Father Thames' in Pope's *Windsor Forest* one of the parts of the poem 'which deserve least praise', and quotes Addison's objection to loquacious poetic rivers, in 'Pope' 316 and n. above. Nekayah had in fact apostrophized the Nile in *Rasselas*, ch. XXV, and SJ later justified the personification of a river as 'the tutelary power of the flood' in Shakespeare (*YW*, xvi. 93 and n., vii. 461). For other 'puerile' works, see 45 below, and 'Cowley 6, 'Waller' 123, 'Prior' 59, 'Granville' 26, and 'Pope' 316 above.

For 'buxom health', see *Eton Ode*, l. 45. SJ was particularly exercised by 'buxom'. In his *Plan of a Dictionary* (1747), 27, he wrote that, though used familiarly to mean 'wanton', it 'means only obedient', adding, however, that Milton's use of the word in this original sense is now obsolete. (See *YW*, viii. 577, for his gloss in 1765 of 'buxom' in *Paradise Lost*, ii. 842, v. 270, as 'obsequious'.) In the *Dict.* he repeated that modern usage misunderstood the word's original meaning. As 'Scrutator' (John Loveday) noted in *Gent. Mag.* (1781), 421, after defining 'Buxom' as '1. Obedient; obsequious', SJ had in fact given what is surely G's meaning: '2. Gay; lively; brisk' and '3. Wanton; jolly' (*Dict.*).

For G's assertion in 1742 that 'the language of the age is never the language of poetry', see 5 n. above. For similar comments on affected diction, remote from common or prosaic usage, see 'Collins' **17** and 'Akenside' **19** above. Wordsworth later quoted G's 'Sonnet' on Richard West in the 'Preface' to *Lyrical Ballads* (1802) to prove that he 'was more than any other man curiously elaborate in the structure of his own poetic diction', and that 'there neither is, nor can be, any essential difference between the language of prose and metrical composition' (*Prose Works* (1974), i. 133–5).

In *Poems* (1768), G cited as a precedent for his use of 'redolent' (l. 19) Dryden's 'Of the Pythagorean Philosophy', l. 110: 'And bees their honey redolent of spring.' SJ defines 'redolent' as 'Sweet of scent' (*Dict.*). G had defended Dryden's 'licentious' poetic language to West, 8 Apr. 1742 (*Corresp.*, i. 192–3).

SJ seems in fact to echo *Eton Ode*, l. 48 ('The thoughtless day, the easy night'), in 'On the Death of Dr. Robert Levet' (1782), l. 29: 'The busy day, the peaceful night.' For a later critique of G's ode, see William Parsons, *Ode to a Boy at Eton* (1796), 6–12, 23–31.

31. G's 'Ode to Adversity', ll. 1–8, may echo Horace, *Odes*, i. xxxv. 17–20: see *Poems* (1969), 70. SJ's praise implies that G did not succeed in blending the 'poetical' and the 'rational' elsewhere.

32. SJ alludes to a work such as *The Wonderful Wonder of Wonders* (1721), a pamphlet attributed to Swift but perhaps by Thomas Sheridan: see Swift, *Prose Writings*, ix. 281–4.

For the reception of *Odes* (1757), and for SJ's earlier claim that many readers 'were content to be shewn beauties which they could not see', see **14** and n. above. Cf. also his reference to Milton as 'an universal favourite, with whom readers of every class think it necessary to be pleased' in 'Addison' **162** above. In *Rambler* 135 (1751), he wrote: 'most will feel, or say that they feel, the gratifications which others have taught them to expect' (*YW*, iv. 351); and in *Adventurer* 138 (1754): 'A few, a very few, commonly constitute the taste of the time; the judgment which they have once pronounced, some are too lazy to discuss, and some too timorous to contradict' (*YW*, ii. 496). For his confidence in popular judgement in earlier periods, see 'Smith' **49** n. above.

SJ had an ally in Oliver Goldsmith, who in 1759 blamed contemporary criticism for the recent degeneration of poetry: 'From this proceeds the affected obscurity of our odes, the tuneless flow of our blank verse, the pompous epithet, laboured diction, and every other deviation from common sense, which procures the poet the applause of the connoisseur; he is praised by all, read by a few, and soon forgotten.' In the dedication to *The Traveller* (1764), he exclaimed: 'What criticisms have we not heard of late in favour of blank verse, and Pindaric odes, chorusses, anapaests and iambics, alliterative care and happy negligence. Every absurdity has now a champion to defend it.' In his 'Life' of Parnell (1770), he criticized 'misguided innovators' in poetry who 'have adopted a language of their own, and called upon mankind for admiration. All those who do not understand them are silent, and those who make out their meaning, are willing to praise, to shew they understand' (*Coll. Works*, i. 317, iii. 423, iv. 246).

By 1780 hostility to G's *Odes* was rare. Cartwright in *Monthly Review*, 66 (1782), 124–6, described SJ's discussion of 'The Progress of Poesy' as 'not only hostile but malignant', in 'a dogmatical spirit of contradiction to received opinions'. *Gent. Mag.* (1781), 276, denied that SJ's judgements on the *Odes* were shared by 'the common reader' invoked in 51 below. Mrs Thrale believed that SJ 'always measured other people's notions of every thing by his own, and nothing could persuade him to believe that the books which he disliked were agreeable to thousands' (*J. Misc.*, i. 320).

33. See 'The Progress of Poesy', ll. 7–12.

G alluded to Horace's description of Pindar in *Odes*, IV. ii. 5–8 (see *Poems* (1969), 162 n.). SJ had in fact praised Horace's simile in 'Addison' 132 above: 'When Horace says of Pindar, that he pours his violence and rapidity of verse, as a river swoln with rain rushes from the mountain...the mind is impressed with the resemblance of things generally unlike, as unlike as intellect and body.' For 'broken' metaphors, see also 'Dryden' 320 and n. above.

34. See 'Progress of Poesy', ll. 17–18, 21–4. For poetic 'common places', see also 'Pope' 323 and n. above.

35. For SJ's hostility to the recycling of ancient mythology, see also 34 above and 38, 41, 45 below, and 'Butler' 41 and n. above. He refers here to 'Progress of Poesy', ll. 27 ('Idalia's velvet-green'), 35 ('many-twinkling feet'). Young has 'spreads her velvet green' in *Love of Fame*, V. 230.

something of cant: in *Plan of a Dict.* (1747), SJ had hoped to 'secure our language from being over-run with *cant*, from being crouded with low terms, the spawn of folly or affectation, which arise from no just principles of speech, and of which therefore no legitimate derivation can be shewn' (16). By 'cant' SJ means '2. A particular form of speaking, peculiar to some certain class or body of men', rather than '3. A whining pretension to goodness, in formal and affected terms' (*Dict.*): 'velvet' may have reminded him that G's mother had owned a milliner's shop. Cf. 'Addison' 54 and n. above.

Many-twinkling: Thomson, *Spring*, l. 158, has 'many-twinkling leaves', but in 1768 G cited Homer as a precedent (*Poems* (1969), 166 n.). SJ seems to allude to Arthur Murphy's parody of reactions to G's *Odes* in the *Literary Mag.* (1757), 422–6: 'don't you think they're very unintelligible?—damnably so—what do you think of *many-twinkling feet?*—very affected!' Walpole defended 'many-twinkling' to Lyttelton on 25 Aug. 1757, citing Mrs Garrick's comment that G was 'the only poet who ever understood dancing'. Although he found 'the bright and glorious flame of poetical fire' in the *Odes*, Lyttelton thought that G's compound was 'against all the rules of language' (*Corresp.*, xl. 101–6).

Beattie gave 'many-twinkling' as an example of 'compound epithets', which are 'part of our poetical dialect', although they can appear 'stiff and finical' and should be 'used sparingly' (*Essays* (Edinburgh, 1776), 522). For SJ's objections to compound epithets, coinages, and the use of words 'in senses quite different from their established meaning, and those frequently very fantastical', see *Life*, i. 421, 221 and n. Although SJ himself claimed to have coined only four or five words, A. D. Horgan, *J on Language: An Introduction* (1994), 184–5, listed twenty such coinages noted by the late J. D. Fleeman.

This stanza...has something pleasing: with this concession cf. Mason's claim that it 'is indeed a master-piece of rhythm, and charms the ear by its well-varied cadence, as much as the imagery which it contains ravishes the fancy' (1775 edn., ii. 85).

36. See 'Progress of Poesy', ll. 53–65.

Cartwright in *Monthly Review*, 66 (1782), 124–5, accused SJ of 'a continued tissue of misrepresentation' here. G's ode, 'divesting it of its poetical language', states only that 'there have been poets even among the natives of Greenland and Chili; and that in those breasts, that are susceptible of the impressions of poetry, there is the residence of Glory . . . An assertion not only poetical, but . . . philosophically true.'

In the history of Anningait and Ajut in *Ramblers* 186–7 (1751), drawing on Hans Egede's *Description of Greenland* (1745) and including a 'prose ode' by Anningait, SJ had himself anticipated 'The Progress of Poesy': 'Yet learned curiosity is known to have found its way into these abodes of poverty and gloom: Lapland and Iceland have their historians, their criticks, and their poets' (*YW*, v. 212).

37. See 'Progress of Poesy', ll. 66–9, 75–6, 79–82.

The history of poetry outlined by G to Thomas Warton, 15 Apr. 1770, referred to 'the first *Italian* School (commonly called the Sicilian) about the year 1200 brought to perfection by Dante, Petrarch, Boccace, & others' (*Corresp.*, iii. 1123–4).

38. See 'Progress of Poesy', ll. 83–94, praised by Mason for the 'tenderness and grace' with which G characterizes 'Shakespear's genius' (1775 edn., ii. 86). G told Hurd in Aug. 1757 that 'a lady of quality, a friend of Mason's, who is a great reader . . . never suspected there was anything said about Shakespeare or Milton, till it was explained to her' (*Corresp.*, ii. 520).

For supernatural 'machinery', see 'Milton' **222** and n. above, for 'truth', **39, 41** below and 'Cowley' **14** and n. above, and for SJ's suspicion of 'fiction', 'Cowley' **16** and n. above.

39. See 'Progress of Poesy', ll. 95–106. SJ alludes to Mason's note (1775 edn., ii. 87–8) on G's 'fiction' that Milton's labours on *Paradise Lost* caused his blindness ('Milton' **68** and n. above). Mason pointed out Milton's own statement in 'To Mr Cyriack Skinner upon his Blindness' that he lost his sight 'overplied | In liberty's defence, my noble task, | Of which all Europe talks from side to side'. SJ for once prefers G's 'fiction' to Mason's 'fact'.

G explained in a note in *Poems* (1768) that the 'two coursers' refer to 'the stately march and sounding energy of Dryden's Rhymes'. For Voltaire's comparison of Dryden's versification to 'a coach and six stately horses', see *Life*, ii. 5. According to Beattie, *Essays* (Edinburgh, 1776), 360 n., G told him 'that if there was in his own numbers any thing that deserved approbation, he had learned it all from Dryden', and Norton Nicholls recalled that G 'admired Dryden, & could not patiently hear him criticised' (*Corresp.*, iii. 1290–1)

40–7. Beattie may have alluded to SJ's views on 'The Bard' in conversation when he defended its 'prophetic enthusiasm' in 1776: 'I have heard the finest Ode in the world blamed for the boldness of its figures, and for what the critic was pleased to call obscurity' (*Essays* (Edinburgh, 1776), 559–61). One of David Garrick's party-pieces had been mimicry of SJ's 'uncouth manner' of quoting 'The Bard' by 'growling . . . without articulating many of the words' (Joseph Cradock, *Literary and Miscellaneous Memoirs* (1828), i. 37).

Joseph Warton ended his *Essay on Pope*, ii (1782), 411, by pointedly praising 'The Bard', and referred in *Works of Pope* (1797), i. 143 n., to SJ's 'disgraceful and impotent' criticism of the ode. Reynolds similarly ended his final Discourse to the Royal Academy in 1790 by praising 'The Bard' (cf. **27** n. above). For an extended defence of 'the grandest and sublimest effort of the Lyric Muse', see Robert Potter, *Inquiry* (1783), 30–7.

40. The Italian author Francesco Algarotti (1712–64) (see 'Milton' **230** n. above) compared 'The Bard' with Horace, *Odes*, I. xv, without implying indebtedness, in a letter of 26 Dec. 1762 in Mason (1775 edn.), ii. 83. Goldsmith had in fact already suggested that G was imitating Horace's ode on the destruction of Troy in the *Monthly Review* (Sept. 1757), a debt G himself described in Dec. 1758 as 'falsely laid to my charge' (Goldsmith, *Coll. Works*, i. 116; *Corresp.*, ii. 532, 602; and *Poems* (1969), 182).

to copy is less than to invent: cf. 'Milton' **277** above. Consciously or not, SJ may be resorting to an 'expedient' described in *Rambler* 143 (1751): 'When the excellence of a new composition can no longer be contested, and malice is compelled to give way to the unanimity of applause', the 'charge of plagiarism' is a means 'by which the author may be degraded, though his work be reverenced' (*YW*, iv. 394). Cf. SJ's later comment on G's borrowings from Norse in **46** below: 'Theft is always dangerous', and his remarks in 1763 on the opening of 'The Bard' quoted in **43** n. below. SJ goes on to complain that G has in any case copied from Horace only an incredible 'fiction' or 'falsehood', just as he later took from the Norse 'a fiction outrageous and incongruous' (see **34–6, 38** and nn. above and **46** below).

For 'imagery', see 'Cowley' **154** and n. above, for 'variety', 'Butler' **35** and n. above, and for imitation as 'copying', 'Cowley' **60–1** and n. above. Cf. also the 'irreconcileable dissimilitude' of 'Roman images and English manners' in 'Pope' **372** above.

SJ ends by quoting Horace, *Ars Poetica*, l. 188 ('I disbelieve and detest'): see also 'Smith' **49** and n. above.

41. *the probable...the marvellous*: see 'Milton' **220** and n., 'Butler' **49**, and 'Dryden' **213** and n. above. SJ admitted in 1765 that, 'such is the power of the marvellous even over those who despise it, that every man finds his mind more strongly seized by the tragedies of Shakespeare than of any other writer' (*YW*, vii. 83).

it has little use: SJ stated in *Rambler* 60 (1750) that, 'in the esteem of uncorrupted reason, what is of most use is of most value', 'whether we intend to enlarge our science, or increase our virtue'; and in *Rambler* 208 (1752) that the exaggerated 'pictures of life' offered by some writers, 'as they deviate farther from reality... become less useful, because their lessons will fail of application...the reader ...finds in himself no likeness to the phantom before him; and though he laughs or rages, is not reformed' (*YW*, iii. 320–1, v. 319–20).

we are affected only as we believe: SJ wrote in 'Smith' **49** above, 'What I cannot for a moment believe, I cannot for a moment behold with interest or anxiety.' Cf. also Richard Hurd, *Letters on Chivalry and Romance* (1762), 95: 'we must first *believe*, before we can be *affected*.' For this neoclassical tenet, see e.g. Jean Chapelain in 1623: 'Where belief is lacking, attention or interest in lacking also; but where there is no interest, there can be no emotion and consequently no purgation or amendment of men's manners, which is the end of poetry. Belief, therefore, is absolutely necessary in poetry' (cf. R. Bray, *La Formation de la doctrine classique en France* (Paris, 1927), 207).

improved: William Tindal, *Remarks* (1782), 58, replied that 'We may not be *improved*; but if we are delighted, afflicted, terrified, or soothed, some of the ends of poetry have been hitherto thought to be answered.'

truth, moral or political: see 38 and n. above. SJ said on 26 Oct. 1773: 'Nothing is good but what is consistent with truth or probability' (*Life*, v. 361). Cf. J. T. Callender, *Deformities of Dr. SJ* (Edinburgh, 1782), 20: 'The Bard very forcibly impresses this moral, political, and important truth, that eternal vengeance would pursue the English Tyrant [Edward I] and his posterity, as enemies to poetry, and exterminators of mankind. Johnson, a stickler for the *jus divinum*, did not relish this idea.'

42. *before the ear has learned its measures*: G himself wrote of the use of a complex stanza, 9 Mar. 1755, that, 'setting aside the difficulties, methinks it has little or no effect upon the ear, wch scarce perceives the regular return of Metres at so great a distance from one another. to make it succeed, I am persuaded the Stanza's must not consist of above 9 lines each at the most' (*Corresp.*, i. 421; Mason (1775 edn.), 233). Reviewing *Odes* (1757), Goldsmith complained about 'a natural imperfection' of poems 'composed in irregular rhymes': 'the similar sound often recurring where it is not expected, and not being found where it is, creates no small confusion to the Reader' (*Coll. Works*, i. 113). Dennis had claimed in 1722 that the ear loses rhymes more than three lines apart (*Works*, ii. 238). For another poet whose odes are 'perplexing to the ear', see 'Akenside' 23 above, and, for the importance of metrical regularity, 'Cowley' 140–1 and n. above.

consonance: '1. Accord of sound' (*Dict.*).

43. For praise of the 'inventor' of 'technical beauties', see 'Denham' 28 and n. above.

SJ refers to an anonymous critic (later identified as J. Butler) cited by Mason: 'This abrupt execration ['Ruin seize thee, ruthless King!'] plunges the reader into that sudden fearful perplexity which is designed to predominate through the whole' (Mason (1775 edn.), ii. 91; *Corresp.*, ii. 256–7). SJ had mocked such claims and invoked 'Johnny Armstrong' as early as 25 June 1763: the opening of 'The Bard' 'has been celebrated for its abrupt breaking off and plunging into the subject all at once. But such arts as these have no merit but in being original. The first time is the only time that we admire them; and that abruptness is nothing new. We have had it often before. Nay, we have it in the song of Johnny Armstrong.' SJ then admitted that ll. 3–4 of 'The Bard' were 'very good' (Boswell, *London Journal*, ed. F. A. Pottle (1950), 282–3 and n.; cf. *Life*, i. 403).

'Johnny Armstrong' had appeared in *A Collection of Old Ballads* (3 vols., 1723–5), and Alan Ramsay's *The Evergreen* (1724), and was a favourite of Goldsmith (Reynolds, *Portraits*, 45). Boswell overheard SJ repeat a line from it 'in a kind of muttering tone' in Scotland in Aug. 1773 (*Life*, v. 43).

In *Rambler* 139 (1751) SJ described Milton's *Samson Agonistes* as 'opening with a graceful abruptness' (*YW*, iv. 372). Warton praised the 'striking abruptness' and 'strong image' of the opening of Pope's 'Unfortunate Lady' in *Essay on Pope* (1756), 250.

Archibald Campbell, *The Sale of Authors* (1767), commented on 'The Bard', l. 1: 'Only observe with what sublimity he has expressed the very vulgar phrase of Devil take ye' (*Corresp.*, iii. 1218).

44. See 'The Bard', ll. 1, 5.

For the fashion for alliteration, see 'Waller' **151** and n. above, and for 'sublimity', 'Cowley' **58** and n. above. Cowper stated, 20 Apr. 1777, that G was 'the only Poet since Shakespear entitled to the Character of Sublime' (*Letters*, i (Oxford, 1979), 268).

45. See 'The Bard', ll. 29–30, 33–4.

For 'puerilities' see **30** and n. above; for 'obsolete mythology', **34–6, 40** above and 'Butler' **41** and n. above, and for the importance of holding the reader's 'attention', 'Dryden' **312** and n. above.

46. See 'The Bard', ll. 48–51.

northern Bards: a revision in proof of the more provocative 'northern Barbarians' (see Textual Notes). Cf. SJ's remarks on the Scottish bards in 1775: 'The state of the Bards was yet more hopeless. He that cannot read, may now converse with those that can; but the Bard was a barbarian among barbarians, who, knowing nothing himself, lived with others that knew no more' (*Journey* (1985), 96).

the work of female powers: G's note (1768) to ll. 47–8 stated, 'See the Norwegian Ode, that follows', referring to 'The Fatal Sisters', which he translated from the Norse *c.*1761. Cf. also the Parcae or Fates in Greek mythology. For objections to G's mingling of Welsh bards with Norse mythology, see *Poems* (1969), 189 n.

the woof . . . the warp: see 'The Bard', l. 49. *Critical Review*, 4 (Aug. 1757), 167–70, asked: 'Is not the warp laid, and the woof afterwards woven?' The 'warp' is properly the fixed thread, but by 'weave' G clearly meant 'weave together' or 'interweave'. 'Scrutator' (John Loveday) in *Gent. Mag.* (1783), 48, noted SJ's cautious definitions of 'Warp' as 'That order of thread in a thing woven that crosses the woof', and of 'Woof' as '1. The set of threads that crosses the warp; the weft' (*Dict.*). In proof he revised 'they *weave* the piece' to 'men *weave* the *web* or piece' (Textual Notes).

SJ may be reacting again to the 'anonymous critic' in Mason (1775 edn.), ii. 92: 'Can there be an image more just, apposite, and nobly imagined than this tremendous tragical winding-sheet? In the rest of this stanza the wildness of thought, expression, and cadence are admirably adapted to the character and situation of the speaker, and of the bloody spectres his assistants', etc. When Boswell claimed on 28 Mar. 1775 that l. 50 was 'a good line', SJ replied: 'Ay . . . and the next line is a good one,' (pronouncing it contemptuously;) "Give ample verge and room enough"' (*Life*, ii. 327).

47. SJ's remarks on ll. 81, 87–8 may react to the 'ingenious friend' in Mason (1775 edn.), ii. 93, who claimed that this stanza 'breathes . . . the high spirit of lyric Enthusiasm. The Transitions are sudden, and impetuous; the Language full of fire and force; and the Imagery carried, without impropriety, to the most daring height. The manner of Richard's death by Famine exhibits such beauties of Personification, as only the richest and most vivid Imagination could supply', etc.

For SJ's objections to literary suicide, which may include an allusion to Thomas Warton's 'Ode: The Suicide' (1777), see 'Pope' **52, 319** and n. and 'Young' **162** above; and R. Lonsdale, 'TG, David Hume and John Home's *Douglas*,' in M. Bell et al. (eds.), *Re-Constructing the Book: Literary Texts in Transmission* (2001), 57–70.

48. G's *Odes* (1757) were for SJ a culminating embodiment of the fashionable affectations in poetic language about which he had been protesting since the 1750s, as in

Idler 63 (1759): 'every man now endeavours to excel others in accuracy, or outshine them in splendour of style, and the danger is, lest care should too soon pass to affectation' (*YW*, ii. 198). See also 'Thomson' **50**, 'Collins' **9, 17**, and 'Akenside' **16–18** above, and cf. 'Pope' **350** and n. above.

For 'ornaments', see 'Cowley' **202** and n. above; for other contrasts of the 'striking' and the 'pleasing', see 'Milton' **276** and n. above, and 'Collins' **17** below, where SJ also objects to 'harshness'; and for 'ease' in writing, 'Rochester' **18** and n. above.

Double, double, toil and trouble: *Macbeth*, IV. i. 10. SJ stated of Shakespeare's tragedies in 1765 that 'he often writes with great appearance of toil and study, what is written at last with little felicity' (*YW*, vii. 69). Cf. also 'Prior' **72** above: 'It is said by Longinus of Euripedes, that he forces himself sometimes into grandeur by violence of effort, as the lion kindles his fury by the lashes of his own tail. Whatever Prior obtains above mediocrity seems the effort of struggle and of toil.'

walking on tiptoe: G had himself described 'The Progress of Poesy' as 'a high Pindarick upon stilts' in July 1752 (*Corresp.*, i. 364).

According to Langton, SJ once described G's *Odes* as 'forced plants, raised in a hot-bed; and they are poor plants; they are but cucumbers after all' (*Life*, iv. 13). Steevens heard him compare them to fireworks: 'He played his coruscations so speciously, that his steel-dust is mistaken by many for a shower of gold' (*J. Misc.*, ii. 321: for SJ's refusal to be impressed by fireworks, see Lipking (1998), 86–7).

SJ's attitude recalls that of an earlier generation (cf. **26** n. above): e.g. Wycherley's objections to '*obsolete* Terms', and to the 'Scribbler' who claims 'the Priviledge of minting *Words* and *Phrases*, of tossing about *Metaphors* at Discretion, and making his own *Jargon* the Standard of a *Language*: These are Fops in *Literature*, that make as awkward a Figure as Apes in Humane Cloathing' (*Posthumous Works* (1728), ii. 7).

49. SJ defines a 'Critick' as 'a man able to distinguish the faults and beauties of writing' (*Dict.*), but has given no specific examples of such 'beauties' in G's *Odes*.

50. G's translations of Norse and Welsh poetry date from 1761, when he was planning a 'History of English Poetry' (cf. **37** n. above). Some appeared in *Poems* (1768), and Mason printed other fragments in 1775, praising their 'fire' and 'judgment': 'He keeps up through them all the wild romantic spirit of his originals' (1775 edn., ii. 104). See also **46** n. above and *Poems* (1969), 210–36.

Even in a translation of primitive verse, SJ expects the language to resemble 'the language of other poets'.

51. SJ held back his eloquent tribute to the *Elegy Written in a Country Churchyard* (1751) (see **10** and n. above) in the belief that it would conclude not merely 'Gray' itself, but his entire survey of English poetry. 'Lyttelton' in fact replaced 'Gray' at the end of the rearranged *Lives* (1781) (see headnote).

SJ praised the *Elegy*'s 'dignity, variety, and originality of sentiment' in 'Parnell' **10** above. His comments here are hardly more specific, his main purpose being to contrast the *Elegy* with the affected obscurities of *Odes* (1757), and to summarize some of his convictions about poetry. As he told Boswell bluntly on 25 June 1763: 'I do not think Mr. Gray a first-rate poet. He has not a bold imagination, nor much command of words. The obscurity in which he has involved himself will not make us think him sublime. His *Elegy in a Churchyard* has a happy selection of images, but I don't like his great things' (*London Journal*, 282–3, revised in *Life*, i. 403). Mason (1775 edn.), ii. 94–5, referred to 'the obscurity which has been imputed' to G's *Odes*, and 'the preference which, in consequence, has been given to his Elegy', but defended the 'new' pleasures of such obscurity: 'The lyric Muse, like other fine Ladies, requires to be courted, and retains her admirers the longer for not having yielded too readily to their solicitations.'

Like SJ, Goldsmith believed that G's poetry had deteriorated after the *Elegy*. Reviewing *Odes* (1757), he complained that he was now addressing more specialized 'literary' readers: 'We cannot . . . without some regret behold those talents so capable of giving pleasure to all, exerted in efforts that, at best, can amuse only the few.' In 1762 he published a mock-Pindaric ode obviously aimed at G ('Perdition seize thee, shameless wight') in an essay, and Boswell heard him parody 'The Bard' later in the year (*London Journal* (1950), 105–6). By 1767 Goldsmith had reservations even about the *Elegy*, 'a very fine poem, but overloaded with epithet', although 'The latter part . . . is pathetic and interesting' (*Coll. Works*, i. 112, iii. 190, v. 320). For his apparent preference for Parnell's 'A Night-Piece on Death', see 'Parnell' **10** and n. above. John Langhorne, in *Monthly Review*, 38 (1768), 408, also regretted 'the departure of Mr. Gray's muse from that elegantly-moral simplicity she assumed in the Country Churchyard' for 'the dark diableries of the Gothic times' in his *Poems* (1768).

This is one of SJ's most decisive appeals to the 'common reader' (see 'Cowley' **65** and n. above), anticipated by his earlier references to 'common use' and 'common apprehension' in **30** above. Cf. *Rambler* 52 (1750) on 'the common voice of the multitude uninstructed by precept, and unprejudiced by authority, which, in questions that relate to the heart of man, is, in my opinion, more decisive than the learning of Lipsius' (*YW*, iii. 280); and his note on *2 Henry VI*, III. iii, which 'will continue to be admired when prejudice shall cease, and bigotry give way to impartial examination. These are beauties that rise out of nature and of truth; the superficial reader cannot miss them, the profound can image nothing beyond them' (*YW*, viii. 591). In implicit reply, Warton distinguished 'the higher flights of more genuine poetry' from verse which is merely 'level to the general capacities of men' in *Essay on Pope*, ii (1782), 409.

a mirrour in every mind: cf. Pope's account of 'True Wit' as 'Something, whose truth convinc'd at sight we find, | That gives us back the Image of our Mind' (*Essay on Criticism*, ll. 299–300). See also *Rambler* 60 (1750) on the 'parallel circumstances, and kindred images, to which we readily conform our minds' (*YW*, iii. 319); SJ's comment in 1765 on the 'oldest poets', whose 'descriptions are verified by every eye, and their sentiments acknowledged by every breast' (*YW*, vii. 89); and 'those ideas that slumber in the heart' in 'Dryden' **326** above.

SJ may have had the opening of the *Elegy* in mind in *Adventurer* 108 (1753), when discussing descriptions which will 'flatter the imagination, as long as human nature shall remain the same': 'When night overshadows a romantic scene, all is stillness, silence, and quiet; the poets of the grove cease their melody, the moon towers over the world in gentle majesty, men forget their labours and their cares, and every passion and persuit is for a while suspended' (*YW*, ii. 447).

four stanzas: *Elegy*, ll. 77–92. SJ in fact claimed on 28 Mar. 1775 that 'there are but two good stanzas in Gray's poetry', slightly misquoting *Elegy*, ll. 85–8, and adding,

'The other stanza I forget' (*Life*, ii. 328). Thomas Campbell heard a similar statement two weeks later (*Diary*, ed. J. L. Clifford (Cambridge, 1947), 79). There are in fact several precedents for G's 'notions' (see *Poems* (1969), 132 n.), including a passage from Swift's *Thoughts on Various Subjects* quoted in the *Dict.* under 'Unwillingness': 'There is in most people a reluctance and unwillingness to be forgotten. We observe, even among the vulgar, how fond they are to have an inscription over their grave.' SJ himself wrote in *Rambler* 78 (1750), shortly before the *Elegy* appeared, about 'that desire which every man feels of being remembered and lamented' (*YW*, iv. 48).

I have never seen . . . always felt them: SJ invokes the ideal poetic combination of the 'natural' and the 'new' (see 'Cowley' 55 and n. above). Cf. Dominique Bouhours, *The Art of Criticism* (1705): 'when a Natural Discourse paints a Passion, we find within our selves the Truth of what we heard, which was there before without being taken notice of' (51); 'one would say, that a Natural Thought should come into any body's Mind, and that it was in our Head before we read it' (156). In 'Congreve' 35 above the reader 'feels what he remembers to have felt before, but feels it with great increase of sensibility'.

vain to blame, and useless to praise him: Lipking (1970), 454, described SJ as pronouncing an epitaph on criticism itself, 'resigned before the greater claims of poetry and the common sense of readers'. In his later formulation, SJ 'resigns his authority—and also asserts it, by merging the public judgment into his own': his 'whole career as an author has led to this moment' (Lipking (1998), 263).

Although SJ does not comment on G's influential use of the quatrain in the *Elegy*, Goldsmith wrote that 'The heroic measure with alternate rhime is very properly adapted to the solemnity of the subject, as it is the slowest movement that our language admits of' (*Coll. Works*, v. 320). For SJ's comments on its disadvantages, see 'Dryden' 24 and n. above. Hill (1905), iii. 444 and n., assumed that SJ was parodying G in his translation of Euripides into quatrains in July 1779, but his target was in fact Robert Potter: see *Poems* (1974), 221–3.

GEORGE, LORD LYTTELTON (1709–73)

Composition. SJ wrote to William Henry Lyttelton (1724–1808), Lord Westcote, on 27 July 1780: 'The course of my undertaking will now require a short life of your Brother Lord Lyttelton. My desire is to avoid offence, and to be totally out of danger, I take the liberty of proposing to your Lordship, that the historical account should be written under your direction by any friend whom you may be willing to employ, and I will only take upon my self to examine the poetry. Four pages like those of his works, or even half so much, will be sufficient' (*Letters*, iii. 291–2; a comma has been preferred above to a full stop after 'danger', as in *Letters*, ed. Chapman, ii. 383).

As an old friend of Henry Thrale and a member of the Streatham circle, Lord Westcote was no stranger to SJ. In Nov. 1778 Mrs Thrale had reported his enjoyment of the still unpublished earlier *Prefaces*: 'Lord Westcote who is a good Tory delights in your prefaces, & would read nothing else.' Not long after SJ wrote to him, he would be involved in Henry Thrale's election campaign in Southwark in Sept. 1780 (*Thraliana*, i. 200, 471; *Letters*, ed. Chapman, ii. 266).

Westcote replied to SJ immediately, declining to help and assuring SJ that his anxieties were unnecessary. SJ wrote again on 28 July: 'I shall certainly not wantonly nor willingly offend; but when there are such near relations living, I had rather they would please themselves.' As he told Mrs Thrale on 1 Aug., Westcote had explained that 'he knows not whom to employ, and is sure I shall do him no injury. There is an ingenious scheme to save a day's work or part of a day, utterly defeated' (*Letters*, iii. 292, 294). In a not entirely reliable later note, Mrs Thrale-Piozzi claimed that SJ asked Westcote 'in my hearing, to write this life for him (tho' I am sure he neither loved nor esteemed the man)', and that, when Westcote was outraged by 'Lyttelton', SJ merely 'sate still and laugh'd at my Lord Parenthesis, as he called Billy Lyttelton' (Lobban, 162).

Although SJ's anxiety about giving offence was to prove fully justified, it is also clear that, with the end in sight, he was by now wearying of his task. Almost simultaneously he asked Westcote to suggest a biographer for L's cousin Gilbert West, and succeeded in delegating 'Young' to Herbert Croft (see headnotes to 'West' and 'Young' above). Early in Aug. 1780 he asked Nichols to send him the works of Pope, Swift, and L: 'The first to be got is Lyttelton.' By 16 Aug. he had found that L's *Works* did not contain the prefatory biography he had expected (see below). Two days later he asked Mrs Thrale: 'What shall I do with Lyttelton's Life? I can make a short life, and a short criticism, and conclude' (*Letters*, iii. 300, 301). SJ probably wrote it soon afterwards, given that he had earlier expected to devote to it only 'a day's work or part of a day'.

Sources. In his letter to Westcote on 28 July 1780, SJ claimed: 'For the life of Lord Lyttelton I shall need no help—it was very public, and I have no need to be minute. But I return your lordship thanks for your readiness to help me' (*Letters*, iii. 292). SJ obviously wished to make clear that he had invited Westcote to provide or commission a life of his brother out of tact rather than lack of information. Although L had died too recently to appear in his usual sources, SJ obviously expected to find a biographical account in George Edward Ayscough's edition of L's *Works* (1774), which he requested from Nichols in early Aug. 1780. Nichols must have sent the 2nd edition (3 vols., 1776), since SJ replied on 16 Aug.: 'I expected to have found a life of Lord Lyttelton prefixed to his Works. Is there not one before the quarto Edition? I think there is—if not, I am, with respect to him, quite aground.'

In the absence of any such prefatory biography, SJ no doubt followed his own suggestion to Mrs Thrale on 18 Aug. that he make merely 'a short life, and a short criticism' (*Letters*, iii. 300–1). Although no particular source has been identified, he himself foresaw no difficulty in finding a factual outline of L's public career (such as, e.g, the 'Memoirs of the Life and Writings of the late George Lord Lyttelton' in the *Annual Register for 1774*, ii. 24–9). SJ could also glean information from L's publications and the letters in his *Works*, and had his own memories of L's public and literary career since the 1730s. SJ's account of L's political career in 4–11 is, however, somewhat confused, confirming that he was at his best when reordering and clarifying a detailed chronological narrative by another hand, such as *BB* had so often provided.

Once SJ explained his problem to Nichols, his printer played a significant part in solving it, and not merely by producing some convenient outline of L's career. It was no doubt Nichols who pointed out to SJ the letter from L's father (see 12 below) in T. R. Nash's still unpublished *History of Worcestershire*, vol. i (1781), which Nichols had already enabled SJ to use in 'Shenstone' (q.v. above), and later cited in his own notes on

L in his *Anecdotes of Bowyer* (1782). Nichols may well also have drawn to SJ's attention Dr James Johnstone's account of L's deathbed in *Gent. Mag.* (1773) (see 24–9 below), which, as SJ admits with barely concealed relief, spared him the task of providing his own 'moral character' of L (23 below).

Nichols seems also to have supplied SJ with first-hand information of his own. As William Bowyer's apprentice and later partner, Nichols had been involved in the printing of both L's *History of Henry the Second* and his posthumous *Works*, and almost certainly provided SJ with the material about these works added to 20, 22 below in the proofs. As a result, L's obsessive preoccupation with the printing of his *History* looms large in SJ's otherwise rather perfunctory narrative, almost half of which is taken up by this subject and by Johnstone's narrative of his death. The extent of Nichols's contributions no doubt explains the proprietorial way in which he later reprinted, annotated, and even criticized SJ's 'Lyttelton' in his *Anecdotes of Bowyer* (1782), 425–8 n., and, with further commentary, in *Lit. Anec.*, vi. 457–67 (see 20 n. below).

Even if it ends with an elaborate and pious deathbed scene (23–9 below), SJ would not originally have envisaged 'Lyttelton' as an obvious conclusion to his *Lives*. *Prefaces* (1781) had ended much more resoundingly with 'Gray': since the reordering by date of death in *Lives* (1781), the work has concluded with a poet about whose claims for inclusion SJ is obviously highly sceptical.

Reception. As his letters to Lord Westcote in July 1780 indicate, SJ evidently foresaw that, left to himself, he would inevitably end up giving the offence he claimed to be anxious to avoid. While 'Gray' primarily provoked fashionable literary taste, 'Lyttelton' caused outrage because of its condescending account of a peer and politician widely esteemed for his integrity, benevolence, and piety, as well as his literary achievements. When L died, Edmund Burke wrote to Elizabeth Montagu, 4 Sept. 1773: 'We have lost no common man; either in the Talents he possessd or in the use he made of them. He united the Characters of the publick, the Literary, and the sociable . . . Every part was well filled' (*Corresp.*, ii. 454–6, and cf. 456–8 for her reply, 11 Sept. 1773). William Combe wrote of L in *The R[oya]l Register*, ii (1779), 100–6, two years before SJ's account: 'This Man's extensive learning, indefatigable industry, fine taste, polished talents, and excellent heart, will continue to delight and instruct the World, while any taste for Letters, or any sense of Virtue, remains in it.'

Although SJ's condescending reference to 'poor Lyttelton' particularly irritated L's friends and admirers (see 17 and n. below), reservations about L's politics, literary abilities, and personality are apparent throughout. As Boswell wrote in 1791, SJ's 'expressing with a dignified freedom what he really thought of him, gave offence to some of the friends of that nobleman, and particularly produced a declaration of war against him from Mrs. Montagu, the ingenious Essayist on Shakspeare' (*Life*, iv. 64). SJ's acquaintance Elizabeth Montagu (1720–1800), literary hostess and author of an *Essay on Shakespear* (1769), had been a friend of L since the 1740s, and her outrage was predictable: see *Life*, ii. 88–9, and S. M. Myers, *The Bluestocking Circle* (Oxford, 1990), esp. 181–6. According to Mrs Rose, daughter-in-law of SJ's friend Dr William Rose, SJ had eventually sent the MS of 'Lyttelton' to Montagu, 'who was much dissatisfied with it, and thought her friend every way underrated; but the Doctor made no alteration' (*J. Misc.*, ii. 421). (Although Mrs Rose stated specifically that SJ sent her his MS, this would have been an unusual, perhaps unprecedented, step, and it is more likely that Montagu saw a pre-publication copy: see below.)

Elizabeth Montagu was certainly aware of the contents of SJ's biography, by whatever means, by early 1781. Horace Walpole reported on 27 Jan. 1781 that she 'and all her Maenades intend to tear [SJ] limb from limb for despising their muppet Lord Lyttelton'. On 5 Feb. he described a bluestocking reception at Lady Lucan's, when Mrs Montagu 'kept aloof from Johnson like the West from the East'. In a later account, they 'kept at different ends of the chamber and set up altar against altar there. There she told me as a mark of her high displeasure that she would never ask him to dinner again. I took her side and fomented the quarrel.' By 28 Feb. 1781 Walpole was claiming to find the progress of this quarrel more fascinating than the angry reactions to SJ's 'Gray' (*Corresp.*, xxix. 97, 104, 113, 115–16). By then Lord Hardwicke had sent Mrs Montagu a pre-publication text of SJ's 'unfair and uncandid' account of L on 20 Feb. (R. Blunt, *Mrs. Montagu* [1923], ii. 110).

SJ himself told Boswell on 26 Mar. that 'Mrs. Montagu had dropped him, and that there were people whom one would like very well to drop but would not wish to be dropped by' (Boswell, *Laird of Auchinleck*, 295; *Life*, iv. 73). Hannah More regretted in Mar. 1781 that SJ 'has lost so much credit' over 'Lyttelton': 'he treats him almost with contempt; makes him out a poor writer, and an envious man' (*Memoirs* (1834), i. 206; *J. Misc.*, ii. 193). Mrs Thrale reported on 17 May that the quarrel continued unabated (*Thraliana*, i. 495). On 13 Aug. 1781 Lord Hardwicke wrote to Thomas Percy, deploring SJ's 'spiteful and unjust treatment of Lord Lyttelton. I have been ready more than once to take up the *pen* myself, but that the insolent style of the author rather deserves the *cudgel*' (Nichols, *Lit. Ill.*, viii. 197).

Most striking is Fanny Burney's long account of SJ's violent outburst at Streatham in mid-June 1781, when, 'in a voice the most enraged', he suddenly demanded that Mrs Montagu's ally, William Weller Pepys (1740–1825), explain their objections to his account of L, and forced William Seward to repeat 'fresh Instances' of L's 'illiberal behaviour to Shenstone'. Even Burney thought SJ 'unreasonably furious & grossly severe'. Pepys, who was evidently shaken by this occasion, and Montagu went on brooding over it for the rest of the year, and it was still rankling in 1783: see the letters between Montagu and Pepys of 4, 14 Aug. 1781 (Huntingdon Library) quoted in O M Brack and L. Rothschild (eds.), *SJ in New Albion* (Tempe, Ariz., 1997), 34–5; Burney, *Early Journals*, iv. 366–70, 429–30, and *Diary and Letters*, ii. 235–7; *Life*, iv. 64–5; *J. Misc.*, i. 244–5, ii. 416–17; A. C. C. Gaussen, *A Later Pepys* (1904), i. 121–43; and Blunt, *Mrs. Montagu*, ii. 156–66. Two years were to pass before SJ could tentatively hope in Oct. 1783 that 'peace is proclaimed' with Mrs Montagu (*Letters*, iv. 203, 217).

Although reviewers of *Prefaces* (1781) devoted more attention and emotion to SJ's 'Gray', his account of L (like his earlier remarks about L's alleged envy of The Leasowes in 'Shenstone' 11 above) offended not only a particular coterie. Joseph Warton, who in 1756 had been appointed chaplain to L ('a man of virtue, and ever a defender of religion') (see Thomas Warton, *Corresp.* (1995), 63), went out of his way to praise L in his *Essay on Pope*, ii (1782), 317–20, no doubt in response to SJ's attack. John Nichols, in his *Biographical and Literary Anecdotes of William Bowyer* (1782), 425–6 n., openly regretted SJ's provocation of L's friends and relatives. Yet, while SJ at times unrepentantly boasted about what he had *not* said in 'Lyttelton' (see **23** n. below), he showed notable restraint on one matter mentioned by Nichols, which helps to explain the sensitivity of L's family and friends to bad publicity. L's son, the notorious rake Thomas, Lord Lyttelton (1744–79), mentioned only incidentally by SJ (see **9** and n., **29** n. below), had recently died, and Nichols later referred in 1782 to a secret journal kept by Thomas, which had used the 'grossest terms' to describe facts of which Aretine and 'the most abandoned haunters of the stews' would have been ashamed (455–6 n.).

SJ was unusual, not so much in having reservations about L's personality and literary achievements, as in being prepared to express them in public. As will become clear below, Horace Walpole often commented scathingly on L's 'absurdity' as a man, politician, and author (see *Memoirs of King George II*, ed. J. Brooke (New Haven, 1985), i. 135), but offered a rather different assessment for public consumption: 'Learning, eloquence, and gravity, distinguished this peer above most of his rank, and breathe in all his prose' (*Works* (1798), i. 539–40).

While he had some sympathy for L's politics in the 1730s (see 8 n.), SJ soon came to dislike the aggressive 'Whiggism' of L's early career and writings (see 19 n.), and refused to take seriously an admired but essentially amateur author (see 31 and n. below). There have been, however, more personal explanations of his hostility to L, one going back to SJ's adolescence. In 1725/6 SJ stayed for several months with his cousin, the Revd Cornelius Ford (1694–1731) (see 'Broome' 2 and n. above), at Pedmore, Worcs., where the Lytteltons were neighbours and friends. According to Thomas Percy, it was at this time that SJ and L first met, and that the grammar-school boy, who was some eight months the younger, had 'colloquial disputes' with the Etonian which forever prejudiced SJ against him (*J. Misc.*, ii. 208).

Mrs Thrale believed that the hostility sprang instead from a later rivalry between SJ and L for the affections of the pious Miss Hill Boothby (1708–56) of Ashburne Hall, Derbys., whom SJ had met in 1739, and may in the 1750s have thought of as a prospective second wife: 'You may see (said he to me, when the Poets Lives were printed), that dear B—thby is at my heart still. She *would* delight in that fellow Lyttelton's company though, all that I could do; and I cannot forgive even his memory the preference given by a mind like her's' (*J. Misc.*, i. 257, and cf. *Life*, i. 83). It is unclear whether SJ intended this explanation of the tone of 'Lyttelton' to be taken seriously. Some later, and probably unintentional, discourtesy by L's relatives seems unlikely to have influenced his basic attitude significantly (see 13 n. below).

SJ was probably aware that Archibald Campbell had not merely dedicated to L his parody of SJ's style in *Lexiphanes* (1767), unfavourably contrasting SJ's 'affectation and *Lexiphanicism*' with L's prose (p. iv), but had in a sense predicted what would follow in 1781: 'There is as great an antipathy between a pure and natural writer, such as your Lordship, and a Lexiphanes, as there is between an elephant and a rhinoceros. When they meet, they are sure to fall foul of one another, most commonly the Lexiphanes first, for the other often holds him too cheap, and the contest is never at an end till one is destroyed' (p. xvii). Boswell, for his part, was flattered by L's interest in his *Account of Corsica* (1768), at a time when SJ's own advice was to 'empty your head of Corsica' (*Boswell in Search of a Wife*, ed. F. Brady and F. A. Pottle (New York, 1956), 175, 178), and had prefixed (in large type) L's 'Letter' to him on the subject to the 3rd edition in 1769, pp. iii–viii (see *Catalogue*, L 895, C 2428; *The Lyttelton Papers* (Sotheby's catalogue, 12 Dec. 1978), item 93).

As for L's opinion of SJ, it seems not to have been unfavourable. For his early 'rapture' over SJ's anonymous *London* (1738), see 8 n. below. Percival Stockdale reported that L once said of SJ that he 'regretted the roughness of his manners; and the too frequently uniform, and elaborate structure of his style…"But (said his lordship) notwithstanding the exceptionable parts of his character, as a writer, and a social being; if I had power; there is no man whom I should be more desirous to serve;— on account of his learning; his talents; and his virtue" ' (*Memoirs* (1809), ii. 43–4).

Given his usual policy of not quoting living authors, the inclusion of five quotations from L in the *Dict*. (1755) suggests some continuing respect at that period.

Publication. In *Prefaces*, vol. x (15 May 1781). Pp. 1–16 (of 22) of the proofs are in the Forster Collection.

Modern Sources:

R. Blunt, *Mrs. Montagu, 'Queen of the Blues': Her Letters and Friendships from 1762–1800* (2 vols., [1923])

R. M. Davis, *The Good Lord L* (Bethlehem, Pa., 1939)

L. Dickens and M. Stanton (eds.), *An Eighteenth-Century Correspondence* (1910)

C. Gerrard, *The Patriot Opposition to Walpole: Politics, Poetry, and National Myth, 1725–42* (Oxford, 1994)

The Lyttelton Papers: The Property of the Viscount Cobham (Sotheby's auction catalogue, 12 Dec. 1978), 113–66

R. Phillimore, *Memoirs and Correspondence of George, Lord L* (2 vols., 1845)

A. V. Rao, *A Minor Augustan: Being the Life and Works of George, Lord L* (Calcutta, 1934)

L. M. Wiggin, *The Faction of Cousins* (New Haven, 1958)

M. Wyndham, *Chronicles of the Eighteenth Century* (2 vols., 1924)

1. L was born on 17 Jan. 1709, the son of Sir Thomas Lyttelton (1686–1751) of Hagley, Worcs. (see **4, 12** below), and Christian Temple, daughter of Sir Richard Temple and sister of Pope's friend Lord Cobham. Gilbert West was his cousin: see **4** n. below, 'Pope' **272** and n., and 'West' **2** and n. above. Nichols, *Anecdotes of Bowyer* (1782), 639, added from T. R. Nash's *History of Worcestershire* (1781), vol. ii, Appendix, 24, that L 'was born at seven months, and thrown away by the nurse as a dead child, but upon closer inspection was found to be alive'.

   L entered Eton in 1725. L's biographers have often cited SJ's report of his excellence at school. SJ may have heard this when he first met L in the mid–1720s (see headnote).

2. L matriculated from Christ Church, Oxford, on 11 Feb. 1726. *Bleinheim* (published 23 Apr. 1728) described Blenheim Palace and the Marlboroughs.

3. L inscribed 'Eclogue I. Uncertainty' in *The Progress of Love. In Four Eclogues* (published 25 Mar. 1732) to Pope, who had corrected it (Davis, *The Good Lord L*, 96). For SJ's dislike of modern pastoral, see 'Cowley' **7** and n. above.

   Letters from a Persian in England to his Friend at Ispahan (1735) imitated the device of a foreign observer in Montesquieu's *Lettres persanes* (1721). Although much of the work is social satire, some of the letters, under Bolingbroke's influence, express L's 'headstrong ardour for liberty' by advocating greater freedom of the press and political reform, and were duly attacked as opposition propaganda by Walpole's journalists: see Davis, *The Good Lord L*, 36 ff., and B. Goldgar, *Walpole and the Wits* (Lincoln, Nebr., 1976), 140–1. L later told Warton that he intended to omit the 'juvenile' *Persian Letters* from his *Works* (*Essay on Pope*, ii (1782), 318–19).

   Joseph Towers in his *Essay* on SJ (1786) stated that, 'taken by itself', the meaning of SJ's second sentence is that 'every man of genius must, in the earlier part of his life, be a zealous Whig' (*Early Biographies* (1974), 212–13). This is as close as SJ comes to admitting that he had shared some of L's political 'ardour' in the 1730s. Cartwright replied in *Monthly Review*, 66 (1782), 121, that L had never lost his 'ardour for liberty': 'there is perhaps, no passion, when once it has taken possession of the mind, that burns with more unabating ardour than that which has liberty for its object... liberty is an object that is equally desirable through every period of life.' For SJ's scepticism about 'liberty', see 'Milton' **169** and n. above.

4. L left Christ Church without a degree by Mar. 1728, some months before SJ's arrival at Pembroke College, just across the road. He travelled in France, Switzerland, and Italy in 1728–30: the poems and letters he wrote abroad are in his posthumous *Works*.

Through his brother-in-law Thomas Pitt, L became MP for Okehampton in 1735, holding the seat until 1756. From 1733 he belonged to the political group, known variously as 'Cobham's Cubs' and the 'Boy Patriots', led by his uncle Lord Cobham (see 1 n. above and Davis, *The Good Lord L*, 44–5), to whom he had inscribed 'Eclogue IV' of *The Progress of Love* (1732). His father, MP 1721–41 and a Lord of the Admiralty 1727–41, was a Walpole Whig. As Hill (1905) noted, examples of the opposed parliamentary votes of father and son are recorded in *Gent. Mag.* (1739), 306, 309.

5. Parliament regularly debated excise and the size of the standing army in the 1730s, even after Walpole withdrew his hated Excise Bill of 1733 (Davis, *The Good Lord L*, 83–8, 110). Cf. Pope, *Imit. Horace, Sat. II. ii.* (1734), ll. 133–4, 153–4: 'In *South-sea* days not happier, when surmis'd | The Lord of thousands, than if now *Excis'd* | ... My Life's Amusements have been just the same, | Before, and after Standing Armies came.' SJ notoriously defined 'Excise' as 'A hateful tax levied upon commodities, and adjudged, not by the common judges of property, but wretches hired by those to whom excise is paid' (*Dict.*; see also *Life*, i. 295 n.).

The government-sponsored *Daily Gazetteer* often attacked L, particularly in 1737–9. Lord Hervey said that 'there was nobody more violent in the Oposition, nor anybody a more declared enemy to Sir Robert Walpole' (*Memoirs* (1931 edn.), 386–8), and the Prussian envoy reported in 1737 that 'The King hates him so bitterly that he cannot bear to hear his name mentioned' (Wiggin, *Faction*, 89). Horace Walpole described L as 'a great enemy of, and writer against, my father' (*Corresp.*, xiii. 19), stating elsewhere that L 'spoke well when he had studied his speeches', and was 'a diffuse and majestic' orator (*Memoirs of King George II*, ed. J. Brooke (New Haven, 1985), i. 135–6, ii. 117).

For a version of L's speech supporting the motion to remove Walpole on 13 Feb. 1741, probably revised, if not written, by SJ himself, see *Gent. Mag.* (1743), 172–3; and for SJ's treatment of 'Lettyltno' in reports of the parliamentary debates in 'Lilliput' in *Gent. Mag.*, see Kaminski, 126, 136–7. L was excluded from the Secret Committee appointed by the Commons on 29 Mar. 1742 to investigate Walpole's conduct (Davis, *The Good Lord L*, 78 ff., 118–19).

6. Frederick, Prince of Wales, left St James's in Sept. 1737 (see 'Pope' **217** and n. above). As the Prince's equerry since 1734, L became an increasingly important political and literary adviser, and was appointed the Prince's secretary in Aug. 1737 with a salary of £866 p.a. (*Gent. Mag.* (1739), 309). Pope described him in 1738 as

'the Man, so near | His Prince, that writes in Verse, and has his Ear' (*Epilogue to the Satires*, I. 45–6).

For L's influence on the Prince's literary patronage, see 'Hammond' 3, 'Thomson' 28, 'Mallet' 12, and 'West' 8 above, and Gerrard, *Patriot Opposition, passim*. Thomson first mentioned L in 1735 (*Letters*, 95) and later praised him in *Spring* (1744 edn.), ll. 904–62, and *The Castle of Indolence* (1748), I. lxv–lxvi (referring to his 'Sense refin'd' and to 'his Mind, | As little touch'd as any man's with Bad'). L obtained a lucrative sinecure for Thomson in 1746, and edited his posthumous *Works* (1750): see 'Thomson' 26, 35, 39, 53 above. The financial figures were inserted in 1783 (see Textual Notes).

7. SJ describes *The Trial of Selim the Persian for Divers High Crimes and Misdemeanours* (1748) by Edward Moore (1712–57), poet, dramatist, and journalist, as 'apologetical' because it defended L against Horace Walpole's *Letters to the Whigs* (1747–8), and praised his *Observations on the Conversion of St. Paul* (see 12 below). SJ told Mrs Thrale, 1 May 1780, that he had met Moore 'about thirty years ago' (*Letters*, iii. 249). He had quoted Moore six times in the *Dict*.

In suggesting that L was a typically careless patron, SJ underestimates his various attempts to obtain preferment for Moore. In 1753 he helped to establish him as editor of *The World*, with Chesterfield, Walpole, Soame Jenyns, and others as contributors, but Moore took offence in 1754 when L appointed Archibald Bower (see 15 below) 'clerk of the buck-warrant' instead of himself: see J. H. Caskey, *The Life and Works of Edward Moore* (New Haven, 1927), 51–7, 64, 135–52, and Walpole, *Corresp.*, xxxv. 176.

SJ might have dwelt instead on L's association from the 1730s with Henry Fielding, who dedicated *Tom Jones* (1749) to him, and based his depiction of the 'truly benevolent' Squire Allworthy on L and Ralph Allen. See M. C. Battestin, *Henry Fielding: A Life* (1989), 453–6, 480–2.

8. SJ's vagueness about the date of Moore's *Selim* entails an abrupt return here from 1748 to *c*.1738.

From the mid-1730s the 'Patriots' had appealed to Pope to join the opposition to Walpole, and in 1738–9 he took particular interest in opposition drama: see 'Pope' 217–21, 'Thomson' 30 and n., and 'Mallet' 15 and n. above, and *Corresp.*, iv. 134, 138–9. Pope praised L as 'Still true to Virtue, and as warm as true' in *Imit. Horace, Ep. I. i.* (1738), ll. 29–30, and told him in Nov. 1738: 'I love Virtue, for I love You & such as you: Such are listed under her Banners, they fight for her; Poets are but like Heralds, they can only proclaim her, and the best you can make of me, is, that I am her poor Trumpeter' (*Corresp.*, iv. 142).

Henry Fox, later Lord Holland, denounced L's association with Pope in the House of Commons in 1740 (Phillimore, *Memoirs*, i. 115–16; Davis, *The Good Lord L*, 69; see also 'Pope' 219 above). By then Pope was becoming disillusioned with opposition politics, although as late as 7 Nov. 1741 L told him that 'some sparks of Publick Virtue are yet Alive, which such a Spirit as Your's might blow into a flame, among the Young men especially' (*Corresp.*, iv. 369: see also M. Mack, *Pope* (1985), 726–7, 755–7, 772; Goldgar, *Walpole*, chs. 4–6; and Gerrard, *Patriot Opposition*, ch. 4). Shortly before Pope's death, L told his father, 5 May 1744: 'besides the publick marks he has given me of his esteem, he has lately expressed the most tender friendship for me, both to myself and others' (*Works* (3rd edn., 1776), iii. 319).

Pope's will left to L the busts of English poets the Prince of Wales had given him (Spence, i. 25 n. and cf. 263).

In 1738 L supposedly brought SJ's anonymous *London* to Pope 'in a rapture', believing it, in one account, to be the work of Pope himself (Hawkins, *Life* (1787), 60; Boswell, *Making of the Life*, 105). SJ had praised L's 'vigorous opposition' and selfless devotion to the good of the nation in his *Compleat Vindication of the Licensers of the Stage* (1739) (*YW*, x. 57).

9. It was in fact on 15 June 1742 that L married Lucy Fortescue, daughter of Hugh Fortescue of Filleigh, Devon, and sister of Hugh Fortescue, Lord Clinton. For their son, the debauched Thomas (1744–79), who became a source of great anxiety to L, see **29** n. below and R. Blunt, *Thomas, Lord Lyttelton: The Portrait of a Rake* (1936). Walpole claimed that, before his marriage, L had himself been 'much attached to the sex', going 'to the tavern with a whore in his hand and an Horace in his pocket' (*Corresp.*, xv. 331).

For the brevity of human 'felicity', see also 'Denham' **19** and n. above. The death of L's wife on 19 Jan. 1747, soon after the birth of their second daughter, occasioned L's 'Inscription' in prose and verse for her monument (*Gent. Mag.* (1747), 338), and *To the Memory of a Lady Lately Deceased, A Monody* (1747). Thomson, who also wrote a poem on this occasion, stated: 'He has had the severest Tryal a humane tender Heart can have' (*Letters*, 197; *Liberty*, ed. J. Sambrook (Oxford, 1986), 313). Gray commented on the *Monody* to Walpole in Nov. 1747: 'Nature and sorrow, and tenderness, are the true genius of such things; and something of these I find in several parts of it'; and later that 'Parts of it are too stiff & poetical; but others truly tender & elegiac, as one would wish' (*Corresp.*, i. 288–9, 293). *Gent. Mag.* (1773), 414, claimed that L's *Monody* 'will be remembered whilst conjugal affection, and a taste for poetry, exist in this country'.

L's poem was parodied in *A Sorrowful Ditty; or, The Lady's Lamentation for the Death of her Favourite Cat* (1748), and by Smollett in *Peregrine Pickle* (1751), ch. 102 (later omitted). Gray told Walpole, 3 Mar. 1751, that Smollett's novel contained a character of L 'under the name of Gosling Scrag, and a parody of part of his Monody, under the notion of a pastoral on the death of his grandmother' (*Corresp.*, i. 344–5). Mr Spondy's grotesque elegy is followed by a long tirade questioning Gosling Scrag's literary reputation, and mocking his patronage of talentless scribblers. Shenstone, L's neighbour at The Leasowes, considered such parodies inevitable: 'He is, you know, engaged in a party; and his poem (though an extraordinary fine composition) was too tender for the public ear' (*Letters* (1939), 319). George Butt later defended L's *Monody*, along with *Lycidas* and Gray's odes, against SJ's condescension in *Poems* (2 vols., Kidderminster, 1793), i. 202–3 n.

10. On 10 July 1749 L married a friend of his first wife, Elizabeth Rich (*c*.1716–1795), daughter of Sir Robert Rich of Roos Hall, Suffolk, 'with 20,000 *l*.' (*Gent. Mag.* (1749), 331). This 'experiment was unsuccessful' in that by 1756 L suspected his wife of infidelity, and by 1759 had separated from her, 'on a general charge of misbehaviour, and an impossibility of my living with her either reputably or in quiet'. She received alimony and 'pin-money' of £800 p.a. (Wyndham, *Chronicles*, ii. 279–80; Davis, *The Good Lord L*, 248–56; Walpole, *Corresp.*, xxxviii. 14–15 and nn.). A late marginal note by Mrs Thrale-Piozzi commended SJ's restraint here: 'Very modestly said. Johnson would not suffer his personal dislike to operate upon

character in a work he meant to be lasting. Lady Lyttelton lived to a very great age' (Lobban, 162).

SJ's famous description of a second marriage as 'the triumph of hope over experience' concerned a case in which the first marriage had been unhappy. In 1769 he denied that a second marriage 'shewed a disregard' for the first wife, and showed, on the contrary, 'that she made him so happy as a married man, that he wishes to be so a second time'. On 15 Sept. 1777, however, he argued that we disapprove of a man who forgets the loss of a wife or a friend, 'not because he soon forgets his grief, for the sooner it is forgotten the better, but because we suppose, that ... he has not had much affection for them' (*Life*, ii. 76, 128, iii. 137, and cf. iv. 121). Walpole mischievously reported, 5 July 1749, a lady's comment on L's remarriage: 'When one loses a husband one loves, I don't know, there is such a void, such a space that wants to be filled up' (*Corresp.*, ix. 90–1).

11. Some chronological vagueness is again apparent: SJ had first referred to Walpole's resignation on 9 Feb. 1742 in 5 above. For evidence that L and other 'patriots' had in fact negotiated with Walpole before his fall, see Gerrard, *Patriot Opposition*, 44–5. L subsequently supported the Whig Pelhamite ministry and became a Lord of the Treasury 1744–54.

12. For L's deathbed account of these religious 'difficulties', see 27 below. The 'corrupt conversation' was no doubt that of his uncle, the sceptical Lord Cobham (see 'West' 7 and n. above). Walpole's view was that, 'when he had been forced to quit virtue' (by changing his political allegiance), L 'took up religion' (*Memoirs of George II* (1985), i. 136).

L wrote *Observations on the Conversion and Apostleship of St. Paul* (1747) after the death of his first wife, telling Thomson, 21 May 1747, that it concerned a subject 'which we have formerly talkt of', and had been written 'with a particular view to your satisfaction' (Thomson, *Letters*, 189). He addressed it to his cousin Gilbert West, whose own *Observations on the Resurrection* had appeared in Dec. 1746 (see 'West' 6 and n. above, and Davis, *The Good Lord L*, 148 ff.). Both works were often reprinted, sometimes together. Philip Doddridge's *Corresp.* (1979) lists twenty-five letters to and from L, who had 'so unfashionably become a Christian' (273).

The letter from L's father is in T. R. Nash, *History of Worcestershire*, i (1781), 501: Nichols probably drew it to SJ's attention before its official publication (see headnote above). For other proud parents of authors, see 'Pope' 161 and n. above.

13. On his father's death on 14 Sept. 1751 L inherited his title and the estate at Hagley, with an income of £4,000 p.a. (Wiggin, *Faction*, 159). Thomson had praised Hagley in prose in 1743 and in verse in 1744 (see 6 above, Thomson, *Letters*, 165–6, and Doddridge, *Corresp.*, 220). Serious 'improvements' began in 1747 and work on the new house was carried out in 1754–60. Walpole had described the old house in Sept. 1753 as 'immeasurably bad', but evoked 'the enchanting scenes of the park', which is 'a hill of three miles, but broke into all manner of beauty': 'I wore out my eyes with gazing, my feet with climbing, and my tongue and vocabulary with commending' (*Corresp.*, xxxv. 147–9). See also 'Shenstone' 11 above, Thomas Maurice's *Hagley. A Descriptive Poem* (Oxford, 1776), and Davis, *The Good Lord L*, 165–85.

SJ declined an invitation to Hagley in July 1771 from William Henry Lyttelton, later Lord Westcote (see headnote above, and *Letters*, i. 369 and n.), but visited it with Mrs Thrale in Sept. 1774, after L's death. Although he was impressed by Hagley itself, 'we were disappointed of the respect and kindness that we expected'. Memories of 'a place where all were offended' may have lingered in 1780 (*Life*, v. 456–7 and nn.; *Thraliana*, i. 114, 316; *YW*, i. 217–18).

14. L was Cofferer of the Royal Household Mar. 1754–Nov. 1755 at £2,200 p.a., and became a Privy Counsellor on 21 June 1754. Refusing to join Pitt in opposition to Newcastle's administration, L was Chancellor of the Exchequer Nov. 1755–Nov. 1756.

Walpole more than once mocked L's innumeracy in parliamentary debates: introducing the budget in Jan. 1756, he 'was strangely bewildered in the figures; he stumbled over millions, and dwelt pompously upon farthings', but replied spiritedly to an attack by Pitt (*Corresp.*, ix. 179, xxxvii. 432, 445).

15. Although L's 'Account of a Journey into Wales: In Two Letters to Mr. Bower' was dated '1756' in *Works* (1774), his original MSS are dated July 1755 (Davis, *The Good Lord L*, 180). L described his 'awful astonishment' at mountain scenery. For SJ's own response to the sublimity of Welsh mountains, see his journal of July 1774 (*Life*, v. 433–4).

Archibald Bower (1686–1766), a former Jesuit priest and professed Protestant convert, published a *History of the Popes* (7 vols., 1748–66). Thomas Birch told Lord Orrery, 20 Feb. 1748, that Bower's *History* 'has been encouraged by a very noble subscription, which he owes greatly to the recommendation of Mr. Littleton' (*The Orrery Papers* (1903), ii. 20). In a series of pamphlets (1756–8) SJ's friend Dr John Douglas (1721–1807) exposed Bower as an impostor who was still in correspondence with the Jesuits (Davis, *The Good Lord L*, 224–7; Walpole, *Corresp.*, xx. 531–4).

L, however, supported Bower's claim that the evidence produced against him was forged, and, according to Davies, *Memoirs of Garrick* (1780), i. 270–4, dissuaded Garrick from satirizing Bower on the stage. Chesterfield commented on 15 Jan. 1757: 'Though Archibald Bower, esq., has used a great deal of paper, he has not, in my opinion, wiped himself clean' (*Misc. Works* (1777), ii. 45). An 'Abstract of the Charge and Defence of Mr. *A. Bower*' in the *Literary Mag.* 1 (July 1756), 126–35, has been tentatively attributed to SJ (*Bibliography*, i. 689). See also *Gent. Mag.* (1757), 65–9, 117–21, and (1785), 177–8. Bower gave his own 'summary view' of the controversy in his *History*, vol. v (1761).

16. In the proofs the first sentence originally ended 'though they are the productions of a mind that means well, than that thinks vigorously' (see Textual Notes).

SJ defines 'Effusion' as '3. The act of pouring out words' (*Dict.*).

Dr Maxwell reported SJ's description of *Dialogues of the Dead* (1760) as 'a nugatory performance: "That man, (said he,) sat down to write a book, to tell the world what the world had all his life been telling him" ' (*Life*, ii. 126). In a scathing account of L's '*Dead* Dialogues', 24 May 1760, Walpole identified 'Penelope' in 'Dialogue V' as L's first wife and 'Pericles' in 'Dialogue XXIII' as Pitt (*Corresp.*, xxi. 407–9). Gray mentioned L's 'second-hand Dialogues' in June 1760 (*Corresp.*, ii. 676), and they were also criticized for containing little new in *Candid and Critical Remarks on the Dialogues of the Dead* (1760). For L's correspondence with Voltaire about the *Dialogues*, see *Gent. Mag.* (Feb. 1761), 54–5.

SJ refers to L's original assertion (later omitted) in *Dialogues*, 18, that Fénelon's *Dialogues des morts* (1712) 'are in general as superior to . . . Fontenelle's [1683], as

Reason is to False Wit, or Truth to Affectation'. For L's contribution to the sub-genre, see F. M. Keener, *English Dialogues of the Dead* (New York, 1973), 74–97. There are occasional similarities in the opinions of SJ and L, especially in 'Dialogue XIV' between Boileau and Pope: see notes to 'Cowley' **60–1**, 'Milton' **230**, 'Waller' **128**, 'Pope' **349**, and 'Thomson' **50, 53** above. The fact that Elizabeth Montagu wrote the last three of the *Dialogues* no doubt made her all the more sensitive about SJ's condescension to L, as he himself suspected (see headnote and **17** n. below).

17. L's *Dialogues* were praised in Smollett's *Critical Review*, 9 (May 1760), 390–3. As a Whig, L no doubt expected hostility from this Tory periodical (see *Life*, iii. 32), especially since Smollett had earlier satirized him in *Peregrine Pickle* (1751) (see **9** n. above and **19** n. below). Smollett later referred favourably to L's poetry in his *Continuation of the Complete History of England*, vol. iv (1761): see J. Basker, *Tobias Smollett Critic and Journalist* (Newark, Del., 1988), 215, and L. M. Knapp, *Tobias Smollett* (Princeton, 1949), 125–32.

SJ conceivably saw L's grateful letter in the early 1760s, when he himself occasionally contributed to the *Critical Review*. Boswell later defended the letter against SJ's remarks here (*Life*, iv. 57–8). SJ's only response to the outcry they aroused was to rephrase them more forcefully in 1783: see Textual Notes.

poor Lyttelton: Walpole noted, 3 Mar. 1781, that these were the original 'words of offence' which particularly pained L's admirers (*Corresp.*, xxix. 115). As William Weller Pepys told Mrs Montagu, 4 Aug. 1781: 'what hurts me all this while is, not that Johnson should go unpunished, but that our dear and respectable friend should... be handed down to succeeding generations under the appellation of poor Lyttelton' (*J. Misc.*, ii. 417; see also headnote).

SJ had in fact used 'poor' of other poets, as Mrs Thrale noted in Dec. 1784: 'Mrs Montagu and all *her little Senate*... censured him severely for his Treatment of Lyttelton: he used to tell me that it was only because he had not flatter'd *her* by any notice of her three Dialogues added to my Lord's [see **16** n. above]; but I long thought their Indignation genuine, as they pretended to rest their Cause on the contemptuous Expression Poor Lyttelton! reading over the Lives again however— I find him saying Poor Dryden! in one passage' (*Thraliana*, ii. 622). See 'Dryden' **40**, and, for other 'poor' poets, 'Prior' **51**, 'Gay' **15**, and 'Pope' **145** (of Lewis Theobald) above. For a reference to 'poor Shenstone' in 1774 and Gray's description of Shenstone as 'Poor man!', see 'Shenstone' **14** n. and **19** above; for 'poor Nahum Tate', 'Rowe' **21** above; for 'poor Collins', 'Collins' **8** n. above; and for 'My poor friend Smart' in conversation in 1763, *Life*, i. 397.

18. L was dropped from the Pitt–Newcastle administration when war broke out with France in 1756, and was 'indemnified with a peerage' on 18 Nov. 1756 (Walpole. *Corresp.*, xxi. 18). His later attempts to return to government in the 1760s were unsuccessful.

19. L had started work on his *History of Henry the Second* (4 vols., 1767–71) as early as 1741 (Pope, *Corresp.*, iv. 348–9), with the aim of illustrating opposition ideals of public virtue and patriotism: see Gerrard, *Patriot Opposition*, 82, 101. SJ discussed L's *History* with George III in Feb. 1767, telling the King that 'he thought his style pretty good, but that he had blamed Henry the Second rather too much' (*Life*, ii. 38). On 15 Apr. 1773 he described it more bluntly as 'the most vulgar Whiggism'

(*Life*, ii. 221). Hume also mentioned its 'Whiggery' and 'Piety' to Adam Smith, 14 July 1767 (*Letters*, ed. J. Y. T. Greig (Oxford, 1932), ii. 150).

Walpole often referred contemptuously to L's *History* in 1767–71: 'the poverty and vulgarism of his style', 'such a load of dull lumber', 'fustian and tedious', 'crowded with clouds of words and they are so uninteresting' (*Corresp.*, x. 248, xxxii. 30, 69, xxxv. 327). In public, he described it more circumspectly as lacking 'the vivacity that is admitted into modern history' (*Works* (1798), i. 540). Gibbon referred to it as 'that voluminous work, in which sense and learning are not illuminated by a ray of Genius' (*Memoirs*, ed. G. A. Bonnard (New York, 1966), 143).

SJ discussed L's 'extreme anxiety as an authour' on 10 Apr. 1776, when Murphy suggested that the *History* had been 'kept back several years for fear of Smollet' (*Life*, iii. 32–3; and cf. **17** n. above). For objections (by Duncombe and/or Nichols) in *Gent. Mag.* (1781), 275, to SJ's comment on L's 'vanity', see **20** n. below. Walpole also discussed L's 'timidity' as an author on 3 Sept. 1773: his 'dread of present and future critics ... made his works so insipid that he had better not have written them at all'. Walpole added drily: 'His son does not seem to have equal apprehension of the world's censure' (*Corresp.*, xxviii. 104): see **9** n. above and **29** n. below.

20. When L told Walpole, 30 Sept. 1754, that he expected the *History* to go to press in 1755, he was already 'cautious not to let it come out uncorrect, or without all the perfection that I can give to it' (Walpole, *Corresp.*, xl. 81). Printing started and continued while he was still writing the *History*, which began appearing in 1767 (not 1764). Writing to Joseph Warton, 7 Sept. 1767, to thank him for praising the *History*, L was already referring to corrections to be made in a new edition: see J. Wooll, *Biographical Memoirs of ... Joseph Warton* (1806), 323–4. The 1st and 2nd editions (both 4 vols., 1767–71) were followed by a 3rd (6 vols., 1769–73).

The proofs reveal that SJ originally wrote a single paragraph about the printing of L's *History*, which he later expanded into **19–22** (see Textual Notes). The main source of his new information was John Nichols, who had been William Bowyer's apprentice while the *History* was in the press, and who later recalled: 'I have frequently attended the good Peer with proof-sheets; and was charmed with the condescending manner in which I was uniformly received by him' (*Lit. Anec.*, vi. 464). As H. Kirkley noted in *RES* 49 (1998), 297–8, when Nichols reprinted a version of SJ's account of L in 1812, he quietly but significantly revised the statement that L's 'ambitious accuracy is known to have cost ...' to 'ambitious accuracy, to my knowledge, cost ...' (*Lit. Anec.*, vi. 464).

This explains why Nichols felt entitled to reprint SJ's 'Lyttelton' in his *Anecdotes of Bowyer* (1782), where he repeated the *Gent. Mag.*'s objection (see **19** n. above) to SJ's attribution of L's 'anxiety' to 'vanity', rather than 'his desire to correct mistakes, his fear of having been too harsh on *Becket*, etc. We ... sincerely wish that in this and some other passages Dr. *Johnson* ... had observed his own humane maxim ... of not giving "a pang to a daughter, a brother, or a friend" ' (see 'Addison' **98** above). Nichols also quoted, however, a letter from L to Bowyer, which illustrates his obsessive concern with the legibility of his MS and the printing of his book, and added another note about L's difficulty in paying for the paper required for the *History* (*Anecdotes of Bowyer* (1782), 426–7 n.; *Lit. Anec.*, vi. 462–5). *Gent. Mag.* (1778), 225 n., had earlier reported that L cancelled all the leaves of the *History* in which he had used 'co-' rather than 'con-' (as in e.g. 'cotemporary'). For another obsessive corrector of the press, see 'Savage' 127 above.

21. Andrew Reid (d. 1767?) edited *The Present State of the Republick of Letters* (1728–36). SJ no doubt referred to Reid or to Sanders (see 22 below) when stating in Apr. 1776 that L 'was thirty years in preparing his History, and that he employed a man to point it for him; as if (laughing) another man could point his sense better than himself' (*Life*, iii. 32). Many authors at this period in fact relied on printers and others to punctuate their writings. According to John Wilkes in 1767, L received £3,000 for his *History* (*Corresp.* (1805), iii. 150).

'Pointer' in the sense of 'punctuator' is not in the *Dict.*

For the benevolence of another poet SJ disliked, see 'Gray' 25 and n. above.

22. For Reid's death in about 1767 and the *History* (3rd edn., 4 vols., 1769–73), see 20–1 and nn. above. In 1781 SJ identified the 'Doctor' as 'Dr. Saunders', but his name was omitted in 1783 (see Textual Notes). A remarkable errata list, no doubt compiled by Sanders, of 'False Stops which hurt the Sense', with other sub-categories of detailed corrections, was appended to the *History*, vi (3rd edn., 1773), 481–99, 505–8.

For an account of Robert Sanders (1727–83) by Henry Lemoine, a letter by Sanders himself of 20 Dec. 1768 complaining of his financial problems while working for L, and L's reaction in a letter to John Duncombe in 1768, see *Gent. Mag.* (1783), 311–13, 482, and Nichols, *Lit. Anec.*, ii. 371–2. For a time Sanders seems to have acted as L's secretary, replying on his behalf to a presentation copy of Boswell's *Account of Corsica* (1768) (*Catalogue*, C 2428). Nichols described him in *Anecdotes of Bowyer* (1782), 427 n., as 'a *Scotch* LL.D.'.

Commenting on L's obsession with punctuation, 'Kastril' in *Gent. Mag.* (Nov. 1781), 516, added that L omitted from his *History* 'a curious anecdote reflecting on the character of the Empress Matilda, because he thought it ungenerous to take away the character of a woman; had the Doctor known this . . . Lyttelton had surely felt the most poignant edge of his ridicule'.

23. By comparison with contemporary accounts, SJ's remarks on L's physique are restrained. Lord Hervey described him in the 1730s as 'extremely tall and thin. His face was so ugly, his person so ill made and his carriage so awkward, that every feature was a blemish, every limb an encumbrance, and every motion a disgrace' (*Memoirs* (1931 edn.), 850–1). *A Faithful Narrative of . . . Habbakuk Hilding* (1752), possibly by Smollett, depicted him as 'a long, lean, lank, misshapen Spectre, with an awkward, shambling Goose-like Gait' (see Davis, *The Good Lord L*, 221–2; L. M. Knapp, *Tobias Smollett* (Princeton, 1949), 131–2). Walpole said that L had 'the figure of a spectre, and the gesticulations of a puppet' (*Memoirs of King George II*, ed. J. Brooke (New Haven, 1985), i. 135–6). For a caricature of L entitled *The Motion* (21 Feb. 1741), see *Life*, v. 285 n., and, for other descriptions, Chesterfield's letter of 22 Sept. 1749, in *Letters*, iv. 1402–3 and n., and Charles Churchill, *Independence* (1764), ll. 117–46.

uncompacted: not in the *Dict.*, but SJ defines 'Uncompact' as 'Not compact; not closely cohering'.

SJ told the Revd John Hussey that L was a 'worthy, good man, but so ungracious that he did not know how to be a Gentleman' (*J. Misc.*, i. 257 n.). Discussing his recent quarrel with SJ, William Weller Pepys told Elizabeth Montagu, 4 Aug. 1781, that SJ 'took great credit for not having mentioned the *coarseness of Lord Lyttelton's manners*' (*J. Misc.*, ii. 417). According to Hawkins, SJ 'assured a friend . . . that he kept back a very ridiculous anecdote of [L], relative to a question he put to a great divine of his time' (*J's Works* (1787), xi. 198). William Seward also mentioned a story suppressed by SJ, 'which would have made his memory ridiculous', in *European Mag.* 34 (Dec. 1798), 376. Walpole wrote: 'No man so addicted to wisdom was less wise than Lord Lyttelton; no man so propense to art was less artful; no man staked his honesty to less purpose, for he was so awkward that honesty was the only quality that seemed natural to him' (*Corresp.*, xxviii. 41 n., and see also xv. 330–1).

For the 'very ordinary bedchamber . . . his constant one' in which L died, see Nichols, *Anecdotes of Bowyer* (1782), 597.

'Scrutator' (John Loveday) in *Gent. Mag.* (1781), 421, identified L's physician as Dr James Johnstone of Kidderminster, and noted that his letter of 28 Aug. 1773, printed in *Gent. Mag.* (1773), 604, was addressed to Elizabeth Montagu. (For the original MS, see Davis, *The Good Lord L*, 387–8.) SJ would no doubt have learned this for himself had he consulted Mrs Montagu about L. As it is, his professed relief at being spared 'the task of his moral character' would strike L's friends and admirers as double-edged.

24. *Sunday evening*: *Gent. Mag.* (1773) reads 'Sunday morning'.

25. *hepatic*: 'Belonging to the liver' (*Dict.*).

27. For L's early religious doubts, fostered by Lord Cobham, see 12 and n. above. With L's claim that 'I have endeavoured . . . to do all the good in my power', cf. SJ's own deathbed injunction to Charles Burney: 'Do all the good you can' (R. Lonsdale, *Dr. Charles Burney* (Oxford, 1965), 287).

29. L's daughter Lucy (1743–83) had married in 1767 Arthur Annesley, Vis. Valentia, who deserted her in 1774 (Walpole, *Corresp.*, xxxv. 422–3).

Although Johnstone and the monument at Hagley (see 30 below) state that L died on 22 Aug. 1773, the date of 24 Aug. on the tablet in Hagley Church is more likely (Davis, *The Good Lord L*, 387).

SJ was in Scotland when he learned of L's death, and immediately 'suspected that it had been hastened by the vexation which his son has given him' (*Letters*, ii. 112). For the rakish Thomas, Lord Lyttelton, who died on 27 Nov. 1779, see also headnote and 9 and n. above. Reviewing his posthumous *Poems by a Young Nobleman* in *Monthly Review*, 62 (Feb. 1780), 128–31, Cartwright described him as 'enslaved by vice, and enfeebled . . . by low and sordid enjoyments', and his poetry as 'poor, contemptible, and vulgar'. Walpole later wrote that he was 'a meteor, whose rapid extinction could not be regretted. His dazzling eloquence had no solidity, and his poetry no graces that could atone for its indelicacy' (*Works* (1798), i. 540).

In Oxford on 12 June 1784, six months before his own death, SJ discussed 'Thomas Lord Lyttelton's vision, the prediction of the time of his death, and its exact fulfilment', which he considered 'the most extraordinary thing that has happened in my day. I heard it with my own ears, from his uncle, Lord Westcote. I am so glad to have every evidence of the spiritual world, that I am willing to believe it.' When Dr Adams told him that 'You have evidence enough; good evidence, which needs not such support', SJ replied: 'I like to have more' (*Life*, iv. 298–9). For 'preternatural intelligence', see also 'Roscommon' 5–7 and nn. above.

30. SJ saw the Lyttelton monuments at Hagley in Sept. 1774 (see 13 n. above). For the date of L's death, see 29 n. above.

31. For *The Progress of Love* (1732) and *Bleinheim* (1728), see 2–3 and nn. above, and for SJ's dislike of modern pastoral and blank verse, 'Cowley' 7 and n. and 'Milton' 274 and n. above.

L's 'epistolary pieces' include *An Epistle to Mr. Pope, from a Young Gentleman at Rome* (1730), and poems to Dr Francis Ayscough, his Oxford tutor (1728), Stephen Poyntz (1728), and Lord Hervey (1730). For 'equability', see 'Cowley' 200 and n. above.

SJ finally discovers at least vestiges of the 'elegance' and 'vigour', which are his minimal demand from poetry, in *Advice to a Lady* (1733), in which L in fact complacently recommended modesty and submission to young women ('Make it your pride his *servant* to appear'). In June 1777 Hester Thrale noted that SJ had praised some of her verses as 'very pretty, & much in Lord Lyttelton's Style. a good one says he—for a *Lady*' (*Thraliana*, i. 550).

In contrast to SJ's condescension, Vicesimus Knox proved a model of polite tact in assessing L's verse in his *Essays* (new edn., 1782), ii. 379: 'Force, fire, and an exuberance of invention, were not his excellence; but that equable beauty of sentiment and diction, which results from an elegant mind. The graces distinguish his compositions, as the virtues marked his honourable life.' In private, 25 June 1782, Horace Walpole described L as 'another sing-song warbler' (*Corresp.*, xxix. 255). In public, he stated that L's poetry 'was more elegant than striking. Originality seems never to have been his aim' (*Works* (1798), i. 539–40). Warton, *Works of Pope* (1797), i. 34 n., believed that SJ had underestimated L's verse.

Twenty-one poems by L had opened Robert Dodsley's *Collection of Poems* (1748), vol. ii, and twelve more were added to the 2nd edition later in 1748. L had considerable influence on this popular miscellany, as Dodsley told Shenstone, 10 Nov. 1753: 'Most of those [poems] which compose the three first Volumes, were shewn to Sir George before they were inserted': see Dodsley, *Corresp.*, 162 and n., and *Collection of Poems*, ed. M. Suarez, SJ (1997), i. 178–80, ii. 1–86.

APPENDIX A
SEQUENCES OF JOHNSON'S POETS

Lives (1781–3) (4 vols.)			*Eng. Poets* (1779) (56 vols.)		*Prefaces* (1779–81) (10 vols.)	
1	Cowley	(i)	1 (i–ii)		1 (i)	
2	Denham	"	5 (ix)		6 (iv)	
3	Milton	"	2 (iii–v)		3 (ii)	
4	Butler	"	3 (vi–vii)		4 (ii)	
5	Rochester	"	7 (x)		9 (iv)	
6	Roscommon	"	8 (x)		8 (iv)	
7	Otway	"	10 (xi)		11 (iv)	
8	Waller	"	4 (viii)		2 (i)	
9	Pomfret	"	21 (xxi)		21 (iv)	
10	Dorset	"	12 (xi)		13 (iv)	
11	Stepney	"	14 (xii)		15 (iv)	
12	J. Philips	"	19 (xxi)		19 (iv)	
13	Walsh	"	15 (xii)		16 (iv)	
14	Dryden	(ii)	16 (xiii–xix)		5 (iii)	
15	Smith	"	20 (xxi)		20 (iv)	
16	Duke	"	11 (xi)		12 (iv)	
17	King	"	18 (xx)		18 (iv)	
18	Sprat	"	6 (ix)		7 (iv)	
19	Halifax	"	13 (xii)		14 (iv)	
20	Parnell	"	37 (xliv)		37 (viii)	
21	Garth	"	17 (xx)		17 (iv)	
22	Rowe	"	27 (xxvi–xxviii)		27 (vi)	
23	Addison	"	23 (xxiii)		23 (v)	
24	Hughes	"	22 (xxii)		22 (iv)	
25	Sheffield	"	25 (xxv)		25 (v)	
26	Prior	(iii)	31 (xxx–xxxi)		31 (vi)	
27	Congreve	"	29 (xxix)		29 (vi)	
28	Blackmore	"	24 (xxiv)		24 (v)	
29	Fenton	"	30 (xxix)		30 (vi)	
30	Gay	"	34 (xli–xlii)		34 (viii)	
31	Granville	"	26 (xxv)		26 (vi)	
32	Yalden	"	9 (x)		10 (iv)	
33	Tickell	"	28 (xxviii)		28 (vi)	
34	Hammond	"	43 (xlix)		43 (ix)	
35	Somervile	"	41 (xlvii)		41 (ix)	
36	Savage	"	39 (xlv)		40 (ix)	
37	Swift	"	33 (xxxix–xl)		33 (viii)	
38	Broome	"	35 (xliii)		35 (viii)	

39	Pope	(iv)	32 (xxxii–xxxviii)	32 (vii)
40	Pitt	"	36 (xliii)	36 (viii)
41	Thomson	"	42 (xlviii–xlix)	42 (ix)
42	Watts	"	40 (xlvi)	39 (viii)
43	A. Philips	"	38 (xliv)	38 (viii)
44	West	"	51 (lvi)	51 (x)
45	Collins	"	44 (xlix)	44 (ix)
46	Dyer	"	46 (liii)	46 (x)
47	Shenstone	"	48 (liv)	48 (x)
48	Young	"	45 (l–lii)	45 (x)
49	Mallet	"	47 (liii)	47 (x)
50	Akenside	"	49 (lv)	49 (x)
51	Gray	"	52 (lvi)	52 (x)
52	Lyttelton	"	50 (lvi)	50 (x)

APPENDIX B
SOME EARLY PERIODICAL REACTIONS
1779–1783

[For responses to, and excerpts from, the *Prefaces* and *Lives* in newspapers, see also Helen L. McGuffie, *SJ in the British Press, 1749–1784: A Chronological Checklist* (New York, 1976), 231 ff.]

London Review, 9 (Apr. 1779), 257–67, reviewing *Eng. Poets* and *Prefaces*, listed in both 'Table of Contents' (p. v) and 'Index' (476) as '*Johnson's* English Poets' [by William Kenrick?]:

Some have objected that the *Prefaces* should have been prefixed to the works of the individual poets. This method was avoided 'from motives of convenience', and the proprietors may find it has one particular advantage: 'For as the preface-writer has let slip no opportunity of venting his spleen against characters, celebrated for the love of political and religious liberty [e.g. Hampden in 'Waller' 1], there may be found purchasers who would chuse to have the poets alone, without these *Tory* prefaces' (258 n.). The *Eng. Poets* are 'neatly enough executed, though unequal in point of correctness; the heads are, for the most part, also, good enough for publication':

As to the prefaces, the well-known biographical abilities of the writer have probably excited expectations in the public, which will be very imperfectly gratified. Cobbled up, as a bookseller's job, with that slow haste peculiar to the author, their composition does him little credit, although many judicious, and some splendid thoughts are to be found interspersed among the matters of fact and hearsay, that make up these bits of biographical manufactory. Of the stile it is almost needless to say they are written in that sententious, elaborate, and unidiomatical way, from which the writer is too great a mannerist to be able to depart. A phraseology, pompous even to dulness, and latinized in all its forms, is but ill-calculated for the light and familiar narrative of biography, or even for the purposes of critical observations. (258)

'Milton' **221–52** is quoted without comment. SJ has traced Dryden's character with 'a masterly hand', and **159–73** is quoted, as well as the letter in **406**: 'Who would have thought that Dryden the poet was a calculator of nativities?' The reviewer takes leave of the work 'for the present'.

[The review was not in fact continued. It may have been a parting shot from SJ's old enemy William Kenrick, founder of the *London Review*, who died three months later, on 10 June 1779 (*Gent. Mag.* 327). For his attacks on SJ's edition of Shakespeare in the 1760s, see *Life*, i. 497–8, and J. B. Kramnick, *Making the English Canon 1700–1770* (Cambridge, 1998), 210–27.]

Westminster Mag. 7 (May 1779), 265:

The article concerns only the *Prefaces* and, in detail, only 'Milton': 'The Editor needed not here to have set his *name* to this Work—his *mark* had been sufficient; for the stile and diction of *Lexiphanes* is obvious throughout.' A note contrasts quotations from 'Milton' with 'the unaffected stile and manner in which Mr. Addison had made the same observations long before him'. SJ's criticism of Milton for 'not conforming to the established ritual' (**166–7**) 'betrays a narrow and illiberal mind'.

Critical Review, 47 (May 1779), 354–62, reviewing *Eng. Poets* and *Prefaces*:

This is a project of national importance: 'As the general character of every polished nation depends in a great measure on its poetical productions, too much care cannot be taken, in works of this nature, to impress on foreigners a proper idea of their merit. This task was perhaps never so well executed as in the performance before us.' The reviewer praises *Eng. Poets*, though the type is rather small 'for eyes turned of fifty'. The *Prefaces* should have been prefixed to the poets' works and printed in the same type. The booksellers will no doubt explain their decision to do otherwise 'in due time'.

Without offering much new information, SJ 'has proved, indeed, that a man of genius, penetration, and sagacity, can always, even from old and worn-out materials, strike out something new and entertaining'. There is little of SJ's 'pompous phraseology'. While biographers of poets usually become panegyrical, SJ may err on the other side, as when dealing with the politics of Milton and Waller, but both lives are quoted approvingly. SJ quotes too much from Cowley.

Critical Review, 47 (June 1779), 450–3 (cont.):

'Dryden' is just and impartial: 'Any man who writes the life of another may settle dates, and relate facts; but every man cannot, like this entertaining biographer, draw out from little circumstances such remarks as these on men and manners.' On the other hand, we 'almost wonder' how Sprat, Yalden, King, and Stepney 'found a place in this collection': they 'are not poets of sufficient note or estimation to deserve the pen of a Johnson to transmit their lives to posterity'. Oldisworth's account of Edmund Smith ('Smith' 3–**26**) is 'a very dull ill-written encomium'. SJ is now at work on lives of Pope, Prior, and other poets, 'which will probably make their appearance in some part of the ensuing winter'.

Gentleman's Mag. (June 1779), 312–13, reviewing *Eng. Poets* and *Prefaces* [by John Duncombe?]:

From such a critic and biographer as Dr. Johnson, much on this occasion has been expected by the public, and, we may add, their expectations will not disappointed. He has the art of working up old materials so as to make them appear new; and, though he cannot give us much new information as an historian, that deficiency is compensated by his sagacity as a moralist and critic.

The reviewer questions SJ's definition of wit as a blend of the 'natural and new' ('Cowley' **55**), since it apparently equates Euclid and Cowley [echoing Addison in *Spectator* 62 on Dryden's earlier equation of 'wit' and 'propriety']. The account of Cowley's *The Mistress* (**123**) is quoted. SJ's reference to Hampden as 'the zealot of rebellion' reveals the 'zeal of his party' ('Waller' 1). His argument about sacred poetry in 'Waller' **135–42** is 'solid'.

Gentleman's Mag. (July 1779), 362–4, review of *Dr. Johnson's Lives of the English Poets* (cont.):

'Milton, as a republican, cannot expect much quarter from his present biographer.' Passages on Milton as a schoolmaster (**36**) and his falling on 'evil days' after 1660 (**134**) are quoted. 'In the examination of Milton's poetical works, whatever censure has been provoked by the impudence or insolence of the republican, due praise is bestowed on the scholar and the poet.' SJ's main points, including his reservations about 'Lycidas' (180–4), are summarized. He does full justice to *Paradise Lost*.

SJ explains Butler's beauties and faults 'with great precision'. Dryden 'is everywhere mentioned with becoming reverence', but SJ might have spared the 'illiberal abuse of Settle, now obsolete, and ever disgusting' (34–41). Dryden's 'perversion to popery is ingeniously extenuated' (118–20). The reviewer objects to the hearsay evidence about Dryden's funeral (153), which SJ's own 'Advertisement' (here placed in vol. ii) now admits is false. SJ draws Dryden's character 'with the hand of a master' (159–92). The reviewer contributes two further anecdotes about Dryden and Tonson. SJ does 'ample justice' to Dryden's prose as well as his poetry: 'on this article, if on any, [he] writes *con amore*'.

Gentleman's Mag. (Sept. 1779), 453–7, on *Dr. Johnson's Lives of the English Poets* (cont.):

The reviewer quotes and adds to SJ's anecdote in 'Sprat' 18 about humming during sermons. Since 'Smith' is the most 'original' of the lives, virtually the whole of SJ's part in it (28–76) is quoted: 'the conclusion in particular, in which the author comes home to himself and his friends, must be admired by all who have taste and sensibility.'

A small grammatical error ('both' used of three) in 'Hughes' 10 is noted. 'Dryden perhaps excepted, Dr. Johnson cannot be charged with bestowing, in any instance, more praise than is due', and on John Hughes has bestowed much less. SJ has 'unfairly quoted' dismissive references to Hughes by Pope and Swift (19–21), while ignoring evidence of Pope's good opinion of him elsewhere, e.g. in *Letters, By Several Eminent Persons Deceased* (1772–3) [edited by John Duncombe, the presumed reviewer, who was Hughes's nephew].

The reviewer mentions SJ's anecdotes about [Reynolds] and Jonathan Richardson in 'Cowley' 3, and about his own father as 'an ancient bookseller' ('Dryden' 109; Cf. 'Sprat' 19). He is pleased to report that the later lives 'are actually preparing for the press'.

Monthly Review, 61 (July 1779), 1–10, review of *Eng. Poets* and *Prefaces* [by Edmund Cartwright]:

[Edmund Cartwright (1743–1823), identified by Ralph Griffiths, the editor, in his copy (Bodleian Library), published *Armine and Elvira, A Legendary Poem* (1772), *The Prince of Peace and Other Poems* (1779), *Sonnets to Eminent Men* (1783), and other works. He later invented a woolcombing machine widely used in Yorkshire mills. His elder brother John Cartwright (1740–1824) was a prominent political reformer.]

This 'long-expected beautiful edition' does not disappoint: 'We must ingenuously confess, that, from the first of its being advertised, we considered Dr. Johnson's *name* merely as a lure which the proprietors of the work had obtained, to draw in the unwary purchaser.' His original plan of giving each poet only a short 'advertisement' would 'have conferred not much reputation upon the Writer, nor have communicated much information to his readers'. As it is, 'In the walk of biography and criticism, Dr. Johnson has long been without a rival. It is barely justice to acknowledge that he still maintains his superiority. The present work is no way inferior to the best of his very celebrated productions of the same class.'

'In the narrative of Cowley's life there is little, except the manner in which it is told, that is new', but 'the review of his poetry . . . abounds in original criticism'. SJ's account of 'Metaphysical' poetry is quoted at length ('Cowley' 50 ff.) In view of Cowley's praise of Crashaw, his omission from *Eng. Poets* is regrettable. Cartwright quotes SJ's attack on 'Pindarism' (142–4), but regrets his failure to comment on 'the present affectation of dividing the English Ode into Strophe, Antistrophe, and Epode' on Gray's precedent: 'no authority can sanctify absurdity ... what both common sense and reason are compelled to disapprove.' He quotes SJ's discussion of Cowley's *Davideis* (145–70), while noting that he and [Hurd] both ignore David's beautiful ode to Michal (quoted), and the preceding 130 lines about Merab and Michal. For more on Cowley's 'poetical merit', Cartwright refers to [Langhorne's] article in *Monthly Review*, 48 (1773), 10–18, on Hurd's edition of Cowley's *Select Works* (1772). SJ's final assessment of Cowley (202) shows 'no marks of partiality'.

In 'Waller',

The moral and political character of this applauded writer are developed with great skill and acuteness. Ever attentive to the more important interests of mankind, and sensible that biography ought to be a lesson of virtue, Dr. Johnson never omits to intersperse, amongst the different parts of his narration, either maxims of prudence or reflexions on the conduct of human life: something that may either direct the judgment or meliorate the heart.

SJ does, however, make the lives of Waller and his contemporaries 'the vehicles of his political orthodoxy. As we profess the principles of universal toleration, we shall leave his political opinions to themselves ... There will never want combatants to attack a man of Dr. Johnson's reputation, when the attack is to be made on a vulnerable part.' SJ's discussion of 'sacred poetry' (135–42) accounts 'very properly' for Waller's failure, and his comments on Fenton's remarks on 'intellectual decay' (132) are approved. SJ himself betrays 'no abatement of intellectual abilities: his imagination still retains the full vigour of youth'. 'Waller' 150, 153 are quoted.

Monthly Review, 61 (Aug. 1779), 81–92 [by Cartwright] (cont.):

Milton's public career 'will ever subject him to the misrepresentations of partiality or prejudice', from which SJ himself is 'not totally free'. Cartwright notes the disparity between SJ's comment on Christopher Milton's 'compliance' under James II ('Milton' 4) and Fenton's earlier account, implying that SJ is indulgent only because 'he adhered, as the law taught him, to King Charles's party'. The 'construction' placed by SJ on Milton's alleged 'corporal correction' at Cambridge is noted (11), as is his unnecessary 'merriment' at the dwindling of Milton's concern for 'liberty' into schoolteaching (36). Cartwright quotes SJ's account of Milton's scheme of education (37–41), while doubting that the 'poets, orators, and historians ... commonly read at schools' in fact teach prudence and moral principles. Socratic 'methods of instruction' differ as much from those SJ defends as from Milton's. The educational innovators SJ opposes had only the 'rational idea of uniting the study of nature with the knowledge of life'.

Cartwright replies at length to SJ on 'the liberty of the press' (58), defending 'the liberty which every one enjoys of diffusing his own opinions'. He is unconvinced by SJ's 'illiberal and indecent' account of Milton's 'atrocious villainy' over *Eikon Basilike* (64–5). Milton appears to have been most culpable in his adulation of Cromwell. On the influence of the seasons on the soul (118–22), Cartwright suggests that Milton's problem may have been gout, which usually abates in the spring. He commends SJ's discussion of the 'slow' sale of *Paradise Lost* (135), and his evocation in 138 of Milton calmly awaiting his future fame: 'an image more exquisitely pleasing can hardly be presented to the mind!' The discussion of Milton's religion (165–7) is 'justly founded'. Whatever its temperamental basis, Milton had better reasons for his republicanism than the frugality of a popular government (**168–9**): an extravagant court *can* injure the nation.

SJ 'seems to have no great partiality for Milton as a man: as a poet, however, he is willing to allow him every merit he is entitled to'. On the subject of Latin poetry (**176**), Cartwright praises Gray's noble ode on the 'Grand Chartreuse'. He quotes 'Milton' **177–9** without objection. On 'Lycidas' (**180–4**) SJ's 'censures are severe, and well enforced', and the dramatic deficiencies of *Comus* are 'unfolded in a masterly manner' (**196–201**). SJ's objections to Milton's sonnets, and to English sonnets in general (**206**), are summarized. There are in fact 'beautiful examples' even of the 'legitimate' sonnet, such as 'Mr. [Thomas] Warton's'. Cartwright does not agree that the sonnet is 'ill adapted to the English language': 'By uniting the elegance and dignity of the ode with the simplicity and conciseness of the ancient epigram, it seems to be a species of composition well suited to convey effusions of tenderness and affection.' Noting that SJ devotes some fifty pages to the 'immortal' *Paradise Lost*, Cartwright quotes **229–33**:

Of this truly excellent analysis and criticism, it is scarcely hyperbolical to affirm that it is executed with all the skill and penetration of Aristotle, and animated and embellished with all the fire of Longinus. It is every way worthy of its subject: the Paradise Lost is a poem which the mind of Milton only could have produced; the criticism before us is such as, perhaps, the pen of Johnson only could have written.

Monthly Review, 61 (Sept. 1779), 186–91 [by Cartwright] (cont.):

The life of Dryden is traced with 'great minuteness', with interesting anecdotes of 'much of the literary history of his time'. Cartwright praises 'the diligence' and 'the abilities' of his 'learned *Reviewer*' (186), and quotes **214–16** on Dryden's neglected prose, **216–22** on the 'new versification', and Dryden's appended letter (**406**).

Cartwright is, however, sceptical about the '*mob of Gentlemen*' in *Prefaces*, vol. iv:

if Denham (their leader) and a few others, be excepted, it may admit of a question how they came intitled to such a respectable situation. That it may not, however, be attributed to the partiality of the *ostensible* Editor, let him speak for himself.

He then illustrates SJ's low opinion of Sprat, Otway, Duke, Halifax, Stepney, and Hughes. Some explanation should have been given for the inclusion of 'men of such slender pretensions', when such poets as Sedley, Marvell, and 'the immortal Spenser' are omitted. 'Butler', accidentally overlooked earlier, provides a 'faithful exhibition of genius struggling with penury and dependence' and **22, 42, 45–6**, and the 'conclusive' **52** are quoted.

Town and Country Mag. 11 (Aug. 1779), 437, reviewing *Eng. Poets* and *Prefaces*:

SJ's name is 'sufficient to give a sanction to any work: that before us has a considerable degree of merit, and plainly evinces, that this gentleman still retains his mental abilities in their greatest perfection', a claim briefly illustrated from the character of Dryden. 'Dr. Johnson is now engaged in writing the lives of Pope and Prior, and many others, which will complete this extensive work.'

Gentleman's Mag. (Oct. 1779):

(1) 492–3: 'J. Boerhadem' deplores SJ's 'stooping to throw the dirt of party' in 'several ill-natured misrepresentations' in 'Milton', especially the claim that he omitted all family prayer (**166–7**), a distortion of statements by Toland and Newton.

(2) 493: a letter from 'Verax' (reprinted from the *St James's Chronicle*, 4 Sept. 1779) notes that the statute permitting corporal punishment of Oxford students under the age of 16, though never enforced, remains unrepealed, and that an earlier correspondent had suggested Thomas Warton's *Life of Bathurst* as SJ's source for 'this dainty biographical morsel' in 'Milton' 11.

(3) 493: A correspondent adds an anecdote about Dryden to those sent earlier.

Gentleman's Mag. (Oct. 1779), 505–7, review of *Eng. Poets* [by John Duncombe?]:

[This, the only serious review of *Eng. Poets*, is largely concerned with the additions made to the works of individual poets through the 'laudable industry of the super-intendant of the press', i.e. John Nichols, who no doubt helped the reviewer with some of the specific detail. Here, at least, it is made clear that SJ had not supervised the edition. Only points relevant to SJ or his biographies are noted below.]

The *Mag.* has so far concentrated on the *Prefaces*: 'though we found much to admire and commend, we have not scrupled to point out the small blemishes observed in those elegant productions of the great luminary of literature.' The reviewer adds that our expectations will increase as SJ approaches his contemporaries, and looks forward eagerly to his accounts of Prior, Pope, Dyer, and Somervile in particular.

Eng. Poets is 'in general correctly printed' and 'very elegant', and its 'decided superiority' [i.e. to Bell's *Poets of Great Britain*] is emphasized. Over the text of Milton 'uncommon pains' have been taken, even if *Of Education* is surprisingly omitted; Rochester's verse has been pruned by 'the judicious hand of Dr. Johnson'; Thomas Yalden, now first collected, has 'abundant merit'; Richard Duke 'deserves a place in a volume of the minor poets'; the absence of notes on Dryden's verse is regretted; William King, 'that genuine son of harmless raillery, appears in a very conspicuous light'; SJ's anecdote about Atterbury's inscription for John Philips ('J. Philips' 8) is apparently new.

Gentleman's Mag. (Nov. 1779), 549–52, review of *Eng. Poets* [by John Duncombe?] (cont.):

Some of Edmund Smith's university verses might still be discovered in Oxford (two examples were in fact to appear in Nichols's *Select Collection*); Swift's dismissive comments on Pomfret are quoted; new poems by John Hughes (probably passed to Nichols by Duncombe, Hughes's nephew) are listed; the earlier complaint about the absence of notes is renewed, with the suggestion that 'some intelligent writer' should 'add a volume of annotations'; SJ's complaint about the *Biographia Britannica's* ignorance about Hughes's schoolmaster ('Hughes' 1) is noted, and relevant information cited from [Duncombe's own] *Letters, By Several Eminent Persons Deceased*; although SJ's attitude to Hughes has been explained as hostility to a 'staunch Whig', his early affection for the Whig Gilbert Walmesley is noted ('Smith' 73); a new edition of Addison's works is needed; the reviewer was 'astonished' to learn of Blackmore's inclusion in *Eng. Poets*, but this is confined to his 'admirable' *Creation*; the Pope volumes, which include the poet's own 'variations', are well edited; Swift benefits from [Nichols's own] 'late excellent SUPPLEMENT' to his *Works* (1779).

Gentleman's Mag. (Dec. 1779), 598–601, review of *Eng. Poets* [by John Duncombe?] (cont.):

Some recent fraudulent attributions to Gay are condemned; William Broome's MS 'alterations' to his poems in 1743, printed as 'Variations', were 'communicated by

Dr. Johnson' [as Nichols would have known]; the posthumous poems condemned by SJ in 'Parnell' **13** are surely genuine, and Pope no doubt embellished what he included in his edition of Parnell (1722); Savage's *Progress of a Divine* has been omitted, presumably because the poet himself wanted it 'suppressed, as a small atonement for his follies' (cf. 'Savage' **196**); two new *Volunteer Laureats* by Savage have been discovered, although another remains untraced; Watts has 'long stood the test of criticism', and his 'Songs' are by no means too puerile for a collection 'particularly intended for the amusement and instruction of youth'.

While *The Chace* and *Hobbinol* 'have long been the subject of admiration', the reviewer is astonished by the 'unparelleled *naivete*' of Somervile's miscellaneous poetry and its current neglect; he discusses the identifications in Thomson's *The Castle of Indolence*; regrets that the original painters of the engraved portraits are not named; notes the additions to Lyttelton's 'few very beautiful poems' (while pointing out that one of them was in fact by [Duncombe himself!]), and the omission of Gilbert West's *The Order of the Garter*, which is in Dodsley's *Collection*; is surprised by the 'partial selection' from Gray's poems, speculates that this was due to questions of 'literary property', citing the 'chancery-suit' mentioned in *Gentleman's Mag.* (1777), 331, and concludes that it is discreditable either to the 'undertakers' or to whoever refused permission.

'On the whole, this collection does equal honour to the English genius and the English press. The Parnassus of the poets is here realised.'

London Review, 10 (Nov. 1779), 350–2:

'A New Correspondent' objects to SJ's claim that Dryden's 'Anne Killigrew' is 'the noblest ode' in the language ('Dryden' **278**), rather than Milton's *Nativity Ode* (ignored by SJ) or Dryden's own *Alexander's Feast*. Gray's *The Bard* is 'infinitely superior', as are 'most of Gray's poems, as well as a few of Mason's'. Why have Chaucer, Spenser, Jonson, Shakespeare, May, Beaumont and Fletcher, Southerne, Farquhar, Goldsmith, and Churchill (and other poets, some of whom would in fact appear in the later *Prefaces*) been omitted?

Westminster Mag. 7 (Nov. 1779), 591–2:

'B.S.R.' asks about SJ's character of Gilbert Walmesley in 'Smith' **71–6**, as quoted in Aug. 1779, 413–14: 'What is meant by Literature [in **72**]?—Is it simply a knowledge of the dead languages, or an acquaintance with the whole circle of letters?' SJ's reference to Walmesley as a Whig ('Smith' **73**) is offensive:

I stopped a moment to see this literary Genius enlisted under the banners of Jacobitism, and vomiting out *anathemas* and damnation against the assertors of religious and civil liberty; against men to whom we are indebted for every blessing of life, and enabled by them, even in these dark and perilous times, to contemplate with the most exquisite pleasure the noble fabric of British freedom.

He objects to SJ's claim, 'in that disgusting pomp of stile which he has ever affected', to have benefited from Walmesley's friendship, and to his phrase about Garrick's death eclipsing the gaiety of nations.

The Annual Register . . . For the Year 1779 (1780), ii. 179–84, review of *Prefaces*, i–iv:

The reviewer refers to 'the many and essential benefits, that English literature hath already derived' from SJ's labours, which have given English 'precision and stability' and, 'as it were, connected his reputation with the very existence of our language'. His new task is 'to form the judgment and taste of the nation on the same solid basis, on which he had established its vocabulary'. Different kinds of critic are categorized. The critic as 'man of taste' is acquainted with authors and men of genius, as well as having his own natural abilities and powers of discrimination; the critic as 'philosopher' investigates the effects and rules of art; the 'general' critic 'traces the progress and improvement of taste and comprehends the interconnections of the arts and sciences'; and the 'occasional' critic analyses literary beauties and defects, and the development of genius.

Long excerpts from SJ's discussions of 'Metaphysical' poetry in 'Cowley' and of *Paradise Lost* and *Paradise Regained* in 'Milton' have already appeared in an earlier section entitled 'Characters' (ii. 27–39). To these, the reviewer now adds the discussions of versification from 'Waller' 142–53 and of *Hudibras* in 'Butler' 23–7, as well as 'Dryden' 214–22, which describe his prose and poetical language with 'great spirit, learning, and penetration'. SJ characterizes lesser poets with 'great judgment and precision'. As for the 'historical' aspect of the *Prefaces*, SJ has 'great reputation . . . as a moral and biographical writer': 'authentic materials' have been carefully selected, previous errors and prejudices corrected, with frequent 'beautiful effusions of moral sentiment, and remarks on the manners of mankind, which distinguish him beyond any writer in the English language'.

Yet 'many parts of his work bear strong marks of those political prejudices, under the influence of which it is well known his mind unfortunately labours'. 'For his own sake', SJ should have 'repressed an useless zeal':

We should be sorry to think, with him, that *virulence and malevolence* really belong to any party:— he has taught us that they certainly do not belong to one alone.—*If faction*, (i.e. the party we oppose) *seldom*, as he says, *leaves a man honest, however it may find him* ['Milton' 64], how will the jealous dignity of Doctor Johnson's character brook the suspicions of, perhaps, the greater part of readers? The bad men of both sides, who have an interest in the destruction of all character, will be glad to make use of his authority; and he cannot complain if those of the adverse party bring his own example as one proof of his rule.

Milton's politics make him 'particularly obnoxious' to SJ. As for SJ's tendentious interpretation of his 'corporal punishment' ('Milton' 11), the reviewer points out that Milton was certainly not the last university student to be so beaten. SJ's account of Milton's attitude to family prayer is a 'calumny' drawn from Toland and Newton (166–7) (as already noted in *Gent. Mag.* (Oct. 1779), 492–3.)

Monthly Review, 62 (June 1780), 479–83, review [by Edmund Cartwright] of Francis Blackburne's *Remarks on Johnson's Life of Milton*:

'The acrimony with which Dr. Johnson has permitted himself to treat the character of Milton is well known', and the 'more particularly obnoxious' parts of his account were noted in the *Review* (Aug. 1779). Blackburne traces SJ's 'malevolence' to Milton back to the 'dirty business' over the Lauder forgeries, in which it is to be hoped that SJ was less involved than Blackburne believes. Cartwright quotes Blackburne's defence of Milton's 'attachment to Cromwell' and willingness to serve under what SJ called 'a manifest usurpation' ('Milton' 73). The author

seems actuated by a generous concern for the reputation of an injured individual, and by a truly patriotic regard for the general liberties of mankind; which he thinks, and perhaps not without reason, have been insidiously attacked by a masked battery directed at the moral character of Milton, one of Liberty's most zealous and respectable advocates.

Blackburne's discussion of SJ's motives in writing a speech in 1777 for the ill-fated forger William Dodd (see i. 16 and n. above) is 'a subject which will naturally excite much *curious* speculation', but seems irrelevant in this context.

Gentleman's Mag. (May 1781), 224–7, on *Prefaces*, vols. v–x [by John Duncombe?]:

As with the earlier *Prefaces*, 'we know not which most to admire, the sense or diction, the elegance or penetration, of the writer'. Some particular points in a detailed discussion may be noted: the long quotations from Dennis on Addison's *Cato* (**139**–**52**) could have been omitted; SJ proves to be a 'sagacious moralist' when discussing Blackmore's character (**41**–**3**); the reviewer thinks more highly of Tickell than SJ; SJ treats Congreve's immorality 'with his usual acuteness' (**22**); 'Prior' contains 'nothing new'; SJ's 'original' character of Warburton is quoted from 'Pope' **184**–**5**; the parallel of Pope and Dryden is masterly ('Pope' **303**–**11**); and SJ examines Pope's works 'with equal ingenuity and candour'.

Gentleman's Mag. (June 1781), 271–6, on *Prefaces*, vols. v–x [by John Duncombe?] (cont.):

The reviewer offers two anecdotes of his own about Richard Bentley, the first concerning his opinion of Pope's *Homer* (see 'Pope' **285** n.). In 'Swift', 'there is little new, except in the mode of narration', and 'Broome' adds only the details of his and Fenton's contributions to Pope's *Odyssey* (**6**); Joseph Warton supplied all that is new in 'Pitt'; the admirable 'Savage' is 'already well known to the publick'; SJ rightly objects to the use of Lyttelton's revision of Thomson's *Liberty* in *Eng. Poets* ('Thomson' **26**), but fails to realize that Lyttelton also revised *The Seasons*; the 'general opinion' of Hammond is 'much more favourable' than SJ's; Croft's 'Young' is taken seriously, and some information added; 'Dyer' derives from [Duncombe's own] *Letters, by Several Eminent Persons Deceased*; SJ was surely misinformed about Lyttelton's envy of The Leasowes in 'Shenstone' **11**, 'as we cannot easily be persuaded that a mind so pure and benevolent . . . was ever debased by such unworthy passions'; SJ unfairly attributes Lyttelton's anxiety over the printing of his *History* to 'vanity' ('Lyttelton' **19**); the 'Blackbird' elegy appended to 'West' **15** was in fact by Richard Jago.

    'Gray' is 'epitomized' from William Mason's *Memoirs* (1775). In 'Gray' **32**–**48** SJ 'proceeds to fritter away the beauties [of *Odes* (1757)] by a verbal discussion, a literary ordeal which even Pindar could not pass unhurt'. Contrary to 'the opinion of the common reader', Gray's shorter poems are also 'more censured than praised':

> The whole of these Lives, which, with a few abatements, we have perused with much pleasure, and now close with regret, must confirm the public in the opinion which they have long entertained of the vigour of the writer's mind, and of that happy art of moralisation by which he gives to well-known incidents the grace of novelty, and 'grapples the attention' by expressing common thoughts with uncommon strength and elegance of diction. We have only to lament (but who is perfect?) that, in some instances, his criticisms are too minute and too severe to be approved by 'readers uncorrupted by literary prejudices'.

    The two-volume 'Index' (compiled by Alexander Macbean), ignored by other reviewers, is 'uniformly given in the words of the poets', and offers

> a good synoptical view of English Poetry, in prudential, moral, and religious sentences, remarkable proverbial sayings, characters of celebrated persons, descriptions of places and countries, and of remarkable events in natural history, antiquities, criticism, or politicks, with strong

remonstrances against the vile prostitution of the gift of heaven to impure and immoral purposes. In short, this Index, independent of the great work it belongs to, is a valuable poetical treasure.

Monthly Review, 65 (Aug. 1781), 100–12, review of *Prefaces*, vols. v–x [by Edmund Cartwright]:

SJ has now 'amply fulfilled his engagements to the Public'. Critics are divided about Addison's 'literary character', and SJ's view of 'this agitated question' is illustrated from 'Addison' 124–30, 136–8, 155–68 (100–5). Blackmore's 'exalted station' in *Eng. Poets* will surprise those familiar only with 'the ludicrous representations of contemporary wits'. SJ is 'the rescuer of his fame', and the merits of *Creation* are made clear in a 'poetical character, which, if not justly, is at least very ingeniously drawn' ('Blackmore' 41–8 are quoted).

Neither Sheffield nor Granville merit their 'present elevation'. Cartwright quotes 'Granville' 25–32, and, on 'a more respectable name', 'Rowe' 30–5. SJ gives 'a lively and entertaining account' of the Collier controversy in 'Congreve' 19–24. A moralist like Collier who, 'in opposition to wit, ridicule, and the depraved passions of mankind, is able to reform one article of the national taste, is certainly entitled to high praise' ('Congreve' 18–23, 34–6, 43–4 are quoted). The final paragraph concerns 'Fenton'.

Monthly Review, 65 (Nov. 1781), 353–62 [by Cartwright] (cont.):

Although SJ's discussion of Prior's poetry 'deviates from the general opinion of its excellence', the poet's public career may have led to overestimation of his achievement. SJ is severe on his love poems and, on the whole, 'justly so': a poet who associates with drabs will lack the warmth or refinement of true passion. SJ may be right about the 'tendency' of 'Henry and Emma' (57), but few will agree that this 'most generally read' of Prior's poems is 'dull and tedious'. 'Prior' 71–3 and the 'striking and just' final 79 are quoted.

SJ views Pope 'with singular complacency'. Cartwright quotes 'Pope' 71–2, 80–8 on the *Iliad*; the 'masterly sketch' of Warburton (184–5); the character of Pope himself, which shows SJ's 'usual acuteness and discernment' (293–8, 303–11); and the critique of the *Essay on Man* (363–7). In 373 and 382 SJ apparently has 'an eye to' Joseph Warton and other critics who have questioned Pope's achievement in 'the most excellent species of the poetical art'.

Monthly Review, 65 (Dec. 1781), 408–11, on *Prefaces*, vols. v–x [by Cartwright] (cont.):

There is 'little that is new' in *Prefaces*, vol. viii (containing 'Swift', 'Gay', 'Broome', 'Pitt', 'Parnell', 'Ambrose Philips', and 'Watts'). SJ's 'unmanly' reference to Colley Cibber in 'Savage' 57 is apparently new [a mistake]: SJ's 'acrimony' to Cibber is a 'stale' topic. SJ's unfavourable account of Thomson represents him as servile when young, and later 'grossly sensual', the latter charge resting on the testimony of the 'unprincipled and profligate' Savage ('Thomson' 45). Cartwright rises to SJ's gibes about 'liberty' in 'Thomson' 22, suggesting that he should make up his mind as to whether or not tyranny has any evils.

Cartwright replies at length [having been briefed by Ralph Griffiths, editor of the *Monthly Review*] to SJ's account in 'Hammond' 1 of the contributions of Robert Shiels and Theophilus Cibber to the *Lives of the English Poets* (1753), published by Griffiths himself. He points out (as SJ had not) that Hammond's elegies closely imitate Tibullus.

SJ's comments on Hammond are 'certainly the height of prejudice': some will read his poetry with 'greater avidity' than SJ's own *London* and *The Vanity of Human Wishes*. SJ's characterization of 'elegy' as 'gentleness and tenuity' ('Hammond' 8) is 'imperfect and mistaken'. In contrast to SJ's dismissive judgement in 'Collins' 17, Cartwright claims that Collins's 'imperfections and peculiarities are lost in the blaze of genius'.

Monthly Review, 66 (Feb. 1782), 113–27, on *Prefaces*, vols. v–x [by Cartwright] (cont.):

Cartwright gives extended treatment to the 'well-written' 'Young', in which Herbert Croft has 'taken off the manner' of SJ so well that only a 'shrewd critic' would notice the difference. The 'impartiality and precision' of SJ's critical paragraphs on Young are illustrated by quotation of 154, 160, 163, 168. SJ's reference to 'a lady' in 163 prompts a comment on his other references to

the Fair; with whom the Doctor takes frequent opportunities, as in the passage above, of hinting that he lives in the greatest familiarity . . . and why may not the Critic be permitted to go a little out of his way to pay a compliment to the anonymous Ladies, by whose smiles and approbation he appears, and, we presume, not without reason, to be so highly gratified?

SJ's joke about *The Fleece* in 'Dyer' 12 is 'as lame an attempt at wit as ever disgraced the vilest pages of the vilest jestbook'. Neglect of *The Fleece* is evidence of 'a decline of poetical taste', and SJ's objections to it ('Dyer' 11) would apply equally to Virgil's *Georgics*. Cartwright quotes 'Mallet' 1–2, 9, but finds it 'wonderful' that SJ passes coolly over the pension he received for his part in the 'diabolical' and 'fiendlike' persecution of Admiral Byng ('Mallet' 21). He contrasts Shenstone's benevolence, humanity, and blameless life with SJ's 'splenetic remarks' on his rural pursuits ('Shenstone' 10), which justify his use of the pastoral mode SJ mocks in 25.

Cartwright is even more provoked by 'Akenside' 3: 'This *unnecessary* and *outrageous* zeal for LIBERTY seems to have given his Biographer (who seldom overlooks THAT object) great offence, as he has stigmatized it in almost every page of this short history.' He also reacts to SJ's condescending comments on youthful 'ardour for liberty' in 'Lyttelton' 3: 'There is, perhaps, no passion, when once it has taken firm possession of the mind, that burns with more unabating ardour than that which has liberty for its object: and for this very obvious reason; liberty is an object that is equally desirable through every period of life.'

After brief comments on 'West', Cartwright devotes 'more than usual attention' to 'Gray', on whom SJ 'deviates so widely from the general opinion'. He concentrates on his treatment of *Odes* (1757), which is quoted at length (32–49). In 32, SJ is 'less desirous of finding the meaning of [the opening of *The Progress of Poesy*] himself, than of preventing others from finding it. Nothing can be more obvious and intelligible.' SJ 'spares no pains to avail himself' of a 'minor inaccuracy' in Gray's expression. He offers 'a continued tissue of misrepresentation': the stanza criticized in 36 in fact contains 'An assertion not only poetical, but, if taken with that degree of latitude with which a general assertion ought to be, philosophically true'.

Only 'singular ingenuity' will find any resemblance between the opening of *The Bard* and the ballad 'Johnny Armstrong' (43). The comments in 48 are 'severe' and 'more than severe'. Gray's 'professed admirers' understandably find SJ 'not only hostile, but malignant', and will even suspect that 'there is treachery in his praise', as in his approval of Gray's allusion to Milton's blindness (39), which is in fact 'forced and unnatural', 'one of those false and hyperbolical thoughts . . . under the class of the false sublime'.

Of the *Prefaces* as a whole,

notwithstanding they contain a fund of profound and original criticism, which, perhaps, no other pen but the Doctor's could have supplied ... some caution is, nevertheless, required to peruse them with advantage. Instances too frequently occur, in which the Critic's judgment seems altogether under the dominion of predilection or prejudice ... this privilege of critical independence, an affectation of singularity, or some other principle, not immediately visible, is for ever betraying him into a dogmatical spirit of contradiction to received opinions.

Examples are his consistent depreciation of blank verse and his 'rough treatment' of Gray. SJ's taste is limited,

method, ratiocination, and argument, especially if the vehicle be rhyme, oftentimes obtaining his regard and commendation, while the bold and enthusiastic, though perhaps irregular, flights of imagination are past by with perverse and obstinate indifference. It is no surprise that the panegyrist of Blackmore should withhold from Collins and Gray what he has bestowed upon Savage and Yalden. Through the whole of his performance the desire of praise, excepting in the case of some very favourite author, is almost always overpowered by his disposition to censure ... the slightest blemish is examined with microscopical sagacity.

Once SJ reaches 'his cotemporaries; for whom, indeed, he appears to have little more brotherly kindness than they might have expected at Constantinople', the 'fastidiousness of his criticism' only increases, and 'his Readers will scarcely forbear exclaiming, with [Voltaire's] honest Candide, what a wonderful genius is this Pococurante! Nothing can please him!'

Critical Review, 52 (Aug. 1781), 81–92, on *Prefaces*, vols. v–x (described in the 'Contents' as 'Prefaces to the Works of the English Poets', but indexed as '(Dr.) *Johnson*'s Lives of the English Poets'):

These volumes continue 'a most learned and ingenious work', and complete the 'elegant edition' of the *Eng. Poets*. SJ is

already too well known and established in the republic of letters, to make any farther recommendation necessary ... we meet with the same critical penetration and sagacity, the same accurate knowledge of men and manners, judicious reflections, nervous style, and manly sentiments, that distinguished the former volumes.

The new biographies concern recent authors, whom some of us knew personally. The reviewer wishes that 'Young' had been more informative about the poet's 'public and private character'. Herbert Croft seems concerned to vindicate Young's son and treats the poet himself unfavourably, but his 'careful and studious imitation' of SJ's 'style and manner' has 'some degree of success'.

While it is difficult to select from SJ himself, 'Pope', 'Addison', and 'Thomson' in particular seem 'written *con amore*'. 'Addison' **165–8** are quoted as 'equally just and delicate'. On Thomson, 'that amiable man and excellent poet', **46–51** are quoted as 'elegant, candid, and judicious; the praise is not (as praises often are) vague, general, and indiscriminate, but founded on true taste and reason; nor is the censure less just'. Although SJ's 'critical determinations will always be received with deference and respect', he places Prior, 'that great favourite of the ladies', in a noticeably lower scale of merit than usual. Prior's admirers will dispute SJ's judgements on his love poetry and use of mythology (**56**), 'Henry and Emma' (**57**), the imitations of Spenser (**59, 75–6**), *Alma*, and *Solomon* (**63–9**).

SJ has also 'boldly steered against the tide of popular opinion, by calling in question the transcendent excellence of our modern Pindar, Mr. Gray, whom he has dethroned and degraded' (quoting 'Gray' **27–42, 48**). Although the reviewer will not decide whether SJ's objections are 'strictly just and well founded', he believes that 'no man ever acquired a high reputation at so easy a rate, or received such *great wages* for so *little work*, as Mr. Gray'. He agrees with SJ's praise of the *Elegy* ('Gray' **51**), but also that his odes and 'little performances' 'have been much over-rated'. While Gray has been compared to Dryden and Pope, SJ levels him 'with the minor bards of a much inferior rank', and such corrective criticism may lead to a more balanced assessment.

SJ bestows 'extraordinary pains and industry' on Pope: 'every part of his character is delineated with the greatest accuracy, and every part of his writings criticised by the nice hand of taste, judgment, and impartiality'. His 'just and sensible' discussion of Pope's letters, 'the result of good sense, and a knowledge of mankind' ('Pope' **273–6, 284**), and the 'masterly' character of Warburton (**184–5**), are quoted. On SJ's claim that Ralph Allen influenced Warburton's career (**194**), the reviewer comments that he was in fact rewarded for 'his own literary merit' by William Pitt, later Lord Chatham. He admires SJ's comparison of Pope and Dryden (**303–11**), and discussions of the *Essay on Criticism* and *Rape of the Lock* (**328–41**), but he may overpraise the Homer translation: a 'better and more faithful translation' is possible, but would have to be in blank verse.

In general, 'this performance is one of the most acute, agreeable, and entertaining works that has passed under our inspection'. Had the *Eng. Poets* been still more inclusive, we would have benefited from more of SJ's biographies.

Gentleman's Mag. (Oct. 1781), 463–7, 'Remarks on Dr. Johnson's *Lives of the Most Eminent English Poets—2d edition*', by 'W.B.' of 'A—', dated 27 July 1781 [by Robert Potter]:

[The Revd Robert Potter (1721–1804) later revised these articles, which break off in Feb. 1782, in *The Art of Criticism; As Exemplified in Dr. Johnson's Lives of the Most Eminent English Poets* (1789). For SJ's low opinion of Potter's translation of Aeschylus in 1778, see *Life*, iii. 256.]

Although 'Cowley, on the whole, is pourtrayed with great ingenuity and penetration', 'Milton' **185–93** illustrate SJ's 'caprice and singularity', 'general aversion to nature', ridicule of love, and willingness to attack 'the whole fraternity of poets whilst he is writing their lives':

the elements of poetry are, or seem to be, uncongenial to him, and only excite his laughter. One would think the smoke of London was as pleasant to him as a coal-pit to a neighbour of Newcastle, who has hardly ever seen the sun. How different is the *Rambler*! Surely a fictitious Johnson is palmed upon me . . . some of the finest strokes in the *Penseroso* are here stripped of their colouring . . . Reciting a poem in such a detached manner, is like expecting a clock to strike when taken to pieces, or beholding a celebrated beauty, not in dishabille, but dislocated.

Yet 'In regard to Milton's *epic*, our author seems to have discarded his partiality, and to be himself, which is the best praise which can be given him', and 'The observations on "versification" are . . . just and pertinent.'

'Butler' prompts Potter's own somewhat entangled discussion of burlesque. 'I agree with our author in making Roscommon some parting amends. A learned and worthy nobleman is a phaenomenon.' Discussing 'Waller', he notes that SJ often mentions his biographical sources only 'by circumlocution', and, of his aphorisms, that 'Such strokes as these discriminate the man of genius, and enliven a narration.' In 'Waller' **63–7** SJ 'mentions Cromwell with a moderation I should not have expected'. On the subject of love poetry, he notes that 'The ladies never meet with much favour from Dr. Johnson.' SJ's biographical and critical sections are not rigidly distinguished: 'Our biographer, I think, sometimes gives a half account of his authors' works in the course of their lives.' His discussion of sacred poetry exhibits 'an astonishing exaltation of style, and justness of sentiment' ('Waller' 135–8).

Potter hopes finally,

that every one who makes the most distant pretensions to reading will purchase the entertaining labours of a writer to whom all lovers of polite literature, his countrymen in particular, are so greatly indebted; I am not afraid of being taxed with flattery, if I describe him, in poetical terms, as armed with the two-edged sword of knowledge (the gift of all the Muses) sharpened by wit, embellished by language, and directed by judgement.

Gentleman's Mag. (Nov. 1781), 506–10, 'Remarks' on the *Lives* by 'W.B.' [Robert Potter] (cont.), dated 5 Aug. 1781:

Potter's opening reflections on 'genius' should have prefaced his first article. On SJ's reference to 'my father, an old bookseller' in 'Dryden' 109, he comments: 'An odd description this. One would suppose the son was born when the father was in years' (Michael Johnson was 53). Although it is not easy to deduce from 'Dryden' 208–12 'whether Dryden was learned, or not', SJ 'has, on the whole, written this great poet's life with candour, and analysed his character with great ingenuity.'

In 'Smith' 47, 49, SJ confusingly asserts successively that Edmund Smith's tragedy pleased only 'the criticks', was rejected by the learned 'as a school-boy's tale', and was 'a scholar's play'. On 'Halifax': 'I am at a loss why the author should give the history of this nobleman, whose poetry he despises, as of an "eminent poet".' Rowe 'has escaped well, considering he was a Whig'. The anecdote of Addison's 'execution' on Steele must be 'a mistake, or a misrepresentation' ('Addison' 7). Other comments on 'Addison' include the complaint that SJ 'strikes at the root of metaphor' (129), and an enquiry whether his use of 'superficial' (162) means that Addison's criticism 'wanted depth'.

That John Hughes 'was a Whig' explains some of SJ's irony about him, but it is 'injurious' to base a 'character' of the poet (18–21) on selective quotation of comments by Pope and Swift (which, as an editorial footnote points out, SJ had in any case misquoted).

Gentleman's Mag. (Dec. 1781), 561–4, 'Remarks' on the *Lives* by 'W.B.' [Robert Potter] (cont.), dated 27 Aug. 1781 (this time from 'U—'):

Potter discusses briefly 'Prior', 'Congreve', 'Blackmore' (with an editorial correction by Nichols at 561 n.), and 'Fenton'. Of 'Gay' 27 he comments: 'He was not a great genius, but a witty and adroit writer; and had much nature as well as true burlesque. It is observed, that Pope has remarked his simplicity, and Johnson his vanity.' Gay 'was a pretty writer, but much inferior to Tickell', who also excelled Addison as a poet.

Of 'Savage' he notes that 'Prudence and genius are seldom united. By culling this biography, and arranging the selections, an excellent account of genius might be obtained'; and of SJ's comments on Anne Oldfield in 'Savage' 45, that 'The liberality of this actress deserves to be recorded in a work that bids fair for immortality. These lives, in the ease and familiarity of the manner, much resemble those of Plutarch, and much exceed them by the vein of pleasantry interspersed.' 'Savage' is more copious than the later lives, but 'entertaining and discriminating... Most writers would have found the life of Savage a maze in which they would have nearly been lost. Our author has, with great skill, divided the wheat from the chaff.'

SJ 'seems at a loss how to criticise' *Gulliver's Travels* ('Swift' **85**). On Swift's 'strange, cruel, and mysterious' treatment of 'Stella' (**91–3**) he comments that SJ 'writes, which is very unusual with him, without imparting knowledge'. Like SJ, he doubts that Swift needed to learn 'nastiness' from Pope ('Swift' **137**). He observes finally that,

by adopting a style familiar and nearly colloquial, Dr. Johnson rather talks than writes to his reader; that he directs him on a new-made road to knowledge as if present, informs him of the characters, circumstances, and incidents of the inhabitants as he passes along, and stops with him now and then for refreshment, becoming his friend as well as fellow-traveller.

Gentleman's Mag. (Jan. 1782), 19–21:

'H.' observes that 'The late poetical biography of Dr. Johnson has transformed all his readers into critics':

If the pedantry and old age of Dr. J. have taken away his relish for pastoral pleasures, shall the world, for that reason, be blind to the beauties of Shenstone... or, shall the superlative merit of Gray himself be overlooked and forgot, because the jealousy of Johnson would not suffer him to see such merit in his contemporaries?

A detailed discussion of Gray's poetry follows.

Gentleman's Mag. (Jan. 1782), 22:

'Philo-Lyristes' is 'hurt by the liberties' SJ has taken with 'two of our most celebrated Lyric Poets'. Gray's *Odes* (1757) are 'by far the two best in the English language... And let Dr. Johnson, with all his reputation, produce me another Lyric ode equal to Collins on the Passions [ignored by SJ]: indeed the frequent public recitals of this last-mentioned poem are a mark of its universally-acknowledged excellence.'

Gentleman's Mag. (Jan. 1782), 24–6, 'Remarks' on the *Lives* [by Robert Potter], cont., but without initials or date:

Discussing 'Pope', Potter comments that John Dennis 'was a man of letters and acute criticism, with a competent share of envy and malignity. His taste exposed him continually to the vexation of being pleased.' Pope's 'Unfortunate Lady' and 'Eloisa to Abelard' are 'replete with poetical fire, and strike the imagination with a captivating horror. A person endued with a true relish of poetry can never be tired of reading them... Pope's poetry has certainly a charm hardly to be equalled.' His 'Pastorals', however, are generally thought to be 'too polite; and to contain too many borrowed plumes.' Of Pope's Homer he asks:

What glory was this, for one to translate, or preside over the translation of, all Homer's works! Perhaps it would puzzle a much better critic than me to determine which was superior, Addison's pre-eminence in prose, or Pope's in poetry. Sitting one against the other, the *Latin* poetry of the former turns the scale. Addison's life was shorter by nine years.

Of Lady Mary Wortley Montagu Potter comments: 'I believe women of education more ready at their pen, as well as at their tongue, than men.' Her letters have 'exemplary fluency and carelessness'.

Gentleman's Mag. (Feb. 1782), 116–18, 'Remarks' on the *Lives* [by Robert Potter] (cont.):

After discussing the theory of the 'Ruling Passion' ('Pope' **202–6**), Potter comments that SJ's remarks on Pope's letters (**273–5**) amount to 'a satire on friendship, deeming it a childish weakness'. His comparison of Pope and Dryden ('Pope' 303–11) prompts Potter to make a case for Addison, who

must certainly yield the palm of poetry to either of them; but may contest it as a writer. His prose has universality of perusal on its side, and carries the prize from both. It is remarkable that Pope could not support an epic poem or play; which must be attributed to scantiness of invention. *The Rape of the Lock* was a piece of good luck. Prose too is in itself more valuable than poetry. The former may be compared to necessities, the latter to dainties. One is for use, the other for entertainment.

Although SJ objects to confusion of the metaphorical and literal by Dryden and Pope ('Pope' 326), 'unnecessary restraints are wrong. Metaphor is interwoven with language, on which basis numberless beauties of thought have their foundation.'

[Although the article was 'To be continued', no more followed. Potter evidently decided to discuss the remaining *Lives* in his *Inquiry into Some Passages in Dr. Johnson's Lives of the Poets: Particularly His Observations on Lyric Poetry and the Odes of Gray* (1783), favourably reviewed in *Gent. Mag.* (Aug. 1783), 684–6.]

London Mag., 50 (Dec. 1781), 593–6, review of *Lives of the Poets* (4 vols. 1781):

Although he is a 'truly original' writer, offering 'a rich fund of sublime entertainment',

Dr. Johnson, like his friend Sir Joshua Reynolds, occasionally feels too much his established superiority in his profession, and condemns the very faults in others, which are the most conspicuous blemishes in his own character. Independent of dictatorial arrogance, his remarks and criticisms are the strongest proofs that can be given, that he has no equal in the science of polite literature.

While the reader is not to expect 'many new anecdotes' in SJ's biographies, he will meet a kind of 'critical scrutiny' not previously attempted. 'Cowley' 51 is quoted. Although SJ shows that the Metaphysical poets are vulnerable to 'the rigid rules of classic criticism', he also 'condescends to make such allowances in their favour, as, from the pen of any other critic, would perhaps be called self-contradiction'. In the case of 'Milton', 'the charge of illiberality, party rancour, and wilful misrepresentation has been so aggravated' that the reviewer will say no more. 'Milton' is in fact 'one of his most laboured criticisms, and contains more of his original spirit, manners, and diction than any other of the collection'. In his discussion of *Areopagitica* ('Milton' 58) SJ 'pays his court to the prejudices of the times' by giving his authority to the administration's wish 'to abridge the liberty of the press'. He is too severe on 'Lycidas' in 'Milton' 180–4, but 'energetic and convincing' on *Paradise Lost*.

SJ's objections to 'sacred poetry' in 'Waller' 135–42 are one of his 'singular opinions', supported only by 'a few weak arguments': they are contradicted by Young's *Night Thoughts*. Although SJ damns most of his verse with faint praise, Waller might have been 'the English Pindar of Johnson', had he not eulogized Cromwell. SJ bestows his 'usual precision, ingenuity and learning' on Dryden, Rowe, and Addison in particular. He gives an 'exalted character' of Dryden as critic, poet, and refiner of the language. His account of Gilbert Walmesley ('Smith' 71)

is one of those masterly strokes of composition which render Dr. Johnson superior to any other prose writer in the English language: he has frequently the happiest manner imaginable of combining elegant diction with refined sentiment and of affecting the heart by this natural union.

The reviewer disagrees with 'Rowe' 32 by recalling that Mrs Cibber used to give Alicia in *Jane Shore* 'real sorrow and natural madness'. No English dramatist excels

Rowe in displaying 'passion in its progress'. SJ's exaggerated praise of Rowe's *Lucan* illustrates his 'pride of singularity in opinion': '*So little sometimes is criticism the effect of judgement*' (turning 'Addison' **15** against SJ). As 'a firm friend to the civil rights of mankind', the protagonist of Addison's *Cato* inevitably meets the same fate as Milton and Waller ('Addison' **55, 60**). SJ's remarks on *Cato*'s poetical merit are outweighed by his long quotations from Dennis's 'ill-natured criticism' (**139–52**), no doubt added merely to 'swell the volume'. The reviewer breaks off: 'to criticise such a critic is surely an Herculean labour.'

London Mag., 51 (Jan. 1782), 35–8, review of *Lives* (cont.):

Returning to 'this celebrated performance', the reviewer finds 'Prior' 'singular and untrue in some particulars': SJ's censure of 'Henry and Emma' is particularly cool, if not degrading ('Prior' **57**). His comments on Congreve's fertility and originality seem to be self-contradictory. He receives 'severe censure' for a grammatical slip in 'Somervile' **2** (a sequence of 'was...is...was said to be...was...was...was'): 'The Dictator, the Judge, the Preceptor, should never be found writing as incorrectly as a schoolboy... Almost every rule of Syntax is here violated.' 'Savage' provides 'a fund of instruction and entertainment'.

The best of the later *Lives* are those of Pope, Thomson, Shenstone, Young, Akenside, and Gray. The reviewer protests about 'Pope' **363–7** on the *Essay on Man*:

the Doctor has passed such censures upon it, as no man, who did not feel his power too much on the throne of letters would have dared to avow. Can he prove before any body of learned men the following bold assertion [quoting 'Pope' **365**]? In reply, we will take the liberty to say that Johnson himself cannot read the *Essay on Man*, as it ought to be read, without learning many things that he ought to know, and which would render him a social being.

SJ criticizes Pope's epitaphs, although, 'in the opinion of most men, they are models of excellence'. His censure of the epitaph on Gay ('Pope' **427–36**) is 'unpardonable, because it is untrue'.

In discussing Thomson as 'a writer' SJ is 'a great master, neither obscured by dogmatism, nor sullied by private prejudice'. 'Watts' does honour to his 'judgement and candour'. Croft's 'Young' is 'remarkably well executed', and SJ's appended criticism 'equally excellent'. SJ describes *The Pleasures of Imagination* as giving 'poetical delight', but then claims that it leaves the reader with 'nothing' ('Akenside' **16–17**). Gray's works 'are degraded beneath the rank they are certainly entitled to in the scale of poetry; some unknown prejudice has warped the judgement of the critic upon this occasion'.

Although no one could have a 'more rational esteem' for SJ, the reviewer

cannot join with that herd of flatterers, whose indiscriminate adulation has rendered him careless and incorrect in many parts of this work, which is extremely unequal. Insomuch, that one page suggests the idea that no man living but Johnson could have composed it, while another makes one doubt if a single line could claim him as its author.

The New Annual Register...for 1781, 3 (1782), iii. 225–34, review of *Lives* [by Andrew Kippis?]:

Long extracts from the 'incomparable Lives of the English Poets' ('Addison', 'Tickell', 'Pope', 'West', and 'Mallet') also appear under 'Biography' (iii. 43–61), with further passages from 'Addison', 'Thomson', and 'Young' under 'Criticism' (iii. 105–12), and the review under 'Domestic Literature'. The work has been 'universally read, and almost as universally praised', for 'the strength and dignity of its style, the originality of its sentiment and composition, and the perspicacity of its observation'. Some 'smaller poets' receive 'very short' treatment, but SJ exerts his 'full strength' on Pope and Dryden.

SJ is no 'biographical flatterer': 'There is much in him of the spirit of diminution and satire, we will not say of malignity; for, notwithstanding Dr. Johnson's severity, we do not think that he is ill-natured in his real disposition.' The reviewer doubts whether SJ has 'indisputable evidence' for some of his anecdotes, perhaps remembered from his youth. He should have investigated them properly, and have 'condescended' to reveal his sources. Although he delivers his judgements with 'great weight' and 'an air sufficiently imposing', the literary world will not submit tamely to such 'dictatorial authority'. Yet he remains 'the first biographer of the age . . . always entertaining, always instructive, always masterly; and his invariable attachment to the cause of religion and virtue deserve high commendation; though it would be better if that attachment were never mixed with the prejudice of education.'

The *Lives* 'form an illustrious addition to critical, as well as to biographical know-ledge'. SJ is 'one of the first critics of the age', and 'the strength and penetration of his understanding' and 'his original cast of thinking' are displayed in 'full vigour' in 'Pope'. Even so,

the general tendency of Dr. Johnson's work is rather to diminish than to exalt our writers; and he hath an unreasonable dislike to some kinds of poetry, which do not coincide with his own turn of mind. Much as the world is disposed to submit to the Doctor's authority, it will not in every case bow down to his judgment. It is almost universally agreed that he hath not done justice to Prior and to Gray.

The Annual Register . . . for 1782 (1783), ii. 203–8, reviewing *Prefaces*, vols. v–x:

The reputation of this 'learned performance' is already 'established on the most universal applause':

Perhaps no age or country has ever produced a species of criticism more perfect in its kind, or better calculated for general instruction . . . for whether we consider it in a literary, philosophical, or a moral view, we are at a loss whether to admire most the author's variety and copiousness of learning, the soundness of his judgement, or the purity and excellence of his character as a man.

It is surely of importance to the rising generation to be supplied in the most elegant walk of literature with a guide, who points out what is beautiful in writing as well as in action, who uniformly blends instruction with amusement, who informs the understanding, and rectifies the judgement, while he mends the heart.

Yet no literary work can 'pass totally without exception, or without censure'. That SJ has at times 'divided the opinions of the learned' and 'provoked the severity of criticism' is clear from various pamphlets defending Gray, to whom he is 'not over zealous' to allow the praise 'pretty universally assigned him'. The *Elegy* may have earned Gray a poetic rank above his 'general merits', and no doubt SJ's object was 'justice', but resistance to error can go to the opposite extreme. SJ also gives 'hyperbolical praise' to some neglected names:

That our learned author's judgement has been warped on some subjects, where party has an influence, is the opinion of probably the greater number of his admirers; and if it be true, it is a decisive argument to show the prevalence of prejudice, and that the strongest understanding is not always proof against its inroads.

SJ gives a 'very copious and minute narrative' of Addison's career, and his conclusion (168) 'exhibits, with a peculiar happiness, the character of a masterly writer, drawn by a masterly hand'. He offers a 'minute and ingenious investigation' of Rowe's works, and characterizes Tickell, Congreve, and Prior 'with great truth and accuracy'. 'Pope' is

eminently distinguished by the minuteness with which it has been traced, by the variety of information it contains, and the valuable criticism it abounds with. The curiosity of the biographer has followed him through the shade of retirement, through the pleasantry of convivial society, and the tumult of his literary warfare; and the whole is interspersed with relations peculiarly interesting to the scholar and the moralist.

SJ's comparison of Pope and Dryden ('Pope' 303–11) is quoted.

Is any other English biography 'calculated so powerfully to awaken the reader's feelings, to excite his compassion on the one side, and his detestation on the other' as 'Savage', which is 'told in a manner strikingly pathetic'? 'Swift' is 'well executed', but 'little new was to be expected'. Croft's 'Young' is written 'in no indifferent stile of imitation' of SJ.

SOME VISUAL RESPONSES

The *Lives* inspired several ingenious caricatures of SJ, including an anonymous depiction of 'The Ghost of the Poet Blackmore Appearing to Dr. Johnson', James Gillray's 'Old Wisdom Blinking at the Stars' (1782), and his 'Apollo and the Muses Inflicting Pennance on Dr. Pomposo Around Parnassus' (1783), in which SJ in a dunce's cap confesses to 'criticism without judgement' and begs forgiveness for 'defaming that genius I never could emulate'. See M. R. Brownell, *SJ's Attitude to the Arts* (Oxford, 1989), 96–7, P. Smallwood, 'The Johnsonian Monster and the *Lives of the Poets*: James Gillray, Critical History, and the Eighteenth–Century Satirical Cartoon', *BJECS* 25 (2002), 217–45, and the headnote to 'Gray'.

SJ's reaction when told about 'Apollo and the Muses' no doubt applies to any of the less favourable reviews summarized above: 'Sir, I am very glad to hear this. I hope the day will never arrive when I shall neither be the object of calumny or ridicule, for then I shall be neglected and forgotten' (*J. Misc.*, ii. 420, and cf. ii. 207).

APPENDIX C
SPELLING AND CAPITALIZATION
IN THE PREFACES AND LIVES

Examination of these features of SJ's text reveals a mild underlying anarchy which will come as no surprise to students of the text of his earlier works. While some effort was evidently made in *P79–P81* and *L81–L83* to 'normalize' or 'modernize' spelling and capitalization, at no stage was consistency achieved, exceptions to any apparent trend can always be found, and in some cases the later editions tend to reverse earlier standardizing policies. Among the factors contributing to this situation are SJ's own idiosyncrasies and inconsistencies, including a failure to conform to his own orthographic prescriptions in the *Dictionary* (1755); the general fluidity of certain spellings in the period; a lingering tendency to give significant nouns initial capitals, a practice which had been diminishing since the mid-century, but which both SJ and his printers continued unsystematically; the different habits of the compositors who worked on *P79–P81* and *L81–L83* over a period of several years, and a failure to impose rigorous consistency in the printing house; SJ's own variable attention to such matters when reading proof and when correcting the text for *L83*; and the fact that quotations transcribed by hands other than SJ's, or set up directly from printed sources on his instructions, introduced variant accidentals, which would themselves be less attentively corrected than SJ's own text at various stages.

This situation is not confined to SJ's last major literary work. The Yale editors of *The Idler* concluded in 1963 that spellings in the early editions varied according to the 'caprice of the compositor' rather than any discernible policy of SJ himself: words appeared in variant spellings, which might later be differently revised. Some of the most frequent variant spellings in *The Idler* reappear later in the *Lives* (*YW*, ii, p. xxv and n.; for a similar list for *The Rambler*, see *YW*, iii, p. xxxix n.).

Some examples will illustrate this aspect of the text in 1779–83:

(i) Apparently random variation in the use of initial 'e' or 'i' in such words as 'increase' and 'enquire', already found in SJ's earlier texts (see *YW*, ii, p. xxv n., iii, p. xl n., and *Journey* (1985), p. xli), persists in *P79–P81* and *L81–L83*. The *Dictionary* includes 'Intrust' rather than 'Entrust', 'Entitle' but not 'Intitle', and under 'Intire' SJ comments 'better written *entire*, which see, and all its derivatives'. Although SJ wrote 'Encrease' in the MS of *The Vanity of Human Wishes*, l. 40 (*Poems* (1974), 417), the *Dictionary* includes only 'Increase' (with a cross-reference to a non-existent entry for 'Encrease'). The evidence of the MS of 'Pope' suggests, however, that SJ usually preferred 'en-' to 'in-' in such cases: e.g. 'entirely' (**67, 238**), 'entitled' (**31, 125, 196, 261**), 'entreated' and 'entreaties' (**159, 265**), 'enquire', enquiry', and 'enquired' (**9, 204, 232, 282**), and 'encreased' (**271**), although, as in the *Dictionary*, he also favoured 'intrust' (**9**) and 'intrusted' (**288**).

An apparent preference for 'in-' in the printing house was inconsistently imposed, sometimes with perplexing results, as shown by some of the more common cases:

(*a*) In 'J. Philips' **22** 'entirely' in *P79* became 'intirely' in *L81*, but in **29** 'entirely' survived in all editions. In 'Rowe' **24** and 'Thomson' **42** 'intirely' in *P81* became 'entirely' in *L81*.

(*b*) In 'Cowley' **134** 'entitled' appeared in the proofs and *P79*, but was revised to 'intituled' in *L81* and *L83*. Both 'entitled' in 'Dryden' **317** and 'intitled' in 'Dorset' **2** survive in all editions. In 'Fenton' **7** 'intitled' became 'entitled' and in 'Savage' **4** 'intitle' became 'entitle' in *L81*.

(*c*) In 'Milton' **132**, **136**, 'encreased' and 'encrease' in *P79* became 'increased' and 'increase' in *L81*, but 'increase' in 'Mallet' **12** was revised to 'encrease' in *L83*. In 'Prior' **17** 'increasing' appears in all editions.

(*d*) In 'Dryden' **189** and 'Swift' **20** 'intrusted' survived in all editions, but 'intrust' in 'Pope' **9** and 'intrusted' in 'Mallet' **4** became 'entrust' and 'entrusted' in *L83*.

(*e*) Although the *Dictionary* includes only 'Entreat', and SJ wrote 'entreated' (**159**) and 'entreaties' in the MS of 'Pope' (**265**), 'intreated' and 'intreaties' appear in all printed editions, as does 'intreaties' in 'Prior' **98**.

(ii) In *L83* there was fairly consistent revision of the '-cies' ending evidently favoured by SJ, as in 'elegancies' and 'excellencies' in the MS of 'Pope' **348**, **374**: these survived in *P81* and *L81*, but were revised to 'elegances' and 'excellences' in *L83*, presumably with SJ's acquiescence. These two words are the most common cases, but similar changes were carried out in *L83* (if not earlier), so that 'deficiencies' became 'deficiences' ('Milton' **36**) and 'exigencies' became 'exigences' ('Waller' **42** and 'Dryden' **183**, **227**). There are the usual variations: 'exigencies' survived in 'Dryden' **187** in *L83*; 'deficiencies' in the MS of 'Pope' **126** survived in all editions; 'Prior' **73** already had 'elegances' in *P81*, and the MS of 'Pope' already had 'delinquences' (**290**); and in 'Savage' **226**, 'exigences' in *P81* unusually became 'exigencies' in *L81* before reverting to 'exigences' in *L83*.

(iii) Final '-ic/-ick' is the most common spelling variant in SJ's earlier texts, with no discernible pattern to the variations (see *YW*, ii, p. xxv n., iii, p. xxxix nn., *Journey* (1985), p. xlii). While the MS of *The Vanity of Human Wishes* reveals some inconsistency in SJ's own early practice (see e.g. *YW*, iii, p. xxxvi), the *Dictionary* usually prescribed final 'k' for such words: 'Epic' is an exception, although SJ wrote 'Epick' in the MS of 'Pope' (see below). Bennet Langton claimed that SJ emphatically preferred final '-ick', asserting that 'English . . . should always have the Saxon *k* added to the *c*' (*Life*, iv. 31; see Boswell's note objecting to the 'curtailing innovation' of omitting *k* in such words as 'critick' and 'publick').

SJ's spelling in the MS of 'Pope' is relatively consistent in such words as 'Epick' (**20**), 'criticks' (**26**), 'publick' (**29**), 'pedantick' (**37**), 'frolick' (**53**), 'encomiastick' (**69**), 'Ethicks' (**173**), 'romantick' (**141**, **199**), 'tragick' (**141**), 'topicks' (**210**), 'Physick' (**242**), 'scholastick' (**308**), 'didactick' (**328–9**), 'heroicks' (**329**), 'majestick' (**333**), etc., although 'Classics' appears in **16**, 'critics' in **122**, and 'heroic' in **348**.

There seems at first to have been somewhat confused resistance to SJ's inclinations in the printing house. Final 'k' was often omitted in *P79–P81*, only to reappear in *L81* or *L83*. For examples of the restoration of final 'k' in *L81*, see 'Cowley' **36**, 'Milton' **176**, 'Butler' **34**, **50**, 'Waller' **128**, and 'Dryden' **279**, **282**, **294** (although 'public' appears in 'Dryden' **144**, **281** in all editions). Final 'k' was restored with noticeable consistency in 'Savage' (e.g. **80**, **100–1**, **104**, **120**, **125**, **129**, **138–9**, **141**, **146**, etc.), with only occasional exceptions (**174**). By the time 'Pope' was printed, final 'k' appears to have won the day, appearing consistently in all editions, with only an isolated 'Public' (133) in *L83*. Elsewhere, however, final 'k' could still disappear in *L81* or *L83*, as in 'Cowley' 68, 107, 144, 'Milton' 147, 220, 222, 265, 'Dryden' 6, 13, 133, 137, 140, 'Prior' 7, 13, 28, and 'Blackmore' 4, 26, 28, 32, 36.

There are also the usual variations and inconsistencies. In *L83* 'epick' appears in 'Milton' 208, 214 but 'epic' in 211. Although 'publick' became 'public' in *L83* in 'Addison' 43, 58, 'publick' survived in 75, 77; and although final 'k' in 'physick' in 'Blackmore' 2 was removed in *L81*, it was restored in *L83*, but with 'physic' surviving in 4. 'Akenside' includes both 'physic' (2) and 'physick' (5) in *L83*. (As a further variant, 'epique' appears in 'Smith' 6, 16 in a quotation from another author.)

(iv) SJ himself tended to favour final '-our' rather than '-or', as in 'authour', 'authours', and 'authour's' in the MS of 'Rowe' 18, 22, 35 (printed as 'author', and 'authors', and 'author's' in all editions), and in the MS of 'Pope' *passim*. The *Dictionary* had, however, prescribed 'Author', but also 'Horrour', 'Inferiour', 'Splendour', and 'Terrour'. Both forms occur apparently at random in SJ's earlier works, but with a general trend from '-our' to '-or' in early editions of *The Idler* (see *YW*, ii, p. xxxix n., ii, p. xxv n., and *Journey* (1985), pp. xli–xlii).

When '-our' appeared in *P79–P81*, it was more often than not reduced to '-or' in *L81*: thus, 'authours' and 'horrour' were revised in *L81* to 'authors' and 'horror' in 'Cowley' 61, 80, 'inferiour' to 'inferior' in 'Milton' 170, 'splendour' to 'splendor' in 'Waller' 62, 'terrour' to 'terror' in 'Dryden' 369, 390, and 'horrours' to 'horrors' in 'Hughes' 15. In 'Pope' the spellings 'author' and 'authors' were already consistent in *P81* (e.g. 24, 26, 32, 37, 53, 77, 84, 107, etc.).

Yet the usual variations also occur: 'terror' had already appeared in *P79* in 'Dryden' 363, 366, 372–4, 378, 389, 391 (in a quoted text), and 'splendor' in 'Milton' 189, 'Dryden' 277, 279, 304, 'Gay' 29, 'Akenside' 20, and 'Gray' 37 in *P79–P81*. On the other hand, 'terrour' and 'superiour' in 'Dryden' 42, 318, 'authour' in 'Dorset' 1, and 'splendour' in 'Addison' 126, 167, 'Prior' 32, and 'Watts' 6 were to survive in all editions. In 'Savage' 1 'splendor' was actually revised in *L81* to 'splendour', which also appeared in 137 in all editions. 'Pope' has 'splendour' in 74, 328, 365, but also 'splendor' in 122, 412, in all editions. (In the first four cases the compositor followed SJ's MS; in 412 he followed the printed text of the 'Essay on Epitaphs'.) SJ's 'errour' in the MS of 'Pope' 20 survived in all editions.

(v) The *Dictionary* favoured 'Cheerful' (cross-referring from 'Chear' to 'Cheer'), 'Complete' (cross-referring from 'Compleat'), and 'Extreme'. In 'Dryden' 376 'extreamly' was revised to 'extremely' in *L81*; in 'Savage' 257, 312 'chearfulness' became 'cheerfulness' in *L81*, although 'chearfully', 'chearfulness', and 'chearful' in 311–12 were not revised until *L83*; in 'Savage' 279 'compleated' became 'completed' in *L83*; and in 'Swift' 73 'chearful' became 'cheerful' in *L81*. The trend was thus towards the more 'modern' spelling, and 'complete' and 'completed', SJ's normal spelling in the MS, duly appear in all editions in 'Pope' 11, 122, 172, 222, 299, 329, with 'extremely' and 'extreme' in 190, 278. Even so, 'compleat' survives in 271 (as, exceptionally, in the MS), and 'Chear'd' in 332 in all editions (again as in the MS).

Lest this appear a relatively simple case, 'completed' in 'Halifax' 8 was revised to 'compleated' against the trend in *L81*; 'chearful' and 'chearfully' in 'Thomson' 38, 41 and 'Collins' 5 survive in all editions, as do 'compleat' and 'chearful' in 'Pitt' 2, 6, but with 'complete' in 9. In 'Watts' 10 'compleated' and in 'Akenside' 20 'completed' are found in all editions. In 'Savage' 230, 257, 266, 291 'cloaths' was revised in *L81* to 'clothes', the spelling favoured in the *Dictionary*, but 'cloathing' is found in 'Dyer' 11 in all editions.

(vi) There is similar diversity in the use of final '-ise' and '-ize'. The *Dictionary* had favoured the spellings 'Aggrandize' and 'Apologize', on the one hand, and 'Comprise' and 'Surprise' on the other. In the MS of 'Pope', however, SJ himself wrote 'methodize' (86), 'sympathises' (147), 'satirised' (151), 'apologise' (154), 'authorised' (163), and 'aggrandised' (329).

Although in 'Dryden' 350 'surprised' became 'surprized' in *L83*, 'surprises' in 'Dryden' 349 survived in all editions. In 'Tickell' 10 'surprize' occurs twice in *P81* (in a quotation), but in only one case was revised to 'surprise' in *L81* and *L83*. In 'Savage' 61 'surprize' was revised to 'surprise' and in 319 'surprized' became 'surprised' in *L81*, although 'surprize' in 319 was not revised till *L83*. In 'Swift' 113 'surprize' became 'surprise', but in 'Lyttelton' 31 '*surprizes*' survived in all editions. In 'Swift' 45 'aggrandise' was revised to 'aggrandize' in *L81*. In 'Denham' 31 'comprised' became 'comprized', and in 'Pope' 154 'apologise' became 'apologize', in *L83*.

(vii) For other examples of variant spellings see:

(a) *Allege*. The *Dictionary* includes only 'Allege'. SJ wrote 'alleged' in the MS of 'Pope' 260, and it survives in all editions, as also in 'Milton' 52. In 'Milton' 46, however, 'alleged' 46 became 'alledged' in *L83*, and in 'Dryden' 388 'alleged' had already been revised to 'alledged' in *L81*. In 'Savage' 114, 130, 284 'alledged' in *P81* had been revised to 'alleged' in *L81*, and 'alledge' similarly became 'allege' in 'Savage' 271 in *L83*.

(b) *Borne*. In the Berg copy of *L81* SJ altered 'borne' (in the sense of 'carried' or 'endured') to 'born' in 'Cowley' 179, which appears in *L83*. In the *Dictionary* he had prescribed the spelling 'Born' for 'The *participle passive of bear*'. The same revision occurs in *L83* in 'Savage' 232 and 'Swift' 53, and cf. the spellings 'forborn' in 'Denham' 38, 'Milton' 102, 105 and 'Pope' 349, and 'over-born' in 'Dryden' 222. However, 'borne' survived in 'Dryden' 276, 'Rowe' 1, and 'Savage' 145 in *L83*.

(c) *Crowd*. Although the *Dictionary* included only 'Crowd', SJ himself seems usually to have favoured 'croud': see e.g. the MS of *The Vanity of Human Wishes*, ll. 4, 24, 73, 250, 273, 337 (*Poems* (1974), 415–27). This helps to explain why both 'croud' and 'crowd' appear in early editions of *The Idler* (*YW*, ii. p. xxvi n.). His preference is also visible in the MS of 'Pope', in e.g. 'crouding' (83), 'croud' (213), and 'crouded' (361). In *P79–P81* the spelling was usually normalized as 'crowd', 'crowds', etc., as in 'Waller' 114, 'Congreve' 38, and 'Savage' 160. In 'Swift' 51, however, 'crouded' was not revised to 'crowded' until *L81*; 'croud' in 'Parnell' 5 and 'crouded' in 'Pope' 361 survived in all editions; and 'crowds' in 'Milton' 235 actually became 'crouds' in *L83*.

(d) *Despatched*. The *Dictionary* includes 'Despatch' but not 'Dispatch' and the MS of 'Pope' confirms that SJ himself normally wrote 'despatched' (19, 89) and 'despatching' (81). Of these cases, 'despatched' in 89 survived in all editions, but so did 'dispatched' in 19 and 'dispatching' in 81.

(e) *Dutchess*. The *Dictionary* favoured 'Dutchess', found also in the MS of 'Pope' 208, and it is the more common spelling in the printed texts, as in 'Waller' 98, 120, 'Dryden' 188, 'Sheffield' 20, and 'Pope' 208. Yet both 'Duchess' and

'Dutchess' appear in SJ's note to 'Savage' **61**; 'Swift' **26** has 'Duchess' in all editions, and in 'Swift' **75** 'Dutchess' actually became 'Duchess' in *L81*.

(*f*) *Falsehood*. The *Dictionary* included only the spelling 'Falshood', as in the MS of 'Pope' (e.g. **164, 180, 281**). The usual spelling in *P79–P81* is 'falsehood', but in 'Savage' **81** the spelling was revised to 'falsehood' in *L83*. While 'falsehood' survived in 'Pope' **281**, the more common 'falshood' or 'falshoods' appeared in 'Pope' **148, 164, 275** in all editions.

(*g*) *Parsimony*. An individual compositor may have been responsible for the consistent revision of 'parsimony' in *P79–P81* (found in the MS of 'Pope' **267**) to 'parcimony' in *L81*. With one exception, the spelling reverted to 'parsimony' in *L83*: see 'Addison' **161** n.

(*h*) *Pursue*. Although the *Dictionary* included only 'Pursue' and 'Pursuit', SJ himself tended to write 'persue', as in the MS of 'Pope' **99, 229** ('persue'), **203, 329** ('persuit'), **338** ('persuits'). (For similar variants in his earlier works, see *YW*, iii, pp. xxxvi, xl and n., and *Poems* (1974), **76** n.) An attempt to standardize the spelling in *P79* was carried out inconsistently: 'pursue' and 'pursued' appear in 'Milton' **102** and in 'Denham' **25, 37** in all editions, but 'persued' in 'Denham' **33** and 'Milton' **128** was not revised until *L81*. While 'Smith' **56** has 'pursue' in all editions, 'Dryden' **132** retains '*persues*' in all editions (in a quotation). (For an objection to the spelling 'persue' in *P79*, see *Gent. Mag.* (1779), 363 n.)

(*i*) *Restoration*. The *Dictionary* includes both 'Restauration' (from Latin 'restauro') and 'Restoration', SJ stating in the second case that 'This is properly *restauration*'. He may initially have intended to use 'Restauration' for the events of 1660, and it survives in all editions in 'Milton' **71** and 'Waller' **68**. SJ either desisted in the face of resistance in the printing house or relapsed into inconsistency, and 'Restoration' is much more common: see 'Milton' **71** and n.

(*j*) *Scribbler*. Although the *Dictionary* includes only 'Scribbler', SJ's own spelling was usually 'scribler/scriblers' (as in the MS of 'Pope' **27, 146, 230**, etc.), which survived into *P79–P81*. It was consistently revised in *L81* or *L83* to 'Scribbler' or 'Scribblers'.

(*k*) *Spritely*. Both 'spritely' and 'sprightly' appear in early editions of *The Idler* (*YW*, ii, p. xxvi n.). Although the *Dictionary* distinguishes adjectival 'Sprightly' (= gay) from adverbial 'Spritely' (= gaily), SJ in practice usually favours 'spritely' for the adjective, as in 'Cowley' **202**. His revision in 'Roscommon' **23** of 'sprightly' to 'spritely' in the corrected Berg copy and *L83* brought it into line with 'spritely' in **35** (all editions). In 'Cowley' **162**, however, 'spritely' became 'sprightly' in *L83* (albeit in a quotation); and 'Rochester' **27** and 'Pitt' **10** retain 'sprightliness', and 'Savage' **13** 'sprightly', in all editions. In contrast, 'Pope' **120** (as in the MS) and 'Watts' **35** have 'spriteliness' in all editions.

(*l*) *Style*. Although the *Dictionary* gives only 'Style', SJ himself usually preferred 'stile', as in the MSS of 'Rowe' **15** and 'Pope' **8, 20, 32, 172, 185**, etc. (but with 'style' at **309**). (This no doubt explains why 'stile' predominated in the earliest text of *The Idler*, but tended later to be revised to 'style': see *YW*, ii, p. xxvi n.) Although *L81* often altered 'stile' to 'style', such revision was typically inconsistent. Thus 'stile' or 'stiles' in *P79* in 'Cowley' **40, 63, 102–3, 115, 139, 142, 200** became 'style/styles' in *L81*, but both 'stile' and 'style' appear in 'Cowley' **63**. In 'Milton' **136** 'style' already appeared in *P79*, but a few paragraphs later 'stile' in **142** was not revised till *L81*, as also in 'Prior' **30**. Later, 'style' appeared more consistently even in *P79–P81*, as in 'Dryden' **78, 225, 294**, 'Smith' **37–8**, and 'Savage' **231, 271**. In 'Pope' **8, 20, 32, 172, 185** revision to 'style' or 'styles', perhaps by Nichols, in visible in the proofs of *P81*. As a predictable exception, 'stiled' survived unobtrusively in SJ's note to 'Prior' **1** down to *L83*

(*m*) *Visitor*. The *Dictionary* includes only the spelling 'Visiter', but 'visiters' in 'Milton' **112** was revised to 'visitors' in *L81*. In 'Milton' **124**, however, 'visiter' survived in all editions, as did 'visiters' in **159–60**, and 'visiter' in 'Dyer' **7**. Strangely, Christopher Smart's *Universal Visiter* is inaccurately entitled *'the Visitor'* in 'Pope' **384**.

(viii) Some of SJ's more idiosyncratic spellings in the MS of 'Pope' did not reach print: e.g. 'Pamflet' and 'pamflets' (**67, 86, 216, 232, 235–6, 239**, etc.), 'stockens' (**257**), 'literall' (**326**) and 'phantome' (**336**). The *Dictionary* does, however, include both 'unkle' ('Pope' **48–9, 51–2, 319**) and 'uncle'. Elsewhere, 'voluntier' and 'voluntiers', not found in the *Dictionary*, appeared in 'Sheffield' **4** and 'Granville' **6** in *P79–P81*, but were normalized in *L81*. SJ's spelling 'Ideot' in MS of 'Pope' **159**, not in the *Dictionary*, survived in *P81* but was corrected in *L81*. Although the *Dictionary* favoured 'Cipher', both 'ciphering and deciphering' and 'cyphering and decyphering' appear within a few paragraphs in *P79* in 'Cowley' **12, 24**, before *L81* settled for 'cyphering and decyphering'. ('Pope' **151** has 'decypher' and 'Pope' **254** 'cypher' in all editions.)

The title of a literary work sometimes varies unpredictably: although 'Eneid' in 'Cowley' **145** and 'Denham' **7** became 'Æneid' in *L83*, 'Eneid' survived in 'Dryden' **147, 203, 304, 309–10, 345–6**, and in 'Pitt' **8–9** 'Æneid' was actually revised to 'Eneid' in *L81* and *L83*.

(ix) For some other variant spellings, only selectively and briefly illustrated here, see: 'ancients/antients' ('J. Philips' **36**, 'Smith' **11, 19**, SJ himself preferring 'ancient' in the MS of 'Pope' **34, 210**); 'awkward/aukward' ('Addison' **106**, 'Prior' **36**); 'connection/ connexion' ('Pope' **400**); 'dissension/dissention' ('Swift' **58**); 'dulness/dullness' ('Granville' **3**, 'Pope' **238, 358**, SJ himself preferring 'dulness' in the MS of 'Pope' **156, 238, 358**); 'groveling/grovelling' ('Addison' **167**, 'Gay' **5**); 'irreconcilable/irrecon- cileable' ('Swift' **57**, 'Pope' **372**); 'judgement/judgment' ('Waller' **43**, 'Savage' **280, 331**, SJ himself usually preferring 'judgement' in the MS of 'Pope' **38, 302, 305, 307, 310**, but with 'judgment' in **86, 373**); 'past/passed' ('Dryden' **294**, 'Rowe' **24–5**, 'Prior' **55**); 'recompence/recompense' ('Savage' **315**, 'Swift' **15**); 'secrecy/secresy' ('Savage' **319**); 'shew/show' ('Cowley' **1**, 'Smith' **2, 6, 51**, 'Savage' **125**); 'solicit/solicite' ('Rowe' **17**, 'Swift' **137**), 'suspence/suspense' ('Pope' **51**); 'vicious/vitious' ('Cowley' **101**, 'Dryden' **320**).

(x) *Names*. Although SJ himself wrote 'Bolinbroke' (as in the MS of 'Pope' **172, 191–3, 245, 272, 289**, etc.), it usually appeared as 'Bolingbroke' in the printed editions. His favoured spelling of 'Cromwel' for 'Cromwell' often survived into *P79* (e.g. 'Waller' **65–8**, but with 'Cromwell' in **63–4**), but was usually normalized later. SJ probably used the spelling 'Cleveland' for the 17th-century poet, as in *P79–P81*, but it was regularly revised to 'Cleiveland' in *L81* (e.g. in 'Cowley' **63, 79, 86** and 'Parnell' **11**). SJ also seems to have used the spelling 'Southerne' for the dramatist, but *L81* standardized this as 'Southern' (e.g. 'Dryden' **87, 90, 177**, 'Congreve' **2, 7**, and 'Fenton' **7, 11**). SJ presum- ably also wrote 'Vanbrug', which appears in *P81* in 'Congreve' **21**, revised to the more common 'Vanbrugh' in *L81*. The spelling 'Wicherley' in the MS of 'Pope' **26–7** was repeated in *P81* in **26**, but was corrected to 'Wycherley' in **27**.

'Shakespeare' is a special case. SJ told Boswell in Aug. 1773: 'there had been great disputes about the spelling of the Shakspear's name; at last it was thought it would be settled by looking at the original copy of his will; but, upon examining it, he was found to have written it himself no less that three different ways' (*Life*, v. 124). SJ himself evidently preferred 'Shakespeare', as in the MSS of 'Rowe' 15, 18 and 'Pope' 125–6, 186, 210, 264 (but with 'Shakespear' in 145), and usually in *P79–P81*. In *L81*, however, 'Shakespeare' was systematically revised to 'Shakspeare', and reappeared in *L83* only by oversight, as in 'Granville' 9. 'Shakspeare' in fact already starts appearing as early as 'Smith' 18 in *P79*, and does so erratically in *P81*, as in 'Pope' 210, 264, although not before *L81* in 'Pope' 125, 357, and 'Shakespeare' in 126, 186 actually survived into *L83*.

It seems likely that it was decided to bring *L81* into line with the title pages of George Steevens's recent revision of SJ's *The Plays of William Shakspeare* (10 vols., 1778). Although 'Shakespeare' appears consistently in SJ's 'Preface' and often elsewhere in this edition, Steevens explained that the dramatist's will made clear that the correct spelling was 'Shakspeare' (i. 199 n.), a conclusion reached, however, too late for use throughout the edition. Malone's *Supplement to the Edition of Shakspeare's Plays* (2 vols., 1780) also adopted this spelling, as John Nichols, involved in the publication of both works, would have known.

Steevens, Malone, and/or Nichols presumably persuaded SJ to adopt the supposedly definitive 'Shakspeare' in *L81*, and he made no attempt to alter it in *L83*. It will be noted from the quotation above that Boswell also used 'Shakspear' in the *Life* in 1791. (The spelling of 'Shakespeare' in the entries for *Plays* (1778) and Malone's *Supplement* in *Bibliography*, ii. 1118, 1122, is inaccurate.)

(xi) *Initial Capitals*. The MSS of 'Rowe' and 'Pope' indicate that SJ usually favoured initial capitals for titles of rank or office. Thus the MS of 'Rowe' has 'Duke' and 'Earl' (19), and 'Queen', 'Prince', 'Clerk', 'Lord Chancellor', and 'Secretary of the Presentations' (21). Similar practice is visible in the MS of 'Pope' (e.g. at 169, 197, 208, 211, 217, 257, 260, 279, etc.). While *P81* consistently lowered SJ's initial capitals in 'Rowe', the policy in *P79–P81* and *L81–L83* is elsewhere inconsistent. In 'Cowley', the lower-case initial letters for titles in *P79* were raised (presumably recapitalized) in *L81* in e.g. 'King' and 'Lord' (11), 'Lord', 'Earl', 'King', and 'Queen' (12), and 'Lord' and 'Earl' (17), etc. The same tendency in visible in 'Milton' (e.g. 4, 21, 25, 28, etc.), 'Butler' (e.g. 6–9, 11–14, etc.), and 'Waller' (e.g. 4, 6, 7, 9, 11, 13, 15, etc.). Hopes of identifying a clear policy are, however, dashed in 'Denham', in which 'king' appears in all editions in 10, 12–13, with 'King' in all editions in 15; and 'queen' in 12, with 'Queen' in all editions in 14.

The relatively consistent restoration of SJ's (presumed) initial capitals for titles in *L81*, vol. i, is much less apparent in vol. ii, in which the lower-case initital letters found in *P79* were more often than not retained and duly survived into *L83*. Thus, in 'Dryden' in *L81–L83* 'king' or 'king's' appear in 4, 8, 118 (but with 'King' in 35, and 'king' lowered from 'King' in 44). Other examples are 'earl' in 20, 25, 62 (though in *L81* both 'Earl' and 'earl' are found in 62), 77, 86, 93, 100–1; 'duke' in 27, 43, 69, 77, 93; 'dutchess' in 72; 'princess' in 72; and 'marquis' in 85. A similar policy is visible in the shorter lives in *L81*, vol. ii (e.g. 'King', 'Sprat', 'Halifax' 'Parnell', etc.). In *L81*, vol. iii, however, initial capitals for titles of rank and office tend to be retained or restored, though without full consistency (cf. 'Granville' 3, 5–7, 14–15, 17–18, 22, 26).

Later in the printing of *P81*, policy may appear to have stabilized: capitals for titles of rank appeared in all editions of 'Swift' as in 'King' (8–10, 19–21), 'Earl' (10), 'Dutchess'

(26), 'Queen' (26), 'Bishop' (50), etc. (though both 'bishop' and 'Bishop' appear in 25 in all editions). In 'Pope', the initial capitals in the MS usually survived into *P81* and the later editions. Yet practice remained unpredictable to the end: while 'duke' in 'Mallet' 3 and 'prince' in 12 in *P81* were capitalized in *L81*, 'duke', 'dutchess', and 'lord' in 14 survived into *L83*.

(xii) SJ often gave initial capitals to significant nouns in his MSS. Thus the opening paragraphs of the MS of 'Rowe' (disregarding for this purpose SJ's sometimes ambiguous initial 'S') contain 'Ancestor', 'Line', 'Father', and 'Law' (1), 'Father' and 'Law' (3), 'Father' and 'Poetry' (4), 'History' and 'Conqueror' (5), 'Tragedy' (6), 'Poet' (7), 'Eagle' (12), 'Comedy' (14), etc. Whatever his own habits and inclinations, SJ apparently viewed the removal of all these initial capitals in *P81* with equanimity. Elsewhere in the MS of 'Rowe', however, he failed to provide initial capitals when they might have been expected, as in 'second' and 'church' (1), 'temple' (3), '*ambitious stepmother*' (4), '*eighth*' (13), 'preface' (16), 'whig' (20), 'forest' (27), 'unities' and 'nature' (31). In all these cases *P81* supplied initial capitals, SJ again apparently acquiescing in 'house style'.

The MS of 'Pope' reveals inconsistent initial capitalization of such words as 'pastorals', 'poets', 'criticks', and 'authour' (24–6, 30–1, 33, 37, 39–40, 65, 68, etc.), 'History' (87) and 'history' (225), and many other cases. While particular contexts may have prompted the instinctive added emphasis of an initial capital, no clear pattern is easily discernible. Faced with a sequence in the 'Pope' MS such as 'Editors, Collaters, commentators, and verbal criticks' (127), or 'wit, a Wit' (213), the compositor in *P81* chose to lower the initial capitals. Elsewhere he also lowered all the initial capitals in such sequences in the 'Pope' MS as 'Comedy ... Tragedy ... Epick Poem' (20), 'Bridge ... Postilion ... Manner' (139), 'Man ... Clergyman's ... Lawyer's' (163), 'Asthma ... Physicians ... Physick ... Jalap' (242), and 'Scithe ... Roller' (309).

Elsewhere, however, the compositor (if not SJ himself in some missing set of proofs) decided to supply initial capitals in *P81* in such cases as 'Epistolary Powers' (29), 'Pastorals ... Peace ... Tories' (65), 'Prologue ... Remarks' (66), 'Painting ... Poetry' (69), 'Letter of Consolation' (140), and 'System of Morality' (176), all of which survived in later editions. While the compositor faithfully reproduced SJ's own wavering between 'Ruling Passion' and 'ruling Passion' in 202, 204–5, 'Letter' and 'Letters' were consistently capitalized in 'Pope' from *P81* on (e.g. 83, 87, 115, 132, 140, 142, etc.), in spite of SJ's visible inconsistency in the MS.

In both *L81* and *L83* initial capitals can come and go at different stages: 'royalists' became 'Royalists' and 'tenor' became 'Tenour' (in a quotation) in 'Cowley' 39, 76 in *L83*, and 'lover' and 'love' received initial capitals in a quotation in 'Cowley' 87 in *L81*. On the other hand, 'Lady' in 'Cowley' 71 became 'lady' in *L83* and 'Wit' became 'wit' in *L81*. Similarly, *L81* added initial capitals in 'Milton' 38 ('Schools'), 39 ('Justice'), 51 ('Peace'), 52 ('Lady'), 87 ('Mysteries'), 122 ('Nature'), 196 ('Lady'), 200–1 ('Brother') in *L81*, although 'Lady' already had a capital in 200–1, 203 in *P79*. Taking the opening of 'Swift' as a final sample, 'university' (4), 'parliaments' (10), 'tory' (42), and 'emperor' (45) all lost initial capitals in *L81*, as did 'primate' in *L83*, although in 21 'Clergyman' acquired a capital in *L83*.

Inconsistency in the printed texts can be partly explained by SJ's own variable practice, as with 'nature/Nature' (e.g. in MS of 'Pope' 69, 204–5, 291, 296, 373). As noted above, the word acquired an initial capital in 'Milton' 122 in *L81*, 'Nature' having already appeared in 124 in *P79*. In 'Addison' 143 and 'Shenstone' 10 'Nature' lost its capital in *L81*, but in 'Swift' **93** this was delayed until *L83*. 'Pope' has both 'Nature' (**291**) and 'nature' (**296**) within a few paragraphs, as in the MS. As J. D. Fleeman concluded of similar inconsistency elsewhere with 'Nature/nature', SJ was evidently 'not careful of such a distinction' (*Journey* (1985), 148 n.).

(xiii) Contractions such as 'tho' ', 'thro' ' and 'heav'n' occur frequently in quotations of verse in *P79–P81*, no doubt because of the small page size, but were usually expanded in *L81*. *L81* also used quotation marks more consistently.

(xiv) *Hyphens*: Fleeman, *Journey* (1985), pp. xlvi–xlviii, suggested that, since hyphenated words are infrequent in SJ's MSS, medial hyphenations in the printed text of the *Journey* might have been 'end-of-line forms' in the (missing) MS, i.e. end-of-line hyphens in what SJ intended to be single words, which were mistakenly preserved by the compositor. The evidence of the MS of 'Pope' does not confirm this hypothesis. SJ rarely hyphenates, and 'self-defence' in **370** is unusual. A number of unhyphenated words in the MS were in fact hyphenated in *P81* and later editions: e.g. 'nearsighted' (**69**), 'tomorrow' (**89**), 'lifetime' (**114**), 'overruling' (**205**), 'lowborn' (**218**), 'Postoffice' (**282**), 'teatable' (**336**) and 'partycoloured' (**372**). None of these cases in fact involved the retention of an 'end-of-line' hyphen within a single word in the MS. (SJ's 'twenty five' **283** also acquired a hyphen in *P81*.)

A final case involving hyphenation further illustrates the mild perplexity SJ could cause compositors. In **326** in the MS of 'Pope' 'common places' is clearly two separate words, but this is less obvious in **323**. *P81* accordingly printed 'common-places' in **323**, as did *L81–L83*. In **326**, however, both *P81* and *L81* printed 'common places', which was not hyphenated until *L83*. In 'Pope' **413**, **421** (in the 'Dissertation on Epitaphs', not present in the MS), all editions have 'common places'. Elsewhere, 'common places' in 'Shenstone' **28** in *P81* and *L81* was finally hyphenated in *L83*, but in 'Gray' **34** 'common places' appears in all editions.

INDEX

Jane, William, 1645–1707, Professor of
Divinity, Oxford ii.168, 378 n

Jedburgh, Roxburghshire iv.96, 364 n

Jeffreys, George Jeffreys, Baron, 1645–89,
judge ii.102, 108, 329 n

Jeffreys, George, 1678–1755, poet and
dramatist iii.12, 253 n

Jeffreys, John Jeffreys, Baron,
1673?–1702 ii.108–10, 336–7 nn

Jemmat, Catherine (Yeo), 1714–66?, poet and
autobiographer iii.370 n

Jennens, Charles, 1700–73, librettist i.346 n

Jennings, David, 1691–1762, dissenting
clergyman and author iv.382 n

Jenyns, Soame, 1704–87, author i.76 n;
iv.509 n

Jermyn, Henry (later Earl of St. Alban's),
1605?–84, courtier and official i.193–4,
198, 313 n, 320 n; ii.31, 47, 269 n, 278 n

Jersey, Edward Villiers, Earl of, 1656–1711,
Secretary of State iii.50, 295 n, 358 n

Jervas or Jarvis, Charles, 1675–1739, painter,
translator and friend of Pope iv.12, 25,
62, 137, 256 n, 259 n

Jodrell, Richard Paul, 1745–1831, dramatist
and friend of SJ iv.80, 237 n, 350 n

Johnson, Elizabeth, 1689–1752, SJ's wife i.3,
388 n; ii.408 n; iii.351 n; iv.301 n

Johnson, Esther or Hester ('Stella'),
1681–1728, friend of Swift iii.22, 192,
198, 200–1, 203–5, 265 n, 434 n, 447 nn,
449–50 nn, 460 n

Johnson, Michael, 1656–1731, Lichfield
bookseller, father of SJ i.93; ii.101, 188,
328 n, 399 n; iv.522 n

JOHNSON, SAMUEL, 1709–84

THE LIVES OF THE MOST EMINENT ENGLISH
POETS (PREFACES, BIOGRAPHICAL AND
CRITICAL, TO THE WORKS OF THE
ENGLISH POETS, 1779–81)

(See also entries for individual poets)

'Advertisement' to i.189; textual
notes i.296; commentary i.305; i.86,
92 ii.311 n, 336 n, 374 n

origins i.1–14, 78

Bell's Poets of Great Britain threatens
London trade i.5–9, 13, 14, 21, 24, 34–5,
356 n

'Committee of the Poets' i.47, 73, 356 n

SJ's involvement with English Poets
(1779) i.1, 4, 5–7, 9, 10–11 n, 11, 12–13,
20, 24, 61–8; iii.463 n; iv.105, 362 n,
380 n, 400 n, 525–6 n

remuneration i.13–14 and n. 51–2 and n,
182

spelling and capitalization i.177, 179–80,
181–2, 184, iv.539–47 n

Prefaces, I–IV (1779) i.14–37; 'little Lives,
and little Prefaces' i.15; enquiries at
Cambridge i.17 and n; visits
Oxford i.17–18 and n; at Ashbourne with
Boswell i.19–23; starts work
('Cowley') i.22; returns to London i.23;
trade advertisements i.24, 31; ill
health i.24–5; enlarged conception of his
task i.25, 27–8; as response to Warton's
History i.27–8 n; pre-publication
volumes i.28, 35, 306 n, 356 n; ii.226 n,
264 n; iii.237 n; iv.234 n; completion of
Eng. Poets i.29; SJ's slow
progress i.30–1; 'Milton' and shorter
lives i.31–2; Vols. I–IV published
separately i.32, 35; iv.237 n, 520–1 n;
available only with Eng. Poets i.35;
Dublin piracy i.35, 47, 50; Whig
reactions i.36–7; early
reviews iv.520–7 n

Prefaces, V–X (1781) i.37–47; delayed
resumption of work i.38–40, 57; the
Spence MSS i.40, 47–8 n; iv.235–6 n;
later lives (Feb.–Aug. 1780) i.40–4; pre-
publication volumes i.43, 45; iii.310 n,
353–4 n; iv.477 n, 505 n; 'Young'
delegated to Croft i.44; concludes with
'Swift' and 'Pope' i.45–6;
publication i.47; early
reviews iv.528–32 n, 537–8 n

Lives (1781) i.47–50, 73; reordered
sequence i.48, 180–1; iv.482 n, 500 n,
504 n; new title devised i.48–50; earlier
references to SJ's 'Lives' i.48–9, 49 n;
SJ's late style i.50 and n; iv.520 n, 526 n,
534 n, 535 n; early reactions iv.532–7 n

revised Lives (1783) i.50–2

pressed to write life of Spenser i.52 n

SJ's 'assistants' i.52–80; Hester
Thrale i.53; John Nichols i.53–72; Isaac
Reed i.72–6; George Steevens i.76–80,
189

political implications i.76, 118–19, 132,
166–75, 368–9 n; ii.266 n; iv.520–4 n,
526–8 n

BIOGRAPHY i.80–103

anecdotes in i.93 and n

appeal of i.80–1, 106

art and life, connection of i.83–4, 94;
iv.103, 373–4 n

authors, lives of i.82–4

autobiographical verse i.94, 268, 285;
ii.262–3 n; iii.461 n; iv.46, 77, 293 n, 427 n

autobiography i.82